The Invaded

The Invaded

*How Latin Americans and Their
Allies Fought and Ended
U.S. Occupations*

ALAN McPHERSON

OXFORD
UNIVERSITY PRESS

OXFORD
UNIVERSITY PRESS

Oxford University Press is a department of the University of Oxford.
It furthers the University's objective of excellence in research, scholarship,
and education by publishing worldwide.

Oxford New York

Auckland Cape Town Dar es Salaam Hong Kong Karachi
Kuala Lumpur Madrid Melbourne Mexico City Nairobi
New Delhi Shanghai Taipei Toronto

With offices in
Argentina Austria Brazil Chile Czech Republic France Greece
Guatemala Hungary Italy Japan Poland Portugal Singapore
South Korea Switzerland Thailand Turkey Ukraine Vietnam

Oxford is a registered trade mark of Oxford University Press
in the UK and certain other countries.

Published in the United States of America by
Oxford University Press
198 Madison Avenue, New York, NY 10016

Library of Congress Cataloging-in-Publication Data
McPherson, Alan L.
The invaded : how Latin Americans and their allies fought and ended
U.S. occupations / Alan McPherson.
p. cm.
Includes bibliographical references and index.
ISBN 978–0–19–534303–8 (hardcover : alk. paper); 978–0–19–049876–4 (paperback : alk. paper)
1. Latin America—Relations—United States. 2. United States—Relations—Latin
America. 3. Anti-Americanism—Latin America—History—20th century. 4. Nicaragua—
History—1909–1937. 5. Haiti—History—American occupation, 1915–1934.
6. Dominican Republic—History—American occupation, 1916–1924. I. Title.
F1418.M3729 2014
327.8073—dc23
2013023259

To Cindy, my love

CONTENTS

ACKNOWLEDGMENTS

This book was a decade in the making, and many are to thank for making it my most rewarding, personally and professionally.

Funding the research was arduous and precarious, but eventually many generous sources came through. My former employer, Howard University, provided me with a New Faculty Research Grant that allowed travel to Nicaragua, France, and England. The federal government awarded the project a Fulbright to the Dominican Republic. The Franklin and Eleanor Roosevelt Institute of the Franklin D. Roosevelt Library, the Hoover Presidential Library Association, the University of Florida's Center for Latin American Studies, and the Duke-UNC Consortium for Latin American Studies kept my spirits buoyant with research grants. Harvard University's David Rockefeller Center for Latin American Studies, where I was the Central American Fellow for a semester, finally allowed me to write the manuscript.

Archivists and colleagues at home and especially abroad helped me find and understand a multinational set of sources. Archivists and reference librarians at all institutions I visited in the United States, France, and England were invariably courteous and resourceful.

In the Dominican Republic, Roberto Cassá and Quisqueya Lora proved that professionalism and a boost from the state could rehabilitate Caribbean archives. The Universidad Autónoma de Santo Domingo was helpful with the papers of Tulio Cestero. Vetilio Alfau opened his father's collection to me. "Natacha" González showed me how to teach Dominican students. Hamlet Hermann helped me understand Dominican politics. Federico "Chito" Henríquez y Vásquez, the grandson of Federico Henríquez y Carvajal, provided family documents over a *cafecito*. Also helpful were Salvador Alfau, Julio del Campo, José del Castillo, Emilio Cordero Michel, Dantes Ortíz, and Alejandro Paulino. The US embassy's cultural staff, especially Rex Moser, gave me the opportunity to share my findings at public universities throughout the Dominican Republic.

In Nicaragua, Margarita Vannini of the Instituto de Historia de Nicaragua y Centro América not only allowed me access to her center's archive but also facilitated entrance into the jewel of Sandino history in Nicaragua, the Centro de Historia Militar. There, Soraya Sánchez did the hard work of digging up relevant materials.

I owe a special debt of gratitude to graduate assistants who brought me mountains of materials, to which I responded with demands for bigger mountains. Among these were Sarah Chancy, Joseph Hartman, Christina Violeta Jones, John Kitch, and especially Glenn Chambers.

Colleagues provided advice and feedback as I made presentations and wrote short pieces. Thanks to John Britton, Roxanne Dunbar-Ortiz, Max Friedman, Michel Gobat, Michael Kazin, Hal Jones, Joseph McCartin, Marisa Navarro, Mary Renda, Yannick Wehrli, and John Womack. Jeffrey Taffet was most helpful by reading the entire manuscript.

My present employer, the College of International Studies at the University of Oklahoma, has been more than generous, giving me time, resources, and encouragement to bring the book to completion. Thanks especially to Zach Messitte and Mark Frazier and to fellow Latin Americanists John Fishel, Robin Grier, Erika Robb-Larkins, and Charlie Kenney. Special thanks go to Sandi Emond and Ronda Martin.

Susan Ferber at Oxford University Press was an attentive editor, giving my originally bloated manuscript two thorough, fastidious readings that slimmed it down and improved its accessibility. Oxford also sent the manuscript to the two best anonymous readers I have ever experienced, greatly enhancing the finished product.

Finally I owe my greatest debt to my family. Work on this book overlapped with the birth of my two lively, lovely boys, Luc and Nico, who bring joy into my life every day—even though that day starts earlier than I'd like. The project germinated before I even met my wife, so since she has known me, Cindy has been married also to this book. With all its demands on my time, this project was most challenging for her, and she responded with patience and encouragement. To her I dedicate this book.

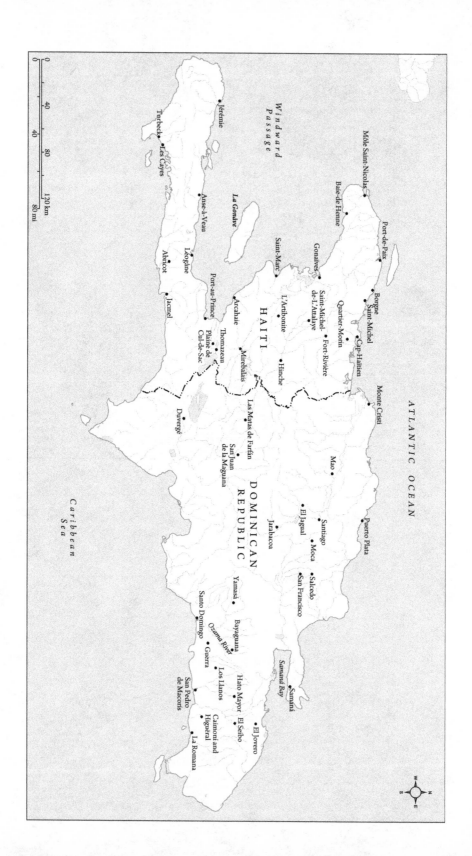

Introduction
Occupation: Why Fight It?

Shortly after the 2003 US invasion of Iraq, a *Washington Post* reporter tagged along with a US Army company in Baghdad. He asked the troops if the people of Baghdad wanted them to stay. "Oh yeah," responded a twenty-year-old specialist from Louisiana. Assessing the friendliness of the neighborhood they were about to enter, he offered, "95 percent." The *Post* man asked a staff sergeant from Minnesota the same question. "Maybe 10 percent are hostile. About 50 percent friendly. About 40 percent are indifferent." Around the block, an Iraqi offered his own statistic: "We refuse the occupation—not 100 percent, but 1,000 percent."[1] In fact, polls throughout the occupation indicated that around three quarters of Iraqis wanted the occupation to end.[2]

A lot can account for these wildly varying assessments. Surely nationality, but rank, region, religion, education, past perceptions of the war, and self-images also play a role. Such markers of identity always lie at the heart of resistance movements to military occupations and determine both their motivations and effectiveness. They were certainly salient during US occupations in Latin America in the first third of the twentieth century. Depending on how one defines interventions, there were from 40 to 6,000 south of the Rio Grande between the Civil War and the 1930s.[3] Three of them—Nicaragua (1912–1933), Haiti (1915–1934), and the Dominican Republic (1916–1924)—are the subjects of this book.[4] There were other occupations—Puerto Rico, Veracruz in Mexico, Chiriquí in Panama, and several in Cuba—but these three were the longest and most complex.[5] They involved large numbers of US troops—2,000 in Haiti, 3,000 next door, and well over 5,000 in Nicaragua. Intended to be temporary, they were neither annexations nor colonizations.[6] Neither were they mere interventions. During occupations, US Marines took over many of the functions of the state—least so in Nicaragua, where politicians invited the occupation; more so in Haiti, where the marines ruled indirectly through a treaty; and completely so in the Dominican Republic, where Washington ran a military government.

Marines also policed a large portion of these territories and interacted with every social group.

Haiti, the Dominican Republic, and Nicaragua were all small, poor, agricultural nations with only incipient industrial sectors. In Haiti, French and Kreyol were spoken; in the others, Spanish, with some indigenous languages, and English in Nicaragua. Haiti was the smallest in area and had the densest population, including a capital, Port-au-Prince, of as many as 100,000 souls. Dominicans were a third of Haiti's population and far more dispersed, and only 21,000 to 35,000 lived in Santo Domingo during the occupation.[7] Nicaragua was about three times the size of the Dominican Republic, but with a population of only 400,000 concentrated on its coasts.

In all three countries, those who resisted invasion were motivated not primarily by nationalism but by more concrete, local concerns that were material, power-related, self-protective, or self-promoting.[8] Resistance to these occupations proved effective at bringing about an official US policy of nonintervention, the Good Neighbor Policy.[9] This book argues that resistance was the most important factor in ending occupations precisely because it reflected concrete grievances and also because it spurred transnational resistance movements. Latin Americans were at their most effective (determined, united, persistent, persuasive) when their interests (personal security, land, culture, local autonomy) were most threatened.

While most studies of occupation focus on occupiers, this book views events through the eyes of the invaded.[10] To do so, it draws on a score of state and personal archives in five countries and three languages, engaging specific events on the ground and emphasizing similarities and differences among these three occupations.[11] Some of the similarities are well known: each occupation confronted a rural insurrection, motivated partly by marine brutality. Less known is why the Haitian and Dominican insurrections failed while the Nicaraguan one outlasted the marines, or why the Dominican occupation ended in 1924 while Haitians lived through another decade of occupation. This book also distinguishes between two waves of resistance, a first against the fact of occupation and a second against its conduct.

Past studies have also limited a comprehensive understanding of resistance to occupation in Latin America by emphasizing the actions of peasants and rural guerrillas. But, with notable exceptions, peasants put up relatively less resistance to marine rule than all other groups save merchants. Once violent insurrections ended and occupations continued in Hispaniola, contact between the military and peasants declined. Several other underprivileged groups—workers, prostitutes, other urban "untouchables"—had more than their share of encounters with occupiers, many of them unpleasant. The process of occupation also threatened the status and wealth of prominent groups. Unemployed politicians, landowners, lawyers, and journalists became second-class citizens under US rule and engaged in everyday acts of resistance. The invaded were already engaged in contested, violent processes of centralization, which occupation both accelerated and placed in the hands of foreigners, prompting further contestation and violence. This book gives peasants and rural insurgents their due while adding weight to the resistance of other groups, especially peaceful ones, which were ultimately more effective than guerrillas, save for Nicaragua in 1927–1933.[12] It also uncovers links between rural folk, urban resisters, and other groups.

Among those other groups were anti-occupation allies abroad. Unlike in traditional war, anti-occupation activists cannot use their nation-state to resist and instead resort to insurgency, civil disobedience, sabotage, and defiance of censorship. They also operate above the state, appealing to overseas civil societies that collaborate as transnational networks of resistance. In Latin American occupations, links forged in Santiago de Cuba, Tegucigalpa, Mexico City, Buenos Aires, New York, Washington, and elsewhere allowed those living under occupation to communicate their grievances to the Americas, Europe, and beyond. The progressive movement, the growth of higher education, the war in Europe, improvements in communications and transportation, and the global expansion of US power helped spur the creation of overlapping and interlocking transnational networks made up of activists, writers, scholars, religious leaders, and government officials who argued that the era of occupations should come to an end. From 1912 to 1934, these networks helped amplify the messages of the invaded through their informational power and political freedoms as well as an increasingly coherent pan-hemispheric identity. While not supplanting occupied activists, transnational networks provided crucial links to an anti-occupation chain that began with the invaded and ended with policymakers in Washington.[13]

The battle over occupations was primarily a struggle over political culture. The beliefs and practices of politics were what occupiers wanted to change and what the occupied wanted to protect.[14] The repertoire of political culture during US occupations in Latin America included elections, to be sure, but also other goals ranging from a narrow insistence on constitutional forms of rule to efforts to broaden socioeconomic equality, depending on occupiers' own beliefs and prerogatives and on local conditions.[15] In addition, large gaps existed between the rhetoric and practice of political culture. Rhetorically, clear differences over political assumptions distanced occupied Latin Americans from US occupiers. The former spoke of violence as a legitimate tool for achieving political legitimacy; the latter preferred constitutional means. The occupied were personalists, believing in following leaders and parties regardless of ideology; occupiers emphasized platforms and programs. The occupied believed that the state existed mainly to enrich officeholders; occupiers saw government as a collective service. The occupied often operated without an opposition, preferring to repress it; occupiers claimed that occupations should respect civil liberties.

In reality, the occupied cherished their peaceful independence, distrusted their leaders, and knew little about their governments. US occupiers meanwhile pursued peace through war, pluralism through dictatorship, civic responsibility through relieving the occupied of responsibilities, and civil liberties through censorship and repression. This book upholds the central proposition of occupiers—that their primary purpose was to "improve" Latin American political culture—yet takes exception to the assertion that the United States did so for "idealistic" reasons.[16] Equally important, it asserts that political culture, while not originally the primary stake in interventions, became so as other reasons faded to the background.

Resistance to political cultural change emerged from the fact that, in the decades leading up to the Great War in Europe, US policymakers concluded that political culture was the connecting tissue of geopolitical, economic, and cultural rationales for occupation. Stabilizing politics was not necessarily the most urgent problem, but it proved the most convenient rationale. When military fears of European intervention turned out to be exaggerated, US policymakers fell back on their political altruism. When economic rapaciousness could not be admitted or did not exist, the desire for political change did and could. And when policymakers proved unable to recognize their prejudices, they explained culture through identifiable political behaviors. Occupiers stated clearly and often their intent to transform the politics of the occupied.[17]

To be sure, these other motivations may have been sufficient to prompt at least short-term military interventions. Geostrategically, the US Navy wanted to secure the Windward Passage—the natural shipping lane from the Atlantic to the Caribbean that runs between Cuba and Haiti—and partly for that reason acquired a naval base at Guantánamo Bay after the War of 1898. In 1891 and again in 1913, US administrations also tried to buy Haiti's Môle Saint-Nicolas, which stood on the other side of the passage.[18] Dominican leaders offered Samaná Bay, the most attractive spot in the Caribbean for a naval base. By 1914, with war brewing in Europe, the US Navy was even more eager to secure lanes to the newly opened Panama Canal. During the war the United States purchased Mexican oil and Chilean nitrates, crucial for its allies, so keeping enemies out of the Caribbean was crucial.[19] Washington had long wanted a canal in Nicaragua instead of—then in addition to—Panama, and in 1914 it signed the Bryan-Chamorro Treaty, which gave it the right to dig in exchange for $3 million to the Nicaraguan government.[20] Part of Washington's reason for deposing Nicaraguan President

José Santos Zelaya in 1909 was to keep him from selling the canal rights to another power, perhaps Japan.[21] Another common strategic argument was that the United States landed in Haiti in July 1915 because the French cruiser *Des Cartes* arrived in Port-au-Prince and the Germans plotted to do the same.[22]

While geostrategies may have justified interventions, they were insufficient to explain the transformative occupations that followed. The Japanese had no intention of taking Nicaragua or digging a canal. The French merely wanted to protect their lives and property in Haiti and retreated as soon as they saw the US Navy doing the job for them. "Anything likely to cause difficulties with [the] United States should be avoided," ordered the Quai D'Orsay.[23] During World War I, German submarines never operated in the Caribbean.[24] When Robert Lansing, Woodrow Wilson's secretary of state, once explained the Haitian occupation on the basis that he suspected a German move, the *New York Times* responded that that "scarcely justifies" occupation.[25] Naval planners in 1904 did foresee "advance bases" in Haiti and the Dominican Republic that might require occupation, but the idea largely lost its appeal by the late William Howard Taft administration.[26] The navy never acquired the Môle nor Samaná Bay yet continued occupying Haiti and the Dominican Republic after the war.

The marines also protected and promoted US economic interests.[27] By 1912 the United States bought a third of Latin America's exports and sold a quarter of its imports.[28] The Panama Canal opened its locks to many more trading vessels than gunboats.[29] Economic motives got their own policy moniker—"dollar diplomacy." Begun under Theodore Roosevelt and flourishing under Taft, the policy gave out Wall Street loans to Latin American governments in exchange for the right of marines to control the customs houses to pay back those loans. In 1907 the Dominicans signed over their customs in a treaty that became the legal justification for the 1916 landing, and in 1910 the United States set up a collectorship in Nicaragua, the Dawson Pact, modeled after the Dominican one.[30] A $1.5 million loan soon followed, giving Wall Street ownership of the national bank, the national railroad, and a steamship company.[31] Wall Street also muscled its way into Haiti, taking half the national bank and the entire national railway in 1910–1911.[32] All this demonstrated the US intent to expand its economic and financial power in Latin America through intervention.[33]

However, military occupations were far more costly than any investments they might protect. In 1913, Nicaragua, Haiti, and the Dominican Republic together made up less than 1 percent of US investments in the Caribbean basin.[34] In Nicaragua in 1912, US assets amounted to only $2.5 million, 90 percent of them on the sparsely populated east coast.[35] In Haiti pre-occupation investments probably did not rise to $15 million.[36] Further, investments and loans were virtually always secured *before* occupations.[37] Heads of state were only too happy to hand over financial oversight if they could get more loans from the deal, and Haitian elites clamored for financial tutelage like the Dominicans and Nicaraguans had.[38] Occupations, moreover, turned out to be bad for business. Investors stayed away from any place foreigners with guns antagonized natives with guns. In 1910, one US mine manager in Nicaragua discussed how the previous year's revolution had driven away "practically all the native Nicaraguan or 'Spaniards' who are the only men practically suitable for underground work."[39] Finally, virtually no private interests pressured State Department personnel into ordering occupations. The main exception was businessman Roger Farnham, but he scared Wilson with tales of French and German intrigue in Haiti, not of economic catastrophe.[40] The goal of dollar diplomacy therefore was not to enrich US corporations—though that did occur—but to transfer debt from Europe to Wall Street and thus bolster regime stability. As the State Department's Dana Munro wrote, dollar diplomacy's "purpose, under Taft as well as under Wilson, was purely political."[41] Wilson, especially, refused to send troops "at the beck and call of the American dollar."[42] In a speech in Mobile, Alabama, on October 27, 1913, Wilson foresaw the end of unfair loans and subsequent land grabs and predicted Latin America's coming "emancipation from . . . private enterprise."[43]

US cultural rationales also played an undeniable though not primary role in military interventions. The main statement of the progressive movement, Herbert Croly's 1909 *The Promise of American Life*, advocated armed policing of the hemisphere.[44] The racist paternalism of US policymakers even more clearly justified military intervention. In the late nineteenth century the drive began to define the US role in the world as advancing white Anglo-Saxon civilization overseas. In 1886, Josiah Strong's best-selling *Our Country* linked these sentiments to a divine plan for spreading Protestantism. Missionaries were especially imbued with cultural Americanization ideals and unleashed them on Puerto Rico.[45] So were bankers and soldiers. In 1898, the desire to "help free little Cuba" compelled Smedley Butler, at sixteen, to lie about his age so he could fight Spain.[46]

Yet no single policymaker made a case for landing marines primarily on the basis of US cultural superiority or Latin American inferiority.[47] Rather, progressives' morality often led them to counsel restraint in international affairs. Secretary of State William Jennings Bryan concurred with Wilson on this, calling colonialism an "inexcusable blunder."[48]

The desire to remake political culture, however, did compel occupations after short-term rationales for landing faded.[49] Occupations were uniquely intended to reform permanently the institutions, practices, and beliefs of governance.[50] In the narrowest argument, a Latin America in which leaders passed on the reins of government peacefully and contracted no outrageous debts would keep

Europeans at bay. Broader US visions included weeding out corruption and teaching industry and sanitation in ways that would induce foreign investment, eviscerating the need for dollar diplomacy. To many, too, political culture reform was about transferring US values to the hapless poor and the clueless rich. Good culture made for good politics, and good politics made for good business.

Wilson was the prime exponent of political reform, dubbed "constitutionalism" for the president's determination to support only Latin American leaders who won power through constitutional means. "I am going to teach the South American republics to elect good men!" Wilson supposedly said when he refused to recognize Mexico's Victoriano Huerta.[51] Political reformism applied to most US policies and predated Wilson. In 1907, the US government justified the customs receivership by saying that Dominicans spent a full 80 percent of their revenue on government salaries.[52] In lieu of such corruption and waste, Wilson wanted "orderly processes of just government based upon law."[53] Wilson's Mobile speech counseled restraint but also suggested spreading "constitutional liberty" throughout the hemisphere—a contradiction he failed to acknowledge.[54] Six weeks later he specified that "the Wilson doctrine is aimed at the professional revolutionists, the corrupting concessionaires and the corrupt dictators in Latin America. . . . It is a bold doctrine and a radical doctrine."[55] Munro agreed that the first goal of occupations was not to make a profit but to "discourage revolutions." He found the objective "neither sinister nor sordid."[56]

Some within the US government disagreed with coercive political reformism. "You shall not push your remedies for wrong against these republics to the point of occupying their territory," Secretary of State Elihu Root warned during the Theodore Roosevelt administration.[57] Others realized the paradox of occupations that sought self-government by Latin Americans by sapping self-government from Latin Americans. When in 1916 Wilson circulated a speech that included the line, "It shall not lie with the American people to dictate to another what their government shall be," his own secretary of state scribbled in the margin, "Haiti, S. Domingo, Nicaragua, Panama."[58]

Yet the desire for reshaping Latin Americans' political behavior rode an unstoppable momentum, especially in response to events in small republics in the circum-Caribbean. In 1915, Haiti had had seven presidents assassinated or overthrown in four years.[59] The Dominican Republic was also caught up in rapid revolutionary cycles after the death of President Ramón de Cáceres in 1911.[60] And Nicaragua degenerated into civil war in 1912. Such events tended to simplify rationales for occupation and draw US gunships.

Although the motivations of occupiers were important, those who most tried to stop the coming of occupations were Latin Americans themselves, who often reminded US policymakers that they had signed on to peaceful resolution methods, such as in the 1907 Dominican treaty.[61] When diplomacy failed, the threat of occupation bristled Latin Americans; occupation itself enraged them. A US major general spying in Mexico in 1911 reported that when a mere rumor of an invasion spread, "Mexicans of the better classes did not hesitate to inform American residents that not a 'Gringo' would escape assassination."[62] When the US government took over Veracruz in 1914 for seven months, riots erupted throughout Mexico. Eggs, rocks, and tomatoes rained on the many US citizens who fled.[63]

Resistance to gunboat threats also arose in Nicaragua, Haiti, and the Dominican Republic. In the first, President Zelaya and memories of his overthrow were the primary obstacles to a landing. Initially pro-United States, in 1906–1907 Zelaya opposed US meddling in a war between Guatemala and El Salvador, seeing it as a threat to his own hegemony over Central America.[64] There were other issues—loans contracted outside the United States, the slow settlement of claims, flirtations with Germany and Japan, the execution of two US adventurers, and especially the US decision not to build a canal in Nicaragua. In late 1909, Secretary of State Philander Knox, whose former law firm represented US mining interests in conflict with the Nicaraguan president, broke diplomatic relations and sent a thousand marines to overthrow Zelaya. The Nicaraguan fled to Mexico, where shouts of "Death to the Yankee!" greeted his every appearance.[65]

Haitians' bloody eighteenth-century revolution against the slaveholding *blancs* and the century-long diplomatic isolation that followed convinced them that no white man valued Haiti's welfare. Haitians encoded within their constitutions prohibitions against white, later foreign, landownership and rejected Washington's attempts to buy the Môle Saint-Nicolas. In the 1910s, anti-foreign sentiment swelled, targeting first Syrians and then the French, Germans, and Dutch.[66] In 1915, a rebellion broke out against the MacDonald railroad concession in the north.[67]

After the 1907 customs treaty, which banned new loans without Washington's approval, Dominicans also resisted additional encroachments that might lead to occupation.[68] In 1911, the Dominican Congress rejected a US project to install a US director of public works and financial advisor with expanded powers. Wilson soon threatened a marine landing if his conditions were not met. In 1912, Santo Domingo declared Spanish the national language.[69] In November 1915, after taking over Haiti, Washington increased its demands on Dominicans, including replacing their military with a US-led constabulary. The administration of President Juan Isidro Jimenes rejected what it called "an abdication of national sovereignty."[70]

And so, in the early 1910s, Washington stood ready to reform through occupation the political culture of its southern neighbors, a political culture that degenerated into violence partly because of previous US intervention. The paradox was obvious to many Latin Americans, but the enormous power differential between the United States and the small nations of the circum-Caribbean easily overwhelmed the will to resist.

The Invaded is organized largely chronologically so as to capture an evolving multinational story of opposition and US response from the landing in Nicaragua in 1912 to the withdrawal from Haiti in 1934. The first three chapters relate Latin American responses to initial landings, arguing that these interventions prompted a first wave of violent and peaceful revolts based largely on national strongmen's fear of losing political power. The next five chapters examine a second wave of resistance, made up of longer revolts by regional and local strongmen, their followers, and ordinary people, against the style of occupation rather than the fact of intervention. Part III, consisting of thematic chapters on culture and politics, shows how occupations threatened values and practices that had little to do with nationalism but rather with concrete ways of life that would not easily be transformed by reformist marines. The final four chapters focus on peaceful resistance movements, including transnational networks, that followed the defeat of insurgencies in Haiti and the Dominican Republic, as well as the final years of the struggle of Augusto Sandino.[71]

The major claims of this book—that the invaded resisted because of local autonomy rather than nationalism; that resistance was effective for this very reason; that peaceful activists were as central to the struggle as were violent guerrillas; and that transnationalism amplified all these struggles—contribute to a historical narrative of the era of occupations that is still, a century later, incomplete, misunderstood, and romanticized. These cases were specific to their time, space, and culture, and a familiarity with Nicaragua, Haiti, and the Dominican Republic is essential to grasping both their uniqueness and their similarities. These cases also show that the first third of the twentieth century stood neither as an aberration of US expansion nor as an exemplar of timeless US behavior in times of occupation. While the conclusion draws present-day lessons from these occupations, the specific circumstances of every US occupation should be kept foremost in mind. Falling short of respecting the local and the concrete would dishonor the memory of the invaded.

PART ONE

INTERVENTION RESISTANCE

1

Nicaragua, 1912

So bitter as to be scarcely understood by civilised people.
—Smedley Butler, on Nicaraguan political parties

The US intervention of 1912 in Nicaragua was a typical case of first-wave intervention resistance, with a distinction. Behind the resistance lay a long-simmering distrust of US dollar diplomacy in Nicaragua, and militarily the intervention was swift and effective. What distinguished Nicaraguans' anger from that of subsequent invaded peoples was the intensity of their attachment to political parties. It colored all their political decisions, including their resistance to debarking marines. Paradoxically, that distinction drove US invaders to try to change Nicaraguan political culture permanently, laying the groundwork for a generation-long occupation.

In seeing so-called national or federal *caudillos* displaced from power, Nicaragua in 1912 shared a key characteristic with the Haitian and Dominican resistance to landings in 1915 and 1916, respectively. Strongmen who practiced politics through violence dominated Latin America in the nineteenth century, aided by weak nation-states after the departure of European colonizers. That weakness was evident in the state's inability to raise enough taxes or provide services, its lack of national consciousness, and especially its inability to monopolize force. National caudillos sat atop a precarious pyramid of authority, with most of the political loyalty and military force at the bottom, in towns and provinces. Caudillos who held on to power in the capital were vulnerable to foreign intervention, especially if competitors called on the marines to provide the required monopoly of force.[1] In the early twentieth century, while this state of affairs dissipated in larger, more industrializing nations such as Venezuela and Argentina, in Central America and the Caribbean, nation-state formation remained embryonic.[2]

A major reason for the bottom-heavy allocation of pyramidal power was the clientelist nature of *caudillismo*. From the pampas of Argentina in the 1840s to the partisan towns of Nicaragua in the 1910s, strongmen, whether national party leaders or local chieftains, mobilized followers largely through a two-way exchange of favors. Followers' interests could certainly be emotional and political, but they were often also hardheaded and material: they risked their lives and butchered their leader's enemies for rewards of all kinds, including protection, sociability, promotions, a political voice, even a steady supply of shoes and beef.[3] The first wave of US interventions offered only a glimpse of these relationships, but their potential for resistance became more salient as interventions settled into occupations. Initial interventions also presaged a more popular resistance outside the purview of caudillos: one equally material, partly nationalist, yet devoid of partisan interest.

In Nicaragua, caudillismo expressed itself in the form of political parties more than in the Dominican Republic and Haiti. Before the land consolidation of the 1920s and 1930s led by sugar and cattle, coffee was Nicaragua's economic driving force. Largely cultivated on small, independently owned farms, it brought relative equality, social mobility, and stability.[4] Such attributes may have driven Nicaraguans to follow family-oriented, non-ideological Conservative and Liberal parties, whose personal and political vendettas tended to overwhelm antagonisms to the United States.

In 1912, invading marines struggled to grasp such complexity. But intervention contained a paradox: meant to stabilize political culture through strengthening the nation-state, it instead made state-builders appear to be collaborators, destroyed incipient processes of centralization under national caudillos, and encouraged further rebellion from local caudillos.

The military intervention of 1912 ended in a quick, decisive victory for Washington and its Nicaraguan allies.[5] In the midst of a civil war, on August 3, Nicaraguan Minister of Foreign Relations Diego Chamorro warned of a danger to US lives and property in Managua and asked Washington for an intervention force.[6] The following day, 100 bluejackets or navy sailors went to the capital to guard the US legation. In mid-August Major Smedley Butler joined them from Panama with 354 marines.[7] Within a few more weeks there were 2,350 US forces in Nicaragua, more than enough to overtake any Nicaraguan challenger.

Overtake they did. On September 24, the leader of the rebellion, Secretary of War General Luis Mena, surrendered to Butler and his marines. Two days later he was on a ship to Panama, promising never to return.[8] On October 4 came the decisive defeat of one of Mena's generals, Benjamín Zeledón. Two days later the marines took the town of León. On October 8, the war was over.[9] By the end of 1912, only 120 marines were left.[10] "The disturbance of the peace in Nicaragua has now ceased," cabled Admiral William Southerland, who commanded the navy forces, "and public feeling is quieting down."[11]

Had it? What had disturbed the peace and how did that disturbance portend resistance to the remaining force of 100?

Before the intervention, Nicaraguans, among all Latin American peoples, perhaps most resented the long-term economic and strategic control that Washington and Wall Street arrogated over Latin America. Nicaragua was deep in debt after the José Santos Zelaya dictatorship and the 1909–1910 civil war, and by 1913 foreigners owned 40 percent of that debt.[12] In 1911 and 1912, the US State Department brokered classic "dollar diplomacy" bargains in which Nicaragua got $2.25 million in loans from bankers Brown Brothers and J. and W. Seligman, in return for which the two corporations received a 51 percent share of the National Railway and the country's steamers and wharves.[13] Mena seized the company's steamers during his rebellion.[14]

The deals united Nicaraguans in hostility, a stunning feat considering their extreme partisanship. In 1911, the US minister found "an overwhelming majority of Nicaraguans . . . antagonistic to the United States" because of the loans.[15] When Secretary of State Philander Knox visited in March 1912, rumors of an assassination attempt abounded, and President Adolfo Díaz jailed demonstrators and muzzled the press.[16] Knox still met with hostility from both parties. Liberals, then out of power, greeted the secretary with violent demonstrations while Conservatives engaged in angry speeches, accusing fellow Conservatives who signed the loan deals of an "Americanizing mania."[17] The assemblyman who introduced Knox to the National Assembly sarcastically derided US meddling.[18] Part of the suspicion centered on the deal-brokers themselves: Knox was the former lawyer of the La Luz and Los Angeles Mining Company, prominent in Nicaragua, and Díaz was its former bookkeeper, and everyone knew it.[19]

Nicaraguan opposition to the deals went even deeper. In September 1912 Liberal delegate and revolutionary Leonardo Argüello expressed to Admiral Southerland his three-fold opposition to the landing. Argüello argued that any intervention weakened Nicaragua's sovereignty and independence. He also rejected the right of the United States to defend its property—the banks' railroad—since it rested on land owned by the Nicaraguan people. Finally he questioned the concept of a government intervening on behalf of a private company.[20] Although Argüello articulated a thorough rejection of dollar diplomacy shared by Mena and others, Butler dismissed such arguments as "rot."[21]

There were other reasons for the temporary Nicaraguan unity. Mena posited a popular, non-Spanish, mixed-race identity for Nicaragua. He also marshaled a bipartisan alliance, naming a Liberal, Zeledón, as co-commander. When Mena launched his rebellion in July 1912, he fled with 600 troops to the Liberal town of Masaya, set up an alternate National Assembly, symbolically deposed Díaz, and later bombarded Managua. On August 3 it was US minister to Nicaragua

George Weitzel who prodded Díaz to request intervention.[22] The State Department's Dana Munro recalled that "North Americans were in real danger because Mena's followers as well as the liberals were resentful toward the United States." Two US citizens apparently died in the bombardment of Managua and many more petitioned for succor.[23]

Partisans, however, exaggerated the danger of violence against US citizens. One member of the American colony in Matagalpa attended a ball in 1912 at which "we all learned that there never had been danger or threat of massacre or molestation of foreigners." Furthermore, "the whole massacre story was an arrant hoax, sent out, as was openly avowed to me, for the purpose of bringing US forces into Nicaragua so as to cow and overawe the Nicaraguan liberals."[24]

Indeed, after the landing of 1912, US forces identified with Díaz and against the Liberals. Butler naïvely thought he was a peacemaker and expressed surprise when he received an order "virtually changing our status from neutral to partisanship with the Government forces. This goes back on all the things I have told the rebels."[25] Late in his life the US military court-martialed Butler when he implied that the Department of State had rigged the elections of 1912 in favor of Díaz by proscribing most Liberal politicians from participating, a move that engendered further opposition to US intervention.[26] Once president, Díaz understood his marching orders in favor of US investors. As one US mine manager wrote in December 1912, after the rebellion, "If those people out there [US investors] want mines, I should think that now would be the time to get them—That [Díaz] Government will be run from Washington more than from Managua."[27]

Before such a US-friendly government could function, however, Mena had to be conquered. The landing marked the first time marines walked into Managua and was the largest US force to date in Central America. Two to five thousand Nicaraguans died during the civil war and US intervention.[28] Butler wrote that the enmity between Nicaraguans was "so bitter as to be scarcely understood by civilised people."[29]

There was plenty of bitterness left over for the invaders. The first incidents of resistance in spring 1912 were attacks on Granada, a Conservative town. After a drought, hungry farmers overcrowded cities, including Granada, and many blamed the United States, saying, "The Conservatives sold the country and the gringos don't care if the people of Nicaragua die of hunger."[30] More specifically, a US official in charge of Nicaragua's custom duties held up government imports of grains. In June, when the government did buy grains, the move brought inflation and a more dire situation. Hunger and crime soared. To make matters still worse, Zeledón and his rebels—the majority of them dissident Conservatives— blamed Granadan elites for the fall of Zelaya, so they tortured and humiliated the town's men and women for two months.[31]

Early September 1912 brought a second episode of violence in Granada, focused on foreigners, especially US citizens. Artisans and peasants locked victims
in dark, filthy cells, forced them to sleep on manure, and starved them for days.
They dunked heads into filthy toilets and reportedly raped women. Lower-class
Nicaraguans were especially invested in symbolic humiliations, such as stripping
elites naked in public and hurling insults such as "Yankee pigs!"[32] Some victims
"went into hysterics" while others became "temporarily insane."[33] The violence
ended only when US troops entered.[34] The troops found Granadans close to
starvation, one woman planning to put her five children in a boat and drown
them rather than see them perish from hunger.[35]

This situation reinforced the US sense that the marines were undertaking a
purely humanitarian mission.[36] Marine dispatches never took responsibility for
the hunger and revolution but merely noted "the most terrible destitution" of
Granadans.[37] Some townspeople contributed to this misperception. One letter
signed by sixty-one self-described representatives of "the highest social, political
and financial standing not only of Granada but of the country" thanked Butler
and his troops for putting an end to "the horrors of an organized anarchy." "The
lamentable condition of these [Central American] countries, perturbed by constant uprisings, is all the sadder when we consider their proximity to the great
American nation, which founded on wise institutions and inspired by the spirit
of liberty and justice, marches at the head of the destiny of humanity."[38] Two
hundred and sixteen "ladies of Granada" expressed similar gratitude.[39] Such sentiment prompted one US officer to write to the secretary of the navy, "Though in
theory Nicaraguans hate Americans, they actually have a child-like faith in our
kindness, helpfulness, and innate fairness."[40]

A further episode of resistance was the "martyrdom" of General Benjamín
Zeledón. Butler described the thirty-three-year-old as "a short plump man with
a dark mustache" who "didn't look very military in his Panama hat and civilian
clothes."[41] Nevertheless, on August 11–13 Zeledón bombarded Managua and
by September had retreated to two fortified, never-taken hills outside Masaya,
some fifteen miles north of the capital, which stood in the way of the US-owned
railroad from Corinto to Granada. Butler had orders to clear the railroad and
remove Zeledón as an obstacle.

Formerly a judge, attorney general, and the president of the National Liberty
Club, Zeledón had married the great-granddaughter of a former president of Nicaragua and founder of the Liberal Party. Zeledón's ideal democracy was a highly
partisan one in which political parties alternated power but meanwhile ruled
without opposition. "We should not try to fool ourselves," he once wrote, "with
tales of national administration, national politics, and national government."[42] It
was ironic, then, that he would now be allied with a Conservative. Nevertheless,
in the heat of resistance, Zeledón wrote to US officers expressing his nationalism

and his anti-imperialist understanding of Nicaragua's place in the world.[43] His narrow legal claim was that the loan agreements of 1911–1912 suspended all transportation in case of war, obviating the need for the marines to clear the railroad. More broadly he cited international rights for small nations, the latest press attention to pan-Americanism, former secretary of state Elihu Root on fraternity in the Americas, and even George Washington on being noble toward other nations. All this meant to accuse the United States of acting "outside accepted norms of civilization." The ouster of Zelaya, he recalled, had set "a unique precedent in international law: the suppression of internal despotism by external despotism." Finally, like the Granadan elites, Zeledón expressed his admiration for a nation "that I admire and respect for its size and power; but that I do not wish as my country's conqueror."[44]

On October 3 Zeledón, surrounded, refused to surrunder to Colonel Joseph Pendleton and pledged to fight to the death for "the dignity of Nicaragua."[45] "We lack everything: provisions, arms and munitions, we are surrounded by cannons and thousands of men ready to pounce," he wrote the same day to his wife. "It would be madness to expect a fate different from death."[46] He met that fate the following day. Based solely on the fact that he refused to surrender on paper, Nicaraguans embraced Zeledón as a hero killed by the United States.[47] Yet nowhere does the record show that US troops killed Zeledón. Hours after the Nicaraguan's death, Minister Weitzel wrote that Zeledón fled with twenty generals even before the fighting began, that it was Nicaraguan government forces who shot at Zeledón's party, and that Zeledón died from his wounds shortly after.[48] Adding to the confusion, Butler wrote to Southerland that same day claiming that government forces were holding Zeledón for rendition to Butler. "Personally would suggest that through some inaction on our part some one might hang him," added Butler.[49] Zeledón's band was further rumored to be fleeing toward Costa Rica and to have killed three women along the way so as to keep their whereabouts secret. Others still said Zeledón did not sneak away but hid in a church in Masaya.[50] No matter the truth, the legend of one Nicaraguan leader resisting US invasion for non-partisan reasons struck a chord.

Many ordinary people did the same, resisting US troops apparently against the will of their superiors—an indication of their incipient independence from caudillos. Rebels in mid-September attacked a train occupied by Butler's men, four of whom were injured.[51] As the engine rolled into Masaya, a man on horseback thundered toward the train and shot at Butler himself. Then six or seven others "started to blaze away at the train," soon backed by firing from surrounding streets and houses, "everybody shooting in every direction." A delegation from Zeledón explained that the attack was by "unauthorized" rebels, and Zeledón let the train pass.[52]

The greatest instance of mass resistance to the US landing occurred in León, a Liberal stronghold and a stop on the railway that Washington wanted cleared. In mid-August, rebels trapped a Conservative detachment in a square and massacred it. A few days later US Captain Nelson Vulte was in town with his troops but could not get his train out through the barrage of fire. He wrote in his diary: "All along the streets they showed their hostility, even women spat at us, many women were armed with rifles and machetes, it was a crazy mob."[53] On August 21 another determined group forced Commander Warren Terhune and his men to get off their train and walk the fifty-five miles back to Managua in pouring rain. León's leaders privately told Terhune they could not restrain the mob.[54] "Oh, you don't know that crowd," said Terhune after the ordeal. "They're bloodthirsty."[55]

Butler, on a quest to recapture the train, told a similar tale of popular resentment. The people of León—notably, angry women—threatened violence and placed themselves before the slowly advancing engine. "As we came into the city about 1000 excited men, women and children surrounded our train, all armed with various instruments of torture, from rifles to razors." Butler, brash as ever, defied them to shoot and obtained their acquiescence.[56]

Throughout September, a diary likely belonging to marine Lieutenant Colonel Charles Long reported continuing anger in the populace. As marines moved material from one train to another, "there were perhaps 300 armed men in the vicinity but many women and children were also present. The people appeared to suspect our object and to resent our appearance in such force. The movements and gesticulations of the crowd were decidedly hostile." Some explained that they feared US-controlled trains would help the Conservatives.[57] He also asked a Conservative general to help him secure workers, assuring them that they "would not be compromising themselves by working for us."[58] One telegraph operator in León took his own life rather than compromise himself.[59]

The US occupation of León after Zeledón's death gave rise to more violence, this time a mixture of partisanship and popular anti-interventionism. The commander of a thousand-man battalion marching into town on October 6 reported that "firing began almost immediately from the brushes." "Serious opposition" grew as 200 León inhabitants fired from churches and private homes. They killed three marines, who shot back 5,000 rounds and killed fifty inhabitants. Marines arrested several men but found no evidence of their firing weapons. They encountered for the first time the Nicaraguan tradition of mutilation: rebels hacked one marine's corpse with machetes and took his clothes and shoes.[60]

Long was correct that the hostility was political in nature. Liberals had long stoked anti-US sentiment in León by associating Conservatives with external rule. One León poet warned in 1912 of "the blond pigs of Pennsylvania advancing on our gardens of beauty."[61] The town quieted down after Mena's surrender on September 24 and even more so after US troops took León on October 7.[62] Fearing massacres by Conservatives after the war, Southerland ordered Managua evacuated of *leonses* or inhabitants of León. "Any slaughter would be on our shoulders, and the brute in these people is too strong to let such a chance of getting the blood of their enemies go."[63]

Another type of resistance was more grassroots and spontaneous. After Liberal chiefs surrendered, they told the US commander that "they could not control all their soldiers as many had refused to give up their arms and had decided to fight us to the bitter [end should] we attempt to disarm them and take over the city."[64] Troops in Chinandega met similar resistance.[65] Perhaps more illustrative was the rejection of the material consequences of the US presence. According to Long's diary, two Nicaraguan women, helped by a longtime US citizen living in Nicaragua whom the troops called "the negro Thompson," complained that navy and marine troops had stolen "wood and boards . . . from their houses and grounds." Another Nicaraguan sought his cattle, allegedly stolen by the invading US troops. Another wanted to be paid for marines drinking his water. Few Nicaraguans would lend the foreigners their bull carts.[66]

For all the popular resistance, the accusation of collusion between Conservatives and Washington remained accurate, and the invasion widened political divides. After marines landed, the workers of a sugar mill in Chichigalpa became more strongly Liberal and identified the owners of the mill more strictly as Conservatives. On the day of Zeledón's death, Chichigalpans attacked Long and his troops, again disregarding orders from their officers.[67]

Long described the politicization of León as an outgrowth of social categories. "It was the people known as Artesanos who rose and took Leon," he wrote. "They do not leave town and are quite capable of repeating such uprisings frequently." Urban artisans, not rural peasants, were most tied to political violence.[68]

Most US officers and diplomats failed to understand the popular sources of resistance or suggest remedies in tune with Nicaraguan sovereignty. Their perspective was jingoistic and often racist. Butler, an exemplar of this group, said one hostile Nicaraguan group reminded him of his son Tommy "playing Indian." Butler disrespected Nicaraguan traditions and insulted their honor by disdaining all ceremony.[69] Southerland, while more diplomatic, saw only the similarities with China's Boxer Rebellion, an analogy also drawn by the newly created Latin American Division at the Department of State and President William Howard Taft.[70] This discourse suggested that the brutal war in the Philippines and experiences in China at the turn of the century had darkened the mood of US foreign policymakers toward anti-interventionism in the developing world, leading marines and diplomats to associate rebellions exclusively with xenophobia and danger to foreign lives and property.

The political consequences for Nicaragua soon came. Long rejected the Liberal request for elections under US supervision.[71] He suggested instead "the just despotism of an American Governor General."[72] The State Department instead chose to restore Conservatives under Díaz and exclude Liberals from power sharing. If Washington hoped to erase its footprint after most troops withdrew, it failed. For years afterward, Nicaraguan mothers invoked Butler to frighten their children: "Hush! Major Butler will get you."[73]

2

Haiti, 1915

That we are here, whose fault is it?

—Candio, "On the Convention"

In Haiti as in Nicaragua, the first wave of resistance to US occupations was largely in response to the fact itself of occupation. Political "disorder," in US eyes, prompted the landing, and the political system reacted strongly to the threat of Yankee centralization. Haitians who resisted feared losing a decentralized political system with caudillismo at its top. In Haiti the top was unusually precarious, even for the Caribbean area, and a remarkable number of Haitians agreed with the intervention in July 1915. That would change as the wave of intervention resistance receded at the end of that year.

In Haiti, Rosalvo Bobo both embodied the fragility of national caudillos and caused the breakdown that prompted intervention. Bobo was among the most unsteady of caudillos. Secretary of State Robert Lansing called him "mentally unbalanced and brutally savage in his treatment of his enemies when they fall into his hands."[1] A dandy with light skin, blue eyes, and a Paris doctorate, Bobo married the eloquence of the Haitian elite with the passion of a revolutionary.[2] His chief of staff boasted that 3,000 to 4,000 men followed the fiery redhead, and he did have at least 500 adherents.[3]

Transborder support was one source of Bobo's power. His cacos, or private fighting force, rural and uneducated, obtained their weapons and ammunition in part from the neighboring Dominican Republic, contraband bringing in hefty profits for Dominican provincial officials far from their own capital. It was to that mountainous border that Bobo's forces ran when government troops chased them.[4]

Bobo claimed to harbor no anti-US sentiment but plenty of nationalist defense of sovereignty. In early June 1915 he signed a public placard in Cap-Haïtien "to explain to you my sentiments towards Americans. There is no people whose genius and industrial activity I admire more than theirs. To

introduce into our country its industries, its capital, its methods of work—
is one of my most ardent and constant dreams. But to turn over to them our
custom houses and our finances, to put ourselves under their tutelage, never,
never, NEVER."[5] Bobo once suggested during a Cabinet meeting that Haitians
could avoid a US fiscal protectorate if government officials, himself included,
accepted a reduction in their salaries. The Cabinet responded by throwing him
out, whereupon he embarked on his revolution. Bobo was the only Haitian
willing to undertake a reform propounded by Washington, yet Washington
drove him from power.[6]

The US Navy identified Bobo as counter to US interests because he threatened the centralization of power around the government of President Vilbrun Guillaume Sam. Captain Edward Beach, chief of staff for Admiral William
Caperton, who ran the early occupation, thought that Bobo was personally fit to
be president—but the fact that he led an insurrectionist caco army disqualified
him. The navy landed at Cap-Haïtien, Haiti's second biggest town, in early July
1915 to drive out Bobo. On July 4, Beach walked with a small party from the Cap
to Bobo's camp. "A more villainous appearing set of men were never gathered
together" is how Beach described the first meeting of cacos with US citizens.
"All were but slightly clad, and each was armed with a musket, a pistol, a sword,
and a long, vicious-looking knife." Beach delivered Caperton's warning of US
intervention if cacos entered the Cap, which failed.[7] Caperton would later post
a larger force in Cap-Haïtien than in Port-au-Prince "on account of its being the
center of all revolutionary activities."[8]

The belief that US forces protected President Sam—unwarranted, since Sam
had failed to negotiate such protection—precipitated the takeover of the entire
country.[9] Opponents of Sam—some followers of Bobo, others not—wanted
to depose the president before he could gain Caperton's protection. Sam attempted to stop this cycle of coups by jailing opposition leaders. Then he had
167 of them shot and bayoneted through the bars of their cells.[10] On July 27,
furious anti-government forces looking to avenge this massacre stormed the
National Palace. Sam's guard deserted, forcing him to flee. The mob looked for
the president and his allies first in the Dominican, then the French legation,
where they found Sam cowering behind a bathroom dresser. A group of forty—
some politicians, some relatives of slain prisoners—dragged him into the street,
killed him, and literally tore him to pieces, parading the body parts on spikes
through Port-au-Prince (see Fig. 2.1).[11] Caperton cabled, "No government or
authority in city. Many rival leaders in town."[12] Centralization had backfired with
a gruesome vengeance.

Though there were no threats against foreign lives or property, even during
the storming of the French legation, the diplomatic corps requested the landing of troops.[13] The grisly lynching of Sam prompted foreigners and especially

Figure 2.1 An alleged photo, perhaps taken from the US legation, of the mob dragging the body of President Vilbrun Guillaume Sam through Port-au-Prince, July 1915. The body is at center left. Folder "Haiti: Officials," USMC Historical Division, Marine Corps Base, Quantico, Va.

US citizens to discuss their rationale for occupation. In a cable, Caperton judged poverty to be an important factor but mainly a byproduct of the political vacuum left by Sam's assassination. "One element dangerous Port au Prince is large number unemployed men and disarmed soldiers. . . . Treasury totally without money and there are no Government officials."[14] Secretary Lansing saw as a primary goal to "conserve the customs and prevent their receipt by irresponsible persons" and saw the humanitarian motivation—to save starving Haitians in Port-au-Prince—as a convenient "excuse" for economic and political stabilization.[15] He wrote to President Woodrow Wilson that a "high handed" occupation was warranted "if we intend to cure the anarchy and disorder which prevails in that Republic."[16]

At the State Department's Division of Latin-American Affairs, talk was also primarily about political reform. An unsigned memo, likely written by division chief Boaz Long, observed "a chronic political unrest" evident in

  I. A lack of public opinion,
 II. No sense of public responsibility,
III. Complete political incompetence,
IV. Growing demoralization generally.

"These facts," the memo continued, "all point to the failure of an inferior people to maintain the degree of civilization left them by the French, or to develop any capacity of self government entitling them to international respect or confidence." The memo recommended "complete forcible intervention" and an initial stay of thirty-three years, renewable for another thirty-three.[17] To Long, the control of customs was a means to this political end, not the other way around. Taking the customs "would remove from the reach of Haitian politicians the prize in money for which all wage war."[18] Wilson agreed to a "long programme" of legislative and treaty changes.[19]

The arrest of a former senator, Joseph Dessources, illustrated the on-the-ground complications inherent in attempting to change political culture. Upon the landing of troops, the hastily formed Revolutionary Committee, composed of elite Haitians wishing to choose the next government, imprisoned Dessources for allegedly "fomenting feeling against America."[20] A quick navy investigation revealed that Dessources was in fact "agitating against the Revolutionary Committee," not Washington. Navy Captain George Van Orden pledged to arrest any Committee member arresting *its* opponents. The Committee's General Ermane Robin was furious: "that method of doing business in Haiti would never be successful," he told Van Orden, warning that Washington was "courting trouble." Van Orden responded that his "duty" was to meet that trouble head-on. Robin retorted that "perhaps we would not meet again in friendship."[21] Soon after, a Wesleyan Mission was mobbed and Haitian soldiers secreted arms despite the call to disband and disarm.[22]

Select Haitians' fear of losing—or not gaining—political power primarily motivated resistance to intervention. "Men who won Revolution," Caperton cabled about Bobo and the Revolutionary Committee, "fear action of United States may prevent them from securing to them result of overthrow of government." Beach concluded: "these rapidly succeeding revolutions do not possess a spark of patriotism."[23]

Bobo was but the most recent figurehead representing entrenched networks of political interests and practices. Cacos were little invested in the public good since observers universally noted that many were mercenaries or forced conscripts, yet they were motivated by political power.[24] Caperton called the Haitian cacos "professional soldiers . . . organized in bands under irresponsible and lawless chiefs who side with the party offering greatest inducement and only nominally recognize the government." He noted their effective political clout by the fact that Bobo's cacos made it impossible for the "terrorized" Haitian Congress to choose anyone else as president.[25] Marine Brigadier General Eli Cole distinguished between "good Cacos" and "bad Cacos," the former being farmers who engaged in revolution "from time to time," while the latter were "objectors to work" who robbed and extorted when not fomenting revolution (see

Figure 2.2 Caco chiefs or generals, about October 1915. Folder "Haiti: Officials,"
USMC Historical Division, Marine Corps Base, Quantico, Va.

Fig. 2.2).[26] The bottom line was, to Caperton: "A stable government in Haiti is
not possible until Cacos bands are broken up and their power broken."[27]

On one hand, these insurrectionists resisted centralization: before 1915, for
instance, cacos rebelled against the planned construction of a US-sponsored
railroad.[28] On the other hand, they contributed to it. All had networks of leaders—some nearby, others in faraway towns—and were connected to elite politicians. Some identified with the elite and likely wanted to gain state power for
themselves or someone else. President Sam was such a man. In March 1915 the
former life convict paid 3,000 lumberjacks and other cacos in northern Haiti
to march south and install him as president.[29] Lesser caco chiefs tended to be
peasants with some contacts in towns, some land of their own, some leadership
qualities, and some ability to read and write.[30] Others still, as journalist Harry
Frank wrote, were "merely the mouthpieces of disgruntled politicians or influential 'respectable citizens' of Port-au-Prince or several others of the larger cities,
who secretly supply funds to the active insurrectionists."[31]

The first wave of resistance—the first months of the intervention—involved
fiercer fighting than US Marines let on in their memoirs. It reflected the primary
motivation of caudillos and their insurrectionist army—to defend regional and
local autonomy from a central administration strengthened by an occupation
force.

To be sure, there was little resistance to the initial landing in the capital, reflecting the fatalism of the body politic in Port-au-Prince. Haitian statesman
Dantès Bellegarde recalled that in July 1915 no one "organized resistance. None

of our political men dared take on that responsibility," judging it "useless." The occupation should have been "a national question" but was instead "an *affaire* of domestic politics."[32]

Still, US officials reported that the first 330 sailors and marines to land on July 28, 1915, met with "considerable sniping . . . from civilians and soldiers," which continued for two more days.[33] On August 6, Caperton ordered all cacos out of the capital. Then his troops began to round them up, prompting Haitians to fire on marines. When the prisoners escaped, the crowd panicked, and Caperton declared a curfew.[34] The *New York Herald* described the riot as fomented "by men of the lower classes" after they realized "that the occupation of Port au Prince by the American forces is complete."[35]

Haitians also practiced non-violent forms of resistance. Sergeant Faustin Wirkus recalled "walls of human silence and dead-eyed stares" greeting him and other arriving troops.[36] Haitians dumped their waste from second-story dwellings onto curfew patrols.[37] The first few days also saw large demonstrations, notably to welcome Bobo to Port-au-Prince.[38] Some circulated the rumor that the Yankees' true aim was to secure Môle Saint-Nicolas for a naval base.[39]

Yet the resistance was disorganized and ineffective. No US troops were even hit during the first clash.[40] Two sailors died later that day, but from friendly fire.[41] On August 4 the Second Marine Regiment arrived, taking the fight out of most Port-au-Prince cacos.[42] By the end of the month, 2,000 marines occupied Haiti.[43]

Bobo's incompatibility with US political culture sealed his own fate. In early August, Caperton met with him and Sudre Dartiguenave, the other Haitian he considered for president. Caperton asked both if they would support the other as president. Dartiguenave said yes. Bobo shouted: "No, I will not! If Senator Dartiguenave is elected president I will not help him." His narcissism getting the better of him, he continued, "No one is fit to be president but me; there is no patriotism in Haiti to be compared with mine; the Haitians love no one as they love me."[44] The non-ideological regionalism of caudillo rule also became clear when Caperton invited Bobo's generals to accept Dartiguenave as president and surrender their weapons. "They said Bobo . . . was the favorite of all the North, that he was entitled to a majority vote, that they would remain loyal to Bobo, that if he were President they would cheerfully acquiesce in any concessions he made to the United States."[45]

Bobo might have secured the presidency had he understood the importance the United States placed on peaceful political opposition. But since Bobo stood his ground, Caperton chose Dartiguenave instead and planned for his election by Congress, which Bobo's allies there failed to prevent.[46] Disheartened and broke, Bobo boarded a United Fruit ship to Jamaica on October 7, 1915.[47]

Although Bobo ordered his men to disarm, few obeyed. Instead, they broke into small groups and pillaged and burned plantations. They cut off food and water supplies to towns, held up the coffee crop—the country's largest export—and committed "acts of depredation against foreign property, the farmers, and the market women." Their cause was that they had not been "given money for rations."[48]

Unlike the reception in Nicaragua in 1912 and a year later in Santo Domingo, some marines reported Haitians welcoming the landing force. Beach described crowds near the presidential palace as filled with "relief and joy." It was the trust by elites, who asked US forces to supervise elections, that convinced Beach and Caperton to claim the authority to choose a president.[49]

Haitians described such responses as reflecting resignation. A palace guard remembered that when he saw the USS *Washington* and the flotilla of launches dropping off men with guns, "Everyone fled. Me too. You had only to see them, with their weaponry, their massive, menacing appearance, to understand both that they came to do harm to our country and that resistance was futile." He returned the following day and saw even more men land. "I understood then that something new in our history had begun. With these people, I could not live. I took to the woods."[50] The French minister to Haiti, Girard, saw a more complex reaction—"a minority that, chastened by these last years, overtly recognizes the incapacity of Haitians to govern themselves, and an anti-American majority, composed in large part . . . of people interested in not seeing too much order in the administration of the country." Many in the latter group, he continued, looked to the US occupation of Veracruz the previous year, where troops pulled up stakes after six months, as what they could expect.[51]

Some politicians mobilized immediately. The day after Dartiguenave's "election," they founded an opposition newspaper. Two more soon followed.[52] It was partly for that reason that Caperton declared martial law: "The newspapers were defaming us and me individually, and everything was running riot."[53] Many of these newspapermen, led by lawyer Georges Sylvain, banded as the Patriotic Union (UP), with the explicit mission of spreading propaganda in Haiti and beyond.[54] The UP held courses on patriotism that focused on land issues, corporate abuses, unfair laws, and incidents of violence against the occupied.[55] In November 1915 young professionals founded the Haitian Youth League, which was less overtly political at first but taught propaganda to a new generation.[56]

This political class protested the landing and the subsequent formal usurping of sovereignty. On August 12 the Haitian Congress, surrounded by marines who physically held its doors open and let in only those with cards signed by Dartiguenave, elected Washington's man president. Beach held Dartiguenave's hand, literally, during his inaugural.[57] On August 21, US officers took charge of Haitian customs, and almost all employees resigned.[58] The following month the United States and Haiti signed a convention providing for a US-supervised constabulary and US control over the customs receivership, sanitation, and public works.

This speedy takeover of state institutions necessitated a majority to proceed, but not all Haitian representatives bowed to US hegemony. In early September Solon Menos, the Haitian minister in Washington, formally demanded "assurances from the United States that the integrity and independence of Haiti would not be impaired by the American occupation."[59] On October 6, 1915, Gonaïves deputy Raymond Cabèche, a thirty-seven-year-old doctor who had studied in the United States, denounced the convention from the floor of the Congress. Cabèche decried the hypocrisy of imposing a convention on Haiti by quoting Wilson's Mobile promise of sisterly equality for the Americas.[60] Why were Haitians sacrificing their patriotic dignity? asked Cabèche. "*Order* within shame? *Prosperity* within gilded chains?" Disgusted at his country's "moral servitude," he threw his deputy's badge in the middle of the assembly and stormed out. Another deputy did the same, and several more either voted against the convention or left the room without voting.[61] Only the US withholding of congressional salaries secured the House's approval.[62]

Xenophobia and anti-white sentiment: these two themes, distinct in their Haitian forms, emerged in the rhetoric of this early resistance, both rooted in the independence and anti-slavery struggles of the revolutionary era. Nineteenth-century Haitians had included a constitutional provision banning the sale of land to whites while describing the law as merely anti-foreign. Yet black foreigners could still own land and white foreigners found loopholes such as marrying Haitian women in whose names they bought land, so Haitians revised the rule to strip citizenship from women who married foreigners. The 1918 constitution, written under US supervision, reversed all this legislation by giving property rights to foreigners.[63]

Many Haitians were quick to see in US occupation a return to bound labor. In late August 1915, circulars in Cap-Haïtien warned that "American annexation means slavery."[64] A caco chief in l'Artibonite, Benoît Rameau, made anti-slavery his rallying cry. Two days after the signing of the Haitian-American convention, his followers in Gonaïves opened fire on US soldiers disembarking from the USS *Castine*.[65]

After US troops secured the cities in late summer 1915, caco resistance continued in the countryside, suggesting the deep entrenchment of caudillo political culture. A navy captain reported "a growing feeling of opposition to our forces" three days after Caperton declared martial law.[66] Caco rhetoric told Haitians in Port-au-Paix "that the war was no longer against Haitians but to drive out the invaders, and called all patriots to arms."[67] Caco leaders now called their struggle an "international war."[68] Yet their enthusiasm quickly waned. After devastating engagements with marines, most Haitian chiefs accepted bribes and formally surrendered on October 1, 1915, at Quartier-Morin (see Fig. 2.3). Many had entered the war only when the invasion had disbanded the Haitian army, throwing 308 generals and 50 colonels off government rolls.[69]

Figure 2.3 Haitian caco leaders discussing a peace treaty with Colonel Littleton W. T. Waller, USMC, commanding officer of the US Expeditionary Forces in Haiti, seated at right, October 1915. Photo # 31F-517445, folder 31F Haitian Leaders, box 7, RG 127G, NARA II.

Yet many others failed to disarm, illustrating, as in Nicaragua, the independence of popular troops from even their leaders. It remains unclear why cacos fought on. Caperton said some avaricious chiefs held out for bigger bribes. "They know no patriotism, no country, and the gourde [Haitian currency] is what they are looking for." Regular cacos seemed to feel betrayed by their chiefs.[70] A few of the chiefs corresponded about the possibility of surrender, and disagreements abounded. One of the more reticent, General Jac Marcelin, complained of being "worn out with the fever and my wife is sick with the tooth-ache," but refused to surrender until all the other camps did. "I am wholly Caco," he proudly wrote.[71]

The cacos fought on until marines, 1,000 strong in the north by October, crushed their stronghold at Fort Rivière on November 17.[72] This sealed the pacification of the north, but not the south. From there, politician Antoine Pierre-Paul and caco general Mizaël Codio, with financing from southern political figures, perhaps also German merchants, aimed to install Pauléus Sannon in the presidential palace. They attacked Port-au-Prince on the night of January 4–5, 1916.[73] According to Pierre-Paul, a recidivist plotter for the presidency, his army was massive but one of his sixteen column chiefs "betrayed" him by colluding with the marines and "paralyzing the other fifteen" by lying to them that Pierre-Paul had delayed the attack by a day.[74] Pierre-Paul's lone column stormed the capital shooting and yelling "Long live the cacos!"[75] The marines rapidly beat back the charge and Pierre-Paul escaped while his colleagues were tortured and killed. After the botched assault the marines closed all bars and restaurants at 6 PM and set a curfew at 7 PM. There were so many arrests that Colonel Littleton Waller, the senior officer in Haiti, publicly apologized.[76]

"The natives down here are all bad, and irresponsible and we are having trouble with them constantly," observed marine company commander William Upshur in a letter to his mother in March 1916, reflecting the frustration of marines with sporadic street-level violence and non-violent resistance against occupation, which continued, unorganized but consistent, for months after the caco defeat.[77] Marine Colonel Frederic Wise confirmed that "we encountered passive resistance from the start." Haitians "were afraid to take jobs with us, lest they get in bad with the Haitian government later on."[78] They greeted Dartiguenave's election with silence as the new president walked through town under a marine escort.[79] When the church finally sanctioned Dartiguenave with a Te Deum in late September, the pews, usually overflowing, were nearly empty.[80] Minister Girard of France noted that all Haitians resented intrusions in their daily freedoms, especially the curfew. Trigger-happy US soldiers on patrol also exhibited, according to Girard, "an extraordinary lack of discipline and in certain cases, an incredible disdain for propriety."[81] The French were particularly insulted that marines burst into their legation looking for prison escapees.[82] Noting how bandits attacked marine outposts and Haitian guards abandoned their posts, Upshur concluded, "These people are no more fitted to govern themselves than a tribe of apes," and recommended for Haiti "a white man's government."[83]

Given such perceptions, tensions ran high. Shortly after the landing, some marines rescued one of their own from drowning and pushed a gathering crowd away, shouting, "Give him air! Let him breathe!" Twenty-four-year-old Valcourt Mauclair shoved back. His brother Lucien, a machete strapped to his trousers, slashed a marine in the ensuing violence and caused a riot. A provost court sentenced Valcourt to life imprisonment and Lucien to death, but the brothers had already "taken to the woods." They roamed the countryside for seventeen years until pardoned.[84]

Haitians' outrage against their own politicians, whose infighting they blamed for bringing on the occupation, was greater than their anger against invaders. On October 17, 1915, a local singer called Auguste de Pradines, known as Candio, introduced a new parody in Kreyol called "On the Convention." Its lyrics condemned the so-called patriots who fought each other for years and now denounced the occupation's order:

> Scream as you will, protest
> But suffer, immobile, your Convention!
> The negro always scorned the negro

Now it's the 'Merican's turn
That we are here, whose fault is it?[85]

Continued resignation, even fatalism, only deepened after the caco war. It blended guilt over bringing about the external force with acceptance of the inability to resist effectively. African American writer Zora Neale Hurston visited Haiti in the 1930s and heard of a peasant woman who, after the Sam massacre of July 1915, "fell upon her knees with her arms outstretched like a crucifix and cried, 'They say that the white man is coming to rule Haiti again. The black man is so cruel to his own, *let the white man come!*'"[86] Several prominent Haitians privately confided similar feelings. "The occupation was a *fait accompli*," said future president Louis Borno to Solon Menos. After the "shameful" events of late July, "it was pure madness to suppose that our country could get out of this one."[87] "There is nothing left to do," said Charles Zamor to an editor friend.[88] Haitians repeatedly blamed the political culture of caudillos, cacos, and revolution for bringing about the occupation. "I hate the insurrection with all my nerves, all my mind, all my blood," ranted journalist Constantin Mayard in September. "I prefer everything to this anarchy that almost killed our nationality."[89] Dartiguenave's minister of finance summed up, "We did nothing but exchange one sorrow for another."[90]

Regardless of US pressure, majorities in the Haitian Congress backed Dartiguenave for president and voted for the convention. This emboldened US administrators to push through further reforms. In 1917 the Congress refused to pass the US-sponsored constitution and drafted its own, but Major Smedley Butler, a prominent presence also in Haiti after his adventures in Nicaragua, presented deputies with an order for the dissolution of Congress signed by Dartiguenave through coercion. In June 1918 US officials committed massive voter fraud to pass a plebiscite in favor of the constitution, 98,225 to 768.[91] In this context, Haitians remembered the few acts of individual resistance. In Port-au-Prince much was made of a soldier named Pierre Sully, sometimes called Joseph Pierre or, endearingly, *le petit Sully,* whom marines killed because he refused to surrender his post despite the army's collapse.[92] It was a chimerical victory amid defeat and despondency.

There was indeed significant pro-occupation sentiment in Haiti, especially in the first year after the breakup of caudillo resistance. Social peace also stemmed from high agricultural prices brought on by the war in Europe, which benefited Hispaniola's exports. Others prized stability over national sovereignty. Charles Moravia's *Le Matin,* a pro-occupation paper, paradoxically praised the new censorship rules for freeing the press from the clutches of government, newspapermen no longer having to take positions for or against it. "Transcending our national pride is a convention that brings us peace, security and work," wrote *Le*

Matin.[93] Throughout the fall of 1915, it urged marines not to be "soft" and called for more coercion against the cacos.[94]

Many Haitians also set aside their outrage and shame when individual US citizens treated them with courtesy and respect. Caperton and Beach were some of the most-liked *blancs* in Haiti. Aware of the resentment against US troops, they instructed them to be friendly to Haitians.[95] They also both spoke French well and, as one Haitian historian wrote, showed "a courtesy so perfect that one saw nothing American in them."[96] Popular US officers socialized with the elite, attending dances and mingling in mixed-race company.[97]

The defeat of caudillos and cacos and the acceptance of the occupation by many might have signaled a change in Haitian political culture. Secretary Lansing had given as his first reason for taking Haiti "to terminate the appalling conditions of anarchy, savagery, and oppression which had been prevalent in Haiti for decades."[98] President Wilson also pledged to "put men in charge of affairs whom we can trust to handle and put an end to revolution."[99] Instead US occupiers found widespread regionalism, personalism, clientelism, partisanship, corruption, strict social hierarchies, authoritarianism, and disrespect for the rule of law and for press freedom. Nepotism, too. One Haitian senator named Pouget congratulated Captain Beach on electing Dartiguenave, and incidentally recommended his brother-in-law as consul general in New York. When told no, "Pouget became a determined opponent of President Dartiguenave."[100]

As a result, US occupiers far from Washington grew disillusioned. The administrator of customs wrote to Caperton, a year into the occupation, that "all ideas relative to assisting or advising [Haitians] in running their own Government, which ideas I was inclined to favor at first, I now regard as entirely hopeless. There is not a man in the Government who is concerned with anything except his private gain and with finding places for his friends. Force and force alone can control the situation." Beach agreed. "The patriotism of leading Haitiens [*sic*] vents itself in political discussion and political combinations. It does not take form in buying seeds, of tilling and planting the land, or providing employment for the idle poor."[101] Because neither the Navy Department nor the State Department drew up specific plans for political cultural change and State washed its hands of the occupation until the 1920s, US administrators called for the continuation and entrenchment of occupation in a futile search for what existed nowhere in Latin America: "a stable, unifying cross-class nationalism."[102] The navy kept the lid on.

3

The Dominican Republic, 1916

Has the United States sent people down here to teach us how to behave?

—Desiderio Arias

Barely nine months after taking Haiti, in May 1916 the US Navy and Marine Corps landed in Santo Domingo, on the other side of Hispaniola. The US decision to intervene in another power struggle with a caudillo presented many similarities with Haiti and Nicaragua, most salient being the desire to erase a revolutionary political culture. Dominican resistance emphasized the persistence of caudillos' defense of local autonomy, again at the national level during the first months. In contrast to Haiti, Dominican leaders and followers of both violent and peaceful resistance movements put up a more determined front, as did unorganized resisters.

"The danger to our sovereignty is within," warned Federico Antonio García a few months before the United States military landed on Dominican shores. "We do not want American intervention, but with each of our revolutions, we do nothing but invite it."[1] Desiderio Arias, the minister of war, embodied that internal peril. Arias was similar to Haiti's Rosalvo Bobo in being a constant irritant to those who wanted centralized elite rule in the Dominican Republic. A classic caudillo, he represented the poorest, most infertile region called the Línea Noroeste. Tall, thin, and of mixed race, Arias was beloved for his humility and generosity, and many Dominicans claimed to know or to be related to him. He banned his troops from taking or stealing food from the poor, a rare trait among caudillos.[2] A former cart-driver with little education, Arias chose the only profession that afforded social mobility—war. He excelled at it—unlike peers, he neither drank nor cavorted—and attracted a following of darker-skinned peasants, soldiers, and urban poor.[3]

After the assassination of President Ramón Cáceres in 1911, Arias competed for power against two other caudillos, Horacio Vásquez and Juan Isidro Jimenes, his former boss. Arias's political savvy and his ability to "blackmai[l] every Dominican president during the past thirty years," as Dana Munro put it, forced national figures to recognize him as a delegate in the national legislature. From this perch he paid back followers by handing out railroad jobs, which stoked the envy of the *horacistas*, as the followers of Vásquez were known.[4]

When Jimenes took the presidency in December 1914, Arias made him his favorite target. Jimenes proved an easy one since his tax men collected only from political enemies.[5] Spurred in part by Arias, the Senate charged the president with misuse of funds, illegal imprisonment, and abuse of power.[6] Jimenes took revenge by ordering the arrest of Arias's aides on April 14, 1916. The aides fought back, getting the House and Senate to impeach Jimenes in early May.[7] Arias added muscle to the impeachment by taking the capital.

This internal struggle overlapped with an external one against US hegemony. In late 1915 the United States had demanded of Jimenes that he accept US control over Dominican finances and customs and a constabulary to replace the existing guard.[8] Jimenes declined, but the humiliation of being asked harmed his prestige and fortified Arias's audacity.[9] When Arias took Santo Domingo, the marines landed on May 4 to protect foreigners but did not take the city. Jimenes resigned three days later, accepting but then rejecting a US intervention, which would taint his office, he said, if "regained with foreign bullets."[10]

Admiral William Caperton, in charge of this expedition, presented Arias with an ultimatum to surrender. Colonel Frederic "Dopey" Wise, along with US Minister William Russell, delivered the ultimatum in person to Arias, who was holed up in Ozama Fortress. Wise described Arias's men as "fired with the fresh enthusiasm of a revolution that looked successful."[11]

"These revolutions have got to cease and you Dominicans have got to run a good government," Wise ordered Arias.

Arias looked at him and smiled. "Has the United States sent people down here to teach us how to behave?"[12]

While US officers waited for a response, Arias hoisted Dominican flags rather than white flags, and, in the ensuing confusion, pulled up stakes, enlisted prisoners from the nearby jail, and left the city headed north with some 300 followers. Six hundred US troops occupied the capital (see Fig. 3.1).[13]

A month later a poster in Santo Domingo, signed by Arias, rejected the label of partisan revolutionary given to him by Jimenes and US officers and presented him instead as a unifying figure. "Mine is an Army of Patriots, fired up by sacred love for the Republic, which has no other cause but Legality, Honor, and National Independence." He swore to surrender his arms only to a duly elected president. "Would US troops not do the same?"[14]

US officers saw things differently. Looking back on the landing a few years later, Joseph Pendleton, a veteran of the 1912 Nicaraguan campaign, wrote to

Figure 3.1 Contrary to what the caption suggests, marines were on their second day occupying Santo Domingo on May 15, 1916. Photo #30B-521582, folder 30B Patrols/ Skirmishes etc., box 7, RG 127G, NARA II.

a friend that Arias was deeply flawed. He was a man of the masses, "a very magnetic chap" and "particularly popular with the poorer and more ignorant class all through the country." "Educated men who were far greater scoundrels than Arias" took advantage of him, however, and Jimenes "wouldn't stand for quite all the graft." Pendleton's primary reason for "going into Santo Domingo" was "because the United States was tired of revolutions."[15]

US officials thus took over the Dominican Republic because of seemingly intractable political problems that ran far deeper than Arias. President Woodrow Wilson called the occupation "the least of the evils in sight in this very perplexing situation."[16] As in Haiti, one evil was disregarding democracy. Minister Russell, for instance, refused to recognize any president elected by the Dominican Congress "because it is probable that Arias or his candidate will be elected."[17] Secretary of State Robert Lansing agreed.[18]

Occupiers also took over the country for an indefinite period. When Caperton took Santo Domingo he said "it should be for ultimate occupation."[19] The French minister, the Comte d'Arlot de Saint-Saud, also believed the intervention "could last, given that Mr. Russell and Admiral Caperton refuse to authorize presidential elections as long as there are in the country armed revolutionaries who could affect the result. That refusal has driven Dominicans to exasperation."

De Saint-Saud correctly predicted how the caudillo war would proceed. "Many speak of taking to the woods, as they say here, and of joining the ranks of Desiderio Arias."[20] The Frenchman was privy to a meeting with Arias at his camp along with the Italian chargé and the Dominican archbishop. After hearing their terms of surrender, Arias lectured them that he had animosities toward none but would "prefer to be killed leading his men rather than to see his fatherland handed over to the Americans."[21] Others reported that Arias's men were growing in number and receiving guns and ammunition from Puerto Plata on the north coast.[22]

Too few voices of the followers of Dominican caudillos survive to characterize their relationship with their leaders. But local caudillos long held the bulk of the power in the pyramid on top of which sat men such as Arias, and they defended their local autonomy against any effort at centralization.

In the Dominican Republic caudillo followers often took the form of small semi-political bands loosely tied to a national leader rather than large ad hoc armies as in Haiti. Before the 1916 intervention, roaming bands had long taken part in civil wars. They formed a continuum that ranged from *gavilleros*, or pure bandits, to revolutionaries who fully demobilized after war.[23] As early as the 1880s, bands resisted national modernization plans and the increasing spread of sugar capitalism.[24] They rose again after the death of dictator Ulises Heureaux in 1899 and especially in response to President Cáceres's tightening of central power. From 1904 to 1916, more than twenty groups targeted representatives of national authority such as provincial governors and the new police force.[25]

These insurrectionists were neither inherently against foreigners, whom they often protected for cash, nor defenders of the poor, whom they robbed and impressed into their ranks.[26] Although most were originally peasants, they did not become insurrectionists because they were poor. While many had lost land due to the expansion of sugar cane growing, they usually sold it cheaply and bands never demanded the return of such land.[27] They most likely organized because they remained isolated in regions, which gave them a measure of protection from national representatives.[28] Thus Dominican rebels could be considered "social bandits," but their social qualities were fraught with political self-interest.[29]

To survive at the national level, caudillos had to buy the cooperation of regional or local leaders backed by bands. The price was usually a government concession or the military command of a province or garrison of a town.[30] The pecuniary nature of the relationship failed to foster loyalty between national leaders or institutions and caudillos. Some were turncoats, as in the case of a Dominican lieutenant arrested for communicating with Arias after Arias fled Santo Domingo in May 1916.[31] Others were independent of any patron, entering into deals with wealthy landowners or politicians when it suited them.[32] In the turmoil of the 1910s, bands would ally with *jimenista* or *horacista* leaders, and, when the violence ended, would return to the hills and become hostile to the new government.[33]

Dominican responses to US intervention, as in Haiti, initially featured a painful self-examination of the country's political failures and a willingness to blame Dominican politicians for the country's ills. Yet resistance to the landings was more uniform, nationalistic, and relatively effective than in Haiti, reflecting the greater level of Dominican centralization achieved by 1916.

Once Desiderio Arias decamped with his troops to the country's second city, Santiago, US troops took the capital in May 1916 without violence. Marines noted "very few cases of hostile feeling displayed" but some mistook the quiet for lack of opposition.[34] In fact, the city was in mourning. As marines walked down the street, they saw only men, servants, and dogs. Stores, social clubs, and theaters were closed, and Dominicans flew their flags at half-mast or covered them with crepe.[35] Newspapers called the reaction a "silent protest."[36] Meanwhile, teachers had pupils sing the national anthem, and petitions protesting the landing garnered thousands of signatures. Town councils organized "Patriotic Commissions" and then sent one overall commission to Santo Domingo to warn the marines of an "international war" if troops moved into the interior.[37] Young women, used to dancing and promenading with naval officers, stayed indoors and hummed a tune whose refrain went, "I don't love you anymore."[38] Playwrights put on shows with titles such as *The Intruder* and *No More Yes*, and poets published verse evoking founding father Juan Pablo Duarte:

> Does Duarte no longer live in our consciousness?
> Has the light of patriotism been extinguished?[39]

The political class feared being too closely associated with central government once it was under US auspices—the supreme irony of an occupation meant to strengthen central government. The governor of Azua province, one of the few collaborators, reported that "all the towns of the South are greatly alarmed" because commissioners were telling peasants to rise up against invasion. "We must proceed energetically to avoid any proceedings that threaten the friends of the government." Town councillors were divided sharply between followers of Jimenes and Arias, he explained. The governor understood early the catch-22 of occupation: such "propaganda," he wrote, "prejudices public order and tends to prolong American occupation."[40]

Yet US officials did not appreciate the delicate balancing act of Dominican politicians. One recalled how the mayor of Santo Domingo very likely had the telegraph wires cut after the marines landed. Asked if the mayor was "in cahoots with the rebels," he answered, "Oh, no. They just didn't like Americans, period. Well, anybody will resent his city being invaded, you know. Who knows what their sympathies were."[41]

As in Haiti, there was significant acceptance of the occupation among Dominicans, but not nearly the same fatalism. "*They intervened, with authority, and for our benefit*," claimed one leaflet distributed in Santo Domingo in May 1916. The landing was "the natural result of our *antipatriotic, unspeakable* Conduct. . . . *We are the authors of our disgrace and we should have the courage to admit it*."[42] One prominent Dominican intellectual, Pelegrín Castillo Agramonte, published a series of pro-intervention articles in 1916, arguing for a strong central state that would banish forever the cycle of revolutions. He saw altruism in US occupation and rejected the absolute sovereignty of nations. Castillo saw himself—and US citizens—as fundamentally democratic while he believed anti-occupation intellectuals to be elitists aligned with revolutionaries.[43] In an article entitled "The Need for the Americans in Santo Domingo," another Dominican argued that government employees could finally count on steady salaries and widows on pensions, something no Dominican-led government ever secured.[44]

Shortly after the marines secured the capital in the south, various groups prepared to defend the north coast, where Arias was holed up in the stronghold of Santiago. The first burst of resistance on the north shore took place in Puerto Plata, where local politicians tied to a caudillo took the lead. In Puerto Plata province, Governor Apolinar Rey, a follower of Arias who stayed on the job despite being fired by Jimenes, denied any anti-US sentiment but promised "he would kill all Americans" if they landed on his shores.[45] As he told another governor by phone, Rey expected military defeat because most Dominicans around Puerto Plata were disloyal.

> As this is a town of eunuchs, with its men castrated who are good for nothing, if they cry too much, I will have to deliver, because I can count on no one here, but anyway, as I obey orders of Desiderio to hold on until the last moment, I will do all that I can. . . . It will be in Santiago that we will make our resistance.

Townsfolk were not with Rey, nor were they with the marines. When about twenty US citizens including the consul evacuated on the eve of the landing, a mob tried to prevent their departure and others sacked the consulate. "Popular meetings" took place in which city council members tried to soften Rey's obstinacy, primarily to avoid a marine landing.[46] Rey was unmoved. He claimed that Arias was to have the city of Santiago declare him president.[47]

Figure 3.2 Mounted Dominican guerrillas, perhaps fighting for Governor Apolinar Rey.
Puerto Plata, Dominican Republic, undated. Photo # 30E-521559, folder 30E Guerrillas,
box 7, RG 127G, NARA II.

Unable to round up enough free citizens, Rey used rural guards and, like
Arias, put guns in the hands of prisoners (see Fig. 3.2). At 6 AM on June 1, 1916,
he waited for the US gunboats with a few hundred men. Against US artillery,
Rey's men fired "a storm of bullets, coming from the water front, and streets in
town, and practically every house near the water front." They continued shooting, allegedly using civilians for cover, as the marines landed at 6:30 AM. The
Dominicans killed one US captain with a bullet to the head but then retreated to
a hilltop hospital.[48] US forces advanced steadily, and it was all over by 9 AM.[49] A
simultaneous landing in Monte Cristi, near the Haitian border, saw no organized
resistance, but several days later 200 men attacked the marine camp at Monte
Cristi before being driven off.[50]

For Dominicans, such defeats could be as glorious as victory if intentions were
noble and execution dramatic. Carlos de León saw the marines disembark in
the northern town of Sánchez and recalled the "teary-eyed," "stupefied," "deeply
mourning" population. What lifted their hearts was an effort by General Manuel
de Jesús Pérez Sosa, known as "Lico," to board his troops onto a train headed to
where the marines were landing. The mission failed: marines were already on
the ground and they easily surrounded Lico. To De León, however, "it matters
not . . . that the patriotic act of the general . . . did not achieve the end promised.
What history will never forget is that [Lico] was of the few Dominican generals
who defied the arrogance of the North American forces of occupation."[51]

The proudest Dominican moments of resistance were the futile but valiant battles against marines while they marched from Monte Cristi and Puerto Plata to converge on Arias in Santiago. Along the way, Dominicans tore up the railroad tracks, forcing marines to walk.[52] They also burned bridges and "sniped constantly," delaying the march.[53]

The real northern resistance came first at "Las Trincheras" (the trenches), a defensive position long used by revolutionary armies. Dominicans imagined it so impregnable they called it "Verdun."[54] A bigger engagement occurred on July 3, 1916, at La Barranquita, when eighty Dominicans dug trenches on two hills blocking passage to Santiago and kept up single-shot fire against the automatic weapons of US troops (see Fig. 3.3). Legend has it that Dominicans even released bees against the marines.[55] The marines, however, used Dominican guides and eventually drove off the entrenched warriors.

Dominican motives for such a suicidal stand varied.[56] Teenagers particularly participated out of patriotic ardor.[57] Others, following personalist political codes, had pledged loyalty either to Arias or to his subordinates.[58] Ranging in age from fourteen to eighty, Barranquita combatants were almost all peasants and clients of Arias. Their arid, cattle-ranching region was isolated, so caudillo power was deeply entrenched. Enerio Disla, sixteen at the time, fought because "Maximito" Cabral, an Arias man, rode in on a horse and distributed rifles. Priests and other community leaders also stoked the martial spirit.[59] Many others cited

Figure 3.3 What Dominicans faced at the Battle of La Barranquita near Guayascanes, July 3, 1916. Photo #30B-516879, folder 30B Patrols/Skirmishes etc., box 7, RG 127G NARA II.

family connections to commanders or others who fought. Luis Disla, a farmer, described Arias affectionately as "the Chief of Mao [Disla's town]. . . . He was one of us." Máximo Muñoz joined the fight because he was a soldier doing his duty. Francisco Gutiérrez described his patriotism as the protection of the land he toiled. "I was not going to let them, as they say, put a yoke around my neck. . . . I grabbed my carbine and preferred to die rather than see mine become theirs." Rafael Reyes explained, drawing on Dominican imagery, that no one wanted "another's cock in his henhouse, right?"[60]

None cited anti-US sentiment as a motivating factor. When asked if it mattered that the invaders were US troops, Demetrio Frías responded, "Oh no, no, no, no, that did not matter to me at all; that they be American, no matter who they were." When troops moved into Mao and other towns to disarm them, Barranquita survivors handed guns over peacefully. Some went to work for the marines.[61] One veteran of La Barranquita even showed up at the marines' sick bay to have his wounds dressed.[62] The astonishing ease with which these Dominicans switched allegiances spoke not only of continuing isolation from state affairs and the lack of programmatic ideology but also the absence of any cultural markers identifying US citizens at the outset of the occupation.

All that mattered to "Uncle Joe" Pendleton, who led the marine march, was that the defeats took the fight out of Arias. The caudillo was hoping to wage a "National War" from Santiago and was "taxing" its merchants $500 a day to prepare.[63] Pendleton wrote that La Barranquita "completely crushed the spirit of resistance and as we proceeded on our march the next day, we were met by a party of prominent men from Santiago, asking for peace terms."[64] The men accepted surrender on July 5—the key term of which was a pardon for Arias—and retracted their threat to set their town ablaze. When marines arrived the following day, according to a British diplomat, Santiagans "warmly welcomed" them and Dominicans showed "little or no animosity against them in any of the other towns with the exception of the Capital where the predominant interests are political rather than commercial."[65] Arias wrote to one of his generals that he was laying down his arms "because of the indifference of the great majority of the country."[66] Those who fought also noted the acquiescence of the mass of Dominicans.[67] Arias himself turned surprisingly docile. He opened a small cigar store and called himself "a Dominican friend of the United States."[68]

After Arias's forces surrendered, however, proportionately more Dominicans than Haitians demonstrated hostility to the US presence. This is likely because on November 29, 1916, Rear Admiral Harry Knapp declared a direct US military government over the country. The "Knapp Proclamation," as it came to be called, eliminated even the pretense of Dominican self-government. With next to no Dominicans left in government, the populace found itself free to unite in opposition.

Perhaps the most common resistance by regular Dominicans was their refusal to disarm. In Haiti, dawdling on disarmament was mostly confined to cacos and seemed linked to obtaining more attractive bribes. Far more Dominicans, in contrast, attached cultural value to their weapons. One provincial governor complained in June 1916 that US forces disarmed even those who had licenses to carry weapons. He suggested reversing the trend, thus restoring "the respect for being governed by Yankees."[69] Instead, on September 14, the order came from US officials to revoke all permits. Dominican officials were unenthusiastic.[70] The governor of Monte Cristi province wrote to prominent Dominicans urging them "to keep [their arms] hidden."[71]

No one knows how many failed to turn in arms, but by the end of the occupation, the marines seized 53,000 firearms, 200,000 rounds of ammunition, and 14,000 cutting weapons from a population of 750,000.[72] US officials partly insisted on disarmament because they wanted to reform an unnecessarily violent society, and in this narrow sense, disarmament worked: in the province of Santiago, homicides declined from 300 to 50 per year.[73] But the fact that most surrendered firearms were obsolete suggests that Dominicans kept serviceable weapons and that marines collected objects with little practical value while inciting significant cultural resentment.[74] To be sure, a significant minority kept their weapons because they were members of bands. Rebel leaders came to associate the concealment of weapons with patriotism. In January 1917, for instance, band leader Vicente Evangelista let it be known through a popular poem that

Is considered enemy of Dominicans
he who, having arms
denies them to a compatriot
to combat a Yankee[75]

Carrying a weapon also served as a measure of manhood. Fathers tended to give sons revolvers when they reached puberty.[76] A poor peasant who worked twelve-hour days, ate poorly, and had "barely two shirts to wear" saved up for years to "buy a good revolver," so he could, gun in belt, "stand face to face with the local braves" and respond to insults.[77]

Street brawls were the more immediate reason for the Knapp Proclamation. Fights were related to disarmament since Dominican resistance in late 1916 stemmed mostly from the marines' probing for weapons.[78] Searches multiplied after the September disarmament order. As the Dominican press published accounts of forcible home entries by marines, provincial governors claimed they could not muzzle press freedoms. Marines grew frustrated that Dominicans chose to obey only this law. "The laws have *never* been obeyed in this country!" shouted Marine Major H. I. Beers.[79]

To have the laws obeyed, as in Haiti, marines paradoxically muffled Dominican democracy. The struggle to oust the Dominican head of state provoked another column of resistance before the Knapp Proclamation. On July 25, 1916, the Dominican Congress elected Francisco Henríquez y Carvajal their provisional president. "Don Pancho," as Henríquez was called, was a French-trained doctor from a prominent family. Congress claimed the new president was nonpartisan—he had never belonged to a faction or held office and he lived in Cuba—but Caperton held out, seeing in Don Pancho a reluctance to give in to US wishes.[80] The president did agree to almost all US demands, yet Caperton and Russell identified too many *desideristas* in Henríquez's cabinet.[81] Russell's own choice for president, Federico Velázquez, was unacceptable to Dominicans precisely because they perceived him as Washington's man.[82]

"These politicians seem to be, if possible, more untruthful, more unreliable, and greater schemers, than our friends, the Haitiens [*sic*]," Caperton fumed.[83] "I fail to find one spark of patriotism in [them]. Each and every one is for the graft, the money and power that he can get out of the country for himself and his party."[84] "I have come to the conclusion," he wrote in July, "that the only thing for these Republics, is a strong United States Military government. . . . They will never be able to govern themselves, that is, not for several generations, if ever."[85]

Overcome by frustration, on August 17, US occupiers struck a mortal blow against Henríquez by withholding customs receipts, thereby suspending all public salaries until Henríquez caved. For over three months, public employees worked for no salary, pensions went unpaid, businesses lost contracts, and charitable groups fed prisoners in the jails and patients in the hospitals.[86] The suffering was too much. "American pressure had reached a limit unknown in our history," wrote Henríquez to confidant Tulio Cestero.[87] The *Listín Diario* of Santo Domingo blamed "revolutionaries" for fighting and then surrendering, leaving the hard work for peaceful government workers. "*We* have to deal with the invaders."[88]

While the Henríquez standoff dragged on, other Dominican political leaders showed that centralizing authority would be difficult. Several provincial governors disobeyed orders from Santo Domingo.[89] Those who agreed in private often did not cooperate in public. Four cabinet ministers, for instance, refused to request a US troop movement, telling Caperton, "while they believe and all feel it for the good of the country, that they could not put it in writing and afterwards live in the Dominican Republic."[90]

There were also numerous popular manifestations of discontent. Throughout the summer of 1916, gunfire pierced nighttime quiet.[91] By October, minor incidents of harassment multiplied as marines took over policing duties.[92] Rising anti-marine sentiment culminated with one violent clash. On October 24, a small group of marines from the capital crossed the Ozama River on their way to the suburb of Villa Duarte, where they planned to arrest Ramón Batista, a party boss whose job was to collect weapons from fellow Dominicans and who was suspected of harboring weapons instead.[93] Marines found his house, informed him of the arrest order, and grabbed him.

"Help! They are killing me!" cried the Dominican to friends who had been milling about. Batista called on them to kill the "Yankee cowards," and the arrest turned into a shootout. Out of nowhere dozens of men with guns blasted away at the marines. People ran screaming in all directions. One woman took a marine bullet to protect a sniper. The marines managed a fatal shot at Batista, but they fled the scene, crossing the river by boat while bullets whizzed by and plopped into the water around them. Two marines died in the riot.[94] Soon after, 100 marines occupied Villa Duarte, breaking down doors, detaining anyone looking suspicious, and burning down homes.[95]

The next day, a "considerable number of Dominicans" attacked two marines on patrol near a Santo Domingo café called Polo Norte. The marines fired back, killing a waiter, the owner of the café, and a nineteen-year-old student.[96] One Dominican immediately called these men "innocent victims of American brutality."[97]

"Former feeling of sympathy for Americans here changed to one of hatred," cabled the legation back to Washington. The *Listín* exemplified that shift, editorializing that "just nations" did not scorch and kill as the Yankees did in Villa Duarte. "The United States have knocked on the wrong door, and instead of going to Africa to crush tribes for the expansion of their empire, they enmeshed themselves in free Republics like Mexico, Nicaragua, Haiti, and the Dominican Republic."[98] The *Listín* printed similar comments every day, as did other newspapers.[99]

President Henríquez y Carvajal and two of his ministers blamed US officials for interfering in police business. The attorney general added that the marines were abusing the *ley fuga*—the right to shoot escaping suspects—by using it in common arrests.[100] The incidents accelerated the coming of the Knapp Proclamation because US officials assumed that Henríquez would be even more intransigent.[101]

Popular resistance turned out to be just what the marines were waiting for. In May, Caperton had hoped that "in case of any sporadic outbreak, I think the situation would be greatly relieved as then I would feel in duty bound to take military possession of the City and place it under martial law."[102] The State Department concluded that the Batista and Polo Norte incidents called for precisely that remedy.[103] Lansing agreed.[104] At a decisive October 31 meeting in Washington, Navy, State, Knapp, and Russell agreed that the stubborn Henríquez y Carvajal "apparently cannot be broken by diplomatic methods." As for public order, they agreed to "legalize our military action in keeping order and putting down any revolutionary activity." To both problems the solution was the same: martial law.[105]

So on November 29, Knapp issued his "Proclamation of Occupation." It imposed martial law under a US military government headed by marine officers. It gave legal teeth to the existing customs receivership and resumed payments to the government from the coffers of those customs offices. It never denied Dominican sovereignty, called the country a colony, or removed Dominican flags from public buildings. It left untouched the courts, schools, and churches. Citing the need for "internal order" to ensure "domestic tranquility," Knapp simultaneously banned firearms and imposed censorship and soon suspended the Congress and declared there would be no further elections.[106] Knapp and the military governors who succeeded him ruled by executive order. President Wilson authorized it all, he wrote, "with the deepest reluctance."[107]

Some Dominicans, usually ones with whom Knapp interacted, welcomed the proclamation. Santo Domingo's chief of police, for instance, called it "news from heaven."[108] US officials widely reported that "the people have accepted the new order of things," many expressing great satisfaction, although privately.[109]

Of course, dissent did not die with the Knapp Proclamation. To be sure, most newspapers immediately silenced their political coverage and four suspended publication altogether.[110] But on December 8, the Cabinet resigned en masse and Don Pancho sailed back to his home in Santiago de Cuba. Knapp noticed that the executives cleaned out their desks, and he had the temerity to call this act of civil disobedience "desertion."[111] The day after the proclamation, Lico, the northern general, barricaded himself with troops in San Francisco de Macorís's fort until the marines rushed the door, and eleven Dominicans died in the fighting (see Fig. 3.4).[112] Other governors refused to serve under US rule and one later joined insurrectionists.[113] As in Haiti, the occupation celebrated a Te Deum at which few showed, perhaps finding the timing—on Dominican Independence Day, February 27, 1917—in poor taste.[114]

Also as in Haiti, the Dominican Republic found its lone resister to elevate as a conscience for the quiescent. On December 10, 1916, in coastal San Pedro de Macorís, sixteen-year-old Gregorio Urbano Gilbert, a local shopboy indignant at the lack of resistance to the occupation, put on his finest hat, strapped on a .32 caliber pistol and a knife, and headed for the wharf where marines were docking. He had wanted to join the cacos in Haiti the previous year, but had no money for the trip.[115] Now, in his own town, he found a group of marines sitting at a table. "¡Viva la República Dominicana!" shouted Gilbert as he rose and surprised the men. He shot two officers, killing one lieutenant. Gilbert had no connection to

Figure 3.4 Dominicans taken prisoner by marines at the fort of San Francisco de Macorís, November 1916. Folder "Dominican Republic: Early 1900s," USMC Historical Division, Marine Corps Base, Quantico, Va.

caudillos or insurrectionists, but he fled back into town, where, according to him, "I received the congratulations of Macorisians, especially the women, who also blessed me and commended me to the Virgin of Altagracia of Higüey." A wanted man, Gilbert ran into a cane field and joined the band of caudillo Vicente Evangelista. He was eventually arrested and sentenced to death, but later pardoned.[116]

Especially noteworthy for its contrast with Haiti was the fact that Dominican diplomats abroad made a substantial show of resisting the theft of their national sovereignty—and of their jobs. On December 4, 1916, the minister in Washington, Armando Pérez Perdomo, enumerated ways the military government violated international law, among these, there was no state of war between the two nations that could warrant an occupation. This became the formal protest of the Dominican government.[117] Soon after, Manuel Morillo, the chargé in Havana, organized protests in the legation and circulated a petition accusing marines of "assassinating old men, women and children and razing innocent populations," a reference to the Villa Duarte and Polo Norte shootings, and calling on American republics to denounce "crimes that affront modern civilization."[118] "Your authority is usurped and criminal," he wrote to a US official in Santo Domingo, "derived from an odious piratical act by a powerful country against a weak and indefensible people."[119] By June, Dominicans in Havana were raising funds for a war of reconquest, claiming Haitians were on board.[120] Murillo even asked for

British intervention.[121] Nothing came of these strategies but the early transnational effort set a precedent.

All US occupiers were left with, it seemed, was sweeping up the last remnants of insurrectionism. In January 1917 Salustiano "Chachá" Goicochea gave up his band more easily than Haitian caco leaders did, allegedly for $500.[122] Marines released Chachá on a suspended sentence but refused him the customary reward of a governorship or even a job with the police.[123]

Though many caudillos continued operating after the Knapp Proclamation, one of Chachá's lieutenants, Vicente Evangelista, immediately rose as the dominant leader in the east. "Vicentico" represented a transition between caudillos fighting internal enemies and those focused on US occupation forces. From a well-to-do rural family of El Seibo, Vicentico apprenticed as a tailor in San Pedro but went into politics early, becoming a *horacista*.[124] After seeing relatives' property sacked and burned by occupation forces, he vowed to kill any US citizen he encountered.[125] Knapp called him "a man of more commanding personality than Cha-chá."[126]

Vicentico continued to use caudillo tactics, including violent property seizures from ordinary Dominicans. Those in the east supported him because of his active use of *parentesco*, ties forged through direct family and extended through godparents. Fear was also a factor in attracting recruits. One marine, pursuing Vicentico, grew frustrated because the people "will not give us information of any value. The[y] lie deliberately and the fear of Vicentico is greater than the fear they have of any punishment we are likely to inflict."[127]

Others, however, conceived of Vicentico as something new. Rather than let his followers loot freely, in the first half of 1917 Vicentico had all requisitions of property flow through him and insisted on respect toward peaceful peasants.[128] His bare-bones state-making included trying to get town councillors on his side and building a main camp that included women domestics, ironworkers, carpenters, and tanners. When he found two US engineers surveying land for the sugar company Central Romana, Vicentico had them tied to trees. When one pleaded with him, he responded "that he would spare no Americans." His men chopped off their heads and hacked them to pieces.[129]

Vicentico's real crimes against the occupation was that he remained armed and wedded to regional politics, despite calling himself an "avenger of the fatherland."[130] Vicentico wanted to rule, in the name of the new military government, the eastern provinces of Seibo and Hato Mayor, but the marines would have none of it. He said he was "fighting on account of his Dominican enemies and that he had nothing against the Military Government or the American Government." He blamed all crimes attributed to him on rival caudillo Pedro Celestino Tolete. The caudillo was even more passionate about killing another rival, Fidel Ferrer, a former governor turned band leader who took money from marines to turn again, this time against Vicentico. Evangelista demanded Ferrer's head as a condition of surrender; the marines refused.[131] In early July 1917, the marines tricked him into surrendering and then shot him while "trying to escape." Rather than the jobs they were promised, his men received long prison sentences.[132]

To Knapp, the death of Evangelista and simultaneous imprisonment of Tolete meant that there were no more insurrectionists in the Dominican Republic.[133] A year after the Knapp Proclamation, a British vice-consul agreed: "Politics, so far as I could judge, have fallen into the background and are little discussed. . . . Relations between Dominicans and Americans appear to be improving."[134]

While open tension receded, however, many noted that the problems of political culture that initially attracted the marines still plagued the Dominican Republic. Those who praised the occupations, for instance, generally had a personal interest, usually in a government job. Manuel de Jesús Galván, for instance, became minister in Washington, and Félix María Nolasco went from a clerk to the *síndico* or chair of the Santo Domingo town council.[135] As they offered their services to the new rulers, some wrestled with their choice. "Some do not consider me a good Dominican," said Eligio Vidal, asking for a job, "because, on more than one occasion I have refused to sign protests against the Government; but I am a good Dominican when I have to be." Occupation, he said, "helps us to put an end to a few bad things in our country."[136] It did not help the cause of unity that few in the cities were proud of the rural resistance to intervention. To novelist Federico García Godoy, none of the caudillos in 1916 was a true "nationalist." "On the thermometer of national dignity we have descended almost to zero."[137] As in Haiti, therefore, US officials began to foresee "a prolonged occupation," wrote Chargé Perroud of the French legation in Santo Domingo, "to modify the mentality of the Dominican people, the cause of all their problems."[138] One US military governor called his subjects "a backward people who need an object lesson in modern ideas and ideals."[139]

PART TWO

OCCUPATION RESISTANCE

4

Nicaragua, 1913–1925

[The marines] have on more than one occasion made Nicaraguans
their victims.
> —*El Comercio*, Managua

The wave of resistance against the marines that washed over Nicaragua, Haiti, and the Dominican Republic for years after the original caudillos suffered defeat represented far more than a response to intervention. The second wave responded violently to the behavior of US troops and US administrators. During this more protracted period, concrete abuses committed by marines against ordinary people—drunken brawls, forced labor, torture, land grabs, concentration camps—motivated the invaded to oppose marine authority. The struggle for local autonomy against marine encroachments in Nicaragua from 1913 to 1925 was unique for not sparking organized violence, either by national or regional caudillos, largely because of the small size of the occupation force. Yet many Nicaraguan dynamics would be repeated in Hispaniola, including the secondary position of nationalism among rationales for resistance. The problems of political culture still hindered unity and altruism. A deeper look at day-to-day resistance illuminates why so many revolted as the occupations settled in.

With the Luis Mena-Benjamín Zeledón rebellion of 1912 suppressed and President Adolfo Díaz safely in power, the United States left a legation guard in Managua, thus turning intervention into occupation. The goal of the force—merely 100 in a town of 40,000—was to back Conservative rule and foster peace through the implicit threat of another mass landing. It worked in that there was no civil war during these thirteen years. Martial law prevailed most of the time and the marines kept parties from fighting, notably quelling a fortress takeover in May 1922.[1]

Occupiers shared the broad goals of dollar diplomacy—to meet the twin desires of investors and diplomats. Investors wanted their loans paid back and so they controlled the national bank, the railroad, and the receipts from the custom service. Diplomats sought a stable political situation that would lead to responsible lending to other nations and to US monopoly rights to a canal through Nicaragua. For this reason Washington endorsed US control over the customs service and the claims commission.[2] The occupation brought no great foreign investment or public works project, which suggested that more energy was channeled toward the goal of political stability than to socioeconomic improvement.[3] Several US citizens in Nicaragua stated that they aimed for a permanent transformation of Nicaraguan political culture. On the very day that Zeledón wrote his final letters, Lieutenant Colonel Charles Long predicted, from his conversations with US citizens and other foreigners in Nicaragua, that "even if we stop fighting and establish the present Government in power the same thing will break out again after our troops leave the country." Foreigners, he added, described Nicaraguans as an easily fooled "unruly mob" who "enjoy fighting" and "have no idea of the value of life, even their own lives." To institutionalize the concept of a loyal opposition, Long suggested a US-supervised election in which Liberals "could have a voice in the Government."[4] Six years later, after little progress in this direction, Dana Munro of the US legation wrote that Nicaraguans still joined political parties because of "petty prejudices and loyalty to individuals rather than political principles."[5]

Nicaraguans themselves had little good to say about their political culture. José María Moncada, in 1912 a dissident Liberal, wrote to the State Department to request that Washington simply take over the Bank of Nicaragua rather than extend a loan. "As a general rule, the Central American is hypocritical." If a loan comes through, he warned, "the money will be wasted and the American Government will have to intervene to pay the debt. What hard work! . . . In Nicaragua between the two factions there exists only hatred and only vengeance moves them to act."[6]

Crude nation-building through nominal pacification and democratization thus became the mission of the hundred-man occupation. In mid-November 1912, Admiral William Southerland, now the commander in chief of the Pacific Fleet, laid out elaborate flaws that forced US troops to remain:

a. Party spirit takes the place of National spirit, men of each party giving no consideration to the country but only to the party.
b. The feeling of each party against the other is so bitter—in fact, malignant—as to dominate all ideas of civilization and humanity—even family ties are forgotten during the frequent revolutions, and the rank and file of both sides actually revert to a semi-savage type.
c. The peon class is ignorant and brutal—practically less than semi-savage and with no National feeling—ready to take part of either side according to which offers the most promising results.

d. There is not a good road in the country.

e. There is no regular and permanent newspaper.

f. The Government treasury is practically empty.

g. There are no educational institutions worth mentioning.

Southerland's reading was brutally simplistic, but it summarized all the avenues for nation-building through political culture that the United States would pursue in most occupations—road building, fiscal responsibility, a "responsible" press, education reform, and, perhaps most surprising, the encouragement of "National feeling."[7] In essence, this was the US rationale for occupations, repeated often. In 1916, the US collector-general of customs in Nicaragua listed political culture as one of the reasons for ratifying the Bryan-Chamorro Treaty, which promised $3 million in exchange for exclusive US rights to build a canal through the country. As a result of that deal, he somehow reasoned, "professional revolutionists will become extinct, and revolutionary movements from personal ambition will be discouraged."[8]

Given the mixture of disdain, paternalism, and genuine commitment to reform of US occupiers, the record of nation-building over the dozen years of the hundred-man occupation is mixed at best. On the positive side, Washington righted Nicaragua's finances, introducing a stable currency in 1913 and keeping its military spending to a fraction of that of its neighbors.[9] It also cut back on graft. Lewis "Chesty" Puller, quartermaster in Nicaragua at the time, ended the system by which local political bosses and mayors rented barracks to the constabulary even though the barracks were public property.[10] Washington also successfully pressured Managua to outlaw forced labor by the 1930s.[11] Yet the marines built no road, ran no school, erected no public building, and did nothing to improve agriculture or sanitation.[12]

The two most concrete efforts at political cultural change floundered from a lack of US will and from Nicaraguan political self-interest. The first effort—to lower the claims made by natives and foreigners during the upheavals leading to the 1912 intervention through various mixed commissions—was intended to teach Nicaraguans to liberate the treasury from political considerations. But US officials allowed Managua to nominate the Nicaraguan member and one of the two US members of the commissions, and local authorities with political interests screened claims before they were considered. As a result, the claims richly rewarded the supporters of former president Adolfo Díaz. The commissions also rejected the claims of Conservatives who backed alternate factions and failed to pay claims immediately that it did approve.[13]

The goal of the second effort, founding the constabulary or National Guard (GN), was to encourage an apolitical, US-trained and Nicaraguan-manned professional quasi-military, which would replace the police, army, and navy.

Resistance, incompetence, and bad timing marred the effort. The training did not begin until the eve of the departure of the US legation guard on August 4, 1925, leaving little overlap between forces.[14] The Nicaraguan Congress insisted that the Nicaraguan army also be maintained as a parallel force and that US instructors of the GN be under the command of the Nicaraguan minister of war. The GN's recruitment budget was also tiny.[15] Initially, few Nicaraguans wanted to join the GN because, in the old army, officers kept troop salaries for themselves, and so Nicaraguans assumed the same of the constabulary.[16] Those recruited tended to be impressed into the GN from the ranks of *mozos* or agricultural laborers by Liberals and Conservatives.[17] As a result of all these weaknesses, the GN collapsed during the 1926–1927 civil war.[18]

Rather than discourage partisan ardor, then, the post-1912 occupation stoked it, as the British legation noted. Liberals "have an overwhelming support of the country at their backs and have especially gained in power since the action of the present Government in inviting and submitting to the intervention of the United States."[19] The hundred men in Managua, Munro recalled, were merely there as a dam holding in swelling political waters.[20]

Despite its size, the legation guard still made an impression on Nicaraguans, especially Managuans. To be sure, many locals had no contact with the marines and perhaps no opinion of them. Among those who did, the evidence suggests that negative impressions outweighed positive ones. Since the marines played no direct political or governing role—say, in building roads or policing Nicaraguans—their impact was almost entirely an expression of cultural tensions.

The marine guard partly helped to Americanize Nicaraguans.[21] Centralization of government in Managua during the occupation also concentrated cultural life in the capital. After the 1916 death of León's legendary poet, Rubén Darío, literary magazines tended to migrate to Managua. In the mid-1920s a Managua paper reported that a ten-piece orchestra "in the Yankee style" was formed. Around that time, moving pictures made their appearance, and magazines advertised US goods from Arrow shirts to Vicks VapoRub.[22]

In 1923 a marine major concluded that popular sentiment among Nicaraguans was "utterly different" from Mexican anti-Americanism. Nicaraguans, like Haitians, saw US citizens as no different from other foreigners, were cordial toward them, and "the majority . . . are very glad of American intervention and would like to see it continued indefinitely." "The effects of the revolution of 1912 and the short campaign of the marines in that year are about forgotten," he added.[23] Months later he reported that news that the marines were not leaving soon "seems to have met with general approval by Nicaraguans of all classes."[24]

This was not the opinion of all. Some Nicaraguans remained outright opposed to the occupation, especially when news of the Bryan-Chamorro treaty spread in 1914. Three Nicaraguans living in New Orleans at the time published a *Public Appeal of Nicaragua to the Congress and People of the United States,* a 185-page pamphlet in English reproducing documents and petitions from compatriots in Managua and New Orleans and from other Latin Americans.[25] Augusto Sandino's father, Gregorio, went to prison for protesting the treaty.[26]

Some Conservative oligarchs especially resented the spread of Protestantism and of the idea of the modern woman.[27] In July 1925 marine intelligence reported that Catholics led by "Mexican Jesuit priests" stoned the Protestant church in Granada "and otherwise threatened the lives of the American missionaries and their followers."[28] No one knows for sure what the elite as a whole thought of occupation. The closest evidence to a poll was a series of interviews conducted by prominent Nicaraguans in the summer of 1925. Interviewees said that they generally enjoyed the lack of party violence made possible by the legation guard but regretted the affront to sovereignty that the guard's presence implied.[29]

A marine major observed in 1923 that regular people who disliked the occupation—a minority, in his eyes—did so for concrete personal reasons. They "have lost money, or have been deprived of certain rights, or have been denied certain demands."[30] The record of the post-1912 occupation is rife with instances of day-to-day anger among Nicaraguans at the indignities visited upon them by the occupation. The episodes speak to the will to resist that met the presence of US troops in Latin America and suggest how that resistance multiplied when troops numbered not 100, as they did at this time, but several thousand as they would later in Nicaragua and elsewhere.

One marine intelligence captain recalled that, up to 1917, "there was no friction between the marines and the population other than small fights in canteens and an occasional rub between individual Marines and police."[31] Yet a Nicaraguan memoirist recalled that the legation guard "when off duty frequently caused a ruckus in the cantinas of Managua, sometimes assaulting peaceful Nicaraguan citizens, without any authority daring to stop them." Nicaraguan police eventually lost patience with the legation guard, and in January 1917 it jailed three troublesome marines. From their cell, the three banged on doors until guards subdued them with cudgel blows. The chief of police heard of the fracas, got on his horse, and stormed into the jail with hanging nooses. "Thinking they'd be hanged," the marines "fell on their knees, begging forgiveness."[32]

In December 1921, one or perhaps several clashes with marines ended with the death of Nicaraguan policemen.[33] To the occupation, the broad cause was obvious. "There is nothing for [marines] to do in town except to visit the numerous cantinas where prostitutes and vile liquor are cheaply obtainable," explained a navy captain. "The evidence presented before the board of investigation [of the police murders] is a constant tale of wanderings from cantina to cantina." He pointed to the humiliation suffered by police, soldiers, and artisans, who all made less money than Nicaraguan prostitutes. He also noted the "racial feeling, . . . which leads to the assumption of an air of superiority on the part of the marines."[34] In response, authorities aimed to minimize contact between marines and Managuans, thus contradicting the argument that a marine presence was enlightening to Nicaraguan political culture. In the midst of Nicaraguan congressional calls for withdrawal, the US minister requested that Nicaragua provide space for a canteen, dancehall, motion picture theater, and other buildings "with a view to keeping the marines from visiting Managua." He asked Managua to choose saloons where marines could be segregated.[35] Marines began to police themselves, raise morale, and enforce standards of conduct. The navy handed down sentences ranging from eight to forty years in prison for those convicted of killing the Nicaraguans, and the legation replaced the entire guard.[36]

Yet not all damage was undone. In 1924 the Liberal *obrerista* movement called for the overthrow of the Yankee-friendly government.[37] That same year a navy major described "a noticeable increase in the anti-American feeling, shown both by individuals and newspaper articles."[38] In 1925 he reported again on six "unprovoked and unpunished attacks on Marines in the streets of Managua" in less than four months. He blamed this "epidemic" entirely on Nicaraguans and their "violent and slanderous attacks on the Legation Guard in the press" and noted that "in no case has the police shown any initiative in bringing the offenders to justice."[39]

Nicaraguan accounts of some of these events were quite different. The navy major described one incident in which two marines pushed a Nicaraguan who was insulting them and blocking US citizens from leaving a reception, then saw him later with friendly police who did nothing. According to this navy version, the police drew their pistols against the marines. The Nicaraguan press reported instead that twenty marines, not two, "without reason" assaulted an innocent Nicaraguan with belts. The police brandished their weapons as "the only way to subdue them [*sic*] who have on more than one occasion made Nicaraguans their victims, and who offer the public these kind of spectacles." Another episode described a marine at a bullfight who was suddenly stabbed in the leg, suffering a "severe wound." *La Tribuna* instead characterized the assailant as a "compatriot" and said the knife "only managed to cut the trousers."[40]

As in other occupations, it remained difficult to parse the truth. Each side had reasons for distorting the facts—the marines to protect themselves while committing abuses, the Nicaraguans to prompt the departure of the guard. Compared to the Haitian and Dominican occupations, the years from 1913 to 1925 in Nicaragua were largely bloodless. Yet they demonstrated a similar desire on the part of the invaded to be free of the day-to-day consequences, as well as the pressure for political and cultural change, brought on by the presence of foreign troops.

5

Haiti, 1916–1920

How can we justify the thousand and one whims and harassments to
which is subject the stunned and stupefied peasant?
—*Le Matin*, Port-au-Prince

In 1921, writer-diplomat James Weldon Johnson testified before congressional
hearings. He had visited Haiti and was asked if Haitians resented "the fact of the
occupation or the method in which it has been conducted?"

"The fact in some degree, and the method in a greater degree," he responded.[1]

Johnson correctly identified how Haitians, like Nicaraguans, grew more irri-
tated as intervention turned into occupation and the small-scale, usually private
abuses of occupiers blended with the larger, more publicized encroachments to
move the invaded toward organized violent resistance. To be sure, some conti-
nuities carried over from pre-1915 social and political articulations. But the increased popular resonance of resistance and its support from many urban elites
spoke volumes about the added resentments resulting from the "method" of the
occupation. Abuses in Haiti were far more serious and widespread than in Nicaragua from 1913 to 1925, and as a result a new brand of caudillo emerged to lead
revolts. All analysts at the time and since noted the growth in size and strength of
the second wave of insurgencies compared to the first. Ensuring their surrender
consumed more time, treasure, and lives.

In Haiti, about 1,000 US troops along with 2,700 gendarmes, or Haitian constabularies, fought thousands of cacos in 131 engagements from April to October 1919, the bulk of the fighting. The pace dropped significantly after the death
of caco leader Charlemagne Péralte and then ended almost completely after the
killing of his successor Benoît Batraville on May 19, 1920.[2] Despite comparable
numbers of combatants on each side, marines benefited from superior weaponry, training, and medical facilities. They saw only ten of their own die versus
1,861 Haitians.[3]

Leaders of this second wave of violent resistance showed some rhetorical nationalism in speaking of uniting Haiti against foreign invaders. However, they operated within regional political settings and had next to no state-building programs in mind.[4] The motivations they articulated were largely a reflection of the parochial—though no less legitimate—issues of their followers.

The definition of "leader" was itself vague. In Haiti, no fewer than 488 Haitians who surrendered or were killed called themselves "chiefs." Of these, 308 were "generals."[5] Still, the leaders who emerged after the surrender of 1915 were better educated, had higher social status, and were younger than the previous wave.[6] A rare pamphlet allegedly from a group of leaders, circulated in late 1919, recalled bitterly "the generals who once were a part of the Revolution and who surrendered to the American Officers," calling them "none else then robber [sic], that did nothing but pillage private families and houses." In contrast, the pamphleteers described themselves as "upright of Character not having the intention to wrong our country men to the contrary we try to protect them." After threatening to kill all Haitian marine guides, the pamphlet ended with the words, "WE CRY VIVE CACOES, VIVE THE CACO GENERALS, VIVE THE REVOLUTION, DOWN WITH THE AMERICANS."[7]

The pamphlet responded to the marine killing on October 31, 1919, of their own leader, Charlemagne Masséna Péralte, the most important anti-occupation insurrectionist leader of his generation after Nicaragua's Augusto Sandino. Before the occupation, Péralte's life had followed a typical political arc. He described himself as "a young man from a good family, belonging to Haitian high society, friend of progress and of good civilization."[8] He was the legitimate child of a "general" and a seamstress, born into one of two dominant families in the Central Plateau town of Hinche.[9] A French priest who taught him as a boy described him as "not bad, but haughty and quick to take offense."[10] Péralte grew into a tall and thin man with large eyes and a powerful voice.[11] To an eighth-grade education he added the skills of a surveyor and made a living managing his and his mother's properties. He was a *griffe*—only three quarters black—which also elevated him above the masses.[12] Like many of the landed in Hinche, Péralte entered politics at an early age and enjoyed a social status between the urban bourgeoisie and the rural masses. When his mentor and brother-in-law Oreste Zamor became president, Péralte landed the job of commander of an administrative zone. After Zamor's overthrow, Péralte switched allegiance to Vilbrun Guillaume Sam, who rewarded him with a similar privilege.[13]

The occupation transformed Péralte from a political operative into a fighter. The July 1915 prison massacre by Sam's henchmen, which prompted the US intervention, included one of Péralte's relatives, an incident that might have forever disillusioned the thirty-one-year-old about Haiti's political culture and transformed him into a supporter of Rosalvo Bobo and a member of his Revolutionary Committee.[14] When US troops disembarked at Léogâne, which Péralte then commanded, they demanded he pull back his troops. Exelman Christophe witnessed the scene: "I could not make out his [Charlemagne's] words, but the conversation seemed rather lively. Charlemagne at times raised his voice, moved brusquely, displayed a hostile body language. Finally the whites left."[15]

Soon after, President Sudre Dartiguenave fired Péralte, who went to Port-au-Prince for a few days and swore he would "raise up the people and send the Americans home." "I will never remain under white domination," he informed his followers. "You will hear from me."[16] Charlemagne was different from his brother Saül, a caco chief who laid down his gun in 1915 for $20. Péralte emphasized how the foreign invader had created new priorities: national unity among blacks and mulattoes and an end to divisiveness and to elite-only political parties.[17] Some recalled that Péralte, unlike his peers, was free of color prejudice.[18] Yet he relied on the traditional animosity of northerners against southerners such as Dartiguenave, and he began his revolt by returning to Hinche.[19]

Péralte's popularity rose after his persecution by marines. On October 11, 1917, after a failed attack on marine barracks in Hinche in which Péralte may or may not have participated, a marine provost court condemned him to five years' hard labor. Gendarmes torched his house and pillaged his brother's. His friends were tortured, hung by their genitals, and forced to swallow water through a funnel.[20] In prison, said a French chargé, "his American guard soaked a mop in a pail of garbage and daubed the prisoner's face with it. The latter suffered the affront in silence."[21] Marines then made a crucial mistake by having Péralte sweep streets in full view of the Cap-Haïtien townsfolk, a disgrace difficult to overcome for an educated Haitian.[22] When Péralte broke out of prison eight months into his sentence, the word immediately spread through the Cap: "Péralte has escaped!"[23]

A year after the first Hinche attack, Péralte was firmly in charge of an incipient rebellion. On October 15, 1918, he recruited 300 workers who had not been paid by the occupation in three months and led a second attack on the town. It failed again since traitors warned the marines.[24] But Péralte was not captured, and from then on he called himself a caco.[25]

At the height of his insurrection, in 1919, Péralte deployed his most expansive ideological vision, seeing himself as a revolutionary and a leader of all Haitians against the Yankee occupation. He spoke of US occupations as behaving outside the accepted norms of "an era of light and progress" and tried to isolate the United States by proposing an alliance with the British. Claiming to command "more than thirty to forty thousand men" in every region save the south, he described the struggle of "Haitian people" as "only for the defense of its territory and of its flag."[26] When a fellow Haitian vacillated, he reminded him, "We are in an international war."[27] To the French Minister René Delage he wrote, unlike any other caco leader to that point, of "the principles of President [Woodrow] Wilson himself concerning the rights and sovereignty of small peoples."[28] He signed his correspondence: "Chief of the Revolutionary Forces against the American nation on Haitian soil."[29]

Péralte denied any anti-white racism or anti-US prejudice and cited his education by white missionaries as evidence.[30] In March 1919 a poster addressed "to the American authorities" explained, "We do not hate foreigners, but our country is ours, come peacefully, develop agriculture and Commerce, bring us trade and industry and we are with you, you will have our esteem."[31] The poster suggested that Péralte never rejected foreign economic and financial domination, not even the loss of administrative and political independence. Leaders during this second caco war limited their grievance to the presence of the marines. In fact, Péralte and his successor Batraville both believed that the withdrawal of US forces would deepen foreign influence, helping Haiti to develop.[32]

Péralte attracted not the 30,000 to 40,000 he claimed, but perhaps 15,000 at the height of the insurrection, still an awe-inspiring number given that adherents came from a limited region. Haitians who followed Péralte described him as sociable, fair, unpretentious, and, unlike many peers, opposed to corporal punishment.[33] He also chose his geography well. The hilly area around Hinche was long a destination for escaped slaves, and because of its isolation it largely eluded the 1915 order to disarm.[34] Its remoteness also allowed marines and their subordinates to abuse a system of forced labor that caused the rebellion.[35] As a result, Péralte presented a formidable obstacle in the countryside, raiding several towns, even the capital in October 1919, often defeating gendarme detachments.[36] His military combined modern guerrilla techniques of surprise and concealment, Catholic symbols such as the crucifix, and traditional Haitian instruments of communication such as drums, smoke signals, and conch shells.[37]

But Péralte's cacos were badly trained and armed mostly with crude rifles and machetes against US machine guns.[38] They never triumphed in open or urban warfare against the marines and gendarmes. Péralte's nationalist rhetoric and military power also have concealed major contradictions. For one, he did single out not only the US government but all US citizens as evil, writing that "in the world, Americans alone have the capacity" for the cruelty they displayed in Haiti. He pointed particularly to US hypocrisy and "unscrupulousness," calling les Yankees "cruel and unjust."[39] He targeted foreign corporations, such as the Haitian-American Sugar Company (HASCO).[40] Péralte also used the bogey of les blancs to scare up adherents. As a female family member wrote to him triumphantly, "Everyone [in the north] is bursting against the whites, no one accepts this condition. They are saying they would rather rebel than be under the white orders."[41] In appealing to gendarmes to turn against their US rulers, Péralte deployed racialist ideas: "You are *blacks*, my brothers, I love you all."[42] In the same vein, an unsigned caco placard included the following entreaty: "Let us chase that ravenous people whose ravenousness is represented in the person of their President Wilson, traitor, vagabond, rioter, thief, you will die with your country. . . . Down with the Americans!"[43] Péralte conformed to a common rhetorical tradition in Haiti, seeing whites and foreigners as hostile to the country.

Péralte's narcissism likely rendered him satisfied with military leadership but unprepared for national political leadership. In a speech in Léogâne he told troops, "I feel happy and proud of being again at your head, like a good father who feels happy among the beloved children who surround him!"[44] His recruiting pitch was, "The gods have willed that the people of Haiti should rule the world and Charlemagne shall be their king!"[45] He never talked of democracy but rather declared his intent to rule by force: "military administrations belong to us, because the country is ours."[46] Péralte's most momentous failure was that, like Vicentico in the Dominican Republic, his state-building efforts were minimal.[47] While he commanded thousands of troops and named generals and a cabinet, and while his movement touched a quarter of Haiti's territory and a fifth of its population, these were all purely military moves.[48] His only ministers were of war and finance. He proposed absolutely no political program beyond "drive the invaders into the sea."[49] Although he enjoyed popular support, Péralte never enacted reforms for the betterment of the masses. He boasted of being a godsend—literally—and claimed immunity to bullets.[50] When the marines tricked him and shot him dead, they made sure to broadcast photos of his corpse so as to puncture the myth of his invulnerability (see Fig. 5.1).[51]

Péralte's brief successor was Benoît Batraville, his first lieutenant and a former schoolteacher. From peasant origins, *Ti-Benoît* was believed to possess even more astonishing magical powers. Haitians swore that Batraville could disappear when on his horse and ride through town unseen; could dodge bullets, sensing they were coming; and could heal with natural medicine.[52]

Batraville's ideology, meanwhile, differed little from Péralte's. Like Péralte, he was in the military when the 1915 invasion force landed and, as his division disbanded, it swore "never to rest until all the whites had been driven from Haiti."[53] After the chiefs elected him to replace Péralte, Batraville also spoke of an "international war" and of the threat of slavery if the Yankees remained.[54] He was in fact more aggressive than Péralte, stepping up the pace of attacks. He personally engaged in these assaults, hacking away at the *blancs* with his machete. A follower described how, after taking a marine prisoner, "Benoit split the head of the White man open, and ordered all of us to grease our ammunition with his brains.

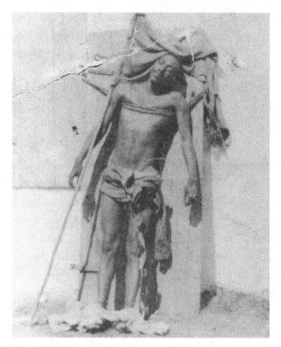

Figure 5.1 Charlemagne Péralte after US forces killed him and tied him to a door, taking a photo to prove to Haitians his death, November 1919. Folder "Haiti: Officials," USMC Historical Division, Marine Corps Base, Quantico, Va.

This is done so that when we fire at Marines we do not miss them."[55] Batraville, too, attacked Port-au-Prince and failed to do much damage, since his force was reduced from 15,000 to 2,500.[56] On May 19, 1920, a patrol found Batraville and killed him.[57]

Once the caco revolt was over, marines distributed *bon habitant* cards to Haitians as badges of their newfound loyalty to the occupation. Of the 36,000 handed out in late 1919 and early 1920, one district commander estimated that 85 percent of the Haitians holding them—a whopping 30,600—"were active as Bandits, at one time or another during the last revolution."[58]

While the motivations of these masses who resisted are hard to discern, many must have been attracted by Péralte's defense of their rights. He explained the simple needs of his followers: "to be protected, to work and to live in peace." He also railed against the corruption of Haitian politicians and the brutality of gendarmes.[59] In his letter to René Delage, Péralte outlined abuses committed by US troops, which would have rung true to his followers: "perpetual humiliations, unbelievable crimes, assassinations, robberies and acts of barbarism."[60] Caco leaders also lobbied for peasant loyalties. Batraville's followers recalled twelve rules that their leader handed down to them. Most were tactical, but one decreed: "After each victory, the caco chief, before leaving, assembles the population and explains the motives and the goal of the battle. Convincing the people of the justice of our cause . . . is the first task of education. The caco war is also a war for hearts and minds." Another said: "The caco is the protector of the poor peasant. Any abuse against a farmer (robbery, rape) is a capital offense. The caco war is a war in defense of oppressed workers."[61]

The few traces of actual peasants in the historical record suggest a variety of peasant motivations stemming from parochial self-interest rather than nationalism. Like traditional caudillos, Péralte and his aides maintained a close relationship with local civil authorities while abhorring Dartiguenave, continuing the tradition of pitting local political figures against national ones. Dozens of "guarantees" speak to the commitment of cacos to informing "authorities civil and military" to protect and aid those who had sold or given goods to the cacos.[62]

In return, the caco caudillos enjoyed the loyalty of many. Farmer Solon Virgile recalled a spontaneous sympathy for Batraville:

> Here, we were all cacos. It was not an individual choice. I mean that the community, in the majority, was spontaneously against the arrival of the *blancs* in the region. . . . My father had a field that I helped to till. During the harvest, the cacos came armed, and we invited them to take what they needed. They did not abuse. We planted for the market; we planted for them too. My father even fought for them. From time to time, he would vanish for a few days and go fire his carbine or distribute machete blows.[63]

Batraville's niece agreed: "Gendarmes and marines . . . knew that responses to all their demands would be courteous but negative; there was no cooperation. We said nothing about what we knew of the cacos."[64]

Many cacos joined the fight for the basest of reasons. Some saw Péralte as the latest incarnation of a leader who would let them plunder. Decils Defilise admitted he "heard stealing was going on and that he came to Hinche to steal because it was in his heart to steal." Raymond Marcelina joined the fight because his chief "told him that it was necessary to kill all of the whites so that Charlemagne could be chief."[65] Only Caludius Chevry, seventeen at the time, recalled joining Batraville because of "nationalism," and still he had an additional motive: "a taste for adventure."[66]

Non-combatants also contributed to the revolt for concrete reasons. Admitting that cacos "have the population with them," marines regularly reported on the thousands likely feeding and sheltering the rebels.[67] Many aided out of fear. In fall 1919 the Vatican's chargé took a trip through the interior and noticed "an unusual agitation, that the inhabitants, ordinarily very calm and hospitable, appeared fearful and fled at the sight of strangers. The cacos threaten to massacre all those who helped the Americans."[68]

Other Haitians opposed the dangers and annoyances of modernity. The *New York Times* reported that some peasants resented US-built roads because they "involved the destruction in many instances of their shady trails, and also because automobiles killed their burros."[69] A California traveler confirmed that Haitians, unused to the speed of cars, dodged them only at the last second, often jumping in front of vehicles instead of away. "One would think they never had seen an automobile before."[70]

The overwhelming reason for following Péralte, however, was the corvée. The unfree labor system was already on Haitian law books in 1915 but Haitians ignored it.[71] In summer 1916, marines revived the program in order to build roads. At first it was unproblematic, even popular, because it required that Haitians volunteer a few days' work per year, close to home, in camps providing free food, shelter, and entertainment. Well-off Haitians could avoid the work by paying a fine.[72]

Then some Haitian gendarmes and mayors, overseen by marines, began to abuse the system. French Consul Delage summarized the "clumsiness" of the US troops in enforcing the corvée.

> Desirous of building roads quickly, the Americans stopped people, peasants tilling fields or going to market, servants, etc. and made them work . . . not around their village, but wherever the new authorities wished, locking them at night in enclosures under the watch of gendarmes, feeding them poorly and forcing them to work beyond their abilities. Many who had given the required number of days saw their paper guarantees torn and they were forced to begin anew. Many peasants, to avoid this forced labor, fled to the mountains and joined the cacos. [73]

In order to recruit still more corvée laborers, marines sacked and burned homes, often of poor farmers hiding from the cacos.

The navy ended the practice in July 1918 and investigated its abuses. In early 1919 the new brigade commander, Brigadier General Albertus Catlin, personally visited a corvée site. "Catlin asked those who had been forced to work and wanted to return to their farms to step to the front," recalled another marine. "Practically the entire gang stepped to the front."[74] Despite the order to end the corvée, it continued for another eight months near Hinche, Péralte's hometown.

Haitians did not need Péralte to tell them to resist. In early 1917 one city council—in Hinche, no less—protested recruitment, the gendarmes having to forcibly escort the mayor to round up laborers.[75] Later that year *Le Matin* enquired rhetorically, "How can we explain these manhunts, slave-catcher style? These multiple taxes and fines to corvée workers? These nighttime arrests and imprisonments, these incarcerations of workers night after night, etc, etc? How can we justify the thousand and one whims and harassments to which is subject the stunned and stupefied peasant?"[76] Kernisan Isodore remembered gendarmes taking him and his brothers and others to a chapel to work the corvée near Laborde. When the order came to march to the site, the men refused. The gendarmes shoved and hit the crowd and began to rope the men together. The laborers hit back with their fists. Women shouted for help. The flustered gendarmes sought a marine who arrested Isodore and the others and then occupied the town.[77]

Others resisted once they were integrated into the work camps. A man called Estimon got into a dispute with a marine over whether he had been paid (labor was forced but paid $0.20 per day). Seeing no resolution, the marine "hung him by the wrists . . . and beat him, beat him without pause. Blood ran down Estimon's body. He clenched his teeth but did not cry. Then the white had enough and sent him, naked, back to work. . . . When he was offered food, he refused his portion; it was his way of defying the white. Soon after, he escaped."[78]

Nestor Dorsica recalled Péralte as a literal savior because he burst into corvée camps, broke down doors, and invited workers to join him. Some used the opportunity to flee. Termitus Michel, tired of the abuse, joined the cacos. "My place was beside the Haitians, my peers, and not the whites. I chose my camp."[79] The identification of the corvée with occupation abuse was so strong that, years later, Haitians gladly worked for foreign corporations but refused to build roads for them.[80]

The second wave of Haitian violent resistance was not only longer, more popular, and more violent than the first, but its motivations stemmed far more from the suffering and the ambition of those living under occupation, thus deepening the two-way collaboration between leaders and followers of caudillo revolts. For all the nationalist rhetoric of the leaders, the motivations of most were more prosaic. Rather than take away from their legitimacy, this reality, in their eyes, reinforced it by strengthening their anti-occupation resolve.

6

The Dominican Republic, 1917–1922

With their lack of education and the life they live it can hardly be
doubted they turn bandit.

—A marine

The simultaneous experiences of Dominicans were similar if somewhat less tragic than those of Haitians: fewer died over a longer period, and fewer joined the equivalent of the cacos. Yet Dominican resistance proved longer lasting because it was even more decentralized. Atomized roaming bands, long established in the sugar producing east of the republic, shifted their rhetoric and tactics after 1917 to focus on the methods of the occupation, which, in a vicious circle, became more sweeping and brutal as more rebels rose up against them. More so than in Haiti, Dominican insurrectionist leaders, with some exceptions, proved largely devoid of nationalistic ideology or alternatives to marine-led state-building, which reflected their continuing attachment to local autonomy and caudillo politics.

The peace that the US-proclaimed military government thought was secured for good in mid-1917 after the killing of Vicente Evangelista broke less than a year later with the resumption of "banditry," this time largely confined to the east.[1] From then until 1922 there were always at least a few hundred rebels in arms, under five to ten leaders, and mostly in Seibo and Macorís provinces, but some also in western Azua, central Santo Domingo, and the north.[2] Military governors minimized the resurgence for months as evidence of attacks mounted, insisting on calling rebels "lawless and work-avoiding criminals."[3] They also suspected German machinations but found no hard evidence.[4] By 1919 the violence grew so generalized in the east that marine numbers tripled, to 1,480 men, then to 2,500 in 1921–1922.[5] With these reinforcements the military government cordoned off areas and used a systematic "dragnet" in addition to spies, amnesty, and search-and-destroy missions to finish off the rebellion.[6] All leaders and their remaining followers surrendered in April and May 1922, the second wave of rebellion having lasted over two years longer than in Haiti.[7] In 467 contacts, 1,137 rebels died compared to 16 marines.[8]

Some "banditry" survived the death of Vicentico after July 1917, but only a year later did marines notice a sharper definition of the leadership, with new names such as Martín Peguero, Nicolás Pimentel, and Carlos Chavaría achieving prominence.[9] "The situation is quite serious," wrote a Dominican called "Pina" in July 1918. Groups of 150 were roaming "publicly by roads, killing without mercy." These, he said, "are not yesterday's gavillero bands who numbered 8 or 10."[10] Yet Dominicans, while unleashing violence on others beyond their traditional political enemies, were never united behind any one figure. There were no strategic goals, no coordination, and no national reach.[11] Decentralization even within regions was stronger in the Dominican Republic than in Nicaragua or Haiti, and partly for that reason the rebels, though fewer, were harder to decapitate than the cacos.

Among the great majority of band chiefs there was little politicization of leaders as the marine occupation spread to the east. As in the Haitian case, the extent of politicization for most reflected their fear of centralization, of an occupation that would transform the state into a permanent far-reaching engine of repression.[12]

Sugar estates were favorite targets of the rebels. Their properties had increased in size and number before the occupation, and owners often paid bands for protection. When the marines came, typical payments fell to about $1,000 per year from each sugar estate because marines offered competition to rebel chiefs.[13] Plantation managers actually asked marines to delay their deployment into the east because they intuited that the presence of US troops would intensify attacks rather than discourage them. Yet there is little evidence that leaders targeted sugar corporations as revenge against the US troop presence; they did so because that was where the money was. Any link between attacking plantations and harming the occupation was indirect in that plantations were a sign of globalization and aggressive land acquisition spreading into the countryside. In the same anti-centralization vein, bands tended to cut off the tentacles of transportation and communication such as railroads and telegraph lines.[14]

Most leaders evinced no nationalism or other ideological goals. Pedro Celestino Rosario was typical. Known as "Tolete" and turned in by Evangelista in 1917, he was back in the saddle soon after, leading one of the most feared bands. Tolete expressed no political convictions or goals but did fancy himself a defender of public virtues. He once ranted that he, "with an honorable guerrilla," would kill all who robbed bodegas and raped women. On the bloodied body of one of his victims he left a note explaining that the man had been shot because Tolete was "cleansing all evil and not hurting anyone."[15]

A few Dominicans attacked marines with the goals of national caudillismo in mind. One marine explained that "General B." was planning to attack his troops because "he will then, truly be a general in the eyes of his people, and will have no difficulty in augmenting his forces, raising his own prestige and increasing the morale of his followers with the idea of ultimately capturing the Capitol."[16]

The most politicized leader, and perhaps the only one, was Ramón Nateras, who emerged from behind the shadow of Evangelista in 1917. Unusual because he "thought like a state," Nateras may have been the only rebel leader to integrate national symbols and practices into his rituals. Every day he had the Dominican flag hoisted and the anthem played.[17] He operated a nascent system of justice in which he punished followers for stealing or undertaking raids without permission, and he used a rubber stamp on correspondence.[18] He considered protection payments a form of taxation or fine.[19] He often wore a red sash around his shoulders.[20] Unlike other chiefs, Nateras made his "army," as he called it, conduct regular military-style drills. They saluted their "general" by genuflecting and raising their right hands.[21]

Nateras's boldest statement of national goals was his attack on the Italian-owned Angelina sugar estate in September 1921 after he mistakenly thought it failed to pay him a "tax."[22] With the Angelina's British manager Thomas Steele as his hostage, Nateras wrote to all sugar companies in the country demanding they pressure the United States to withdraw. He wanted "the complete restoration of my Country" and threatened the lives of all other managers. He indicated his power over sugar laborers by saying he could "prevent the grinding of cane this year" if the managers failed to comply (Steele, once free, fled the country without paying; it is unclear if others paid).[23] Yet Nateras had limits as a nationalist. He stamped correspondence partly because he could neither read nor write.[24] And he ran protection rackets just like other caudillos.[25]

Dominican followers, meanwhile, also harbored a variety of motivations for resisting, although marines often assumed that they were either criminals, sugar workers, or simple peasants forced to join.[26] No Dominican leader, reported a marine, had "what we term personal magnetism, the adherence of their respective followers resting solely on what the chief promises to pay or give or do."[27] Few of their voices have survived, but it seems that followers joined for either symbolic or material benefits. Some, for instance, joined to fortify their political standing within their village or locality.[28] Many were sugar workers. From June to October, rebel activity tended to rise along with unemployment as the plantations stopped cutting and grinding cane. Followers also flocked to the rebels when the economy nosedived.[29] One knowledgeable marine related how Nateras's followers were "voluntary recruits from the riff-raff among the unemployed who were hanging around the Sugar Estates . . . and . . . those who were being forced from their lands, where they had lived for years, by the expansion of the Sugar Estates."[30] "During the quiet spells," another explained, most rebels were "living in the houses of the sugar cane workers, some of them even working in the sugar mills. It is a certainty that they are being supplied with rum, clothes and all sorts of supplies by their friends around the mills."[31]

A second lieutenant reported on the town of El Jagual, whose inhabitants "do not appear friendly to the marines, in fact some might be called hostile." El Jagual's sugar workers had family connections to Nateras.[32] The caudillo used to work for the nearby sugar estate and so locals likely provided him with services in return for "good clothes." The estate paid little and there was little work to be paid for. Many had owned their own land but moved to town either because they feared the rebels or wanted the higher wages of the sugar estate. When work became sparse, they found themselves stuck in a wage economy with no savings to return to the land. The marine ended with the candid observation, "With their lack of education and the life they live it can hardly be doubted they turn bandit."[33]

On and off the sugar plantations, Dominican peasants, like Haitians, were reluctant to share information with marines, either identifying with rebels or fearing reprisals.[34] Some were told by rebels, "Now that you have been fighting the Americans you have got to remain with us as, otherwise, they will kill you."[35] Nateras was reportedly "the most vicious of the bandit chiefs and is the one most dreaded by the inhabitants."[36] Others had family members among the rebels, and when these relatives were killed by the occupation, they joined.[37] Many claimed to want to help the marines but rarely did.[38]

As one former marine who served in all three occupations said, peasants were stuck "between the Devil and the deep sea"—the occupation and the resistance—and they adopted survival strategies in response.[39] One district commander wrote in frustration that Dominicans reported robbery, arson, and murder by rebels, but never sooner than two days after the fact, and usually a week later, thus rendering the information useless—and keeping themselves safe from rebel retribution.[40]

Finally there were followers who joined, or at least said they joined, free from self-interest. A marine commanding officer reported on "a class of bandits who gave as an excuse patriotic motives. These bandits boast that they have driven the Spanish and the Haitiens from the Republic and will soon drive the Americans out. They look upon themselves as heroes, and the food and clothing that they steal as prerogatives of their position."[41]

Like their Haitian counterparts, Dominican insurrectionists operated largely at two levels—one for leaders, who occasionally expressed nationalistic ideals and deployed the rudiments of state formation, another for followers who sought more prosaic ends and rarely expressed a thought beyond the needs of themselves, their family, and their community. Although the rebels eventually surrendered, they forced the occupation to spend far more time and money than it planned to, without any evidence of achieving a permanent change in Dominican political culture, and only after the occupation promised it would begin to withdraw. Ramón Nateras surrendered on May 4, 1922, with twenty-three men.[42]

Nicaragua, 1927–1929

Although you state in your letter that the continuation of my armed resistance will serve no purpose, I declare to you that only the continuation of my armed resistance will bring about the benefit to which you allude.

—Augusto Sandino to Rear Admiral D. F. Sellers

Although the rebellion led by Augusto Sandino against the marines in the Segovia mountains of northern Nicaragua began in 1927, after all other insurrections in Nicaragua, Haiti, and the Dominican Republic ended, it shared many characteristics with its predecessors, among them rebel motivations stemming from both social inequalities and US behavior. More deliberately than any other guerrilla leader, however, Sandino marshaled markers of identity into effective asymmetrical warfare. He was also more of a social revolutionary than any other resisters. Sandino, finally, expressed the most developed, persistent, and effective nationalism of any anti-occupation leader, though his nationalism was merely one among a constellation of motivations. In fact, his movement was most compelling when it was least ideological and most focused on fighting for concrete improvements in the lives of his followers. From 1927 to 1929 especially, Sandino appeared as if he could be everything to everyone. He combined effective guerrilla warfare with the Segovias' political traditions while remembering whom he was fighting with and why.[1] Yet by 1929 the uprising ran up against its own limitations.

Compared to other insurrections, the Sandino revolt attracted a larger force of marines, fought them longer and more ferociously, and reached a peace deal rather than surrender. Sandino's success highlighted a dilemma of the era of occupations: while marines claimed that resistance only brought more US troops, Sandino, as in the opening epigraph, countered that only resistance could bring about lasting independence and peace through the departure of those troops. Sandino was also effective because, while the benefits to which the US naval commander alluded included ending the cycle of political revolutions, Sandino also opposed this very cycle. Occupiers as well as resisters wanted a deep change in political culture in Nicaragua but never perceived each other as sharing this goal.

Two and a half months after the small US legation guard withdrew from Managua in August 1925, a bipartisan coalition fell to the Conservatives. In May 1926, marines returned to Nicaragua, first landing on its isolated Caribbean shore to put down a Liberal uprising. They withdrew in August, but when the insurgency spread, they returned. By January 1927, US mediation failed and the marines returned to Managua, with the limited mission of safeguarding foreign lives and property.

At the start of the war there was one clear difference between the parties, sharpened by the 1913–1925 occupation. Liberals identified Conservatives as *yankistas*, sellouts of the nation. When the US chargé paid a social visit to Liberals in León in August 1926, he was the first US diplomat to be entertained there in twenty years.[2] The east had always been majority Liberal and the west was now, too.[3] Washington supported President Adolfo Díaz reluctantly, but it did support him.[4] "I am afraid the USG[overnment] have made rather a mess of this," noted a British observer weeks before the marines took Managua again.[5]

The occupation of Nicaragua in 1926–1927 was again by Conservative invitation, unlike in Haiti or the Dominican Republic, a fact that threatened the very political reformism behind the occupation. On November 15, 1926, Díaz asked for a full-scale US intervention and Washington actually demurred for a while. It was aggression against US citizens—"annoying taxes on American firms" and the murder of a US citizen at Puerto Cabezas on the Atlantic coast—that moved President Calvin Coolidge to order the marines back in.[6] With Mexico arming the Liberals, Coolidge also lifted an embargo that allowed Conservatives to buy weapons from the United States.[7] This made clear to all that Washington chose—again—the least electable party.[8] US invaders had woven their own web of geopolitical self-interest, democracy promotion, and plain naïveté, and were now tangled in it. In 1926, when US Chargé Lawrence Dennis reversed the US stance and refused to support a Conservative because the 1923 Central American treaty forbade the recognition of coup-elevated presidents, *The Nation* called Dennis a "big bully."[9]

The price for opposing Liberals was high. One marine described how Managuans greeted arriving troops: "The sidewalks were crowded with natives. Some cheered, the majority passively looked on with contempt in their eyes for the 'gringo invader,' and some of the bolder ones even went as far as to hiss at the procession." After a bloody US fight in La Paz Centro, inhabitants of Liberal León reacted to marines moving fallen comrades with "cheers, cat calls, and boos." Marines punched them in the face.[10]

Washington recognized its error in choosing sides yet remained in Nicaragua and attempted further reforms of the country's political culture by sending Henry Stimson in April 1927. A protégé of empire builders such as Theodore Roosevelt and Elihu Root and secretary of war in 1911–1913, Stimson talked to warring Nicaraguan parties and brought along Brigadier General Logan Feland, who had been in the Philippines, Cuba, and the Dominican Republic.[11]

Stimson's diary of the trip revealed that Nicaraguans presented him with non-ideological, self-interested views of the war. Stimson's wife, meanwhile, listened to Nicaraguan women tell her that all were sick of the fighting. Stimson himself concluded the same, seeing little to distinguish the parties.[12] The Nicaraguan minister of foreign relations freely admitted that governments in power regularly stole elections. He asked for US supervision, using the analogy of Washington as a baseball umpire, to which Stimson "remarked jokingly that the players at times tried to kill the umpire."[13] Liberals told him the same and even spoke of the United States as a "big brother."[14] Stimson was "surprised to find that as great manifestation of friendship was shown . . . by the Liberals . . . as by the Conservatives."[15] Liberal leader José María Moncada even praised US protection of Liberals in a US magazine, foreseeing "a period of twelve or more years under the supervision of the American Government" because "Nicaragua stands in need of republican education."[16]

On May 4, 1927, under a black hawthorn tree—the *espino negro*—in the town of Tipitapa, Stimson had Liberals accept Díaz as president in return for government jobs and US-supervised elections in 1928 and 1932. Both sides also accepted the re-establishment of a constabulary, the National Guard. Disarmament for $10 a gun was part of the pact, resulting in a hefty haul: 11,600 rifles, 303 machine guns, and 5,500,000 cartridges.[17] "We figured out that we had risked our necks fighting for a lousy ten dollars," said one disillusioned Nicaraguan.[18]

"The civil war in Nicaragua is now definitely ended," cabled Stimson on May 15, 1927.[19] Two thousand fighters accepted amnesty.[20] All thirteen Liberal generals, including Moncada, signed the Pact of Espino Negro.[21]

All except for one. Few knew anything about him. Stimson dismissed him and spread the false rumor that he had fought with Pancho Villa in Mexico.[22] A US diplomat called him "Sandina."[23] A marine reported that he was "slightly crazy" and could not survive in the mountains, much less hold together his primitive, multinational band (see Fig. 7.1).[24]

Though he himself thought his chances remote, Augusto Sandino appears never to have hesitated. He allegedly agreed with US-supervised elections since these would likely elect Liberals, but his personal animosity toward Moncada changed his mind. "They want to install a Yankee as president," he told supporters,

Figure 7.1 Augusto Sandino. Folder "Nicaragua; Sandino," USMC Historical Division, Marine Corps Base, Quantico, Va.

"and in my opinion it should be a son of the nation, be he Liberal or Conservative, but a son of the nation—but a Yankee, never."[25] In early May, while feigning to prevaricate on signing Espino Negro, Sandino retreated to the small town of San Rafael in the department of Nueva Segovia. With all his men before him, he slammed a bullet onto the middle of a table and told them to choose sides. "From here to there: Yankees; from here to *there*: Sandino. All those who want to follow me, raise your hand." Nine of every ten deserted.[26] The twenty-nine who followed took off to what would become Sandino's remote mountain hideout.[27] From then on, Sandino taunted Moncada. "I don't know why you keep ordering me around," he wrote his former superior. "Indubitably you know my temperament and you know that I am unyielding. . . . I DO NOT SELL OUT, I DO NOT SURRENDER, you must defeat me."[28]

Sandino's life had prepared him for his stand against the Yankee troops.

Augusto Calderón Sandino was born in Niquinohomo, between Managua and Granada, probably in 1895.[29] His classical name, and even more that of his brother Sócrates, suggested the Sandino family's belief in "the great ideals," which instilled in Augusto a "great will."[30] Unlike Sócrates, Augusto was a "love-child," the product of a Spanish-descended middle-class Liberal coffee land-owner, his father Gregorio, and Gregorio's Indian servant Margarita.[31] Because

Sandino was illegitimate, Gregorio's wife, América, kept him out of his father's house. Augusto grew up in dire poverty as a second-class family member, an experience he recalled instilling in him a hatred of "misery and impotence."[32] At four or five he accompanied his mother to the fields to pick coffee and corn. He rarely attended school and stole food for his house.[33] At nine, his mother left for Granada to join a lover but Sandino stayed behind. His father recognized him but América continued to ostracize him, forcing him to eat with the help. At sixteen Sandino briefly left town after an altercation with América. Even as a teenager he was bent on owning land like his father.[34]

In 1920 Sandino shot a man and had to escape.[35] "My honor was at stake" is all he ever said of it.[36] Going on the lam began Sandino's years abroad, which gave him a unique perspective among leaders of insurrections.[37] Sandino traveled through Central America and Mexico, toiling at working-class jobs.[38] Perhaps most meaningful were his experiences working for US fruit and sugar corporations in Honduras and then a precursor of the United Fruit Company in Guatemala.

Mexico, where he arrived in May 1923, was his most formative stop. The oil fields of Veracruz and Tampico offered not only generous salaries but also a political education. The Mexican Revolution was identifying its enemies—racism, imperialism, great landowning. Sandino imbibed a variety of intellectual and spiritual traditions, even practicing yoga and vegetarianism.[39] "I confess that in our profane world I never found happiness," he later wrote of those days, "and because I was in search of spiritual consolation, I read mythological books and searched for teachers of religion."[40] Most influential, however, was anarcho-syndicalism, more popular than Marxism at the time. From it Sandino borrowed, among other things, the red and black colors of his future flag.[41] Yet living among workers, whom he found to be undisciplined, vice-ridden wastrels, was also difficult. "This life is not for a man who wishes to distinguish himself in something," he wrote his father.[42]

On May 14, 1926, Sandino "suddenly resigned, stating that he had urgent business at home in Nicaragua," according to his boss in Tampico.[43] He was perhaps homesick, perhaps in love, or perhaps the statute of limitations on his attempted murder charge had expired.[44] "My Liberalism screamed from within me" is apparently what Sandino recalled.[45] He went to the San Albino gold mine, owned by Charles Butters of California, who, like other employers, noticed nothing distinctive about Sandino—a responsible, intelligent employee, but physically unimpressive at 5' 5" and 125 pounds.[46] As assistant paymaster at San Albino, Sandino learned of the unfair system of pay and told workers to ask for cash wages rather than company scrip that could only be redeemed at the company store, with prices triple those of competitors.[47] "I explained to them that I was not a communist, but a socialist," he later told an interviewer.[48] Sandino was also partisan, recruiting Liberal soldiers while at the mine.

Unlike Dominican or Haitian insurrectionist leaders, who embraced ideologies—if at all—after being caudillos for years, it was Sandino's early political awakening against Conservatism and imperialism that made him a caudillo. Sometime in late 1926, with $300, some weapons from Honduras, and workers from San Albino and elsewhere, Sandino raised an army and joined the Liberal cause.[49] In March 1927 he scored his greatest coup of the war, taking Jinotega. Otherwise he was little noticed by other Nicaraguans or US officials.[50]

In the first two years of his revolt, Sandino made tactical mistakes, perhaps born of his outsized ambitions. Yet he quickly adjusted his fighting style to focus his goals not on military but political victory through sympathy for guerrilla warfare.

Sandino dated the birth of his revolt against Moncada and the Yankees to May 4, 1927, the signing of Espino Negro. He was thirty-two or thirty-three. His father tried to dissuade him from taking on the marines. Upon seeing his son's resolve, however, Gregorio advised him: "If you are ready to sacrifice yourself, you must do it with utmost honor. After firing the first bullet against the invader you should expect nothing less than death or victory. . . . Better you commit suicide than to fall into shameful surrender."[51]

The Sandinistas had several advantages starting off. Perhaps more than 100 who had defected, seeing Sandino's army survive, re-joined after a few weeks.[52] They possessed arms, including four machine guns.[53] To defeat Sandino, meanwhile, marine commanders had limited authority. They could impose no martial law countrywide nor send troops outside areas under rebellion. Finally, Sandino's army was 100 miles from any railroad, straining the supply chain.[54]

Yet the marines were better trained and equipped than any fighting force in Latin America, and Sandino made a grievous error by taking them head-on. On May 19, he sent out a circular warning that he intended to wage violent warfare until the marines left or replaced Díaz with a representative president, neither of which the invaders would do. In mid-June he seized Jícaro, renaming it Ciudad Sandino, and the San Albino mine to fund his rebellion as well as surrounding towns.[55] On July 16, 1927, in the first major battle of the rebellion, Sandino, with 400 to 500 men, attacked the 87 marines and guards at Ocotal, a small town a dozen miles from the Honduran border. The attack came as a surprise, and the battle lasted sixteen hours. But the marines rallied, calling in bombing raids that terrified the townspeople.

The day after the "rout," the US minister figured Sandino was finished.[56] The marines recorded "a complete silence regarding him" and sent half their force home.[57]

But Sandino was merely regrouping and processing two lessons from Ocotal. One was to shift to guerrilla warfare. New tactics included temporary recruitment so that campesinos could return to their farms after engagements; ambush, cover, and retreat; taking the wounded away so as to distort body counts; and persuasion or intimidation of non-combatants.[58] The Sandinistas had no choice but to embrace guerrilla tactics since the marines occupied all the towns around Nueva Segovia province.[59] The other lesson was to use any battle, even a defeat, to attract public opinion. "We learned the tremendous value of publicity in terms of world opinion," Sandino later told an interviewer about Ocotal, "and it convinced us that our main goal should be to prolong the war as long as possible."[60] He retreated further into the mountains, about thirty miles from the Honduran border, to El Chipote—"the slap."[61]

In mid-August the marines dropped leaflets around Ocotal offering amnesty to Sandinistas but "nothing substantial" came of it.[62] They again offered $10 per gun, which this time yielded "practically no results." Complicating the marine mission in the Segovias was that many other bands—Liberals, Conservatives, and Hondurans—existed alongside Sandino's in the fall of 1927.[63] Even after November, when marines found and bombarded El Chipote, Sandino could not be routed (see Fig. 7.2). By January 1928, when marines took the hideout by foot, Sandino and his army had slipped away.[64]

Figure 7.2 A US plane flying over El Chipote, Sandino's mountain hideout, right before the marines attacked it in November 1927. Photo # 56A-515025, folder 56A Scenes—Rural, box 15, RG 127G, NARA II.

From then on, battles increased in frequency and intensity. Everything Yankee was fair game, said Sandino. He attacked and occupied several mines. In the first half of 1928, the marines doubled their number to 5,692.[65] By mid-April they had lost twenty-one of their own.[66] Before the Sandino rebellion was over they would lose more than in all the occupations of Haiti, the Dominican Republic, and Nicaragua in 1912–1925 put together.[67]

Many, perhaps a majority, of the four Segovian departments—Nueva Segovia, Jinotega, Matagalpa, and Estelí—supported Sandino. Internal marine reports spoke for themselves. Three months after Ocotal, estimated one, one town was friendly "in public" but "privately at least half the population are friendly to Sandino." Around nearby Jícaro, "all surrounding country is at least 95% Sandinista."[68] Anecdotes confirmed the numbers. One marine recalled his trek to northern Nicaragua. "The natives were very suspicious of us, they were afraid of us. They were also afraid of the bandits, but they just naturally were more responsive to their own people."[69] A sergeant noted the "cold, icy stares that the Marines received from the Nicaraguan natives as they patrolled many of the villages in and around Ocotal."[70] Even Nicaraguan guards recalled the difficulty in telling Sandinistas apart from sympathizers since most lied about their knowledge of rebels and hid their wounds.[71] Non-combatant *segovianos*, like Haitians and Dominicans, placated both sides by giving the marines detailed information on the Sandinistas, but only days after the event.[72] Campesino disinformation convinced one major, for a while, that El Chipote did not exist.[73]

To be sure, the Segovias held a relatively small proportion of Nicaragua's population, less than 30 percent.[74] Nueva Segovia, the most supportive department, accounted for no more than 4 percent.[75] Sandino found little open support in the rest of Nicaragua. Although, as in other occupations, the merchants and bankers were happy because the presence of marines on highways and in ports reduced the insecurity and the incidence of bribery in getting goods to markets, few other Nicaraguans were enchanted with US troops. One senior officer remarked "that the United States were more hated by the population of Nicaragua than they had ever been in Hayti."[76] In 1931, 6,000 in Managua protested the presence of the troops, but not one sign or speech mentioned Sandino.[77] The press was so partisan and removed from the Segovias that it filled its pages with infighting and treated the Sandino rebellion as a mere "bandit" annoyance.[78] Largely because it was aimed at the oligarchy regardless of party, the Sandino cause rarely moved the elite, even in Nueva Segovia.[79] More than in other occupations, Sandino's was a strictly regional resistance movement.

Yet the Sandino rebellion kept thousands of marines busy for the better part of six years. Trying to understand what motivated Sandino in early 1928, the

Dayton, Ohio, *Journal* defined him as "a combination of Trotsky, Sitting Bull, and Aguinaldo."[80] The paper was not far off.[81] Sandino distinguished himself from other insurrection leaders such as Charlemagne Péralte and Ramón Nateras by the protean nature and explicitness of his political ideas. Like the Russian revolutionary Leon Trotsky he represented the working class and championed socialist solutions. Like the Sioux chief Sitting Bull he addressed the needs of indigenous peoples who feared threats to their communally defined land. And, like Filipino rebel leader Emilio Aguinaldo, he saw himself as a freedom fighter against empire.[82]

Sandino's ideas resonated with followers by speaking to their concrete fears, aspirations, and identities. Those group beliefs in turn influenced Sandino to sustain, adapt, and refine his motivations.[83] Sandino claimed that, at the height of the insurrection, those who shared his ideas included 2,000 troops in arms plus 1,800 farmers who could be quickly mobilized. Those he called "partisans" totaled 180,000—a clear exaggeration, and perhaps not coincidentally the population of the four departments in rebellion.[84]

Sandino was primarily an anti-imperialist, and within his anti-imperialism resided most of his nationalism. Few campesinos understood what Sandino meant when he spoke of defending the fatherland. "No, no, I didn't know what *la patria* meant at the time," responded Eudiviges Herrera Siles after much prompting years later.[85] Followers did understand, however, when Sandino spoke of a land free of foreign troops, and it is around this fundamental grievance that Sandino, in September 1927, formed his Army for the Defense of the National Sovereignty of Nicaragua (EDSNN).[86] US troops embodied his definition of imperialism—foreign investment and diplomatic arm-twisting were peripheral. He never argued for Nicaraguan exceptionalism and perhaps never believed his nation could truly be united. He not only advanced no social or economic program for the benefit of most Nicaraguans but also denied such a program vehemently.[87] His only consistent demand was the withdrawal of the "Yankee invaders."[88]

In targeting foreign troops so clearly, Sandino did everything he could to eliminate the reasons for their presence, among which was the protection of foreign property. On December 14, 1927, Sandino suspended all guarantees to foreign nationals and their property.[89]

Members of the EDSNN absorbed the anti-occupation message. Asked why Sandino refused to surrender like Moncada, Francisco Ceteño Fonseca explained plainly that "the general was the enemy of the Yankees."[90] Magdaleno Matute Rodríguez agreed: "We did not fight for money, but rather to defeat the enemy, to drive the Yankee out of Nicaragua."[91] Asked decades later why he and his comrades fought, Calixto Tercero González, nicknamed "Death," did not hesitate: "pure patriotism to drive the empire out of Nicaragua."[92]

An area long subjected to vicious inter-party feuds, the Segovias had long been isolated from centralizing authority. The national state only touched this region remotely through the personal, violent rule of caudillos and their private armies.[93] Conservative abuses also made Sandinista recruitment easy. One miner who later joined Sandino in his rebellion remembered how Conservative troops in 1927 were "killing and robbing and taking advantage of the poor women."[94] Conservative bands roamed the Segovias, confirmed many others, killing, raping, and destroying their property, even after the "peace" of Espino Negro.[95] In fact, the "free and fair" elections called for in Espino Negro signaled to Conservative patriarchs—all large landholders—the urgency to reduce the influence of Liberals, leading to twenty to thirty bands inflicting atrocities almost exclusively on Liberals.[96] "All had debts to pay off. Old blood-feuds with the hated Conservatives" is how one British soldier of fortune fighting for Sandino described the Liberals.[97] One *segoviano* joined Sandino because "he wanted to drive out the Conservatives."[98] When asked what he did for a living before he joined Sandino in 1927, Tiburcio Zelaya answered without hyperbole that he was "fleeing" the Conservatives.[99] To be sure, Liberals committed their own depredations, but Conservative terror primed the Sandino following before there was a Sandino to follow.[100]

Family honor was intimately tied to party terror. Many who joined Sandino did so because Liberal family members either prodded them or suffered violence from the Conservatives.[101] Engracia Uriarte and Anastacio Rodríguez Casco both said they joined because their family were Liberals.[102] Juan Pablo Ramírez was fourteen when the Conservatives tortured him to find out where his father, a Liberal, was hiding. He revealed nothing, so the Conservatives took their land and killed their pigs.[103]

Marines stumbled into this political culture of retribution. They also identified family members as sources of information and committed abuses against them, prompting them to join the EDSNN. "I felt obligated to join the army," Gabriel Cruz recalled, "because the Yankees had assassinated the family of my *mamá*."[104]

Sandino needed little convincing that hating Conservatives dovetailed nicely with hating foreign troops. The words "Conservatives" and *"yankistas"* were interchangeable to him.[105] There is significant evidence that Liberal Party leaders in Managua who broke with Moncada gave aid to Sandino, at least in his early phases.[106]

The more Sandino became disenchanted with *moncadistas* who saw him as a threat to their electoral success in 1928, however, the more the Liberals and Sandinistas diverged. "The partisan struggle for me has ended," Sandino proclaimed as early as June 1927.[107] By 1929 he identified only as an anti-imperialist and dated his correspondence as of the seventeenth year of the "anti-imperialist struggle in Nicaragua," signaling his identification with the resisters of 1912.[108] "We do not care to treat with the Yankees, nor with Diaz, nor with Moncada, nor any of their crew," wrote Sandino's surgeon, Domingo Mairena Hernández.

> Ours is not a revolution in favor of some particular leader, who drops his plans when they meet his price and pay his men. No. Ours is the hurricane; it is going to tear up the forest by the roots and level right down to the floor the temples of corruption, in order to sow and build anew and let the sun's rays fall on a purified landscape.[109]

Sandino knew that he also had to appeal to his many specific downtrodden constituencies, key among them workers and peasants, to associate a social revolution with his definition of nationalism.[110] Nine of ten *segovianos* were impoverished, illiterate, and barefoot—almost all peasants.[111] They paid fewer taxes than other Nicaraguans, and they produced largely for themselves. The region was overwhelmingly rural, with few roads, no railroad or industry, and no river navigable by vessels larger than a canoe. But the creeping presence of wage work threatened local independence and patriarchal order.[112] In January 1929 Sandino demanded that Managua deregulate tobacco farms, a long-standing desire of *segoviano* farmers.[113]

Sandino also wanted workers on his side, but there were few full-time wage earners in the Segovias. A rural proletariat of sorts worked on coffee farms, mostly owned by US and British interests, but it largely identified as campesinos, not workers.[114] Even though artisans backed him, Sandino was never able to organize them in León and Chinandega because of partisan warfare and repression.[115] There were those miners who had joined him at first.[116] No one knows how many workers joined but Sandino once claimed that "the chiefs and officers of my soldiers are mostly artisans and workers."[117] On the Atlantic coast, where the labor movement was stronger because of larger foreign interests, US officials in 1927 linked labor trouble at the Standard Fruit Company to Sandino's provocations, one employee reporting that workers "are in communication with Sandino" and "are not given light, water and other things which will be the cause of the uprising."[118] Sandino followers allegedly camped next to Standard Fruit plantations and recruited and armed workers whose wages had been cut.[119] Dana Munro of the US legation also believed that "elements in Western Nicaragua, friendly to Sandino, were largely responsible" for a strike by customs and wharf workers in Corinto in January 1928.[120]

To be sure, these allies were strategic. Marines were not after Nicaraguan land, yet Sandino told his soldiers and chiefs to be "lovers of the campesino." If not, "the battle will be lost" since the cooperation of peasants provided food and clothing to the EDSNN.[121] The workers were also important as propaganda since Sandino wanted support from working-class organizations outside Nicaragua.

Yet Sandino still felt the pain of the poor and their anger toward the rich. "The rights of the weak are more sacred than those of the powerful," he wrote a friend, "who in their arrogance disavow them and whose violation should be punished with their blood."[122] He tried to blend seamlessly the interests and identities of peasants and workers. He explained to both groups that they should fear two forces: Yankee imperialism and "the native bourgeoisie or exploitative national capitalists," and for that reason he rejected alliances with US labor unions.[123] Sandino also respected the harvest schedule, allowing peasants to plant their crops, join his army while the food grew, then return to their farms to harvest it and give a portion to the EDSNN.[124] Benigno Ortiz's participation was typical: "It was not full time, but part time, because I had my work cutting cane, making sugar."[125]

The poor who followed him grasped Sandino's message of class warfare. Secundino Hernández Blandón joined as a thirteen-year-old peasant, seeing Sandino's as the first ever peasant movement in the region. He interpreted the "free country" that Sandino spoke of as one where "all would have somewhere to work."[126] Gerardo Rugama also believed that Sandino would give him "somewhere to work," as opposed to the United States, who would "take" his land.[127] Mercedes Rivas remembered Sandino promising he would multiply ten times their daily wages.[128]

Sandino made class grievances concrete by focusing on the injustices perpetrated by US mine owners and landowners. In a public "statement about the causes" of his rebellion, Sandino drew on his own experiences at the San Albino mine, criticizing the practices of paying miners in store credit and of forcing them "to work twelve hours a day." The US owner *thinks himself authorized by his nationality* to commit such abuses," he added.[129] Sandino understood the concept of added value and for that reason wanted Nicaraguans to own their own mines. He once complained that US mine owners "take the gold, take the wood. Then the gold comes back as watches, in jewelry, and we have to buy it more dearly. And why are we not owners of Nicaragua, we sons of Nicaragua?"[130] The message came through to followers. José Flores Gladys reiterated it almost verbatim: "What the Yankees wanted in Nicaragua was to exploit our country, take the gold, the silver and wood and everything our country had."[131]

Sandino backed actions with words. San Albino's owner, Charles Butters, had introduced the hated company scrip in 1926 and the workers had already gone on strike in 1927 when Sandino asked for cash payments to the workers in compensation.[132] When Butters did nothing, Sandino took the mine in summer 1927 and held it for forty-two days. The Sandinistas mined $5,000 of gold and minted their own coins, giving half to the workers.[133] The marines eventually took back the mine but then, called to patrol other territory, abandoned it. Sandino took it again, "wrecked the property and took away everything movable." Butters claimed a loss of $914,000.[134]

Sandino was not done with the mines. On April 24, 1928, with twenty-five cases of dynamite, he "reduced to ashes" the La Luz and Los Angeles mines, nearer the Caribbean coast. He wrote to their manager that the act was symbolic punishment against all US capitalists and even all US citizens.[135] Behind it were real political and economic interests. Sandino netted $50,000 in cash, gold, and mercury from the mines.[136] Their owners, the Fletchers of Pittsburgh, had backed warring politicians to retain their concession and had employed the hated Adolfo Díaz. They also worked the miners ten hours a day and paid them "thirty cents a day, thirty lousy cents," recalled miner Eudiviges Herrera Siles. "It was nothing, you couldn't buy anything with so little, the food was bad, everything was bad, working day after day without rest, without land, without anything; we were all slaves to the rich, the rich had everything around here, everything; the poor, we had nothing, nothing."[137] An engineer who investigated the La Luz affair concluded that "the seizure and blowing up of the mines was not alone a political action, but was a result of insane labor conditions and corruption in the mine management. . . . The miners in this and many other ways deprived of making even a modest living have had good reason for revolt and found in Sandino's movement a splendid opportunity to take revenge over their former superiors." He advised keeping the episode as quiet as possible.[138]

In the end, however, Nicaragua, like Haiti, was not a fertile field for contesting US investment since it had so little of it compared to Mexico and Cuba. To be sure, US and other investors supported the marine presence, hoping it would end epidemic warfare.[139] US investors were certainly the largest foreign presence, though they controlled only $12 million, $9 million of which was in two banana plantations on the Caribbean coast.[140]

During his struggle, there is a single instance in which Sandino addressed specific Indian concerns—a letter in early 1932 foreseeing public schools that would give all indigenous peoples "the opportunity to be managers and bankers of your communal cooperatives and shipping companies."[141] But his broader battle on behalf of workers and campesinos potentially resonated also with indigenous groups. By the mid-1920s Indians in Nueva Segovia had lost a fifth of their land. They may have also feared the encroachments of wage labor since they accounted for about 80 percent of the rural inhabitants around Jinotega and Matagalpa and served as an extra workforce during coffee-picking season.[142] Other problems were political. Caudillos often expected that Indians, like other peasants, would join small wars and terrorize other peasants lest they be terrorized themselves.[143]

Among his 180,000 supporters, Sandino claimed to have 100,000 indigenous Nicaraguans.[144] This was surely an exaggeration, and there were tensions between the two. The Miskitu of the Atlantic Coast were thought to harbor "an inborn hatred of the Spanish-speaking Nicaraguans."[145] One Sandinista confirmed their cultural distance from the "Spaniards": the Miskitu spoke their own language, ate mostly rice and snails, and "had no Sandinista culture at all."[146] Even on the Pacific side, Sandino refused to recognize the local autonomy of indigenous communities because they clashed with his nationalist modernization project.[147] Yet there is a record of Indian help to the Sandinistas.[148] Some from indigenous communities of Jinotega and San Lucas, who shared enemies with Sandino, joined his army.[149] Others ran mail to Honduras for him and helped guide visitors to his hideouts.[150] In the east, indigenous river guides helped Sandino navigate the Coco River to purchase weapons.[151] There is at least one report of "several Sumu Indians armed with shotguns and machetes" helping to sack a district for Sandino.[152]

The participation of children in the rebellion confirmed the broad resonance of Sandino. The so-called *palmazones*, named apparently after three young brothers who died from machine-gun fire, referred to anyone under thirteen or anyone who needed basic training.[153] Those forty to fifty children not ready to fight helped with chores, spied, or belonged to the "Choir of Angels," which, with shouts, tin pans, and firecrackers, would raise a cacophony in the forest during an ambush to create the impression that there were more Sandinistas than there really were.[154] Some former *palmazones* recalled grimmer roles. Calixto Tercero González joined when he was twelve and claimed that, when a prisoner was captured, he pleaded with a general, "Leave him to me," and finished off the prisoner with his machete.[155]

The accumulation of grievances resulted in a Sandinista ideology uniquely filled with a hatred of US citizens and justifying murder and destruction of property. Shortly after Ocotal, Sandino declared "his intention of cutting the throat of every American and other foreigner with whom he came in contact."[156] Over a year later, having lost fourteen pounds, he still felt "vigorous enough to catch Coolidge and [Secretary of State Frank] Kellog [sic] by the throat and make them smash each other's nose shaking one against the other until we can present to humanity the flesh remnants of two imperialists who dream to deviate with blood and gold the future of men."[157] Sandinistas called marines "blonde beasts," "degenerate pirates," "paid assassins," "hired thugs," "morphine addicts," "murderers," "criminals," and "the enemy of our race and language."[158]

When Sandino was in Mexico in 1929, attending a dinner party with supporters, he was introduced to a US citizen named George Moreno. "What!" said Sandino angrily. "You're North American?"

"*Sí, señor*," answered Moreno. "I am North American, an enemy of the imperialism of my country and an admirer of yours."

Sandino raised his voice. "I don't believe in your admiration because you're a *gringo* and all *gringos* are enemies of freedom."

Moreno explained that many in the United States were sympathetic, but Sandino would have none of it. Several Latin Americans in attendance tried to calm the Nicaraguan down. The party ended there and its Mexican hosts later expressed their apologies to Moreno.[159]

"The North American people," Sandino told the *New York World* while in Mexico, "is as imperialist as its leaders. If in the United States there exist anti-imperialist organizations, it is not because their members are North Americans but because they are in majority Russians, Lithuanians, Germans, Spaniards, Italians, Latin Americans, from all over the world. Few are the exceptions to this general rule."[160]

Such virulent hatred for US citizens was rare among anti-occupation leaders. Others had gone to pains to at least feign admiration for ordinary *americanos* and for US heroes and ideals. Sandino, in contrast, claimed to have been disabused of such naïveté. "In the beginning, I confided in that the people of North America would not be in accord with the abuses committed in Nicaragua by the Government of Mr. Calvin Coolidge but I am now convinced that the North Americans in general uphold the attitude of Coolidge in my country and it is for this reason that all that is North American that falls into our hands surely has arrived at its end."[161] Throughout the first years of his struggle, he expressed unwavering distrust of US promises and refused to negotiate.

Especially early in his struggle, Sandino reserved a perhaps equal hatred for the Moncada Liberals, those in whom he had once believed and who now sold out the nation. He lambasted them as "servile traitors" and threatened them with death.[162] He listed clearly the behaviors making up a *vendepatria*: requesting US invasion, making secret pacts with the enemy, helping the enemy assassinate patriotic Nicaraguans, submitting official reports against said Nicaraguans, and asking for protection from the invaders.[163] Such statements were meant to strike fear in the hearts of Nicaraguans who sat on the political fence.

Yet, again, Sandino integrated his own beliefs with the political culture of the Segovias. One of his followers was only too glad to acquaint marines with "the mountain system of our country," by which he meant the breaking of necks, the chopping of ears, and the infamous *cortes* or machete cuts to the body, including the "jacket cut," obtained by slicing off the arms, legs, and head.[164] Among the verses celebrating decapitation, one poem sarcastically recalled "Poor Mister Bruce," referring to Lieutenant Arnold Bruce, whose head the Sandinistas lopped off as revenge for Bruce's own atrocities.[165] They "stuck a wire through his nose and strung him up on the main road, so everyone could see him," recalled with satisfaction Calixto "Death" Tercero.[166]

The most fearsome exemplar of Sandinista violence was Pedro Altamirano. A quarter-century older than Sandino, Altamirano knew little of the world outside the Segovias. He learned to read and write only during the anti-occupation campaign. With a barrel chest, tousled hair, thick eyebrows, a large mustache, and a hoarse voice, "Pedrón"—"big Pedro"—approximated a gray bear to one interviewer (see Fig. 7.3). A cigar forever hung from his lips, a scar marked his face, and nicotine permanently colored his teeth. The hardened warrior spent his nights on a leather hammock with a .44 Winchester by his side, his black dog under him, and a wooden board over his chest to ward off machete attacks while he slept. Pedrón had over sixty severed heads to his name.[167] Sandinistas credited him with inventing the jacket cut, which he instructed a subordinate to use on "every man you meet in the roads who seems to be suspicious of being an enemy, and set fire to his belongings."[168] The only act Pedrón rejected was stealing from the poor.[169]

"Who began the atrocities?" Sandino once asked rhetorically. "No matter. What matters is that the marines are more guilty for considering themselves educated and civilized and for being the intruders."[170] Sandino's seal, used on

Figure 7.3 Pedro Altamirano, second from left, with family. CHM.

Figure 7.4 Sandino's seal, used on much of his correspondence. Photo # 56Q-515402, folder 56Q Sandino Flags, etc. Copy of Sandino seal for Lieutenant D. H. Boyden, box 15, RG 127G, NARA II.

his coins and his correspondence, featured a Sandinista beheading a marine (see Fig. 7.4). Near the end of his life, the battle over and sick in bed, Sandino expressed a tinge of regret at so many decapitations. "It is a terrible thing to take a man's head. But," he caught himself, "those dogs forced us into that kind of tactic."[171]

Sandino partly spoke of hatred for US citizens because it contrasted with the love within his own community of resistance.[172] Unlike other insurrectionists in Nicaragua and abroad, Sandino believed in the purifying effect of brotherly love and wanted his followers to set an example of "moral uplift" in order to counter accusations of banditry.[173] "I sleep with the sweetness and tranquility of a healthy child," he once wrote. "Does the same occur with the directors of international politics of North America?"[174]

Sandino also preached and practiced behavioral purity. While in the Segovias Sandino drank nothing but "the clear water of the mountains."[175] He never gambled. He meditated almost daily. He used Western medicine only for malaria—other ailments he healed with herbs, yoga, and "selfsuggestion."[176] Among his troops he banned drinking while on duty, selling alcohol, and stealing animals. Rape was especially *prohibíssimo*.[177] He once executed one of his generals for the crime, and Pedrón did the same to a captain. Sandino claimed that homosexuality and other "urban degenerations" did not exist in the EDSNN.[178] Also reflective of his image of purity was his white horse, its ornate saddle, and his practice of wearing silk underwear.[179] Charles Butters, briefly his captive, described him as "exceptionally neat and clean [in] appearance, with highly polished boots and well-groomed clothes, always shaved and washed, an unusual trait in the Nicaraguan wilderness."[180]

To be sure, Sandino's men committed some of these forbidden acts behind his back; after all, Sandino decreed these prohibitions for a reason.[181] Yet their existence spoke to the unique identity of the Sandinistas and explained their unusual effectiveness.

The "manifesto" that Sandino published at the San Albino mine on July 1, 1927, most clearly expressed how, even early in the struggle, his many ideological strands could intertwine successfully to envelop his supporters. In the two-page letter he spoke of geopolitical concerns, saying that the world would be "imbalanced" if the United States controlled a canal in Nicaragua. He railed against Díaz and Moncada. He boasted of his "Indian blood" and "artisan" identity, adding that "emerging from the bosom of the oppressed" was his greatest honor. And he wrapped it all up in an inspiring underdog pugnacity when he claimed that although his army was small, its heart was large and it would never surrender.[182]

Brambles and Thorns

Where troops have been quartered, brambles and thorns spring up.
—Lao Tzu

Nicaraguans, Haitians, and Dominicans shared many day-to-day frustrations under occupation. Most experiences did not drive them to join or help insurrections, but the typical invaded Latin American was not shy about complaining about marine abuse. In late 1921 the marines themselves grumbled about what had become the Dominican habit of "sending in daily protests against everything."[1] The record of these protests is rife with instances of clashing interests and pent-up emotional frustration that erupted into violence, largely results of the behavior of occupiers, even when occupiers sought to check the exploitation of the poor by the rich. The overall style of US occupation in Latin America—brutal, acquisitive, disrespectful, and racist—transformed much of the initial relief and hope of some occupied peoples into disappointment, fear, and eventually rage.[2] The episodes suggested a correlation between the length of an occupation and the discontent it engenders.

One marine, Ivan Miller, who served in all three occupations, later attempted to place complaints of abuse in cultural context. "What we consider brutality among people in the United States is different from what they considered brutality. . . . They treated their people the same way as they treated their animals. Their animals, they let them starve, they wouldn't treat them for injuries or anything like that."[3] Yet the occupied did consider sub-human violence by marines and by constabularies to be horrendous. It was by far the most consistent and passionate cause of discontent.

Abuses were particularly frequent and grave either when no marines supervised constabularies or when a single marine—often a non-commissioned officer elevated to officer status in the constabulary—unleashed a "reign of terror" in a small town or district (see Fig. 8.1).[4] The residents of the Haitian town of Borgne, for instance, hated a Lieutenant Kelly for approving beatings

Figure 8.1 *The Crisis* magazine published this grainy photo, saying it was sent from Haiti with the following caption: "St. Michel (Artibonite), February 1919. Two wrists cut off and an amputated leg prior to execution by a gendarme. The work of the American officer." The photo at once indicated the reign of terror that could be inflicted by the occupation as well as the conflation of torture by US forces and constabularies. *The Crisis*, November 1920, 38.

and imprisonments for trivial crimes—such as selling "a bundle of wood"—or for no apparent reason. The mayor pleaded with the attorney general of nearby Cap-Haïtien for something to "be done as soon as possible regarding Lieutenant Kelly, because the evil is growing."[5]

The particular bane of Hinche's existence, Charlemagne Péralte's hometown, was Freeman Lang, whose three-month rule in 1918 so terrified the town that in the 1970s his name still sent "shudders up the spine of the townsfolk."[6] Haitians long remembered marines and gendarmes freely shooting cattle or fellow Haitians who might in some way be of service to the cacos.[7] In Saint-Marc, Captain Fitzgerald Brown allegedly whipped a seventy-five-year-old woman, hanged a fifteen-year-old boy for petty theft, and had an innocent man's whole body seared with hot irons, among other atrocities.[8] The Reverend Ton Evans, a Baptist minister, was jailed in Saint-Marc. Asked if he had witnessed "any acts of cruelty and ill treatment in there," he answered, "Yes; while night after night, as well as during the day . . . I could hear the yelling and groaning of native prisoners, as well as their being cruelly beaten and pounded by gendarmes. Many a time these yells and moans would suddenly cease, and then a scuffle, whispering, and the sound like if they were carrying out a dead body or bodies."[9]

Around Hato Mayor, in the Dominican Republc, Captain Thad Taylor, who briefly captured Ramón Nateras in 1918, terrorized the area.[10] As one marine described it, Taylor "believed that all circumstances called for a campaign of frightfulness; he arrested indiscriminately upon suspicion; then people rotted in jail pending investigation or search for evidence. His policy sooner or later would have found nearly everyone in jail." Marines who investigated at once reduced the town's inmate population from 269 to 95. Taylor's "braggadocio" had a "bad effect upon other officers" by encouraging some to join in the abuse while others longed to be reassigned. Taylor also "utilized too freely" the "services" of cruel Dominicans. Under his watch his lieutenant executed eleven rebels in jail and then "conducted a campaign of severity in Seibo province, burning houses, treating the inhabitants arbitrarily, taking horses, etc."

Taylor worked alongside Captain Charles Merkel, who, according to a marine, acted "without regard for feelings of natives, with no attempt at courtesy, and with a good deal of arbitrariness."[11] On September 13, 1918, Merkel cut off the ear of a prisoner, beat him with a stick, and "did maliciously cause the said prisoner to be cut across the breast and salt to be put in his wounds." He ordered the other ear lopped off and the prisoner kept without food and water for four days. The same day he had four other prisoners executed by machine gun. His own men reported him. While marines investigated, Merkel blew his brains out with a gun secreted to him by marine officers.[12]

Nicaragua provided less evidence of abuses, yet *segovianos* believed them to be legion.[13] Most stories focused on one National Guard (GN) company, "La M," and its notorious Lieutenant William A. Lee.[14] "This man finished off half of Nicaragua," said Luisa Cana Araúz of the one they called "The Butcher."[15] Lee stood accused of group assassinations, mutilations, and killing animals for pleasure. A handbill circulated in early 1932 showing Lee "announcing to the peasant rebel, Jose Montero, his death sentence" (the GN called it a fraud) and holding three severed heads (the GN confirmed that it executed the men). The handbill concluded sarcastically, "This is the result of the American intervention and civilization in our country."[16] The M company was widely accused of violence against children, especially throwing them into the air and spearing them with bayonets (see Fig. 8.2).[17] One Nicaraguan author claimed that Lee pulled out a child's Achilles' heel with his bare hands.[18]

Such brutality was a recruiting bonanza for insurgents. Little useful information, and even less military advance, was gained from abuse and torture in Nicaragua, but they did drive peasants to help Augusto Sandino.[19] Elsewhere, too: in Hato Mayor, Dominican Republic, "the inhabitants suddenly felt a great change in the conduct of the 11th Co[mpany after Thad Taylor took command], and a number of unsteady ones joined the Gabilleros [rebels]."[20] Adolf Berle, who witnessed the Dominican occupation as a young lawyer hired by the sugar

Figure 8.2 Nicaraguan illustration from 1961 of William A. Lee of the dreaded "M" Company. Cover of Frente Unitaria Nicaragüense, *Intervención sangrienta: Nicaragua y su pueblo* (Caracas: FUN, 1961).

estate Central Romana, noted that "in the neighborhood of Macoris the whole occupation is frankly and undeniably unpopular. . . . The people seem afraid of the military . . . and it is partly due to this that the bandit activity in the Province of Seybo has continued at all."[21]

The leading nationalist group in Haiti, the Patriotic Union (UP), described the pervasiveness and wantonness of torture under interrogation. "Internal peace could not be preserved because the permanent and brutal violation of individual rights of Haitian citizens was a perpetual provocation to revolt."[22] The UP presented a *mémoire* while on a mission to Washington, listing twenty-five "abominable crimes" against Haitians.[23] A marine inspector of roads gauged "illegal executions" in the north of Haiti at "400 at least," which he called "a low estimate."[24]

Nicaraguan guard Manolo Cuadra recounted an incident when two marines severely beat a suspect and then electrocuted him. "A satanic look of pleasure marked the face of Phillips. Hays just smiled." Phillips and Hays then shot the man while his son looked on.[25] A British consul visited the Caribbean coast of

Nicaragua and reported that "there can be no doubt but that the Marines have in a number of cases abused their position and used unnecessary violence in dealing with the Indians and negroes of that region."[26] There were rumors of marines killing West Indian prisoners and machine-gunning an Indian village. One US doctor in Bluefields charged "all sorts of inhuman beatings and unmentionable tortures by our marines, in which an electric chair figured." The marines shot one survivor in front of "a score or more of witnesses in the center of the town."[27] Benito Vargas, a forty-four-year-old farmer, had informed US forces of arms caches during the civil war but they suspected that he knew of others.

> He was struck in the face and on the head and body repeatedly by the clenched fists of four marines . . . ; his hair was pulled, his head forced back and his throat choked by the hands of these beasts until he spat blood . . . ; his head was forced into a barrel of water and held there until he thought he would strangle; water was dashed into both ears, forcefully, from full buckets; he was given the "water cure"; ropes were twisted about his wrists . . . ; he was tied to a scantling so that he could not move and rifle barrels were forcibly rubbed up and down over his shins . . . ; and his testicles were grasped and twisted until he nearly fainted from pain.

The doctor, hearing of several more cases, estimated them to be "occurring by the hundred right along on the Atlantic Coast to-day."[28] Captain Donald J. Kendall, who took over the police in Bluefields in 1927, oversaw the torture done by a Lieutenant Carroll, whom a fellow marine described as "a bit subnormal mentally." A naval investigation eventually disciplined Kendall for seizing arms in an unorthodox fashion but praised him for bringing peace to Bluefields.[29]

Such terror may have been the work of a minority, and it was punished—but only when thoroughly proven.[30] The marines also issued orders, for instance, "to avoid the use of physical force, the inflicting of physical or excessive mental suffering or what is spoken of as 'being hard on the natives.' "[31] But they usually attempted to shift blame onto native constabularies.[32] In Nicaragua, they recorded only one report of an unjustified killing by one of their own.[33]

Occupied peoples were not fooled. "Whether it was the Gendarmerie or Marine Corps is immaterial," wrote one Haitian. "It was the Marine Corps policy."[34] He and others argued that constabularies committed atrocities because marines either ordered them to do so, looked the other way, or were too few to police their subordinates. Marines had also trained these constabularies and put guns in their hands. There were cases in which constabularies refused to follow marine orders on moral grounds, in addition to several episodes of mutiny.[35]

The arbitrariness and randomness of the violence was most frightful. "The *machos* here grabbed and beat anyone," recalled Nicaraguan Heriberto Toruño Reyes. "Who was going to talk back to those despots if they ruled? They killed whomever, and they killed for pleasure."[36] They shot Santiago Herrero because he "refused to speak" when they barged into his house; he turned out to be mute.[37] In early 1928 one peddler of maize cakes walked past the marine barracks in Ocotal. A competitor shouted, "He's a Sandinista! He's a Sandinista!" Immediately, four marines fell upon him, punching and kicking, despite his insisting that he knew nothing of Sandino. He fled, but the marines pursued him with guns blaring and shot him several times. They took him to the hospital, where he died.[38]

Of all three countries, the event eliciting the most outrage was the torture of Dominican Leocadio Báez, known as Cayo Báez. A peasant from Salcedo, Báez recounted that when he was sixteen, occupation forces kidnapped him and forced him to act as a guide against rebels. When they suspected him of knowing the location of an arms cache, a combination of US and Dominican forces seared him so severely with a red-hot machete that Báez could never walk again. They tortured sixteen others but also shot them; only Báez survived.[39] For decades thereafter, Dominicans considered him a cause célèbre of marine abuse.[40]

Dominicans suffered an additional torment: the *desalojo* or policy of concentrating rural inhabitants into a confined space in order to both identify rebels among them and sweep surrounding lands. Many abuses—notably by Charles Merkel—occurred during these roundups, which took place in August 1918, April 1919, and October 1921. These swept up both criminals and prominent citizens without distinction—a direct affront to social hierarchy. In the 1921 *desalojo* of Los Llanos, for instance, all men—including the mayor, city council, and schoolteachers—were arrested, tied together, and forced to walk for six hours. A complaint related how "the poor families in the town, full of anguish and terror, did not sleep that night, for they knew not [what] was going to happen to their husbands, fathers, sons and brothers."[41]

The *desalojos* themselves were a result of resistance because marine commanders suspected town leaders of helping insurrectionists.[42] As the head of the occupation wrote to a protesting Dominican, "The Military Government has tried in every way to obtain the co-operation of Dominicans in the suppression of banditry and, failing in this, the measure now being taken is the only means at the disposal of this government."[43] The government nevertheless soon ended the practice.[44]

Former Sandinista Santos López accused the US-led National Guard of reconcentrating Nicaraguan families in Yalí, resulting in hundreds of deaths.[45] In mid-1930 an effort to relocate families in the departments of Jinotega and Nueva Segovia did occur, but US diplomats quickly saw confusion and miscommunication causing a "distressing stampede" of 6,000 to 10,000 souls toward a town of 4,000 and called off the *desalojo*.[46]

Rape added an element of gendered terror to abuses. It does not appear that sexual assault was systematically practiced as a tactic of war. Yet the cases that appear in the historical record—many more likely went unreported—indicate an attitude of permissiveness, fed by the occupations' monopoly of force, that bred widespread fear among occupied women. Writer John Houston Craig, who caricatured Haitians as savage cannibals, minimized rape, calling it being "waylaid." "The *tiefies*" or young women of Haiti, he claimed, "apparently enjoyed being waylaid. Rape, I believe, implies lack of consent. I never heard of a case where consent was lacking in Haiti's black belt."[47] Yet assault was so dreaded that Haitian women stopped bathing in rivers. Duversel Rafaèl, a teenager at the time of the occupation, recalled her fear of "all foreign men in the neighborhood. Whites, especially, had a bad reputation. When they came to town, we would be hidden out of sight, tucked away in attics" until they left.[48] Elanor Charles was not so lucky. As she walked home from the Gonaïves market with her mother, a marine private "caught her, dragged her into the bushes, violated her and then inserted his penis into her mouth." The doctor who examined her confirmed that "she has bruises and lacerations on her body and that her maidenhead has recently been broken" and assessed that Elanor was between fourteen and sixteen years old. "She did not know her age."[49] Rape appeared to be among the least punished offenses. Future Dominican dictator Rafael Trujillo began his rise to notoriety in the Dominican constabulary when a commission of marines acquitted him of rape charges.[50]

In all three occupations, marines on duty also destroyed homes and animals. One marine under investigation defended the practice of killing oxen by saying his troops needed the meat. It was "a practice well known to higher authority and condoned."[51] Occupied peoples hated losing the little property they had. Few lodged complaints with the marines, partly because they were illiterate. Those who did protest tended to know how to write or had others write for them. Gilbert Kuant wrote to the head of the occupation force in April 1928 that marines had stolen his mule. He unsuccessfully tried to get the beast back, or at least the $70 it was worth.[52] Of those who joined Sandino, Pastor Joya Dávila did so because "they took my beasts, they took my cows, everything."[53] Engracia Uriarte and her two brothers joined because the marines burned down their father's house.[54]

Marines were none too careful about keeping abuses quiet and perhaps wanted them to be widely known so as to terrorize the populace. They repeatedly beat and hanged occupied peoples in town plazas, walked them down country roads with ropes around their necks, and ordered them to dig graves for others. In August 1918 Captains Merkel and Taylor assembled over 2,000 Dominicans in a plaza and, in front of them, Merkel shot dead a drunk who had insulted him.

Terror may have silenced some, but in the long term it hardened the population against the occupation. Many in the Dominican Republic later testified with disgust to having seen lynchings with their own eyes. There and in Haiti, newspaper editors braved prison sentences to publish tales of atrocities. Dana Munro observed that occupation abuses especially "gave the Dominican patriotic groups much material for propaganda."[55]

In Pacificador Province, revelations of the abuses committed by constabulary Captain Charles Buckalew, or "Bacalú" as Dominicans called him, divided Dominicans who opposed and supported the occupation. Newspapers were up in arms and social clubs shut down as a consequence.[56] Dominicans claimed Buckalew ordered the torture of Cayo Báez.[57] Marine investigators exonerated Buckalew of all offenses, praising him for "spread[ing] terror in the hearts of lawbreakers, high and low, rich and poor."[58] He soon retired and settled down, incredibly enough, in Santo Domingo.[59]

Some opponents distorted or fabricated tales of depredations. The most important of these was the lie that 5,475 Haitians died at the Chabert "concentration camp."[60] Haitians who made the original accusation later admitted "that it was necessary to exaggerate in order to attract public attention."[61] Sandino also used tales of abuses to paint a distorted picture of warfare against innocent civilians.[62] Few marines grasped that distortions stemmed from the urgency the invaded felt to stop atrocities, which were perhaps the greatest impediment to imparting to occupied peoples the "civilizing" example of US behavior. A marine captain trying to restrain his subordinates' abuses said it best: "We are here to implant in the Haitian people, by our own example of living and conduct, the highest and best ideals of Americanism rather than the worst."[63]

After physical abuse, a second category of grievances was the culturally offensive behaviors of marines in daily interactions with ordinary people. Some transgressions were relatively innocuous, such as the refusal to speak Spanish. One lieutenant refused to learn it even when ordered by the Marine Corps, explaining to the US legation that "when the Spaniards conquered what is now Latin America they compelled the natives to learn Spanish and that we should adopt the same attitude and compel the inhabitants to learn English in those countries in which we intervene." The State Department felt that the marines' intelligence service was their "weakest feature" because several of its spies spoke no Spanish.[64]

Other insults were rarer but more serious. A marine who went to Nicaragua three times recalled darkly "the narcotics condition down there. A man can get it [sic] very easily and cheap, and we found that a whole bunch of them were taking it and we had to get rid of them." He did not specify which narcotics.[65] Sandino did, calling the marines "morphine addicts."[66]

Alcohol was by far the favorite intoxicant of marines and the one that caused the most clashes with the invaded. Its tales were countless. In 1922 a drunk private walked into a Port-au-Prince bar, and when the owner, a Puerto Rican, refused to serve him, the marine grabbed him and labeled him a "high yellow spick" and raised his fist against his wife, whom he called a "Dominican whore."[67] Reviewing such cases, a commanding officer assessed that 90 percent of his "troubles with the men" stemmed from alcohol.[68]

One Nicaraguan clerk reported that his office received repeated complaints of marines barging "into houses without any regard for strange property nor with the owner's consent, late at night and in a state of drunkenness."[69] Café owners wrote to the occupation, asking that marines be banned.[70] Ramiro López of La Concordia, near Jinotega, reported on a rash of drunken home invasions in March 1929, "the Chief being drunker than the soldiers."[71]

In the most terrifying "drunk and disorderly," in 1927 private Mike Brunski left his Port-au-Prince legation post at 6 AM and started shooting Haitians "apparently without provocation," killing one and wounding others. He walked back to the legation "and continued his random firing from the balcony." Medical examiners pronounced Brunski "sane but drunk." The next day the chargé commented dryly on "an increased antipathy on the part of the Haitians toward Americans wearing the uniform of the United States."[72]

A US journalist explained how inebriation especially insulted Dominicans. "The Dominican is seldom a tee-totaler, but he is even more seldom seen under the influence of liquor, at least publicly." Dominicans also considered US citizens to be "hypocrites" because they drank so much abroad while living under prohibition at home.[73]

In Nicaragua, marines found themselves in the Segovias, a remote rural region where violence commonly accompanied drinking. On August 16, 1928, two US lieutenants in the GN looked on as a fistfight broke out among Nicaraguans in Juigalpa. Five hundred people soon gathered and a panicky captain feared "a general free for all, having had previous experience with drunken Latin people." After the riot, he found that the GN "had an agreement with the fiesta committee that fistfights would be permitted."[74] The following January, a Nicaraguan invited two marine privates to a fiesta. When one stepped outside, an uninvited local called Vicente Aguado socked him in the jaw and twenty "of his friends formed a circle," inflicting several cuts on the marine's "neck, arms, thighs, and legs." Other Nicaraguans came to the marine's rescue. It turned out that Aguado had a reputation for slashing faces.[75]

Dominicans and Nicaraguans particularly tended to rise up against moral offenses against women, the result of occupiers' drinking, boredom, monopoly of force, and sense of cultural superiority.[76] In November 1916, drunken marines chasing two teenage girls caused "a great disorder" in Santo Domingo.[77] The day after Christmas 1920, at least fourteen drunken marines took revenge on Dominicans who had defended a woman slapped by one of the marines. Not content to throw punches, they torched a shopkeeper's store and adjoining houses, firing shots as it burned to the ground so as to prevent anyone from putting out the flames.[78] In 1930, one Nicaragua newspaper article titled "Marines who Abused Countrywomen" described how "a group of Americans" demanded "obscene services from the women folks for which reason many of them ran away." The writer denounced "the acts done by persons who believe themselves superior to our race and who call themselves heralds of civilization."[79] Accusations of rape of Nicaraguan "margaritas" or young women became a staple of the propaganda of Sandino and his defenders.[80] Marine files on Nicaragua contain no evidence of rape.

Perhaps because of the greater resistance to moral offenses in the Dominican Republic and Nicaragua, occupations regulated morality there differently than in Haiti. In 1917, the city of Santo Domingo relegated seventeen whorehouses to a "Zone of Tolerance" where liquor was banned and ordered all prostitutes to move there or pay a fine. On July 1, 1918, the military government ordered that no "intoxicants" be sold to US troops in uniform.[81] In Port-au-Prince, rules were much looser. While streetwalking and bordellos were uncommon, prostitution abounded in bars and private homes. Alcohol prohibition was non-existent, rum selling for five to ten cents a drink. The chief of police assessed that it would take "several hundred men" to keep marines from drinking and cavorting, an impossible task.[82] In Nicaragua the Corps warned all arriving marines against "venereal disease."[83] Most of the onus, however, was on prostitutes, who, as of 1928, needed to register and undergo weekly medical exams. Those failing to do so were to be "confined and treated in prison."[84]

Resistance likely explains why marines made efforts to reform enlisted men's behavior as occupations dragged on. In late 1922, Brigadier General Harry Lee wrote an "Indoctrination" to "not be misunderstood by the dullest of intellects."

> Every time a member of this brigade commits an act of abuse upon a citizen or resident of this Republic he brings forth the criticism of the Dominican people. And where does that criticism fall? Upon the man who committed the abuse? No, but upon the United States and its officials and officers, your president receives the blame; your whole government receives the blame; your Marine Corps and my Marine Corps receives the blame, and especially your commanding general and officers of this brigade.

Knapp admonished his men to "seek clean amusement instead of trying to paint the town red."[85]

Land disputes were a third cause of discontent. The struggle for the land took on more than a figurative form in some occupations. Nicaragua's land grievances against the occupation were limited: although US corporations did own some mines and plantations that benefited from marine and guard protection, the marines did not pass laws in their favor. "In Nicaragua," Sandino further explained, "property is very divided and is mostly small landholding. There are few large properties, and these are not very big. . . . The few who do not have land do not starve."[86]

Elsewhere, occupations did transfer land. In Haiti, taking land from peasants was difficult because, after its revolution, the state redistributed 66 to 90 percent of its land to small farmers but kept the legal title.[87] In ensuing years, squatters often insisted that the land was theirs but produced no documents and had little idea where individual properties began or ended. When the US-owned Mac-Donald railroad project began in 1911, farmers responded to ensuing dispossessions with cries of "Down with MacDonald!" and "Down with the railroad!" and attacked the company's buildings.[88] In the constitution of 1918, US authorities allowed foreigners to own land and made it easier for the state to re-acquire land from peasants.[89] Estimates vary of how much land passed from Haitian to US hands during the occupation, but one reliable source added up 43,100 acres by 1927.[90]

In the Dominican Republic, sugar corporations since the 1870s already had set a land-grabbing precedent with their capitalization and enclosure movements. By 1915, the largest seven of these corporations had already acquired 36,271 acres, some of it allegedly by force or forgery. A decade later their property had quadrupled to 124,148 acres.[91] There, too, the occupation was partly to blame. It decreed a Land Registration Act in 1920 that created a centralized land tribunal, obliterating the authority of local officials over such matters.[92] The occupation also moved to survey Dominican lands, which tended to lead to enclosure, which in turn threatened the collective-use tradition of cattle ranchers.[93]

Passage of the 1920 law encouraged at least one company to use terror as a means for expanding its landholdings. In 1921, Central Romana, which harvested 30 percent of the country's sugar cane, evicted the entire population of Caimoní and Higüeral, two hamlets adjoining its plantations. It claimed the towns were diseased; Dominicans and others shot back accusations of naked expansionism. Days later Central Romana burned both towns to the ground and 150 families fled to nearby woods.[94] Central Romana even threatened small landowners with its own police and jails unless they accepted below-market offers for their land.[95]

In Haiti, a January 29, 1926, law speeding up evictions prompted an energetic effort—by both foreigners and Haitians—to take over poor peasants' land in the northern plains. Estimates of the dispossessed range from 200 to 700.[96] "Some Haitians," confirmed US investigators in 1927, "indeed tend to believe that the nub of the whole American policy toward Haiti was the desire to open up Haitian land for foreign land speculation and see in this its chief purpose and its greatest menace."[97]

Haiti's Nationalist Union (UN), an organization similar to the UP, took up the fight against evictions. In a rare elite interaction with the poor, one UN member lived with peasants for twenty days, polling and interviewing, and concluded that "thousands" were robbed of land. The UN accused agents of US companies of showing up at small farms, demanding to see titles. When these could not be produced, the companies, without legal procedures or eviction notices, returned to destroy the peasants' homes and fruit trees. Courts proved unresponsive to peasants' complaints. When they turned in receipts to show they paid taxes on the land, the receipts were conveniently lost. The UN claimed that US administrators, not just US companies, participated in this illegal activity, which put the burden of proof of ownership on the state, not the squatter: "it is impossible today for the State to prove its ownership of the lands it claims."[98]

The possibility of losing land perturbed many. Le Nouvelliste suspected the intent of the new land laws, assessing that the typical Haitian peasant, "no longer enjoying a hearth and plot of land, will return to slavery."[99] In 1929, seventy-seven squatters in the north, "mainly State farmers," petitioned the occupation against the Haitian government, which had threatened them with eviction the next day unless they paid not only current land taxes but all back taxes at higher rates and a penalty of 100 percent for late payment. They expressed shame at having to ask the occupation for protection.[100]

The UN argued that all blame rested with US landowners, yet new land laws also unleashed land hunger among Haitians. In 1929, locals in Mirebalais challenged the right of Martiche Blaise to property allegedly inherited from his father. A US investigator found in favor of Blaise. He called the case "a deliberate spoliation of a prosperous peasant by a combination of townspeople" and suspected that a local judge and the man who handed out the eviction order would both gain materially. Blaise was not blameless either because "he was occupying a much greater area than that covered by [his] documents." The case illustrated how difficult it was for an individual landowner to resist eviction, even one literate and richer than most.[101]

Yet resist is what occupied peoples did. One Dominican provincial governor reported, only two months after passage of the 1920 Land Registration Law, "numerous . . . grievances received by this ministry." "Unscrupulous individuals" dragged into courts simple peasants who "see themselves caught up in judicial proceedings by speculators and because they have no resources are forced to accept, to receive anything, some disastrous offer."[102] "The land grabbers are abroad in hordes and are measuring and fencing land in all directions, respecting nobody's rights and properties," one man complained from Los Llanos. In the last three years, he added, thirty-seven roads had been closed and fenced in. The peasants couldn't afford wire to fence in their farms so they sent a delegation to speak to the marines.[103]

In the Dominican Republic, small farmers also banded into "Committees for the Defense of the Water" to prevent the US-owned Barahona Company's irrigation project around the Yaque del Sur, which they claimed would divert the river's water from their already arid land. "The Barahona Company," wrote a local paper, "is a powerful fiefdom that... takes over by violence and terror some of the best and largest arable land, reducing to powerlessness the small farmers who dare oppose its designs."[104]

Some resorted to outright crime to evade evictions or cover up forgeries. In January 1928, after US authorities signed a contract for a dam to irrigate 30,000 acres in Haiti's Artibonite Valley, someone broke into the public works building and set fire to aerial photos and negatives of the valley. The loss, estimated at $40,000, was complete. Despondent and with no suspects, the head of the occupation called it "probably the greatest blow that has been given to the American Intervention in Haiti."[105] In the Dominican Republic in May 1918 a group of rebels rode for a day out of their district to burn down an archive of land titles in Bayaguana, apparently so that the forgeries of their urban patron Abelardo Elandino could not be exposed.[106] Dominicans even concocted an ink out of avocado seeds to render fakes more authentic.[107] When marines audited some 4,000 titles, they found a forgery rate hovering at 90 percent.[108]

Although US authorities abused peasants in other ways, they did at times protect them against undue land loss. The chief of the Gendarmerie complained that "abandoned land, state lands, communal properties, estates in litigation etc., are being claimed daily by citizens with or without justice." He ordered gendarmes to investigate, try to settle matters out of court, and "not evict unless the trespass is very recent or the transaction is *plainly one of fraud or theft*," an order obviously directed at those overzealous in their eviction orders.[109] Rather than do the bidding of US investors, occupation authorities saw their mission as serving political culture: to modernize land transfer so that occupied peoples could buy and sell in a predictable, fair way.

In the Dominican Republic the military government also came to the aid of small landholders while it encouraged land purchases in principle. It arrested the Central Romana official who ordered the razing of Caimoní and Higüeral.[110] A few months after setting up the land tribunal, the military governor ordered authorities to "stop this fencing in of land on public ways and around other people's property" by simply tearing down others' fences.[111] While some Dominicans assumed that the military government would back the Barahona Company's irrigation project, it instead halved the project's size.[112]

Occupation authorities were perplexed that Haitians, especially, refused to participate in the modernization of their own country by taking cadastral surveys, acquiring legal titles, and making it easier for foreign corporations to invest and create jobs.[113] Proponents of land reform argued that Haitians were too dependent on coffee and that foreign investment and surveys would diversify agriculture.[114] Even President Calvin Coolidge, usually completely unaware of Haitian events, expressed befuddlement when a senator wrote him of land resistance. "It seems to me it would be much better policy to leave the natives in possession of the real estate than to try to bring it into larger holdings," the president responded. Coolidge reiterated his intent to change Haitian political culture: "The only benefit we derive from [our occupation of Haiti] is to prevent it being an island given over to all of those disorders, physical, mental, moral, economical and political, to which it would otherwise be a prey."[115]

Overall, however, resistance to evictions never became a major concern of any organized group. The Nationalist Union published only one pamphlet on it. The cacos never discussed it. Perhaps this is because the US footprint was so small. The 43,100 acres purchased by US corporations constituted only two thirds of 1 percent of Haiti's land. Of ten companies that bought land during the occupation, only two turned a profit, partly due to resistance: sugar plantations never worked, investigators wrote, "because peasant proprietorship has resisted all attempts to break it up or make it produce one crop on contract."[116]

Other economic issues contributed to resistance. Estimates vary, but 300,000 to 400,000 Haitians found their way to Cuba, especially Oriente province, from 1915 to 1930, with countless others walking over to the Dominican Republic.[117] The UN claimed that occupiers encouraged this emigration so as to weaken the small farmer's hold on the land.[118] To be sure, US authorities in no way obstructed Cuban recruiters in Haiti. In fact, for years, taxes paid by migrants were the main revenue of Port-au-Prince, and emigration may have acted as a safety valve for poor young peasants.[119] More likely, Haitians simply went abroad where wages were higher.[120]

The installation of US and other foreign corporations in Haiti also prompted a nascent proletarian identity there, and with it came the country's first labor protests. Sugar, pineapple, and sisal entrepreneurs not only bought up land but also hired thousands of Haitian peasants as workers. US occupiers considered this progress. But wages were low—20 to 30 cents a day for men and less for women—and work, whether on plantations or railroads, tended to be temporary.[121] Wage workers also were inclined to move to towns, overcrowding them.[122]

In 1919, the workers of the Haitian-American Sugar Company demanded higher wages and shorter hours after HASCO lowered the former and lengthened the latter. HASCO refused, so workers launched the first strike in Haitian history.[123] "We certainly wish to work here, in our country," they explained, "but on the condition of being well paid. If not, we will be forced to abandon said Company for the Dominican Republic and its better conditions."[124]

In the Dominican Republic, meanwhile, the occupation intensified a labor movement already formed during an earlier development of capitalist agriculture. "The very large financial interests," explained a lieutenant colonel, "make the situation difficult for one thing because they trouble the labor class who, in turn, estimate the foreign sugar centrals as representing Americanism, and, so in their minds their grievances against these hard employers are grievances against the US—therefore against the Military Government."[125] Trouble came in many forms, reported another marine. "The abuse of laborers by cheating them out of their wages and then maltreating them by illegally arresting them, beating them and placing them in stocks on Sugar Plantations is altogether too common a practice. This is one of the principal methods of driving recruits to the 'gavilleros.'"[126]

Overall, economic grievances came in a distant second to abuses because economic hegemony was not the defining motivation of occupiers. In 1917 the military governor of the Dominican Republic, Harry Knapp, wrote that he was "very much pestered by would be concessionaires, almost invariably Americans," who wanted "to exploit Santo Domingo."[127] In the 1920s Haiti occupation officials refused "tax exemptions and other privileges" for foreign investors, arguing they would not benefit Haitians enough.[128] Eventually this technocratic approach helped ward off many investors. Over the entire Haitian occupation US investment totaled $15 million while the occupation itself cost $50 million.[129] The American Chamber of Commerce in Haiti voted to dissolve itself in 1927, citing insufficient stimulus by occupation officials.[130]

Much of the hostility to both occupations resulted directly from the creation of constabularies. The Gendarmerie and (as of 1928) the Garde in Haiti, the Dominican National Guard (GND) and (after 1921) the Dominican National Police (PND), and the Nicaraguan National Guard, revived for the Sandino revolt, constituted arguably the most serious US effort at changing political cultures during occupations. Constabularies were meant to be apolitical, professional, national armed forces that would break the cycle of personalist, regional revolution. They were especially intended to centralize force. The GND fused the functions of the old army, navy, and frontier and republican guards. The

Gendarmerie not only replaced the disbanded army but also managed prisons, coastlines, traffic, and electricity.[131]

In Haiti, US State and Navy insisted that the Gendarmerie be part of the 1915 Convention. In the Dominican Republic the constabulary was a demand of the navy as soon as the marines landed, though it was not formed until 1917.[132] Marines often praised the service of gendarmes. Smedley Butler, their first commander, never had a case of disloyalty.[133] Marines judged Dominican guards to be effective fighters when properly trained and equipped, losing only one battle against rebels.[134]

Because of poor funding, however, gendarmes were often not paid their promised measly 50 gourdes ($10) per month, and they complained.[135] They also smuggled, moonlighted, stole, and took bribes.[136] In the GND, salaries were higher—about $15 a month—but also often unpaid, and the force remained underfunded, understaffed, and less able than its Haitian counterpart.[137] US officials complained that "discipline" tended to break down as soon as no marine officer was present.[138] In one typical year of the Gendarmerie, 992 enlisted but 757 were discharged and 170 deserted.[139]

Most constabulary-induced resistance was not internal, however. Guards and gendarmes engendered hatred by abusing the population they were supposed to protect. Two years into the Haitian occupation, a French envoy noted that no sooner did peasants feel free from local political chiefs and obligatory military service than they had to contend with gendarmes stealing their crops.[140] Haitians complained that gendarmes taxed market women unfairly. They killed pigs arbitrarily. They arrested innocents at night. They confiscated. They assaulted. And they tortured.[141] One Haitian gendarme officer, Jules André, recalled decades later how his men transformed peaceful peasants into insurgents with their brutality and pillage.[142] After his unannounced tour of the Haitian countryside in 1920, Knapp reported that the only complaint of peasants was the Gendarmerie. "I have no doubt that this fear of the Haitians is too well founded," he grumbled.[143]

Dominican peasants in Seibo Province refused to come to town for meetings for fear that guards would "borrow" their horses and never return them.[144] The governor of Puerto Plata Province reported that guards hung suspects from the roofs of their own houses until, "bursting with desperation and pain," they confessed to owning a revolver. He identified a "general hatred of this institution" in his province.[145]

The corruption of Haitian and Dominican men with arms had a long pedigree. James McLean, a veteran US officer of Dominican missions, reported that many guards were transplants from the old republican guard, "men who had been encouraged in the art of maltreating inhabitants." The marines felt they had no choice but to hire them since they alone had military training.[146]

Many from the elite resisted the authority of constabularies. The crème of Haiti refused to mingle with the lower classes.[147] Dominicans mocked the PND with an alternative acronym: *pobres negros descalzos* (poor shoeless negroes).[148]

In the midst of the insurrection, the US minister characterized the Dominican Guard as an "absolute failure." Marine officers commanded no respect from enlisted men, he wrote, and Dominican lieutenants "brought discredit on the organization by their high-handed and brutal methods." The fundamental political problem: "Every Dominican is more or less under the influence of some political party whose leaders would do anything to injure American prestige in the Island."[149]

Alongside this disillusion remained, remarkably, an abiding belief in the reform capabilities of empire. It surfaced when Knapp lectured guards after three of them were acquitted on a technicality of killing prisoners. "The action charged was wrong, criminally wrong," he wrote in a letter widely distributed to the GND, warning them not "to let wrong traditions start."[150] Marines seemed to have no idea that these traditions were not starting but rather continuing. In all occupations authorities complained throughout of constabularies' incompetence and inability to learn, predicting that chaos and disorder would return if the marines ever left.

A final dynamic of day-to-day resistance emerged around the borders between the Dominican Republic and Haiti and between Nicaragua and Honduras. In border regions, the invaded crossed both ways in their struggle to preserve the decentralization that the occupations threatened. The intensification of cross-border activity after the arrival of marines also seemed to create a new identity, or at least strengthen an old one, among border dwellers. They became more aware of the importance of their shared interests and freedoms as uniquely transnational groups.[151]

Commerce across the border had always existed, and it continued during the occupations. As the state extended its reach and imposed new or increased taxes on trade, more commerce took on the name "contraband." In 1918, the Dominican constabulary caught and tried around 150 smugglers.[152] As contraband increased in response to taxes, more occupied peoples became outlaws because they traded in such goods. Some of these outlaws became cacos or traded with them, thus increasing the need of the state to raise taxes.[153]

Because of the border, from 1916 to 1919 the Haitian and Dominican insurgencies overlapped, occasionally sharing commanders and information and trading resources.[154] Dominicans, notably Ramón Nateras, enlisted Haitians.[155] A few voluntary Haitian insurrectionists in the Dominican Republic are known by name—Novilis Gil and a man named Louis.[156] US reports often complained of weapons coming from the Dominican side.[157] Marines tracked down one transnational network of ordinary border denizens, including several women, who relayed information to insurrectionists "personally and verbally."[158] Insurgents also crossed over either to escape prosecution for crimes or to rob and then cross back.[159] One Haitian corporal fleeing Haiti allegedly said, "I'd rather die or go to the Dominican Republic than to suffer the presence of *blancs* in the country."[160] A group of seventeen Haitians—including two gendarmes—killed a marine first lieutenant and relieved him of a "large sum of money." They went in and out of the Dominican Republic as they tracked the marine, and finally pounced at a site that "from the most reliable information at hand is Haitian territory, however both countries claim it."[161]

Dominican officials meekly reported that they could do little. A mere sixty Dominican guards patrolled the 241-mile line. These guards filed no reports nor did they "pretend to stop men from crossing with individual arms" because the Dominican government itself long profited from the Haitian hunger for weapons.[162] Cross-border resistance so repeatedly foiled occupation plans that the desire to seal the border was a prime motivator for the US seizure of the Dominican Republic in 1916.[163]

The consolidation of the frontier into a border—marines themselves used the two terms interchangeably—increased the political cultural space between denizens of the border and "modernity" or the services of a central government: schools, roads, prisons, and post offices. Those who were modern looked different, more homogenous—guards, for instance, wore a uniform—and drew their legitimacy from the central state, not from their reputation in the community.[164] When marines burned down Dominican houses in which Haitians had long lived, they characterized the dwellers as "questionable characters who want to live between the lines."

Dominicans and Haitians who enjoyed the "statelessness" of the frontier resisted its militarization and centralization. After the marines landed in Haiti, the Dominican minister of foreign affairs, B. Pichardo, complained that marines were coming from Haiti to beat up Dominicans trying to cross with twist tobacco and otherwise prevented "Dominicans from entering Haitian territory with any kind of produce."[165] Félix Magloire, the Haitian minister to Santo Domingo, complained of the reverse.[166] Both officials made the not too subtle point that US forces disrespected the very borders they imposed on others.[167] In 1920 the town of Monte Cristi petitioned Santo Domingo for "the free passage of Haitians through this part of the border," deeming it "indispensable for commerce."[168] After the occupation imposed land taxes on Dominicans, Haitians who owned land that overlapped both countries refused to pay it, claiming they were exempt and in any case did not recognize the border.[169]

The Nicaragua-Honduras border was even more central to the anti-occupation struggle. Lying a few miles away from his headquarters, Honduras provided an escape valve for Sandino and a path for weapons and men to the Segovias. The marines had little idea where the border was and even those who lived there disputed its exact location.[170] Henry Stimson characterized the border as "the most lawless parts of the entire isthmus of Central America. It is a sort of bi-national lawlessness."[171] *Segovianos* disobeyed labor laws, ignored taxes, made their own alcohol, grew their own tobacco, and slaughtered cows without permits.[172]

Sandinistas later recalled that Honduras was crucial to the struggle. From it they received clothes, money, guns, dynamite, medicine, information—"all we needed."[173] The other way went stolen cattle and goods, which Hondurans could resell at a healthy profit.[174] Danlí, the closest border town, was the hub for most goods and services, and its post office held Sandino's mail.[175] Honduran stores sold guns from Mexico to Nicaraguans.[176]

Men also crossed over—in both directions. Dana Munro sent dispiriting reports that 600 Hondurans joined Sandino in a matter of months.[177] Other Hondurans promised to walk across and vote in Nicaraguan elections.[178] Sandino's men, too, crossed into Honduras, notably when their leader went to Mexico and they needed safe havens.[179] Some, like Juan Pablo Umanzor, had second families there.[180] Many Hondurans fought for revenge, since neither Conservative raids nor marine bombardments respected the border.[181] Smugglers had obvious pecuniary rewards in mind, and Sandino's men were careful not to steal from them. "Self-interest, therefore, would not tend to create any spontaneous opposition to banditry," noted the US legation.[182]

As along the Dominican-Haitian divide, there was little the marines could do to police the 500-mile Nicaraguan-Honduran border.[183] Allegedly they emulated the rebels and crossed the border in pursuit of them.[184] Honduran governments claimed the inviolability of sovereignty and were generally lackluster in sharing information.[185] The State Department, unwilling to expand the war, avoided clashing with Tegucigalpa.[186]

Besides, reported Marine Major P. C. Geyer after a surprise visit to Danlí in early 1931, "the main stumbling-block to perfect collaboration is not the President of Honduras, nor his Government, but the mental attitude of the majority of the Hondureans [*sic*], of some Governmental officials and or nearly all Nicaraguans living within [Honduran] territorial limits. These people believe in Sandino."[187] A Nicaraguan guard went to Danlí as a civilian and reported on "the intense hatred that people, rich and poor, express toward the guardia . . . and the marines."[188] The result of not patrolling the border was a psychological victory for Sandino: "In Choluteca [Honduras]," reported the navy, "every home has a picture of Sandino decorated with colored paper, etc. In the movies, they play Sandino's song and everyone is speaking about him as the national hero, as a second Simon Bolivar."[189]

Alongside resistance, pro-occupation sentiment also existed in later occupation years, belonging increasingly to social groups with a concrete stake in the presence of the marines. Almost uniformly, US observers reported that merchants in both countries were in favor of the occupation. According to Harry Knapp, the Dominican intervention was "approved by 90 per cent of the republic's business men."[190] Adolf Berle, working for a law firm, agreed that "the shopkeepers and merchants" approved of occupation.[191] Others reported that merchants feared giving such approval in public, but continued to do so in private even at the height of public protests.[192] Forty-six merchants in Port-au-Prince openly petitioned the marines for the continuation of the occupation, praising "the security to persons and property, the fair and honest administration of the Customs, the placing of business on a sound foundation." Since the occupation defeated the cacos, they explained, "even the women can carry all their money on their person" and "the merchant does not need to sleep in his shop to feel sure that thieves will not rob him."[193]

Berle added a second group of satisfied occupied peoples: small farmers, the vast majority of inhabitants in all occupations.[194] "These men suffered bitterly under the old disorders," Berle wrote, "and have frankly regarded the Americans as their rescuers. . . . Since the advent of the Americans it was now safe to plant where the farmers never would have dared to plant before."[195] A US inspector in the Dominican Cibao region noted that small farmers placed their *conucos* or plots "as close as possible to the travelled roads, so as to be able to get their produce to market," indicating the shared economic interest of merchants and farmers.[196] Haitian peasants were allegedly relieved to no longer fear caco impressments and to have 1,200 kilometers of national highways in addition to secondary roads on which to bring goods to market.[197] One old man told a US treaty official in 1928, "Do you know I would fight for you and so would my sons? Formerly we had no peace. My sons were taken away from me, my crops were destroyed. You have come and given us peace. . . . We would fight for you!"[198]

In late 1922, US authorities celebrated the end of organized violent resistance on the island of Hispaniola and noticed the ease with which leaders and followers returned to lawful lives. "No trouble of any sort has been experienced with the bandit leaders who have surrendered," confirmed a marine about cacos, many of whom then became vigilantes.[199] Few, however, fully realized how much their abusive, callous, or negligent behavior during that pacification process and in almost every other interaction with the invaded had eroded their standing in the eyes of non-combatants. Peace had been achieved, but not goodwill.

PART THREE

THE STAKES

9

Cultures of Resistance

> In the 20th century one does not change easily from one day to
> another the religion and language of a nation, no matter how small.
> —French Minister to Haiti L. Agel

Rear Admiral Thomas Snowden, who took over from Harry Knapp as the military governor in the Dominican Republic in 1919, assumed his office determined to change the occupied society despite warning signs from insurrectionists and non-violent resisters that the task was not inconsiderable. Snowden assumed that most of the invaded welcomed the US presence, and he wished to transform their culture as well as their politics. Unlike Knapp, Snowden listened to no prominent Dominicans in making decisions. He spoke no Spanish and read no local papers.[1] On June 28, 1919, at the dedication of a new school for Dominicans, he intoned, "When the youths now in schools are grown, I hope to devolve the administration of government into their capable hands and I am certain that everything will go well in the future."[2] Snowden uttered publicly what peers said privately: that the United States intended to stay for at least a generation and dedicate itself to changing the culture of the occupied. Some warned against such ambitions: "I am more than ever aware that no American ever can or even will know more than a fraction of the thought of the Island," wrote Adolf Berle as he left.[3] Yet top US authorities were headstrong in their projects to transform the values and practices of the occupied so as to make them "capable" of absorbing US ways.

Efforts to effect long-term changes in culture revealed the deeper stakes of the occupations. Culture was not the primary stake for either occupiers or occupied. Washington did not attempt to thoroughly "Americanize" major cultural markers such as schools and language in Haiti, Nicaragua, and the Dominican Republic as it did in Puerto Rico and the Philippines.[4] Yet occupations did impact culture in all countries, and cultural representatives among the invaded—writers, educators, religious leaders—did fight back, often out of a sincere desire to protect beliefs, values, and folkways. But these representatives also often sought to preserve, if not enhance, portions of cultural identity that helped concentrate power in the hands of dominant groups. While they spoke of nationalism, they defended notions of education, religion, and race that excluded large slices of the nation and enhanced the cultural purchase of those already advantaged. Culture was another manifestation of the political struggle at the heart of the resistance to occupations.

Daily contact between US occupiers and occupied peoples, much of it informal and unplanned, meant that occupiers would impact the ways of the occupied. In general, the least intrusive cultural forms transmitted most successfully. Without any apparent encouragement from occupation forces, US-style organizations arose in invaded societies. The Boy Scouts appeared in 1917 in the Dominican Republic and in 1919 in Haiti. That same year the Rotary Club founded a chapter in Haiti.[5] Those who adopted Yankee ways seemed to do so freely. Women engaged in US dances "cheerfully and innocently," said a Dominican who disapproved.[6]

Unobtrusive promotion of other cultural forms yielded even greater imitation, baseball being the prime example. In Nicaragua and the Dominican Republic, marine officers organized games among troops to conquer monotony, and those troops in turn played the invaded. Baseball already existed in both countries before occupation, but the sport grew dramatically when the marines arrived.[7] Spreading baseball among the invaded was not a systematic effort to change fundamental habits or beliefs, yet in Nicaragua the sport practically replaced cockfighting as the national pastime by the early 1920s.[8] In a 1916 article titled "Americanizing Nicaragua," US customs collector Clifford Ham claimed that the middle class used to be anti-occupation but then "got interested in seeing the marines playing baseball. A few got balls and bats, and soon others joined."[9] A navy rear admiral was amused at how a "little team" in Chinandega "licked the pants off us."[10] "People who will play baseball and turn out by the thousands every week to see the match games, are too busy to participate in revolutions," concluded Ham.[11] In the eyes of many occupiers, therefore, baseball was a way to pacify the occupied while also displaying evidence of their cultural superiority through the mere acceptance of the game.

However, perhaps Dominicans and Nicaraguans played baseball in part because it gave them a site in which they could defeat the occupation, if only symbolically. At times, baseball games could reflect underlying tensions. One marine described a Nicaragua scene: "At the slightest dispute among the players the people would rush on the field with sticks and stones and assume the most threatening attitude towards our men. Natives in the grand stands were exceedingly rude and discourteous, sometimes their conduct towards marines and other Americans were bordering on insults."[12] In general, however, the invaded seemed to enjoy the bragging rights that the game offered. In one season, Dominican teams flogged the marines eighteen times while losing only three games.[13] "It has now been proven," boasted an anonymous Dominican, "that all the Dominican teams are stronger than any of the Yankee teams that we have met until now."[14] Pitcher Enrique Henríquez's no-hitter against a navy team caused a nationwide sensation.[15] Dominicans' prowess only heightened their zeal for playing, suggesting that the love of *la pelota* was likely the primary motivation. One Dominican who played during the occupation recalled decades later that baseball was only partly about resistance yet infused with nationalism. "Sometimes we felt humiliated by the occupation, but in sport, we fraternized. The crowds were full of this fervor and wanted us to win because we were their team and because we represented the Dominican flag. But there were no demonstrations or rock-throwing, anything like that."[16] By 1918 a Dominican resigned himself to the fact that "baseball has been naturalized in the Dominican Republic and has become part of our customs." He suggested, in vain, that its lexicon be at least "Castillianized"—*home plate* changed to *plataforma, shortstop* to *sitiador, strike* to *golpe, home run* to *carrera de los cuatro bases,* and so on.[17]

Marines encouraged other US cultural forms as entertainment, for themselves and the occupied. Jazz entered Haiti during the occupation, some of it from the presence of marines and from the first phonograph and radio station, Radio HHK, which went on the air in 1927 under marine management. Broadcasts were live and the Gendarmerie band was the first on the air. The occupation put speakers out on the Champs-de-Mars outside the presidential palace and later elsewhere in the country. Illustrated magazines also came to Haiti during the occupation.[18]

Language enjoyed perhaps the most widespread informal impact. Occupations did not systematically spread English in these three countries. Yet while occupation personnel used translators when they had to, they used English almost exclusively for daily administration, forcing the invaded who interacted with them to learn a minimum of vocabulary.[19] Not surprisingly, many of the terms adopted by the occupied denoted the trappings of modernization and organization—*boss, payroll, djob* (job) in Haiti; *suape* (swab, from a mop), *zafacón* ("safe can," for trash can), and *mitín* (meeting) in the Dominican Republic.[20] In the Dominican Republic, words that remained after occupation included some unmodified English words such as *pic-nic* and *usa,* the latter denoting a saddle blanket since marine blankets were marked "USA."[21] The town of San Francisco de Macorís, generations later, still used insults such as ¡*sanibobiche!* (son of a bitch) and called a small street *Bacafar,* from "back far," where prostitutes serving marines congregated. Marines also gave the merengue dance a new style, which Dominicans labeled *pambiche* or *apambichao,* after Palm Beach. Insults, prostitution, and dancing: such were the nodes of contact between occupier and occupied.[22]

Some were horrified by linguistic encroachment. It was said that in 1915 Haitian poet Edmond Laforest drowned himself by hanging a Larousse dictionary around his neck.[23] Haitian poets became purists of French vocabulary and grammar during the occupation, and novelists portrayed occupiers as having no appreciation for the intellectual and artistic values of Haitians.[24] In all countries, especially in Haiti, occupiers who refused to speak the vernacular—such as Colonel Littleton Waller and Major Smedley Butler—were despised.[25]

Cultural resistance came mostly from the elite, especially in Haiti, where class differences coincided sharply with culture. When William Scott, an African American painter, visited in the 1920s, he was shocked that no Haitian painter had taken as a subject the rich natural beauty of the island. Haitian artists were stuck in a formalism inherited from pre-modern Europe and unable to appreciate abstraction or realism. When a US lieutenant named Perfield put on an exhibit of his own in 1932 clearly reminiscent of the Ashcan School, Port-au-Prince newspapers derided it for portraying "the most villainous kind of Haitians, sometimes poor and sickly." President Louis Borno, buckling to elite pressure, deported Perfield.[26] In the Dominican Republic, the *gente de primera*, as a portion of the elite was called, distinguished itself from both the riff-raff and the growing merchant and foreign bourgeoisie through consumption of European rather than US clothes. In the face of growing incivility by the masses who watched motion pictures and the effort by marines to show them to poor children, the elite called movie houses "salons" and divided showings into "acts."[27]

Perhaps the greatest resistance came in response to women's liberation. The Dominican military government, enjoying a legislative monopoly, decreed several reforms to the status of women. It allowed women to practice law, medicine, dentistry, and pharmacy, permitted them to manage their own finances, employed them in government offices, made divorce easier, and forced parents to support all offspring, including illegitimate children.[28] All occupations, by lowering trade tariffs, also eased the import of consumer goods aimed at women.

Women's already changing behavior, now sanctioned by invaders, drew the disapproval of cultural patriarchs. Dominican novelist Horacio Read described how US dances in his country were scenes of motorcars "vomiting bare breasts and backs, pink perfumed flesh flapping lustfully." Once inside the ballroom, "the *fiesta* continued as a bacchanal devoid of art or literature, only mechanics: fox-trots, one-steps and shrieks. No beautiful words. No dignified movement." Such behavior, Read concluded, led naturally to adultery and emasculation.[29] Another witness to a Dominican dance, shocked at the fox-trot, advised, "Our women should distance themselves completely from it and strictly keep to our native dances (the waltz, the *danzón*, etc.) which in no way affect the delicateness, the decency and the modesty of Dominican feminism."[30] Jazz in Haiti also competed with more genteel French parlor dances like the mazurka, the waltz, and the quadrille.[31] Nicaragua witnessed the most organized opposition to women's social liberation. There, prominent men founded the Catholic Knights in January 1918, perhaps not coincidentally at the same time as Nicaraguan women founded the country's first feminist organization. The Knights succeeded mostly in their own homes but also convinced Catholic priests and bishops to refuse sacraments to women who attended services in sleeveless blouses or skirts above ankle-length. Even Augusto Sandino agreed that US-style music was too "sensuous" for Nicaraguan women.[32]

At times, occupiers could do little if occupied governments chose not to enforce their culture. In Nicaragua, especially, there was no censorship in much of the country. In 1932, marine frustration was palpable when one reported that a Chinandega music distributor sold copies of "Sandino's march" yet there existed "no order prohibiting their sale."[33]

Education reforms occurred in the Dominican Republic and Haiti and constituted the most systematic effort to transfer US culture onto the occupied. Reforms were not as far-ranging as in Puerto Rico, which spent 29 percent of its budget on education in the late 1920s compared to 10 percent in Haiti.[34] Yet education reformists in Hispaniola met with determined resistance from elites.

In the Dominican Republic the military government changed the educational system to a limited degree yet made key mistakes and drew significant opposition. In 1918 only 18,000 out of a possible 200,000 children aged seven to fourteen were even registered for primary education, all in private schools. Of those, maybe four out of ten showed up on a given day, and most who did failed to complete primary school. Knapp took the system out of the hands of the city councils and centralized it under a Commission on Education and a general superintendent of education. The commission instituted obligatory primary school assistance, doling out punishments to parents of truants. It hiked teacher salaries.[35] It also standardized curricula and equipment, built new facilities, created parent associations, ordered inspections, set promotions based on daily work, gave special attention to reading and writing, standardized diplomas and degrees, and cut summer vacations from three months to forty days. By 1920, attendance was up to 120,000. Literacy, previously negligible, jumped to 20 percent.[36]

Some US observers argued for also changing the content of education to alter political behavior. "Santo Domingo has always run more or less wild," noted US journalist Harry Frank, who mirrored Snowden by calling for "at least twenty-five years of good elementary schooling." He suggested that Dominican textbooks be rewritten to enumerate the "chief faults of Dominicans," "caudillismo" being the first.[37] Yet the occupation made no efforts to Americanize the content of education, the reason likely being that Dominicans, who liked what students learned and just wanted more of it, staffed the Commission on Education.[38]

Initially, US education reforms attracted little national attention, yet small-town administrators were none too happy to see the capital's authority grow at their expense. An incident in the town of Guerra, a dozen miles outside Santo Domingo, illustrated how the musical chairs of reform stoked political jealousy. In mid-1920 twenty inhabitants of Guerra assaulted the new schoolmaster, Carlos Concha, ostensibly because he enforced the school attendance policy and called former city councillors "dishonest" in a newspaper article. The latter sin was a clue to the real stake in the matter. The rebellious group included former members of the city council, whom the occupation had replaced the previous year for stealing from the till. The ousted head of the council, Angel Delgado, accused his replacement of being "nothing but a supporter of the Americans with their laws and Executive Orders who are doing in our people." His son called for Concha and the new city councillors, whom he called "foreigners" because they were not from Guerra, to leave "because Guerra must be exclusively of the guerreros."[39]

The financing of schools eventually grew into a serious problem. With the US reforms, the per-child cost of Dominican education skyrocketed, doubling that of Mississippi.[40] Up to 1919, local businesses shouldered the burden through a tax, but centralization tied school budgets to national revenues, which were dependent on customs receipts. In 1920–1921 a sharp drop in export prices gripped the nation. Dominicans opposed the floating of a large loan as a remedy for financing the schools, so in May 1921 the military government responded by closing all public schools indefinitely.[41] Dominicans were up in arms. How ironic, wrote the *Listín Diario*, to see "the total suppression of Public Instruction" under "our WISE AND CIVILIZED TUTORS."[42] Some teachers and principals continued to teach pupils in their homes.[43] In 1922, to revive the schools, the military government tied their financing to an unpopular and boycotted property tax, hoping to make boycotters feel guilty that they robbed local schools of income. Dominicans expressed no guilt. In 1924, when the marines departed, the local tax returned to fund the schools, and attendance dropped to half that of 1920.[44]

"These people have no incentive to work," reasoned a marine officer in Haiti as he laid out the case for a reform of education there that would prompt some of the more passionate resistance of that occupation. "Their wants are limited to food, and a simple shelter from inclement weather. . . . Education with its accompanying creation of needs and desires beyond a mere animal existence is the sole remedy."[45] The US minister to Port-au-Prince agreed, wishing to impart "the language of mind, of morals" to Haitians. New schools were to be the means to that end.[46]

Even more so than in the Dominican Republic, it was no wonder that schools in Haiti elicited calls for reform. Fewer than five out of every thousand school-age children even showed up, and most of these were in Catholic schools.[47] Four years into the occupation the education budget was still a mere $340,000, a pittance compared to the $7 million spent in Cuba, a country with the same number of inhabitants, or even to the $1.5 million in the Dominican Republic, with a third of Haiti's population. It was widely reported and admitted that "schoolteachers" drew their pay but often only sat at their desk, "taught" children who did not show, and were often themselves illiterate.[48] Haitians had no objection to increasing the number of students served, yet they rarely engaged the deeper problem of political culture: education as a vehicle for distributing spoils.

Unlike in the Dominican Republic, however, US forces in Haiti had no direct authority over education. Up to the early 1920s, the occupation only built new schools under its Public Works service. Controversy arose nevertheless, first over Haitians' own reforms. Dantès Bellegarde, the Haitian minister of Public Instruction and Agriculture in 1918, was the instigator. In 1904, as an education bureaucrat, Bellegarde had attempted to bolster rural schools and to shelter education from political upheavals. He fought for improved buildings, good salaries for teachers, overhauled curricula, and regular inspections. His efforts resulted in new textbooks, but politicians opposed his merit-based reforms.[49]

When he rose to the rank of minister under the occupation, Bellegarde tried again. Traditionalists accused him and others of being *anglo-saxonistes* who advanced the materialist and racist educational program of the occupation, and Bellegarde was himself torn because he loved Haiti's French culture. He won pay raises for teachers, but the occupation, which controlled the purse strings, opposed all his other proposals, and—interpreting loosely the Treaty of 1916—instead imposed on Haiti a Louisianan, Lionel Bourgeois, as superintendent of public education, who proceeded to change nothing at all.[50]

Bellegarde later blamed "the Americans" who "opposed this project because it was originated by Haitians."[51] He also fingered "the peculiar psychology of the Haitian mass at this time which unaccustomed to disciplining itself does not tolerate the attempt coming from its own race."[52] The head of the occupation countered that Bellegarde behaved as a typical elite, arguing that "his one desire was to make addresses to the schools on ceremonial occasions, and that the efficiency of public instruction did not particularly interest him."[53]

A second controversy sprang up after 1923, when the occupation created the Technical Service of Agriculture and Professional Education, giving itself the authority to offer industrial and agricultural training as an alternative to religious education. The director of the Technical Service, George Freeman, explained that since 90 percent of Haitians lived off the land, the same proportion of education should cater to them. "We find that we can give the child a great deal of training so that he may better help himself in his work, such as for instance, how to count his chickens and pigs and care for his garden."[54] In early 1926, Freeman shut down forty low-attendance traditional schools and replaced them with twelve industrial schools, eight for boys and four for girls, each with 500 students.[55] The schools taught, in addition to English and French, botany, engineering, agrarian chemistry, entomology, land surveying, horticulture, zoology, and cattle raising.[56]

"Everybody is indignant about this action," wrote anti-occupation activist Perceval Thoby, especially since the new buildings occupied two century-old public squares.[57] More surprising to the occupation was that peasants also resisted. Many thought only "of going to the city and taking what we call 'a white-collar' job." "The average country father and mother," explained Freeman, "feel they have always lived under the most barren circumstances in country and rural life and they say 'I want to send my boy to school so that he may learn to read and write so that he may go to the city and get a job' and when we start to teach them agriculture they say 'what do we want with agriculture—you can't teach us that because we already know it.'" Parents also kept children on the farm to work. Sometimes attendance to agricultural schools was "as low as 60 per cent," and those who did show were often undernourished.[58] Graduates of the Technical Service, sent to rural schools to teach, hated the monotony of the countryside and resigned after a few months.[59]

But most resistance came from supporters of traditional *belles-lettres* education focused on literature, law, and medicine. Freeman hoped to re-educate some elite Haitians "to get them away from that 'gentleman' idea that they were not supposed to even carry a package down the streets in town, and to make them leaders of actual work."[60] In 1923, in response to a suggestion that they close down high schools and libraries, Haitians created the Society of History and Geography to promote Haitian culture.[61] There were also practical arguments: Haitians denounced the scale of expenditures of the Technical Service as these could not be supported after the occupiers left; the lack of French spoken by officials, who turned classes over to interpreters; and the threat they posed to other schools and to Haitian artisans, who competed with the service's offerings.[62]

The Haitian elite also associated vocational training with African Americans, whom they disdained, an antipathy most in evidence during the visit of the Moton Commission, which President Herbert Hoover sent to Haiti in mid-June 1930 to review and recommend changes to Haitian education.

African Americans dominated the commission, starting with its head, Robert Moton, president of Tuskegee Institute.[63] In response to the announcement about the commission, Raoul Lizaire, the Haitian chargé in Washington, feared that African Americans would recommend "a program of agricultural and vocational rather than cultural education."[64] The Moton Commission, whom few Haitians took seriously, was to reform an area that few Haitian wanted reformed.

The commission went ahead with its work for twenty-four days in Haiti, and gave its report to Hoover on October 1, 1930. It agreed that private, religious education was elitist and unsuited to the needs of the country. It also argued that the Technical Service "represents a pressing need," that "real progress has been made," and that its "motives . . . can not be questioned." Yet it sympathized "with the Haitian view point concerning the charge that the service is over-staffed and extravagant." The report's sixty-one recommendations advocated a third way, public education for all: a centralized system, higher salaries, more farm and educational programs, a national university and library, foreign study, Haitian rather than US administrators, and more.[65] The Department of State said the report was badly informed, and it made no announcement to the public when it was published in April 1931. No recommendation saw the light of day.[66]

There were, again, political ramifications to this resistance. "The elite" in Haiti, noted Dana Munro, "were cool to the idea of building up a middle class which might challenge their own political and social ascendency."[67] At the end of the 1920s there were still no more than 101,150 Haitian pupils in schools out of 450,000 school-age children. Half were in towns, where attendance was high, which meant that, after a decade of reforms, almost no rural children got any formal schooling.[68] In the 1960s, 90 percent of Haitians remained illiterate.[69]

Occupations attempted much less to reform religion in all three countries, but their behavior still aroused opposition. Religion, however, was a more ambivalent site of resistance than was education because faith services were a major point of contact of the masses with occupations, and the masses tended to be more acquiescent than the elite. Religion also pitted communities of faith against each other. Overall the role of religion in resistance confirmed that groups of believers, like others under occupation, fought for their own ways of life rather than for an abstract national good.

The 635 priests and nuns of the Haitian Catholic Church largely desired to see the US goal of modernization do away with old habits of state corruption, violence, and poverty. Also motivating the priests, mostly white Frenchmen, was that the occupation did not at first threaten the primacy of the French language or of Catholicism. Priests and occupiers saw each other as partners in bringing civilization to Haiti.[70] "It is time to open our eyes," is how the archbishop of Cap-Haïtien responded in 1919 to the fait accompli of occupation. "Those whom it oppressed directly are the revolutionaries. . . . Those are our enemies, not the Americans."[71] In Hinche, priests campaigned for the repression of Charlemagne Péralte.[72] Also pleasing the church was that the occupation vowed to eradicate Vodou.[73] Along with devout lay Haitians, Catholics snitched on peasants who organized Vodou's *rara* dances on Good Friday, judging the practice "a profanity on that holy day."[74] Marines suspected that one Catholic priest at Mirebalais "was poisoned on account of his activity against Vaudoism."[75]

As abuses in most occupations became legion, however, even friendly Catholics seemed to abandon the occupiers. Priests in small, faraway parishes where single marines or small groups imposed reigns of terror usually turned first. Since priests were close to the masses, said one, "we know the mind of the poor people, its misery, its spirit, its revolt against foreign occupation, its hopes, and often its secret thoughts of revolution."[76] At Thomazeau, Haiti, Abbé Louis Marie Le Sidanier testified in 1921 how his parishioners were at first in "full sympathy with the American occupation" but now "no longer have confidence." A company of gendarmes and marines had burned down 250 to 300 homes in his parish, including his own and by error the chapel, all because cacos had camped across the road. The "terrified" inhabitants fled to nearby woods and a half-year later only a handful of families had returned.[77] Discontent eventually percolated up to the bishops.[78]

Much of the Haitian Catholic Church's resentments came from educational reform. In 1918 François-Marie Kersuzan, the bishop of Cap-Haïtien, implored Secretary of State Robert Lansing not to reduce school budgets.[79] The church had enjoyed state funds to run schools since an 1860 Concordat with the Vatican, but the arrival of Lionel Bourgeois, who wanted to separate church and state, set off a panic. The church also opposed agricultural and industrial schools for their alleged control by Protestants and the fact that they made religious schools look passé.[80]

In early 1930, Haiti's five bishops declared that the church officially opposed the occupation.[81] "The clergy will rejoice with all its heart when the present situation is ended," wrote a group representing "the Clergy of Haiti" in an open letter.[82] Vocational schools were the ostensible issue, but the church also must have sensed the shifting political winds with free elections coming up and the anti-occupation party strongest. In addition, the Concordat stipulated that the church had to support the government in power, in return for which the priests lived on government salaries.[83]

In Nicaragua, in contrast, there was little repression of folk spirituality, priests were largely Nicaraguan, and the church retained influence in a government not overtaken by occupation forces.[84] As a result, although the church itself was close to US-friendly Conservatives, Catholic opinions converged against the US presence. Granada's Catholic Knights dominated this anti-intervention stance, rejecting the "waves of immorality" washing over Nicaragua.[85] Apart from their repression of "Americanized" women, the Knights feared urbanization, economic modernization, consumerism, popular mobilization, and the expansion of the state. The film, record, magazine, and radio industries were equally foes. The Knights also felt threatened by the proliferation of Protestant missionaries since the 1912 arrival of the troops, even though Baptists had converted only 735 Nicaraguans by 1933. The Knights published tracts and demonstrated to shut down Protestant churches, schools, and health clinics or to prevent their opening. They blacklisted those who sold them goods. Some attacked US missionaries and Nicaraguan followers with stones and machetes. By 1926 the violence led the American Baptist Home Mission Society to brand Nicaragua as perhaps the most dangerous site of missionary work in Latin America.[86]

The Nicaraguan Catholic Church itself spread anti-US sentiment. In 1927 the Bishop of Granada sent around a pastoral letter—read as a sermon in all churches—deriding "the corruption of manners ... among the people, who have departed somewhat from the primitive simplicity of Christian life. . . . This is evident in the immoral moving pictures, the indecent theatrical spectacles and clothes, and all that mass of worldly diversions." That same letter spoke also to the partisan nature of the church in Nicaragua, long tied to the Conservatives, who had increased its funding. It warned against "above all ... the extremely serious evil ... [of] belonging to the party and sect of Liberalism."[87]

In the Dominican Republic, the Catholic Church was united in its opposition to occupation, though more subtly so because it lived under a US military regime. The country was Catholic through and through—98.6 percent in 1920—and unlike in Haiti, more of the clergy were Dominicans than foreigners.[88] Perhaps more than in any other occupation, Dominican believers used Christian symbols, liturgy, and rhetoric to suggest their discontent without openly voicing it.[89] Women stood at the forefront of this subtle resistance. Barely a month into the occupation, a religious women's society marked the anniversary of the country's Restoration from Spain in 1863 to call for "a restoration of the ideas and sentiments that might save the Republic from total ruin. . . . Judases today are legion."[90] Dominican women also organized a 1920 fundraising week for anti-occupation activists, which they couched in religious analogies: "During this week of blessings, hopes, and faith, foreigners, mendicants, lepers, the wealthy, children, women, and the elderly turned out in haste to lay down before the altar of the subjugated Fatherland the sacred donation."[91] Others spoke of their experience since 1916 as a *via crucis*, the Stations of the Cross.[92] Dominicans fondly remembered the pious outrage of

Judge Juan Pérez, who, unable to prosecute marines torturing Dominicans, slammed his hand on a table and shattered a cross.[93] Pérez was forever known as *el hombre del cristo*.

As protests against the occupation mounted, the Dominican Church grew bolder. Dominicans had long "despised" their priests for being drunkards and fornicators.[94] In contrast, they revered Archbishop Adolfo Nouel, who had briefly been a beneficent president of the country and who, in spring 1920, publicly presented charges of abuse to the marines.[95] Nouel's move placed the church squarely in the camp of the resistance, most likely convincing many of the pious also to turn against occupation. The French chargé in October described Nouel as "the champion of independence, the symbol of resistance against American intervention. He is today the most popular citizen in the country."[96] In early 1922, 30,000 Dominicans crowned the Virgin of Altagracia, the patron saint of the republic, typically a purely religious ceremony. The French chargé that year noted "a certain political connotation," with speeches alluding to the restoration of sovereignty.[97]

Catholic opposition was, overall, motivated by both a concern for parishioners and the welfare of Catholicism itself. In no case was the church a vanguard of the resistance; instead it joined anti-occupation protests once they had become difficult to resist.

While Catholicism skirted the edges of resistance, Vodou's resistance was unequivocal but clandestine, in keeping with its pariah status among spiritual practices. A syncretic African religion blended with Catholic symbols and unique to Haiti and to some border regions of the Dominican Republic, Vodou was derided as obscure peasant occultism, but national elites as well as local politicians joined in celebrations or went to Vodou healers for treatment.[98] Vodou seemed disproportionately popular among those who resisted the occupation. Some cacos apparently mutilated captured marines out of the belief that if they ate the heart of a white man they would have his courage, that his liver would provide them with wisdom, and that rubbing his brain on a gun would sharpen their aim.[99] Caco chief Benoît Batraville was a *hougan* or Vodou priest who apparently used his powers to frighten the Haitian aides of US forces.[100] Péralte, Batraville's predecessor, had a Dominican mistress well practiced in healing.[101] "Probably all of the caco chiefs are Vaudoux priests," assessed one US observer.[102] Vodou-motivated resistance, however, was not always successful. Elite opponent Placide David once sprinkled cornmeal in a doorway through which President Louis Borno was to walk, an apparent *ouanga* or curse. Borno "did a little jig in it and snapped his fingers" at David. "See what I care about your ouanga," he blustered.[103]

Vodouisants also opposed the occupation because the occupation opposed them. The marines aimed to crush Vodou in Haiti, destroying its talismans, stopping its dances, and forcing it underground. The ban continued long after the insurrections expired and grew out of the desire to rid Haiti of its "savagery."[104] But Vodou survived. One US author in 1921 said the practice disappeared from the cities but thrived in towns, "where they dance the weird 'bambeula' to the beat of a tom-tom very much as they do at the real Vaudoux meetings."[105] In November 1924, US Gendarmerie officials tried to sweep up the country's Vodou leaders, which proved difficult because Haitian courts, hostile to the occupation, freed those arrested.[106] In Hinche, reported a marine, *hougans* no longer called forth their believers with drums but now merely clapped hands or slapped banana leaves.[107] A report from Le Trou assumed "that most of the haitien [*sic*] people" took part in Vodou dances. "However, when authority appears this immediately changes into the dances that are allowed."[108] Smedley Butler, who headed the Gendarmerie, himself cheated by allowing corvée workers to "carry on with their drums and snake symbols and closed my eyes to the Saturday jamborees."[109]

One case of Vodou that the marines did pursue demonstrated the tragedy of banning a religion both feared and defended by the elite. Cadeus Bellegarde was arrested in December 1919 for practicing human sacrifice, an extremely rare form of Vodou. Bellegarde had apparently murdered twelve to fifteen children—some claimed fifty—including one of his own. He was also wanted for cannibalism, burning down the houses of Catholic priests, and "aiding and abetting an armed uprising against the United States."[110] Twenty-seven witnesses gave statements to the police: they called Bellegarde a "Demon" and accused him of forcing them to join the cacos and to work on his lands for free.[111] The marines asked President Sudre Dartiguenave if native courts would try Bellegarde, but the president begged off, saying first that Bellegarde would surely be found guilty, then that he would be acquitted.[112] Dartiguenave's real reason was probably that some of the elite feared Bellegarde. Bellegarde claimed the marines destroyed his property and that the testimony against him was obtained through torture, yet he denied no charges. The *Courrier Haïtien* fell for Bellegarde's strategy of associating himself with the resistance and reiterated its belief in violence as legitimate in Haitian politics. "Revolutions will remain the decisive argument against the bad faith and oppression of venal and inept leaders."[113] The last recorded mention of Bellegarde, months after his release, reported that "the natives are greatly alarmed" because he threatened those testifying against him. The marines could do little but send a patrol to observe.[114]

Another case of Vodou-like resistance and persecution was that of Olivorio Mateo. Soft-spoken, pleasant, with cotton threads and knots in his hair, looking much like an African "witch doctor," Mateo was known alternatively as Liborio, Dios Olivorio, Papa Livorio, and El Maestro. He gained a cult-like following in the Dominican border province of San Juan de la Maguana for predicting the coming of Halley's Comet in 1910. Among his followers were polygamists, out-laws, and traders newly defined as outlaws by a 1907 agreement that allowed the United States to patrol the border. *Liboristas* syncretized African, indigenous, and Catholic beliefs and practices and probably borrowed their dances from Haitian *rara*. In 1909 and 1910 Mateo ran into trouble with local authorities for practicing medicine illegally, but in 1911 he entered into an informal agree-ment with them giving him virtual local autonomy provided he undertake no insurrection.[115]

US authorities resented that autonomy when they aimed to centralize the Dominican Republic. The occupation pursued Mateo as a threat both to modern social mores and to political stability.[116] In April 1917, a joint marine-guard patrol destroyed his hideout, but the *liboristas* took to the mountains in this most inaccessible region.[117] In January 1918 the marines again found Mateo's camp, but only after locals warned him of their presence, allowing him to escape. The movement spread throughout the southwest, partly because the occupation de-stroyed property while hunting Mateo.

When the marines threatened him, Mateo likened them to Satan.[118] Yet anti-occupation activists also denounced Mateo because *liboristas*, in sharing food, drink, money, and land and in practicing sexual liberation, challenged bourgeois notions of propriety and property, not to mention land concentration in his region. Mateo also threatened both groups as a caudillo when in 1912 he raised an army for an assault on national government.[119] In 1920, when a smallpox epi-demic threatened the border area, Mateo preached "antivaccination and caused quite a commotion." Partly in response, the Dominican occupation banned folk healing or *curanderismo*.[120]

Marines chased Mateo for five years, urban Dominicans offering assistance, peasants refusing to provide it.[121] In 1922, another patrol went after him. On June 27 it surrounded his camp and shot him "15 times before he fell."[122] The marines exposed Mateo's body in San Juan's central square to make clear to ev-eryone his mortality. People stood all afternoon, staring at the body. Schools let out so that children could see. Decades later, many Dominican peasants still considered the man a "living god."[123]

Pervading almost all interactions between occupiers and occupied was the marker of race, which emerged most strongly in Haiti but suffused the resistance in all three countries.[124] US occupiers were almost uniformly contemptuous of non-white Latin Americans, and not only Haitians. Marines often called Do-minicans "spigs" or "niggers," even more so in the east, which had more inhabit-ants of mixed and African blood.[125] In Nicaragua a marine doctor attended a ceremony with well-dressed Nicaraguans but admitted, "I can't overcome my prejudice toward them and the feeling that they are 'negroes' which they are not in the African sense. But their Indian blood makes them about as dark. . . . Our little brown brothers and sisters! Huh!"[126] The resistance also often used racial differentiations in divisive discourses that argued against national and nationalist movements.

Augusto Sandino elevated the identity of the Indian with an essentialist discourse that posited, like Mexico's José Vasconcelos at the same time, that a mixture of Indian and European blood made Latin America unique and superior to racially pure peoples.[127] The discourse cleverly celebrated all who had Indian blood—which, according to a 1920 census, was 71 percent of Nicaraguans.[128] Sandino wrote that, unlike other Latin Americans, he did not seek exemplars of heroism in Europe. Heroes, rather, "always emerge from the people, mostly from the Indo-Hispanic race and I believe that the blood flowing in my veins is Indian blood, which contains the mystery of being heroic, loyal, and sincere." Given such a construct, the "other" became obvious: the "foreign invader enemy of our race and language, in other words the barbarous colossus of the North."[129]

Dominican elites also enlisted a racial discourse, in their case in the service of persuading the invaders. Like Nicaraguans, Dominicans' blood was also heavily mixed, their own 1920 census showing that half were mulatto, one quarter white, and the other quarter black.[130] Elite Dominicans, largely white, often used the trope of "civilization" to distinguish themselves from their neighbors and expressed shock at the possibility of being lowered to the level of Haitians. As troops disembarked in 1916, four Dominicans explained to the US minister that Dominicans were "not a semi-barbaric race needing to be civilized by cannons, but rather a gentlemanly race, peaceful, cordial, enamored of its sovereignty, a lover of science, of letters and of art."[131] One of the most persistent urban advocates for withdrawal, Tulio Cestero, wrote Woodrow Wilson that his country had fought a nineteenth-century war with Haiti for its independence "in behalf of the prevalence of the white race and with the same unswerving will they conserve religion, language, and the racial attributes bequeathed by the Spanish founders."[132] In 1921 another Dominican wondered why occupiers "treated us as though we were Negroes from the Congo."[133]

Dominicans, in contrast to Sandino, tended to see racial admixture as threatening their ideal of "civilization." Novelist Federico García Godoy wrote that "our ethnic reality is a mixture of the blood of the white European of a generally low and criminal nature and that of the savage Ethiopian, full of the fevered and fetishistic superstitions of his African jungles." He blamed this "hybridity of our ethnic origin" for "a society largely opposed to effective and prolific civilization."[134] Américo Lugo, perhaps the foremost anti-American Dominican, in 1916 blended racial and climactic determinism to explain political failure: "Due to the possession of a too fertile territory under a tropical climate, to the deficiency in nourishment, to the excessive mixture of African blood, to anarchical individualism, and to the lack of culture, the Dominican people have very little political aptitude." He did not consider the Dominican people a "nation" until the United States occupied them, after which Lugo and his ilk revived Hispanism, which championed all things Spanish, including whiteness.[135]

Haiti, meanwhile, was in the unusual position of being a "black republic" yet having a color line drawn far more sharply than in either Nicaragua or the Dominican Republic. Before occupation, Haiti's racial dynamics were perhaps the most complex of all three countries. The most obvious of these dynamics was the apparent fear of whites. In 1939, former president Sténio Vincent began his four-volume memoir by discussing "the racial obsession." "No doubt we had good reasons for it. The white, who had oppressed our forefathers for centuries, remained our *bête noire*." The Constitution of 1805 not only prohibited whites from owning slaves or land but also associated citizenship with blackness. Vincent regretted that "this age-old obsessive fear of the white" resulted in "a racial pride that, unfortunately, beyond the glorious but isolated fact of independence conquered by force of arms, nothing yet could justify."[136] The other side of antiwhite racism was an inferiority complex vis-à-vis whites. Travelers noted how Haitian barbershops offered skin bleaching and hair straightening and how Vodou practitioners plastered their faces with white clay to symbolize the importance of whites.[137]

Intersecting and heightening racial tensions were relations between men and women. The marines at first discouraged white wives from accompanying their husbands to Haiti, minimizing opportunities for friction.[138] When wives were allowed in 1916, tensions arose, mostly at dances.[139] "When a Haitian gentleman asked an American woman to dance," reported the *New York Times*, "he usually was met with a polite excuse, only to see her a few minutes later dancing off with an American." Haitians were used to far more cordial gender interactions with Europeans, which explained why one French traveler thought US fears entirely unjustified. "Negroes are indifferent to white women. Never have they appeared to me to be these sex maniacs, these gorillas of which the American newspapers talk."[140]

Marines were not indifferent to black women: they treated them as either lascivious or asexual. In Port-au-Prince, a city of 100,000, there were 147 registered saloons or dancehalls, and prostitutes operated out of all of them.[141] Yet one marine recalled decades later that the "thought of intermarriage" with Haitian women was "horrifying."[142] Faustin Wirkus, the lone marine in La Gonâve who entered into a power-sharing agreement with Ti-Memme, a Haitian "queen," made a visiting US writer promise to report that Wirkus "is not married to the queen; he is not married to anybody."[143] When seeing a shapely black woman Wirkus exclaimed, "What a figure! If that woman were white she'd be a knockout."[144]

In response to US racism, Haitians showed "no subserviency [*sic*] in their attitude toward the whites," investigator Carl Kelsey remarked.[145] Haitians rarely fought back physically because provost courts protected US whites. Instead, they used their own courts, in which judges regularly took the side of Haitians against whites. In one typical case a Haitian lawyer defended his client against an air-tight case of theft by saying, "It is not the poor negro who is guilty, . . . it is the white man. . . . But why, by an absurdity of the law, is it necessary that the American escape from Haitian [justice]?" After seventeen minutes of deliberation, the jury pronounced the defendant not guilty and the court broke out in applause.[146]

By the late 1920s some Haitian intellectuals developed their own version of black empowerment, called *négritude* or *noirisme*, partly in response to what Dantès Bellegarde called the "white dictatorship."[147] Their agenda was mostly to recognize the positive contributions of Africa to Haiti, but some also aimed to de-humanize whites. Émile Roumer, founder of one of *noirisme's* central vehicles, *La Revue Indigène*, explained that "the racial principle of *l'Indigène* consisted in recognizing only two races: *homo sapiens* and the human excrement that is the WASP." Roumer admitted he wanted to "give the bourgeois and the Americans a kick in the ass."[148]

A less intuitive aspect of race for marines in Haiti was the color line between mixed-race and African-phenotype Haitians, or, as Haitians put it at the time, between "yellows" and "blacks." The so-called line, in fact, was more of a ladder with many rungs. Haitians constructed a vast array of miscegenation formulas—four for Indians, ten for whites, and fourteen for blacks.[149] Because of mulatto-black relations, wrote Sténio Vincent, "too many Haitians became hypnotized by race and thus relegated the Nation to a secondary consideration."[150] Many others agreed that the color line undermined political stability, observing that mulatto-led governments tended to be thrown out by blacks and vice versa.[151] At the micro level, the same dynamic operated. One US doctor, about to depart Haiti, recalled being ordered to replace himself with a Haitian and he hired a black doctor. "You can't do that; he's a black man," said his mulatto colleagues, but the doctor insisted that his pick was the best man for the job. One month later, the black Haitian was fired.[152]

Many US visitors were shocked at the pervasiveness of inter-Haitian racism. "It was in Haiti that I first realized how class lines may cut across color lines within a race, and how dark people of the same nationality may scorn those below them," wrote African American writer Langston Hughes in his memoir. "I hated this attitude."[153] Robert Moton and other African Americans came back from the black republic even concluding "that the dividing line between mulattoes and negroes is more sharply drawn than between the whites and negroes in the south of the United States."[154] Yet US citizens did little to discourage the color line. Some reinforced it by assuming that light-skinned Haitians were more competent and honest in government and appointed them disproportionately to positions of influence. President Sudre Dartiguenave, elevated into office by the marines in 1915, was the first mulatto president since 1879, and three others followed. Later in the occupation, US forces tried to blur the color line—for instance, by bringing more educational opportunities to darker-skinned students.[155] They also invited light- and dark-skinned Haitians to the same dances. High Commissioner John Russell, observing "mulatto girls dancing with the blacks," thought such mingling "will finally lead to true democracy."[156]

Race, religion, education, and other cultural forms proved highly resistant to change during the occupations, partly because occupiers were not intent on deep cultural change and mostly because the invaded wanted next to none. Schools were the only cultural institutions the occupations founded, and even they were meant only to compete with existing models, not replace them. In 1922, French Minister to Haiti L. Agel recalled that, upon taking his post three years earlier, he feared that the United States tried to "sap our intellectual and moral influence in this country." Now, he wrote, "[US authorities] realized that in the 20th century one does not change easily from one day to another the religion and language of a nation, no matter how small."[157]

10

Politics of Resistance

There were two truths: the official truth and the truth of the
Dominican people.

—Horacio Blanco Fombona

While the invaded clung to cultural identities they felt the occupations threatened, invaders aimed reforms far more directly at politics. They had more legal
authority to do so, especially in Haiti and the Dominican Republic, and political
groupings were easier to alter than massive cultural institutions such as schools
and churches. But mostly, occupiers saw political behavior rather than cultural
markers at the core of their problems in Latin America. So it was to be expected
that occupied peoples would most resist change in their political process.

Politics was also the site where one would expect the most nationalism. Although occupied peoples—especially the politically engaged elite—talked a
good nationalist game, their actions betrayed more local political and economic
interests. No matter how poor the occupied were or how well intentioned some
occupation reforms might have been, small-town Haitian, Nicaraguan, and Dominican power holders, as well as big-city activists, refused to accede to changes
in their political systems. Political resistance, large and small, was the heart of the
anti-occupation phenomenon.

Unsurprisingly, peaceful political resistance emerged in urban areas. The small
size and social cohesion of elite and middling groups, along with their physical
concentration, proved advantageous to organizing against occupation in capital
cities. The Haitian elite was perhaps 3 percent of the population, or 150,000.[1]
Within the elite, resistance leaders tended to be professionals—writers, journalists, politicians, and lawyers. In Port-au-Prince, professionals numbered a few
thousand, and in the Dominican Republic the 1920 census listed professionals
as 0.1 percent of the population—around 750.[2]

These small groups dominated politics to the exclusion of the large majority
and had more to lose in a foreign takeover. Before 1915, Haiti masqueraded as

a democracy but was in essence "a military oligarchy," as the State Department noted.[3] "A few hundred men" there organized political parties only as temporary political groupings that followed a strongman-candidate.[4] Dominicans also gathered around personages: the *jimenistas* behind former president Juan Isidro Jimenes; the *horacistas* behind Horacio Vásquez, former president and vice-president and longtime king-maker; and the newer and weaker *velazquistas* under Federico Velázquez.[5]

Not surprisingly, those in the elite who most opposed occupations were those who lost jobs to them. The Haitian occupation threw out of office about 500 heads of families.[6] No similar accounting exists for the Dominican Republic, but the 1920 census counted 2,803 government employees, so a similar number as in Haiti likely went without state salaries.[7]

These "outs" elicited little pity, at least from foreigners. In December 1916, French Minister Dejean de la Batie reported that Haitian groupings described themselves as "progressive" or "nationalist" but in reality had no ideology, no program. The opposition "picks quarrels, opens up more or less scandalous old wounds. In sum, Haiti has not changed. Its only politics is culinary: everyone fights over the 'butter,'" meaning the state treasury.[8] Marines made the same argument, that the elite only wanted back its "graft."[9] To such accusations *Le Nouvelliste* retorted that the label "professional politician" to tarnish all opposition "is a little too convenient."[10] Yet one of the major grievances of the opposition *was* the loss of well-paying positions, whether acquired by skill, social status, or political contacts.[11] Haitians argued that the loss of government jobs threw families into "near misery" since most government workers had no other training. Compounding the pain felt by Haitians fired for alleged budgetary reasons was the hiring of marines at much higher salaries.[12] In May 1918, with the legislature dissolved, Haitian outs formed a party opposed to both President Sudre Dartiguenave and US occupiers.[13] Throughout the 1920s they protested the end of the spoils system.[14] Dominicans did not organize politically against their thinning "butter" but did offer piecemeal protests. One journalist called for a boycott of lottery tickets when a US citizen took over as Collector of Lotteries.[15]

The outs failed completely to convince occupiers of their cause, but the persistence of their arguments indicated that political values in no way changed by minimizing the spoils. Journalist Charles Moravia fully backed the occupation at first in his newspaper *La Plume*, but when President Louis Borno kept him out of government in the 1920s he founded *Le Matin* and turned against Borno.[16]

More difficult for occupations to process was that those who held on to or acquired new jobs also resisted the will of the occupier. There was practically no internal government resistance in the Dominican Republic because of the US-run military government. But in Haiti the occupation initially kept all branches of government intact and pledged only to "recommend," not impose, laws. So Haitian "ins" at first considered US treaty officers as mere advisors to Haitians—until they grasped that the opposite was the case.

Before the dissolution of the Haitian Congress in 1917, the legislature presented the keenest opposition to US initiatives. After the January 1917 election, marines labeled only seven out of thirty-five deputies as "unfavorable to Occupation," yet these seven could paralyze the legislature.[17] They managed to get the Congress to refuse to declare war on Germany and maintained the prohibition against foreign ownership of land.[18] Other Haitian officials obstructed US administrators, refusing to spend treasury funds on marine projects, or they dawdled, promising action then blaming subordinates for inaction.[19] "These wretched politicians do not intend to fall in with our American plans and ideas for their betterment," grumbled Smedley Butler.[20] Secretary of the Navy Josephus Daniels shared Butler's frustration, saying of Haitian politicians, "they talk honesty, efficiency, etc., can write well, but the next minute you find them involved in some petty graft or deceit. Whenever American control ceases in any particular, it will be followed by a resumption of former conditions."[21]

Dartiguenave remained courteous with the occupation throughout his presidency, from August 1915 to May 1922, yet he, too, nibbled at the hand that fed him. Less than a month after marines elevated him to the Presidential Palace, Dartiguenave expressed displeasure with marines' control of customs and threats of martial law.[22] Believing that marine authority should not exceed that given in the Convention, he opposed their plans to control the postal service, telegraph, public works, and records.[23] When negotiating the treaty of occupation in 1916–1917, he leaked the correspondence between his government and the marines, exposing a US effort to dictate the document.[24] In 1918 Dartiguenave packed his Cabinet with ministers willing to confront the marines.[25] Even in 1920, with no legislature, no caco war, and practically alone against the marines, Dartiguenave refused to recharter the National Bank, now in the hands of the US National City Bank.[26] He also opposed placing the US dollar on the same level as the gourde, fearing it would replace the Haitian currency.[27] His most public act of defiance was writing to President-elect Warren Harding, listing seven grievances of his government and proposing a remedy to each.[28]

Defenders of Dartiguenave went too far in admiring his resistance, much of which intended to encourage graft, harm political enemies, or, as he confessed, protect his personal assets from seizure.[29] Yet Dartiguenave felt genuinely betrayed by occupiers as he recalled his agonizing years as president:

My compatriots failed to understand my painful sacrifice: they attributed what I accomplished in suffering and often in patriotic revolt to selfish motives. I believed in the American government; I was often misled. Now, it's over: I have suffered too much. If you want your country take it. I will not hand it over.[30]

Dartiguenave left office after his minister of finance and foreign affairs, Louis Borno, won the 1922 election. Before leaving, the departing president begged the secretary of the US Navy to protect him from internal enemies.[31]

Neither the outs nor the ins made up the lion's share of urban anti-occupation activism, however. The writers of Port-au-Prince and Santo Domingo took on that task—enthusiastically, bravely, selfishly, and irresponsibly, often all at once. Poets, novelists, and especially journalists were the leaders as well as the rank-and-file of opposition parties. Georges Sylvain, for example, founded La Patrie in 1915 and later the Patriotic Union (UP).[32] The first anti-occupation paper, Haïti-Intégrale, directed by Elie Guérin, emerged within days of Dartiguenave's "election" in August 1915, and by the early 1920s Haiti had twelve anti-occupation papers.[33] Especially in Haiti, newspapermen were generally not trained as journalists, however admirable their literary erudition and prose. They traded in rumors and exaggerations rather than fact and analysis, and their biographies and personalities colored many a story. Yet because their words were recorded on paper, editors and journalists left a larger historical imprint on the resistance than anyone else.

The press used every weapon at its disposal. Dominican papers exposed every detail of US abuses but suppressed news of attacks on occupation forces. They also defended almost anyone arrested by the marines, even common criminals.[34] In Haiti the press gave prominent placement to stories on the violence, corruption, and racism of US society, easy targets in the 1920s.[35] And it undermined the occupation in material ways, such as spreading rumors of its withdrawal, which prompted merchants to tear up customs invoices under the assumption that they would soon be invalid.[36] In 1917 the Nicaraguan press called the marines "barbarian oppressors" and accused them of bringing sexually transmitted diseases to Managua, claiming thirty-five marines had syphilis or other diseases. On February 6, twenty-three US forces responded to the slander by sacking the offices of La Tribuna.[37] Following the retribution, the press called not only for the punishment of the guilty but also the removal of the entire command. Commanders court-martialed the marines, giving them each two years' confinement and a dishonorable discharge.[38]

Newspapermen also voiced opposition beyond their publications. Dominicans banded as a Press Association in October 1916 to defend press freedom, then into a more robust Press Congress in 1920 numbering thirty-five media.[39] In February 1921, all but one of the Port-au-Prince newspapers did the same.[40]

That grouping was short-lived, suggesting the relative atomization of the elite in Haiti.[41] Organizing public protests or subverting official ones was another common press tactic. In 1921 the Haitian press invited US officers to a patriotic ceremony in Arcahaie. Its commemoration of revolutionary Jean-Jacques Dessalines tearing the white off the French flag to indicate the new Haitian colors should have tipped off the officers to the tenor of the ceremony. Welly Thébaud, a young editor, mounted the stage and called a new generation of Haitians to arms by intoning, "If might rules over right, youth will not hesitate to make the supreme sacrifice. . . . The enemy eagle will not soar over our cities in ashes and our deserted countryside." "Down with the Occupation!" the crowd chanted. The marines, though oblivious to the French slogans, got the gist. They broke into Thébaud's home at night and arrested him.[42]

The motivations of editors were as diverse and complex as those of insurgents. All expressed patriotism and nationalism as their prime motives and many expounded on various grievances done to their nation.[43] Many were also interested in gaining political office or else whipped up public frenzy over minor scandals to sell newspapers.[44] At least one editor took bribes: on August 16, 1927, Luc Dorsinville of *La Lutte* abruptly ended his support for the Borno government when his monthly $50 from that government ceased rolling in.[45] Writers, finally, generally agreed on the need for withdrawal of occupation forces but not democracy or equality. Américo Lugo, among the most prominent Dominican writers, believed a "cultured" aristocracy should lead the mixed-race and illiterate masses through an expanded state apparatus.[46] He founded the Nationalist Party in 1923.[47]

One sign of the effectiveness of the written word was the censorship imposed by the occupations. Marines repressed journalists through the Haitian government as of 1915 and through their provost courts as of 1921, over the objections of Dartiguenave and Haiti's highest court.[48] Dominican censorship came sweepingly with the Knapp Proclamation of November 1916. Knapp notably ordered the seizure of *El Derrumbe*, Federico García Godoy's novelistic denunciation of the occupation.[49] Dominican censorship lasted until 1919, when marines lifted it but then re-imposed it later that year, only to loosen and tighten again in 1920.[50] In 1922 the marines abruptly shut down Santiago's *La Información*.[51] At least twenty-seven Haitians and twenty Dominicans saw the inside of a cell for their writings.[52]

Occupiers—along with some occupied peoples—justified censorship on the political cultural grounds that Haitian and Dominican editors engaged in libel and sedition.[53] "The Haitians cannot enjoy freedom of speech and of the press without outrageous abuse," wrote one, "and any attempt to punish newspaper editors or politicians for offences which would render them liable to imprisonment in the United States gives rise to charges that the American occupation is throttling the press."[54] It was true that newspapers called political figures names that would land them in jail in any country.[55] Some Dominicans published "open appeals to prepare to take up arms against [the occupiers]."[56] Haitians suggested poisoning Borno and plotted to assassinate him.[57] Yet marines also fined and jailed editors who published accurate facts. Such was the fate of Ernest Chauvet, perhaps the only Haitian newspaperman with a professional pedigree, having worked at the *Brooklyn Daily Eagle*.[58]

Because of its brutish application, censorship often resulted in political victories for the opposition to occupation. The experience of being imprisoned for one's words became a rite of passage of sorts for anti-occupation newspapermen. Prison produced martyrs, potent symbols in Catholic cultures, especially if they managed to write while in prison.[59] While confined, many appealed to the highest US authorities, even the president, with denunciations of poor prison conditions and demands for clemency.[60] Elites invariably complained of having to share cells or courtyards with non-elites and of having to do hard labor.[61]

In 1920 Fabio Fiallo, a prominent Dominican writer, editor of *Las Noticias*, and co-founder of the Press Congress, received a one year sentence and a $2,500 fine.[62] His article "Listen All" had called the United States a "most cruel civilization that, bayonet at the ready, invaded our backyard on a dark night of betrayal, surprise, and cowardliness, and that has caused us countless tears, countless homes in ashes and countless starving orphans." It ended with, "The order is RESISTANCE; RESISTANCE until victory or death!"[63] Fiallo wore his prison term like a badge of honor. He called the persecution of journalists "the most resounding victory of Dominican patriotism" and proclaimed his own satisfaction at being jailed despite the "fetid water," "wormy meat," and "dirty, evil smelling and depraved men" around him. Not only Dominicans but also Cubans, Spaniards, and others throughout the world celebrated him.[64]

Américo Lugo used the opportunity of his prosecution to question the legitimacy of the occupation. During his trial he declared, "As a Dominican citizen, I cannot recognize in the Dominican Republic any sovereignty but that of my fatherland. . . . As a result, and since I believe I have committed no crime, I cannot recognize this court's jurisdiction over me."[65]

Horacio Blanco Fombona, editor and owner of the literary magazine *Letras*, also garnered attention against the occupation. On November 7, 1920, *Letras* featured a photo of the Dominican peasant Cayo Báez showing his burn wounds with a short text that accused "American officers and soldiers of the Guardia" of torturing him.[66] The occupation, judging the statement that US officers tortured him false, shut down *Letras*, confiscated all circulating copies, and tried Blanco. Under oath, Báez admitted that his torturer was a Dominican who took no orders from US officers, but to Blanco this was hair-splitting.[67] When the occupation explained that the accused Captain Charles Buckalew was not guilty of burning Báez, Blanco "answered that there were two truths: the official truth and the truth of the Dominican people."[68] He was motivated, Blanco said, as "a Latin-American subject and as a newspaperman and as a man of civilization."[69] Like Lugo, Blanco refused to put up a defense before a US judge. "Condemn me," he said.[70] Since he was Venezuelan, the court deported him instead. A Dominican writing for the successor of the banned *Letras* called Blanco's ordeal a "glorious martyrdom."[71]

Among newspapermen, Joseph Jolibois Fils excelled at using prison as a political stage. By the late 1920s the editor of the scurrilous *Courrier Haïtien* had either been accused of, indicted for, or had charges pending for petty graft, perjury, sedition, outrageous conduct to police, libelous complaints, defaming the president, libeling the president, defamatory and scandalous remarks against the diplomatic corps, swindling, and attempted murder.[72] He spent a total of four years and seven months in seventeen separate incarcerations.[73] In 1930 he ran for a deputy seat in Port-au-Prince using his time in prison as campaign propaganda: his electoral flyer featured obviously staged photos of Jolibois handling a broom and piling up rocks, dressed in overalls.[74]

A minor but revealing facet of the urban resistance was its covert support of the rural insurgents.[75] In all three occupations, the instinct to back rebels emerged in elite individuals, likely members of small cells, who seemed to cling to the idea that a rural defeat of the marines—a chimera in itself—would bring back the days of caudillo rule.

In Nicaragua, some Conservative Party members lent support to Sandino. Before its collapse the Autonomist Party contained many Conservatives and supported the rebellion. One of its leaders, José Coronel Urtecho, explained that Sandino was "anti-Yanquista like us. Although we were rooted in North American culture . . . we opposed US domination over [Latin] America and the things they sought to impose: commercialism, capitalist industrialism, capitalism." The Autonomists distributed pro-Sandino handbills and secretly painted slogans on facades.[76] Many Conservative coffee planters also got deep in debt during US occupations since only the US-controlled National Bank gave large loans and did so sparingly.[77] Politically, Conservatives could only benefit from Liberal voters being split over support for Sandino. Former Conservative president Emiliano Chamorro, whom US occupations had not treated kindly, reared his divisive head again in the late 1920s to express delight at the quagmire in the north.[78]

There were fewer rural-urban connections in the Dominican Republic. Dominicans in the cities abhorred the rural insurgents and had little contact with them.[79] But there were contacts. Marines highly suspected the *horacistas* in the east of being "mixed up with [rebel chief Vicente] Evangelista."[80] They sometimes heard rebels shout "Long live Horacio Vásquez!" along with "Long live the Revolution!"[81] In 1918 marines arrested "Cipriano Bencosmé, the principal 'Horacista' in the North, . . . charged with encouraging the banditry and aiding it with arms and ammunition."[82] In 1920 they reported that the *horacistas* had created a "revolutionary organization" to negotiate with rebels.[83] The following year rumors abounded that arms from Mexico landed at Monte Cristi, "arranged by prominent men of San Pedro de Macoris." "Hoping for the early departure of the Americans," said a US investigator, they "were starting their old games."[84] In a rare direct correspondence, the obscure National Defense Council wrote to rural rebel leader Martín Peguero, promising "provisions and arms" meant to "incite you to continue on the path which you have traced," a path described as a "heroical task" for "the integrity and liberation of the home ground from the Invaders of the North."[85]

From Port-au-Prince, newspaperman Auguste Magloire almost surely corresponded with Charlemagne Péralte, as evidenced by letters found on Péralte's dead body. Addressing Péralte as "My Dear General," one unsigned letter said Magloire urged Péralte to attack the capital as soon as possible, promising aid from "inside the city." Another missive three days later urged Péralte to strike with all his might but foolishly advised him not to fear marine counterattacks on the grounds that marines only protected their barracks. Another unsigned letter, perhaps from Péralte's brother, claimed that a man called Sausarierz in the Haitian government would help with strategy and informed him that "your friends are expecting a victorious entrée on your part in Port au Prince."[86] Months later a woman, arrested for transporting ammunition to the cacos, identified her source as salt merchant and former caco chief Saint Julien Noel, of the capital. Noel denied everything but the police kept a close eye on him.[87] Marines later concluded, hyperbolically, that urban Haitians were "really the directing head" of the Péralte movement. "A large percentage of the population of Port au Prince," said High Commissioner John Russell, "namely those not making money at this time and including disgruntled politicians and most of the lawyers, were at heart in sympathy with the bandits."[88]

The revelation that Magloire likely helped Péralte with "exceedingly good military advice" shocked Haitian high society.[89] The Magloires were a prominent conservative family who had benefited from the occupation. Auguste was a police commissioner who wrote for the pro-occupation *Le Matin*.[90] Perhaps these were fronts. Perhaps the correspondence was a forgery.

Benoît Batraville, Péralte's successor, also received support, perhaps enough to convince him to unsuccessfully attack Port-au-Prince in January 1920. In the wake of that failed assault, the occupation arrested Salomon Janvier, a Port-au-Prince merchant, for supplying Batraville.[91] Salomon was likely "Intérior," the pseudonym of the person who corresponded with Batraville in December 1919. Intérior wrote the caco at least twice that month, informing him that he used to supply Péralte, exhorting him to attack as soon as possible, and giving "very pre-cise details as to the enemy's intentions." Later he confirmed having sent Batraville ammunition and promised "a ready-prepared depot" when Batraville pounced on Port-au-Prince. Intérior apparently never met Batraville since he looked for-ward to "shaking hands" with him, yet he expressed "perfect confidence in your energy, in your bravery and in your patriotism" and received at least one written response from him.[92] Rosalvo Bobo, the exiled challenger to the presidency in 1915, also wrote to Batraville.[93] The thirst for revenge was strong in these letters: "The perfidy of the enemy who does not hesitate to adopt any means must be punished, and that severely," wrote Intérior. "It is necessary that Port-au-Prince, which is infested by vices of every kind, be entirely burned down."[94]

The occupation was aware of urban backing for both Péralte and Batraville, increased its troops in the capital to resist the latter, and captured Janvier during the January attack.[95] Yet it could rarely track down leads. Occupation head Rus-sell confided to his diary right after the attack, "It is well known that there are many persons in Port au Prince who assist the bandits but it appears to be almost impossible to obtain defining proof against them."[96] Frederick "Dopey" Wise confirmed that "we knew pretty well who they [urban supporters] were, but we never were able to arrest them, for we didn't have enough evidence to prove the case in court."[97] The Magloire case remained cold. Its only evidence were the two letters on Péralte's body, which compared favorably with Magloire's handwriting. Marines eventually sent the letters to a handwriting expert in the United States, who was "positive" that Magloire was the author. By the time the expert could visit Haiti, the caco war was over and the expense seemed pointless.[98]

Though these various plots were small and unsuccessful, they indicated that some elites engaged the rural insurrections of their own free will. Mostly they confirmed the ongoing refusal to abandon the traditional political culture of revolution.

More typically and openly, elites formed organizations to denounce occu-pation peacefully. In Haiti, George Sylvain's 1915 Patriotic Union (UP) lasted only a few months, crushed by the passage of the Convention. On November 17, 1920, Sylvain and seventeen other Haitians met in his law office and revived the UP. This time, rather than merely decry the loss of territorial integrity, the UP's grievances targeted the abuse and authoritarianism of the occupation. The UP demanded the suppression of provost courts and martial law; the reorganization of the Gendarmerie followed by the withdrawal of the marines; the end of the 1915 Convention; and a reconstituted national assembly.[99] Its first large meet-ing drew an audience of 1,000, whom speakers and poets overwhelmed with emotion. "Long live national Sovereignty and Independence!" they shouted. "Long live Haiti!" The organization, though providing a forum for campaign-ing members, remained non-partisan and independent. Dartiguenave offered it a donation of $1,000 along with a representative, but the UP demurred.[100] UP members created fourteen chapters and soon claimed representation in all twenty-nine districts in Haiti and "virtually the unanimous support of the entire Haitian people."[101] In the Dominican Republic, the anti-occupation elite formed the Dominican Nationalist Union (UND). Like the UP, the UND coupled calls for independence with denunciations of abuses.[102]

More than elites in capitals, political leaders in small towns suffered the brunt of the political changes wrought by occupation and countered them with the most robust—and most largely unexplored—resistance.[103] Partly, mayors, members of city councils, and other local guardians of authority most fiercely defended against the loss of their—and their constituents'—autonomy because the occupations had little legal authority over municipalities. More fundamentally, small towns under occupation rejected the claims of the central state on the most peripheral of political peripheries.[104] Generally, communities with slimmer differences in social status among its inhabitants were more prone to resist centralization because these suffered economic shocks more equally and reacted more uniformly, as in one case where a marine described how men in a small Haitian town were "for the most part very democratic in their relations to each other."[105] Yet rural political leaders also saw themselves as intermediaries between the central state and the rural poor. They were humble in their means, but not as humble as peasants, and many of them were literate and owned property or businesses. Centralization often threatened to obliterate leaders' own claims on peasants' resources.

In Haiti, marines made important changes to municipal government.[106] Marines sent Gendarmerie commanders to sub-districts, each sub-district encompassing several communes, or counties, which were further divided into sections. The commanders had to deal with the commune's *magistrats*, who combined the functions of "mayors, county judges, court officials, tax collectors [and] surveyors." The occupation exercised no "direct authority" over the *magistrats* but did pay their salaries, which provided leverage for centralization.[107] A marine assigned to a Haitian town was, as one US critic noted,

> clothed with almost unlimited power in the district where he serves. He is the judge of practically all civil and criminal cases, settling everything from a family fight to a murder. He is the paymaster of all funds expended by the National Government; he is ex officio director of the schools, inasmuch as he pays the teachers. He controls the Mayor and the City Council, since they can spend no funds without his O.K. As Collector of taxes, he exercises a strong influence on all individuals of the community.[108]

In January 1916, Port-au-Prince stripped the communes of all their military and police powers, explaining that local military commanders "have not produced . . . all the benefit that we hoped." New rules reduced magistrates' purview to gathering and sending information to the central government. They were also to submit weekly "surveillance" reports, thus pitting them against their constituency.[109] Magistrates continued to collect funds from merchants and pay out collections for births, deaths, and weddings. They also took a percentage of fines levied by local courts.[110] In the sections, the occupation abolished the rural guards and their chief of section, again centralizing military power.[111] In addition the occupation gave itself the sweeping prerogative to replace any local official.

Demoted or dismissed Haitians especially rejected a centralization that robbed them of local authority. "Dopey" Wise recalled taking over Jérémie and dismissing a hundred soldiers "barefoot, clad in ragged shirts and cotton trousers," and the magistrate, all of whom "didn't particularly fancy our arrival." The mayor "had been stealing all the money he could get his hands on. . . . This was just one of innumerable such cases."[112] Marines found that, with corrupt officials removed, ordinary Haitians easily transferred to them their trust in—or fear of—the state. In Hinche, people "come to the Officers with all their troubles, however small. It is not known why they do this unless because they are sure of justice or that they have more confidence in us than, perhaps, their own judges."[113]

Overall, marines spread themselves thinly over Haiti. One district commander had authority over thirteen communes, including Aux Cayes, a town of 15,000, paid the salaries of 500 people, and approved the ordinances and budgets of each. He felt dispirited by Haitians' lack of basic accounting practices and judges too willing to take bribes. With no clerk, he wrote and typed up by himself thirty-two monthly reports.[114]

The Dominican occupation was even more intrusive, and evidence of small-town resistance, more plentiful. The country was divided into twelve provinces, each headed by a governor and separated into communes. Each *común* was further divided into *secciones* but the commune was the main administrative unit. Each had its *alcalde* or mayor, its *ayuntamiento* or town council with a president, and an additional official called a *síndico*, the elected head of the ayuntamiento and often more powerful than the appointed mayor. In addition were *alcaldes pedáneos*, or sheriffs appointed by the ayuntamiento; and regional and local military officials called *jefes comunales, jefes de sección,* and *jefes de orden.*[115] The Dominican constitution provided for the communes' independence, and Executive Order #44 decreed that town councils, or ayuntamientos, retained their corporate identity.

The occupation, however, took that de facto identity and independence away because #44 also contained the sea-change proviso that the military government could change the personnel of small-town government.[116] The change began at the provincial level, where the occupation stripped governors of their armies, striking a major blow against caudillismo by making governors mere civil representatives responsible only to the central government. At the municipal level there were 1,216 municipal employees in 1920, so any "reorganization" affected many families.[117]

Local resistance arose in no time. After Governor Lico Pérez of Pacificador failed to stop the 1916 marine landing, the occupation declared him an "outlaw," telegraphing to other local authorities the new centralization.[118] Governors, mayors, síndicos, and others silenced their guns but continued to resist. "Under the best conditions we have some insubordination," observed Military Governor Thomas Snowden in 1920 of local officials. He affirmed the need to flout the constitution since the ayuntamientos "are becoming more and more dependent upon the general government," without recognizing that he engendered that very dependence. Snowden did realize that centralization "is rather against the Dominican idea and also against the intent of Dominican laws," yet he persisted.[119] Snowden even opposed local elections because they would revive "the old political parties, a mercenary, grafting, vicious, office-seeking clan."[120] Logan Feland, briefly military governor before Snowden, complained that Dominicans in charge of relations with towns were too independent of him, even finding it "absurd" that one considered himself a "Dominican Official."[121]

The occupation sank into local political quicksand by attempting to replace uncooperative locals. It encountered widespread and persistent passive resistance, ayuntamientos and especially síndicos all but ignoring orders from Santo Domingo.[122] As late as 1921, Dominican aide Manuel Lluveres identified numerous problems in the northern Cibao region. Governors complained of tight budgets and insufficient control over appointments of city councillors and municipal police. In the town of Moca, "the President [of the ayuntamiento] is not a competent man and the Sindico is the disturbing and principal element in the Ayuntamiento," yet no one could suggest replacements.[123] In 1922 a second lieutenant in charge of Seibo expressed frustration that town officials, "instead of enforcing the laws that the duties of the Office requires, are the first and foremost in violating them." He recommended appointing a síndico "that is not a native of this place" because "with very few exceptions, the people living here are all of one family."[124] Some Dominicans agreed with the effort to purge political offices of those who resisted centralization.[125] W. Ramírez, whose son suffered a "violent death," pleaded for all heads of public offices to be US citizens. "This is the only possible means by which we may evade the uneasiness in which we live, due to the old hard feelings and political antagonism of the past which does not occur among the Americans whose one idea is to give us peace."[126]

Even in Nicaragua, the US presence applied political pressure on small town politicians and faced an unwillingness to alter political culture. As in other occupations, centralization had begun beforehand, Managua asserting its fiduciary and military authority over Granada.[127] The expansion of coffee for export also brought forth a new commercial bourgeoisie that sought a state more responsive to its needs.[128] Marines, dominating the constabulary, reinforced the central state through strengthening police functions, collecting taxes, and persecuting smugglers.[129]

There were ironies to centralization and resistance. President José Santos Zelaya, ousted by Washington in 1909, embodied much of the centralization that Washington would itself encourage in Nicaragua. August Sandino similarly advocated a "National Government" "to put an end once and for all to *caciqueism*," or the rule of caudillos, yet he also fought the marines, who were the main force strengthening the central state.[130]

In all three occupations, several motivations lay behind the revolt of the ayuntamientos. During rural insurgencies many local officials were enmeshed in rebel networks and aided them out of fear, economic opportunity, family loyalty, or other motivations. A captain in the Dominican Republic recalled that he stopped hiring local officials as guides "as they would invariably advise the fugitive that the Guardia was in pursuit."[131] In 1919 a judge named Nestor Febles of San Pedro was "captured" by rebels when his chauffeur drove into bushes, whereupon Febles waited for the rebels to take him, along with the enormous sum of $2,000 he happened to be carrying, and was later seen roaming with them, unrestrained. In Guerra in 1919, a band of thirty-three held up the town for an hour. At the municipal treasurer's house they took $1,500, then barged into the mayor's house and took his revolver, belt, forty rounds of ammunition, and even a $10 bill on his desk, a recently collected fine. Guard Director James McLean was suspicious. "The local police were not molested, neither did they do anything to the bandits. . . . Someone from the inside furnished the information."[132]

Local officials also resisted occupations based on their history of partisan and personal bitterness. Some Dominican towns were loyal to caudillo Desiderio Arias, such as Yamasa, where alleged Arias men shot and killed the síndico and the justice of the peace soon after the marine landing.[133] The occupation exacerbated vendettas. One administrator of a sugar estate explained how a rival administrator was a mortal enemy for organizing armed bands to defend against bandits while *he*, calling himself "a good servant of the Government," collected their weapons.[134] Altidor Kersaint, apparently "continually under the influence of liquor," used his new appointment as the new *commissaire du gouvernement* in Anse-à-Veau, Haiti, in 1922 to replace all public officials with friends.[135] That same year a Dominican síndico in San Juan described a newspaperman as a "personal enemy of mine, and we are political opponents."[136] At times marines got unwittingly involved in local intrigue, investigating innocents whom political rivals accused of malfeasance.[137]

Reflecting the national trend, partisanship ran especially deep in local Nicaraguan politics. In 1929, marines deemed a police chief, Indalecio Pastora, "a failure. No discipline is maintained in the force itself, and he allows politics to enter into his administration of justice to a great extent." A Conservative, Pastora refused to help the Liberal *jefe político*—an appointed departmental governor of sorts—and allowed gambling and knife fights in the streets, molesting or beating up Liberals who opposed.[138] Bluefields, on the Caribbean Coast, was even worse. A US citizen there described an "almost unbearable state of affairs" as the newly appointed Liberal jefe político faced a mutiny by his Conservative subordinates, where the police chief in Bluefields "flaunts publicly his non-subservience." Even the Court of Appeals of Bluefields, dominated by Conservatives, rejected the authority of the politically mixed Supreme Court.[139]

Partisanship brought on more centralization. Dana Munro of the US legation in Managua argued in October 1927 for the constabulary to take over local police forces for political reasons. He understood that police chiefs often overwhelmed the jefes políticos and arrested political opponents on trumped-up charges. Yet a dilemma remained: if the opposite situation arose and police chiefs and jefes were of the same party, they would have a monopoly of force and punish opponents.[140]

In Nicaragua, too, marines saw in the constabulary their vehicle for introducing a less partisan, middle class democracy through the ballot box, but not without great resistance.[141] In fall 1927, municipal elections took place and the legation reported widespread fraud and intimidation.[142] After the Nicaguan Supreme Court voided the "unfair and illegal" Conservative victory in Mateare, two marines went there to oversee a new election but immediately stumbled by accepting lodging and translation services from a leading Liberal. From Managua, party head Emiliano Chamorro sent word "'instructing' the local chief of police to win the election at all costs." Liberals won with a "small majority" but local Conservatives kept them from power. The mess in Mateare, reported Munro, was "but one of a large number of municipal elections in which somewhat similar events have occurred."[143]

After 1927 the marines mobilized to dominate elections in Nicaragua. The US chief of the electoral mission, who was also the president of the national board of elections, supervised elections in 1928, 1930, and 1932 with some fifty officers, 550 to 900 enlisted men, and 1,800 guards. Acting boldly to strip power from electoral caudillos, they blocked some presidential candidates from running, suspended thousands of rural sheriffs, sandbagged indigenous authorities who controlled Indian votes, removed ballot boxes from large private haciendas and placed them in public areas, and ended the practice of giving away state resources in return for votes. Results seemed promising. In the presidential contests of 1928 and 1932, voting rose 20 percent from pre-occupation levels, and Nicaraguans both times chose a Liberal president.[144] One marine praised the constabulary for "inculcat[ing] in the citizens of the rural districts a knowledge of the principles of sanitation, public education and representative government."[145]

Yet Nicaraguans came to resent the electoral missions. Some rejected the mere presence of foreigners or non-locals giving orders. The guards, especially, tended to become permanent fixtures overlooking schools, baseball tournaments, radio networks, spies, and most nefariously, police and judiciary bodies. Some locals came to depend too broadly on the marines, asking them to arbitrate in social matters.[146] Electoral interference, in short, created another kind of corruption—the central state arrogating municipal authority. In late 1929, a year after his "successful" election to the presidency, José María Moncada replaced entire municipal governments in one department with Liberals. Secretary of State Henry Stimson judged this to be an "unwarranted interference in the normal political and administrative activities of the Republic."[147] He failed to notice that he had done the same with the Espino Negro accords.

More typically than partisanship, occupations encountered local resistance because of deep corruption and incompetence ingrained in political culture. Local officials were used to graft, with profits made especially on procuring weapons for the army and police and in financing revolutions.[148] The Dominican mayor of San Pedro, by the name of Aybar, stole from the till and was infamous as "a grafter and totally unreliable."[149] Some officials wanted to keep jobs that allowed them to extort constituents, and they abused the privilege of funding their salary with fines.[150] Others expected kickbacks. Again in San Pedro, marines judged the síndico to be "a shrewd, scheming lawyer with a bad reputation" whom the courts had disbarred. He collected money for roads that remained "in the worst possible condition" and refused to build sewers unless he received his cut.[151] One US inspector described how Dominican officials' "principal efforts are to see how many of their friends or relatives they can get on the Municipal pay-roll," adding that they hired several men but worked them only two hours a day. He did not appreciate how, for Dominicans, this might be a way of spreading a small pot of spoils as widely as possible.[152]

Dominicans, too, complained of corruption and authoritarianism. In 1922 the Dominican occupation decreed a Law of Communal Organization, giving office seekers the opportunity to expose officeholders for illiteracy, corruption, or lack of property. Denunciations rolled in. An Arab-Dominican named Juan Herrera excoriated the ayuntamiento of Duvergé, the president of which in turn accused Herrera of using a banned gun to force villagers to pay up debts incurred in his cock pit.[153] Another asked the military governor to replace all civic leaders

in the capital. The síndico, he said, "is an archetypal speculator-adventurer... en-
riching himself with funds destined to public health, to development, to beauti-
fication." "The majority of aldermen in this ayuntamiento are venal and sell their
votes for money." He accused them of "pilfering" 200,000 pesos every year and
blamed them for the city's poor sanitation and public works.[154] Fifteen residents
of San Pedro reported on a police commissioner who pulled a suspect out of jail
and shot him in the street.[155] The sharpest description of local incompetence and
corruption came from Manuel Lora, the governor of Santiago Province, who
explained the impact of centralizing military functions.

> When political-military attributions are taken away from those Chiefs
> they become nullities. The civil regime suffocates them, they are lost,
> and as they have no skills they do not know and are not able to know
> what they can and should do. They are decorative figures if they do
> nothing, and if they do something they interrupt all work toward the
> organization of the commune.

Lora reported, commune by commune, that rural authorities were illiterate,
too numerous, and completely unaware of their job requirements. They had no
desks, no furniture, and no working telephones. "Entirely incompetent," their
personnel occupied no office, kept no books, estimated no budgets. City halls
were in "complete disorganization." Grafting was the motive of many, concluded
Lora: "To be an official was for them something like a pirate flag."[156]

Cases of corruption and incompetence were so numerous that the Dominican occupation came up with a form letter that district commanders could send
to presidents of ayuntamientos, asking them to advise Santo Domingo whenever
a síndico needed replacement because of "advanced age," "lack of competence
or laboriousness," or "their desire for personal enrichment, conducting private
deals in municipal venues." The letter requested recommendations for replacements, suggesting marines' awareness of their insufficient ability to find honest
or competent administrators.[157]

Much local resistance was passive. The jefe comunal of El Jovero, Dominican
Republic, promised to give information and supplies to the marines but never
delivered.[158] In La Romana, the ayuntamiento and police force did little at all,
the síndico spending his time on his dentistry practice and not on building roads
with money from the capital.[159] Nearby in Seibo the police commissioner shot
and killed a policeman and claimed it was an accident. Hours after his arrest—
while he was drunk at 7 AM—someone paid his $400 bail and reinstated him as
commissioner.[160]

Some resisted the usurpation of traditional channels of command that protected the initiative and independence of local authorities. In Cap-Haïtien,

Joseph Augustin Guillaume, a *commissaire du gouvernement* and nominally a representative of the central state, refused to replace a town official, claiming he would comply only at the behest of the minister of justice. After more pressure, Guillaume quit and explained—to the president of Haiti, no less—that he had suffered enough "humiliations of this sort."[161]

Marines shook their heads at the non-ideological, self-interested rule of local officials. Military Governor Snowden identified "lack of education, and in many instances, lack of public spirit," primarily political cultural factors, for "retard[ing] the progress of civic improvement." Notable also was Snowden's conviction that democracy—a reliance on "elective officials"—was a distant possibility.[162] Another marine privately hoped that "at no distant date even the nominal independence [of municipal governments] will disappear."[163]

What few occupiers noticed was that towns presenting the greatest resistance suffered both a history of internecine political violence and a reign of terror by marines. Hato Mayor del Rey, in the Dominican east, was a notorious example. Before the occupation, both decentralizing caudillos such as Fidel Ferrer and centralizing military chiefs such as Rogelio de la Cruz terrorized the town. They extorted and killed political enemies, usually local civil and military figures. The 1914–1917 period was especially divisive, as *horacistas* and *jimenistas* both fought at the ballot box—the former besting the latter two to one—and through the barrel of a gun. Many leaders of anti-occupation bands, including Vicente Evangelista, Ramón Nateras, Ramón Batías, and Tolete, emerged from Hato Mayor or operated around it.[164]

At sunset on January 12, 1917, the marines rode in to the troubled town and soon imposed their own brand of terror. As a result, many fled to larger towns, selling their land cheaply to sugar estates.[165] In such a situation, local officials were political survivors who could help rebel leaders while holding on to power by any means necessary, including intimidation and dissemblance. One marine described how "there is constant bickering between these people and they do not hesitate to lie about each other with great fluency."[166] Even the town priest extorted a hefty $12 from poor families for burials during a typhoid epidemic lest their loved ones be "condemned to hell."[167] The marines made resistance the only recourse by targeting everyone of prominence. The day before taking the town, they fought the employees of the nearby Consuelo sugar estate. Then they disarmed the municipal authorities. The ayuntamiento suffered the humiliation of having to do manual labor, cutting grass and carrying water for US troops and their animals.[168]

Twenty miles away, Los Llanos was a more unique case, having previously lost its economic livelihood. The town of 300, surrounded by a común of 12,000 and set amidst a fertile plan fine for grazing horses and cattle, saw its share of violence, including shootouts among family members of the ayuntamiento.[169]

Before the occupation, the central government marched its troops through town and depended on bandits to raid its cattle for meat. In early 1918, marines rode into Los Llanos and sent pathetic reports—of 98 percent illiteracy, of drinking water coming only from stagnant ponds, and of inhabitants slaughtering animals in their homes for want of a market or slaughterhouse. "The inhabitants all have a sallow color and appear to be suffering from fever. Typhoid is prevalent."[170] Still, municipal leaders resisted any change. "Stone deaf" Mayor Rafael María Vallejo ran the town like his fiefdom: he fined inhabitants without charges, without summons to appear in court, and largely without keeping books. Vallejo's wife rented out his mayoral office, and, against regulations, his son acted as his secretary. Mother and son "seemed to officiate" when a rare case went to trial. Major McLean reported that Vallejo "was known locally as a 'Guapo' (Bully) and he knew that the majority of the inhabitants were afraid of him." When McLean attended a meeting of the ayuntamiento—which McLean called "a do-nothing body"[171]—Vallejo barged in and, without seeing McLean, "in a very loud voice began to threaten any member of the Ayuntamiento who would dare to denounce him." Spotting McLean, Vallejo "bowed and excused himself." The marine called for his replacement.[172]

Perhaps the greatest tension came from municipal politicians who resented the newfound but ill-defined authority of the constabularies, who went beyond instructions and attempted to take over local sources of revenue and influence.[173] In Haiti's Saint-Michel de l'Attalaye, after the gendarmes took over the town, a member of the *conseil communal* or town council complained that gendarmes treated locals "disrespectfully" and used "very unseemly language." "They even have the pretension to subordinate to their caprice the authority of the Communal Board."[174] The Haitian Secretary of the Interior wrote to General Butler that gendarmes were particularly abusive to municipal magistrates, "who represent Haitian authority."[175]

The very presence of constabularies reflected a power shift away from towns. A Dominican governor, recalling the "abuses" of the pre-occupation republican guard, pleaded with the occupation not to place a provincial police force under the National Police, the Dominican National Guard's successor. After all, the ayuntamientos were "called to recruit it, organize it, regulate it and pay it with municipal funds." Shouldn't they have a right to direct it?[176] "I respectfully inform you of the immorality of the Juge de Paix," Benjamin Bordnave, a gendarme corporal sent to Baie de Henne, wrote to his commander. The justice of the peace ruled the town's tribunal with his two brothers-in-law and told townsfolk to disregard all Bordnave's orders. The justice, described by Bordnave as "always intoxicated, ... immoral and unfitted for duty ... positively refused to have any contact with us saying that he is the only authority of the locality."[177] Such communal leaders must have understood their conundrum: the only redress against centralization through the constabularies was to complain to an even higher centralizing agent, the marines. Haitians had no choice but to ask that other gendarmes be sent to replace those now oppressing them.[178]

On December 14, 1919, a US corporal with his company of guards burst through the doors of a small café in San Pedro and caught five "well known gamblers" playing cards with wads of bills stacked before them. Two of the men leaped out the window but the guards quickly seized and arrested them, as well as the owner of the café. All admitted to gambling. Five days later the accused appeared before the Court of First Instance, run solely by Dominicans. The prosecution had an airtight case: eyewitnesses, confessions, the cards, and the money.

The judge acquitted all the men "on account of lack of evidence."[179]

The case was typical of local resistance around gambling, an activity that revealed interrelated networks of power. In occupied small towns, gambling was often the favorite—if not the only—pastime. US journalist Harry Frank described cockfighting in the Dominican Republic as existing in every town, out in the open, and involving significant sums of money.[180] A visiting scholar to Haiti in 1921 reported that "cock pits are found everywhere. Gambling is universal."[181]

Some occupiers vowed to fight the immorality of gambling. One US officer called horse racing "one of the most insidious forms of public corruption" and cockfighting, "brutal and degrading." He proposed banning all games of chance, even the lottery. "With these reforms accomplished, an important step will have been taken for the moral benefit of the Dominican people."[182] In early 1918 the military government outlawed cockfighting except on holidays, and months later enforced other laws against betting on horses unless at the track. By late April 1918, Major McLean proudly reported that "nothing but authorized cock-fights were in operation [and] a short campaign against gambling checked that vice and more than one hundred professional gamblers received prison sentences."[183] Cockfighting was further restricted to towns that had a police force to respond to the brawls that regularly broke out around the pits.[184] The US occupation of Haiti never tried to ban gambling there.[185]

Resistance to these restrictions to gambling revealed three layers of motivations among Dominicans. The first was cultural: cockfighting proved central to the identity of Dominicans. The General Receiver of Customs in Santo Domingo concluded that "[to Dominicans,] patriotism and love of country are unknown things; to them the sum total of existence is a little work, a little rum, lots of fiestas and a cock-fight every Sunday."[186] Despite this crude characterization, occupied peoples indeed blanched when they saw their precious cockpits threatened with closure. Several *rematistas* or cockpit owners wrote to the Dominican occupation with lists of reasons why their pits should stay open, and most had to do with protecting Dominican culture. Mario Otero petitioned with five colleagues, arguing that "the cockfight is not a corrupting vice, but rather a mere diversion."[187] Santiago Carbonell and his eleven co-signatories argued that cock-fighting was, along with Catholicism and Castillean, "one of the few relics that the Motherland bequeathed to us." Dominicans also advanced a traditionalist appeal, explaining that "these cockfights have been celebrated year after year."[188] Failing to convince occupiers, Dominicans instead moved cockfighting under-ground.[189] The governor of Santiago Province also reported that, since cock-fights could now only be held on holidays, several town councils simply declared new holidays.[190]

A second threat that anti-gambling efforts posed was, logically enough, to economic power. Pits existed almost exclusively in towns and therefore were more likely to attract townspeople, but peasants came to town on weekends to place bets or just watch the show. Cock pits in the Dominican east notably at-tracted workers of the sugar estates.[191] Haitian and Dominican cock pits also at-tracted the many poor who behaved as if rich. "It always amazed me," one marine recalled, "that you would find a Haitian who didn't have a pair of trousers to wear, but he could always dig somewhere or other and come up with one or two gourdes to bet on a cock fight."[192] If cockfights were financially important to those who placed the bets, they were doubly so to those who owned or ran them. Pit owners tended to be "wealthy merchants and men high in local affairs," wrote a US journalist.[193] By gambling, Latin Americans funneled their scarce re-sources into the hands of the owners of cock pits, saloons, and other sites where simple folk played games of chance. In the town of El Jaguel one Dominican told a marine that he "conducted a gambling house Saturday night to obtain suf-ficient money to add to his weekly wage to enable him to buy a pair of shoes."[194] Petitioners Carbonell and his friends argued that town councils could tax the cockfights and thus bring in revenue.[195] Otero's petition specified that his own pit could generate "THREE HUNDRED PESOS IN GOLD next year."[196]

Finally and most subtly, restrictions on gambling revealed a resistant political order. Gambling created a space in which political ideas and hierarchies could be elaborated, disputed, and in the end usually reinforced. A typical town coun-cil, especially in the Dominican Republic, had members tied to gambling estab-lishments. "These authorities are the bosses of the towns: the gambling houses belong to them . . . , they administer Justice and they are sometimes surveyors," wrote Santiago Governor Manuel A. Lora.[197] Even ayuntamientos who banned gambling could harbor ulterior motives: the San Pedro síndico abolished cock-fighting in 1918 in order to eliminate competition to his horse racing associa-tion.[198] In addition, as the card game acquittal indicated, a disregard for gambling required the collaboration of either local police or courts. One hand washed the other: gambling put pesos in the pockets of officeholders, and political power (and bribes) kept the cops and judges away. When occupations moved to ban gambling while they simultaneously threatened to replace local officials, they endangered every avenue of income and influence for small town rulers.

If cock pits were filled with men who rejected the occupation, it followed that they would use the pits for organized political action. In June 1920 marines reported that Dominican anti-occupation leaders gave political speeches at cockfights and "collect[ed] some money from the people there for the Junta Nacionalista."[199] In one of the Haitian towns most responsible for insurrection, another report stated, "the only recreation engaged in is cockfighting and dancing."[200]

Equally problematic for the occupations, flouting anti-gambling laws led to what McLean called "a general disregard for law in minor things." He described gambling as the tip of the iceberg of a chaotic situation in which the invaded continuously violated the *Ley de Policía* or police law. "To add to this disorder," wrote McLean, "native officials, almost in their totality, countenanced, connived at, or openly aided in . . . violations."[201] Gambling illustrated important dynamics that helped doom the reformism of US occupations in Latin America.

Causing perhaps more local resistance than gambling were the myriad regulations of occupation, which telegraphed concretely the desire to centralize authority in ways that frightened, frustrated, or inconvenienced small towns. To be sure, some regulations impacted the capitals. In March 1919 an unsigned placard went up in Port-au-Prince griping that the marines were "preventing people to rebuild [their houses] in wood under the false pretense to beautify the town."[202] Henri Brisson of the Port-au-Prince Chamber of Commerce similarly complained that gendarmes arbitrarily fined peasants who brought their goods to market if their packhorses bore "the tiniest injury."[203] Mostly, however, opposition to regulations came from ayuntamientos, who saw what may have been beneficial to the nation at large as annoying and oppressive to locals. A French chargé described resistance to regulations as "sometimes small incidents that, from a distance, seem insignificant, but that are nonetheless a good indication of the growing antipathy against the American military element."[204]

Regulations clashed with the perspectives of autonomous agricultural peoples, and many of these, as in Port-au-Prince, had to do with animals. In Haiti marines required that animal property be ascertained by proof of ownership. In Belladere, marines accused magistrate Charles Rimpel of having "fraudulently acquired" six horses across the Dominican border, and Rimpel admitted having no ownership papers. Instead, speaking of himself in the third person, he invoked community-defined property: "The whole population of this commune knows that these horses are the product of two mares, one of which has belonged to him for six years, and the other to his brother who has owned her for fifteen years."[205] In 1919 the Dominican occupation decreed that all hogs in a border town called Las Matas de Farfán should be slaughtered, perhaps to stanch a ty-phoid epidemic. In response, a petition signed by 140 persons—probably every adult male in this hamlet of 100 houses—settled on a tone that praised the in-tentions of the military government while it also argued for flexibility within centralization: "A law may be excellent for a populous center such as Santo Do-mingo, but would be of less importance for Azua [a mid-size town], and null or disastrous for Las Matas de Farfán."[206] Two years later, Jarabacoa's síndico complained of a new regulation forcing inhabitants to kill animals at least a day before selling them, likely to allow for sanitizing the slaughterhouse before the sale. This síndico reiterated the argument that such laws were too strict for small, remote towns. "As this village is small, a cow cannot be sold in a day, but rather takes two days to sell, and if you butcher the cow one day before selling it, after three days it won't sell because it is in a bad state."[207]

As sanitary officers fanned out to the countryside armed with regulations, complaints kept coming. Why did peasants in Samaná have to pay $5 twice a year for a permit to sell bread? They bought flour in large bags and needed to unload the surplus.[208] Did San Juan's midwives really need to pass an exam, be literate, and also pay $5? "Since the discovery of the island midwives have prac-ticed their profession without any regulations," complained the síndico, José Peguero. If this rule persisted, "our souls will weep to see many women die in childbirth because no one would dare assist them, and that would be anti-hu-manitarian."[209] Was it necessary, again in San Juan, for a marine officer to shoot all the loose pigs? "The people were too poor to build enclosures for their pigs," explained a local official.[210]

The regulation that aroused the most—and the most effective—resistance was pharmaceutical. In 1918 came its first iteration: taxes on drug imports, inspections on pharmacies, and criminal penalties for buying (and therefore selling) large quantities of drugs such as opium.[211] In response, all the pharma-cists of Santo Domingo sent a protest to the head of the occupation positing that the regulations were "useless and inefficaciously too strict, contradictory to the liberty of commerce, . . . and contradictory to individual and economic rights." The pharmacists feared being drowned in litigation and, less convinc-ingly, argued that opium needed to be imported in large quantities because it evaporated easily. Overall the pharmacists resented "constant inspection from the Government."[212] Military Governor Knapp suspected the petitioners of being motivated by "private interests as compared with the public welfare" and lectured the druggists, calling the law "consonant with enlightened practice in countries where a high degree of intelligence, education and humanitarianism prevails."[213]

In 1922 came a more sweeping drug regulation, which placed a prohibitive stamp on medicine and other products sold by pharmacists, effectively ending their monopoly and allowing physicians also to sell drugs. Regulators argued that the rule ended the doubling of fees for patients (to both physicians and pharmacists) and simplified patient care in emergencies, and they predicted that prices would come down and medicine would reach the countryside.[214] This time the pharmacists of Santiago banded together. They declared a boycott of "all American drugs and chemical products." "Taxes are never acceptable to anyone," commented an occupation inspector, rather dismissively. "But in the case of the Military Government anything they do will be wrong in the eyes of at least a part of the people."[215]

Land taxes were also "never acceptable," especially to the well-off in small towns. Taxes were largely unknown to Latin Americans, especially taxes on land.[216] Before 1916 Dominican landowners moved to more remote arable land if the state attempted to tax them, and coffee and cocoa were largely tax-exempt crops.[217] As a result, "the old taxes bore far more on the poor man than on the man of property," explained a US journalist.[218] To occupation officials, therefore, taxes were a means to a fairer economy. Collecting more taxes, and honestly, would pay for the expansion of the state into public works, education, and other common goods. The occupation also wanted to shift the tax burden away from customs collection, a dependence that helped bring on the occupation. A final motive was to substitute central land taxes for municipal ones such as levies on imported merchandise and on inter-municipal trade.[219] President Wilson himself described his goal as "placing the burden of the taxes upon property owners and eliminating a multitude of small, nagging and inadequate taxes."[220] Faustin Wirkus doubled tax collections in La Gonâve, a place notoriously resistant to taxation.[221]

As a result of its complexity and of resistance, the Dominican land tax took over two years to materialize, becoming "the greatest problem confronting the government."[222] On April 10, 1919, the occupation decreed a Land and Property Tax Law that placed a tax of 0.5 to 2 percent of the assessed value on properties with 0.25 percent on permanent improvements.[223] Since half the Dominican Republic's lands were uncultivated, the marines hoped that installing an incentive for making land productive, along with clearing up land titles, would attract foreign investment.[224]

In response, the towns clung to their revenue sources. A year into the occupation, Knapp noted that he received "a number of requests from different Ayuntamientos to establish what are virtually surtaxes for the purpose of raising municipal revenue." Local officials were not opposed to taxes per se, but to their loss of control over them.[225] Dominican sugar estates fought the Tax Law first, forming the Sugar Association of Santo Domingo and even lobbying in Washington, but to no avail.[226] Soon after the law's passage, the end of war in Europe sparked a Dominican recession. To make matters worse, in 1921 a hurricane in

Samaná destroyed crops, making taxes even more burdensome.[227] Landown-ers panicked.[228] In 1920 they called for a boycott of the tax. They banded as *juntas patrióticas* in almost every province to spread the rumor that taxes should be withheld since the occupation would leave soon.[229] Party leader Horacio Vásquez supposedly signed a protest while assuring the occupation that he sup-ported the tax.[230]

Landowners made concrete arguments, largely shorn of nationalism. A Do-minican pamphleteer explained that a tax on property could be devastating in bad economic times whereas a tax on income or production would rise and fall. He added that the tax upset traditions and "it is impolitic to brusquely over-throw the customs of a people." Since North American colonists had revolted because they were taxed without representation, why not Dominicans?[231] The Santo Domingo Chamber of Commerce, along with several petitions, added that recent boom times had overvalued land.[232]

Marines also confronted the combined forces of landowners and ayunta-mientos. The few town officials who did not oppose the land tax, one reported, were those who owned no land and proposed that they themselves do land as-sessments and receive in return 5 percent of all values. Disgusted, the marines blocked their measure.[233] More typically, town officials practiced passive resis-tance by failing to show up at meetings with governors.[234] One governor failed to pay his own tax, as did all but two town councillors in Seibo.[235] In the same town one treasurer told landowners who came to pay him their tax, "*Señores* do not be stupid, do not pay these invoices because no one in the country is paying them and here we also do not pay them."[236] Many ayuntamientos wrote to Santo Domingo that their constituents simply did not have the money. One suggested donating animals instead.[237]

The boycott did not reverse the tax, but together with the downturn it pre-vented the raising of revenue. Military Governor Samuel Robison admitted in October 1921 that in the north, "the richest half . . . have very largely failed, or re-fused, to pay their property taxes."[238] In November 1921 the occupation reduced the tax by half and later promised that the tax would go to fund education.[239] It mattered little. By mid-March 1922, marines in several provinces reported a widespread refusal to pay on time or at all.[240] In 1922, of almost $1 million due in land taxes, only $390,000 was paid, and $230,000 of it by foreigners, leav-ing only $160,000 or 16 percent paid by Dominicans.[241] In 1923 the mayor of Santiago said property taxes equal to the entire revenue of the town had not been paid that year.[242] Tax collectors reported being beaten by Dominicans who swore their innocence on the basis that they were "men of property, family and standing in the community." The tragedy, thought US officials, was that three quarters of the tax would have been administered by Dominicans and gone di-rectly to ayuntamientos.[243]

The Dominican occupation also imposed a Dominican *corvée* of sorts, as in Haiti, but it became more of a tax revolt since most resisted paying the four pesos per year in lieu of labor. Arguing against the corvée, merchants in San Francisco complained that such taxes were being spent on roads outside their district. They wanted better roads close to home to help bring their goods to market and as a reward for cooperating against the rebels.[244] No nationwide numbers on road tax resistance exist, but in one común over 27 percent refused to work or pay.[245] The ayuntamientos, charged with collecting the road tax, largely did not. Marines reminded the president of San Pedro of his dereliction of duty because he raised only a third of the tax.[246] An investigation found that over $5,200 of the road tax went instead to "other municipal services without proper authorization."[247] In Los Llanos the síndico reported slightly better numbers for 1922: half paid rather than worked; the other half registered to work, but almost a third of those did nothing. He explained that the loafers were "Haitians, Englishmen (*cocolos*), and Dominicans from other communes" who moved to other towns when asked to labor on roads.[248]

The Dominican occupation also ordered a tobacco tax, a business tax, and a tax to fund education.[249] In 1919 it revised the tariffs of the country, slashing 700 of them and eliminating completely 245 others, and abolished revenue taxes on imports. These executive orders chiefly harmed producers of shoes, apparel, furniture, hats, shirts, soap, hides, cigarettes, and matches.[250] Six Dominican shoemakers wrote to the military governor warning that these orders would "smother" their industry. Several small manufacturers closed shop.[251]

US officials denied that they imposed land taxes in Haiti, but they did, and taxes "raised much criticism in the north," according to a Cap-Haïtien consul. Like Dominicans, Haitians cited overvalued land and prohibitive rates.[252] One lawyer in 1917 resented the lifting of the prohibition on foreigners to own Haitian land not out of xenophobia but because "if foreigners come here house rents will be raised and the house he now pays twenty gourdes for will probably cost twice as much or more."[253] To avoid paying property taxes, large landowners colluded with Haitian sub-collectors, who purposefully undervalued their land.[254] In 1930, 2,000 demonstrated in front of the presidential palace in the capital, with more in Cap-Haïtien. Near Abricot, a US Garde (the successor to the Haitian Gendarmerie) officer with his troops trying to collect a land tax "was stoned by a large crowd of natives."[255] Additional income came from new excises on alcohol and tobacco. In 1917, for instance, sixty-six alcohol stills in the north generated only $15,000 in monthly taxes, until an occupation official concentrated them into nine and drew from them $35,000 per month.[256] Haitians particularly resented the alcohol tax because it raised the cost of making tafia, a local fermented drink.[257] In 1923, 3,000 Haitians, allegedly instigated by newspaperman Jolibois Fils, gathered in Jacmel to illegally protest the tax.[258] In 1931, 600 in Léogâne attacked three government inspectors and tore off the seals they placed on stills.[259] The occupation in Haiti also backed down somewhat from its taxation, promising not to force the payment of back taxes and to protect landowners against eviction.[260] But it refused to lower the alcohol tax, claiming that a diminished tax would not be worth collect-ing.[261] By the end of the occupation, non-customs revenues climbed from 53 to 72 percent of the government's budget.[262]

In the end, the effort to reform politics—whether national, provincial, or local—failed, primarily due to resistance from those who held office or wished to. Fail-ure should have indicated to invaders that all politics of resistance are local. The great majority of political players among the invaded responded to the central-ization of political power with some nationalism, to be sure, but also a great deal of regionalism and localism, and much of it self-interested rather than responsive to constituents. Safeguarding their interests is what the elite, the "ins" and "outs," the journalists, the mayors, the landowners, the taxpayers, and countless others did all along. It was the essence of the politics of resistance. Given such a chal-lenge, changing personnel failed to effect measurable change in political culture. Late in the Dominican occupation, marines complained of being unable to trust even the ayuntamientos and police forces they had themselves appointed.[263] They attributed municipal resistance to faulty "character" and "attitude" on the part of Dominican officials rather than self-interest.[264] They also lost sight of the fact that occupations whose purpose was to teach self-government undercut that purpose by replacing local officials. "It is typically American," one marine later mused, "to believe we can exert a subtle alchemy by our presence among a people for a few years which will eradicate the teaching and training of hundreds of years. . . . It is a hopeful theory, but it lacks common sense."[265]

PART FOUR

TRANSNATIONAL NETWORKS
AND US WITHDRAWALS

US Responses, Haitian Setbacks, and Dominican Withdrawal, 1919–1924

> On the international scene there has now appeared a new actor: solidarity.
>
> —Tulio Cestero

The accumulation of violent and peaceful, cultural and political resistance took its toll by the early 1920s in the Dominican Republic. The country's liberation from occupation, agreed to in 1922 and accomplished in 1924, presaged successful strategies of resistance movements. While urban resistance was key to this success, so were the persistent transnational efforts by Dominicans and other Latin Americans to create networks of propaganda and lobbying.[1] US officials and the US public began to recognize and even embrace the arguments of the resistance against occupation.

Dominicans were bitterly divided on strategy but able to paper over their differences for the sake of international allies and US occupiers. Their self-proclaimed national unity proved to be a show of short-term political expediency that ran against US hopes that the occupation had created a stronger national identity that would lead to political stability. Haitians, too, built a transnational network, claimed national unity, and prompted US administrators to consider withdrawal. But all three developments were significantly weaker in Haiti, all partly because of race. Anti-black racism, among both US and Latin American citizens, proved the most consequential reason for continuing the Haitian occupation while ending the Dominican one.

Anti-occupation groups began to communicate with those outside their occupied land following the interventions of 1915 and 1916 and intensified their transnational activism with the end of the Great War in 1919. Besides withdrawal, activists abroad achieved a more inchoate though longer-lasting result: the strengthening of a pan-Latin American identity of independent republics fighting for one another against a common US enemy. The fight against occupation, more than anything, shaped this shared identity.

After the marines forced Dominican president Francisco Henríquez y Carvajal from office on December 8, 1916, he wrote to his former lover Marie Fache. He would try to speak directly to President Woodrow Wilson, "Don Pancho" pledged. If unable to reach Wilson, he would defend his country "before the Hispanic-American Embassies and Legations. If I receive funds from my country, I will undertake a voyage throughout the Americas." Yet Henríquez feared the apathy of fellow Dominicans along with "the indifference of the Americas toward a country that it judged too insignificant to risk anything for it."[2] Early on in the resistance, therefore, its leader imagined the opportunities in using other Latin American countries as a propaganda lever as well as the odds against success. He was prescient on both counts.

During and immediately after World War I, activism abroad was the only option for anti-occupation activists because widespread censorship in Santo Domingo created "a cemetery silence," wrote Henríquez's son, Max Henríquez Ureña.[3] In 1916 lawyer-journalist Luis del Castillo dreamed of "establish[ing] in the main cities of Europe and the Americas an association of citizens of all countries of Latin America . . . that will respond in the press against imperialist practices" because those still in the country, "submitted to the tutelage of the invader," were hopeless.[4]

After a few weeks in New York in December 1916, Don Pancho traveled to Washington in January 1917, where he presented the Department of State with a detailed proposal for withdrawal. Washington, focused on the war in Europe, gave no response.[5] The next stop was Santiago, Cuba, where Henríquez's family and medical practice awaited. The exiled president and his sons understood that one of his weaknesses in attempting to hold out against US pressures in the fall of 1916 had been the lack of an office of international public relations. He vowed to create one in Cuba.[6] However, after the military government in Santo Domingo dismissed Dominican diplomats who vowed to help him, Henríquez, broke and caring for an ill son, largely stopped writing and did no public speaking.[7]

The end of war in Europe signaled a renewed transnational "Indo-Spanish campaign" in the Caribbean, as Henríquez called it.[8] On Armistice Day, November 11, 1918, three Dominicans and eight Cubans formed the Society of the Eleven, which gave birth to several Pro-Santo Domingo Committees.[9] The first committee, founded in Santiago de Cuba on December 30, drew donations from several nationalities and pledged to use only "legitimate means" in Cuba and the United States to communicate Dominican grievances.[10] Committees held concerts, lectures, and other entertainments, and Cuban papers advertised them vigorously.[11] Most leaders of the committees were the former Dominican diplomats who had organized in 1917. Others were respected

Cubans such as scholar Emilio Roig de Leuchsenring and rum magnate Emilio Bacardí.[12] Don Pancho went to Cuban meetings, drumming up support by re-calling the two nations' ties—Dominican Máximo Gómez leading the Cuban fight against the Spanish in the 1890s, Cuban José Martí living in exile in the Dominican Republic. The Cubans, angry that the United States had made their island a protectorate, needed little convincing.[13] Bacardí and friends consid-ered themselves bound to Dominicans by "the powerful ties of blood, religion, and language."[14]

The committees mostly raised funds to send Henríquez to the Versailles peace conference, and at first, the chances of a hearing by US delegates looked good. Henríquez recalled how Queen Wilhelmina of the Netherlands, surrounded in the grand salon of her palace in The Hague by representatives of large and small nations, addressed only the latter.[15] Henríquez was also markedly moderate in Paris. One US diplomat appreciated that, despite his exile, he was "not rabidly anti-American and that he recognizes the necessity of the step which the United States has taken in Santo Domingo but desires that some of the functions of the Government be turned over to the Dominicans."[16]

Yet signs quickly pointed to Don Pancho's ostracism. He complained that delegates were so busy with European affairs that "they will see no one."[17] Hen-ríquez never saw Wilson but did have a meeting with J. H. Stabler, head of the Latin-American Division, on April 10, 1919. He gave Stabler several versions of his official demands, promising in return to resign as provisional president.[18] Stabler countered with the crushing news: the United States would not discuss the matter further.[19] The Dominican had crossed the ocean for nothing.

For the invaded, however, the end of the war offered an opportunity to refine anti-occupation ideas. Like many self-identified victims of imperialism around the world, Henríquez seized on Wilson's wartime promotion of self-determina-tion in Europe to question the US president's scuttling of self-government in the Americas. In Havana, Roig de Leuchsenring spoke in January 1919 of Wilson's contradiction. "How is it," he asked rhetorically,

> that President Wilson, after having declared . . . the right of small na-tionalities and having presented it as one of the reasons for which the United States entered the War . . . allows . . . in his own Continent to exist a small nation from which his government has taken the very free-dom and the sovereignty which, in his actions in the Old World, he pro-tected for small European nationalities?[20]

Many compared the Dominican Republic to the trampled minorities of Europe.[21] "The hour has come not only for the small nationalities of Europe but also for the Americas; not only for Belgium and Poland but also for Santo Domingo," wrote Santiago's *Diario de Cuba*.[22] Others placed the United States within the family of traditional imperialist European powers. Dominican poet Fabio Fiallo called Versailles "nothing more than a second Vienna Congress, and the League of Nations another Holy Alliance."[23] Deputies brought up the issue in the British Parliament, one British diplomat admitting privately that "this is rather a delicate question. It is one of those cases in which President Wilson has conspicuously omitted to practice those views about the rights of small nationalities which he is preaching."[24] US diplomats in Paris admitted that the end of war removed an "excuse" for the continuation of the Haitian occupation, "particularly, as the rights of smaller nations are being kept to the fore and in the light of the President's utterances."[25]

The Henríquez clan nevertheless claimed to share political values with the very US officials who stonewalled them.[26] Tulio Cestero, one of its most important operatives, wished that US occupiers could help instill among Dominicans the desire for hard work, honest government, and universal schooling. "We have to . . . eliminate the parasitism of bureaucrats and semi-intellectuals."[27] One of Don Pancho's instructions to Cestero was to achieve "the institutional reforms to which Dominicans aspire [and that] will almost surely bring on the death of *caudillismo*."[28]

The Henríquezes were also persistent and developed alternative lines of diplomatic attack. In late July 1919 the Dominican Nationalist Commission (CND) was founded, likely when Henríquez returned from Paris. Francisco presided and brother Federico was a member, along with Francisco's sons Max and Pedro, and Cestero, a distant relative. René Fiallo joined, as did his father Fabio. The commission acted simultaneously in New York, Cuba, and Washington.[29]

In September, Henríquez had a rare meeting with US officials in which, again, he pleaded for moderate reforms and gradual emancipation. He proposed replacing US-controlled provost courts with Dominican judges who would also take cases away from the police and municipal officials, and called for a body to revise organic laws on elections, reorganize municipalities and provinces, regulate the budget, and rethink the executive and other branches of government.[30] In October 1919 he made an eloquent and convincing case for withdrawal to Secretary of State Robert Lansing:

> The situation in which the Dominican people finds itself is unjust from the legal point of view, intolerable in practice, unnecessary for any end that may be pursued, illogical in its results, and absolutely discordant with the ethical and legal principles of international life which prevail to-day. . . . The time is ripe to undertake there a number of institutional reforms which may insure the stability of its national government and the progress of the people.[31]

The State Department sympathized with some of Henríquez's proposals, yet reforms under the direction of Dominicans themselves seemed unacceptable. State thought that to form any consultative body would signal to Dominican political leaders "that the American authorities in control of the Government were to be withdrawn," resulting in these Dominicans "working up the political factions with a view to controlling the situation."[32] This argument would be repeated throughout US occupations: setting withdrawal target dates only encouraged political jockeying and discouraged real reform. Henríquez's contacts with State also prompted panicked letters from the US Navy predicting "chaos" and "anarchy" if independence came to the Dominican Republic.[33] Military Governor Thomas Snowden wrote that self-government was impossible "until such time as the people of the Dominican Republic have developed the character and ability to govern themselves, handle their finances properly, and maintain a permanently stable government." He and State agreed that this would take "a minimum of twenty years."[34]

From New York and Washington Henríquez and others from the CND returned, deflated but not defeated, to their homes in Santo Domingo and Cuba, while Cestero stayed behind as Don Pancho's "personal representative." In April 1920 Cestero met with Secretary of the Navy Josephus Daniels, but Daniels was largely noncommittal.[35] Perhaps feeling that Henríquez's moderation was getting nowhere, Cestero went on a propaganda offensive. He wrote directly to President Wilson, calling for investigations into various acts of torture and mistreatment by marines and guards.[36] On April 3 he sent two similar letters listing grievances against the occupation, one by himself and the other by Dominican Archbishop Adolfo Nouel, to every member of the US Senate. They garnered attention from the US press but produced no action.[37] The occupation responded by discrediting Cestero because of the misdeeds of his family members.[38] In September, Daniels refused to meet at all. So did the new secretary of state, Bainbridge Colby.

Henríquez's disillusion in France and the United States nevertheless made him aware of the broad interest in Dominican matters among a potentially useful group of outsiders, Latin American diplomats. At Versailles, no Latin American officially spoke out in his favor, but they all granted him audiences.[39] In New York and Washington in late 1919, Cestero also attempted to garner the support of South American diplomats. He lectured a group in New York on his belief in hemispheric brotherhood. "On the international scene there has now appeared a new actor: solidarity," he said. "No nation, no people, can realize by itself its destiny." To Cestero, "nationality" encompassed transnational identity. "We are citizens of twenty nations," he said, "but in one language, with the same soul, we feel nationality."[40] On December 16, 1919, he spoke to an audience that included the ambassadors of Argentina and Peru, the ministers of Colombia, Ecuador, and Venezuela, and Herbert Hoover, a wartime hero for delivering food to starving Europeans.[41] Uruguayans were particularly receptive to the Dominicans abroad, their minister in Washington setting up meetings between Henríquez or Cestero and US officials.[42] By May 1920, US officials in Havana reported that Cestero was there attempting to convince senior Cuban officials to officially denounce the occupation.[43] The Cuban town of Ardilla witnessed "acrimonious pamphlets and public meetings," very likely the result of the Pro-Santo Domingo Committees.[44]

As early as 1919, Cestero and the Henríquez family began conceiving of a tour of South America to cement hemispheric allegiance to the Dominican cause.[45] It took until October 1920 to raise enough money to undertake it, and in Havana, the CND chose three envoys: Federico, Max, and Cestero. "Your mission will assume two guises," Don Pancho instructed Cestero: "One of them public, whose end will be to persuade host peoples of the need for the freedom and independence of the Dominican people; the other, confidential, secret, whose end will be to interest Heads of Government in every country in favor of the Republic's cause." The patriarch had written to all Latin American heads of state three times already, with little to show for his efforts.[46] Up to then the only Latin American activity in favor of Dominicans were the Cuban and Uruguayan efforts and a resolution of sympathy—though stripped of any reference to US occupation—from the Colombian Congress.[47] The tour meant to light a fire under others.

The three men boarded a ship from Brooklyn on December 29, 1920, sailed through the Panama Canal, and disembarked in the capitals of Peru, Chile, Argentina, Uruguay, and Brazil, returning on May 26, 1921. At least one of them met with the minister of foreign relations in every country and with the president in all but Peru. Upon their return, Cestero filed a fifty-three-page report declaring the public mission fully realized and expressing satisfaction with the private mission. The voyage indeed received cordial and enthusiastic public support, drawing large public gatherings everywhere and friendly articles in every country's press—some were so anti-US that the Dominicans pleaded with editors for restraint.[48]

The results of the "secret" campaign were more mixed. Friends and family, printing handbills from the CND and placing articles in newspapers, predicted sanguinely that getting heads of state to lobby Washington would "be unbearable for the American government, which will need to resolve matters to our advantage."[49] But few South American presidents wanted to confront Secretary Colby, who ended his own tour of Argentina, Brazil, and Chile right before the Dominicans came.[50] The Brazilians, tussling with US counterparts over commodity exchange rates, said they would only lodge a complaint with Washington if everyone else did (they eventually reversed their stance).[51] The Chilean minister, who remained standing as Cestero sat in his office, expressed discomfort at the suggestion that he write a letter that "would equal reminding Mr. [President Warren] Harding of 'the fulfillment of his duty.'" More encouraging, Argentine President Hipólito Yrigoyen said he would speak to the US minister "without waiting for other governments and without fearing a negative response from Washington." Uruguayan President Baltasar Brum was even more supportive. He had spoken to his congress about the Dominican situation, and when Colby asked him, during his visit, what Washington could do for Uruguay, Brum answered, "We need nothing, we only desire that you reestablish the Dominican Republic."[52]

The trip may have been unnecessary. Secretary Colby had returned from South America convinced that the United States should withdraw from the Dominican Republic. Wilson, as a lame duck, issued a statement to this effect even before the Dominicans left.[53]

Yet the tour helped stiffen the solidarity of South American publics and perhaps the backbone of some of their officials. Numerous Latin American and European organizations responded favorably to the Dominicans' pan-Hispanic rhetoric and to postwar notions of international solidarity and self-government. US intelligence officers often complained of the effectiveness of "the sympathetic underground advice from the Spanish speaking countries" on sustaining Dominicans morally if not otherwise.[54]

Above ground, newspaper editors led the offense. About sixty Latin American and Spanish newspapers reproduced the pamphlets of the Santo Domingo–based Dominican Nationalist Union (UND), many also editorializing in its favor.[55] They paid special attention to cases of torture.[56] Latin American editors may have even saved Fabio Fiallo's life: US occupiers considered the death sentence for the poet, but after Havana and Montevideo press clubs appealed to Wilson, Fiallo's sentence was reduced and then suspended. Colby admitted that the reason was anti-occupation propaganda.[57]

In Europe, Spaniards were the most active. The former Dominican consul in Madrid, Enrique Deschamps, representing Henríquez and apparently funded by the CND, lobbied in Spain, France, Belgium, and the League of Nations, where a Chilean presided and a Brazilian chaired the Assembly.[58] He published articles in Spanish newspapers in the hopes that "racial solidarity" would motivate Spaniards to help him. "For us Spaniards, this issue has the singular spiritual reach of an outbreak of the soul of the race in the Caribbean. The incarnation of this outbreak is the moral triumph of one of the smallest peoples of our race against the largest of the Anglo-Saxon race."[59] One Deschamps visit to Madrid resulted in the Spanish government forwarding to Washington a request for the restoration of Henríquez's government.[60] In 1919 and 1921 the Spanish Congress sent messages of sympathy, an event reported in 3,600 newspapers in the United States and Canada.[61]

Beyond cultural sympathy, Europeans and others also may have resented their war debts to the United States, or they may have wanted to act as a mirror to US occupiers, showing the error of their colonial ways. The press in France, Great Britain, Russia, and Italy seemed gleeful to see the anti-colonialist moralists caught red-handed. Japan justified its own "Monroe Doctrine of the Orient" by citing the Dominican occupation.[62] Barcelona's *Mercurio* editorialized that continuing the occupation would cost the United States more in prestige than it could possibly gain otherwise.[63]

By mid-1921 Henríquez initiatives were piling up. A buoyant Don Pancho wrote to his nephew in May: "Today we can count on all of the public opinion of the world and on that of America. The latter was largely hostile, before; today, it is either favorable or indifferent."[64] Without polls it is impossible to tell if his optimism was warranted. But his and Cestero's tireless activities had garnered allies who could broadcast their cause to the most important audience—the US public and policymakers.

Cestero found in the US Congress willing instruments of resistance. Félix Cordova Dávila, the Puerto Rican delegate, introduced him to Congressman William Mason, who agreed to introduce a resolution on April 7, 1920, calling for an investigation into the situation in the Dominican Republic. At seventy years old, Mason wrote to Cestero, "I want to live long enough to see my country free from colonies and all kinds of slavery. This will mean self-determination for the Philippines, Porto Rico and Sandomingo [sic]." Cestero called Mason a "friend" and gave him stories of oppressed Dominicans and censorship as grist for the propaganda mill.[65] The Mason resolution never came to a vote, but months later Representative Oscar Bland introduced a similar resolution.[66]

The real Henríquez coup in Washington was to hire Horace Knowles, a former US minister to Bolivia and the Dominican Republic and an insider who could work his peers. Presidents and secretaries of state read Knowles's letters to keep abreast of abuses and censorship in the Dominican Republic. Knowles asked State Department officials during Wilson's lame-duck months to order a full withdrawal before president-elect Harding instituted the more generous policy he had promised. Knowles reminded Colby of his promise to Uruguay's Brum to withdraw "within a period that will not exceed five months the last of the American troops." To Harding himself Knowles warned that Latin Americans "will organize themselves in a movement of hostility toward our country" that would harm US relations with Europe and Japan.[67]

Knowles helped Dominicans partly for the money. In 1920 the CND paid him the enormous sum of $25,000 to $35,000.[68] A Republican working for the Harding campaign and desirous of an ambassadorship to Chile, Knowles may have also harbored political interests.[69] Overall he seemed sincere in his conviction that the United States was doing itself more harm than good through occupation. Knowles embodied the populist anti-imperialism of many US citizens, who saw empire as anathema to US values and experience. "The bully is not a becoming part for our Government to play," he once wrote Senator William Borah, "and any attempt to do it will not win the admiration of true Americans." He labeled a proposed $10 million loan "taxation without representation," adding that it threw the Dominican Republic "to the wolves of Wall Street."[70]

Knowles drew the attention of the *New York Times* and other newspapers to Dominican matters, organized a major rally in Carnegie Hall, and helped convince the Harding campaign to make a statement on the Dominican Republic.[71] He was also apparently instrumental in identifying—and perhaps coaching—witnesses for US senatorial investigations in 1921–1922.[72] The US occupation was concerned with Knowles's activities to the extent of spying on him during his stays in Santo Domingo, recording his every visitor.[73] Like the Henríquez clan, Knowles began his activism trying to persuade Washington, ran up against a wall, then chose outright dissent.

US scholars and labor leaders also became active for the Dominican cause, many through the Henríquez-Cestero group. On May 20, 1920, Clark University held a conference on the matter, featuring Dominican expert Otto Schoenrich.[74] Months later New York's Hotel Commodore was the site of another conference, organized by the League of Free Nations. Schoenrich and scholars from Columbia University attended, as did special guest Don Pancho.[75] The conference also highlighted abuses in Haiti and the ongoing hundred-man occupation in Nicaragua.

Tulio Cestero also encouraged the labor organizing of José Eugenio Kunhardt of San Pedro de Macorís. Kunhardt wrote as early as 1916 to Samuel Gompers, president of the American Federation of Labor, who championed organizing Dominican workers along AFL lines.[76] Kunhardt created a nationwide organization that defended Dominicans not only as workers but also as occupied peoples. The US military government, he said, claimed to control all docks—where most workers were employed—and tolerated no strikes, ignored labor petitions, and considered labor activism, alongside journalism, as sedition.[77] When Kunhardt threatened a general strike in 1919, the military governor judged it a ruse by Dominicans, "a prelude to active revolution to obtain the restoration of their government."[78] In late 1920, the Pan American Labor Congress in Mexico passed a resolution against the Dominican occupation.[79] By then Kunhardt, along with delegates of other Latin American labor organizations, pressured Gompers to push for immediate withdrawal, not simply an accelerated marine departure.[80] The AFL president demurred, but Wilson still called Gompers's letter "extraordinary," adding, "apparently the American Federation of Labor is as willing to rule the world as the Soviets are." Acting Secretary of State Norman Davis advised the president not to respond.[81] By 1922 Kunhardt was a full-blown internationalist, committing the sin among Dominican politicians of proposing an alliance with Haitians. He also "called upon the workingmen of Porto Rico, Cuba, and all other Latin-American countries to flock to the banner of their Dominican brothers and expel the invader."[82]

Fissures of race and class marred the landscape of transnational solidarity networks, as Marcus Garvey's United Negro Improvement Association (UNIA) demonstrated when it attempted to find adherents in both the Dominican Republic and Haiti. Dominican political elites and US occupiers both disliked Haitians and other black workers, yet sugar corporations needed the labor, and the occupation saw the corporations as agents of development. A legal tug of war thus ensued. In 1912, before the occupation, Santo Domingo required authorization to introduce non-Spanish speaking workers into the country and declared Spanish the official language. In 1919 the occupation countered by giving the *braceros* or migrant manual laborers temporary residency, nullifying the requirement for authorization and prompting migration around San Pedro, where most sugar plantations were. Since West Indians congregated there, San Pedro saw the establishment of one of the first UNIA chapters in the Caribbean in December 1919.[83] A mutual aid society "for all Negroes irrespective of nationality," the San Pedro UNIA took care of its ailing, buried its dead, and taught its illiterates.[84]

The occupation still shut it down, not because the UNIA opposed the occupation but rather because of its supposed Bolshevism and anti-white racism.[85] A white Episcopal minister, Archibald Beer, told occupation authorities, "The negroes are as jealous as can be of one another and continual trouble and contention arises," accusing them of unspecified labor agitation and, ironically, "Klu [*sic*] Klux Klan methods."[86] In September 1921 the San Pedro police burst into UNIA headquarters, arrested its leaders, and deported them for "not observing an irreproachably moral and legal conduct according to law."[87]

In Haiti the UNIA also made a brief appearance, though its activism had even less traction. A UNIA-connected business was apparently established in summer 1920, but there exists no trace of its survival.[88] For "Haitian Independence Day" on October 26, 1924, the elite's Georges Sylvain allied with the UNIA to parade banners announcing "Down with the Occupation, Long live Haiti," "Long live the Negro Improvement Society," and "Long live Government of the People, by the People, and for the People." Occupation authorities reported that 90 percent of attendees were "of the lowest class" and that in Cap-Haïtien, a town of 20,000, only 200 took part.[89] The crowds were exclusively black and urban, meaning that peasants, mulattoes, and the elite stayed away. A Cap paper, *Les Annales Capoises*, denigrated Garvey as a "workman who does not possess . . . that beautiful Latin culture, that civilization of which we are so proud and which distinguishes us from all the other Negroes in the world."[90]

Despite the discrimination they faced, African Americans played a disproportionate role in transforming nation-based anti-occupation movements into transnational crusades. Haiti was a major concern for a diverse group of African American leaders, from communists such as Cecil Briggs of the African Black Brotherhood, to capitalists such as Robert Moton of the Tuskegee Institute, to feminists such as Addie Hunton, who in 1919 founded the International Council of Women of the Darker Races (ICWDR), which investigated the lot of Haitian women and children. Those traveling, writing about, or otherwise defending Haiti were a veritable who's who of postwar black America. In 1919 Madam C. J. Walker allied with A. Philip Randolph to found the short-lived but important International League of the Darker Peoples to oppose the occupation. Margaret Murray Washington, the wife of Booker T., presided over the ICWDR. Visitors to the black republic included some of the brightest lights of the Harlem Renaissance and 1920s civil rights—Langston Hughes, Zora Neale Hurston, William Scott, and Arthur Spingarn. They linked the cause of Haitian independence to larger struggles for racial justice.[91]

"I am an American citizen, though of the colored race, which means that I am little, or not at all regarded at home; yet I cannot help to be loyal to the mother country." So wrote James Blackwood to the US chief of the Haitian Gendarmerie to denounce its abuses.[92] Blackwood's letter demonstrated that, for African Americans, patriotism meant pressuring their nation to meet its own standards. The only African American working for the occupation in Haiti, Napoleon Marshall, became a critic of the occupation and helped connect Haitians and US citizens.[93] Back in the United States, 143 members of a Harlem church asked for the recall of the US head of the occupation after reading an article in the *Courrier Haïtien*.[94] The African Episcopal Church in New York, under Reverend John Hurst, a Haitian native, also spoke out for the 500 or so New Yorkers from Haiti.[95] Through much of the 1920s, a sleeping car porter, Joseph Mirault, wrote tirelessly to US officials and prominent African Americans.[96]

The National Association for the Advancement of Colored People (NAACP) contributed most to making Haiti a US cause.[97] From 1915 on, the NAACP's co-founder, W. E. B. Du Bois, whose grandfather hailed from Haiti, editorialized against the occupation.[98] Du Bois urged Wilson to send African Americans instead of whites if an occupation had to occur and called on "we ten million Negroes" to write the president. In the following years, the NAACP denounced violations of human rights in Haiti.[99] When three Haitian delegates presented a memoir to the US government in 1921, the NAACP's white former president and last president of the Anti-Imperialist League, Moorfield Storey, was there and wrote to Secretary of State Charles Evans Hughes.[100] Haitian anti-imperialists also used the NAACP's New York office as their headquarters.[101] In 1923 Perceval Thoby and Georges Sylvain used their friendship with Spingarn, also of the NAACP, to seek justice when President Louis Borno persecuted editors.[102] The NAACP also met Haitian diplomat Dantès Bellegarde at Versailles. During Bellegarde's 1927 US visit the *Philadelphia Tribune* proclaimed, "At last Haiti has come home."[103]

Transnational networks were most effective when investigating, exposing, and advocating, all the while nurturing links with occupied peoples. These postwar anti-imperialist muckrakers appealed to a US public opinion increasingly interested in Latin America. The study of the region was spreading and institutionalizing. In 1910 a mere 5,000 US high schoolers studied Spanish. A decade later, 260,000 did. The foremost journal of the region's history, the *Hispanic American Historical Review*, first appeared in 1918, and historians such as Herbert Bolton of the University of California wrote popular books on Latin America. Interest in the region partly reflected US disillusionment with Europe as "spiritually and intellectually bankrupt" after the horror of the war. Latin America also looked to overtake Europe as a trading partner.[104] Many US citizens found themselves moving permanently to Mexico as part of what radical scholar Joseph Freeman called "an exodus of bored and unhappy Americans south of the Rio Grande."[105]

Like Dominicans abroad, muckrakers fell silent during the war, but out of disinterest or patriotism rather than censorship. Although the marines controlled cable traffic in occupied lands, journalists could have traveled to Latin America or published or reproduced occupied people's articles. In fall 1915, Haitian journalist Ernest Chauvet returned from New York complaining that the press there was "radically opposed to all protest."[106] Humorist Will Rogers first performed for President Wilson the day after the US landing in the Dominican Republic. Rogers hated the intervention but refrained from denouncing it in front of the president.[107] US publications in 1919 were largely in favor of the Haitian and Dominican occupations, expressing belief that self-government was impossible among people of color, disgust at the history of violent insurrection, fear of European intervention, and concern for protecting US investments.[108] "As for Blacks in the United States, it is useless to look to them," added Chauvet, indicating that Booker T. Washington had condoned the occupation early on.[109] More accurately, African American editors were split, reflecting their divisions on Wilson's war policy, sharpened by the administration's stick-and-carrot strategy of threatening to suspend mail privileges of some while appointing others to cushy positions.[110]

In 1916 the NAACP hired its first black field secretary, the writer and former diplomat James Weldon Johnson. With a great-grandmother from Haiti, facility in Spanish and French, formative days in France, and diplomatic experience in Venezuela and Nicaragua, Johnson felt a kinship to the region.[111] Like many

African Americans he originally thought that strategic interests justified the occupation of Haiti. But the constitution of 1918 imposed on Haiti changed his mind. Johnson also wanted to enlarge the scope of the NAACP by making it more international.[112]

Johnson headed to Haiti in March 1920 and stayed two months.[113] He talked to marines, some of whom, drunk, admitted to the worst abuses. He also met with the most prominent Haitian activists, prompting the rebirth of the Patriotic Union (UP). One Haitian later boasted that Johnson's resulting articles were "the almost literal translation" of the notes he gave the African American.[114] Johnson would stay in contact with Haitians, especially UP founder Georges Sylvain, and even helped it create a US branch in 1923.[115] Johnson's resulting exposés in *The Crisis* and *The Nation* and his speeches got the attention of the US public.[116] He made arguments that shocked the conscience of progressives— namely, that economic interests had plotted the invasion of Haiti and that atrocities and racism were rampant.

Johnson also made little-noticed arguments about political culture. Some of what he claimed was tendentious or flat-out wrong, but overall his intent was to show that Haitians had achieved a high level of civilization, with no crime, no homelessness, and no "filth and squalor," and so had nothing to learn from US invaders.[117] Often explicit was a comparison to the US South with its underdevelopment, disfranchisement, and lynching.[118]

Johnson also did as much as, if not more than, Horace Knowles to insert Haiti into presidential politics. His trip to Haiti was politically motivated since Johnson, a member of the Republican National Advisory Committee, asked for Theodore Roosevelt's advice before boarding his ship.[119] It is also likely that the Republican Party financed the trip in order to dig up a scandal against Democrats.[120] In 1920, too, the NAACP polled African Americans on their concerns and Haiti came in at number four. So to cement the alliance between the GOP and blacks, Johnson set up a meeting with candidate Warren Harding on August 9, 1920, in Marion, Ohio. The meeting prompted Harding to make a front-page speech on August 28 denouncing "the rape of Haiti and Santo Domingo" and forcing the Democrats to respond.[121]

The Nation magazine, an anti-imperialist force since the War of 1898, arguably played as weighty a role as did Johnson and the NAACP, often in collaboration with them.[122] It was one of few US publications during the war that spoke out against the Dominican intervention.[123] It helped found, along with Johnson and the UP, the Haiti-Santo Domingo Independence Society (HSDIS) and housed its headquarters in *The Nation's* New York offices. The weekly also allied with Francisco Henríquez y Carvajal in calling for congressional investigations.[124] In 1920, following the Johnson articles, some Haitians founded a newspaper called *La Nation*, which reproduced articles from the New York magazine.[125]

Like Johnson, *The Nation* warned of the foolishness of US efforts at reforming political culture. As early as December 1916 it called censorship in the Dominican Republic "un-American" and asserted that "no man is good enough to govern others without their consent."[126] Especially after 1918, when pacifist, radical, and NAACP co-founder Oswald Garrison Villard became its editor, *The Nation* portrayed Haiti, Nicaragua, and the Dominican Republic as glaring contradictions to US rhetoric about self-determination.[127]

In their efforts to portray occupations as irredeemable, *Nation* reporters sometimes distorted them. Herbert Seligmann, a freelance journalist and former NAACP staffer, sailed to Haiti along with Johnson.[128] He got permission in early April 1920 to don a marine uniform and "embed" himself with a patrol through Haiti's mountains.[129] Marines described him as devious, unethical, and biased, reporting that Seligman admitted to a marine captain his intention of "getting" the administration, all the while assuring other marines that he supported their work. When his patrol interrogated a peasant woman by putting a noose around her neck and swinging it around a branch, she repeatedly denied knowing anything and Seligmann shouted, "Shoot her God damn her, she has lied to you four times now!" The marines refused, explaining that these were only scare tactics. Perhaps Seligmann acted as an agent provocateur, goading the marines into abuses that he could then report.[130] Perhaps the marines lied about Seligmann. In any case, the article Seligmann produced stuck to the script of the anti-imperialist movement: racism, colonialism, economic self-interest, and atrocities were the essence of the occupation.[131]

The Nation was particularly meaningful in this propaganda war because it bridged the worlds of progressive whites and blacks. The magazine not only published Johnson's investigation but also publicized a 1921 visit by three Haitian delegates and published their report.[132] When the Senate investigation took place in 1921–1922, Villard and his successor, Ernest Gruening, who previously ran New York's only Spanish-language daily *La Prensa*, organized the presentation of the Haitian case.[133]

By 1920, largely because of the work of Johnson, Villard, and Gruening, the majority of US publications had swung from pro-occupation to anti-occupation.[134] Occupation officials stopped trusting visiting US journalists and began spying on them.[135] The Marine Corps also identified a newfound spunk in the Haitian press, which they explained "partly as a reflection of race disturbances and agitation in the United States."[136]

Like Don Pancho, Haiti also made an appearance at Versailles. Seven Haitians attended the parallel Pan-African Congress and attempted, unsuccessfully, to meet with Wilson and US diplomats.[137] The episode illustrated well the contrast between the two countries' fortunes: whereas Dominicans abroad were clear-eyed and supported by their hosts, Haitians were disunited, ostracized, and ineffective.

Haitians too sought allies abroad, but largely after being prompted by the transnational network. The Patriotic Union (UP), which Johnson inspired, devoted most of its energies to funding trips for its delegates. From March to May 1921, Pauléus Sannon, Sténio Vincent, and Perceval Thoby were in the United States and presented the UP's report to the US press, the Republican Party, the Department of State, and the Senate Foreign Relations Committee.[138] In August, Vincent returned to Washington to give a statement at Senate hearings.[139] Like those produced by Henríquez and Cestero, the UP report was well argued and specific, but unlike Dominican reports, it advocated quick withdrawal and no US supervision of a transition, indicating that Haitians wanted none of the reforms advocated by Washington.[140] The radical stance of the Haitian resistance earned it much less traction with US audiences.[141]

A few years later, Dantès Bellegarde, twice Haitian delegate to the League of Nations in Geneva, had an equally ineffective experience. Since Haiti was nominally sovereign, it carried on diplomacy but in a muted fashion. Bellegarde broke with the pattern, making passionate speeches in Europe, especially in 1924 and 1930, that drew more attention from Europe than any other Haitian action. Borno recalled Bellegarde so as to silence him, but Bellegarde persisted. He intoned, "So long as there is military and civil occupation of the Haitian Republic—unjustified by law and resting upon a treaty imposed by force on the Haitian people—fear and suspicion will continue to exist among the American nations."[142]

Bellegarde found some friends abroad. The League of Nations in 1924 accredited him despite protests from his own government.[143] A speech in Lyon on July 1 to a pacifist organization garnered applause for "several minutes, punctuated by cries of 'Bravo!'" and when he returned to Port-au-Prince he got more of the same.[144] Bellegarde reached out to several audiences at once, particularly by flattering the French.[145] He also appealed to the League's self-interest, saying it would bolster the League's standing by inducing the United States to join and then pressuring it to end occupations.[146] In 1930 Bellegarde returned to France to speak to the League of Nations Assembly.[147]

Haiti nonetheless failed to obtain much support from the international community. Woodrow Wilson admitted that he had occupied the republic partly because, in the rest of Latin America, Haitians, "being negroes . . . are not regarded as of the fraternity!"[148] In the 1920s Pierre Hudicourt went to the United States, Peru, and Cuba. He also attended the Fifth Pan-American Conference in Chile but was escorted out of the conference.[149] A lone State Department bureaucrat met with him, and on his return home, Hudicourt lied that the president and

secretary of state had received him.[150] In Geneva, British delegates, with US assistance, diluted a request for the immediate withdrawal of troops to instead
simply reaffirm Haiti's nominal independence.[151] The Quai d'Orsay also refused
to advocate for Haiti on the technicality that Haiti was independent and could
fend for itself.[152] Perhaps for these reasons Le Nouvelliste called Bellegarde's 1924
speech in Geneva a "moral victory."[153] It was little else.

One of the reasons for Haitians' difficulty in raising support from abroad was
the expense. The UP's major fundraising drive in 1920–1921 raised less than
$10,000.[154] Dominicans raised over ten times that in one week.[155] In 1925 the
UP began another subscription drive, but after several weeks Jacmel had raised
only $50, Aux Cayes $100, and several other towns nothing at all.[156] Haitians
also had few friends overseas. Unlike Dominicans, Haitian diplomats abroad
largely toed the line of occupied Port-au-Prince.[157] There was not yet much of
a Haitian community in New York and even less of one in Florida. Even Paris
was quiet. Only The Nation's Villard made an effort to welcome the Haitians in
1921.[158] The Courrier Haïtien took notice of the Dominicans' better organization, having an "intelligent, tireless" network in Europe and the Americas.[159]
The Courrier's editor, Joseph Jolibois Fils, spent September 1927 to March 1930
touring Latin America but encountered widespread indifference, some of it
based on language and race.[160] Costa Ricans said that "his color and his complete appearance are against him . . . he speaks Spanish so brokenly as scarcely
to be able to make himself understood . . . even those who know French in this
country have difficulty in understanding him."[161] As a US officer noted in 1922,
in contrast to the Dominican Republic, "no criticism has been directed in Latin-
America against the action of the United States Government in intervening in
Haitian affairs."[162]

Despite Haitian shortcomings, transnational activism by occupied peoples and
their US allies did prime the US public and Congress to seek answers from the
executive and the military when serious charges arose. The chain of resistance
was such that occupied peoples prompted the activism of US muckrakers and
others, who then stimulated investigations by the US government.

Investigations began when, on October 13, 1920, the US Navy made public
a letter, marked "personal and confidential" and written a full year before, by
former Marine Major General Commandant George Barnett and accompanying a report about Haitian abuses.[163] Reviewing the evidence, Barnett concluded
that "practically indiscriminate killing of natives has gone on for some time."[164] In
both the report and subsequent statements, Barnett heavily qualified his finding
and even said he thought the occupation should continue since Haitians were
childlike and unable to self-govern.[165] But the phrase "practically indiscriminate
killing" stuck with the US public. The New York Times joined The Nation and

the NAACP in calling for an inquiry. Candidate Harding demanded that the navy publish everything on Haiti, essentially forcing it to investigate.[166] Navy Secretary Daniels denied three times that he had seen Barnett's letter before its publication.[167]

The Barnett letter illustrated that investigations were an unwelcome intrusion into the insular worlds of the US Marine Corps and the US Navy, who insisted on policing their own. Their instructions on killing occupied peoples—a prisoner could be shot "to prevent his escape," for instance, and an unarmed peasant should be left alone "unless it is positively known that *he is* a bandit"—contained the giant loophole that a marine's word on who was escaping or was a bandit was final.[168] Congress was not necessarily much better unless the public kept an eye on it. In 1917 the chair and seven members of the House Naval Affairs Committee visited the Dominican military government, and after one day of observation they declared themselves satisfied and left.[169]

A first public investigation, conducted by the navy itself, demonstrated this insularity clearly. Rear Admiral Henry Mayo headed the court of inquiry, which landed in Port-au-Prince on November 8, 1920.[170] Haitians anticipated, the UP wrote, that "a work of truth and justice was at last going to be carried out." Alas,

> Not a single rule was ever established for the inquiry, and no form of procedure was indicated. The Court never made known where it would hold its sessions, on what days they would take place, whether they would be public, whether the Court itself would call in witnesses, whether the people who were acquainted with the whole thing, or who were victims of acts at the hands of the forces of Occupation, could go and testify freely before the Court, or what guaranties of safety it offered to Haitian citizens who wished to prove charges of criminal acts against officers who still had military authority, knowing well the cruelty of martial law in the country for the past five years.

Anti-occupation Haitians learned from the papers that, to their surprise, the testimony had already begun, and on the first day the first witness was President Sudre Dartiguenave, whom they considered a puppet. Others considered the act of deposing a head of state a great humiliation.[171] It also quickly became apparent that the Mayo inquiry was only interested in evidence of abuses, not in a larger discussion of occupation problems, so it largely dismissed the civilian elite, who had no eyewitness reports of abuse.[172] Mayo and his crew left on November 30 with the majority of witnesses still unheard.[173]

On December 21 the inquiry announced its conclusions—reached before it even went to Haiti. It found only two unjustified homicides and sixteen incidents of severe violence. All were "isolated acts of individuals," all duly brought to trial. It also made sure to undermine Barnett's accusations, express anger at the US media, and justify torture against "savages."[174]

Despite the Mayo whitewashing, public investigations were crucial in the development of resistance movements. Their very existence resulted from the hard work of transnational networks and so strengthened their resolve.[175] Their visits to occupied countries compelled resisters not only to clarify their arguments against occupation but also to set aside divisions and organize demonstrations, testimony, and press coverage. Witnesses whom Mayo declined to hear, for instance, published their testimonies in Haitian newspapers.[176] Unpleasant findings might have convinced occupied peoples to fight even harder for withdrawal. After Mayo, Haitians and Dominicans were suspicious of investigations, but they—joined by the US press—continued publicizing abuses and preparing for the next inquiry. The *Washington Post* called for a broader investigation to include the Dominican Republic.[177] A few months after the release of the findings, marine intelligence complained that the press "is excessive against the occupation and principally originating in result of the Mayo Court of Inquiry and propagation by the Union Patriotique."[178]

Resistance movements revisited many of these formative processes during much more comprehensive investigations headed by Medill McCormick, chair of the Senate Select Committee on Haiti and Santo Domingo. The committee held months of hearings in Washington starting in August 1921, then in late November and December went to Haiti and the Dominican Republic for several days; then, from February to June 1922, it heard more testimony in Washington, some of it from the invaded. The hearings included representatives of groups who both supported and opposed the occupations—even firebreathers like Jolibois Fils.[179]

The testimonies also prompted coverage from the US press, advocacy groups such as the NAACP, and the occupied press, which printed almost every word of the hearings.[180] Almost all observers at the time agreed that the work of James Weldon Johnson and the NAACP, *The Nation*, the speeches of Harding and members of Congress, and the UP's visit to Washington in spring 1921 had prompted McCormick to correct the mistakes of Mayo.[181] The Cestero group in New York City set up a Dominican Republic Information Bureau at 280 Broadway that churned out press releases, as did the NAACP.[182] Ernest Angell, a US citizen, represented the HSDIS, the NAACP, and the UP in Haiti and not only testified but arranged for others to do so.

The coming of the committee to countries under occupation prompted all stakeholders on the ground to prepare for a propaganda showdown. The military government drew up lists of allegations and investigated all possible witnesses so as to accurately answer—or deftly dodge—difficult questions.[183] Dominican Military Governor Samuel Robison even warned Knowles, in Santo Domingo for the hearings, "to refrain from creating enmity toward the United States or the Military Government by his speeches or activities."[184] In 1921 Ernest Gruening, fluent in French and well traveled in Haiti, went there to screen those scheduled to testify before McCormick, mediated between Haitian opposition groups, and served as a witness.[185] When the committee landed in Port-au-Prince they were met by 10,000 Haitians carrying forty-two banners, eight of them in English and suggested by Gruening (see Fig. 11.1).[186] When the senators moved to the Dominican capital, a demonstration of five to six thousand met them.[187] To make sure the poor were not left out, the Dominican *Listín Diario* offered to pay any witness's travel expenses to the capital.[188]

All in all, Dominicans seemed better prepared than Haitians. To be sure, committee members were better disposed toward Dominicans if only because of their race. But Knowles also earned his salary by testifying himself and being present for every statement given by a Dominican. He may have coached them, too, because their arguments were shrewdly focused on diplomatic and financial

Figure 11.1 Haitians, including schoolchildren, welcoming the McCormick Committee with forty-two banners. The mobilization was massive but somewhat diffuse, as the variety of themes suggests. From the Edmond Mangonès Collection, published in Georges Corvington, *Port-au-Prince au cours des ans.* Vol. 5: *La capitale d'Haïti sous l'occupation, 1915–1922* (Port-au-Prince: Henri Deschamps, 1984).

causes of discontent that would appeal to US senators and the press. Moreover, almost all Dominican witnesses began their testimony with a suspiciously similar statement of opposition to the occupation while at the same time stating their experience living in the United States, if any, and/or their admiration for some US occupiers and/or US institutions and ideals.[189] Haitians, by contrast, mostly revisited episodes of abuse that the Mayo inquiry had already dismissed, at times embellishing with lies or exaggerations.[190] Senators and other US officials tended to conclude that all Haitians were liars, so they required indisputable evidence for all allegations.

Revealingly, most witnesses glossed over the argument that occupied peoples had nothing to learn from their occupiers' political culture. When senators asked Gruening if Haitians would meet a withdrawal with yet another revolution, he contradicted himself, first saying they preferred "their own tyranny to alien tyranny," then promising they had "learned their lesson" and would "adhere strictly to constitutional forms." Even more ominously, "one of the best-educated men on the island" explained the spoils system to visiting scholar Carl Kelsey.

> Those of us who have been trained have never been trained to work physically. We do not believe in it. We have no respect for it. We have to go into the Government service. . . . It does not make any difference whether the lowest type of man gets into office or the highest type in this country; the moment he gets in and appoints his assistants there are many more disappointed people than satisfied ones. And the disappointed ones immediately begin to counsel together to know how they can get rid of him. That has been true all through our history, and it will be true the minute you leave.

Kelsey, who had investigated both Hispaniola occupations, suggested that the marines should stay in the Dominican Republic "if the reasons that led us to go in there in 1916 were the ones stated. We have not yet developed a functioning government in Santo Domingo."[191]

Yet the testimony taken in Hispaniola, in contrast to the Mayo inquiry, still impacted investigators. Committee member Atlee Pomerene said his colleagues and he were "very much distressed" to learn of so many abuses.[192] "We sent here very poorly prepared agents," McCormick confided to a Frenchman in Port-au-Prince.[193] While still in Santo Domingo, Pomerene wrote to Secretary of State Hughes confirming a widespread "change of sentiment" from pro- to anti-occupation, coming about two years after the marines landed in each country.[194]

While the commission was in Santo Domingo, Francisco Henríquez y Carvajal set foot on Dominican soil for the first time in five years. The presence of a returning exiled president further legitimated the Dominican cause in contrast to the Haitian one. In Monte Cristi and Puerto Plata, delegations showered Don Pancho with flowers while the national anthem played in the background.[195] In the capital, Henríquez stood on a balcony of the city hall to oversee processions and in the following days virtually held court for prominent visitors.[196]

Yet anti-occupation activists were not as united as they seemed. Fissures especially appeared among Dominicans, who could taste the coming withdrawal. Rumors abounded that Knowles, the agent of Henríquez, kept the partisans of Federico Velázquez from testifying to the committee. A handbill circulated accusing Henríquez of being "against any plan or plans other than the reinstatement of the Government of 1916"—that is, his return as president.[197]

As the senatorial committee's work came to a close, Dominicans swiftly proceeded with negotiations for withdrawal, so the committee, at the request of State, withheld its Dominican report.[198] On June 26, 1922, however, it made its Haiti recommendations. Those expecting withdrawal should not have been surprised to be disappointed. McCormick had written in *The Nation* in 1920 that US policy in Haiti had been a "failure" but also that "We are there, and in my judgment we ought to stay there for twenty years."[199] President Harding, also writing to *The Nation*, confirmed.[200] McCormick identified the problem as merely one of maladministration—there were too many US cooks in Haiti's kitchen. He recommended appointing the present head marine, Brigadier General John Russell, as high commissioner directly answerable to the State Department, thus handing to State authority over all US matters in Haiti.[201]

To prevent this colonialism masquerading as reorganization, the National Popular Government League (NPGL), an ally of the NAACP, and the Foreign Policy Association (FPA), a grouping of twenty-four prominent US lawyers including Moorfield Storey, launched a last ditch attempt at convincing Secretary Hughes to evacuate Haiti. Gruening wrote the FPA report. Reflecting elite US sentiment, the NPGL report abjured the very notion of political reformism because the United States had "enough of racial troubles at home without seeking to infinitely multiply them by gratuitously assuming the task of regulating the affairs of the 30,000,000 colored and mixed peoples of the Caribbean region and Mexico."[202] Another politically popular argument was that the estimated $50 million already spent in the previous six years in Hispaniola could be better spent on domestic issues. Overall the NPGL argued that imperialism was contrary to US national identity.[203]

Other denunciations poured in. The Anti-Imperialist League of Boston and the Progressive Friends made statements against the Dominican and Haitian occupations.[204] The HSDIS suggested that a civilian, perhaps James Weldon Johnson, should be high commissioner.[205] Weeks later, on May 1, Senator Borah delivered a speech at New York's Carnegie Hall that was written by Knowles at an event organized by Gruening. Knowles reserved box seats for journalists and

Latin American ambassadors. In addition to the 3,500 in attendance, radio stations broadcast the speech live nationwide.[206] Speaking of Hispaniola as a whole, Borah warned presciently, "We are in to stay unless American opinion brings us out." The *New York Times* called the speech "sensational."[207] Meanwhile, in the Senate, William King tried to stop the confirmation of Russell as high commissioner in Haiti.[208]

The main reason the Dominicans moved toward independence while the Haitians did not was the judgment by US policymakers and observers that Haitians, primarily because of their race, had a long way to go to absorb modern political culture. In typical remarks, the Latin-American Division urged the Department of State

> to distinguish at once between the Dominicans and the Haitians. The former, while in many ways not advanced far enough on the average to permit the highest type of self-government, yet have a preponderance of white blood and culture. The Haitians on the other hand are negro for the most part, and, barring a very few highly educated politicians, are almost in a state of savagery and complete ignorance. The two situations thus demand different treatment.[209]

The McCormick Committee agreed that "early withdrawal of or drastic reduction in the American marine occupation force in Haiti would be followed certainly by brigandage and revolution."[210] W. E. B. Dubois was furious: "If ever a Senator deserved defeat for betrayal of the Negro race, Medill McCormack [*sic*] is that man."[211]

As a result, Haiti degenerated into a pseudo-colony. Its undemocratic Council of State chose as president Louis Borno, a former minister who pledged closer collaboration with High Commissioner Russell. US officials openly regretted not having installed a military government from 1915 on, having secured greater loans, or having sufficiently organized their own treaty officials. And they blamed Haitian resistance for obstructing almost all their projects. The solution was typical occupation reformism—to impose stability and development against the will of the invaded.[212]

While in the early 1920s US policymakers were not ready to give up on occupations, part of the public was. This anti-imperialist US public was not swayed by arguments about race or geopolitical self-interest, nor was it dissuaded from caring about the suffering of those under occupation by investigators who denied all but the most fastidiously documented abuses. For this small but increasing slice of the US public, moral arguments won the day. These arguments held that the very practice of occupation, in every case, brought about evils incompatible with the identity of the United States.

A 1924 article published in the *Atlantic Monthly* by Samuel Guy Inman, a missionary who had traveled with the marines to Haiti and the Dominican Republic, proved a landmark in the evolution of the US public's thinking about empire.[213] The article posited not only that imperialism was contrary to US values but also that US exceptionalism was a farce, that US values did not rise above base imperial practices. Inman also emphasized foreign public opinion. "We are piling up hatreds, suspicions, records for exploitation and destruction of sovereignty in Latin America, such as have never failed in all history to react in war, suffering and defeat of high moral and spiritual ideals." Such blowbacks were "not worth the surrender of American principles, the bowing before materialistic gods, the hatreds and the sacrifice of the spiritual."[214] Some Department of State officials called Inman a "Bolshevist" and tried to get his article pulled before publication, and the United Fruit Company threatened to sue. The article ran anyway and had a massive impact throughout Latin America.[215] Haiti's Pierre Hudicourt, who met Inman in Chile, read it and responded by expressing "hope and confidence" that at least someone in the United States cared about his country.[216]

The Department chose Sumner Welles as the best person to respond to Inman. Welles was a transitional figure in the abandonment of occupation as a US policy for the hemisphere. In 1920, at twenty-eight, Welles had become the acting chief of the Latin-American Division. Like his friend Franklin Roosevelt, he bridged two worlds as a firm believer in US exceptionalism and practitioner of imperialism yet also a progressive liberal internationalist.[217] Dominican Fabio Fiallo called him "an official endowed with rare sagacity and subtle skill."[218] Under Welles, the new Latin-American Division understood that the hemisphere's increasing solidarity against intervention harmed US commercial and geopolitical interests.[219]

Welles's response to Inman reflected his transitional status. He resorted to some shopworn arguments, such as the one that anti-imperialism represented only a "small group" of US opinion and "a small proportion of the inhabitants of any of the republics on this Continent." "Ninety per cent" of anti-imperialists, he added rather cruelly, were those in the United States "who promote racial or religious antagonism for personal or political ends." Yet, somewhat contradictorily, Welles posited that the United States was becoming less imperialistic: "dollar diplomacy" was in decline, US troops would leave Nicaragua after 1924, and Washington was mediating rather than invading. Most important, Welles reaffirmed the US willingness to occupy as long as failures of political culture remained. The United States wanted to "strengthen the foundations of constitutional and stable government" and would remain "until certain of these countries have developed a firm tradition of orderly, constitutional government."[220]

The greater openness to world criticism at State coincided with an upsurge in anti-occupation activity among the Dominican middle and upper classes. It was they, not the Henríquez and Cestero expatriates, who in 1922 secured the Hughes-Peynado agreement for withdrawal, which incorporated few of the political cultural reforms instituted by the occupation and instead legitimated the traditional practices that had helped bring about the occupation. US negotiators were fully aware of this. In a preview of other occupations, they shook their heads at the persistence of the old ways, washed their hands of the dark days to come, and patted themselves on the back for deferring to "public opinion."

It was not nationalism but the economic self-interest of the elite that brought about definitive movement toward withdrawal. The imposition, relatively late in the occupation, of the property tax drew fire from the elite, especially in the Cibao region, which had been theretofore relatively quiescent.[221] Protests continued even after the occupation revised the tax to eliminate all its progressive features and levy all lands at the same 0.5 percent rate.[222] In February 1922 one landowner predicted countless foreclosures, after which "we shall be reduced from property-owners to mere wage earners, the black wave of civilization which has wrought so much evil in Santo Domingo continuing mercilessly on its way."[223] Merchants also complained of the sweeping tariff reductions on US goods coming into the country while increased tariffs weighed on Dominican exports. "At this present moment," wrote the Chamber of Commerce, Industry and Agriculture of San Pedro in late 1921, "the planters and merchants are in a worse economic condition than ever."[224] Future President Juan Bosch recalled that his father José had to close down his import-export business in 1921 due to the tariffs.[225] The south, more dependent on global economic conditions, had it even worse. The price of sugar plummeted from an astronomical 22 cents per pound at the end of the war in Europe to 1.8 cents per pound, less than its selling price. "Unless sugar sells here at about 3 cents," wrote the military governor, "the whole southern half of the island will gradually become bankrupt."[226] In 1920, sugar producers lost $1,125,000.[227] As a result, merchants went from supporting to opposing the marines, and when the marines lost the merchants, they lost the occupation.

Even if he became president again, warned Don Pancho in December 1920 from his exile in Washington, "the struggle of 1916 will begin again. Those who led then are still there, ready to reengage in their pettiness and despicable acts."[228] Horacio Vázquez, Federico Velázquez, Elías Brache—the three political leaders who represented the national extension of regional caudillismo—indeed still controlled the parties and their voting machines. They no longer split among them the bulk of military force—that was now the Dominican National Guard's (GND) prerogative. But party heads assumed that development to be temporary and were singularly focused on regaining national office and redistributing its spoils.

The first glimpse of movement toward withdrawal came on October 27, 1919, when State ordered the military governor, Thomas Snowden, against his will, to form an Advisory Council of prominent Dominicans on how to transition out of occupation. The council included political figures such as Velázquez and Jacinto de Castro but also the widely respected Archbishop Adolfo Nouel and prominent lawyer Francisco Peynado, well liked among US diplomats. Henríquez had proposed something similar and was surprised that State now adopted his plan. State invited him to join the council, but, in a major misstep, he refused.[229]

The Advisory Council's recommendations stated that their purpose was to rewrite "laws regarding political organization that constituted the joint cause in a very great degree of our revolutionary upheavals." To avoid "a return of personalism," they recommended registering every voter and disenfranchising the military. They suggested handing back to municipalities "that independence given them by the Constitution" and making conscription voluntary so as to prevent caudillos from raising armies. They also recommended preventing fraud in government finances. Finally, they asked for the end of censorship and US provost courts.[230]

Snowden, declaring this reasonable advice "unadvisable," said that "the time was not ripe" for such reforms. He instead proposed a loan of $5 million, to which the council agreed in principle, but then it rejected the loan by putting short-term class interest first, saying the loan would likely increase property taxes.[231] The impasse drew the ire of the press against the council, to which Snowden responded by tightening censorship. Two months after its formation, the Advisory Council resigned en masse.[232] The State Department judged that "political motives dominate to a great extent [the council's] members, also each being, if not active, passive aspirants [to the] presidency."[233] Snowden himself blamed Cestero and Henríquez who "stirred up" some "very vicious" agents in Santo Domingo.[234] "Entire affair another instance of inability majority Dominicans work in unselfish harmony even under present conditions for public welfare," State cabled.[235]

A month after the Advisory Council quit, Fabio Fiallo, Américo Lugo, and other writers and activists formed the National Dominican Union (UND). It drew "the almost unanimity of DOMINICANS from all corners of the island," reported the French chargé, claiming 3,000 members within a month.[236] The UND may have held the potential for reforming Dominican political culture, but instead it called exclusively for "pure and simple" withdrawal and placed no trust in diplomacy. It implored all Dominican provincial governors to resign their positions, and two of them did.[237] The UND also thwarted a proposed trip to Washington to form a second Advisory Council.[238] Individual Dominicans and US citizens suddenly stopped socializing, the latter losing their invitations to clubs.[239] "The schism between Dominicans and the military government is complete," wrote the French chargé in early April.[240]

Francisco Henríquez y Carvajal then entered the domestic fray by instigating Patriotic Week, a successful fundraiser held in June 1920. A group of women from Santiago organized artistic and literary events in all the country's main towns to appeal to both men and women. Dominicans read poems, sang patriotic odes, put on dances, showed movies, and auctioned off jewelry, flags, money, clothes, dishes, cigarettes, toys, and chickens. Organizers capped the week with a tremendous Catholic mass.[241] An aura of Catholic celebration and sacrifice surrounded the entire week. Pledges ran as high as $300,000 and the UND eventually collected about $115,000.[242] Marines circulated rumors about missing funds, graft, and arms purchases, but found no hard evidence.[243] The funds went to sustain the propaganda of Cestero in New York, fund his trip to South America with Federico and Max, and hire Horace Knowles. Patriotic Week's success again marked crucial differences between the Dominican and Haitian resistance: Dominicans were wealthier, (somewhat) more united, and more transnational.

For a time, the flow of money placed Henríquez on an equal plane with other Dominican political voices and allowed him to shape the international image of the Republic. The UND meanwhile represented internal radical demands. *Horacistas* behind Vásquez, the most redoubtable political machine, still held sway among armed factions. The late summer of 1920 was the opportunity for these three actors to come to a power-sharing agreement. The marines admitted that the groups' interests were mutually reinforcing: every time more journalists from the UND were arrested, more Latin American pressure piled onto Washington, helping Don Pancho. Instead, the Dominicans exacerbated their differences. While Henríquez wanted to continue the "diplomatic drive," Vásquez said he wanted "more drastic action under a joint organization"—that is, demands for withdrawal followed by war.[244] The UND, meanwhile, refused to back down from its "pure and simple" slogan.

In the absence of Dominican agreement, President Wilson proposed a new plan in December 1920, written by Sumner Welles: a commission to write up amendments to the constitution and the election law and have them ratified by both the military government and a Dominican convention. For its rationale, the Wilson Plan cited "the substantial accomplishment" of the occupation but failed to mention that these accomplishments—the protection of the country from Europe, the stability of its finances—had been achieved three years earlier.[245] Secretary of State Colby stated a more likely explanation—"the increasing agitation among the Dominicans during the last two years for the right of self-government, and the anxiety expressed by the governments of other American republics as to our intentions in Santo Domingo."[246]

The Wilson Plan, however, satisfied almost no one. Occupation officials and pro-occupation Dominicans found it "premature." Activists opposed it because the military governor would have to endorse the Dominican code before the convention.[247] Henríquez disliked US supervision of the Dominican constitution and again refused to be on the proposed commission. The only Dominican who liked it was Velázquez.[248] Vásquez, the most powerful man in the country, vacillated and, "beyond a reasonable doubt," according to the marines, funded insurrectionists such as Ramón Nateras. As one intelligence officer explained, insurrectionists "will be able to pose as heroes and patriots for they can point to the fact that they were conducting active operations against the occupation even to the end. As a remuneration they will accept positions with the government."[249]

"We all awaited with anxiety the advent of Harding who, during his electoral campaign, had morally obligated himself by the most explicit declarations to rectify the arbitrary conduct of his predecessor in Santo Domingo and Haiti."[250] So recalled Fabio Fiallo, who soon shared his disillusion with fellow Dominicans—and even more with Haitians. To be sure, Harding was no moralistic interventionist like Wilson.[251] He had no intention of starting new occupations and believed rather in the natural harmony of US-Latin American trade. Once president, in 1922 he removed US troops from Camagüey, leading to the normalization of relations with Cuba.[252] But his boldest move in the Dominican Republic was to replace Snowden with the only slightly less intransigent Rear Admiral Samuel S. Robison.[253] Navy Secretary Josephus Daniels wanted "no great change in Dominican affairs even under the new administration."[254]

Inside Dominican politics, meanwhile, there was rapid movement toward ostracizing Henríquez—a development crucial not only to who would be president after withdrawal but also, more profoundly, to reaffirming the rejection of US political reformism. Skeptical Dominicans spoke of the end of occupation as a *rancho* or fixed horse race in which the marines came first, followed closely by *concho primo*, or personalist politics. Third was Don Pancho. Henríquez was indeed losing his grip on a fast-moving process. According to him, Vásquez spread malicious rumors that Henríquez intended to trade Samaná Bay for US withdrawal.[255] Anti-occupation groups failed to consult him before filing protests. "Above the principles that each sustains, passions and the abandonment of patriotic interest always prevail," bemoaned Don Pancho.[256] Disillusioned and desperate, by March he switched stances and aligned with the *pura y simples*.[257] In mid-April Washington abandoned the Wilson Plan.

On June 14, 1921, Military Governor Robison announced a revamped plan for withdrawal. It required that Dominicans ratify all acts of the military government, accept a $2.5 million loan, extend the US receivership to internal revenues, retain US officers in the GND, and hold elections under US tutelage on August 13 in exchange for withdrawal in eight months. The Harding Plan abandoned the Wilson Plan's right to intervene.

If the Dominican political chiefs were divided, the Harding Plan united them, at least in rejecting it. The new Advisory Committee rebuked the plan "as a whole."[258] The press did so, too, as did youth and women's groups.[259] One governor resigned.[260] "Down with Americans!" "Eradicate the White Blood of the Republic," and "To the Devil with the Khaki Uniform," shouted San Franciscans at an anti-plan rally.[261] Five days after the announcement, 3,000 marched to Robison's residence to express their rage.[262] On July 3, delegations from throughout the Cibao met and adopted a common script. In the week or so that followed, dozens of municipal councils sent written protests to Santo Domingo, all with only slight variations in the wording.[263] "More United Than Ever," crowed the *Listín Diario* about Dominican activists.[264]

The occupation feared chaos. It forbade government employees from engaging in political activism and fired those who signed petitions.[265] In mid-August US troops whipped Dominicans who threw stones at them.[266]

The UND formed the Committee for Electoral Abstention, whose slogan was, tellingly, "Elections mean slavery and death for the Fatherland."[267] Party chiefs, though not *pura y simples*, instructed followers to obey the call and abstain.[268] One pamphlet, called the "Lugo Protest" and signed by seventy-five Dominicans, breathlessly enumerated their grievances, denouncing the

> pirates who, under orders from the filibuster [Admiral William] Caperton landed on sacred Dominican soil, taking possession of it, supported only by machine guns and bayonets, killing, burning, reconcentrating entire regions of unhappy peasants, robbing them of their lands and their water for the benefit of Yankee corporations, weighing down the people with terrible taxes, squandering and sacking the treasury into the most horrible bankruptcy, eliminating public education throughout the country, and, finally, realizing all sorts of iniquitous assaults, before the eyes of the entire world, which contemplates it, shocked.[269]

The Dominican political class's response to the Harding Plan was much more immediate, consensual, and implacable than it had been to the Wilson Plan. Dominicans characterized that response as "spontaneous," saying they had enough of US proposals that assumed a continuation of US power over Dominican military and financial matters.[270] Yet scholar Carl Kelsey suspected that the political chiefs knew of the plan in advance and prepared their response. He may also have been correct that the chiefs feared that a successful Harding Plan would associate Don Pancho with the departure of the Yankees, ensuring his return as president.[271] The Harding Plan, after all, called for elections in which no incumbent could ensure fraud and did not specify who would eventually control the GND. As a friend wrote to Cestero, the GND was sure to be another prize for the parties to covet. "While Horacio Vásquez and Fed[erico] Velázquez live," he despaired, "it will be impossible to realize such a well-meaning plan."[272]

One thing was certain. The response to the Harding Plan was the urban Dominican resistance as its best organized—presenting its strongest arguments, streamlining its message, and enforcing unanimity. The *Listín Diario*, usually a calming influence, published lists of prominent Dominicans and called on them to publicly denounce the plan. Several of these men privately agreed with it, the French chargé reported, but could not say so in public. "To adhere to the 'Harding Plan,'" he explained, "is to be banished from the Republic; to abstain is to betray!"[273] Allegedly the party chiefs originally agreed to meet with Robison to discuss the plan but then backed off in the face of public outcry.[274] Six weeks after the occupation proposed the Harding Plan, it suspended the elections proposed in it.

After the Harding debacle, the Dominican press painted Don Pancho, still in Washington, as out of touch.[275] Manuel de Jesús Lluveres, a true believer in the reformism of occupation who worked for its Ministry of Interior and Police, asked the chiefs to propose alternatives to the Harding Plan but reported "a negative result. The leaders instead of undertaking the patriotic work have given themselves to reorganize their parties and to hold certain positions politically that may assure advantages to them in the future."[276] One US officer noted a glimmer of good news for his peers: "Political activities are becoming more and more a campaign of some Dominicans against other Dominicans, thereby causing less agitation against Americans."[277] "As much as Dominicans distrust Americans, they distrust one another more," observed another.[278] Washington followed prevailing political winds. In July 1921 Sumner Welles told Henríquez that he would no longer discuss Dominican affairs through him but would do so directly with party leaders in Santo Domingo.[279] The following month he stopped talking to Knowles.[280]

The culmination of Dominican counterproposals was a convention held from December 3 to December 9, 1921, in Puerto Plata. Henríquez presided and Vásquez signed on to its documents, as did two other party chiefs. Also represented were the *pura y simples*, women, lawyers, church and Masonic leaders, and the press. While they reiterated their rejection of the Harding Plan, delegates planned for a significant democratization of Dominican politics by eliminating presidential reelection, creating a vice-presidency, ensuring representation for minorities, holding elections at the provincial level, and increasing municipal authority. They also vowed to write basic laws for all branches of government.[281] Henríquez wrote to Cestero that Puerto Plata had written a page of Dominican history "impossible to erase."[282]

The impossible occurred. Dominican chiefs opposed the very holding of the Puerto Plata convention.[283] Vásquez's party quickly reassured Robison that "his signature did not mean that he was in accord with all of the resolutions adopted."[284] Velázquez did not even show up, claiming, "The Political Parties are those meant to intervene directly in everything related to the Restoration of the free and sovereign Republic, because it is they, in reality, who represent the different opinions of the Dominican people."[285] Francisco Peynado was also absent. These men and others instead met on December 30 with Robison.[286] As a result, reported Santiago's La Información, "partisan committees and sub-committees are being set up, with the immediate goal of seeing to the interests of the CAUDILLO rather than the interests of the enslaved Fatherland."[287]

Don Pancho gave up. He had remained in Washington until he had only a few hundred dollars. International donors promised to sustain his campaign but none came through. Henríquez could not inspire anyone to organize another Patriotic Week. He had cataracts in his eyes and suffered facial paralysis, treated with electric shock therapy.[288] In early February 1922 he returned to Cuba for good.[289]

Secretary Hughes, meanwhile, dug in his heels. He insisted that occupation acts be ratified since property had changed hands and bonds had been issued under those acts. If the marines simply withdrew, all law would collapse.[290] Robison further explained the ratification of acts as a technicality—a Dominican congress could always rescind any law but government would keep functioning in the meantime—and despaired that no "thinking men" could be found to grasp this reality.[291] In February 1922 Hughes threatened to continue the occupation indefinitely.[292] On the 23rd Robison proposed to replace the military mission with a 600-man legation guard. The Dominicans rejected the proposal outright.[293] The occupation was partly stalling so that it could finish building a few major roads to ensure a freer market and the ability of the GND to repress regional rebellions.[294] Eventually the occupation built 240 miles of first- and second-class roads and 155 miles of third-class roads.[295]

Negotiations in Washington cleared their own figurative road to disoccupation. Welles—to whom Hughes later ceded "the principal credit" in these negotiations—played the chiefs ably during negotiations.[296] He approached them all simultaneously since "so long as one of the important leaders holds out, his political opponents will be afraid to accept the plan proposed for fear of the political effect which such action would have, when one of their opponents has refused to accept it on alleged patriotic grounds."[297] Welles was also tough. On March 6, he and Hughes rescinded the Harding Plan and soon after approved a $2.5 million loan for the occupation. The loan pulled the Republic out of the financial abyss but, as Knowles remarked, burdened Dominicans with an outrageous 19 percent rate pocketed by Wall Street. Had they negotiated on their own, Dominicans could have gotten 4 percent.[298] Welles's tough stance was a bluff; he badly wanted negotiations. But it worked.[299] On March 27, 1922, Vásquez and Velázquez announced that their parties would make counterproposals.[300]

Independently, Francisco Peynado, a prominent lawyer who spoke English, had contacts in Washington, and had worked on land issues with the occupation, also began serious talks with State.[301] He had been Don Pancho's minister of finance in 1916 and also enjoyed the blessing of the chiefs as a neutral figure. In March 1922, through Senators McCormick and Pomerene, Peynado began negotiations with US officials and members of Congress.[302] "It's useless to pretend that the Americans will depart Santo Domingo vanquished, convicted of having committed any crime or even error in having occupied our country," he concluded. They would never agree to a return of Henríquez as president. Washington was also unmovable on the loan and the ratification of occupation acts.[303]

The Hughes-Peynado agreement that resulted from these talks was a compromise between US and Dominican positions. Washington won the argument for a larger loan and road-building program, in addition to continuing supervision over finances. Dominicans won a provisional government before elections under occupation and scrapped any kind of military mission. Despite Peynado's involvement, the accord was a party construction. Henríquez was not invited to the negotiations. Velázquez held his own talks in Washington in March, independent of Peynado.[304] He, Vásquez, and Brache, who by mid-1922 headed the three main parties, went to Washington in mid-June to sign the accord. As a measure of the chiefs' power, suddenly all the major newspapers lauded the accord.[305] Tulio Cestero, now a newspaper editor in Cuba, also accepted Hughes-Peynado.[306] The only holdouts, it seemed, were those not associated with parties: the Henríquez brothers and the *pura y simples*.[307]

Lugo's criticism of the process as "three of four citizens . . . exploiting the personalism of the political parties" was fair warning.[308] Welles himself noticed the persistence of personalism when he visited the Dominican Republic in July 1922 to sell the project to Dominican audiences.[309] "In the country districts," he explained, "the people are almost entirely illiterate and vote in accordance with the instructions which they may receive from the local bosses, who are, without exception, affiliated with one of the major parties." To Welles, however, this was evidence of Dominican democracy, not the lack of it.[310]

The politicking that accompanied campaigns in the last two years of the occupation was the final evidence that Dominicans had absorbed few of the so-called lessons that US occupiers wished to impart. In mid-1922 this was not obvious.

Hughes-Peynado called for a provisional president, and the party chiefs, in a rare consensual move, agreed to appoint Juan Bautista Vicini Burgos on October 21, 1922. Vicini's main function was to oversee the presidential election, which took place on March 15, 1924. After a few shifts, the major parties gelled. Vásquez headed the National Party, Velázquez the Progressive Party, and Peynado the National Coalition.

The campaign showed that, in four distinct ways, political culture was largely unchanged. First, Dominican leaders still proved incompetent administrators. Welles was constantly frustrated by the delays in implementing Hughes-Peynado, including an inexplicable five-month delay between designing and signing the election law. Even then, the party chiefs, "too much occupied with their own political interests," had made "no effort . . . to obtain any part of the physical material required for registration of the elections such as ballots, registration certificates, etc."[311] At another point Welles gathered party aides to appoint a new minister of the interior. They began with a list of no fewer than 250 names and agreed on only two, both of whom refused to serve.[312] Welles stayed in the country for much of the campaign to micromanage these problems.

Second, Dominican political identities still did not reflect any program, ideology, or loyalty to any group of voters such as peasants or artisans. Instead, they remained singularly concerned with personal self-interest. Peynado, long touting himself as a disinterested party, instead ran for president. In December 1922, as the campaigns kicked off, Velázquez himself laid out the political failures of his compatriots—"the lack of preparation of our people for civil struggles; the partisanship that reaches considerable proportions while these struggle go on; the desire for rebellion and fits of passion that persist deep in the soul of our masses."[313] Yet, like the others, he proposed nothing beyond the usual call for unity—behind his candidacy.

Third, the constant threat of the return of violence and fraud hung over the electoral process. "The political situation is bad," wrote the US legation in the summer of 1923 as political leaders imported arms and twelve men were killed in "political rows."[314] The Dominican National Police (PND)—the new GND—seized 600 revolvers and rifles.[315]

Fourth, presidential candidates harmed their nationalist credentials by continuing to seek the backing of Washington privately while publicly rejecting it. Their obsequiousness was partly Welles's fault. He pledged to all parties—and reiterated in private—his neutrality in elections, while insinuating that Washington had favorites and pariahs in mind. In April 1923, as former caudillo Desiderio Arias considered joining the Velázquez party, Welles feared that Arias would monopolize patronage appointments if the Progressives won. So in a delicate conversation with Velázquez, Welles restated his position of non-interference but then added that Washington obviously disliked Arias just as Velázquez used to.[316]

In the end the campaign revolved around trumped-up accusations of pro-Yankee dispositions rather than platforms for future change.[317] In April 1923 Vásquez and Velázquez accused Peynado of being the candidate of the occupation and of taking funds from sugar corporations or *ingenios*. They falsely charged that Peynado's wife was a US citizen who could not speak Spanish.[318] Even the British chargé believed Peynado had US support, claiming he received as much as $100,000 from the *ingenios* to buy votes.[319] Américo Lugo breathed that same fire up to the eve of the election, calling Peynado "a friend who speaks English, an experienced lawyer and counselor for important North American corporations interested in this country; a well-to-do *business-man*, in sum."[320]

The winner of the election was undisputed: the Vásquez-Velázquez alliance swept 70 percent of the votes, with Vásquez as presidential candidate and promising 30 percent of spoils to his new running mate.[321] Vásquez then welshed on his promise, gave jobs to friends, and fired competent bureaucrats.[322] After the election, Dominican party operatives refused to show up at meetings and failed to draft the laws to which they had agreed. Cabinet members were dismissed for misconduct or improper use of funds.[323] Guards went underpaid. US scholar Charles Chapman, in Hispaniola in December 1924, worried that "the story of the past six months would seem to indicate that the Dominicans have learned nothing from their long era of loss of independence. . . . As many as 80% of former government employees ha[ve] been removed and replaced by personal or political favorites of the administration. Still, there are not jobs enough, so new posts are being created."[324]

On July 12, 1924, US troops lowered the Stars and Stripes at Fortress Ozama in Santo Domingo before a jubilant Dominican crowd and then left the country (see Fig. 11.2). In Port-au-Prince *Le Nouvelliste* observed this as a most egregious instance of a double standard of the era of occupations.[325] The United States had intervened at both ends of Hispaniola less than a decade earlier for ostensibly the same strategic, financial, and political reasons, but now declared that the strategic and financial no longer applied. Political instability continued to haunt Haiti enough to justify the occupation. The injustice was not simply due to US racism but also demonstrated the United States' inability to recognize that political instability also continued in the Dominican Republic. Within a half-dozen years, the PND's new commander, Rafael Trujillo, would rise to end that instability and install one of the most ruthless and personalistic dictatorships in the history of Latin America.

Figure 11.2 Dominicans raise their flag on July 12, 1924, the last day of the occupation.
Folder "Dominican Republic: Santo Domingo (early 1900s)," USMC Historical Division,
Marine Corps Base, Quantico, Va.

One of the unsolved questions of US occupations in Latin America is
why occupiers acceded to self-government when they believed occupied
people were not ready for it. In late 1921 Marine Colonel L. H. Moses enumerated the limitations to Dominicans' ability "to maintain a just and stable
government":

> the large percentage of illiteracy and the backward state of education in
>   general;
> the unsatisfactory administration of justice in the courts;
> an irresponsible[,] conscienceless and large uncontrolled press;
> the universal lack of mutual trust and confidence between Dominican
>   leaders of all classes, and the personal ambitions of these leaders;
> the poor organization and discipline and the uncertain loyalty of the
>   military and police forces as at present constituted;
> the low standard of public ethics, and the lack of any effective
>   condemnation of moral turpitude by public opinion;

the unwillingness to assume responsibility and the inability to firmly
  grasp the essential facts of a situation so characteristic of the great
  majority of Dominican leaders;
the inherent weakness of the political structure due to the fact that
  inasmuch as the civil governors now possess little real authority the
  Ayuntamientos are largely independent of any control except such as
  can be exercised by the Central Government.[326]

Even if exaggerated, these were massive shortcomings, almost all connected to political culture. The occupation was supposed to correct these but several factors derailed it. Some, such as the sharply declining market for agricultural goods after the war, were beyond its control. Others, such as personalism and regionalism, proved resilient. Yet invaders and invaded also missed several opportunities to end the occupation early and on terms that would herald at least some change toward a modern, centralized, democratic nation-state. The very nature of occupation made changes in political culture nearly impossible. John Vance, a US citizen who lived in the Dominican Republic, summarized much of the tragedy of the occupation by noting the "illogical" nature of teaching self-government "through the instrumentality of a military government." "The Dominicans have not had the slightest instruction in self-government," he added. "On the contrary, they have had a very strong lesson in government by force, something they were already well schooled in, from a people who they thought were the champions of freedom throughout the world."[327]

12

The Americas against Occupation, 1926–1932

> In spite of the long months of American occupation, our concern has
> not been blunted. . . . Rather have we suffered greater humiliation
> as the months have passed and as our government has so conspicu-
> ously failed to bring about any civilized and intelligent solution to
> this problem.
> —Dorothy Detzer, Women's International League for Peace
> and Freedom, speaking of Nicaragua in 1928

While the transnational activities of Dominicans and their allies helped spark the
withdrawal process in the Dominican Republic, in the late 1920s and early 1930s,
a more expansive shift in public opinion in the United States and other American
republics had an even greater impact upon US policymakers. That shift strengthened the network that linked the invaded to sympathetic non-state actors outside
occupied countries to policymakers in the United States. Without that network,
it is likely that occupations would have lasted far longer than they did.

Several qualitative changes in the late 1920s made it easier for the message of
the invaded to reach the US public. New media, newly emboldened politicians,
thicker transnational networks of resistance, and the inauguration of a new president combined to break down the obstacles to greater communication and solidarity among those in the Americas who rejected occupation. More than ever,
US officials admitted that the pressure became too great to withstand. "Armed
intervention in Haiti and Nicaragua," one US ambassador recalled, "kept us in
hot water not only with other countries of Latin America but also with a sizable
sector of our own public."[1]

Both creating and reflecting the change in US public opinion was the shift in
media coverage of the Nicaraguan—and to some extent the Haitian—situations. US newspapers and magazines began to resemble the press in Latin America by echoing the arguments of the resistance. US occupiers heard the echo.

One marine recalled that in 1920s Haiti, "American newspapers were raising hell. Marked copies kept coming to us."[2]

In May 1927 President Calvin Coolidge sent a telegram to the president of Haiti that marked the opening of the first commercial cable line to the country.[3] This signaled the culmination of a postwar sea change in hemispheric communications, when the State Department enforced an "open door" policy on cables, pressuring Latin American governments not to grant monopoly concessions and getting the British to drop theirs.[4] The war also made Washington aware of the importance of radio, and in 1921 it obtained dominance over Europe of an open radio network in the Americas.[5] In 1929 International Telephone and Telegraph inaugurated the first radiotelephone communications between the United States and Latin America.[6] This meant that US news agencies could compete with Europe in providing foreign news to Latin American newspapers. By the late 1920s United Press fed news to more than eighty Latin American papers and the Associated Press could send a cable to Latin American capitals in two to three minutes.[7] Other communications flows increased. By 1922, US movies made up 95 percent of the Latin American market.[8] In the late 1920s, direct steamship lines to both coasts of South America departed from San Francisco and New York.[9] In 1928 Pan American-Grace Airways inaugurated direct flights between New York and Buenos Aires, and the following year it and another airline flew mail to and from Latin America.[10]

News came not only to but also from Latin America on established channels. Muckraking about imperialism and tales of battle involving US soldiers made for thrilling copy, and the topics converged over Nicaragua. Augusto Sandino's ability to draw ever greater numbers of US forces into the Segovia mountains without being caught attracted the most media attention. One of his interviewers recalled how Sandino's rebellion sparked "a never before seen explosion of global publicity."[11] Even before Sandino burst onto the scene in mid-1927, the US press expressed doubts about the occupation. The 1926 US intervention into the Nicaraguan civil war, for instance, did get support from the *Washington Post, New York Tribune,* and *Philadelphia Public Ledger,* but the *New York Times, New York World,* and *Baltimore Sun* suspected "imperialistic motives."[12] When Washington pressured the Nicaraguan congress to accept Adolfo Díaz as the new president, humorist Will Rogers scratched his head: "We say that Díaz is the properly elected president of Nicaragua, but Brazil, Argentina, Peru, Chile, Mexico, Ecuador, Costa Rica, Cuba, Guatemala, Colombia, Uruguay, Paraguay—all those say that the other fellow is the properly elected president. It's funny how we are the only ones that get everything right."[13]

The US press broke most meaningfully with previous coverage by considering seriously the Latin American view that Sandino was not a "bandit" but instead a "patriot" or "revolutionary."[14] The US practice had long been to fight insurrectionists with dismissive labels. In July 1919 the First Brigade in Haiti instructed its men to use the term "bandits" instead of "cacos."[15] The semantics mattered. Calling Sandino a bandit denied that he represented a political position and constituency and thus closed the door to foreign states recognizing him.[16] The debate over "bandit" versus "revolutionary" or "patriot" reflected the myriad Latin American motivations for opposing occupation. Was Sandino in it for the money? Personal power? Could he really be altruistic? US citizens had rarely encountered an insurrectionist who displayed civic virtue.[17]

Sandino's political consciousness, however, was obvious to many who knew the Nicaraguan situation. One marine met an elite Salvadoran on board a Grace Line cruise ship headed to Nicaragua and asked the Georgetown University student what his compatriots thought of Sandino. "Well," he responded, "you people think he is a bandit, but we regard him the same way you used to regard George Washington in the United States. He is a patriot."[18] One US adventurer who went to Nicaragua in 1926 and met Sandino denounced "the slush that has been written about him by the American papers" and called Sandino "a figure that commands a considerable amount of admiration."[19] Even one marine lieutenant confided to his diary that "the forces opposed to the government are revolutionists—regardless of the fact that we call them bandits as an excuse—an effort to screen our actions—to fool the public of the United States whose opinion would demand our immediate withdrawal were they to realize the facts."[20]

In 1927 Secretary of State Frank Kellogg unwittingly made public the semantic debate by telling a member of Congress that Sandino's "activities cannot be considered to have any political significance whatsoever," calling his men "nothing more than common outlaws." Immediately after the battle of Ocotal in mid-July of that year, the New York Times responded by criticizing the intervention.[21] The dichotomy set in. "Sandino is not a bandit," argued Salomón de la Selva in The Nation the following January, invoking Latin American public opinion: "If Americans read the Latin-American press they would realize that to a growing population of Latin-American opinion Sandino is of the breed of Bolívar and Sucre and San Martín and Martí."[22] That same month the Washington News editorialized that "the inspiration to make it appear that he [Sandino] and his followers are mere bandits was equally ridiculous. Any further attempt to keep up this fiction becomes an insult to the American public."[23]

One journalist stood out for his ability to make the US public—and policymakers—question their assumptions. Carlton Beals, a native Kansan, was a conscientious objector during the Great War. Then, in an experience parallel to that of Sandino, he worked for the Standard Oil Company but got disillusioned and moved to Mexico, joining other US bohemians and intellectuals of the 1920s.[24] Also like Sandino, Beals was a critic of imperialism and communism. "Both," he said, "are dogmatic, demanding, sincere, sentimental."[25] In late 1927, prompted by Oswald Garrison Villard of *The Nation*—and perhaps, against his own stated beliefs, funded by Mexico City and Moscow—Beals set off to find the reclusive insurrectionist.[26] When he arrived in Nicaragua, Beals recalled, there were two accredited US reporters, but, being the US collector of customs and his assistant, they merely parroted the US line.[27] By finding Sandino, Beals gained fame as the only journalist to interview him in the Segovias before Sandino reached a peace deal.

Beals's *Nation* interviews with Sandino hammered a final nail in the coffin of the "bandit" label by demonstrating that Sandino and many of his followers harbored well-defined political motivations and goals. Beals subtitled one of his interviews, "Sandino—Bandit or Patriot?"[28] His articles also appeared in the *Herald Tribune* and forty other US newspapers, in addition to *La Nación* of Buenos Aires, Latin America's most influential daily, and Australian and European newspapers. All Latin American countries, he claimed, published translations of his articles.[29]

As Beals himself noted, there were repercussions in the Senate. In February 1928 Henrik Shipstead, a Minnesota senator from the Farmer-Labor Party, asked General John Lejeune, who testified before Congress about the Nicaraguan "bandits," whether Lejeune had read Beals.[30] Lejeune said no. "I have read it," said Shipstead.

> General, these people are called bandits down there, are they bandits in
>   the same sense as the word is used in European countries?
> LEJEUNE: I was just saying that they are called bandits for lack of some
>   other word. While Sandino's force is made up partly of a criminal ele-
>   ment, they are not all bandits in the sense that they are in the field solely
>   for the purpose of robbing people.
> SHIPSTEAD: You remember that the Cacos in Haiti were called bandits.
> LEJEUNE: Yes.
> SHIPSTEAD: Are these people bandits in the same sense that they [Cacos]
>   were called bandits?
> LEJEUNE: The Cacos of Haiti were utilized by revolutionary leaders when
>   they wanted to overthrow the government, in the old days . . . . They
>   were not bandits in the Italian sense you speak of—bandit in the Old
>   World sense; men whose only mission in life was to rob people in order
>   to live. I could not say that Sandino is that kind of a bandit either.[31]

Another general, Logan Feland, told Beals he was using the term "bandit" in a "technical" sense since Sandino was the leader of a band.[32] Henry Stimson, who early on called Sandino an "outlaw," later admitted that he was instead a "skillful guerrilla."[33]

To be sure, the debate proved far too narrow since it tended to apply only to Sandino and not his supporters and because insurrectionists could be both bandits and patriots. But the simplicity of the dichotomy allowed a slice of the US public to question the motivations of their own government. "For what are the marines in Nicaragua to die?" asked *The Nation*.[34] "What is all this fighting about? Why are these young men in marine uniforms being killed?" echoed the *Boston Globe*.[35] Will Rogers probably best expressed the populist anti-imperialism of US citizens: "Why are we in Nicaragua, and what the Hell are we doing there?"[36]

"Tell your people there may be bandits in Nicaragua, but they are not necessarily Nicaraguans," Sandino instructed Beals, suggesting like many others that the criminals in his country were in fact the marines.[37] By 1929 even a journalist as sympathetic to US aims as Harold Denny of the *New York Times* struck a balance: "At times the United States has been a noble and unselfish hero to Nicaragua; at times it has been the villain who would let nothing thwart his purpose. And often it has been both hero and villain at once."[38] Such equivocation was a far cry from the unquestioning support of a dozen years prior.

As always in US debates over imperialism, the press suspected that occupation eroded the moral fabric of US diplomacy by forcing Washington to lie.[39] The Washington *News* wrote that the US public was "shamelessly deceived by its officials."[40] It did not help that Smedley Butler, now a major general, admitted on January 5, 1929, in a Pittsburgh speech, that "the opposition candidates in Nicaragua were declared bandits when it became necessary to elect our man in office."[41]

Many, finally, noted the accumulation of negative press from around the world—mainly Europe and Latin America. Shouts of hypocrisy came from the former; anger from the latter. Titled simply "Why?" a *Boston Globe* editorial showed the extent of world criticism:

> Comment bitter, sarcastic, and distrustful fills the press of Brazil, Argentina, Chile, Peru, Salvador, Uruguay, Costa Rica, Bolivia, and Ecuador.... While this reaction stirs, in Europe our Nation is being pilloried from the Baltic to the Straits of Gibraltar, from London to Angora. The painfully developed prestige, the tradition of American disinterestedness toward and support of small nations in their rights to sovereign independence, has received a blow from which it will require years to recover.[42]

The battle of "bandits" against "patriots" brought out several of the themes that would mark the late-1920s surge in criticism of the occupations throughout the Americas.

The *Globe* did not exaggerate. In the late 1920s Latin Americans expressed the broadest, most culturally infused criticisms of US occupation, almost solely regarding Nicaragua. Guatemalan students demonstrated against the US intervention in the 1926–1927 war at the US legation and "all the local newspapers, with the exception of the semi-official government organ," editorialized in favor of the students.[43] US and British officials in Argentina, Uruguay, Costa Rica, El Salvador, the Dominican Republic, and elsewhere reported near-universal press condemnation of the marines in Nicaragua.[44] In Chile even the government's *La Nación* penned hostile editorials.[45] In 1926, especially, Latin Americans saw Mexico as defending the weak in Nicaragua while Washington bolstered the strong.[46] By the end of the decade, tracts with titles such as *Barbaric Yankeeland* and *The White House Shadow* were devoid of any hope of pan-American solidarity and painted US intentions as unabashedly evil.[47]

For Latin Americans, some motivations were more important than others. Landing in Nicaragua in 1932, one Buenos Aires reporter communicated some of the themes of the continent's opposition. One was a seething animosity toward the marines themselves, whose blood, apparently hotter even than the weather in sultry Nicaragua, needed "some kind of escape valve." When he and his shipmates disembarked, "the Yankees looked over our papers with their notorious bad tempers, angry with everybody and nobody. Surely they must have guessed how much we hated them." He also painted Sandino as a noble savage of sorts, a man with "rustic intelligence" and "the courage of a wild animal." Mostly he heeded Sandino's warning "that the Yankee menace is a danger to all of our America."[48] In 1929, Buenos Aires's *La Prensa* declared that "the Latin-American protest seeks to create, and in large measure has succeeded in creating, public consciousness regarding the rights of weak States and the necessity that they be respected and that right must be defended against force."[49] The establishment of non-intervention as an inviolable principle of inter-American affairs was the primary motivation of Latin Americans who rejected US occupation.

The impact of Latin American opposition could be material. A Salvadoran newspaper called for "a campaign for the boycott of everything belonging to the United States."[50] Others reported on boys "fifteen and sixteen years of age, who have run away from home with the intention of joining Sandino's forces."[51] The former president of Chile, Arturo Alessandri, warned Senator William Borah that "an unstoppable wave of resentment and distrust against the American people in all Hispanic America" would harm "the commercial, intellectual and moral relations between those countries and the United States."[52]

For all these reasons, the influence of Latin Americans on US occupations concerned US officials. These convinced the Salvadoran and Honduran governments to censor pro-Sandino stories.[53] (Salvadoran papers responded by reproducing anti-occupation items from the US press, embarrassing censors.)[54]

In 1927 US officials feared visits to Nicaragua by anti-imperialists such as Mexico's José Vasconcelos and Peru's Raúl Haya de la Torre as well as by other Latin American delegations.[55] Secretary of State Frank Kellogg had his legation in Buenos Aires "discreetly" request that the Argentine government refuse a visa to Alfredo Palacios, the president of the Latin American Union, who also threatened to visit.[56] US diplomats corrected careless reporting, such as an Associated Press story out of Buenos Aires claiming there were 24,000 US troops in Nicaragua when there were in fact only 2,400.[57] Or when another Buenos Aires paper published a photo of a charred body with the headline and caption:

Yankee Barbarity in Nicaragua
The Height of Atrocity!

"In Nicaragua there are no prisoners of war"—the Yankees have said! When one of the rebel patriots fighting for the sovereignty of his fatherland falls a prisoner to the Yankees the latter burn him on a pyre in the public square, so that he may serve as a lesson to others. The picture shows a "rebel" being burned alive.

The photo, it turned out, was unrelated to the US intervention. Editors lamely explained that it was "published inadvertently" and refused to print a retraction.[58]

In a 1927 article titled "What the World Thinks of America," *The Nation* cited dozens of newspaper criticisms of US occupation in Nicaragua. Five were from Latin America. Another seven were British, five French, two German, two Italian, and one Spanish. The enumeration drove home the point that Europe's disapproval may have mattered as much as Latin America's.[59] Europeans tended to frame the occupation as old-world imperialism, seeing US actions in Nicaragua as hypocritical because Washington denounced European colonies. A Leningrad paper countered Secretary of State Stimson's complaints about violations of the Kellogg-Briand Pact on the Soviet-Manchurian border by citing Haiti as an example of using war as "an instrument of national policy."[60] There was a more cultural threat, especially from "Latins" such as the French, Italians, and Spaniards, but also from Germans, who had well-developed cultural institutions in South America. Unlike US citizens, prominent French and Spanish intellectuals wrote articles for dailies there and gave well-attended talks to the Spanish Club, the Latin American Union, and the Hispanic American Atheneum.[61] Spaniards were "our bitterest and most relentless foe in Latin America," observed *Foreign Affairs* in 1927, since they aimed to revive Hispanic influence by arguing that occupation threatened the cultural resonance of the Spanish language, Catholicism, and social conservatism.[62]

In addition to the press, other non-governmental groups in the late 1920s formed the main transnational anti-occupation movements, providing the press with much of its content.[63] US activists were exceptionally robust partly because of their interactions with counterparts in Latin America.

"There have been few public questions in this country which have received more attention in the past few years than the policy of intervening in the affairs of the Latin-American countries." So wrote Lamar Beman, who reproduced a series of anti-imperialist essays in 1928.[64] Beman and other scholars were largely responsible for bringing such attacks to the public as their interest in Latin American occupations rose sharply and US campuses offered more than 135 courses in Latin American history. Yet up to then the dominant narrative depicted Latin America as a place doomed by climate, race, and culture. As doubts about US superiority blended with a more open anthropological pluralism and progressive-era reformism, interpretations morphed.[65]

Books—rather than magazine articles as in the early 1920s—led the way. Focused on economic and military imperialism was a series published by the American Fund for Public Service, and five of its volumes targeted Latin America: Bolivia, Colombia, Cuba, Puerto Rico, and Melvin Knight's 1928 *The Americans in Santo Domingo*, a searing indictment.[66] Scott Nearing administered much of the fund that supported publication. He formed an Anti-Imperialism Committee within the fund and wrote, with Joseph Freeman, his own sweeping study, *Dollar Diplomacy*. They interpreted "armed intervention" in Haiti, the Dominican Republic, and Nicaragua as symptoms of economic imperialism.[67]

By denouncing loans and occupations as twin features of US imperialism and especially by arguing that underdevelopment was not a result of culture but rather of financial interference, these scholars undermined much of the rationale for occupations.[68] But economic arguments fell on deaf ears at the State Department. Dana Munro, as close to an intellectual as the Latin-American Division had at the time, believed that "the motives that inspired [US] policy were basically political rather than economic" and that "discouraging revolutions" was the first of these motives.[69]

The surge in scholarship also included more centrist works, such as Clarence Haring's *South America Looks at the United States* (1928). Haring spent a year in Latin America in 1925–1926, funded by Harvard's Bureau of International Research, and came to mourn the enthusiasm sparked by Woodrow Wilson's 1913 Mobile promise never to take land and by his defense of self-determination during the war. Books such as Haring's, aimed at a middlebrow audience, tended to bemoan the harm to the US image brought about by occupations or haughty tourists.[70]

These US scholars followed in the footsteps of progressives and muckrakers from the early century—Nearing had lived on a farm with Upton Sinclair—but they also derived inspiration from readings and contacts from Latin America. Latin Americans were now regular contributors to US anthologies, and Fred Rippy, author of the American Fund tome on Colombia, also edited Manuel Ugarte's *The Destiny of a Continent*.[71] There were also increasing numbers of Latin American students in the United States. In 1919 several private institutions created the Institute for International Education (IIE), and, by 1930, 1,455 Latin Americans studied in US universities. The following year the director of IIE found that South Americans increasingly traveled northward rather than to Europe, their traditional destination.[72]

Faith-based organizations, entering the fray in the late 1920s, emphasized the ethical costs of occupation. "We believe," read one protest signed by three organizations, "that moral and humanitarian considerations rather than purely political and financial should hold the dominant place in the determination of our relations to the Republic of Haiti and to the Dominican Republic." To this end they subtly warned policymakers that a potentially large group—"Christians in America"—was "watching the attitude of our Government towards those Republics with deep concern."[73] Similar warnings came from the National Catholic Welfare Association.[74]

Non-church-based pacifists advanced similar arguments. The first, a leading peace movement in the 1920s, was the Women's International League for Peace and Freedom (WILPF). Jane Addams led it for most of the 1920s, but toward the end of the decade subordinates Dorothy Detzer and Emily Balch focused the organization more on occupations. Villard of *The Nation* judged that Detzer did more to end Nicaragua's occupation than any other US citizen.

Balch, a professor of economics at Wellesley before being fired for opposing the Great War, joined the staff of *The Nation* in 1919 and led a bi-racial investigation to Haiti in 1926 that led to a seminal book, *Occupied Haiti*. The group presented its findings to Coolidge and later influenced President Herbert Hoover's policies on Haiti. Balch shared the reformism of the occupations but feared that the occupation was not preparing the Haitians for self-government. Her recommendations would be very close to those adopted by the US government in 1930, but in 1926, her group had little impact. Some smeared it as defending the same cause as communists.[75]

Philosopher John Dewey, in 1930 the president of the non-partisan People's Lobby, wrote Hoover that to send US troops abroad, "at best an anachronism," "belies the sincerity of our good will toward those countries, and raises the pregnant question of the validity of our good intentions."[76] The National Council for Prevention of War, whose vice-chairmen included Addams, Louis Brandeis, and William Allen White, attempted to transform Dewey's moral imperatives into political ones. Claiming to represent "a large section of thoughtful and fairminded American people," they wrote to Kellogg in 1928 about the "slaughter" of 600 Nicaraguans and warned of the public opinion backlash. "The result is more hatred and more resistance in Nicaragua, fear of our aggression now throughout Central America and loss of honor, prestige and trade for our nation as far as Cape Horn, while imperialists in Europe rejoice in our bungling in the very territory we guard under the Monroe Doctrine. Can this be denied?"[77] It could. "These societies," said Kellogg, "are like blowholes for whales": "never in favor of their own country."[78]

In November 1927 in New Orleans a motley group boarded a United Fruit Company ship bound for Nicaragua. It included Robert Cuba Jones, a twenty-eight-year-old graduate student from the University of Chicago; Carolena Wood, a Quaker of independent means; and Dr. Elbert Russell from the Duke School of Religion. Their leader was John Nevin Sayre, a Princeton graduate, Episcopal minister, son of a wealthy Bethlehem Steel entrepreneur, and secretary of the Fellowship of Reconciliation (FOR), an interfaith pacifist organization founded in 1915. The four called themselves the "FOR-Quaker Mission of Peace and Good Will to Central America" and set off on the most sanguine faith-based enterprise of the era.

FOR was a mainstay among anti-occupation groups. One of its officers, Harold Watson, had accompanied Balch to Haiti in 1926, and Sayre was later to sign the Dewey letter to Kellogg. In 1927 Sayre had invited Sandino representative Salomón de la Selva to FOR's annual convention. He had also heard of a 1926 trip to Hispaniola by the Quakers so he allied with them.[79]

On board the ship Sayre busied himself reading Nearing and Freeman's *Dollar Diplomacy* and no doubt dreaming of bringing Sandino's war to a close. On Thanksgiving Day, 1927, the party landed in Guatemala and headed to Nicaragua. All the while Sayre failed to tell the others that his secret mission was to find Sandino and persuade him to lay down his arms.[80] This was a few weeks before Carleton Beals interviewed Sandino, when the Nicaraguan refused to speak to any US citizen.[81]

In Managua, Sayre and company met with Chargé Dana Munro, who listened politely to their scheme. They had met with Sandino's wife, Blanca Araúz, and through her sent him a letter, so they expected to be received with open arms. "They appeared to feel that kindness and a manifestation of good will would be sufficient to achieve this," Munro reported. He told them they had "practically no chance of success for their mission and that it was much more probable that they would be captured and held as hostages."[82]

"My argument of course did not convince them."[83] In late December 1928 the group headed into the Segovias, unaware of the mountainous topography. Their car broke down, and two of the members, Wood and Russell, gave up and headed back to the United States. Sayre and Jones continued on horseback. They never found Sandino. He did respond to their letter, denying an interview but reiterating that he would lay down his weapons if the marines left first.[84]

Jones and Sayre returned home disheartened but persisted in fighting occupation with pacifism. Sayre went on a lecture tour and delivered to members of Congress a wise warning: "Irrespective of whether you think that Sandino is a bandit or a patriot or both, it is undeniable that he is a Nicaraguan fighting on his own soil against the soldiers of a power that is a foreign power in Nicaragua. To kill him is to light the fire of war passion and furnish a battle cry that will resound through Latin America. The United States will not make peace by shedding Nicaraguan blood. Do not exterminate Sandino."[85]

Civil society activism reflected the concerns of a number of US citizens with occupation. The late 1920s witnessed growing appreciation among ordinary people for the wisdom of non-intervention and for the opinions of foreigners living under occupation. Demonstrating the former, one thirteen-year-old girl wrote Senator Borah in early 1928 that "in our civics class almost every day the Nicaraguan question is brought up and vigorously discussed." In debates she took the side of non-intervention and only three classmates disagreed.[86] Showing a no-nonsense appreciation for the hatred of foreign troops, a US businessman lectured Hoover that "[Nicaraguans] do not want order maintained by marines any more than would Californians want order maintained by Japanese soldiers."[87]

The Congress of the United States eventually included a significant minority of anti-occupation voices that placed consistent pressure on the president, resulting in a tangible impact on the Nicaraguan occupation. Munro recalled that "domestic criticism probably actually had more effect on American policy [than hostility in South America]."[88] By the 1920s there appeared especially in the Senate a group shaped by a generation of events to oppose occupation. Most, channeling Midwestern or Western progressivism, combined, in different degrees, the parochialism and xenophobia of populism, a moral streak of pacifism, and isolationism.[89]

The senator most enmeshed in the transnational network of resistance was William Borah, who as far back as 1913 opposed the US presence in Nicaragua.[90] During the Great War he played the archetypal isolationist and helped squash Wilson's peace treaty and US entry into the League of Nations. His "irreconcilable" stance earned him the moniker "The Great Opposer." By the 1920s Borah suspected dark financial motivations behind all marine landings, seeing loans as an instrument of permanent occupation not just in Latin America but also in Siberia, Syria, and Iraq.[91] Friends of Haitians and Dominicans organized his lecture at Carnegie Hall in 1922. In 1925 he penned an article arguing that the Monroe Doctrine did not give Washington the right to depose foreign governments and establish new ones.[92] He would learn Spanish in order to speak with Latin Americans.[93]

Anti-occupation senators such as Borah came from both parties and at times railed against administrations of their own party. They spoke of US hypocrisy, economic imperialism, and damage to the national image. "It is positively discouraging to know the things which are being done in the name of Americanism," Borah wrote to Moorfield Storey in 1922. "In my opinion, there is very little difference between Japan's actions in Korea and our actions in Santo Domingo and Haiti."[94] Some added that the executive essentially waged wars within occupations without declarations from Congress.[95] In March 1922, Senator George Norris, a member along with *The Nation*'s Villard of the National Citizen's Committee on Relations with Latin America, protested the appointment of a high commissioner to Haiti on the grounds that the Senate had not approved what amounted to an ambassadorial position.[96] Senators also criticized the Stimson mission to Nicaragua in 1927 for this reason.[97]

Senators generally placed too little weight on political culture. Borah's case for economic causes in the Carnegie Hall speech, for instance, was weak. He claimed 200,000 acres of land had passed into US hands under the Haitian occupation—the real figure was closer to 40,000. After blaming greed for going into Hispaniola, he added, "I have been unable to satisfy myself as to why we went in." His most convincing arguments suggested how occupation degraded political practices—both abroad and at home. "We have taken away the freedom of speech and the freedom of the press, and other rights, and what is Japan doing in Korea that excels that in infamy?" Borah warned that marine cruelty lowered Latin America to the level of "India and Siberia," to which a heckler added, "Ireland!"[98]

Many congressional "peace progressives" hardened their determination through direct contact with Latin Americans or occupied peoples.[99] Several traveled to Haiti and Nicaragua in the late 1920s, corresponding with key occupied activists and publishing their speeches in the *Congressional Record*.[100] Borah hosted Haiti's Pierre Hudicourt in 1925, swearing to him that he would withdraw troops in twenty-four hours were he president, while fellow senator William King ushered Hudicourt into a meeting with the State Department.[101] Other trip results were mixed. Shipstead visited Haitians in 1927 and came away with the impression that they lived "carefree and happy lives," yet he still counseled US administrators to minimize loans to Haitians so as to avoid sending marines to get the money back.[102] Meanwhile Senator Hiram Bingham III, an amateur archaeologist who claimed to have discovered Machu Picchu in 1911, wrote *The Monroe Doctrine: An Obsolete Shibboleth* (1915), arguing that the long-standing US policy caused unnecessary anti-US sentiment.[103]

Anti-occupation senators advanced legislation—riders and resolutions—against all US occupations. They demanded cuts or wholesale elimination of occupation budget lines. They also called for investigations into alleged atrocities or the handover of executive documents. Compared to those of the press or civil society, congressional actions began late. In February 1921, Hiram Johnson, an aspirant to the White House, proposed investigations of both sides of Hispaniola, which became reality under the McCormick Committee. Gilbert Hitchcock did the same for Nicaragua.[104] On January 19, 1922, King proposed to cut off all funds to the occupations in Haiti, Nicaragua, and the Dominican Republic.[105] With Borah as its driving force, the King resolution failed 43 to 9 in the Senate, yet King reintroduced it as well as other resolutions perhaps a dozen times.[106] President Louis Borno of Haiti resented King so much that when King announced he would visit Haiti in 1927, Borno instructed the Gendarmerie to physically prevent him from landing. He even banned a song, by Haiti's most popular singer, titled "Sénateur King." Instead King visited Santo Domingo.[107] King's barrages of long-shot resolutions could be seen as mere annoyances, but one lawyer complained that they made a large loan to Haiti less likely because they were "affecting the salability of these bonds."[108]

When senatorial opposition slowed in the mid-1920s, civil society lit some fires. In February 1925, Detzer and Balch worked with Senator Edwin Ladd, a few months before his death, toward a resolution against large loans that might prolong occupation. Borah, chair of the Foreign Relations Committee, agreed to hold hearings at which Lewis Gannett and Ernest Gruening of *The Nation* and James Weldon Johnson testified. The following year, the Women's Peace Union got Senator Lynn Frazier to sponsor a resolution against US armed conflict "for any purpose."[109]

US congressional opposition intensified in response to the second foray into Nicaragua in 1926. In January 1927, after meeting with Coolidge, Borah broke with Kellogg on the issue. "If it had not been for Borah," said his colleague Simeon Fees with some hyperbole, "the country would never have known about the landing of marines in Nicaragua."[110] That same month saw two Senate resolutions: one by George Moses asking for evidence of a rationale for the Nicaraguan landings, another by Burton Wheeler demanding immediate withdrawal. After Stimson signed Espino Negro on May 4, Congress backed off somewhat, but it regained momentum after the mid-July battle of Ocotal.[111] One representative from Wisconsin told Kellogg that "to the citizens of this district" the killing of 300 Nicaraguans "appears as an unnecessary and unwarranted massacre."[112]

Another round of congressional opposition came after the Nicaraguan elections of 1928. Senator Clarence Cleveland Dill, inspired by a Carleton Beals article, saw no reason to stay in Nicaragua after the Liberals won, and he threatened to attach to the 1929 Navy appropriations bill a rider cutting off all funding to the occupation. The Senate first voted for it, then, under pressure from the administration, against it. Even if only temporary, it marked the first time in US history that Congress cut off funding for an ongoing war abroad.[113] At this crucial point Borah dissented from the dissenters. He had long advocated self-rule for Nicaragua. When he saw it coming, he did as Medill McCormick had in 1922 with the Dominican Republic and backed off.[114]

Yet the barrage of resolutions, in addition to mountains of personal letters written by the likes of McCormick and Shipstead to secretaries of state and presidents, eventually had a lasting impact.[115] The key victory came in 1932 when the Senate cut off funding for any further troops, making it impossible for the marines to oversee the Nicaraguan vote.

In May 1928 the Cecil de Mille Moving Picture Company contacted the State Department for permission to shoot a movie about the marines in Nicaragua. Secretary Kellogg's response was unequivocal: no. "This would have a bad effect in this country," he said, "and particularly in Latin America if the film was sent to that region." Since Hollywood movies of the genre—Frank Capra's 1929 *Flight*, for example—tended to depict heroic marines fighting barbarous Latin Americans, the secretary of state wanted in no way to encourage even more negative public opinion in fellow American republics.[116]

The episode signaled that the "criminally stupid young men in the State Department," as *The Nation* called them in 1928, had in fact matured in their appreciation of anti-occupation resisters by the late 1920s.[117] The pressure from the press, civil society, and the Congress got to Kellogg, who wrote to the US legation in Managua in frustration. "There is a great deal of criticism in this country about the way in which these operations are being dragged out with constant sacrifice of American lives and without any concrete results.... People cannot understand why the job cannot be done, and frankly I do not understand myself."[118]

The State Department demonstrated increased interest in Latin America in the late 1920s because US investments there escalated and negative public opinion could endanger them. Between 1914 and 1929, those investments more than tripled and exports to Latin America almost tripled.[119] Of the $10 billion in US investments worldwide in 1926, $4 billion was spent in the region.[120] The following year, US trade to Latin America was greater than trade to Great Britain, Germany, and France combined.[121] According to Munro, Europeans supported criticism of US occupation because they "were trying desperately to recover the preeminent position in the South American market which they had lost during the war."[122]

A first step toward balancing US interests with public opinion was to improve State's personnel by hiring more professionals. Up to the 1920s many US diplomats and consuls received their jobs out of nepotism or political obligation or because they were temporarily available young gentlemen of independent means—and often limited abilities. The problem was in evidence in Nicaragua where chargé Lawrence Dennis, complaining of his inadequate salary, resigned to join a Wall Street bank.[123] To remedy the situation, the 1924 Rogers Act focused on training diplomats for well-defined specialties and longer careers and gave diplomats higher pay, spending accounts, and pensions. The administrations of Warren Harding and Coolidge also provided more room for State to conduct policy, a welcome breather from the micromanaging Wilson.[124]

As a result, recalled Munro, at the Latin-American Division "from 1923 on there was a definite trend toward a policy of less interference in the internal political affairs of the Central American and West Indian republics." Much of this was the work of Francis White, who led the division from 1922 to 1926 and rose to assistant secretary in charge of Latin American affairs from 1927 to 1933. Tellingly, White was away from Washington in 1926–1927 when it again stumbled into Nicaragua.[125] In the spirit of the Rogers Act, the division replaced political appointees with career men, hoping to erase the image of being sent to the region by the State Department as penitence for the untalented. In 1927 Kellogg appointed as ambassador to Mexico Dwight Morrow, whose deep appreciation of Mexican culture and conciliatory attitude immediately mended fences. When Hoover took over in 1929, his secretary of state Henry Stimson replaced the minister to Nicaragua with Matthew Hanna, another competent diplomat with military experience in Cuba.[126]

The second step of the executive was to confront critical diplomats head-on. Inter-American conferences were increasingly the place to embarrass Washington, as early as the 1923 Fifth Pan-American Conference in Santiago, Chile, where fifteen Latin American nations openly defied US occupations and delegates from Haiti and the Dominican Republic joined forces to protest, distributed pamphlets to all the delegates, and aired their grievances in the Latin American press.[127] The 1927 conference of the International Commission of Jurists in Rio de Janeiro passed a non-intervention resolution.[128]

With Sandino bringing anti-occupation activism to a fever pitch, diplomats from all sides prepared for a confrontation at the Sixth International Conference of American States, the so-called Pan-American Congress, to gather in Havana in January and February 1928. Latin Americans arrived ready to go on the offensive, encapsulated by a Dominican paper that editorialized that "proclamations of 'pan-Americanism' are no longer received with naiveté."[129] "Let our voices be heard in Havana," Sandino goaded the delegates from Nicaragua.[130] Mexico's José Vasconcelos answered the call: "The heroic conduct of Nicaraguan patriots could not have been more untimely, more disturbing to the official story and to the unshakable optimism of the foreign ministries."[131]

Bracing his department, Kellogg sent out an advance memo about Havana. "The past year has seen the development of a vigorous anti-American propaganda throughout Latin America based on charges of 'imperialism' and characterized by violent criticism of . . . the American policy in Nicaragua. . . . It is possible that an effort may be made by some delegates ... to bring up controversial matters."[132] Kellogg readied a delegation that included Morrow and former secretary of state Charles Evans Hughes—the man who finalized the Dominican withdrawal. Breaking with precedent, Coolidge himself attended the opening ceremony.[133]

There were other issues—Washington kept out Argentine beef to prevent the spread of hoof and mouth disease to the United States, Mexico had its oil dispute—but Sandino overshadowed them.[134] As Coolidge's ship approached the harbor, Havana police, under strongman President Gerardo Machado, erased graffiti on the city's walls that read "Yankees Out of Nicaragua," "Death to Yankee Imperialism," "Go Home, Coolidge," and especially "Long Live Sandino." From Germany Albert Einstein protested US policies in the region.[135] In a special ceremony, delegates hoisted the Nicaraguan flag.[136] The closing ceremony, usually non-political, became so when El Salvador raised the issue of non-intervention, and thirteen Latin American states, including Haiti and the Dominican Republic, voted for the Salvadoran resolution ordering that no state could "intervene in the internal affairs of the other."[137]

Then came Hughes's moment, his chance to beat back the diplomatic onslaught.[138] He acknowledged the opinions of Latin Americans yet stood his ground. He lectured them that the problem of Latin America was one of internal stability, not external aggression. The secretary also seemed to sense that Latin Americans' racism compelled them to agree on the degenerate nature of Haitian politics and therefore with the occupation. "We would leave Haiti," he promised them, "at any time that we had reasonable expectations of stability, and could be assured that withdrawal would not be the occasion for a recurrence of bloodshed."[139] The Hughes speech succeeded in postponing a final vote on the non-intervention resolution until the next pan-American conference, to be held in Montevideo.

Anti-occupation activists claimed a propaganda victory, but for all their speechifying, Latin Americans had made no show of union.[140] One Nicaraguan delegate—whose nation had voted with Washington—complained privately to his father about the meekness of Latin Americans: "It looked like a Saxon conference."[141] White of the Latin-American Division agreed, concluding that Havana "showed no real united animosity against us, a comprehension of our difficulties in the Caribbean, and a realization of our non-aggressive, non-imperialistic purposes. It also showed the number of friends we can count upon in Latin America." Only Argentina, El Salvador, and Mexico were "out-and-out antagonists."[142]

A much less publicized but more momentous third step in the State Department occurred in 1928 when Kellogg ordered Undersecretary of State Reuben Clark to reexamine the Monroe Doctrine in light of Latin American contentions that it did not justify US intervention. Clark kicked the job down to an assistant, Anna O'Neill, who scoured encyclopedias and law books and cobbled together dozens of interpretations of the Doctrine since its enunciation in 1823. On December 17 Clark added a seventeen-page interpretation of the interpretations. Reading the Doctrine narrowly and defensively, he agreed with Latin Americans: the Doctrine did not in fact justify the takeover of Latin American republics, merely the checking of European invasions.[143] The implication was that it neither proscribed nor condoned occupations. Occupations would have to be individually justified, not grouped as a natural hegemonic prerogative of Washington.

The Clark Memorandum, as it came to be known, had no immediate effect since the incoming president, Herbert Hoover, chose not to publish it for fear of insulting Europeans. Yet it came out in a government publication from 1930. Though Clark responded that the memo was his personal opinion, the *New York Times* leaped at the chance to declare the death of Theodore Roosevelt's reading of the Doctrine, which rationalized "police power" in the Caribbean.[144] By early 1931, in a speech to the Council on Foreign Relations defending US policy, Secretary Stimson repeated Clark's wording that the Monroe Doctrine was "a declaration of the United States vs. Europe, not of the United States vs. Latin America."[145]

As Clark put the finishing touches on his memorandum, Hoover made a more public statement of the executive's resolve against occupation, the fourth step toward ending ongoing occupations. "As Secretary of Commerce," recalled Hoover in his memoirs, "I had developed an increasing dissatisfaction with our policies toward Latin America. I was convinced that unless we displayed an entirely different attitude we should never dispel the suspicions and fears of 'Colossus of the North' nor win the respect of those nations." Hoover understood the power of the transnational network speaking through newspapers. "The German-, Italian-, and British-subsidized South American press constantly encouraged this antagonism as part of their trade propaganda."[146] As commerce secretary, Hoover had chaired the Inter-American High Commission and witnessed the ways anti-US sentiment harmed trade relations.[147]

As a presidential candidate, Hoover navigated political waters while pursuing the ideal of withdrawal. Democratic candidate Franklin Roosevelt advanced his own party's abandonment of intervention in a 1928 *Foreign Affairs* article. The man who in 1920 proudly claimed to have written Haiti's constitution as assistant secretary of the Navy affirmed twice that "the world ought to thank us" for the Hispaniola occupations. "But does it? . . . . The other republics of the Americas do not thank us, on the contrary they disapprove of our interventions almost unanimously." Immediately after tallying the "hate and fear" of the United States in Latin America, Roosevelt proposed "a higher law, a newer and better standard in international relations"—the rejection of occupation.[148] From Hoover's own party Senator Borah pressured him to do the same, but Hoover feared losing the support of Coolidge loyalists, so he hedged. In the end, the Republican platform on Nicaragua "absolutely repudiate[d] any idea of conquest or exploitation, and [wa]s actuated solely by an earnest and sincere desire to assist a friendly and neighboring State which has appealed for aid in a great emergency."[149] Hoover was repeating a US line consistent since 1912: altruism was the only desire of Washington's occupations.

Right after his election, however, Hoover undertook a seven-week tour of nine Latin America countries.[150] Some may have thought that Hoover might have had more serious tasks to prepare for, yet the length of the trip and its public nature were statements of Hoover's foreign policy priorities.

The trip confronted Hoover with some protest against US occupations. "Sandino! Sandino! Sandino!" chanted some in Buenos Aires.[151] A small group unfurled a banner reading, "Long Live Sandino! Long Live Nicaragua! Down with North American Imperialism!"[152] Two days before he got to Buenos Aires, police foiled a plot by "notorious anarchists" to blow up the president-elect's train.[153] Yet Hoover meant to minimize cultural clashes. He employed a disciplined communications strategy, his press man George Baker taking aboard the USS *Maryland* eighteen reporters and seven photographers and signing off on all outgoing cables.[154] Baker further gave his entourage a list of appropriate behaviors, including referring to themselves as *norte-Americano*. "If you carry into these countries any 'nigger-white man' attitude of superiority," he cautioned, "for God's sake forget it or at least have the decency to hide it."[155]

Shorn of overt cultural superiority, Hoover's message was clear: "There is not the remotest idea in the United States in increasing our territorial domain," he told the press.[156] He also used the phrase "good neighbor" on his first stop.[157] In Argentina he explicitly abandoned the paternalistic metaphors that had long poisoned US-Latin American relations. "In the American Continent there are neither big brothers nor little brothers. They are all of the same age from the spiritual and political point of view. . . . No intervention policy predominates or will prevail in my country."[158]

The message got through (see Fig. 12.1). "That intervention is not now, never was, and never will be a set policy of the United States is one of the most important facts President-elect Hoover has made clear," reported the *New York Times*. "The result is that for the first time in a generation, Latin America really understands the attitude of the United States toward Nicaragua, Haiti, and Santo Domingo."[159] Indeed, the press in both the United States and Latin America reflected Hoover's optimism. Latin American newspapers often devoted half their pages to his visit, embraced increased trade and cultural exchanges as common goals for the continent, and made apologies for untoward incidents.[160]

Figure 12.1 Hoover caricatured as trying to remake the US image in Latin America. Thiele, *Culver* (Indiana) *Citizen*, 1928. Used with permission of the Plymouth *Pilot News*.

The official US stance toward occupations had completely changed. Hoover was prepared to move to end both the Nicaraguan and Haitian occupations. When Washington recalled Dana Munro from Managua to head the Latin-American Division in the late 1920s, Munro noted the new atmosphere in Washington: "There had been much criticism of intervention in anti-imperialist circles and in Congress, and the Sandino affair in Nicaragua had shown how unpleasantly action in one Latin American country could affect our relations with the others."[161] Some of the occupied also took great inspiration from the Hoover trip: Haiti's Dantès Bellegarde dedicated his 1929 book to the new US president.[162] In his State of the Union message on December 3, 1929, Hoover noted the presence of US troops in Haiti, Nicaragua, and China, and remarked, "We do not wish to be represented abroad in such a manner."[163]

A will existed to end occupations, but not yet a way. The anti-occupation resistance would do what it could to influence the manner and speed of withdrawal.

13

Nicaraguan Withdrawals, 1925–1934

> You don't understand the Central American way or the Latin American way of doing things.
>
> —Anastasio Somoza to a marine friend

Nicaragua was unique among these three cases of occupation because it lived through two withdrawals of marines, in 1925 and 1933. The first did not respond to any organized transnational network, but rather to the US desire to reform Nicaragua's political culture. The second was very much a response to a movement sustained by international solidarity, yet that solidarity waned in the last years of occupation, and political cultural reformism remained the principal factor contributing to withdrawal. In both episodes, worrisome evidence of persistent caudillismo undermined the occupation's perception that it had brought some stability and democracy to Nicaragua.

Helping to lengthen and isolate from criticism the 1912–1925 hundred-man occupation was the lack of attention paid by surrounding countries. There was some limited agitation in Central America, especially in Costa Rica, where Zelayista exile J. Irías organized protests and petitions.[1] From this neighboring country, Irías attacked Nicaraguan government troops with 2,000 men, lost, then retreated to New Orleans.[2] But Mexico and Spain, the usual dissenters, kept quiet.[3] Even fierce critics agreed that some intervention force in Nicaragua— were it neutral—was legitimate.[4] Surrounding governments only formally resisted when the US presence in Nicaragua infringed on their interests.[5] After the US Senate ratified the Bryan-Chamorro Treaty in 1916, Nicaragua's neighbors asked the Central American International Court of Justice to declare the treaty null and void. El Salvador said it violated its proprietary rights in the Gulf of Fonseca, where the treaty called for a US naval base. Costa Rica, meanwhile, claimed rights to its own canal, which a canal foreseen in the treaty would threaten.[6] The court found in favor of both plaintiffs but also that the United States was not subject to the court's jurisdiction.[7] Nicaragua rejected the decision and the court soon after collapsed.[8]

There was also little criticism of the 1912–1925 occupation in the United States. In the Senate, the only resolution submitted—and not approved—asked President William Howard Taft to justify the intervention, especially one without express congressional authority.[9] A few editorialists warned against the slippery slope of intervention.[10] But few adopted Nicaragua as a cause. The socialist press, for instance, published only one article on the occupation.[11] Otherwise, the press echoed the paternalistic claims to superiority common in US political culture. Nicaragua was "a chronic trouble-maker" that "tries the patience of the big Anglo-Saxon guardian. No one of the baby republics so richly merits a spanking on general principles."[12]

Beyond narrow protests, many of which did not oppose the US presence itself, there was no high-profile international or transnational dissent against the legation guard—no diplomatic speeches, no conferences, no mass demonstrations— any time during the thirteen-year occupation.

Withdrawal came mostly as US observers realized that their legation, in buttressing the Conservative Party, undermined the stability of Nicaragua by depriving it of any semblance of democracy and so constantly threatening a Liberal revolt. In 1922 a navy captain wrote to the secretary that the legation guard was on the wrong side of politics. Conservatives represented only one third of the country and were divided and ruled by a tiny elite. Liberals were far more numerous and represented "the common people and the artisan class and it is with the latter that the marines are mostly thrown."[13] Social tensions also played a role: the December 1921 killing of Managua police prompted the State Department to plan for withdrawal.[14]

Perhaps the most telling sign of the failure of the occupation was that US officials admitted leaving behind a political culture largely unchanged since 1912. Upon the sudden death of President Diego Chamorro in 1923, Vice-President Bartolomé Martínez assumed office, but the State Department opposed him, judging his ascent unconstitutional. Marine intelligence described the political parties as further divided because of the occupation. While the Conservatives welcomed US influence, "the Liberal Party denounces American influence, proclaims American bankers as robbers, speaks of American officials as grafters and men of little honor and is preaching a gospel of national independence which is no longer possible in the world as we find it today."[15]

Wishing to magically erase partisan hatred, Washington backed a bipartisan ticket in 1924, made up of a Conservative presidential candidate, Carlos Solórzano, and a Liberal running mate, Juan Sacasa. In 1916 and 1920, the United States had openly flouted democracy by pressuring Liberals not to participate in the elections of Emiliano Chamorro and then his uncle Diego. There was also little press freedom during those elections. In 1924, however, the appearance of a fair election was crucial to Secretary of State Charles Evans Hughes. Clashes between US troops and Nicaraguan civilians made the difference. Hughes understood that the "continued presence of American troops . . . has at times given rise to the assertion . . . that the United States Government is maintaining in office a government which would otherwise perhaps not be strong enough to maintain itself against the attacks of its political opponents."[16]

The Solórzano-Sacasa ticket won a plurality in an election marred only minimally by accusations of fraud and force. Washington recognized the results but delayed the departure of the hundred-man guard from January to August 1925 to help stabilize the regime. But stability had been an illusion for thirteen years. Lurking in the shadows remained the old war horse, Emiliano Chamorro, who planned for revolution. Dana Munro, soon to take charge of the legation, wrote that the marines knew they were leaving behind a weak coalition government.[17] Solórzano even "sent a strong and very humble plea" for the legation guard to remain, as did "business interests both foreign and native."[18] Right before the withdrawal, Nicaragua witnessed an increase in violent incidents—knifings, beatings, and a stoning.[19] The marines nevertheless left on August 4, 1925. Immediately after, partisanship returned. During Solórzano's first year, Chamorro worked his Conservative allies to purge the cabinet of Liberals, prompting the president to resign and the vice-president to leave the country—a virtual coup d'état. Washington, desperate, gave Adolfo Díaz another chance in the presidential seat. Less than four weeks later, civil war reignited as Liberals under José María Moncada revolted against renewed Conservative rule.[20]

In 1927, after the marines returned to Nicaragua, they faced an opponent who, this time, built the most redoubtable transnational network to sustain him materially, politically, and psychologically. International aspects of the Augusto Sandino struggle were arguably as crucial to it as its regional or local ones. Ideologies and persons from abroad deeply infused the insurrection, providing intellectual and political frameworks to the grievances of the *segovianos* that gave them sustenance in the face of intransigence from the marines and the Nicaraguan government. Allies abroad also broadcast Sandino's messages to those who could persuade the marines to withdraw. When asked what Sandino's purpose was, one advocate admitted, "No, he can't accomplish anything tangible." He posited that winning over world opinion was Sandino's real goal. "Every time there is a battle, every time marines are killed, the attention of the United States and the world is drawn to what is going on in Nicaragua. That is why he keeps on fighting."[21] Willard Beaulac, who replaced Munro at the legation in 1928, understood that Sandino fought two wars—one military, the other "a political war against the United States in the free press of the world."[22]

The socialist ideas Sandino imbibed in Mexico gave structure and legitimacy to his inchoate thoughts about inequality and property redistribution. The vague communism and Mexico-influenced anarcho-syndicalism he would eventually adopt shaped his vision and blended with the grievances of followers. Except for his contemporary enemies, few have called Sandino a communist. While he envisioned a "classless and egalitarian society," he did not call for a state-controlled economy. He would redistribute land, but only uncultivated land and only through cooperatives. Still, on this point among many, Liberals broke with him.[23] Tellingly, so would communists later. When El Salvador's Agustín Far-abundo Martí once tried to preach communism to Sandino, the Nicaraguan cut him off: "If you think that you will seduce me with your ideals, do me a favor and don't stay here one more minute. I am not a communist."[24]

A "foreign visitor" once said to Sandino: "I believe, General, that your strug-gle for the complete liberation of Nicaragua is not just limited to this country, but is rather the beginning of a Race War. You represent in these moments all the energy and all the proud spirit of the Latin soul, the young soul of Indo-America, which has risen against the Anglo-Saxon Imperialism brought to these virgin lands by the brutal and ultra-CIVILIZED blondes."

"Precisely," was Sandino's response.[25]

The exchange encapsulated Sandino's other international core belief. Directly arrayed against US-dominated "pan-Americanism," he inserted himself within a rich intellectual tradition of Latin American anti-imperialists who countered that the oppressed peoples of Latin America had a common destiny—that of resisting the "Colossus of the North."[26] Sandino wrote that "among us [Latin Americans] there should be no frontiers, and that all of us have the clear duty to be concerned with the fate of each of the Hispanic American nations, because all of us face the same danger before the colonizing and absorbing policy of the Yankee imperialists." He then famously declared, "Sandino is Indo-Hispanic and he has no frontiers in Latin America."[27]

Sandino explained to a French writer that his thinking evolved on this front. "At the beginning of my campaign I thought only of Nicaragua. Afterward . . . my ambition grew. I thought of the Central American Republic. . . . Tell Hispano-America that as long as Sandino breathes, the independence of Central America will have a defender. I shall never betray my cause. That is why I am the son of Bolívar."[28]

Sandino translated theory into praxis. He filled his ranks with sympathetic Latin Americans and other foreigners and did not consider a Latin American to be a "foreigner in Nicaragua." He labeled the non-Nicaraguans among his top staff "the Latin American Legion" and called them "eloquent proof of the immense value of the ties of blood, language, and race that unite the Latin American peoples."[29]

Sandino never inventoried his transnational Army for the Defense of the National Sovereignty of Nicaragua (EDSNN), but one former Sandinista tallied, just among officers, eleven Hondurans, six Salvadorans, three Guatemalans, three Mexicans, two Venezuelans, two Colombians, two Costa Ricans, one Peruvian, and one Dominican.[30] Among the more famous of the officers were Farabundo Martí of El Salvador, José de Paredes of Mexico, Estevan Pavletich of Peru, and Juan Pablo Umanzor of Honduras. Less known were soldiers of fortune, including British and US citizens.[31] Sandino's Salvadoran mistress, Teresa Villatoro, administered his camp for a year.[32]

The Dominican was none other than Gregorio Urbano Gilbert, the teenager from San Pedro who had killed a marine in 1917 in protest against the occupation of his own country. In 1928, out of prison and still in his twenties, Gilbert heard of Sandino's struggle in Nicaragua and yearned to join. Various Dominican city councils and political organizations, no longer under US occupation, pitched in a total of 2,400 pesos for his trip, along with letters of introduction.[33] When Gilbert tried to board a vessel for Central America, however, none would take him because he was "colored." He finally found passage to Belize but jumped off ship when it briefly stopped in Honduras. There he met Nicaraguan guides, who he said treated him as an inferior, overcharged him, and tried to lose him in the woods. When he finally got to Sandino's camp, he was called a "Haitian." While racism may have discouraged Gilbert, it also kept him motivated to fight segregationist US soldiers. Sandino's troops eventually accepted him as "the Dominican." Sandino promoted him to captain within three weeks, made him his Dominican liaison, and took him along on his trip to Mexico in 1929. In late August of that year, after 386 days, Gilbert headed back to his homeland.[34]

Arguably as useful to Sandino as his foreign officers were the international intellectuals and activists who formed a network of sympathizers whose nodes were in Honduras, Mexico, and New York City.

The foreigner most responsible for making Sandino a hero abroad was Froylán Turcios, the Honduran owner and editor of *Ariel*, a magazine published twice monthly in Tegucigalpa. Turcios, a former foreign minister, apparently began the magazine without prompting from Sandino. Sandino wrote to him repeatedly, clearly indicating that he had found his political soul mate, and he made Turcios his official spokesperson.[35] By 1928 almost all the content of the eighteen-page *Ariel* was Sandino-related and much of it flowed from Sandino himself.[36] Incredibly enough, the two men never met.[37]

Turcios became the linchpin of Sandino's information network. He developed the underground mail route to El Chipote and other Sandino hideouts. He informed Sandino of outside events and kept up his spirits.[38] It was Turcios who gave Carleton Beals access to the guerrilla along with guides and a "Sandino passport."[39] He was also the conduit for all payments to Sandino.[40]

What motivated Turcios? An insightful German reporter visited the "small man of insignificant appearance, between forty and fifty." He did not question the editor's "patriotism and the sincerity of his motives" but identified in him a misplaced romanticism. "Only by hearsay and from letters does he know his hero, and . . . he will not allow himself to be robbed of his happy illusion. . . . Buried under a mass of manuscripts, newspapers and books, he has created the protagonist of a drama which is imaginary but which the world has taken seriously."[41] The name of Turcios's magazine came from Uruguayan José Enrique Rodó's book-length thesis, *Ariel*, which in 1900 argued for a superior Latin American culture in opposition to US materialism and militarism and went on to influence countless Latin American intellectuals.[42] Turcios saw Sandino as the new Ariel of Latin America, a Shakespearean creature pure of heart, uninterested in earthly rewards, and uniquely unifying for the continent.

Ariel had a resonance far beyond Honduras. The Nicaraguan National Guard (GN) reported it was "read over the whole of Honduras, Salvador, Guatemala, Mexico and Costa Rica."[43] Editors throughout Latin America, Europe, and the United States reproduced its articles.[44]

If Honduras was the conduit for money and propaganda, Mexico was the source of much of the former and the amplifier of the latter. Mexican allies mostly lived in Mexico City, the only major city in Latin America that was both truly international and radical at the same time, combining the populism of the Mexican Revolution, the dogmatism of the Russian Revolution, an artistic and literary renaissance, and the policy imperatives of Mexican presidents. Sandino's experiences with Mexico, both before and during his revolt, helped him to situate Nicaragua within a greater imperialist context, away not only from the Liberal-Conservative partisanship of his own country but far, too, from the romantic, elitist bent of *arielismo*.[45] This added dimension was the most important contribution of Mexico to Sandino.

Hard evidence of aid from Mexico does not exist, and the bulk of Sandino's financing might have come from his own region of the Segovias or the nearby Honduran border area, but Sandino himself told Beals in early 1928 that he received $25,000 per month from a prominent Mexican friend. Mexican President Plutarco Calles refused to send soldiers or direct aid.[46] But US Army intelligence suspected that Calles's own chief of staff raised money through an organization and sent it through the consul general in New York to Sandino's representative there, Salomón de la Selva.[47] Contradictory reports claimed that the organization in question, the Pro-Sandino Committee, was "entirely private" and that the amounts raised were insignificant.[48] But money did flow. At one time Sandino received $9,000 in gold.[49] Medical supplies also went through Turcios (see Fig. 13.1).[50]

Mexican presidents may have stayed aloof of the financing, but they lent moral support. Calles and his successor, Emilio Portes Gil, both refused to recognize

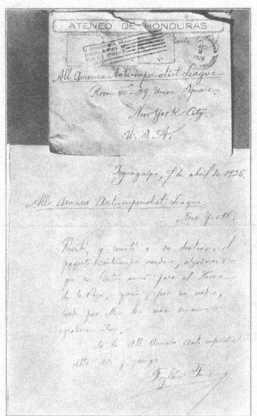

Figure 13.1 The AAAIL of New York advertises Froylan Turcios's letter acknowledging receiving medical aid for Sandino's forces. Folder Nicaragua M.I.D. Reports, box 27, O&T.

Sandino's nemesis, President Moncada, even though all other Latin American nations did. When US Ambassador to Mexico Dwight Morrow pleaded with Portes Gil to recognize the Conservative government in Nicaragua, the president's response was telling: "Suppose for a moment that . . . instead of Nicaragua, the United States were invaded. What would you think, Mr. Morrow?"[51]

Organizations in Mexico City, all transnational and interrelated, also raised funds—and a little hell (see Fig. 13.2). The Pro-Sandino Committee was essentially Nicaraguan in membership and headed by Pedro Zepeda, a former Nicaraguan consul in Mexico City.[52] Money going through Turcios first passed through the hands of Carlos León, president of the Center-South American and Antillean Union (UCSAYA).[53] On January 18, 1928, UCSAYA and ten

Figure 13.2 MAFUENIC ("Manos Fuera de Nicaragua" or Hands-Off Nicaragua) poster, probably from 1929, announcing a bullfight featuring Sócrates Sandino and Gustavo Machado. Folder Nicaragua M.I.D. Reports, box 27, O&T.

other organizations in Mexico City, ranging from anti-clerical groups to labor activists to Joseph Jolibois Fils of Haiti, founded the Hands-Off Nicaragua Committee (MAFUENIC), itself under the umbrella of the All-America Anti-Imperialist League (LADLA), a front founded in 1925 by the Third Communist International (Comintern).[54] Likely one or several of these groups set up a news agency, also called Ariel, that distributed pro-Sandino pieces picked up, among others, by French media. All of MAFUENIC's founders were international in membership and ideology. UCSAYA represented thirteen Latin American countries and MAFUENIC's own secretary general was from Peru.[55] MAFUENIC's leading founder, Venezuelan Gustavo Machado, had formed an Anti-Imperialist League in Cuba in 1924 and co-founded its Communist Party in 1925.[56]

As Machado explained, MAFUENIC's activities included "fundraising, manifestos, cultural events, and conferences." He recruited legendary muralist Diego Rivera to helm the magazine El Libertador, the Ariel of Mexico, but Machado remained its driving force. On April 1, 1928, MAFUENIC organized the largest pro-Sandino rally ever as 5,000 assembled in Mexico City, listened to various speakers including Carleton Beals, and raised $1,000.[57] MAFUENIC also printed flyers and sold postcards reproducing Sandino's writings.[58] In May, Machado and others trekked to Sandino's headquarters, bringing with them medicine, money, and moral support. The Sandinistas "knew that the world was watching and that they had to project a continental image, a revolutionary consciousness," Machado wrote.[59]

Mexico also amplified the lies of the Sandinistas. For instance, Mexican newspapers reprinted LADLA claims of 200 marine deaths in recent encounters with Sandino—an impossibility since only forty-eight died in the entire war.[60] When Machado returned after four months, Sandino entrusted him with an enormous US flag that he claimed his men stole from a marine, and Machado carried it to a talk with Mexican deputies.[61] Marines investigated—no marine flag was stolen and the stars on Sandino's were too small for the flag to be theirs. Most likely the flag was from a US-owned mine (see Fig. 13.3).[62]

New York City became the third vital link in Sandino's transnational network because, like Mexico City, it contained a multinational mass audience ready to participate in radical organizations. New York had a Latin American population of some 40,000 in 1927 and a daily, La Prensa, to service them. It also had its share of artists and radicals. The few Nicaraguan Liberals in town, such as Salomón de la Selva and journalist José Román, imbibed tequila and mescal with the likes of Diego Rivera, Edna St. Vincent Millay, Sherwood Anderson, and Waldo Frank.[63] They rallied around one cause: Sandino.

Many of these New Yorkers belonged to the Communist Party of the United States (CPUSA) and its Union Square-based affiliate, the All-America

Figure 13.3 Gustavo Machado, standing at left in door, giving the All-America Anti-
Imperialist League Sandino's "captured" flag, Mexico, 1929. CHM.

Anti-Imperialist League (AAAIL), the English-language counterpart to Mexico's LADLA. New York hosted smaller Latino workers' associations, such as the
Hispano-American Nationalist Confederation. The most active of these groups
was the AAAIL, which stamped its mail with the directive, "Protest the marine
government in Nicaragua."[64]

New York was also a source and conduit of much of Sandino's transnational
money. The State Department reported that the AAAIL sent $48,000 to Sandino
in April, through Mexico, with an additional $15,000 from the Soviets directly
to Mexico. The CPUSA allegedly financed the AAAIL to the tune of $125,000
but none of it went directly to Sandino.[65]

One significant difference between New York and Mexico City was that
US officials could and did stand in the way. In January 1928, police broke up a
pro-Sandino march of "350 communists" with liberal use of their rifle butts.[66]
In March, New York's postmaster won an injunction against the circulation of
AAAIL handbills raising funds for medical supplies. The AAAIL countersued
both New York and the Postmaster General of the United States, and the Federal Bureau of Investigation quietly agreed that there was nothing illegal about
sending the supplies.[67] A federal judge tried to figure out if the handbill was
fraudulent in claiming Nicaragua was under "marine rule," so he asked Secretary
of State Frank Kellogg for clarification.[68] Meanwhile the persecution continued.
In April 1928 police arrested more than 100 AAAIL picketers in front of the

White House, one of the first arrests for picketing in US history.[69] By May, Kellogg wrote back vaguely to the judge that the situation in Nicaragua could not "properly" be described as "marine rule" since Nicaraguans headed the government, so on May 16 the judge found against the AAAIL, suspecting "a campaign of falsehood and vilification against the American forces in Nicaragua."[70]

Oddly enough, New York gave Sandino a chance to reconnect with his half-brother Sócrates, five years his junior. In 1926, perhaps because of Sócrates's heavy drinking, patriarch Gregorio exiled him to New York.[71] He lived in Manhattan but commuted to a Staten Island shipyard as worker #6498. Sócrates soon changed jobs but complained to his mother of incessant work, even during the Latin American Holy Week. Like most workers in the United States, constant labor brought him barely enough to cover basic expenses. "All I do is work to survive," he reported in shame. "I beg of you, let no one know of my life here, only you and *Papá*."[72]

The Sandino uprising awoke Sócrates from his drudgery, as it did many Latin Americans. At first Sócrates heard of his brother only through local papers and newsreels.[73] After Ocotal, Augusto became a celebrity, appearing on the front page of all the papers, and Sócrates's fellow laborers soon made the connection. "In the factory where I work, where I was an unknown, today everyone knows me," Sócrates wrote his father proudly.[74] By now he had moved to Brooklyn, just in time for the AAAIL to make of him a figurehead. For months he gave speeches and signed handbills. In January 15, 1928, at twenty-nine, Sócrates appeared before the largest crowd of his life. Fifteen hundred in Irving Plaza Hall listened to him describe his brother as the George Washington of Nicaragua. Attendees paid a quarter to hear him and filled hats with spare change to buy bandages.[75]

Then, uncharacteristically, Sócrates joined his brother after the struggle in the Segovias moved him to cure his alcoholism.[76] After his speech, he was deported for signing those handbills.[77] In June he hopped on a steamer and landed in Veracruz, looking for work and a way to get to his brother.[78] A year and a half later he reappeared in Mérida with Augusto.[79] They made their way back separately to the Segovias, Sócrates bouncing around Central American nations with a fake passport.[80] On November 12, 1930, US officials, fearing his propaganda value, refused to let Sócrates disembark in Corinto, seized all his documents, and left him on the ship, broke.[81] He landed in San Salvador, where sympathetic journalists took him in.[82] Some time in 1931 Sócrates reached Sandino's camp, perhaps a mistake since his value diminished once he was there.[83] Upon seeing his brother Augusto exclaimed, "What are you going to do here? There's no hooch here, there's no *chicha*, there's no wine, there's no beer."

"I've come to help you," answered Sócrates. "I want us to fight against the Yankees."

Sandino thought a bit, then turned to an aide. "Give him a gun."[84]

Latin Americans outside of Honduras and Mexico were comparatively unengaged, unseemly, or ineffectual, especially considering their stated pan-Latin Americanism. In March 1929 Sandino tried to engage all American heads of state, including Herbert Hoover, by inviting them to a conference to plan a canal through Nicaragua, and even designed a flag for an imagined "Central American Federation." There was little interest.[85] Argentine President Hipólito Irigoyen spoke of a similar conference, but one Buenos Aires paper called the proposal "an act of political romanticism."[86] In 1929 two conferences did take place, in Buenos Aires and Montevideo, but both were too openly communist to have an impact on public opinion, not to mention on Washington.[87] LADLA had branches in most Central American countries, but they did little.[88] Peru's Popular Revolutionary American Alliance (APRA) fully shared Sandino's international outlook but could never get its leader, Raúl Haya de la Torre, to meet with Sandino. In 1928, APRA broke with the Comintern.[89]

Western Europe's help was mostly rhetorical. Often reported were the inspiring words and slogans of writers such as French mystic and pacifist Romain Rolland and French journalist Henri Barbusse. Europe also hosted two major anti-imperialist conferences. The first, held in Brussels in February 1927, named itself the First International Congress Against Imperialism and Colonial Oppression. Gustavo Machado had the idea of uniting all pro-Sandino organizations in Mexico after attending the Brussels meeting.[90] Yet little resulted. At the Comintern's Sixth Congress in July–September 1928, Chairman Nikolai Bukharin upbraided the CPUSA for not producing an "appreciable reaction" to the US presence in Nicaragua.[91] Little came of a second Congress held in Frankfurt in July 1929. Barbusse presided, Diego Rivera was there, and so was the "captured" US flag.[92] Sandino sent a long letter reaffirming his anti-imperialism, but all the Congress resolved to do was to wish him well.[93]

Beyond the Western world, identification with Sandino was purely symbolic. Old communists such as Japan's Sen Katayama as well as young nationalists such as India's Jawaharlal Nehru and China's Soong Ch'ing-ling, otherwise known as Madame Sun Yat-Sen, sent congratulations to Sandino.[94] In China, a Kuomintang unit called itself the "Sandino brigade."[95]

Despite the limited material value of Sandino's international network, its propaganda value was not inconsiderable. Sandino once demanded from Moncada that the president "rectify his errors" and sent him a clipping from a German newspaper. "The global knowledge of our cause and of the men who defend it," Sandino added, "is what should move you."[96] The clearest testament to the power of propaganda was the discomfort it caused US policymakers. Since their intervention in 1926, US officials reported a decline in their commerce because of Nicaragua. As a journalist explained, "Your Latin-conscious Central American will sell his coffee to a German or an English buyer if the price is anywhere near being equal, and he will buy a German sewing machine in preference to one coming from the country which he thinks is oppressing Nicaragua."[97]

Just as international activism and Sandino's popularity peaked in 1928, Sandino began to suffer setbacks. First, in fall 1928 the marines "drained the sea" of Sandino's supporters by securing the surrender of about 1,600.[98] Second, the marines oversaw presidential elections on November 4, 1928, that were the fairest in Nicaraguan history, and Sandino harmed his populist credentials by attempting to stop the vote through disinformation and terror.[99]

The third event breaking Sandino's stride was his parting of ways with Froylán Turcios. After spying on the editor for years, the Honduran government shut down *Ariel* in the summer of 1928.[100] Both Sandinistas and US officials suspected that Turcios, showing "obvious signs of prosperity," had pocketed more than his fair share of Sandino funds.[101] With no more income from *Ariel* and no more Sandino funds to skim, Turcios resigned as Sandino's spokesperson in early January 1929. For years thereafter Sandino rued what he saw as betrayal by Turcios—"my Judas!"[102] Within a month after his resignation, perhaps as part of a deal with Tegucigalpa and Washington, Turcios was off to Paris as a new consul.[103] The result of the break, Sandino later said, was to cut off his main conduit of information to the outside world and render him isolated.[104] There were also non-monetary issues. Sandino may have wanted to leave Nicaragua to gather his forces in Mexico and Central America for a massive attack, while Turcios encouraged Sandino to surrender and accept Moncada's presidency in exchange for amnesty.[105]

These problems forced Sandino to take a major risk and go to Mexico. On January 6, 1929, he asked the Mexican government for asylum.[106] Sometime in late June, without telling most of his supporters, he left with his senior officials. It was not clear who was left in charge, if anyone.[107] President Portes Gil offered a paid asylum but only after consulting with the US ambassador and secretary of state, who agreed on three conditions: Sandino could not continue his war, could not stay in Mexico City, and had to remain in a "remote state"of Mexico.[108]

Sandino apparently never considered his struggle over. He went to Mexico to revive its transnational network, seeking "moral support, the sympathy that we have always had from all the countries of America. We were overwhelmed by the silence, by the isolation."[109] Yet he was desperate. "Our trip" to Mexico, he wrote in 1930, "was a matter of life or death for our Cause; our leaving was the last card we had to play."[110] Still, marine intelligence considered that Sandino was "finished."[111] After the 1928 election the marines drew down their numbers from over 5,000 to 2,500.

Yet some cautioned that the entire operation against Sandino had failed to address the fundamental cause of instability—the political culture. "No one is more eager than I to see the marines withdrawn," said US Chargé Matthew Hanna, "but we must not forget past experiences. Disorder in Nicaragua is a mushroom growth and can spring up over night."[112]

Latin American solidarity against US occupation suffered a blow during Sandino's year-long sojourn to Mexico.[113] The interests of the Mexican establishment, those who could truly help, were no longer in harmony with the communists and radicals who welcomed Sandino. The appointment of Dwight Morrow as ambassador in 1927 resolved many outstanding issues between the two countries, thus softening Mexico's foreign policy. More seriously, in February 1928 the Comintern dropped its support for non-communist liberation struggles such as that of Sandino, and Mexico City responded to a hardening communist line by ostracizing the Mexican Communist Party (PCM).[114] By January 1929, when Sandino requested asylum, the Mexican government declared the PCM illegal.[115] In early 1930 it brutally repressed the party and drove it underground. On May 1, 1930, police and security forces violently put down worker, student, and peasant marches.[116]

None of this at first halted Sandino's ambitions. Portes Gil provided Sandino with 4,815 pesos (a US dollar equaling about 2.1 pesos) in June 1929 and transportation.[117] Another 2,000 pesos followed in July and perhaps more.[118] Sandino gave dozens of interviews and even wrote a column for the *Diario de Yucatán*.[119] Delegations of workers, students, socialists, and other visitors came to him to pay homage.[120]

Yet Mexico City's assistance was designed to isolate and neutralize the Nicaraguan. When Sandino crossed the border from Guatemala, Mexican generals met him there with bad news: he would not go on to Mexico City.[121] Portes Gil made good on his promise to US officials that he would keep Sandino in a remote region, and on July 11 Sandino and his party arrived in Mérida.[122] When Sandino finally visited Mexico City in January–February 1930 and met with the president, Portes Gil told Sandino what he always maintained—that he had promised asylum and expenses while in Mexico, but nothing else.[123] Sandino was despondent. He did receive weapons from the Mexicans, but the package— apparently two Thompson submachine guns and 4,000 bullets—was so paltry as to worsen the relationship.[124] By early March he wondered where the pension for his entourage was. "The lack of everything is tremendous," he told his agent Pedro Zepeda, in whom he was also losing faith. "My *muchachos* are in a deplorable situation because of the scarcity. We have them at half rations. Some are missing the basics: shoes, underwear, hats, socks."[125]

The worst consequence of the Mexican trip was Sandino's falling out with the Communist Party. On December 25, 1929, Mexico's *El Universal* reported that all three of Sandino's Mexican allies—the PCM, LADLA, and MAFUENIC—were investigating him for allegedly taking $60,000 from Washington to live quietly in Mexico. The communists claimed to have a copy of the check but never produced it, and a later investigation exonerated Sandino.[126] Machado, whom Sandino considered a loyal liaison, apparently designed the smear. There might have been motives beyond the communist falling out with Mexico City. One historian suggested Machado was "apparently bitter at not having been appointed Sandino's general representative." Possibly, the communists were also unhappy with Sandino's proposals for a Latin American confederation.[127] Sandino apparently forced Agustín Farabundo Martí, his liaison to the Comintern, to choose between him and the Comintern.[128] Immediately after the bribery scandal broke, Farabundo Martí harangued Sandino twice while drunk and Sandino had to refrain himself from having him shot.[129] Farabundo went on to his native El Salvador where he founded his own guerrilla struggle and was captured and shot on January 1, 1932. [130]

Sometime in late April 1930, Sandino evaded his surveillance and left Mexico. He arrived in the Segovias between mid-May and mid-June.[131] Sócrates on June 30 reported that his brother, though wounded in the leg by a bomb fragment, had now begun "the second stage of our freedom struggle."[132]

Back in Nicaragua, Sandino made the most consequential metamorphosis of his struggle. When he came back he had no more support from the outside world—for a time, not even mail.[133] "We have come to realize," he wrote, "that we do not have at our disposal one single Indo-Hispanic government, much less any other nation of the globe. Nicaragua is directly and solely represented by our army."[134] Poor Nicaraguans were still not with him anywhere but the Segovias, where he was also losing support.[135] To overcome these crippling losses Sandino turned his movement inward. He altered its ideology by making it militant, mystical, and millenarian.[136] He also expanded the theater of battle. He took the small force he had left and spread it thin, spilling out of the Segovias.

There were novel elements to Sandino's protean ideology. It more than ever championed those who toiled in factories and farms and spent less energy on intellectuals and politicians. On November 20, 1930, Sandino reaffirmed his devotion in his "MANIFESTO TO NICARAGUAN WORKERS AND PEASANTS." "Noble and generous" humble people had always been exploited by professional politicians, who made devilish deals with foreigners, it claimed.[137] Sandino also vented more anger toward the GN, since by 1930 its 2,000 or so men had taken over all combat functions from the Marine Corps.[138]

A few months later, in another manifesto—"of light and truth" this time—Sandino introduced an all-encompassing cosmology. The manifesto explained that "man," insufficiently aware of his "spirit," had brought injustice to a universe of pure "ether." It predicted that the "Final Judgment" would come in the twentieth century and affirmed that Sandino's Army for the Defense of the National Sovereignty of Nicaragua (EDSNN) were the "chosen ones" to bring about that judgment. When they did, "oppressed peoples will break the chains of humiliation with which the imperialists of the earth have wished to keep us neglected" and "the reign of Perfection, Love will be ushered in; with its favorite daughter, Divine Justice."[139]

Sandino's embrace of a tailored spiritual perspective was long in coming. It placed his own extraordinary achievements as an anti-occupation leader above the earthly aspirations of his erstwhile allies. It also explained the loyalty of his followers and justified pressing on. While raised Catholic, Sandino wrote of being disenchanted with organized religion from a young age, doubting God and portraying priests as symbols only of law and authority. The tightening association of the Catholic Church with the Conservative Party intensified his alienation.[140] His years in Mexico began to fill the void with the Revolution's discourse of brotherly love, while its anti-clericalism also confirmed the Nicaraguan's doubts.[141]

On his 1929–1930 trip to Mexico, Sandino joined the Magnetic-Spiritual School of the Universal Commune (EMECU), calling EMECU's founder, Joaquín Trincado Mateo, "one of the great contemporary philosophers."[142] Spiritism was popular in Mexican revolutionary circles, and a friend at the Mérida Masonic lodge introduced Sandino to Trincado's writings. For Sandino, Trincado somehow explained it all—"reincarnation, Rosicrucianism, the spirit, yoga, theosophy, and intuition," according to an interviewee.[143] This mystic belief system bolstered the moral purpose of the insurrection as Sandino spoke to his followers in terms of angels and demons, hell and purgatory. After Mexico, Sandino ordered his men to call each other "brother" and one of their camps was baptized "Joaquín Trincado."[144]

Spiritism also explained Sandino's own role. Although he later said that to call him "a redeemer" was an "exaggeration," the EMECU satisfied Sandino and his followers' need to validate his leadership.[145] Sandino felt that he communicated through magnetic waves with certain people. Others also believed him to have magical powers. Some peasant women and children were known to follow him just to touch him or the things he touched.[146] One Indian kept a Sandino shoelace "as a priceless charm." A student Sandinista told an interviewer, "I'm no ignoramus . . . yet I've seen, as others, a double rainbow descend upon the head of the 'old man,'" as followers called Sandino.[147] For *segovianos*, who long wedded

Catholicism to beliefs in the supernatural and surrounded military chiefs with myths, the EMECU did not seem odd.[148]

Trincado's theories rejected both capitalism and Bolshevik communism, even all organized religion, in favor of a belief in the eventual coming together of all life forms in a communal spirit. Progress was unstoppable and one branch of that progress was economic. Since the original EMECU in Argentina had sustained an agricultural cooperative for twenty years, it confirmed Sandino followers' desires for communal land, and in 1930 Sandino founded such a cooperative.[149] To summarize it all, Sandino adopted the EMECU's motto, "Forever beyond."[150]

As of 1930, Sandino built the embryo of a state. His previous plans for an honorable Nicaraguan president free of partisanship or US input became all but chimerical after the election of the Liberal Moncada under US auspices in 1928. After Mexico, Sandino considered his own army as the microcosm of how Nicaragua should be run.[151] Thinking like a state, Sandino organized. In the first weeks of his insurrection, he had minted gold coins to express his desires for statehood.[152] He then divided the EDSNN not only into military units such as columns, an intelligence service, and even a "fleet" of thirty canoe-like embarkations, but also administrative ones. It had, for instance, a "department of agriculture" devoted to providing the EDSNN with goods and materials. An "education department" aimed to teach to read the 90 percent or so of his followers who were illiterate (it largely failed). A Sandinista archive organized hundreds of pounds of documents, many of them on EDSNN letterhead.[153] From 1930 to 1933 Sandino also appointed local judges and police commanders to extend his authority into Segovian towns.[154]

Also like a state, Sandino took resources from the people and provided them services. He extracted "contributions" and gave "guarantees" in return.[155] Peasants in the Segovias began to think of the Sandinistas as repositories of resources and gatherers of force and therefore began to make (polite) claims on them. In July 1930, for instance, Seferino López wrote to Pedro Altamirano asking for "some cartridges with powder ready to shoot a monkey because this is my remedy." López, sick in bed, explained that monkey innards healed soreness if rubbed on the body.[156]

Finally, Sandino planned, though not much. After his surrender he discussed expropriating US mines and eliminating the Liberal and Conservative parties and founding his own Nationalist Party. He also developed a mini-state around his cooperative at Wiwilí, with training facilities for artisans.[157] But there is no hard evidence—not even a statement from Sandino—that he wanted to rule a separate nation in the Segovias.[158]

Upon his return from Mexico, Sandino also unleashed a bicoastal war, a logical outcome of his new ideology and desperation. With men all over the northern two thirds of Nicaragua, from coast to coast, as early as July 1931 Sandino boasted of the EDSNN having eight columns and controlling eight departments, double the coverage of the pre-Mexico years, and of "maintaining in a state of siege all the cities and towns" in those departments.[159] Despite the exaggeration, his fighting force peaked at 2,000 with another 1,800 in reserve.[160] The first thrust of this renewed war consisted of raiding and temporarily taking towns in the Segovias.[161] The second attacked the west coast, where most Nicaraguans lived.[162] In the third and most sanguinary stage of the post-Mexico war, perhaps 1,000 Sandinistas descended on the Caribbean coast.[163] Before Mexico, when Sandino held a US mine owner captive, friends had asked why he did not kill him. "He's too much of a gentleman," Sandino had answered.[164] In April 1931, however, a statement by Sandino included the order "to kill all Americans and destroy their property."[165] The Caribbean coast was where 369 of the 520 US civilians in Nicaragua lived.[166]

The most ruthless attack on a US citizen was Pedro Blandón's murder of Karl Bregenzer, a Moravian pastor in Musawás. Bregenzer was from Germany but had married a US citizen. On March 31, 1931, two Sumu Indian women breathlessly ran into town yelling, *"Parsen! Ispail kaiwada! Ispail kaiwada!"* (Parson! The Spaniards are coming!)[167] Blandón and his men rode in and accused the pastor of being a GN spy. When Bregenzer unwisely defended his presence by saying that he was sent by the US government, Blandón also judged him "a miserable deceiver of Indians [who] therefore oppressed and exploited them brutally." "I could do no less," Blandón later wrote, "than to ORDER HIS HEAD SEPARATED FROM HIS BODY," and his men forced a Sumu Indian to split Bregenzer's skull open. His wife and two children also were killed. Notwithstanding his methods—and the fact that no missionary apparently informed on the Sandinistas—Blandón was not incorrect about Bregenzer, who oppressed the surrounding Sumus. Even other Moravians considered him a fanatic. After his killing, the Sumus abandoned his colony.[168]

Marines, guards, and other opponents at the time were certain that Altamirano, Blandón, and other chiefs roamed independent of Sandino and fought for "no political interests."[169] Yet their behavior was consistent with his orders. "I firmly believe Pedron is saturated with his mission and faithfully believes he is doing right and that he is absolutely loyal to Sandino," said mine manager W. Pfaeffle, kidnapped by Pedrón for a few days in August 1931. "His troops may share that to a certain degree but my belief is that their animal instinct for loot and murder is more the attraction than anything else."[170] The assessment was similar to those of Dominicans and Haitians: chiefs pursued power, troops sought resources, all within a political culture of violence.

Rather than unite them in nationalism, the fighting divided residents of the Caribbean coast. There was sympathy for Sandino among some workers, especially the Spanish speakers, who engaged in slowdowns coinciding with the Great Depression hitting the coast in 1931.[171] But Indians refused to join them and so did the British-influenced English speakers. Culture on the coast had long been Anglo-American, Bluefields being the first site of baseball in Nicaragua.[172] Terrorizing and kidnapping locals threatened that identity. Decades later *costeños* remembered Sandinistas as dangerous bandits who stole cattle and endangered the wage economy made possible by foreign investments. Many joined the GN after the 1931 attacks.[173]

The offensives of 1930–1932 were nevertheless effective in getting US officials to redefine not only their strategy in Nicaragua but also their approach to occupations overall.

Two things motivated the Department of State and the Department of the Navy to rethink Nicaragua. One was cost. The October 1929 Wall Street crash caused the marines to disengage from the Segovias.[174] It obliterated any chance of building a US canal in Nicaragua, a policy shift made official in mid-1932.[175] After US forces halved their number to 2,500 following the 1928 election, they further reduced it to fewer than 1,000 by mid-1930. The GN was supposed to take up the slack but Moncada promised it $1 million a year while delivering only $230,000.[176]

More decisive, the ongoing struggle caused opposition among the greater public, especially outside Nicaragua.[177] A US diplomat who had been chargé in Nicaragua in 1926 was convinced that public criticism led the marines to withdraw by 1931. He wrote that US opponents of the intervention had "the sympathies of the masses both in Nicaragua and through Latin America."[178] In 1932 the Division of Latin-American Affairs announced that the last of the marines were leaving after that year's election "since public opinion in this country would not understand their remaining there any longer, and their presence there was a fruitful cause of misunderstanding and criticism in Latin America."[179]

One event in particular galvanized negative public opinion and served as the nail in the occupation's coffin: the telephone ambush. On New Year's Eve 1930, ten marines near Achuapa were repairing telephone wires that had been cut, a long-time Nicaraguan form of protest against centralization.[180] A Sandinista band sneaked up on three sides and began firing. The marines fired back, killing eleven Sandinistas. After two and a half hours the Nicaraguans got the best of the marines, killing eight and wounding two. Some were "brutally hacked by machetes after being wounded."[181]

"Public indignation and alarm" followed.[182] Congress was in an uproar.[183] On January 2, William Borah, chair of the Senate Foreign Relations Committee, came out in favor of complete withdrawal.[184] On January 5, 1931, the Senate passed a resolution demanding all the relevant information on Nicaragua from the State Department since 1924, not to mention the withdrawal of the marines. This was in sharp contrast to leading Nicaraguans, mostly Liberals, who argued for *more* marines and guns and ammunition for a "National Army" headed by Moncada.[185] Secretary of State Henry Stimson refused Moncada's request largely based on "public opinion in this country."[186]

A policy shift followed directly. President Herbert Hoover responded immediately and personally to letters about the telephone ambush.[187] The State Department called Hanna and the commanding officer of the GN back to Washington to discuss the response. Following those discussions, on February 13 Stimson announced a plan for the complete withdrawal of the marines. By June he reduced the force from 1,300 to 500 and an aviation section. The rest would leave after the 1932 elections. No marine was left in the Segovias.[188]

Stimson's decision to withdraw the marines came hand-in-hand with another that proved even more of a watershed in the history of US occupations: the end of automatic protection of US property. The cause was, again, anti-occupation activity. EDSNN rampages against US and other foreign properties prompted numerous landholders to demand protection from the marines and guards. As soon as Stimson became secretary of state in spring 1929, it seemed, the petitions increased: twenty owners wrote in June, British diplomats (who were also landowners) did the same in October, and so did a US rancher in December, all this before Sandino even returned from Mexico.[189] The cost to protect private property was rising. One marine calculated that to keep a single detachment in one mine cost US taxpayers "at least $2,000 per month, . . . far in excess, I believe, of the equity in the company held by its present management."[190] Another problem with defending "fixed points" such as plantations or mines was the inability to patrol around them, resulting in "no definite military results."[191] It did not help that Sandino threatened to attack the very properties protected by marines, meaning that the more troops stayed, the more resistance they invited.

Marines also complained about the abandonment of mutual back scratching between military and economic actors that had characterized dollar diplomacy. The Standard Fruit Company, for instance, charged marines to ship their equipment and men to and from New Orleans, and at the most inconvenient times. Company representatives retorted that it had lost "six or seven million dollars" because of violence in Nicaragua. Another company used marine boats to shuttle its own workers, thus saving on labor costs. As early as March 1930 marines considered replacing all of their troops who acted essentially as private security guards with cheaper Nicaraguan guards.[192] In April 1930, citing "no military reason for further retention of marines on East Coast," a GN commander handed mine owners some rifles and a non-commissioned officer and left them to their fate. Other marines simply told landowners to hire private armed guards.[193] US officers even suspected one British hacienda owner of staging an assault on his own property "in order to have a post of Marines or Guardia (preferable to Marines) stationed at his place for the coming coffee season, to take care of what promises to be a bumper crop."[194] As attacks multiplied, so did complaints, one US landowner getting snippy: "I fail to see why our Government cannot give American citizens full protection in Nicaragua. . . . What have you got gun boats *for*?"[195]

Stimson lost patience. In his diary he called US property owners in Nicaragua "a pampered lot."[196] Two days later, on April 17, 1931, the secretary of state announced a formal change in policy: marines would protect US citizens on the coasts but leave property in the interior at the mercy of raiders. Stimson tried to minimize the meaning of the shift, but it was clearly the end of blanket protection of property.[197]

US Marines and diplomats made these momentous decisions despite numerous signals not only that they had not defeated Sandino militarily but also that Nicaraguan political culture had changed little since 1927.

To US officials, by far the most frustrating relic of Nicaraguan political culture was the abiding partisanship among political figures. Years of fighting had not exhausted the parties' passions, nor had Sandino's condemnation of both Conservatives and Liberals helped to unite them.[198] "Nowhere else in Central America has development been retarded to such a degree by deluded political leaders," wrote a visiting German journalist in late 1929. "The desire for a government post is the deciding factor and state considerations of a philosophic nature are of little importance. . . . The spectre of hatred among brothers haunts every hut."[199] The result was social inequality—"a wage of fifty cents a day, long hours of toil, enforced army service, hookworm, malaria, infant diseases, and the oppressions of centuries." "With 71% of the people unable to read and write," he concluded, "political democracy is so far little more than a phrase, while social democracy is a dream in the minds of a few intellectuals."[200] Neither party championed reforms that might help regular Nicaraguans—widows losing pensions, workers with lowered salaries, agricultural laborers fired—all made more precarious by the Depression.[201]

The only difference from 1912 was that, by the 1930s, Liberals, too, wanted US Marines to stay since they now protected *them* from enemies. Increased clientelism was one of the great ironies of an occupation begun with the hopes of creating a more modern, freedom-loving political system. The chief Liberal, Moncada, was increasingly paranoid, strapping two pistols to himself wherever he went.[202] He personally appointed Liberals to replace elected municipal

officials. In early October 1929 he arrested forty political opponents for plot-
ting his overthrow, accusing them of providing weapons for and allying with
Sandino.[203]

Salomón de la Selva was among the arrested. The longtime Liberal was a
classic Nicaraguan political chameleon. He had turned against his party to
handle some of Sandino's affairs from New York. He had also tried his hand at
labor organizing and even worked for Conservatives. Moncada ordered men to
barge into de la Selva's home and search it. They arrested and jailed him with
no charges, no trial, no benefit of counsel, and no due process. He was forced
onto a ship without a passport. He landed in Washington, DC, "a man without
a country."[204]

The presidential elections of 1932 showed all too clearly the depth of the
problem. Jockeying for position inside the Liberal Party displayed the bitterness,
distrust, and naked ambition of potential candidates. The same could be said
for Conservatives and third-party hopefuls, but they had only a slim chance of
electoral victory.[205] Against this partisanship, US officials could do little. Stimson none too subtly threatened Moncada with withdrawing the marines early
and leaving him exposed.[206] In anticipation of the election, Emiliano Chamorro
reappeared and, still controlling an anti-US faction of the Conservatives, told
supporters to boycott the vote. Rumors flew that both parties were regrouping
armies and that poor Nicaraguans were hoarding food to survive another civil
war upon the departure of the marines.[207]

Partisanship worsened every other aspect of political culture that US officials
saw going awry, starting with political freedoms. Moncada disbanded unions
and showed little appreciation for the freedom of the press.[208] Since 1912, US
officials had never imposed censorship, even as the press remained highly partisan. But as the Sandino struggle dragged on, La Prensa, a leading Conservative
newspaper headed by Pedro Joaquín Chamorro, accused both sides of corruption. One man felt his honor so compromised by an article that he pulled a gun
on Chamorro. Chamorro drew his own, and they agreed on a retraction.[209] La
Prensa also called for US withdrawal and drew the admiration of Sandino.[210] In
1929 Moncada considered censoring La Prensa and in November arrested one
journalist for criticizing US actions. Chargé Hanna, though he also disliked La
Prensa's editorial line, showed that he had learned from US mistakes in other occupations and warned the Nicaraguan president of "the grave dangers involved
in the suppression of any newspaper."[211]

Marines found themselves in a paradox as they championed nationalism so as
to minimize anti-US sentiment. Occupiers banned any political talk in the GN,
any flying of partisan flags. Instead they marched young guards, twice a day, with
the blue and white Nicaraguan flag, and had them sing the national anthem as
they raised and lowered it. This was "a ceremony new to a country that for years

has known no loyalties except to clan or party."[212] Yet marines, too, doubted the capacity of the guard to take over. Major General Ben Fuller, the commandant of the Marine Corps, boldly told the House Appropriations Committee, "It takes a good while to make a good soldier out of anybody and it takes much longer to make one out of a Nicaraguan." He added that "those Indians" would be "very likely to mutiny" if officers were no longer from the United States. When pressed to retract his statement, he stood by it.[213]

One Nicaraguan championed the GN like no other. General Anastasio Somoza, subsecretary of foreign relations in mid-1930, argued that the constabulary was ready to take over any and all policing of the country, whatever the cost. A firm believer in centralization, Somoza also proposed identification cards for all Nicaraguans.[214] The United States thus was thrilled to help elevate him to the head of the GN after the 1932 elections. Yet Somoza was also Moncada's nephew.[215] Somoza walked a line between both his patrons—promising professionalization to Washington but politicization to Moncada.

The last years of Sandino's life were a testimony to his dedication and idealism even in the midst of compromise. They also revealed yet again the broader unwillingness of other Nicaraguans to accept any true democratization, social justice, or political freedom. Their implacability led them to paralysis, a condition of which Somoza took advantage.

On November 6, 1932, Liberal Juan Sacasa, the former minister to Washington, won the presidential election, and the marines pledged to leave on January 2, 1933. Militarily weak, low on resources, and having failed to prevent yet another presidential contest, Sandino agreed to peace talks (see Fig. 13.4).[216] The final agreement, signed on February 2, 1933, provided for a "gradual" disarmament of Sandino's troops in exchange for amnesty, some public works jobs for his soldiers, and the right to a hundred-man armed guard in Sandino's cooperative near the Coco River.[217]

Like the Dominican agreement of 1922, this document postponed political solutions to the problems that had brought about the occupation. The agents who negotiated the documents were from the Sandinistas and the Liberal and Conservative parties.

It was the beginning of the end for Sandino. As he surrendered his arms, he told his followers, "Men, I will accept peace, but I will embark on another revolution. . . . This revolution will not be with rifles or weapons, it will be a political revolution."[218] Sandino meant by this that he would influence by example, especially through the development of his agricultural and industrial "Río Coco Cooperative," soon settled by 2,000 or 3,000 workers at Wiwilí.[219] Yet Managua feared that Sandino's revolution would be literally political, as some urged

Figure 13.4 The Sandinos around the signing of the peace agreement, 1933: left to right, standing: Sócrates and Augusto; seated: América and Gregorio. CHM.

Sandino to run for president in 1936.[220] A group of men from Masaya even nominated him to the presidency one year after the peace deal.[221] There were rumors of Sandino joining or heading a National Labor Party and more seriously an Autonomist Party, but both schemes collapsed.[222] Sandino did come down to Managua in May 1933 to discuss leading a new party in collaboration with Conservatives, but he never formally agreed: "I could never be president of Nicaragua because I would immediately become a dictator."[223]

The GN continued to pursue Pedro Altamirano, who had been cold to Sandino's surrender and still headed a band in the Segovias. An attack on Pedrón in July 1933 caused President Sacasa to fear that Somoza was really targeting Sandino, so he declared a state of siege and warned Sandino of an imminent second attack. A clash with Sandinistas occurred in August. By December, Somoza argued that Sandino's cooperative consisted of an illegal state-within-a-state and was still "taxing" peasants, so he called for Sandino to disarm completely. Sandino countered that the GN itself was unconstitutional, also a state-within-a-state.[224] The impasse was complete.

With the marines gone, Somoza talked openly about becoming president and "finishing once and for all with Sandino and his pretensions."[225] In the late 1920s he had bragged to a marine that he would kill Sandino since "you don't understand the Central American way or the Latin American way of doing things."[226] On February 21, 1934, Sandino was in Managua to discuss disarmament with President Sacasa. After dinner and drinks, as Sandino left the president's home with his party, the GN disarmed them at gunpoint and took them to an airfield. There the GN forced Sandino and Generals Francisco Estrada and Juan Pablo Umanzor to their knees, shot them dead, and buried them.[227] Simultaneously, another detachment of guards shot Sócrates dead, along with his son-in-law and a ten-year-old servant.[228] On the same day, the GN descended upon Wiwilí, massacring 300 hundred men, women, and children before destroying the cooperative.[229] Somoza's men then tracked others down in their villages and killed them and their families and burned their fields and houses.[230] Dozens fled to neighboring countries.[231]

With Sandino dead, the stage was set for Somoza's ascent. The GN had practically become the state, consuming half of its budget.[232] Many Nicaraguans expressed relief that the impasse was over, an atmosphere that allowed Somoza to quickly take control of most state institutions and install a dictatorship over the Republic.[233]

As they readied to depart, US officials were dumbstruck by the Nicaraguan desire for them to stay. The "general opinion," wrote one, was that withdrawal was "essentially unfair" to Nicaraguans. Minister Hanna observed that *La Prensa*'s Chamorro chided the Conservatives for their abiding "Americanism" or embrace of US policies. Hanna hoped Nicaraguans would follow Chamorro's advice and be more nationalistic.[234] The marines had assured security for twenty-three years, on and off, and Nicaraguans had lost the self-confidence of an unoccupied republic.

14

Haitian Withdrawal, 1929–1934

It is more difficult to terminate an intervention than to start one.
—Dana Munro

In Haiti as in other occupations, transnational anti-occupation networks played a crucial role in pressuring the US government to speed up withdrawal. But again, it was two forces on the ground—invaded and invaders—who showed that they had the most at stake and therefore held most of the cards in the process of withdrawal. That messy, imperfect process included protest, politicking, negotiation, and reconciliation before the wishes of two US presidents could become reality. Withdrawal also demonstrated how the motivations of those under occupation had less to do with nationalism and more to do with the advantages they could obtain from the retreat of US forces. The resistance in Haiti—far more political than military, in contrast to Nicaragua—severely tested the willingness and ability of US policymakers to follow through on their promises of political cultural reform.

Withdrawal in Haiti seemed nowhere in sight during most of the rule of President Louis Borno from 1922 to 1929. The man who was relatively truculent with US officials while a member of Sudre Dartiguenave's cabinet adopted a far more conciliatory attitude once he moved into the presidential palace. A US journalist who met him described Borno as "a highly cultured, vindictive, patriotic, personally ambitious, shrewd and dictatorial man, lacking in balance."[1] It was an "open secret," said another, that he had bribed the Council of State to make him president in 1922. It was no secret at all that he would replace them if they disobeyed him—as he did with eighteen out of twenty-one to gain "reelection" in 1926. With a $24,000 a year salary and a $12,000 expense account, Borno benefited from the occupation far more than the average Haitian, whose annual income was $20.[2] So did the five US treaty officials who essentially ran the country, along with some 250 US civilians, under the rule of the high commissioner, Brigadier General John Russell, who answered only to the State Department.[3]

In all but name, Haiti became a colony of the United States. Yet unlike other colonies, the empire held on not for economic or military reasons but in the hope that Haiti could somehow become a stable, prosperous, self-governing republic. In 1923, US administrators in Washington and Port-au-Prince informed the *Boston Transcript* they intended to stay another twenty-five years.[4] They built roads, airports, and hospitals; they cleaned up the jails and the bookkeeping; and the Gendarmerie—renamed Garde in 1928—policed the country efficiently enough.

As the occupation dragged on, fewer occupiers remained true believers and more of the invaded lost hope that the occupation might—or even should—try to enhance their political culture. Occupiers rarely explained their crusade for a saner political culture and Haitians grew frustrated at the apparently rudderless occupation. In 1925, Pierre Hudicourt returned from the United States dismayed that "no American, not even in the Department of State, could tell me the reason why Haiti does not share the fate of the Dominican Republic."[5]

Around Borno's inauguration, marines reported that many elites seemed either indifferent or mildly pleased that one of their own—an educated, experienced mulatto—had succeeded Dartiguenave.[6] Some partisans and clients of Borno in 1925 showed their satisfaction by organizing as the Progressive Party, likely a mechanism for enforcing loyalty to Borno: government employees "chose" to tithe, most likely in return for the right to keep their jobs.[7]

Yet in the 1920s, elite resistance shifted from anti-US to anti-Borno and from social and economic grievances to defeating the hated new chief executive. Also diffusing hatred toward the United States, at least at first, was High Commissioner Russell, who was courteous in public and liked by Haitian high society.[8] As Borno's rule grew more iron-fisted and vindictive, the elite became more desperate and recalcitrant. To their great frustration, US supervisors ran the treasury honestly and diverted expenses toward road building and agriculture.[9] "The governing élite have been ousted from their natural function in the state," complained Constantin Mayard, indicating that he and his peers still conceived no other vocation for themselves but government.[10] Mayard himself had been removed from the Council of State. In 1922 he and other former ministers took with them official documents as they departed and published them in order to embarrass Borno. Around the same time someone tried to shoot the mayor of Port-au-Prince and likely also a witness, both of whom were engaged in building a case against grafters in the Dartiguenave administration.[11] In response to such incidents—or merely to insulting editorials—Borno tended to demand arrests and Russell would grant them.[12]

Frustrated, the elite opposition also organized as a party. Since their existing organization, the Patriotic Union (UP), forbade itself from running candidates, UP leaders spun off a faction in September 1922, the Nationalist Party (PN).[13]

There were other short-lived organizations—the League of Public Welfare, the Committee for National Action, the Haitian Anti-Imperialist League, the Constitutional Action Committee, the League of the Flag, and the League for the Defense of the Rights of Citizens and Man, among others.[14] They opposed just about every initiative of Borno in his first year—a new loan, a reorganization of the National Railroad, a concession to the Sinclair Oil Company, a contract to the Haytian Pineapple Company, and a tax on the manufacture of rum and tafia, a local fermented drink.[15] Otherwise the PN advanced no constructive counterproposals. One "plan" of a particularly optimistic PN presidential candidate in 1925 included "fifteen thousand primary schools," "one thousand forts in the mountains and trenches provided with high caliber and long range cannons," "an aerial and naval fleet," and "a loan of four or five billion gold on the Belgian market." The US chargé cited it to give "an idea of the mental and moral value of the so-called Nationalist Party."[16] Eventually UP members—including Pauléus Sannon and Sténio Vincent, who had traveled to Washington in 1921 to argue for more democracy—betrayed the spirit of the UP by campaigning against Borno while declaring they would take his job if the Council of State appointed them.

Throughout the inter-elite struggles, the opposition consistently threatened that if Borno did not restore the legislature, the poor black masses would revolt and all of the elite would suffer. "Our people have come to such a point of exasperation against the protectorate of the United States, disguised as Haitian-American cooperation," said the UP's Georges Sylvain, "that if we did not feed its need for active protest, a revolt would be feared."[17] The role of the elite, Sylvain told Oswald Garrison Villard of The Nation, was "to direct this wave of discontent and to prevent it degenerating into a bloody conflict."[18] This threat assumed that the hoi polloi had a will to rebel, for which there was no evidence in the 1920s, and furthermore that the elite would realize the desiderata of the masses. It was a logic filled with paternalism, fear, and disdain for the masses.

The State Department declined to hold legislative elections. They were constitutionally mandated every even-numbered year, but State interpreted loosely the wording—"an even year"—to mean some years could be skipped. Munro elaborated on the real reason: "the ignorance and illiteracy of the majority of the voters . . . would probably result in a legislature largely anti-American in sentiment." The Borno government acquiesced because it wanted, as the Haitian minister to Washington plainly admitted, "to have its friends elected."[19]

In 1926 and 1927 the fractured opposition strengthened and unified in response to Borno's attempts to monopolize political power. To be sure, most Haitians were still indifferent to the goings on in Port-au-Prince. The closest thing to a poll during the occupation was a local count, in late 1927, of a registration before a possible plebiscite. In it the pro-Borno crowd was "three or four times as numerous as their opponents."[20] That figure, if accurate, may have made the opposition seem hopelessly unpopular. Yet a 20–25 percent anti-Borno rating was far higher than what occupiers imagined, which was usually 2 to 5 percent. In any event, as a result of Borno's power grab, anti-Borno petitions got larger.[21] They also became more alarmist—for instance, spreading the rumor that three years of US Navy maneuvers out at sea prefigured the taking of Môle Saint-Nicolas.[22] UP meetings also improved in attendance, organization, and focus.[23] In small towns, some refused to run for mayor under Borno on the grounds "that they would make too many personal enemies . . . and that the cost would be more than the pay would warrant."[24] Seeing this state of affairs, Russell predicted that it would take "two generations for this backward nation to advance sufficiently to properly handle its own affairs." That was the time required to develop a "middle class, which will be the salvation of the country."[25]

Russell's hope that the next generation would be more favorable to US rule was sorely off the mark. A younger generation of Haitians proved more militantly anti-occupation, while advancing its own race- and class-influenced program.

Jean Price-Mars, author of *Ainsi Parla L'Oncle* (*So Spoke the Uncle*), set the intellectual tone for the new generation. A physician and former minister to Paris, the son of a deputy, and a cousin of former president Vilbrun Guillaume Sam, Price-Mars was fully of the elite, except that he was "a pure black man" and explored seriously Haiti's racial identity.[26] In 1904, Price-Mars had visited the Centennial Exposition in St. Louis and been shocked by its primitivist treatment of Filipinos. He was also disgusted by US segregation. Yet he visited Booker T. Washington's Tuskegee Institute and showed interest in bringing its agricultural techniques to Haiti. Price-Mars returned to Haiti denigrating the superiority complex of mulattoes and other elites and preaching an embrace of the black peasantry and its practices such as farming and Vodou.[27]

Some of the new generation's concerns, coinciding with the rise of a transnational *noirisme* or artistic renewal of the African Diaspora, were largely literary, mostly an effort to pull away from classical French influences.[28] For that reason the occupation, not caring about Haitian art, paid little mind to Price-Mars and his ilk.[29] However, another purpose of *Ainsi Parla L'Oncle* and *La Revue Indigène*, a magazine founded in 1927, was to build up resistance to occupation by reminding Haiti of its unique and meaningful blend of African and Western virtues.[30] Among the many new rebels of *noirisme* were well known anti-occupation activists Léon Laleau, Alfred Nemours, Ernest Chauvet, Georges Léger, and Clément Magloire.[31]

More radical and politicized than the young writers were the young socialists. Marxism made an appearance in Haiti in 1924 when the Workers' Association publicly called on "comrades" to enter politics.[32] Yet socialism was really the souvenir that Jacques Roumain brought back from Europe. The Communist Party recruited the future author of *Masters of the Dew* while he was in France and Switzerland. In 1927, aged twenty, Roumain returned to Haiti and immediately founded the short-lived *Revue Indigène*, then *Le Petit Impartial*, then *La Nation*.[33] He had several run-ins with the Borno government, once starting a wild courtroom brawl with a marine when on trial for libel.[34] He also refused an invitation from the high commissioner with the reply, "The black Jacques Roumain does not dine with the white racist Russell."[35] Roumain founded an underground Haitian Communist Party in 1932, then brought it into the light in 1934.[36]

The labor movement also gathered steam in the final half-decade of the occupation. In late 1929 employees of three US-run treaty services formed another workingmen's association, to, as they said, "end depressions."[37] A year later, longshoremen, pineapple workers, and coffee sorters struck near Cap-Haïtien, some attacking the Garde. Shortly after, workers at a US-owned sisal plantation threatened to walk out. A marine memo noted an "undercurrent of unrest" in the republic.[38]

This new generation of Haitians was clearly more militant than the previous one. A Garde officer commented that Roumain's group were "ANTI EVERTHING. . . . They are against their parents, the Government, the opposition, and the Occupation."[39] A year later the occupation noted that the founding of the Patriotic Youth League advanced "one of the most disturbing and subversive proposals offered in many a day." Louis Mercier spoke to a crowd of 500, aged twelve to thirty, telling them his role models were Charlemagne Péralte and Mizaël Codio, two insurrectionists. "The white man is not necessary," said Mercier, "and we do not need him." He added that "all Haitians are negroes and therefore equal and that there should not be preference or distinction among the citizens of the same country." Mercier then suggested that those who joined the League could be executed if they denounced it.[40] These were indeed fighting words, against both the occupation and the elite.

Because they argued for egalitarianism, young Haitians represented what the elite saw as "the danger of the new middle classes created by the Americans."[41] Yet the youth movements' ideas were confused: they criticized both Catholic and American education; romanticized peasants but failed to communicate with them; and attacked the older generation but had similarly self-interested political goals.[42] They also exaggerated the sharpness of the color line among their elders, since the leadership of the two largest anti-occupation organizations was half-black and half-mulatto.[43] Some young *noiriste* writers berated the elite's belief in free speech, freedom of the press, and representative government as a façade hiding the elite's self-interest, yet as a remedy they advocated a black dictatorship.[44] Even the younger generation's fashion was contradictory. Like the

US troops who oppressed them, Haiti's youth adopted what papers derided as the "military" look: rolled up sleeves, low-heeled boots with rubber soles, and the abandonment of ties and high collars.[45]

Facing this varied and growing opposition, in 1929 Borno and the State Department again had to decide whether to hold legislative elections the following year. "The people of Haiti are centuries behind the people of any of the Central American countries in this respect," observed Munro, as head of the Latin-American Division. In Haiti there was no independent supervision of elections and "at least 95% of the people are not only illiterate but absolutely ignorant of the first principles of representative government." Reflecting State's concern with public opinion, Munro concluded that the status quo was safest. "From the standpoint of hostile propaganda the manner in which the election was conducted would have more news value than would a mere decision to let the present situation continue."[46] At the same time Secretary of State Henry Stimson determined that Borno should "under no circumstances" run again.[47] Contradictions abounded. State wanted public welfare but saw nowhere the roots of democracy. It sought continuity but denied Borno a third term. It wished for an educated peasantry but offered next to no education. In September 1929, Stimson confirmed the status quo while promising the new president, Herbert Hoover, that he, too, wished for "a Commission of highly important citizens to examine into the whole question in Haiti" and to "have a policy mapped out."[48]

While State and the White House inched toward withdrawal, the resistance took a giant leap forward. "Paul," a spy among Port-au-Prince opposition groups, reported in 1929 "that the city is in a turmoil following the decision of the President in regards to the elections. They are enraged. They say there is one thing left for them. To fight. The country will be reduced to cinders and the Americans will reign and rule over the cinders. Of two things possible either that the country will return to normal or will become a colony. Washington will be responsible." Paul concluded that people were "looking for an opportunity to release their rage."[49]

They got it in the students' strike.

On October 31, 1929, students walked out of one of the occupation's new agricultural training schools in the town of Damiens, north of the capital. The Central School was a symbol of the few new reforms under Borno, meant to create a middle class through better farming. In October, schools administrator George Freeman changed the scholarship scheme to divert one fifth of the funds away from the highest achievers and toward those willing to toil at the farming unit in the school. The achievers, unwilling to do manual labor even for pay, protested.

Once they walked out, the students refused to go back and intimidated others who did. In subsequent weeks, student lawyers, doctors, pharmacists, dentists, and nurses struck in sympathy. They marched to Freeman's house, chanting "Down with Freeman!" He responded by shooting off his revolver to warn them away.[50] Girls' schools also joined the walkout. Reform school boys, complaining of their "monotonous menu of cornmeal," refused to eat. Primary and secondary schools wrote letters of support. By late November, thousands were on strike and hundreds demonstrated on a daily basis in Jacmel, Gonaïves, and Cap-Haïtien.[51]

The Damiens strike, spearheaded by the Patriotic Youth League, was the first major appearance of students on the anti-occupation scene and the first student strike in Haitian history.[52] Strikers' motivations were both understandable and disheartening. They resented occupation officials who arrogantly told Haitians how to develop while giving them insufficient tools and disrespecting their culture. French Minister to Haiti Ferdinand Wiet, who publicly denounced the occupation, described Freeman, an Alabaman who spoke horrid French:

> Far below average in education, infatuated with himself, inclined to believe that the economic and financial supremacy of his country confers upon him an intellectual and social superiority over other foreigners, he has shown on many occasions that he is far from blessed with the tact and moderation needed to interact with the inhabitants and authorities of a sovereign State.

Freeman had run the twenty schools of the Technical Service since 1923 and had brought in a few dozen compatriots, the "experts," whose salaries matched those of Haitian ministers. Freeman himself made $10,000 per year plus travel, housing, and a car.[53] When he died in Puerto Rico in 1930, Damiens students expressed "pleasure" that he had "given his soul to Satan."[54]

The strike, however, also laid bare the deepest fissures of race, class, and culture dividing Haitians. Freeman's shifting of scholarships from rich to poor students embodied the reformism of most occupiers, explained the British vice-consul, but the elite "shows as yet little sense of social responsibility."[55] Both elite politicians and students did not "desire to see the peasant educated, and this desire would overcome any thought they might have for the good of Haiti as a whole," wrote a US administrator.[56] Student leader Justin Sam, trying to discourage a prospective student of Freeman's, said, "It is shameful to work as a student alongside derelicts."[57]

A desire to take down Borno and perhaps force out the Yankees also motivated strikers. On November 18 the president actually capitulated to the Damiens students, restoring all their grants and offering amnesty, but the students refused and asked for additional concessions such as replacing US stenographers with Haitians and firing Freeman.[58] What politicians pressing the students really wanted was to prevent a third term by Borno, who had intimated he would seek one and in November postponed the scheduled 1930 elections to 1932.[59] Freeman's moves met with a coordinated effort by the political opposition, organized in 1929 as the National Constitutional Action League, to spread the student strike. League members bought meals for strikers, fed them arguments, and goaded their own children into striking.[60]

Peasants also joined, spurred in their case by a decline in the price of coffee. Borno meant to increase the price by mandating that growers clean and cure their beans before selling them, but the onset of the Great Depression, combined with Brazil dropping a price support program, collapsed the world price. Exports plummeted 31 percent in one year.[61] The peasants blamed Borno and the occupation, and occupiers worried that such discontent could spread strikes "from the cities to the country districts."[62]

In a larger sense, the coming of the Great Depression had an impact on the occupation of Haiti as it did in Nicaragua. US trade with Latin America collapsed generally—imports declined from $2 billion to $500 million—and Haiti was no exception.[63] Although foreign trade was a small component of Haiti's economy, occupation enlarged it and the country arguably suffered more than it otherwise would have. A US interest, the Haitian-American Sugar Corporation, had, for instance, revived the trade in sugar and made it the major export along with coffee, but with the crash, quantities fell by a third. Overall, Haitian trade with the United States fell by about half.[64]

By early December, occupation authorities began to panic. "Not only politicians are behind the disturbance," reported the brigade commander, "but also the elite and educated Haitians of color other than black."[65] The strike spread quickly to all port cities, drawing also "many Haitian . . . business men." Russell judged that even the Garde's loyalty was "very questionable." On December 3, he cabled Secretary Stimson for 500 more marines.[66]

On December 4, at Aux Cayes, a port city where stevedores refused to unload ships, the occupation reinstated martial law. Newspaper editors published names of government workers who stayed on the job, hoping to intimidate them. The Garde, desperate for reinforcements, paid prisoners to help, and guards moved their families into their barracks to protect them. On December 5, the US colonel in charge cabled back to Port-au-Prince: "Request help. Streets full. Attitude menacing." The next day at 6 PM Captain Roy Swink narrated what had just happened:

Patrol sent to meet party of 150 reported headed toward Aux Cayes. Met crowd of about 400 at edge of town. Refused to disperse. Shouted and cursed. Sent burst of fire over their heads. They did not leave. Another burst fired in the ground ahead of them. No effect. Fired into the crowd. Five killed and twenty wounded. Crowd took to the hills. Patrol returned to town. Magistrat returned from Camp Perrin says countryside in revolt. Situation very grave.[67]

Misconceptions abounded after the Aux Cayes incident—"the Massacre at Marchaterre," Haitians called it, where the twenty marines had indeed fired into a crowd of not 400 but 1,500. The Haitian press reported twenty-four dead and fifty-one wounded; more reliable figures from the hospitals were twelve dead and twenty-three wounded.[68] Occupiers thought the mob had received an arms shipment; the mob, in turn, believed Aux Cayes was being bombarded.

Those who descended from the hills around Aux Cayes to taunt the marines were motivated by economics. They looked to abolish an August 1928 alcohol tax that placed seals on their stills.[69] With coffee wiped out, the plain around Aux Cayes had made sugar cane its mainstay. Hundreds of growers had petitioned Borno in May 1929 but he responded with "deep disdain."[70] As one deputy from Aux Cayes explained, distilling was "the base for the subsistence of many families of our town. It allows the maintenance and extension into the plain of Cayes of sugar cane, and with it ensures the living of a host of small artisans who provide it with services." The design and application of the law were also faulty: the same tax applied to all rums regardless of their water content, thus encouraging high alcohol volumes; the salaries of the inspectors, who were subject to bribes, would take up most of the earnings of the tax; and, most egregious to Haitians, small distillers were disproportionately thrown out of business: in one district, eighteen distilleries dwindled to one; in the Plaine de Cul-de-Sac, 100 shrank to three.[71] Distillers in Torbeck told Borno in February 1929 that the tax, if it put them out of business, would not only drive them to a "horrible misery" but also raise *no* income.[72]

Many accurately described Damiens and Aux Cayes as sparks setting off a well-primed fire. "For years we were forbidden to manage our own affairs. Shorn of all dignity, we were no longer citizens, not even men," recalled deputy Edgar Numa. "That is why, when we learned of the Damiens strike, all eyes turned to them with the secret and vague hope that something decisive would come from their action."[73]

In December 1928, Sumner Welles gave a lecture in which he identified Latin America's resistance as the reason for withdrawal everywhere. Occupation, he said, "inevitably loses for the United States infinitely more, through the continental hostility which it provokes, through the fears and suspicions which it engenders, through the lasting resentment on the part of those who are personally injured by the occupying force, than it ever gains for the United States through the temporary enforcement of an artificial peace." That peace, he continued, did "not remove the basic causes for the resort to revolution. These causes, so long as the inhabitants of the nation where intervention takes place remain an independent people, can only be removed by the will of those people themselves. . . . I make no exception to this assertion."[74]

Haiti was certainly no exception. The killings at Aux Cayes, like the attack against the marines repairing telephone cables in Nicaragua, drew blood and so got the attention of the world and especially of US public opinion. The Associated Press and United Press sent special correspondents to cover the aftermath.[75] Senators, major newspapers, and civil society groups such as the National Association for the Advancement of Colored People (NAACP) and the American Civil Liberties Union (ACLU) called for ending the occupation.[76] Protests poured into Washington. The Young People's Socialist League complained from Chicago that "our Might is being employed to prevent organization of labor unions and to crush whatever strikes the workers may engage in."[77] The Communist Party staged rallies in New York and Washington.[78]

Yet Haiti, as always, drew less Latin American sympathy than other occupied countries. Only US diplomats in Uruguay reported any significant protests beyond a few editorials. The Dominican and Chilean governments remained quite cordial to the United States.[79] From Bogotá, the chargé noted how events in Haiti "have aroused but little unfriendly comment here, in marked contrast to the events in Nicaragua of two and three years ago."[80] Even the Cubans, so hostile to the Dominican occupation, barely denounced the massacre in Haiti. Cubans perhaps resented the thousands of Haitians who flocked to their sugar fields every year.[81]

Hoover did not wait for the Haitian events of fall 1929 to act. In Latin America he looked to avoid new occupations or interventions. "It ought not to be the policy of the United States to intervene by force to secure or maintain contact between our citizens and foreign states or their citizens," he had declared in April.[82] He refrained from intervening in Panama, Peru, Honduras, and El Salvador in response to events that in the past would have drawn the marines.[83] Hoover's conviction against occupation stemmed from the Great War, which had shown him the nefarious effects of power politics and the robustness of nationalism. The Quaker saw his presidency as an opportunity to encourage representative democracy and peace as the bases of international relations. He also wanted to encourage trade through expertly trained diplomats, and he reduced the number of political appointees to Latin America from fifteen to one.[84] In Washington, Dana Munro recalled, Hoover's insistence got policy moving.[85] In mid-September 1929, even before the students struck at Damiens, the president proposed a commission to find an end to the Haitian occupation.[86] Three days before the Aux Cayes massacre, he made his idea public, "to arrive at some more definite policy than at present."[87]

Yet transnational resistance was crucial in sustaining Hoover's determination. "It remains probable," said Minister Wiet, "that the President of the United States of America, in sending a Commission of enquiry to Haiti, is mostly wishing to satisfy his domestic opinion and the public opinion of the other republics of the New World."[88] Haitians, too, had an impact. Immediately after the Aux Cayes shootings, Hoover said that the "entire situation should be reviewed in the light of this experience."[89] On December 7, he formally asked Congress for the commission and soon secured $50,000 to fund it. Those moves ended the strike, martial law, curfew, and censorship.[90] Stimson had also been preparing Russell to respect public opinion. He questioned the closing of newspapers in an illiterate society, saying the benefits of martial law were "outweighed by the unfortunate effect produced in the United States." Although he provided a warship off the coast, Stimson warned Russell against landing additional marines or "extending" inland those already there. In a preview of what he would advocate in Nicaragua the following year, he ordered that US citizens in "exposed places" be withdrawn rather than protected.[91] "We are satisfied," declared student leader Justin Sam on January 14, 1930.[92] The pressure from the US public was off, too. "The President has obviously averted a great deal of hostile criticism from the radicals, the churches and the humanitarians, by his prompt move," British officials noted.[93]

The visit of Hoover's commission to Haiti in February–March 1930, more than any event, proved the effectiveness of the Haitian resistance, just as the Dominican response to the Harding Plan in 1921 convinced US occupiers to go. In both instances the key strategy was not to *achieve* unity; it was to give the *impression* of unity. That strategy suggested the larger failings of the political opposition, which were to never accept US entreaties to modernize Haitian political culture and to focus instead on the political battle against internal enemies.

After Congress approved his commission, Hoover's February 4 statement laid out the end game for all concerned. "The primary question which is to be investigated is when and how we are to withdraw from Haiti," he said, breaking with the tradition of sending merely investigative commissions. "The second question is what we shall do in the meantime." The president refused to withdraw immediately because the current treaty gave the United States the right to remain until 1936 and he wanted "to build up a certainty of efficient and stable government, in order that life and property may be protected after we withdraw." The statement confirmed the political reformism that had motivated the occupation and continued to color US rhetoric, albeit limited now to a law-and-order approach rather than the building of democracy or a middle class.[94]

Minimizing the political nature of the commission was its membership, which included neither a member of Congress nor an African American, omissions meant to satisfy, respectively, US and Haitian advisors.[95] Instead, Hoover chose to send what he called "unbiased minds."[96] Cameron Forbes, the chair of the commission, was not exactly unbiased: he hated Wilson for his idealism, for thinking a black republic such as Haiti could be made democratic, and perhaps also for dismissing him from his post as governor general of the Philippines.[97] Along with him went Henry Fletcher, an old friend of Forbes's who had attended the Chile and Havana pan-American conferences and advised Hoover on his tour of Latin America; Elie Vézina, a French Canadian who represented the Franco-American Catholic Federation; editor James Kerney to represent Democrats; and William Allen White, a Progressive editor from Kansas (see Fig. 14.1). All the commission's members spoke French and two were Catholics.[98] Before his departure, Forbes met with Hoover and described him as "not a bit theoretical or visionary. He sees things exactly as they are. He honestly wanted to get out of Haiti and let them run their own affairs; and he honestly doubted whether it would prove possible."[99] The commission was due to arrive in Port-au-Prince on February 28, 1930, and to conclude its work before the elections scheduled for April 14.

In Haiti, the resistance began to plan its strategy the day after Hoover's announcement that a commission would go, and the process showed an abiding concern with appearances. A group in Aux Cayes advised townsfolk to avoid

Figure 14.1 The Forbes Commission, February 28, 1930, upon landing in Port-au-Prince. Photo # 52G-516321, folder 52G Forbes Commission, box 14, RG 127G, NARA II.

Mardi Gras celebrations "as the Americans wish to show tourists that the Haitiens [sic] are still savages because of their manner of dancing."[100] The opposition tried to paper over its internal dissent, but by mid-February it was deeply split on tactics. The more conservative, peaceful faction led by former UP president Perceval Thoby counseled testifying in front of the Forbes Commission "in an orderly fashion, attacking faults, and not individuals." The more radical faction led by Antoine Rigal and Victor Cauvin, informed partly by socialism and perhaps dominated by youth organizations, prepared "a program of demonstrations, propaganda and disturbances."[101] The radicals held a February 12 requiem at the Port-au-Prince cathedral in memory of the Aux Cayes victims. After the service, 500 stood on the steps to hear what French minister Wiet described as "an untimely provocation by the opposition."[102] Cauvin and Sam were arrested along with twenty-nine others.[103] Russell released them two days later, citing the radicals' plan "to lead the Commission to believe that there is violent popular discontent with [the] regime."[104]

The marines, too, prepared. Russell knew that the Forbes Commission was coming to his fiefdom to judge his rule as much as the ability for Haitians to rule themselves. He kept US flags flying only at the legation.[105] The Garde was also to report any instance of "anti-American opposition or hatred" and during the Forbes visit kept its eye on thirty-two "agitators."[106] On the eve of the arrival Russell ordered all US treaty officials and military officers to check their attitudes toward the occupied, ordering them to behave "with a minimum of harshness compatible to the situation."[107]

The very evening of Russell's warning, a "very surly" crowd of 2,000, armed with knives and clubs, gathered at the palace of the Council of State in response to the false rumor of a coup d'état. The Garde descended upon them with its own clubs. The clash produced thirteen arrests and four wounded guards.[108] No one was killed, but the incident confirmed that no one seemed to control events as the Forbes Commission's ship approached the Haitian capital.

On February 20, conservative and radical factions of the Haitian opposition made a pact to reconcile temporarily under an umbrella organization called the Federated Committee of Haitian Patriotic Groups, with Antoine Rigal as its chairman. The committee claimed to represent 100,000 Haitians.[109] The agreement they signed engaged the parties "to take any essential action with a view to obtaining the withdrawal of the Occupation, the reconstitution of the legislative chambers, and of national institution, and the organization of national Haitian power."[110] Perhaps as a quid pro quo for conceding leadership to the radicals, conservatives dominated the public relations side of the federation by presenting a softened but resolute opposition. The day before the commission arrived, Haitians, like Dominicans in 1916, draped Port-au-Prince's homes in Haitian flags covered in crepe. They also distributed thousands of small paper flags to passersby.[111]

The following day, as Forbes and his team docked, a crowd of 5,000 men, women, and children met them in a quiet and orderly demonstration. "Long live the American nation" and "Welcome to the Commission" read their banners. The opposition correctly assumed that Hoover and his commission truly wanted a withdrawal and that they could overrule Russell and Borno. The strategy, therefore, was to flatter the commission and lay out a clear political path for it to embrace. The crowd, informed in advance of the commission's route, followed it from its ship to its hotel, then to the presidential palace where the men visited with Borno. At dusk the commission walked down the palace steps and extended their hands to greet the throng, which responded with a thunderous cheer.[112] "The demonstration," commissioner Fletcher recalled, "had been extremely well organized by the political opponents of President Borno."[113] Forbes himself wrote in his journal that the banners were "all of one tenor."[114]

At the hearings, the opposition was equally "united and organized," as Russell admitted.[115] It packed the meeting halls and took up 90 percent of the hearings' time.[116] It hired Georges Léger, an English-speaking lawyer, to help during all the testimony, which lasted ten full days. At first, Fletcher recalled, the commission heard "rather scattered and not very well supported criticism of the occupation." But then "the opposition concentrated its fire on the political situation." Speaker after speaker demanded, in practically the same words, three political changes: the resignation of Borno, the dissolution of the Council of State, and the holding of legislative elections. These identical three conditions were on banners when the commission landed. No matter who was testifying—labor leaders, women, Masons—all presented these three ingredients for a political solution and left out grievances more germane to their group. The withdrawal of the marines was not their first priority; getting rid of Borno was.[117] The problem was that the proposed solutions satisfied mostly the ambitions of the unemployed political class, to whom legislative elections would give hundreds of jobs.

There was a second crucial element to the witnesses' discourse. Almost all threatened that if these three conditions were not met, the "people" would revolt, the marines would crack skulls, and Washington would be embarrassed. Many used the memory of "the atrocious and purposeless carnage" at Aux Cayes as a warning. "Since October 31 of last year," said one witness, referring to the Damiens walkout, "we have been in full unarmed revolution."[118] In a typical testimony, Léger prompted a witness with just the right question:

LÉGER: Do you believe that a presidential election by the Council of State would be accepted peacefully by the Haitian people?

CAUVIN: I bet that the blood would flow on the Haitian side and on the American side.[119]

Victor Cauvin based his conclusion not only on Aux Cayes but also on the February 27 riot, which he himself likely manufactured. The memory of recent deaths was the collateral for this threat, La Presse cleverly citing the Gettysburg Address's relevant passage about not letting the dead die in vain.[120] This tactic seemed a sop to the radicals, who threatened bloodshed daily, but the argument most benefited the conservatives since there would be no violence.[121]

Outside of the testimony the opposition also presented a disciplined, united face to the commission. On March 2, Perceval Thoby's wife led a religious procession of 1,200 women that drew 15,000 onlookers.[122] Russell put on a formal evening for elite Haitians to hobnob with the commission, but several declined and printed their responses in newspapers, signaling that they welcomed the commission but would not associate with Russell.[123] The commission also gathered testimony in the interior, witnessing additional evidence of unprecedented organization by Haitians. "Everywhere we saw the same banners and heard the same refrains which greeted us on landing: sometimes the same organizers appeared in the crowds," Fletcher recalled. "In every town we went we were greeted with the same reception," Forbes wrote. "No music; everyone with the same paper banners, cut out of the same roll of paper; and with signs carrying the same inscriptions."[124]

Forbes understood this as a strategy, but for the first time in the occupation, the Haitian opposition was, to use modern parlance, "on message." The British chargé observed that the opposition convinced the commission that its case was that of all Haitians. "Undoubtedly popular opinion is now over 90% anti-Borno." The "counter-case"—the bloody history of political mismanagement by these same elites—"is not understood to be relevant at present."[125]

The threat of violence worked. Forbes cabled President Hoover to summarize the three Haitian demands, adding, "Any other course will not be accepted by the people and will be opposed with acts of violence."[126] Russell shared Forbes's fear of real violence, so he urged him to calm the Haitians down.[127] That request led directly to a political solution. Forbes met in his hotel with Léger, two conservatives, Pierre Hudicourt and Seymour Pradel, and two radicals, Rigal and Sam. Forbes admitted the commission members "were impressed by the delicate and dangerous political situation in which Haiti found herself" and he asked for the five Haitians to calm the passions of their followers, which they promptly did, suggesting the extent to which they stoked those passions to begin with. Forbes then overstepped his instructions from Hoover, which were to merely "study and review conditions," and helped nominate a successor to Borno.[128] Hudicourt, painfully aware of how rare a Haitian agreeable to all sides would be, sighed: "Where are we to find this white blackbird?" Still, the opposition produced a list of five names. Borno at first refused the formula, but on March 15 he agreed to Eugène Roy.[129]

The threat of violence worked further. When Borno made the legalistic argument that legislative elections could only be held in 1932, Forbes answered: "The responsible leaders of the articulate elements of the Haitian public have convinced us of their sincerity when they say that if they have to wait for two years more for their legislative assemblies the United States will be held responsible for a period of riots and disorders, to quell which it may be compelled to use the marines." He even urged Hoover to approve the political deal "for our own protection."[130] The White House and the State Department obliged.[131]

The coming of the Forbes Commission gave Haitians the opportunity to vent on a number of matters concerning political culture. US officials countered with their own thoughts. The resulting clash rendered obvious the broad gap between occupied and occupier and cast a foreboding pall over the future politics of Haiti.

Among the strongest arguments of Haitians was the fact that US occupiers gave a terrible example of "self-government" by importing dozens of unnecessary US citizens at exorbitant salaries to do work that could have been done by Haitians.[132] At the Customs office, US citizens earned $250 per month for similar work as Haitians earning $18.[133] Such arguments struck a chord both with the masses, who thought their increased taxes paid these salaries, and with the "outs," who hungered for the very spoils they criticized.[134]

More convincing, but less common, was to argue that the occupation had in fact been a counterexample of democracy. "America's representatives in Haiti have taught us," wrote *Le Nouvelliste*, "to drive our Senators and Deputies out of office, to close down social clubs, to refuse to permit our expenditures being controlled, to pass laws of the utmost stringency against the Press, against the right of holding public meetings, the right of free speech, the right of making public manifestations, the right of holding opinions, the right of suffrage, in brief against one and all of the democratic liberties guaranteed by the very Constitution imposed upon us by Washington."[135] "We have now less knowledge of self-government than we had in 1915 because we have lost the practice of making our own decisions," Georges Léger explained in his testimony.[136] As one group of Haitians summarized, "There is only one school of *self-government*, it is the practice of *self-government*."[137]

In its last years, the occupation did attempt Haitianization, or replacing US with Haitian citizens, in the Public Health Service, Public Works, and Technical Service.[138] Yet the universal US opinion was that Haitians proved resistant to new ways of doing things and dishonest and incompetent when unsupervised, especially when it came to keeping order or counting money. The head of the customs reported that "Haitians have frequently been left in charge of custom houses during vacations of collectors, and in each instance there has been a noticeable letting down in the efficiency of the organization, and a large increase in the number of errors found in customs documents."[139] It did not help that occupiers felt there was "so much to do" and had "no time to waste in debating or explaining matters to the Haitians."[140] The pace and nature of Haitianization remained the main sticking point from 1930 to the end of the occupation.[141]

To school administrator George Freeman, reform came down to a deep cultural change. "What we must have in Haiti is a middle class and it is by this means of education that we are trying to establish that middle class." Russell agreed. "This question is not solely one of technical efficiency," he said, "but it is also one of development of character by indoctrination which is naturally a slow process." Yet the Haitian color line made that change all but impossible, according to US administrators, who cited the Kreyol proverb *Neg' pas ça commande neg* (Negroes cannot command Negroes) approvingly. Russell gave the example that the most competent engineers in the country were black but they could not make a living because mulattoes would not hire them. Russell himself engaged in racially tinged judgments on Haitian political culture, saying for instance that "the negro race . . . will always require inspection by white men" and that "the only power the Haitian recognizes is force."[142]

The elite also continued to argue that it, and only it, should continue to rule the masses. *Le Nouvelliste* warned Forbes and his colleagues that peasants mattered little next to "the Haitians of real worth who compose the class known as the 'élite.'"[143] Even interim president Roy embraced a natural deterministic explanation of Haitian national identity. "The Haitian is good but he is deeply sensitive; the luxuriant tropical nature in the midst of which he lives has not permitted him to do much thinking."[144]

As they saw Forbes hammer out a withdrawal essentially rewarding the elite for their unscrupulousness, US officials on the ground, civilian and military, were outraged. How could fifteen years of work to bring Haiti into the modern era be abandoned and Haiti left to the rapaciousness of its elite? Russell believed there had been sincere efforts "to develop a middle class to bridge over the gulf that now separates the few 'elite' or former controlling class, from the great mass of the Haitian people." The occupation had also tried to create a "land-owning and productive class among the peasants." Yet "the Haitian people are, to-day, but little better fitted for self-government than they were in 1915." He proposed to Forbes that the six years remaining on the treaty of occupation be used to speed up political reforms at every level—legislative, judiciary, and municipal.[145]

Forbes and his colleagues knew that they were leaving behind a highly unequal and undemocratic republic. A withdrawal "would inevitably inure to the disadvantage of these poor country people," wrote Forbes, "and yet they are immeasurably superior to the so-called elite here who affect to despise them and propose to despoil them and, producing nothing themselves are for the most part drones."[146] Fletcher's comments also echoed those of treaty officials: "Haiti really has no artisans and no middle class. Her people have rarely learned to be mechanics, carpenters or plumbers. Even the chauffeurs are usually Jamaicans."[147] Yet Fletcher and his colleagues had abandoned all hope of changing this state of affairs. When a US official expressed dismay to commissioner White that no peasants had been heard, White's response was, "Yes, that is too bad, but if the Haitian peasant is inarticulate so much the worse for him. There is nothing that can be done about it." He added that international public opinion now mattered more than reform. "The goodwill created in Latin America by this change is more important than any obligations, if there are any, we may have to Haiti."[148] The Forbes Commission also kept one foot in Washington as it roamed Haiti. Forbes told Borno that "we had to consider public opinion in the United States and that our people were getting a good deal stirred up over this whole situation."[149] He and Fletcher, recalled a US official, "were both perfectly frank in saying that the action of the Commission was purely a political matter in the sense of politics of the United States."[150]

"Hooray!" scribbled Forbes in his journal upon hearing that his stay in Haiti was over. He and his men wrote up their recommendations on the boat ride home. Besides the restoration of Haitian elections under the temporary presidency of Roy, these included the Haitianization of all services and a phase-out of the occupation until 1936, starting with the recall of Russell and Freeman.[151] Hoover accepted all the recommendations as "along the lines I would like to move."[152] The US press hailed the commission's report. Even *The Nation*, in perhaps its first positive comment on the US government during an occupation, praised the commission for its "astonishingly quick and effective piece of work."[153]

Much of the delay between the holding of Hoover-approved elections in spring 1930 and final withdrawal of US forces more than four years later could be explained by the abiding political perceptions of occupied and occupier. The former proved, not surprisingly, far more divided and self-interested than when the Forbes Commission visited. The latter proved far more recalcitrant to cede any power before reforms were fully implemented.

With elections set for April 1930, enmities among aspirants to the presidency resurfaced, as did broader divisions in Haitian society. Among these, the US chief of police singled out "the question of caste" and "the question of the elite and the common people." An old caco from "the hills," General Emmanuel Thézan, appealed to the masses, and so other presidential candidates kept him out of all their meetings. "The wealthy class place their hopes in the youths and the elite," continued the chief. "For them the common people constitute purchasable slaves." Because dozens in the occupation hoped to be president, they disagreed with minor details of negotiations with Borno and the occupation so as to distinguish themselves as patriots.[154]

During the campaign, an epidemic of politically motivated fires swept Port-au-Prince. One destroyed the brigade commander's house, another the Parisiana Theater, where politicians often met. One life was lost, a dozen suspects were arrested, but no conclusive evidence pointed to a culprit. "The populace is excited," reported the British chargé. "Rumours are as numerous as they are fantastic, and there seems to be no satisfactory explanation of this outbreak of terrorism." Theories flew that someone was unhappy with the election of Roy and that the occupation set the fires as an excuse to prolong its rule.[155]

Things did not settle once Roy took power. "Composed largely of black Haitians, of extreme anti-American antecedents," his cabinet angered "the liberal minded mulatto element." One of these, Hannibal Price, predicted that for this very reason, as soon as the marines departed, "political dissension and civil strife will break out again in Haiti, and Haiti will revert to the chaotic condition which obtained in 1915."[156] Opponents of the occupation were now scattered throughout government. Dantès Bellegarde was back in France as minister. Young radicals Jacques Roumain and Justin Sam, while not ministers, held positions of authority. Roy explained that he awarded them jobs not to reward them but "to avoid the necessity of locking them up."[157]

This jockeying was a prelude to the real prize, the presidential and legislative elections scheduled for October 14, 1930. Seymour Pradel of the so-called Cartel and Constantin Mayard led most other candidates up to a week until the election. Because Mayard promised to collaborate with the occupation until its departure, the Cartel's slogan against him became *Mayard, cé blanc* (Mayard is a white man).[158] Color indeed separated the parties, the "Blacks" behind the Cartel and the "Yellows" backing Mayard.[159] Joseph Jolibois Fils came back to Haiti for the campaign. The newspaperman had been away for a few years on a largely failed continent-wide attempt to find allies against the occupation. He spun yarns to the riffraff in Haitian towns about immediate withdrawal and government jobs for all when the Cartel took the reins. "Jolibois will get rid of the whites" was the word.[160] The only real concern of the people, it seemed, were the alcohol and tobacco taxes, which the Cartel vowed to repeal.[161] French Minister Wiet estimated that no fewer than 60 percent of government employees lost their jobs under Roy, including stenographers, clerks, and office boys, many because of "the color of their skin." Everyone expected another purge when the new president came in.[162]

Dirty tricks plagued the vote on October 14. *Mayardistes* complained that Cartel money bought not only "the various voting booth administrators" but also Mayard's drivers so that they would steer voters to the wrong booths.[163] The Garde observed "wholesale fraud" but did not intervene. As a result, the Cartel won an overwhelming victory. The National Assembly was now anti-occupation and thirty-three of thirty-six House members were black. The president of the House was Jolibois fils. Despite its triumph, the Cartel broke up right after the election because the newly elected National Assembly had to choose a president. On November 18, among the Cartel's leaders, Sténio Vincent, a mulatto and longtime opponent of the occupation, took four ballots to defeat Pradel by "straddling the fence" along the color line and appointing prominent blacks such as Thoby and Pauléus Sannon to his cabinet.[164]

Haitian anti-occupation activists, back in power, fêted Senator William King, who visited for two weeks in 1931 after having been barred by Borno in 1927. Crowds met him with "frenzied ovations," as did representatives of President Vincent, delegates of the Senate and House, and Thoby. Haitians put on several receptions and banquets in King's honor and named a street after him.[165] The warm reception indicated how optimistic Haitians were that the occupation would soon be over.

They were wrong. Secretary Stimson certainly seemed conciliatory and quickly replaced Russell with Dana Munro, a civilian. But a few diary entries by Stimson in 1931 suggested his attitude. "We are trying to give way to the Haitians gradually," he wrote in April, "but of course that is not the way to deal with Negroes." In September he added that Munro, in negotiations with Haiti, "is expecting trouble with his niggers, and I told him that we would back him up at giving back at them as hard as they gave him."[166] No wonder Sannon, minister of foreign relations, noted that US officials were too proud to admit any mistakes and so arrogant as to expect gratefulness from Haitians.[167]

Out of the stalemate emerged, as in the Dominican Republic, what Sannon called a *pure et simples* crowd demanding immediate and complete Haitianization and withdrawal.[168] The hatred of this group toward white occupation was palpable, for example, in an article in Roumain's *Le Petit Impartial* that told whites to "remember the Haitian slaves—remember what they did to the soldiers of Napoleon's army. . . . Fear, insolent whites, that this horde of negroes whom you despise so much will accompany you, one day, at the wharf with a machete on this hip, crying 'Vive Cacos!' . . . Americans, fear the *red fury* of the *negroes of Haiti.*"[169]

For a while, though, things seemed auspicious for those seeking accommodation. On August 5, 1931, the Haitian and US governments reached an agreement on Haitianization that terminated martial law and gave Haiti authority over public works, health, and the Technical Service. The US legation would no longer approve legislation and the financial advisor would stay out of expenditures. Yet the Haitian government still had to get approval for new expenses since the US government wanted its $40 million loan paid back.[170]

The accord further increased the gap between the executive and other political Haitians. In November 1931, the government abolished the UP, citing it
as no longer needed even though the president himself had been a prominent
member. That same month, a pro-Vincent deputy was assassinated, for which
Jolibois and others were arrested.[171] Then the National Assembly unanimously
rejected a convention of September 3, 1932, setting a timetable for withdrawal
while keeping a military mission and financial oversight because the US financial officer would merely change his title while indefinitely capturing greater
powers.[172] Revealingly, the final accord on withdrawal, reached on August 7,
1933, was an executive agreement, exempt from legislative approval.

Seeing Haitians creep back into power was disheartening for many occupiers
and made them ponder the cultural differences between them and US citizens.
Perhaps the most representative rumination came from Stuart Grummon, the
chargé in 1930:

> In general, while the Anglo-Saxon has a deep sense of the value of social
> organization and of the obligation of democratic government to assume
> a large share of responsibility for the social welfare of the masses, . . .
> the Latin mind, on the contrary, is apt to scorn democracy and neglect
> activities looking to the health and educational welfare of the masses.
> This Latin outlook . . . has been impressed upon the Haitian élite in an
> exaggerated form.[173]

Munro actually noted how "the Haitians are totally unlike the Spanish Americans," with whom he had dealt for years.

> With the latter, one can usually appeal to their better qualities and
> count on a certain amount of real patriotism among the more enlight-
> ened leaders. The Haitian seems to think primarily in terms of jobs.[174]

While giving a speech at Howard University in the spring of 1931, Roy's chief
of cabinet Lucien Hibbert said essentially the same, that "the Haitian people are
extremely excitable" and "are anxious to get complete control of the American
Services as quickly as possible in order to secure as many lucrative jobs as they
can."[175] Most worrisome still were the many comments, by President Vincent
and other prominent Haitians, that perhaps Haiti was not ready for democracy
and was better suited for dictatorship.[176] US diplomats predicted that "a military
government" would soon follow withdrawal.[177]

In a December 1933 speech, ironically given at the Woodrow Wilson Foundation in Washington, President Franklin Roosevelt explicitly repudiated "armed

intervention" as a hemispheric policy. More important, he rejected Wilson's constitutionalism, saying the United States would no longer maintain "law and the orderly processes of government" abroad unless directly threatened and foresaw a collective response from the Americas if such occupations recurred.[178] To Roosevelt, Haiti was a fait accompli, and ongoing disputes were just loose ends. Evacuating Haiti cleanly and quickly would signify his intent to pursue with vigor his Good Neighbor policy toward Latin America, and thus Haiti became a symbol of inter-American relations.

Few complained in Port-au-Prince, since further negotiations were in Haiti's favor. Like Dominicans, Haitians got better deals as they held out. The 1933 agreement dropped the military mission and limited financial oversight, substantially similar to the Dominican case, and confirmed that what occupied peoples hated most about military occupations was the military. Yet the remaining financial oversight was a problem. "What the Haitian people will never be able to understand," said President Vincent in a speech, "is a tendency to delay the definitive resumption of its sovereignty over a mere question of money, of interest only to a few dozens of bondholders."[179] Roosevelt and the State Department also got an earful from the ACLU and the NAACP, both prompted by the minister in Washington, Dantès Bellegarde, and by the Women's International League for Peace and Freedom.[180] Bellegarde also worked Latin American public opinion by showing up at the Pan American Union's Seventh Congress in Montevideo in November 1933. When his time to speak came, he raised his hands. "In the name of my little Haiti which has suffered so many injustices on the part of the great powers during the course of her sorrowful history," he implored, "in the name of justice, peace and friendship, I beg the delegates of all our countries" to form a better Union. Then he resigned from it.[181]

A remaining problem with the 1933 agreement was that it did not foresee withdrawal until 1936, when the US-Haitian treaty would elapse. President Roosevelt wanted to push the date up and his secretary of state, Cordell Hull, let it be known that "such a gesture would make a good impression in South America."[182] Ernest Gruening of *The Nation* agreed, calling early withdrawal "conclusive proof of the high purpose and good faith of the New Deal in inter-American affairs."[183] Roosevelt gave in to all of Vincent's final demands, even making less evident the US hand in financial oversight. Also, he sailed to Cap-Haïtien in July 1934 to deliver a speech—partly in French—to celebrate Haiti's independence, to express hope for mutual friendship, and to remind Haitians that the United States "tried to help the people of Haiti."[184] Haitians received the words gracefully. It was the first visit by any foreign head of state in Haitian history.

On August 15, 1934, the last US troops left Haiti (see Fig. 14.2). The *Haïti-Journal* expressed disbelief: "The Republic of Haiti is disoccupied . . . yes, disoccupied. . . . We can now put an end to our eternal stance of resistance and alert."[185]

Figure 14.2 Marines lower US flag in Cap-Haïtien, August 6, 1934, the last day of the occupation there. Troops left Port-au-Prince on August 15. Photo # 52P-51519, folder 52P Official Ceremonies, box 14, RG 127G, NARA II.

As a sign of how little had changed since 1912, at the 1933 Pan-American Congress in Montevideo, Gruening accompanied Secretary Hull as an official delegate. On the ship, the delegation met and Hull said he wanted to avoid signing any non-intervention resolution and just make friends. Gruening urged Hull to come out strongly against intervention.

"Ah'm against intervention," Grunening recalled Hull saying with his Tennessee accent, "but what am Ah goin' to do when chaos breaks out in one of those countries, and armed bands go woamin' awound, burnin,' pillagin' and murdewin' Amewicans? How can I tell mah people that we cain't intervene?"

"Mr. Secretary," responded Gruening, "that usually happens *after* we have intervened."

"Wemember, Gwuening, Mr. Woosevelt and Ah have to be weelected. You don't have to win," was Hull's retort.

Gruening had one of his own: "Coming out against intervention would help you get reelected."[186]

The exchange laid bare what the decades of struggle against occupation, both in Latin America and the United States, and the years of painful negotiations and recriminations among US policymakers, still left unclear. Hull still had not abandoned the principle of intervention to remedy failures of political culture that harmed US interests. And Gruening, an exemplar of the transnational anti-occupation activist, had still not convinced him that occupation had unacceptable political costs. In the end, the convention out of Montevideo banned intervention in all its forms, and Hull signed it.

Conclusion
Lessons of Occupation

Goodness gracious. I don't think any time we've ever gone anywhere
and acted in the capacity of a policeman that we've been overly
popular.

—Lieutenant General Edward A. Craig, USMC (ret.)

Craig served as a marine in Haiti, the Dominican Republic, and Nicaragua and
reflected decades later upon the shadow these occupations cast on US relations
with the world.[1] He and many others agreed that they were largely failures.[2]

To be sure, occupations deserved some accolades. There were numerous acts
of bravery among US troops, who clearly defeated the Haitian insurgency, arguably the Dominican, and perhaps even the Nicaraguan one.[3] The United States
obviated the need for European powers to invade. It also built roads, sewers, hospitals, and schools.[4] Occupations addressed root causes of instability, namely, by
managing debts responsibly and creating national constabularies.[5] Finally, the
costs to the United States were relatively low: seventy-nine US dead and perhaps
$100 million for all three occupations combined.[6]

Yet even these achievements were mitigated. The highest costs were borne by
those who died resisting—estimates are 2,250 Haitians and 1,115 Sandinistas—
not to mention the perhaps thousands who died from incidental violence.[7]
Many would strongly dispute that Sandino was ever subdued. There was also no
evidence of any European intent to occupy. Financial regularity lived on largely
because US administrators kept it under their authority—until 1941 in the Dominican Republic and 1947 in Haiti. The national constabularies, for all their
stabilizing power, became instruments of unprecedented repression under Anastasio Somoza in Nicaragua and Rafael Trujillo in the Dominican Republic. To
these failures can be added that occupations built physical infrastructures that
Latin Americans did not—sometimes could not—sustain, and that democracy
was but a façade of elections, some fair, others not, that failed to protect speech,
assembly, and other civil liberties.

What such debates about successes and failures typically omit are the views of the invaded and attention to matters of political culture. Reviewing a few lessons from these occupations from these points of view may help to make the US occupations in Latin America part of the usable past and not simply the quaint "banana wars" or "small wars" that seem at times to bear little relation to twenty-first-century US operations in which roadside bombs and cell phones have replaced machetes and pamphlets as tools of resistance.

Resistance Begins at Home

Resistance among the invaded played a crucial role in ending occupations in the 1920s and 1930s.[8] The State Department's Dana Munro wrote that "the hostility and distrust that [occupations] aroused, not only in the Caribbean but throughout Latin America, was the worst result of the intervention policy."[9] Without widespread, persistent, and interlaced networks of men and women fighting against the presence of US troops, occupations may have lasted for generations, as occupiers intended. After they ended, there was widespread agreement that the resistance had been, as one marine wrote, "a formidable weapon against which the Occupation seemed powerless to act."[10]

Within the resistance there also existed a dynamic. The causal chain in all resistance movements inevitably began in rural areas, where occupations committed the bulk of their atrocities and most threatened the political fortunes of caudillos. After a few years, resistance usually moved to towns and cities as occupations showed that they were serious about changing political culture and that their reformism threatened the livelihood of the upper classes, bureaucrats, and artisans. Finally, groups of urban activists, led by journalists and out-of-work politicians, spurred the transnational network by writing to sympathetic foreigners, traveling abroad, hosting visitors, and hounding the US government. Haitians, Dominicans, and Nicaraguans could not afford to wait for US allies to rescue them without prompting.

The impact of the occupations on public opinion in the Americas should not be understated. The transformations witnessed from 1912 to 1934 among the US and Latin American press and civil society emerged from and contributed to greater cosmopolitanism among the citizens of the Americas. US provincialism suffered a stinging blow in these years, and the occupations were a primary cause.

Anti-Occupation Does Not Equal Nationalist

Perhaps the clearest pattern in the resistance was that it too easily imagined itself as purely nationalist. Yet the rhetoric and especially the actions of the resistance barely subscribed to any definitions of the term. Few argued for ethnic or racial chauvinism, for superiority above other nations. Few attempted to unite their nation, engaging instead in every intra-national division imaginable. Fewer still worked for the general betterment of their republic. Rather than nationalists, those who resisted were anti-occupation activists who defended an autonomy that was local rather than national.

Perhaps the difficulty in building a truly nationalist front rested on the reality that the instruments of anti-occupation activism remained beyond the nation. Activists, largely excluded from national state power, found themselves forced to resist either below the state—as insurrectionists, caudillos, city councillors, and the like—or above it, as part of transnational networks. Yet the minimal role of nationalism preceded the occupations, a more determinative factor. Resistance during occupations failed to call on nationalism—with the partial exception of Augusto Sandino—because politics in these countries had barely developed national institutions and identities.

It may be best that resistance come to terms with its true motivations. Knowing a movement's true interests allows it to better rally followers, form coalitions, pursue goals, and confront enemies both within the resistance and in the occupation.

If Unity is Impossible, Fake It

Perhaps the most original tactical lesson to emerge from these cases of resistance was the effectiveness of good public relations. Dominican and Haitian activists appeared for years to be disunited and uncoordinated. But in 1921 and 1930, respectively, they presented a united front to occupiers and the outside world, a crucial step in convincing the United States to withdraw. Sandino also survived for years largely through the appearance of uniting Nicaraguan and even Latin American opinion against occupation.

Beware Nation Builders

These occupations were among the first "nation building" efforts by the United States. Yet occupiers sabotaged the trajectory for national institutions and identities by artificially creating the former without the latter existing. The new roads, the telegraphs, the centralized political system, and the constabularies that dominated a disarmed population could easily be used by politicians whose civic irresponsibility, elitism, and violent methods were largely unchanged from pre-occupation days, save for their newfound ability to unleash repression on a national scale. As the marines prepared to leave each occupation, constabularies had absorbed few warnings against politicization. In Nicaragua, for instance, the US legation, as a favor to Liberals and Conservatives, supported the appointment of fifty Nicaraguans, half from each party, into the officers' ranks within the National Guard. None had military training.[11]

Those who fear the negative impact of foreign occupation on their compatriots should be wary of withdrawal as a panacea. A year after the Haitian withdrawal, the National Association for the Advancement of Colored People again criticized the country's lack of civic freedoms—but this time the culprit was the administration of Sténio Vincent. Haitian elites shot back that "here no one any longer bothers about" jailed journalists, and accused African Americans of being manipulated by Haitian communists.[12] In 1942, Howard University historian Rayford Logan visited Haiti for the second time since 1934 and noted a growing disenchantment with democracy. "I was especially struck," wrote Logan, "by the frequency with which I heard the statement: 'What Haiti needs is a dictator like Trujillo.'"[13]

It got one. By the 1950s, the Garde—the constabulary that adhered to US values the longest—was fully enmeshed in political intrigue and coup plots, leading three overthrows in the decade after World War II.[14] Added to this was a growing rift between dark-skinned blacks and mulattoes that ended with the victory of blacks in the 1957 election of Jean-Claude Duvalier.[15]

Reconcile the Soldiers and Diplomats

For the occupiers, the most original lesson from these occupations was that they had to better streamline the objectives and interests of the military personnel on the ground, usually marines, and the diplomats back in Washington. In all three occupations, marines were content to carry on their political reformism, regardless of failures, until the State Department ordered them, often against significant pushback, to heed the resistance and plan for withdrawal. Almost universally, soldiers thought they knew best because they quelled dissent among the occupied, pushed through material improvements, and blocked input from abroad, including their own superiors. The diplomats countered that they knew the US president's wishes, in addition to getting earfuls from US and world diplomats, press, and civil society.

Neither had a holistic vision. While soldiers *were* often better placed to judge events on the ground, diplomats, while caring less about changing political cultures, brought greater objectivity and cosmopolitanism to decisions for withdrawal. It is therefore important to re-situate the State Department at the center of occupations because these were undertakings whose beginnings and ends were primarily political in nature.

Political Culture Is Resilient

Some occupied peoples did claim that political culture changed after occupation. "You taught us how to work," Dominicans told a visitor in 1928.[16] "The Occupation very sensibly marked Haitian mentality," wrote president Vincent. "She impressed upon it a tidier and more practical conception of life, a more developed and surer taste for material comfort, a greater need for peace, security, and work, a more pronounced tendency for fact rather than speech, for results rather than illusions . . . and developed . . . this sentiment . . . that not only in public service can a good Haitian be useful to his country."[17]

Yet there is far more evidence that political culture in all countries largely continued to be anti-democratic, self-interested, and ruinous to the nation. "A realistic examination of Haitian peasant life," wrote a sociologist in 1937, "reveals that the American occupation, the recent work of rural school teachers, public health physicians, agricultural agents, and army officers have not as yet modified appreciably either the objective aspects of the Haitian social structure of the nineteenth century nor the attitudes associated with it."[18] His assessment could also apply to urban Haitians and to Dominicans and Nicaraguans.

Journalist Carleton Beals warned that changes in political culture, slow to occur under any conditions, were almost impossible under foreign rule. "The politician from there has to identify with the reigning social forces and beliefs of his country and know how to use them. The foreign administrator is free of that obligation; and regardless of his good intentions, the system of life and thought that he imposes will never be a welcome graft onto the native stump."[19] Essentially agreeing with Beals, a Haitian told a marine officer near the end of the occupation, "how about if our situations were reversed? If the Haitians came up to the United States and occupied your country. We know how you helped us in so many ways," he said, "and we appreciate that part, but after all this is our country, and we'd rather run it ourselves."[20] Woodrow Wilson himself had come to this realization after he pulled troops out of Veracruz: "If the Mexicans want to raise hell, let them raise hell. We have nothing to do with it. It is their government, it is their hell."[21]

Memories Persist

Part of the reason that the occupations and their resistance had such a lasting impact on these societies was the vivid if sometimes inaccurate images that they burned in the memories of occupation survivors and how individuals and states then turned those memories into official versions of history.

Certainly, there were many personal anecdotes demonstrating concrete, bitter memories from the occupation. In the Dominican Republic, wrote one visitor a few years after the occupation, "practically every person told me that because of the brutalities committed by American soldiers in that country . . . there is implanted in the people of Santo Domingo a deep-seated feeling which borders on hatred towards the Government of the United States, and you cannot imagine the strength or the depth of that feeling until you go to that country and talk to the people concerned."[22] Dominican resistance leader Ramón Nateras was still celebrated in song decades after his death.[23] Former Sandinistas interviewed decades after their own struggle, as old men and women, vowed to fight to the death were the marines ever to occupy their country again.[24]

Several future leaders of these three countries were children during the occupations and harbored painful images. Leftists such as the Dominican president Juan Bosch and the Nicaraguan founder of the modern Sandinistas Carlos Fonseca grew up listening to stories from those under occupation. Fidel Castro once tried to overthrow Trujillo as a member of the Sandino Battalion. And Ernesto Ché Guevara studied Sandino in 1956, saying "I love the land of Sandino and I want to fight there too."[25]

Sandino left the most persistent memory, both because he died a martyr in a time of peace and because he had the greatest influence on the rest of Latin America.[26] One friendly author wrote shortly after Sandino's death that his impact was largely psychological—a refusal to fear the Yankee.[27] A Salvadoran general wrote to Sandino's parents on the fourth anniversary of their son's death that "I have and will always have as a relic the image of the Hero of the Segovias, because the departed General Sandino and his soul will forever be the true personification of the integrity of Nicaragua and Central America."[28] Gregorio Sandino himself considered his son "the first soldier of Spanish America."[29] Perhaps for these reasons the Cuban Revolution in 1962 produced a comic book version of the Sandino struggle as part of an anti-imperialist series for children.[30]

Bias and inaccuracy colored some of these memories. The Cuban comic book, for instance, featured shady Wall Street bankers giving the direct order to assassinate Sandino—a claim for which there is no evidence.[31] One historian in 1944 wrote that public works in the Dominican Republic were simply a way for marines to "justify" their occupation, not an end in themselves.[32] And a Nicaraguan in 1951 argued that political parties had nothing to do with intervention, even though one always requested it to defeat the other.[33]

Other memories reflected the cultures in which they grew into legends. The death of Charlemagne Péralte was an example. When the marines finally tracked him down and killed him, they tied his body to a door, stretched his arms out, lifted him up, and took a photo so that Haitians would believe that he was truly departed. The pose backfired. Writers and painters eulogized Péralte, a Vodou practitioner, as a Christ-like martyr. On his tomb was the poem,

> Dead at thirty three years of age, betrayed like Christ,
> Exposed nude under his flag, crucified;
> As one day he had dared to promise it to us,
> And for our Nation he sacrificed himself.
> Confronting the American, and alone to shout: "Halt":
> Let's bare our head before Charlemagne Péralte![34]

The Haitian painter Philomé Obin used Péralte's "sacrifice" as a model for his painting titled *Crucifixion of Charlemagne Péralte in the Name of Liberty*, which hung in the national art museum (see Fig. 15.1).[35]

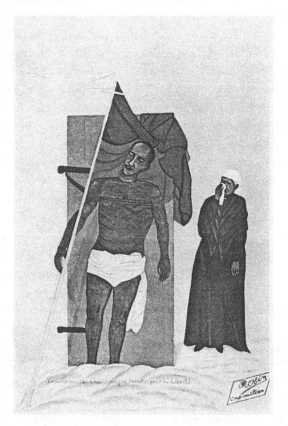

Figure 15.1 Painting by Philomé Obin (Haitian, 1891–1986) of the "crucifixion" of Charlemagne Péralte, with his grieving mother added: *The Crucifixion of Charlemagne Péralte for Freedom [Crucifixion de Charlemagne Péralte pour la Liberté]*, 1970. Oil on Masonite, 19 ¼ × 15 ½ in. (48.9 × 39.37 cm), Milwaukee Art Museum, Gift of Richard and Erna Flagg M1991.139, photo credit Efraim Lev-er.

Regardless of motivations, states kept anti-occupation perceptions alive. The modern-day Sandinistas and their sympathizers produced their own children's literature and textbooks meant to glorify Sandino.[36] Such revisionism worked: in 2000, Nicaraguan educators overwhelmingly described Sandino as a "hero" who "was a defender of democracy" and "drove the marines out of Nicaragua" while only 6 percent thought he was a "bandit."[37] Similarly, after the Duvalier regime finally abandoned Haiti in 1986, "Péralte's face was everywhere," wrote journalist Amy Wilentz. "You could find his likeness on a priest's office door. At a radio station in Cap-Haïtien. In the kitchen of a rich Haitian artist. Painted on a wall in the La Saline slum. On a door in an inner office of the Canadian Embassy. On flyers announcing demonstrations. Even on a new half–gourde coin."[38]

Given that the enterprise of occupation was fraught with muddled intentions, hypocrisy, arrogance, and incompetence on the part of both occupier and occupied, it is a wonder it materialized at all. It is just as awesome to behold how successful the invaded and their allies were at ending all occupations. However belated, however undemocratic, however self-interested, the invaded did, more than anyone else, rid their soils of foreign troops. Almost all states that have undertaken occupation have come to regret it and usually cited their lack of knowledge of resistance as a major factor of their remorse. Understanding the complex and often compromising motivations of that resistance—its sub-national and transnational methods, and its probabilities of success—there lies the path to winning an occupation.

Or to choosing not to start one. Latin America has often been described as a laboratory for US relations with the rest of the world, the place where informal empire, dollar diplomacy, and other policies saw their first attempts.[39] It may also be time to see in the region the first laboratories for *resisting* US power. The greatest lesson then is most likely that occupation is a folly to be avoided at all cost.

ABBREVIATIONS

AAAIL	All-American Anti-Imperialist League (New York)
ACLU	American Civil Liberties Union
ACS	Collección ACS (Augusto César Sandino), CHM
AD	Archives Diplomatiques, Ministère des Affaires Étrangères, Paris, France
AFL	American Federation of Labor
AGN	Archivo General de la Nación, Santo Domingo, Dominican Republic
APRA	Popular Revolutionary American Alliance (Peru)
ASN	FDR Papers as Assistant Secretary of the Navy, FDRL
Bellegarde Papers	Papers of Dantès Bellegarde, MSRC
Berle Papers	Papers of Adolf Berle, FDRL
Borah Papers	Papers of William E. Borah, MD
Butler Papers	Papers of Smedley Butler, MCA
BZ	Collección BZ (Benjamín Zeledón), CHM
Caperton Papers	Papers of William Banks Caperton, MD
Cent. Am. 1918–1940	Centre Amérique, Amérique 1918–1940, Correspondance Politique et Commerciale 1914–1940, AD
Cestero Archive	Archivo de Tulio Cestero, Fondo Antiguo, Universidad Autónoma de Santo Domingo, Santo Domingo, Dominican Republic
Chapman Papers	Charles Edward Chapman Papers, Bancroft Library, University of California-Berkeley
CHM	Centro de Historia Militar, Managua, Nicaragua
Civilian Complaints	Correspondence Relating to Civilian Complaints in the District of Matagalpa at Jinotega, 1928, RG 127, NARA I
CND	Dominican Nationalist Commission
COCP	Correspondence of the Office of the Chief of Police, Gendarmerie d'Haïti, 1927–1934, RG 127, NARA I
Comintern	Third Communist International
Conservatory Papers	Washington Conservatory of Music Papers, Manuscript Division, MSRC
Coolidge Papers	Calvin Coolidge Papers, HHL
Corr. 1915–1926	General Correspondence of the Gendarmerie d'Haiti 1915–1926, RG 127, NARA I
Corr. 1916–1919	General Correspondence of Headquarters, Gendarmerie d'Haiti 1916–1919, RG 127, NARA I

Corr. 1918–1921	Correspondence Relating to Subjects Not in the Regular Series of General Correspondence, 1918–1921, RG 127, NARA I
Corr. 1919–1920	Special Correspondence of the Chief of the Gendarmerie d'Haiti, 1919–1920, RG 127, NARA I
Corr. 1921–1923	General Correspondence of the Chief of the Gendarmerie, 1921–1923, RG 127, NARA I
Corr. 1923, 1925	Correspondence of the Gendarmerie d'Haiti 1923, 1925, RG 127, NARA I
Corr. 1927–1932	Miscellaneous Correspondence of the 2nd Brigade, 1927–1932, RG 127, NARA I
Corr. 1928–1930	General Correspondence of the 2nd Brigade, 1928–1930, RG 127, NARA I
Corr. 1929–1931	Correspondence Relating to Bandit Prisoners, 1929–1931, RG 127, NARA I
CPUSA	Communist Party of the United States
CS	Fondo Colección Sandino, Archivo Nacional de Nicaragua, Managua, Nicaragua
CTP	Campaign and Transition Papers, HHL
Dickinson Letters	Letters of Dwight Dickinson, Hoover Institution, Stanford University, California
DR 1897–1918	République Dominicaine, Correspondance Politique et Commerciale/Série Nouvelle 1897 à 1918, AD
DR 1910–1929	Central Decimal Files Relating to Internal Affairs of the Dominican Republic, 1910–1929, RG 59, NARA II
DR 1918–1940	République Dominicaine, Amérique 1918–1940, Correspondance Politique et Commerciale 1914–1940, AD
EDSNN	Army for the Defense of the National Sovereignty of Nicaragua
EMECU	Magnetic-Spiritual School of the Universal Commune
Exp. Comm.	General Correspondence of the Expeditionary Commander and 1st Brigade, 1915–1920, RG 127, NARA I
FDRL	Franklin D. Roosevelt Library, Hyde Park, New York
First Brigade	Records of the First Provisional Brigade in Haiti, 1915–1934, RG 127, NARA I
FO 370	Foreign Office 370, PRO
FO 371	Foreign Office 371, PRO
FOR	Fellowship of Reconciliation
FPA	Foreign Policy Association
Freeman Papers	Papers of Joseph Freeman, Hoover
GC	General Correspondence, 1907–1936, RG 127, NARA I
Gendarmerie	Records of the Gendarmerie d'Haiti, 1915–1934, RG 127, NARA I
GM	Fondo Gobierno Militar, AGN
GN	Nicaraguan National Guard
GN-2 1928–1932	Selected Correspondence of the Intelligence Department (GN-2), 1928–1932, RG 127, NARA I
GN-2 1932	Correspondence of the Intelligence Department (GN-2), 1932, RG 127, NARA I
GND	Dominican National Guard
GS	Archivo de Gregorio Sandino, IHNCA
Haiti 1897–1918	Haiti, Correspondance Politique et Commerciale/Nouvelle Série 1897–1918, AD
Haiti 1910–1929	Central Decimal Files Relating to Internal Affairs of Haiti, 1910–1929, RG 59 NARA II

Haiti 1918–1940	Haiti, Amérique 1918–1940, Correspondance Politique et Commerciale 1914–1940, AD
Haiti 1930–1939	Central Decimal Files Relating to Internal Affairs of Haiti, 1930–1939, RG 59, NARA II
HASCO	Haitian-American Sugar Company
HHL	Herbert Hoover Library, West Branch, Iowa
Hoover	Hoover Institution Archives, Stanford, California
HSDIS	Haiti-Santo Domingo Independence Society
ICWDR	International Council of Women of the Darker Races
IIE	Institute for International Education
IHNCA	Instituto de Historia de Nicaragua y Centroamérica, Managua, Nicaragua
Intel. Reports 1926–1927	Intelligence Reports from the Department of the North, 1926–27, RG 127, NARA I
IP	Fondo Secretaría de Estado de Interior y Policía, AGN
Kneeland Letters	Kneeland Letters, Hoover
LADLA	All-American Anti-Imperialist League (Mexico)
Logan Papers	Rayford D. Logan Papers, MSRC
MAFUENIC	Hands-Off Nicaragua Committee
Marines 1912–1979	Miscellaneous Records Relating to Marine Activities in the pre–World War II era, 1912–1979, RG 127, NARA I
MCA	Marine Corps Archives and Special Collections, Gray Research Center, Quantico, Virginia
MCARA	Marine Corps Audiovisual Research Archives, Marine Corps Base, Quantico, Virginia
MCH	Marine Corps History Division, Marine Corps Base, Quantico, Virginia
MD	Manuscripts Division, Library of Congress, Washington, D.C.
MGSD	Military Government of Santo Domingo, RG 38, NARA I
Morris Papers	Fred Ludwig Morris Papers, Bancroft Library, University of California-Berkeley
MSRC	Moorland-Spingarn Research Center, Howard University, Washington, D.C.
Municipio	Fondo Municipio, AGN
NAACP	National Association for the Advancement of Colored People
NARA I	U.S. National Archives and Records Administration, Washington, D.C.
NARA II	U.S. National Archives and Records Administration, College Park, Maryland
ND	U.S. Navy Dispatches March 1912–August 1914, FDRL
Newspapers 1914–1923	Original and Microfilmed World War I and Inter-War Era Newspapers, 1914–1923, RG 127, NARA I
Nicaragua 1897–1918	Nicaragua, Correspondance Politique et Commerciale/Série Nouvelle 1897 à 1918, AD
Nicaragua 1910–1929	Central Decimal Files Relating to Internal Affairs of Nicaragua, 1910–1929, RG 59, NARA II
Nicaragua 1927–1932	Reports Received from Marine Units in Nicaragua, 1927–1932, RG 127, NARA I
Nicaragua 1927–1933	Headquarters, Historical Section, Records Relating to Marine Corps Units in Nicaragua, 1927–1933, RG 127, NARA I
Nicaragua 1930–1944	Central Decimal Files Relating to Internal Affairs of Nicaragua, 1930–1944, RG 59, NARA II
NPGL	National Popular Government League

NYHT	*New York Herald/Tribune*
NYT	*New York Times*
OAB	Operations Archives Branch, Naval Historical Center, Washington, D.C.
Occupation 1916–1924	Miscellaneous Collection of Records Relating to the Marine Occupation of Santo Domingo (Dominican Republic), 1916–1924, RG 127, NARA I
OCNO/OSN	Secret and Confidential Correspondence of the Office of the Chief of Naval Operations and the Office of the Secretary of the Navy, 1919–27, RG 80
Operations 1915–1921	Reports Relating to U.S. Navy and Marine Corps Operations in Haiti and Santo Domingo, 1915–1921, RG 127, NARA I
O&T	Operations and Training Division, Intelligence Section, 1915–1934, RG 127, NARA I
PCM	Mexican Communist Party
Pendleton Papers	Papers of Joseph H. Pendleton, MCA
PN	Nationalist Party (Haiti)
PND	Dominican National Police
PP	Presidential Papers, HHL
President's Comm.	President's Commission for Study & Review of Conditions in Haiti, HHL
PRO	Public Record Office, Kew, UK
RG 38	Records of the Office of the Chief of Naval Operations, NARA I
RG 59	General Records of the Department of State, NARA II
RG 80	General Records of the Department of the Navy, NARA I
RG 127	Records of the United States Marine Corps, NARA I
Rhodes Diary	Diary, Charles Dudley Rhodes, Hoover
Road Reports	Road Reports of Headquarters Gendarmerie d'Haiti, 1916–1921, RG 127, NARA I
Russell Papers	Papers of John H. Russell, MCA
Sacasa Archive	Archivo de Juan B. Sacasa, IHNCA
Smith Papers	Papers of Oliver P. Smith, MCA
Spingarn Papers	Papers of Arthur B. Spingarn, 1850–1968, MD
Stern Papers	Max Stern Papers, Bancroft Library, University of California-Berkeley
Stimson Diary	Stimson Diary, FDRL
Storey Papers	Papers of Moorfield Storey, MD
UCSAYA	Center-South American and Antillean Union
UN	Nationalist Union (Haiti)
UND	Dominican Nationalist Union
UNIA	United Negro Improvement Association
UP	Patriotic Union (Haiti)
Upshur Letters	William P. Upshur Letters, Southern Historical Collection, University of North Carolina at Chapel Hill
U.S.-Haiti 1910–1929	Central Decimal Files Relating to Political Relations Between the U.S. and Haiti, 1910–1929, RG 59, NARA II
Welles Papers	Sumner Welles Papers, FDRL
White Papers	Francis White Papers, HHL
WILPF	Women's International League for Peace and Freedom

NOTES

Introduction

1. Shadid, *Night Draws Near*, 238, 241.
2. "Iraqi Public Opinion and the Occupation," *Global Policy Forum* http://www.globalpolicy. org/component/content/article/168/37143.html, last accessed May 20, 2013.
3. A conservative estimate of forty is likely limited to interventions that landed troops. See Gobat, *Confronting*, 3. Grandin reported that the United States sent warships into Latin American ports 5,980 times from 1869 to 1897 and then landed marines thirty-four times from 1903 to 1933, in *Workshop*, 20. The navy in 1929 produced its own list at http://www. history.navy.mil/library/online/haiti_list_exp.htm, last accessed May 20, 2013.
4. Calder called for such a multi-occupation comparison a generation ago, in *Impact*, xx.
5. Castor called the occupations of Haiti and the Dominican Republic instances of the "greatest severity" of US imperialism in the early century, in "Occupation," 253.
6. Edelstein, "Hazards," 52.
7. At the time of the occupation "Santo Domingo" usually stood in for the name of the entire country. I will use it in reference to the capital city only, unless using a quotation. For figures, see Kelsey, "Intervention," 166–7; Derby, *Dictator's Seduction*, 25; Chapman, diary entry of December 20, 1924, folder Diary, 1924–1933, box 2, correspondence and papers—additions, 1920–1941, 83/153, Chapman Papers.
8. Edelstein calls nationalism "the greatest impediment to successful military occupation," yet defines it narrowly as "the desire of a population to govern itself or, put differently, to join an identifiable nation together with the governing institutions of the modern state," in *Hazards*, 10–11. Romanticized and simplified interpretations tended to see in early-century insurrections antecedents to later nationalism. For a Dominican example, see Ducoudray, "Epopeya," 36–43. A Haitian example is Castor, *Occupation*. See also Schroeder's discussion of historiography in "'To Defend,'" 30–1, and Healy, *Rise*, 275–83. For discussions of the nature of nationalism, see Hayes, *Essays*, 6; Gellner, *Nations*, 1; Charles Taylor, "Nationalism and Modernity," in *Morality*, ed. McKim and McMahan, 31–55; and Moore, *Ethics*, 5.
9. Matthews, "Policy," 805–20; Park, *Underdevelopment*, 131. A recent exception is Grandin, *Workshop*, 3.
10. US-focused monographs have been divided into military studies, usually laudatory of the marines, and diplomatic, cultural, and political ones, usually more critical. Among the first category, the one with the most impact was Boot, *Savage*, which argued that the United States should learn from successful past wars against insurgencies. Making a similar point were Best, *Occupation*, and Ferguson, *Colossus*. Critical analyses have been focused on US rather than Latin American actors: Healy, *Rise*; Langley, *Banana Wars*; Macaulay, *Affair*; Perkins, *Constraint*; Schmidt, *Occupation*; Renda, *Taking Haiti*; Brissman, "Interpreting"; Rosenberg, *Missionaries*. Calder stands out for devoting as much space to the resistance as to

the occupation, in *Impact*. Gobat comprehensively examines the agency of the occupied, especially on the 1912–1926 period, in *Confronting*. See also San Miguel, "Resistance," 41–62; Legrand, "Informal," 555–96; Alexis, "Nationalism," and Michiel Baud, "The Struggle for Autonomy: Peasant Resistance to Capitalism in the Dominican Republic, 1870–1924," in *Labour*, ed. Cross and Heuman, 120–40. There are also countless works in French and Spanish on the occupied.

11. Examples include Carlton, *Occupation*; Nabulsi, *Traditions*. For examples of the anthropological reading of resistance adopted by this book, see Anderson, *Java*; Mintz, "Proletariat," 291–325; Steve Stern, "New Approaches to the Study of Peasant Rebellion and Consciousness: Implications of the Andean Experience," in *Resistance*, ed. Stern, 3–25; Scott, *Hidden Transcripts*; Van Young, "Someone," 133–59; Gutmann, "Rituals," 74–92; Fernando Coronil, "Foreword," in *Close Encounters*, ed. Joseph, LeGrand, and Salvatore, ix–xii; Lauria-Santiago and Chomsky, "Introduction," 1–24, and Gudmundson and Scarano, "Conclusion," 335–64, both in *Identity*, ed. Chomsky and Lauria-Santiago.

12. Joseph observes that work on individual bandits and bands took the focus away even from other peasants, in "Trail," 8.

13. Grossman recognizes the success of transnational networks in "setting limits on war-makers" in Nicaragua and divides them into anti-interventionists, who did not support Sandino, and solidarity groups, who did, in "Anti-Intervention," 67–79. My definition of these networks is similar to that of Keck and Sikkink's "transnational advocacy networks" in *Activists*, including the presence of government officials in that network, thus making more explicit the "blurring" of state-citizen boundaries, 1, 9.

14. The concept of political culture, revived in recent years as a repertoire of meanings that political groups appropriate, adapt, and contest accurately describes the stakes in US occupations. The structural-functionalist approach includes Pye and Verba, *Political Culture*; Delos D. Hughes and Edward L. Pinney, "Political Culture and the Idioms of Political Development," in *Comparative Politics*, ed. Pinney, 67–96; and Harris and Alba, *Political Culture*; and to an extent Wiarda, *Soul*. Since the 1990s, constructivists have revived political culture as a dynamic, inclusive process by which social sectors interact with a growing nation-state by defying and negotiating the cultural meanings of political participation. See Gil Joseph and Daniel Nugent, "Popular Culture and State Formation in Revolutionary Mexico," in *Everyday*, ed. Joseph and Nugent, 3–23; Levine, *Constructing Culture*; Holden, "Limits," 455; Alvarez, Dagnino, and Escobar, *Cultures of Politics*. Go in *Empire* attempts to re-insert power struggles within political culture and to appreciate the changing and multifaceted nature of cultural meaning.

15. An excellent primer on democracy promotion in early-century US-Latin American relations is Paul W. Drake, "From Good Men to Good Neighbors: 1912–1932," in *Exporting Democracy*, ed. Lowenthal, 3–40.

16. Perkins, *Constraint*, viii. Boot correctly claimed that the marines occupied to achieve "stability," but he meant it in a largely altruistic way in *Savage*, 160. A thorough study of civil-military relations during the Dominican occupation is Tillman, "Dollar," esp. 14.

17. Other historians have emphasized the desire for a more democratic political culture in US interventions in Latin America: Calhoun, *Power*, 7; Perkins, *Constraint*, ix. Unfortunately, Calhoun adds, of the Dominican Republic, that "the Wilson administration expressed no other interest in the affairs of the country than the desire to help the people grow out of their political immaturity," 75.

18. Schmidt, *Occupation*, 31; Adler, "Bryan," 221–2.

19. Yerxa, "Navy," 182.

20. In the 1880s, the Maritime Canal Company already had a concession for a Nicaraguan canal, O'Brien, *Mission*, 50.

21. Macaulay, *Affair*, 23.

22. Coffey, "Notes on the Intervention in Haiti," Port-au-Prince, February 1, 1916, folder Reports, Miscellaneous (1915–1916), box 3, Caperton Papers; Pierce and Hough, *Compact*, 161; Munro, *Intervention*, 270–1; Beaulac, *Career*, 102.

23. Bertie to Foreign Office, August 7, 1915, file 108600, reference 2370, FO 371.

24. Yerxa, "Navy," 182; Douglas, "Haiti I," 253.

25. Editorial, "Mr. Lansing's Haitian Letter," *NYT*, May 9, 1922, 15.
26. Challener, *Admirals*, 44.
27. The argument for economic imperialism too often rests on a single quotation from Smedley Butler, a disillusioned interventionist who ranted in 1935 about being a "racketeer" for US big business, in Butler, "Armed Forces," 8. For a recent example of this argument, see Dubois, *Aftershocks*, 204–64.
28. Longley, *Shadow*, 133; Schoultz, *Beneath*, 193.
29. Yerxa, "Navy," 182.
30. Munro, *Republics*, 238.
31. Schroeder, "'To Defend,'" 52–3.
32. Langley, *Caribbean*, 70.
33. Macaulay, *Affair*, 23.
34. Juarez, "Withdrawal," 182.
35. Ferguson, *Colossus*, 55; Merritt, "Patrol," 20.
36. Posner, "Marines," 245.
37. Langley, *Caribbean*, 70; Millet, *Paysans*, 30–1; Munro, *Intervention*, 247–58.
38. Moral, *Paysan*, 61.
39. Stanford [to Adler?], [early 1910], folder Nicaragua, Bluefields Topaz Mining Co. Corres. + papers ... (1910–1913), carton 9, Morris Papers.
40. Schmidt, *Occupation*, 52.
41. Munro, *Intervention*, 537.
42. Navy secretary cited in Boot, *Savage*, 160.
43. Wilson cited in *Congressional Record*, 63rd Congress, 1st Sess., vol. 50 (Washington: Government Printing Office, 1913), 5845–6.
44. Croly, *Promise*; Whitaker, *Idea*, 118.
45. Samuel Silva Gotay, "Protestantismo y política en Puerto Rico a partir de la invasión de Estados Unidos," in *Protestantismo*, ed. Gutiérrez, 235–62.
46. Butler, *Gimlet*, 55. See also Hudson, "Dark Finance."
47. Renda convincingly argues for the power of racist paternalism to compel military intervention, in *Taking Haiti*.
48. Cited in Adler, "Bryan," 201.
49. This argument is a key distinction between this book and Calhoun, *Power*, and Perkins, *Constraint*, who conflate intervention with occupation and argue that political culture was a sufficient rationale for the initial landings.
50. Historians have called this the promotion of "technological modernization, organizational efficiency, and the cultivation of pragmatic as opposed to esthetic or spiritual attitudes" and of "a civic culture of democracy," Schmidt, *Occupation*, 13; Derby, "Magic of Modernity," 30.
51. Cited in Munro, *Intervention*, 271.
52. Brown, "Occupation," 395.
53. Wilson cited in Callcott, *Policy*, 314.
54. Adler, "Bryan," 202.
55. Wilson cited in Callcott, *Policy*, 316.
56. Munro, *Intervention*, 533–4.
57. Cited in Callcott, *Policy*, 259.
58. Cited in Ferguson, *Colossus*, 64.
59. Langley, *Caribbean*, 71. A good narrative is McCrocklin, *Garde*, 8–13.
60. For a narrative, see Welles, *Vineyard*, 700–57.
61. Vega, *Derecho*, 343.
62. Rhodes and Malone to chief of staff, War Department, October 27, 1911, Rhodes Diary.
63. Hart, *Empire*, 310–1.
64. Gobat, *Confronting*, 67.
65. My translation. Lefaivre to minister of foreign relations, Mexico City, January 18, 1910, dossier 2, Nicaragua 1897–1918. For narratives of this period, see Macaulay, *Affair*, 23, 34; Buchenau, *Shadow*, 92–6; Gobat, *Confronting*, 67–70.
66. Buell, *Occupation*, 331.
67. Millet, *Paysans*, 45.

68. Lugo, *Intervención*.
69. Derby, "Magic of Modernity," 84.
70. Cited in Calder, *Impact,* 7, 6.
71. See the bibliography under "McPherson" for journal articles related to the topic of this book.

Chapter 1

1. Several writers have explained the characteristics of caudillos: Wolf and Hansen, "Caudillo," 168–79; Burns, *Poverty*; Pfoh, "Formación," 129–48; Castro, "Caudillismo," 9–29; and Ruiz Chataing, "Caudillos," 101–44. On Nicaraguan state-building and caudillos, see Wolfe, *Nation-State*.
2. Holden, *Armies*, 5.
3. The most recent work on caudillos has made this two-way case most effectively: Chasteen, *Heroes*; and De la Fuente, *Children*, especially 94–109; Shumway, "Rosas," 1–14; Morelli, "Régime," 759–81.
4. Charlip, *Cultivating*, makes the case for a coffee-dominated department, Carazo. Gould, *Equals*, examines the sugar and cattle-dominated department of Chinandega.
5. Examples of celebratory accounts include Denny, *Dollars*; Munro, *Intervention*; Kamman, *Search*; Boot, *Savage*.
6. Hill, "Los Marinos," 2–11.
7. Musicant, *Banana Wars*, 140; Munro, *Intervention*, 205.
8. Gobat, *Confronting*, 114.
9. Munro, *Intervention*, 209.
10. Hill, "Los Marinos," 8.
11. Southerland, aboard USS *Annapolis* in Corinto, to secretary of the navy, October 17, 1912, roll 1, film: 10–1, ND.
12. Gobat, *Confronting*, 128.
13. Gobat, *Confronting*, 80.
14. Munro, *Intervention*, 205.
15. Elliot Northcott, cited in Musicant, *Banana Wars*, 143.
16. Langley, *Banana Wars*, 63.
17. Gobat, "Revolutionaries," 7.
18. Langley, *Banana Wars*, 63.
19. Gobat, *Confronting*, 86.
20. Cited in Ghiraldo, *Yanquilandia*, 88–9.
21. Butler, Granada, September 23, 1912, folder Transcripts of Nicaraguan letters, 1912, box 5, Butler Papers. On Argüello and Mena, see Selser, *Restauración*, passim 277–300.
22. Gobat, *Confronting*, 87, 101–3.
23. Munro, *Intervention*, 205, 207; Hill, "Los Marinos," 8.
24. Emerson to Borah, New York, March 23, 1924, folder Nicaragua 1924, box 162, Borah Papers.
25. Butler, September 24, 1912, folder Transcripts of Nicaraguan letters, 1912, box 5, Butler Papers.
26. Asprey, "Court–Martial," 33.
27. Harry Lavering to "Bill," December 3, 1912, folder Nicarauga, Bluefields Topaz Mining Co. Corres. + papers … (1910–1913), carton 9, Morris Papers.
28. Hill, "Los Marinos," 8; Gobat, *Confronting*, 111, 120.
29. Cited in Gobat, *Confronting*, 109.
30. Bartolomé Martínez cited in Gobat, *Confronting*, 95.
31. Gobat, *Confronting*, 95–8, 100.
32. Gobat, *Confronting*, 103–8.
33. George Weitzel to secretary of state, Managua, October 24, 1912, 817.00/2121, Nicaragua 1910–1929.
34. Gobat, "Revolutionaries," 1.
35. George Weitzel to secretary of state, Managua, October 24, 1912, 817.00/2121, Nicaragua 1910–1929.

36. "'Moral Mandate,'" 505.
37. Southerland to Pendleton, September 15, 1912, folder 6, box 1, Pendleton Papers.
38. Juan José Martínez et al. to Butler, Granada, October 9, 1912, folder 7, box 1, Pendleton Papers.
39. Women of Granada, Granada, October 11, 1912, folder 7, box 1, Pendleton Papers.
40. Rear Admiral William Kimball, cited in Musicant, *Banana Wars*, 140.
41. Butler, *Gimlet*, 153; Whisnant, *Rascally Signs*, 344; Gobat, *Confronting*, 117.
42. Zeledón, "Fighting Intervention," 69, 66–8.
43. Amador, *Derrota militar*, 21.
44. My translations. Zeledón to Southerland, Masaya, September 19, 1912, E-001, C-002, 000109, BZ, also published in Selser, *Restauración*, 289–90.
45. My translation. Zeledón to Pendleton, Masaya, October 3, 1912, E-001, C-002, 000076, BZ.
46. My translation. Zeledón to "Estercita," Masaya, October 3, 1912, E-001, C-002, 000082, BZ.
47. See for instance the many poems in BZ. Most famously, a seventeen-year-old Augusto Sandino saw Zeledón's body wheeled by on an ox-drawn cart. He later recalled that, to him, Zeledón was "unbeaten and glorious." Sandino considered his own war against the marines "a continuation of his." Whisnant, *Rascally Signs*, 345.
48. Weitzel to secretary of state, Managua, October 4, 1912, 817.00/2058, Nicaragua 1910–1929.
49. Butler to Southerland, October 4, 1912, folder 7, box 1, Pendleton Papers.
50. Weitzel to secretary of state, Managua, October 6, 1912, 817.00/2065, Nicaragua 1910–1929.
51. Butler, Granada, September 23, 1912, folder Transcripts of Nicaraguan letters, 1912, box 5, Butler Papers.
52. Delegation cited by Butler to Colonel Pendleton, "Beyond Masaya," September 19, 1912 [apparently written September 16 or 17], folder 6, box 1, Pendleton Papers; Butler, Granada, September 23, 1912, folder Transcripts of Nicaraguan letters, 1912, box 5, Butler Papers.
53. Entry for August 20–21, 1912, Vulte, "Expedition to Nicaragua," August 10, 1912 [through September 23], folder Nicaragua-1912, Nicaragua, Geographical Files, Reference Branch, MCA.
54. Gobat, *Confronting*, 112.
55. Cited in Butler, *Gimlet*, 141.
56. Butler, aboard USS *Annapolis*, August 28, 1912, folder Transcripts of Nicaraguan letters, 1912, box 5, Butler Papers.
57. Unsigned [likely Long], "Military Diary," folder Military Diary: U.S. Forces in Nicaragua (1912–1913), box 2, Marines 1912–1979.
58. Long to General J. M. Rivas, León, September 16, 1912, folder 6, box 1, Pendleton Papers.
59. Long to commanding officer, León, September 16, 1912, folder 6, box 1, Pendleton Papers.
60. H. G. S. Wallace to Long, León, October 10, 1912, folder 7, box 1, Pendleton Papers.
61. Cited in Denny, *Dollars*, 117.
62. Long to Southerland, León, September 27, 1912, folder 6, box 1, Pendleton Papers.
63. Southerland to Pendleton, Managua, September 27, 1912, folder 6, box 1, Pendleton Papers.
64. Frank F. Zissa, cited in Zissa, "Nicaragua," 28.
65. Gobat, *Confronting*, 119.
66. [Long], "Military Diary," folder Military Diary: U.S. Forces in Nicaragua (1912–1913), box 2, Marines 1912–1979.
67. Gould, *Equals*, 26.
68. [Long?] to executive delegate, Departments of León and Chinandega, León, September 29, 1912, folder 6, box 1, Pendleton Papers. Confirming this judgment is Wolfe, *Nation-State*, 203, and Gould, *Equals*, 32–3.
69. Butler, aboard USS *Annapolis*, August 28, 1912, folder Transcripts of Nicaraguan letters, 1912, box 5, Butler Papers.
70. Southerland to Pendleton, aboard USS *Annapolis*, Corinto, September 4, 1912, folder 6, box 1, Pendleton Papers; Langley, *Banana Wars*, 65; Munro, *Intervention*, 206.
71. Long to regimental commander First Provisional Regiment in Managua, León, October 4, 1912, folder 7, box 1, Pendleton Papers.

72. Entry from September 22, unsigned [likely Long], "Military Diary," folder Military Diary: US Forces in Nicaragua (1912–1913), box 2, Marines 1912–1979.
73. No title or author, *The Nation*, 278.

Chapter 2

1. Lansing to Woodrow Wilson, August 3, 1915, 838.00/1275 B, Haiti 1910–1929.
2. Brissman, "Interpreting," 111.
3. Healy, *Gunboat Diplomacy*.
4. "History of Flag Career of Rear Admiral W. B. Caperton, U.S. Navy."
5. Cited in "Flag Career."
6. "Factions Push Hayti Nearer American Rule," *NYHT*, August 1, 1915, in folder Clippings 1915, box 2, Caperton Papers.
7. Healy, *Gunboat Diplomacy*, 95–8, 48.
8. Caperton to Benson, August 31, 1915, folder Correspondence 1915, box 1, Caperton Papers.
9. Healy, *Gunboat Diplomacy*, 45.
10. Plummer, *Psychological Moment*, 90.
11. Beach, "Autobiography," 248–9.
12. Caperton to secretary of the navy, aboard the USS *Washington*, July 28, 1915, 838.00/1227, Haiti 1910–1929.
13. Girard to minister of foreign affairs, Port-au-Prince, August 13, 1915, dossier 6, Haiti 1897–1918.
14. Caperton to secretary of the navy, aboard the USS *Washington*, July 30, 1915, 838.00/1233, Haiti 1910–1929.
15. Lansing to Woodrow Wilson, August 3, 1915, 838.00/1275 B, Haiti 1910–1929.
16. Lansing to Woodrow Wilson, Washington, August 13, 1915, 711.38/24A, U.S.-Haiti 1910–1929.
17. Division of Latin-American Affairs, undated, 838.00/1391, enclosed with July 31, 1915, 838.00/1390, Haiti 1910–1929.
18. Long to Lansing, August 5, 1915, 838.00/1426, Haiti 1910–1929.
19. Wilson to Lansing, Washington, August 4, 1915, 838.00/1418, Haiti 1910–1929.
20. Caperton to secretary of the navy, aboard the USS *Washington*, August 2, 1915, 838.00/1236, Haiti 1910–1929. The committee was composed of Charles de Delva, Charles Zamor, Edmond Polynice, Léon Nau, Ermane Robin, Eribert St-Vil Nöel, and Samson Mompoint, according to Corvington, *1915–1922*, 6.
21. Van Orden to Caperton, Port-au-Prince, August 2, 1915, 838.00/1276, Haiti 1910–1929.
22. Caperton to secretary of the navy, aboard the USS *Washington*, August 2, 1915, 838.00/1233, Haiti 1910–1929.
23. Caperton to secretary of the navy, aboard the USS *Washington*, August 3, 1915, 838.00/1236, Haiti 1910–1929; Beach to chief of naval operations, June 3, 1916, folder Correspondence June 1916, box 1, Caperton Papers.
24. An example is Caperton to Benson, November 21, 1915, folder Correspondence 1915, box 1, Caperton Papers. Traditional colorful accounts of insurrectionists include Craige, *Cannibal Cousins*, 22, and Montague, *Haiti*, 20.
25. Caperton to secretary of the navy, aboard the USS *Washington*, August 2, 1915, 838.00/1236, Haiti 1910–1929. Writer Craige estimated between 20,000 and 50,000 cacos in Haiti in 1915, in *Cannibal Cousins*, 62, while Caperton's estimate was closer to 8,000, to secretary of the navy, August 21, 1915, 838.00/1301, Haiti 1910–1929. In the Dominican Republic, Roberto Cassá counted thousands of *gavilleros* from 1916 to 1922, in "Los gavilleros," *Isla Abierta*, in *Hoy*, August 24, 1996, 8–9.
26. Cole statement in Senate, *Hearings*, vol. 1, 709.
27. Caperton to secretary of the navy, aboard the USS *Washington*, August 2, 1915, 838.00/1236, Haiti 1910–1929.
28. Millet, *Paysans*, 45.
29. Beach, "Autobiography."

30. Millet, *Paysans*, 46.
31. Frank, "Death," 23.
32. My translation. Bellegarde, *Haïti Heureuse*, 5.
33. Coffey, "Notes on the Intervention in Haiti," Port-au-Prince, February 1, 1916, folder Reports, Miscellaneous, 1915–1916, box 3, Caperton Papers. See also "Factions Push Hayti Nearer American Rule," *NYHT*, August 1, 1915, enclosed in folder Clippings 1915, box 2, Caperton Papers.
34. Healy, *Gunboat Diplomacy*, 93.
35. "American Forces Fire on Port-au-Prince Mob; Haytian Rioter is Slain," *NYHT*, August 7, 1915, p. 1, enclosed in folder Clippings 1915, box 2, Caperton Papers.
36. Wirkus cited in Boot, *Savage*, 156.
37. Schmidt, *Occupation*, 68.
38. Renda, *Taking Haiti*, 81; "American Forces," *NYHT*, August 7, 1915, 1.
39. Davis to secretary of state, Port-au-Prince, August 9, 1915, 838.00/1242, Haiti 1910–1929.
40. Coffey, "Notes," Port-au-Prince, February 1, 1916, folder Reports, Miscellaneous, 1915–1916, box 3, Caperton Papers.
41. "Two U.S. Sailors Killed by Haitians," *New York Sun*, July 31, 1915, in folder Clippings 1915, box 2, Caperton Papers.
42. McCrocklin reported the first clash as occurring on 30 July, *Garde*, 17, 24.
43. Bickel, *Mars Learning*, 70.
44. Caperton, testimony, Senate, *Hearings*, vol. 1, 315. Caperton mistakenly dates this meeting on October 8, 1915.
45. Caperton to secretary of the navy, August 23, 1915, 838.00/1268, Haiti 1910–1929.
46. McCrocklin, *Garde*, 27.
47. Griffith to secretary of state, October 8, 1915, 838.00/1356, Haiti 1910–1929.
48. Livingston to secretary of state, Cap-Haïtien, August 8, 1915, 838.00/1240, Haiti 1910–1929; Coffey, "Notes," Port-au-Prince, February 1, 1916, folder Reports, Miscellaneous, 1915–1916, box 3, Caperton Papers.
49. Beach, "Autobiography," 254, 261–2.
50. My translations. Gelin Choute interviewed in Gaillard, *Premier écrasement*, 13, 21.
51. My translation. Girard to minister of foreign affairs, Port-au-Prince, September 2, 1915, dossier 6, Haiti 1897–1918.
52. Georges Sylvain, Fleury Féquière, and Marcelin Jocelyn founded *La Patrie* on August 13; on August 18 Elie Guérin, Félix Viard founded *Haïti Intégrale*; soon after Chrysostome Rosemond, Furcy Chatelain, and Constantin Dumervé founded *La Ligue*. See Castor, *Occupation*, 128.
53. Caperton statement, Senate, *Hearings*, vol. 1, 373.
54. "Union Patriotique," *Le Matin* (Port-au-Prince), August 14, 1915.
55. Millet, *Paysans*, 89.
56. Corvington, *1915–1922*, 215.
57. Beach, "Autobiography," 266; Douglas, "Haiti I," 243.
58. Conard, "A Year," 607.
59. "Haiti's Senate Asks Pledge of Integrity," *NYT*, August 8, 1915, 18; Division of Latin-American Affairs to Long, September 9, 1915, 838.00/1295, Haiti 1910–1929.
60. Gaillard, *Premier écrasement*, 140–2.
61. My translations. Bellegarde, *Résistance*, 43.
62. Douglas, "Haiti I," 246.
63. Castor, *Occupation*, 22, 66.
64. "Rebel Circulars Urge Haytians to Expel Americans," *NYHT*, August 28, 1915, in folder Clippings 1915, box 2, Caperton Papers.
65. Gaillard, *Premier écrasement*, 109, 118.
66. Durrell, Campaign Order Number One, Cap-Haïtien, September 6, 1915, folder Correspondence Sept 1915, box 6, Butler Papers.
67. My translation. Girard to minister of foreign affairs, Port-au-Prince, September 2, 1915, dossier 6, Haiti 1897–1918.
68. Caperton to secretary of the navy, USS *Washington*, 17 August [misdated as July] 1915, 838.00/1256, Haiti 1910–1929.

69. Healy, *Rise*, 223.

70. My translation. Castor, *Occupation*, 133.

71. Marcelin to the delegate Basse [Baes?] Bernard, Bassintourque, October 20, 1915, folder Caco Correspondence, box 5, Gendarmerie.

72. Coffey, "Notes," Port-au-Prince, February 1, 1916, folder Reports, Miscellaneous, 1915–1916, box 3, Caperton Papers.

73. Russell to Frank Kellogg, secretary of state, Port-au-Prince, March 22, 1927, 838.00/2302, Haiti 1910–1929.

74. Pierre-Paul, *Première protestation*.

75. My translation. Girard to minister of foreign affairs, Port-au-Prince, January 26, 1916, dossier 6, Haiti 1897–1918.

76. Heinl, Jr., and Heinl, *Written in Blood*, 431–3; Castor, *Occupation*, 131–2; Pierre-Paul, *Première protestation*, 15. See also Corvington, *1915–1922*, 51–6.

77. Upshur to his mother, Fort Liberté, March 29, 1916, folder 1914–1916, box 2, Upshur Letters.

78. Wise, *A Marine*, 133.

79. Bobo to Woodrow Wilson, September 8, 1915, 838.00/1331, Haiti 1910–1929.

80. Girard to minister of foreign affairs, Port-au-Prince, September 26, 1915, dossier 6, Haiti 1897–1918.

81. My translation. Girard to minister of foreign affairs, Port-au-Prince, September 2, 1915, dossier 6, Haiti 1897–1918.

82. De la Batie to minister of foreign affairs, Port-au-Prince, June 1, 1916, dossier 6, Haiti 1897–1918.

83. Upshur to his mother, Fort Liberté, March 29, 1916, folder 1914–1916, box 2, Upshur Letters.

84. Gaillard, *Premier écrasement*, 127–8.

85. My translation from French. Gaillard, *Premier écrasement*, 147–8.

86. Hurston, *Horse*, 92.

87. My translation. Cited in Blancpain, *Haïti*, 81, 82.

88. My translation. Cited in Corvington, *1915–1922*, 12.

89. My translation. *Le Matin*, September 15, 1915, cited by Gaillard, *Premier écrasement*, 106.

90. My translation. Emile Elie cited in Numa, *Antoine Simon*, 76.

91. Schmidt, *Occupation*, 97–9. See also Douglas, "Haiti I," 249–51.

92. Brierre immortalized Sully in a January 14, 1934, speech published as *Le petit soldat*, especially 5–13. See also Sylvain, *Dix années*, 3, and Blancpain, *Haïti*, 59, which falsely affirms that Sully was the only Haitian casualty.

93. My translation. Louis P. Casséus, "Lettre ouverte à Monsieur Charles Moravia," *Le Matin*, September 13, 1915, 2.

94. My translation. "La Situation dans le Nord," *Le Matin*, November 9, 1915, 1.

95. Schmidt, *Occupation*, 78.

96. My translation. Danache, *Président*, 45.

97. Heinl, Jr., and Heinl, *Written in Blood*, 443.

98. Cited in Boot, *Savage*, 160.

99. Cited in Heinl, Jr., and Heinl, *Written in Blood*, 406.

100. Beach to chief of naval operations, June 3, 1916, folder Correspondence June 1916, box 1, Caperton Papers.

101. [Beach] to Caperton, Santo Domingo, July 17, 1916, folder Correspondence July–December 1916, box 1, Caperton Papers.

102. Holden, *Armies*, 47.

Chapter 3

1. My translations. Federico Antonio García, "El asunto americano," *El Tiempo*, December 10, 1915.

2. Nancie L. González, "Desiderio Arias: Caudillo y Heroe Cultural," 199–213, in Ferreras, *Enfoques*, 200.

3. Bosch, *Dictaduras*, 102–9.
4. Munro, *Intervention*; Bosch, *Dictaduras*, 102–9, 113.
5. Mejía, *Lilís*, 114.
6. De Saint-Saud to minister of foreign affairs, Santo Domingo, May 18, 1916, dossier 7, DR 1897–1918.
7. Welles, *Vineyard*, 763.
8. U.S. Army, *Military Government*.
9. Brown, "Haiti," 143; Knight, *Americans*.
10. Cited in Calder, *Impact*, 8.
11. Wise, *A Marine*, 141.
12. Wise, *A Marine*, 143.
13. Calder, *Impact*, 8; Knight, *Americans*, 73.
14. My translations. Desidario Arias, "Actualidades," *El Tiempo*, May 24, 1916, 2.
15. Pendleton to Bishop, Santiago, June 17, 1919, folder 22, box 3, Pendleton Papers.
16. Cited in Ferguson, *Colossus*, 56.
17. Russell to Lansing, Santo Domingo, May 15, 1916, 839.00/1826, DR 1910–1929.
18. Lansing to Russell, Washington, May 17, 1916, 839.00/1826, DR 1910–1929.
19. Russell to Lansing, Santo Domingo, May 6, 1916, 839.00/1818, DR 1910–1929.
20. My translations. De Saint-Saud to minister of foreign affairs, Santo Domingo, May 18, 1916, dossier 7, DR 1897–1918.
21. My translation. De Saint-Saud to minister of foreign affairs, Santo Domingo, May 30, 1916, dossier 7, DR 1897–1918.
22. Caperton to Daniels, aboard the USS *Dolphin*, May 16, 1916, 839.00/1829, DR 1910–1929.
23. San Miguel, "Historias," 123.
24. Cassá, "Movimientos," 177. He adds that *gavilleros* never explicitly rejected modernization.
25. González Canalda, "Incursiones," 103; Franks, "Gavilleros," 161.
26. Miller, "Spurs," 48.
27. "Los gavilleros," *Isla Abierta*, in *Hoy*, August 24, 1996, 9.
28. Calder, "Caudillos," 653; Franks, "*Gavilleros*," 166; Cassá, "Movimientos," 189.
29. For more on social banditry, see Hobsbawm, *Bandits*, 7–8; Calder, *Impact*, 119; and Pérez, *Lords*.
30. Calder, "Caudillos," 653.
31. Pedro A. Pérez to secretary of state of interior and police, Seybo, May 22, 1916, legajo 351, 1916, IP.
32. Calder, "Caudillos," 655.
33. González Canalda, "Incursiones," 104.
34. Hall to Caperton, Santo Domingo, May 15, 1916, folder Dominican Republic, Santo Domingo, 1916, Dominican Republic, Geographical Files, Reference Branch, MCH.
35. Low to regimental commander, Santo Domingo, May 16, 1916, folder Dominican Republic, Santo Domingo, 1916, Dominican Republic, Geographical Files, Reference Branch, MCH; D'Arlot de Saint-Saud to minister of foreign affairs, Santo Domingo, May 18, 1916, dossier 7, DR 1897–1918; Mejía, *Lilís*, 127, 130.
36. Von Zielinski to Lansing, Santo Domingo, May 17, 1916, 839.00/1842, DR 1910–1929. Calder said this was "an officially declared day of mourning" but there is no evidence of such a call, "Varieties," 103.
37. Cited in Caperton to Benson, Santo Domingo, June 15, 1916, folder Correspondence June 1916, box 1, Caperton Papers; Mejía, *Lilís*, 128; Zeller, "Appearance of All," 52.
38. Gómez, "Dominicans," 94.
39. My translation. Emilio Jiménez, "Pro Patria!" *Renacimiento*, November 18, 1916, 819, AGN; Calder, *Impact*, 13.
40. My translations. Roca to secretary of state of interior and police, Azua, May 28, 1916, legajo 347, 1916, IP.
41. Pedro Del Valle, oral history.
42. My translation; emphases in original. M. C. Grullón, "Actualidades," *El Tiempo*, May 26, 1916, 2.
43. Roberto Cassá, "Legitimación intelectual de la invasión de 1916," *Isla Abierta*, in *Hoy*, August 5, 1994, 18–9.

44. Miguel Román Pérez, "Necesidad de los Americanos en Santo Domingo," *Listín Diario*, undated, in Russell to secretary of state, May 4, 1918, 839.00/2090, DR 1910–1929.

45. Henry to Lansing, Puerto Plata, May 18, 1916, 839.00/1836, DR 1910–1929.

46. Henry to Lansing, Puerto Plata, June 3, 1916, 839.00/1860, DR 1910–1929.

47. Abstract of telephone conversation between Rey and Sosa, governor of Santiago, May 29, 1916, in Henry to Lansing, Puerto Plata, June 7, 1916, 839.00/1886, DR 1910–1929.

48. Hatch to commander cruiser squadron, Puerto Plata, June 4, 1916, folder Dominican Republic, Santo Domingo, 1916, Dominican Republic, Geographical Files, Reference Branch, MCH.

49. Henry to Lansing, Puerto Plata, June 3, 1916, 839.00/1860, DR 1910–1929.

50. "Marines Kill 18 Rebels," *NYT*, June 7, 1916, 8.

51. My translation. De León, *Casos*, 23.

52. Langley, *Banana Wars*, 137.

53. Caperton to Daniels, aboard USS *Memphis*, June 30, 1916, 839.00/1930, DR 1910–1929; Crosley, telegram, July 1, 1916, legajo 27, 1916–1917, IP.

54. Pendleton to Bishop, Santiago, June 9, 1919, folder 22, box 3, Pendleton Papers.

55. Guzmán, *Ocupación*, 50. Guzmán cited no source for this story.

56. San Miguel, "Historias," 109.

57. Calder, *Impact*, 9. Calder identified the leader of the La Barranquita as Máximo Cabral, but González argued that he was Carlos Daniel, in *Línea noroeste*, 8.

58. My translation. Arias to General Calú Ares, May 30, 1916, cited in González, *Línea noroeste*, 43.

59. Rodríguez Bonilla, *Barranquita*, 34–6. Dominicans spoke of Haitian "Vega" rifles, but they were originally from Belgium, and "Belga" (Belgian) transformed into "Vega."

60. My translations. González, *Línea noroeste*, 8–9, 72, 78, 83, 97, 87, 137.

61. My translation. González, *Línea noroeste*, various interviews.

62. Smith, oral history.

63. Caperton to Conard, Santo Domingo, June 8, 1916, folder Correspondence June 1916, box 1, Caperton Papers; Caperton to Daniels, aboard the USS *Memphis*, June 26, 1916, 839.00, DR 1910–1929.

64. Pendleton to Bishop, Santiago, June 9, 1919, folder 22, box 3, Pendleton Papers.

65. Fisher to Grey, July 28, 1916, file 165654, reference 2682, FO 371.

66. My translation. Arias to Rivas, Santiago, July 6, 1916, legajo 27, 1916–1917, IP.

67. See, for instance, González, *Línea noroeste*, 80, 88.

68. My translation. Arias to Pendleton, Santiago, September 9, 1916, legajo 27, 1916–1917, IP.

69. My translation. Vasquez to secretary of state of interior and police, Barahona, June 12, 1916, legajo 347, 1916, IP.

70. [Mantero?] to secretary of state of interior and police, Barahona, June 14, 1916, legajo 347, 1916, IP.

71. Adams to district commanders, Northern District, August 21, 1920, legajo 34, 1919, IP.

72. Miller wrote that it was "an appreciable percentage" who failed to turn in weapons or did so reluctantly, in "Spurs," 25.

73. Kelsey, "Intervention," 179. A similar decrease occurred in Duarte Province: Mejía, *Lilís*, 145.

74. Miller, "Spurs," 25, 52.

75. My translation. Cited in Sosa Jiménez, *Hato Mayor*, 311.

76. Mejía, *Lilís*, 145.

77. My translation. Américo Jiménez, "Informe sobre la psicología . . . ," Salcedo, October 10, 1922, in Rodríguez Demorizi, *Lengua*, 205.

78. Henríquez Ureña, *Los yanquis*, 177. Henríquez was writing in 1919.

79. Knight, *Americans*, 78–9.

80. Caperton to Benson, Santo Domingo, June 12, 1916, folder Correspondence June 1916, box 1, Caperton Papers.

81. Henríquez and other Dominicans rejected a US financial advisor to dominate the country's revenues and payments and they accepted a constabulary only if the Dominican president would appoint its officers. Russell to Lansing, Santo Domingo, August 26, 1916,

839.00/1915, DR 1910–1929; Delage to Ministry of Foreign Relations, August 19, 1916, dossier 7, DR 1897–1918. See also Mejía, *Lilís*, 132.

82. D'Arlot de Saint-Saud to minister of foreign affairs, Santo Domingo, June 10, 1916, dossier 7, DR 1897–1918.

83. Caperton to Benson, May 18, 1916, folder Correspondence Jan–May 1916, box 1, Caperton Papers.

84. Caperton to Benson, July 9, 1916, Santo Domingo, folder Correspondence July–Dec 1916, box 1, Caperton Papers.

85. Caperton to Benson, July 9, 1916, Santo Domingo, folder Correspondence July–Dec 1916, box 1, Caperton Papers.

86. Roig de Leuchsenring, *La ocupación*, 38.

87. My translation. Henríquez y Carvajal to Cestero, Santo Domingo, August 31, 1916, legajo Papeles 1919–1920, Tomo 1, Cestero Archive.

88. My translation and emphasis. Imparcial [pseud.], editorial, "La situación," *Listín Diario*, August 22, 1916, in Russell to Lansing, Santo Domingo, August 29, 1916, 839.00/1924, DR 1910–1929.

89. Caperton to Benson, Santo Domingo, June 15, 1916, folder Correspondence June 1916, box 1, Caperton Papers.

90. Caperton to Benson, Santo Domingo, June 19, 1916, folder Correspondence June 1916, box 1, Caperton Papers.

91. Caperton to Conard, Santo Domingo, June 22, 1916, folder Correspondence June 1916, box 1, Caperton Papers.

92. Knight, *Americans*, 82; Calder, *Impact*, 15; Fuller and Cosmas, *Marines*, 24; Henríquez Ureña, *Los yanquis*, 179–80.

93. Mejía, *Lilís*, 131.

94. Case, "Occurrences at Duarte, October 24, 1916," and Trembley, "Statement," both Santo Domingo, October 25, 1916, 839.00/1949, DR 1910–1929. See also Morrison, "Report of Attempt to Arrest Ramón Batista," Santo Domingo, October 24, 1916, 839.00/1949, DR 1910–1929.

95. Henríquez Ureña, *Los yanquis*, 181–2.

96. Brewer to Lansing, Santo Domingo, October 26, 1916, 839.00/1937, DR 1910–1929.

97. Américo Lugo et al., "Temístocles Ruiz ha muerto," Santo Domingo, October 26, 1916, in Alfau Durán, ed. *Incháustegui*, and Delgado *Malagón*, 558–9.

98. My translation. Editorial, "Conceptos cotidianos," *Listín Diario*, November 14, 1916.

99. See, for instance, "De la Capital," *Ecos del valle* (Baní), November 11, 1916, 3; Luis Arquímedes Herrera, "Los horrores de la Intervención," *Ecos del valle* (Baní), November 11, 1916, 2.

100. R. Castro Ruiz, "Procuraduría Gral. de la República," *Listín Diario*, October 26, 1916.

101. Brewer to Lansing, Santo Domingo, October 29, 1916, 839.00/1938, DR 1910–1929; Knapp to chief of naval operations, November 23, 1916, 839.00/1966, DR 1910–1929.

102. Caperton to Benson, May 18, 1916, folder Correspondence Jan–May 1916, box 1, Caperton Papers.

103. Stabler to Lansing, Washington, October 27, 1916, 839.00/1939, DR 1910–1929.

104. Lansing to American Legation, Washington, October 28, 1916, 839.00/1937, DR 1910–1929.

105. Stabler, memcon, Washington, October 31, 1916, 839.00/1952, DR 1910–1929.

106. Knapp, proclamation, aboard USS *Olympia*, November 29, 1916, 839.00/1965, DR 1910–1929; Vega, *Derecho*, 344.

107. Wilson to Lansing, Washington, November 28, 1916, 839.00/1951a, DR 1910–1929.

108. Knapp to secretary of the navy, December 1, 1916, 839.00/1969, DR 1910–1929.

109. Russell to Lansing, Santo Domingo, December 14, 1916, 839.00/1967, DR 1910–1929.

110. Knapp to secretary of the navy, December 5, 1916, 839.00/1969, DR 1910–1929.

111. "Annual Report," July 21, 1917, 839.00/2043, DR 1910–1929, 6.

112. Knapp to secretary of the navy, December 3, 1916, 839.00/1969, DR 1910–1929.

113. Bob Considine, "The Marines Have Landed," *The American Weekly* [*Washington Post & Times Herald*], October 5, 1958: 7; Calder, *Impact*, 19; U.S. Army, *Military Government*, 28.

114. Delage to Ministry of Foreign Relations, February 28, 1917, dossier 7, DR 1897–1918.
115. Ducoudray, *Los "Gavilleros,"* 89.
116. My translation. Gilbert, *Mi lucha,* 7, 11, 13, 44, 46, 47, 139; Calder, *Impact,* 133–4.
117. Knight, *Americans,* 91–2.
118. My translation. "Resolución de Protesta," Dominican legation in Havana, December 17, 1916, 839.00/1977, DR 1910–1929. Eighteen people signed the petition, including Dominicans Román Pérez Cabral, Francisco Henríquez Ureña, and Luis E. Ricart.
119. My translation. Murillo to Chandeles, reproduced in *La Razón,* March 13, 1917, in [Stimson?] to Lansing, Buenos Aires, March 22, 1917, 839.00/2021, DR 1910–1929.
120. "Dominicans Talk of War," *NYT,* June 17, 1916, 1.
121. Fisher to Balfour, October 17, 1918, file 217, reference 3803, FO 371.
122. Sosa Jiménez, *Hato Mayor,* 310.
123. Russell to secretary of state, Santo Domingo, January 29, 1917, 839.00/2002, DR 1910–1929; Delage to Ministry of Foreign Relations, Santo Domingo, January 24, 1917, dossier 7, DR 1897–1918; Cassá, "Vicentico," Isla Abierta, in *Hoy,* May 5, 1995, 8–11.
124. Cassá, "Vicentico," Isla Abierta, in *Hoy,* May 5, 1995, 11.
125. Cassá, "1–La campaña de Vicentico," *Isla Abierta,* in *Hoy,* September 2, 1995, 14–6.
126. "Annual Report," July 21, 1917, 839.00/2043, DR 1910–1929.
127. Davis to regimental commander, 3rd Prov. Rgt, San Pedro de Macorís, June 1, 1917, folder Dominican Republic 1917, Dominican Republic, Geographical Files, Reference Branch, MCH.
128. My translation. Cassá, "Vicentico," *Isla Abierta,* in *Hoy,* May 5, 1995, 8–11.
129. Thorpe to brigade commander, Seibo, July 8, 1917, 839.00/2039, DR 1910–1929; Cassá, "y 2–La campaña de Vicentico," *Isla Abierta,* in *Hoy,* October 7, 1995, 17–20.
130. Perroud to Ministry of Foreign Relations, Santo Domingo, June 10, 1917, dossier 7, DR 1897–1918.
131. Proceedings of investigation, Santo Domingo, July 13, 1917, folder 19; Thorpe to Pendleton, San Pedro de Macorís, July 26, 1918, folder 21, both in box 2, Pendleton Papers.
132. Proceedings of investigation, Santo Domingo, July 13, 1917, folder 19, box 2, Pendleton Papers; Gould to Lansing, Santo Domingo, July 7, 1917, 839.00/2033, DR 1910–1929; Thorpe to brigade commander, Seibo, July 8, 1917, 839.00/2039, DR 1910–1929.
133. "Annual Report," July 21, 1917, 839.00/2043, DR 1910–1929.
134. Fisher to Balfour, November 28, 1917, file 5518, reference 3228, FO 371.
135. Other important collaborators included Mario Fermín Cabral, Haim H. López-Penha, Francisco A. Herrera, P. A. Ricart, Francisco J. Peynado, and Dr. A. Fiallo Cabral. See Calder, *Impact,* 29.
136. My translation. Vidal to Robison, Neyba, September 22, 1921, folder 34, 26–50 Miscellaneous, box 40, MGSD.
137. My translation. García Godoy, *El derrumbe,* 171, 170.
138. My translation. Perroud to Ministry of Foreign Relations, June 10, 1917, dossier 7, DR 1897–1918.
139. Snowden, cited in Grieb, *Harding,* 62.

Chapter 4

1. Hill, "Los Marinos," 10.
2. Musicant, *Banana Wars,* 285.
3. Gobat, *Confronting,* 3, 127.
4. Long, October 3, 1912, folder 7, box 1, Pendleton Papers.
5. Munro, *Republics,* 73.
6. My translation. Moncada to Huntington Wilson, Brooklyn, October 8, 1912, 817.00/2078, Nicaragua 1910–1929.
7. Southerland to Secretary of the Navy, aboard USS *California* off Corinto, 14 November 1912, 817.00/2164, Nicaragua 1910–1929.
8. Ham, "Americanizing," 185.
9. In 1922–1923, for example, Nicaragua spent $132,292 on its army while Guatemala and El Salvador each spent $1.6 million and Honduras $1.1 million. Greer, "State Department," 465. See also Messersmith to Hough, Washington, November 26, 1924, roll 30, OCNO/OSN.

10. Davis, *Marine!*, 57.
11. Dore, *Myths*, 147.
12. Beaulac, *Career,* 120; Schroeder, "'To Defend,'" 53.
13. Gobat, *Confronting*, 128–30.
14. Harrison, *Dollar Diplomat*, 91.
15. Musicant, *Banana Wars*, 286.
16. Nalty, *Marines*, 15.
17. Goldwert, *Constabulary*, 23.
18. Grossman, "'Hermanos,'" 176.
19. Haggard to Grey, February 14, 1913, file A11091, reference 1583, FO 371.
20. Munro, *United States*, 164.
21. Gobat, *Confronting*, 2.
22. Whisnant, *Rascally Signs*, 109, 121.
23. Marston, Managua, September 30, 1923, folder Nicaragua Intell. Summaries (1921–1925), box 7, GC.
24. Marston, Managua, December 31, 1923, folder Nicaragua Intell. Summaries (1921–1925), box 7, GC.
25. Foner, *Labor*, 89.
26. Sócrates Sandino to Doña América de Sandino, El Chipotón, August 20, 1931, GS.
27. Gobat, *Confronting*, 2, 6.
28. Keyser, Managua, July 31, 1925, folder Nicaragua Intell. Summaries (1921–1925), box 7, GC.
29. Kamman, *Search*, 34.
30. Marston, Managua, September 30, 1923, folder Nicaragua Intell. Summaries (1921–1925), box 7, GC.
31. Underhill, Managua, February 28, 1921, folder Nicaragua—Legations, Foreign Correspondence, miscellaneous, box 26, O&T.
32. My translations. Borgen, *Una vida*, 68.
33. Estimates of the number of dead police range from one to six. See "Marines Convicted in Nicaragua Slaying," *NYT*, December 31, 1921, 5, and other footnotes in this paragraph.
34. Taylor to secretary of the navy, Managua, January 27, 1922, roll 30, OCNO/OSN.
35. "Asks Marines' Withdrawal," *NYT*, February 6, 1922, 15.
36. "Marines Convicted in Nicaragua Slaying," *NYT*, December 31, 1921, 5; Nalty, *Marines*, 11; Musicant, *Banana Wars*, 286.
37. O'Brien, *Mission*, 69.
38. Keyser, Managua, November 30, 1924, folder Nicaragua Intell. Summaries (1921–1925), box 7, GC.
39. Keyser, April 28, 1925, folder Financial Reports (1923–1932), box 1, GC.
40. *El Comercio*, January 29, 1925, and *La Tribuna*, April 19, 1925, both in Keyser, confidential memo, April 28, 1925, folder Financial Reports (1923–1932), box 1, GC.

Chapter 5

1. Senate, *Hearings*, vol. 1, 780.
2. Gendarmerie intelligence officer to chief of the Gendarmerie, Port-au-Prince, October 20, 1920, folder Bandits, Reports on—June May 20, 2021, box 4, Gendarmerie; Graham A. Cosmas, "*Cacos* and *Caudillos*: Marines and Counterinsurgency in Hispaniola, 1915–1924," in *Interpretations*, ed. Roberts and Sweetman, 296; Langley, *Banana Wars*, 155.
3. Heinl, Jr., and Heinl, *Written in Blood*, 462; "Casualties," 1067; Schmidt, *Occupation*, 102.
4. Roberto Cassá, for instance, could not find any overtly political programs of *gavilleros* yet warned that such may still have existed, in "Emergencia del gavillerismo frente a la Ocupación militar," *Isla Abierta*, in *Hoy*, March 3, 1995, 6–9.
5. "Bandit Chiefs–1919/1920" October 6, 1920, folder [Action Reports], 1919–1922, box 1, Corr. 1916–1919.
6. Millet, *Paysans*, 90.

7. "THE MINISTERS, COUNSELLORS AND DELEGATES OF THE REVOLUTION ACTUALLY IN NORTHERN HAITI," pamphlet, [November 1919?], folder Bandit Activities and Descriptions, box 3, Gendarmerie.

8. My translation. Péralte to British minister in Haiti, General Headquarters, October 7, 1919, in Delage to minister of foreign affairs, Port-au-Prince, October 12, 1919, dossier 9, Haiti 1918–1940.

9. Michel, *Péralte*, 1.

10. Frank, *Roaming*, 135.

11. Greathouse, "King," 30.

12. Frank, "Death," 26.

13. Michel, *Péralte*, 4–8; district commander to chief of the Gendarmerie, Hinche, December 29, 1918, folder 14th Company at Hinche, Corres., box 10, Gendarmerie; Frank, "Death," 26.

14. Michel, *Péralte*, 13–7; Alexis, "Nationalism," 43.

15. My translation. Christophe cited in Gaillard, *Premier écrasement*, 39.

16. My translation. Christophe cited in Gaillard, *Premier écrasement*, 40.

17. Michel, *Péralte*, 13–7, 66–9; Millet, *Paysans*, 78; Heinl, Jr., and Heinl, *Written in Blood*, 451–2.

18. Marcel Baudin cited in Gaillard, *Premier écrasement*, 66.

19. Heinl, Jr., and Heinl, *Written in Blood*, 463.

20. Here accounts vary widely. See McCrocklin, *Garde*, 103; and Gaillard, *Hinche*, 33–8. Suggesting strongly not only Péralte's participation but his role as an organizer are several documents in folder Department of Cape, Corres. from, box 6, Gendarmerie.

21. My translation. French Chargé d'Affaires Lucide Agel to minister of foreign affairs, Port-au-Prince, November 19, 1919, dossier 9, Haiti 1918–1940.

22. Wise, *A Marine*, 311.

23. M. Dietz cited in Gaillard, *Hinche*, 179.

24. Frank, *Roaming*, 136; Wedor to Williams, October 18, 1918, folder Operations Against Hostile Bandits 1919 + 1920, box 1, Corr. 1919–1920.

25. Gaillard, *Péralte*, 11.

26. My translation. Péralte to British consul in Port-au-Prince, Caco headquarters, June 3, 1919, attached to Wall to Balfour, June 27, 1919, file 105852, reference 3803, FO 371.

27. My translation. Péralte to Riphin Dubuisson, Camp Général, April 18, 1919, folder 8, box 3, Russell Papers.

28. My translation. Péralte to Delage, Camp Général, July 27, 1919, in Delage to minister of foreign affairs, Port-au-Prince, August 8, 1919, dossier 9, Haiti 1918–1940.

29. My translation. Castor, *Occupation*, 134. A longer appreciation of Péralte's nationalism is Alexis, "Nationalism."

30. Péralte to Catlin, Grand Quartier, 1919, folder Caco Correspondence, box 5, Gendarmerie.

31. My translation. [Péralte?], poster, Saint-Michel, March 29, 1919, folder 8, box 3, Russell Papers.

32. Gaillard, *Péralte*, 126.

33. Gaillard, *Premier écrasement*, 30, 32.

34. One marine said 20 percent of the population had a gun. Hill to "My Dear Col. Williams," Mirebalais, February 21, 1919, folder Operations Against Hostile Bandits 1919 + 1920, box 1, Corr. 1919–1920; Niles, *Black Haiti*, 138.

35. Michel, *Péralte*, 23–4.

36. Freeley to commandant, Azua, December 14, 1918, legajo 370, 1918, IP. For detail, see Gaillard, *Péralte*.

37. Michel, *Péralte*, xv; Castor, *Occupation*, 138–43.

38. Military histories and memoirs on the *cacos*: Frank, *Roaming*, 130–1; Inman, "Hard Problems," 338–42; Wise, *A Marine*, 135, 301.

39. My translation. Péralte to Delage, Camp Général, July 27, 1919, in Delage to minister of foreign affairs, Port-au-Prince, August 8, 1919, dossier 9, Haiti 1918–1940.

40. Plummer, *Psychological Moment*, 103.

41. Widow Masséna Péralte to Charlemagne Péralte, undated [1919], folder 8, box 3, Russell Papers.

42. My translation; emphasis in original. Cited in Gaillard, *Péralte,* 214.

43. Bailly-Blanchard to secretary of state, March 18, 1919, 838.00/1566, Haiti 1910–1929.

44. Cited in Michel, *Péralte,* 65.

45. Greathouse, "King," 30.

46. My translation. [Péralte?], poster, Saint-Michel, March 29, 1919, folder 8, box 3, Russell Papers.

47. Schmidt argued that Péralte formed a provisional government in the North but the evidence is scant: *Occupation,* 102.

48. Castor, *Occupation,* 138.

49. My translation. Péralte cited in Millet, *Paysans,* 81.

50. Kuser, *Haiti,* 30; Millet, *Paysans,* 92.

51. Frank, "Death," 22–35; Greathouse, "King," 29–33, and especially Hanneken to chief of the Gendarmerie, Grande Rivière, October 31, 1919, folder Grande Rivière, from, 1916–1919, box 1, Corr. 1916–1919.

52. Gaillard, *La guérilla,* 60–3.

53. Russell, unpublished manuscript, folder 3, box 3, Russell Papers.

54. Batraville to Decès Jean Jules, Camp Général de Bemaco, April 5, 1920, folder Confidential File, box 5, Gendarmerie.

55. Statement of Methius Richard, Hinche, April 18, 1920, folder Bandit Activities and Descriptions, box 3, Gendarmerie.

56. Entry of 11 April, Russell, daily diary report, April 16, 1920, 838.00/1637, Haiti 1910–1929.

57. Russell, statement, [1920], folder Investi[gation] Haitien Affai[rs], box 1, Corr. 1918–1921; Millet, *Paysans,* 90, 95.

58. [Raymond?], memo to department commander, Las Cahobas, June 1, 1920, folder Bandits, Reports on - June 20 - May 21, box 4, Gendarmerie.

59. My translation. Péralte to Catlin, Grand Quartier, 1919, folder Caco Correspondence, box 5, Gendarmerie.

60. My translation. Péralte to Delage, Camp Général, July 27, 1919, in Delage to minister of foreign affairs, Port-au-Prince, August 8, 1919, dossier 9, Haiti 1918–1940.

61. My translations. Chevry cited in Gaillard, *La guérilla,* 68.

62. My translation. For example, [illegible name], handwritten note, September 17, 1919, République d'Haïti, folder 86, box 1, Road Reports.

63. My translation. Virgile cited in Gaillard, *La guérilla,* 82.

64. My translation. Mérianne Batraville cited in Gaillard, *La guérilla,* 82.

65. Doxey to chief of the Gendarmerie, Hinche, March 17, 1919, folder Operations Against Hostile Bandits 1919 + 1920, box 1, Corr. 1919–1920.

66. Chevry cited in Gaillard, *Péralte,* 107.

67. Russell to Johnson, Port-au-Prince, October 31, 1920, 838.00/1664, Haiti 1910–1929.

68. My translation. Delage to minister of foreign affairs, Port-au-Prince, October 12, 1919, dossier 9, Haiti 1918–1940.

69. "Says Natives Ate Marines," *NYT,* November 17, 1921, 36.

70. Chapman, December 18, 1924, folder Diary, 1924–1933, box 2, correspondence and papers—additions, 1920–1941, 83/153, Chapman Papers.

71. Saint-Amand, *Code rural,* 23–5.

72. Bickel, *Mars Learning,* 79; Moral, *Paysan,* 66.

73. My translation. Delage to minister of foreign affairs, Port-au-Prince, March 7, 1919, dossier 9, Haiti 1918–1940; Gaillard, *Hinche,* 58.

74. Interview with Williams, January 6, 1920, folder Investigations, Haiti, extra copies, box 2, Operations 1915–1921.

75. Gaillard, *Hinche,* 30.

76. My translation. "Simples Notes," *Le Matin,* December 27, 1917, 1.

77. Isodore cited in Gaillard, *Hinche,* 147.

78. My translation. Dorsica cited in Gaillard, *Hinche,* 182.

79. My translation. Dorsica and Michel cited in Gaillard, *Hinche,* 225.

80. Frank, "Death," 24.

Chapter 6

1. Russell to secretary of state, August 24, 1918, 839.00/2098, DR 1910–1929.
2. "Quarterly Report," August 28, 1919, 839.00/2153, DR 1910–1929.
3. Cited in "Quarterly Report," April 17, 1919, 839.00/2130, DR 1910–1929; see also "Quarterly Report," February 5, 1919, 839.00/2118, DR 1910–1929.
4. For example, Thorpe to Pendleton, San Pedro de Macorís, August 9, 1918, folder 21, box 2, Pendleton Papers.
5. Calder, *Impact*, 133, 156, 181.
6. U.S. Army, *Military Government*.
7. See "Names of Bandit Leaders . . . ," [May 22, 1922?], folder Miscellaneous Records 1916–1922, 1932–1940, box 1, Occupation 1916–1924.
8. Lee to major general commandant, Santo Domingo, August 24, 1922, folder Santo Domingo, Contacts, Reports of, box 2, Occupation 1916–1924; "Casualties," 1067.
9. Calder, *Impact*, 145.
10. My translation. "Pina" to Williams, Hato Mayor, July 15, 1918, legajo 28, 1918, IP.
11. Lozano, *Dominación*, 222.
12. Roberto Cassá, "Emergencia del gavillerismo frente a la Ocupación militar," *Isla Abierta*, in *Hoy*, March 3, 1995, 6.
13. Harllee to commanding general, San Pedro de Macorís, January 2, 1922, folder 14, 51–75 Commanding General, USMC, box 48, MGSD.
14. Cassá, "Emergencia del gavillerismo frente a la Ocupación militar," *Isla Abierta*, in *Hoy*, March 3, 1995, 7.
15. My translation. "Copia de los documentos encontrados . . . ," San Pedro de Macorís, April 4, 1922, legajo 90, 1922, IP.
16. Unsigned "estimate of the situation," Santo Domingo, July 2, 1921, folder Santo Domingo—Intell. Summaries May–Aug 1921, box 5, GC.
17. Cassá, "Movimientos," 196. Tolete and Martín Peguero also claimed "to be revolutionists and not bandit leaders," but only because they threatened to kill thieves, in Kilgore, March 24, 1921, folder Santo Domingo—Intell. Summaries 1921, box 5, GC.
18. An example of a message he left behind when doing so is Harllee to commanding general, Second Brigade, USMC, San Pedro de Macorís, January 18, 1922, folder 14, 26–50 Commanding General, USMC, box 48, MGSD.
19. Calder, "Caudillos," 661–2.
20. Thorpe to regimental commander, San Pedro de Macorís, July 25, 1918, folder Santo Domingo, Contacts, Reports of, box 2, Occupation 1916–1924.
21. Harlee to commanding general, San Pedro de Macorís, October 1, 1921, folder 14, 476–500 Commanding General, box 37, MGSD.
22. Nateras's men placed the note under Steele's door within hours of the extortion's expiration and Steele did not see the note until too late. He thus never "refused" to pay the extortion: commanding general to Robison, Santo Domingo, October 7, 1921, folder 14, 476–500 commanding General, box 37, MGSD.
23. Nateras to managers of sugar estates, September 30, 1921, legajo 37, 1921–1922, GM.
24. Commanding general to Robison, Santo Domingo, October 7, 1921, folder 14, 476–500 Commanding General, box 37, MGSD.
25. Harllee to commanding general, San Pedro de Macorís, January 18, 1922, folder 14, 26–50 Commanding General, USMC, box 48, MGSD.
26. Gamborg-Andresen to brigade commander, Santo Domingo, February 27, 1919, folder D-40 Dominican Rep. Misc. USMC Reports, box 8, O&T.
27. Gamborg-Andresen to brigade commander, Santo Domingo, February 27, 1919, folder D-40 Dominican Rep. Misc. USMC Reports, box 8, O&T.
28. Franks, "*Gavilleros*," 170. See also Calder, "Caudillos," 662.
29. Kilgore, May 23, 1921, folder Santo Domingo—Intell. Summaries April–June 1921, box 5, GC.
30. McLean, quarterly report, [19 August?] 1919, legajo 9, 1919, IP.
31. Heaton to brigade commander, Hato Mayor, June 11, 1919, folder Santo Domingo, Contacts, Reports of, box 2, Occupation 1916–1924.

32. McLean to commandant, Santo Domingo, June 10, 1919, legajo 382, 1919, IP.
33. Hamet to district commander, San Pedro de Macorís, June 15, 1919, folder Santo Domingo—Operations Reports, 8 Sept 18–15 Jun 19, box 2, Occupation 1916–1924.
34. Kilgore, May 23, 1921, folder Santo Domingo—Intell. Summaries April–June 1921, box 5, GC.
35. Gamborg-Andresen to brigade commander, Santo Domingo, February 27, 1919, folder D-40 Dominican Rep. Misc. USMC Reports, box 8, O&T.
36. Harllee to commanding general, San Pedro de Macorís, January 2, 1922, folder Dominican Republic, Santo Domingo, 1922, Dominican Republic, Geographical Files, Reference Branch, MCH.
37. Calder, "Caudillos," 669.
38. Gamborg-Andresen to brigade commander, Santo Domingo, February 27, 1919, folder D-40 Dominican Rep. Misc. USMC Reports, box 8, O&T.
39. Craig, oral history.
40. Davis to commanding general, Santo Domingo, December 30, 1921, folder Dominican Republic, Santo Domingo, 1922, Dominican Republic, Geographical Files, Reference Branch, MCH.
41. Rogers to district commander, San Pedro de Macorís, April 25, 1919, folder Reports of Operations, Brigade Diary Reports, Santo Domingo, November 9, 1918 to August 31, 1919, box 2, Operations 1915–1921.
42. "Names of Bandit Leaders . . . ," [May 22, 1922?]; folder Miscellaneous Records 1916–1922, 1932–1940; box 1, Occupation 1916–1924.

Chapter 7

1. The best analyses of the Sandino struggle in Spanish agree that his political ideology was pluralist and protean. They include Alemán Bolaños, *Sandino*; Selser, *Sandino*; Wünderich, *Biografía*; Dospital, *Siempre*; and Bolaños Geyer, *Sandino*.
2. Dennis to secretary of state, Managua, July 17, 1926, 817.00/3706, Nicaragua 1910–1929.
3. Comments by Snow, January 3, on Patterson to Foreign Office, December 31, 1926, file A2, reference 11969, FO 371.
4. Kamman, *Search*, 68.
5. Comments by Vansittart, January 4, on Patterson to Foreign Office, December 31, 1926, file A2, reference 11969, FO 371.
6. Nalty, *Marines*.
7. Buchenau, *Shadow*, 169; Salisbury, "Mexico," 324–6.
8. Howard to Chamberlain, Washington, January 6, 1927, file A320, reference 11969, FO 371.
9. Editorial, "Big Brother or Big Bully," *The Nation*, July 14, 1926, 25.
10. Pagano, *Bluejackets*, 74, 90.
11. Bickel, *Mars Learning*, 155; Boot, *Savage*, 234.
12. Stimson and Bundy, *Active Service*, 113.
13. Stimson, April 18, 1927, microfilm reel 1, vol. 7, Stimson Diary, FDRL.
14. Stimson, May 1, 1927, microfilm reel 1, vol. 7, Stimson Diary, FDRL.
15. Stimson to White, New York, September 26, 1927, 817.00/5044 ½, Nicaragua 1910–1929.
16. Moncada, "Nicaragua," 460–2, 477.
17. State, *Brief History*, 53.
18. Martín Tercero cited in Gould, *Equals*, 36.
19. Cited in Ellis, *Kellogg*, 75.
20. Hazlet, "United States," 100.
21. Macaulay, *Affair*, 40.
22. "Brief Notice of Sandino's Career," *Panamá América*, February 24, 1934, in *Sandino*, comp. Arellano, 8.
23. Clancy to Borah, Bluefields, June 4, 1927, folder 1926–1927 (2), box 234, Borah Papers; Davis, memo, July 8, 1927, 817.00/4941, Nicaragua 1910–1929.
24. Frisbie, Managua, July 12, 1927, folder 2d Brigade B-2 Intelligence Reports (1Feb1927–26Feb1928), box 6, Nicaragua 1927–1932.

25. My translation. Mejía, one of the original twenty-nine followers, oral history.

26. My translation. Baylen, "Sandino," 403.

27. Instituto, *Ahora*, 65.

28. My translation. Sandino, "Una digna respuesta al traidor Moncada," [May?] 1927, E-001, C-004, 000201, ACS.

29. Bolaños Geyer claims 1894, in *Sandino*, whereas all others say 1895.

30. My translation. Bendaña, *Mística*, 14.

31. Sandino cited in Román, *Maldito país*, 44; Wünderich, *Biografía*, 38.

32. My translation. Sandino cited in Román, *Maldito país*, 45.

33. Vayssière, *Auguste*, 48.

34. Sandino Pérez, oral history.

35. For differing arguments, see Román, *Maldito país*, 54; Sandino Pérez, oral history; "El drama," E-001, C-008, 000411, ACS.

36. Sandino cited in Navarro-Génie, *Augusto*, 10.

37. Vayssière, *Auguste*, 52.

38. The most likely destinations were Honduras, Guatemala, and Mexico. Others have added Costa Rica, Panama, Venezuela, and even the United States. See Román, *Maldito país*, 54–6; Bendaña, *Mística*, 19–35.

39. Navarro-Génie, *Augusto*, 16.

40. Sandino, "Letter to the Honduran Poet Froylán Turcios, April 1, 1928," in *Sandino*, comp. Ramírez, trans. Conrad, 25.

41. Bendaña, *Mística, passim* 20–56. See also Selser, *Sandino*, 161. Amador asserts that he was a union member, in *Derrota militar*, 33.

42. My translation. Sandino cited in *Pensamiento vivo*, ed. Ramírez, 73.

43. Green to Walker, Tampico, March 15, 1928, 817.00/5465 ½, Nicaragua 1910–1929. Sandino had worked for Huasteca since August 17, 1925, first as a warehouse employee and then in charge of the Gasoline Sales Department.

44. Navarro-Génie, *Augusto*, 20.

45. My translation. Sandino cited in Arrieta, *¡Habla Sandino!*, 12; José Veles, oral history.

46. Green to Walker, Tampico, March 15, 1928, 817.00/5465 ½, Nicaragua 1910–1929. Butters interviewed in Evelyn Trent, "Californian's Mine Is Seized in Nicaragua," *San Francisco Chronicle*, February 19, 1928, 2F.

47. Musicant, *Banana Wars*, 300; Amador, *Derrota militar*, 33.

48. My translation. Cited in Román, *Maldito país*, 57.

49. Baylen, "Sandino," 398.

50. Munro, *United States*, 235.

51. My translation. Gregorio Sandino cited in Augusto Sandino, "Orígenes de nuestra resistencia armada, iniciada el 4 de mayo de 1927, contra la invasión Yankee en nuestra república," *El Chipote*, April 10, 1929, E-001, C-004, 000209, ACS.

52. Schroeder, "'To Defend,'" 262.

53. Sandino, "Orígenes . . . ," *El Chipote*, April 10, 1929, E-001, C-004, 000209, ACS.

54. Gray, "Campaign," 36.

55. Schroeder, "'To Defend,'" 256.

56. Eberhardt to secretary of state, Managua, July 17, 1927, 817.00/4936, Nicaragua 1910–1929.

57. Frisbie, Managua, August 16, 1927, folder 2d Brigade B-2 Intelligence Reports (1Feb1927–26Feb1928), box 6, Nicaragua 1927–1932; "Testimony of the Major General Commandant before the Senate Committee of Foreign Relations," February 18, 1928, folder Nicaragua—U.S. Senate Inquiry, box 30, O&T, 50.

58. Munro, *United States*, 236; Macaulay, *Affair*, 84, 122.

59. Pedro Antonio Araúz Pineda, unpublished autobiography, E-001, C-006, 000323, ACS.

60. My translation. Cited in Román, *Maldito país*, 79.

61. Lejeune cited in "Testimony . . . ," February 18, 1928, folder Nicaragua—U.S. Senate Inquiry, box 30, O&T, 53.

62. Eberhardt to secretary of state, Managua, August 18, 1927, 817.00/4991, Nicaragua 1910–1929.

63. Munro to secretary of state, Managua, September 26, 1927, 817.00/5070, Nicaragua 1910–1929.
64. Schroeder, "'To Defend,'" 256.
65. Hazlet, "United States," 99. For slightly different numbers, see Frazier, "Dawn," 450.
66. Kamman, *Search*, 133, 140.
67. "Casualties," 1067.
68. Peard to jefe director, November 13, 1927, folder 2dBrig—B-2 Int&RPatlRepts-10Sept27–6Jan28, box 3, Nicaragua 1927–1933.
69. Munn, oral history, 8. Munn added that pro-US opinions increased with time.
70. Daugherty, "Reminiscences," 5.
71. Cuadra, "Memorias," 33.
72. Holmes, "Horse Marines," 42. Confirming this is Racicot to Commanding General, Second Brigade, Ocotal, February 28, 1930, folder 2dBrig—B-2 Report, 28Feb30, box 3, Nicaragua 1927–1933.
73. The major was Oliver Floyd, in Nalty, *Marines*, 17.
74. Grossman, "'La Patria,'" 6.
75. "Sandino," *Literary Digest*, February 4, 1928, 42.
76. Edwards to Chamberlain, December 7, 1927, file A349, reference 12746, FO 371; Frisbie, Managua, August 3, 1927, folder 2d Brigade B-2 Intelligence Reports (1Feb1927–26Feb1928), box 6, Nicaragua 1927–1932; London to Henderson, Managua, August 16, 1929, file A6862, reference 13470, FO 371; Larsen to commanding officer, Managua, April 20, 1928, folder 2d Brigade Bandit Reports (April 1928), box 12, Nicaragua 1927–1932.
77. Gobat, *Confronting*, 237.
78. London to Henderson, Managua, August 16, 1929, file A6862, reference 13470, FO 371. See also Gobat, *Confronting*, 236.
79. Schroeder, "'To Defend,'" 526, 502. Gobat gives other reasons for the lack of anti-occupation protest outside the Segovias: there was little terror among popular groups in cities; parties competed for popular support with land and labor reforms; and there was little response to economic nationalism, in *Confronting*, 145–6.
80. Cited in "Sandino," *Literary Digest*, February 4, 1928, 42.
81. It certainly righted the assumption among early opponents of Sandino that he had no political ideals. For example, Moncada said Sandino led "a war lacking in ideals," cited in Linton Wells, "Marine Planes Again Targets in Sandino Attack," *NYHT*, July 21, 1927, 1; "His activities cannot be considered to have any political significance whatsoever," said Frank Kellogg, in "Kellogg's Letter of Explanation," *NYT*, July 19, 1927, 1.
82. Scholars who focused on nationalism include Frazier, "Dawn." Founder of the modern Sandinistas Carlos Fonseca identified six Sandino themes, enumerated in Zimmermann, *Sandinista*, 148. Brooks also identified "a compound of Nicaraguan Liberal ideas and Nicaraguan and Segovian popular practices," in "Rebellion," 25. Schroeder made the case for these diverse motivations, among other places, in "The Sandino Rebellion Revisited: Civil War, Imperialism, Popular Nationalism, and State Formation Muddied Up Together in the Segovias of Nicaragua, 1926–1934," in *Close Encounters*, ed. Joseph, LeGrand, and Salvatore: 214. Yet Schroeder, like Brooks, Fonseca, and Grossman, "'Hermanos,'" thought nationalism the strongest motivator.
83. Grossman has usefully argued that the "Sandinista conscience" (my translation) held the struggle together as much if not more than Sandino's leadership, in "'La Patria,'" 3.
84. My translation. Román, *Maldito país*, 118.
85. The prompting was by Schroeder, "'To Defend,'" 141.
86. Navarro-Génie, *Augusto*, 42.
87. De Belausteguigoitia, *Con Sandino*, 181. Wünderich, *Biografía*, 25, argued that Sandino was primarily a nationalist, not a proletarian warrior. Paige in *Coffee*, 176, argued that Sandino's lack of a social program was a major weakness.
88. Vayssière, *Auguste*, 37.
89. Sandino, "Acuerdo No. 7," *El Chipote*, December 14, 1927, E-001, C-004, 000181, ACS.
90. My translation. Ceteño Fonseca, oral history. Cana Araúz confirmed this early disposition, in her oral history.

91. My translation. Cited in Instituto, *Ahora*, 77.

92. My translation. Tercero González, oral history.

93. Schroeder argued that partisan acts of violence in the region were "exemplars of modes of elite domination and popular struggle, with deep and abiding roots in the political culture of the country and region," in "Horse Thieves," 387, 392.

94. My translation. Tercero González, oral history.

95. González, oral history. On Conservative bands, see Munro, memo to secretary of state, Managua, October 4, 1927, 817.00/5051, and November 17, 1927, 817.00/5145, both in Nicaragua 1910–1929. Wünderich, *Biografía*, 27, said the primary "exterior political motivation" of armed struggle in the Segovias was the 1926–1927 civil war, not the US intervention.

96. According to Schroeder, three Ocotal landowners emerged as the chief proponents of violence: Gustavo Paguaga, Abraham Gutiérrez Lobo, and Pedro Lobo, in "Horse Thieves," 396, 397, 400.

97. Trelawney-Ansell, *Nine Lives*, 162.

98. My translation. Ortiz, oral history.

99. My translation. Zalaya, oral history. Salgado Castellano said exactly the same: oral history.

100. Castillo Castilblanco, oral history. Evidence of both Liberal and Conservative depredations are in Eberhardt to Kellogg, Managua, February 9, 1928, 817.00/5387, Nicaragua 1910–1929; and Stimson, April 24, 1927, microfilm reel 1, vol. 7, Stimson Diary, FDRL.

101. Grossman, "'Hermanos,'" 634.

102. Uriarte, oral history; Rodríguez Casco, oral history.

103. My translation. Ramírez, oral history.

104. My translation. Cruz, oral history.

105. Sandino to Castillo Estelí, *El Chipote*, August 26, 1927, E-001, C-003, 000178, ACS.

106. Eberhardt to secretary of state, Managua, September 11, 1927, 817.00/5027, Nicaragua 1910–1929; Munro to secretary of state, Managua, September 26, 1927, 817.00/5069, Nicaragua 1910–1929; César to Kellogg, Washington, January 12, 1928, 817.00/5259, Nicaragua 1910–1929.

107. My translation. Sandino to Ramires [Ramírez?] Telpaneca, June 17, 1927, E-001, C-003, 000155, ACS.

108. My translation. Sandino, credential, El Chipotón, May 4, 1929, E-001, C-002, 000070, ACS.

109. Mairena Hernandez to Miralda, El Chipotón, August 22, 1928, folder Nicaragua (1927–1928), box 2, GC.

110. Wünderich, *Biografía*, 25.

111. Schroeder, "'To Defend,'" vi.

112. Grossman, "'Hermanos,'" 9, 104–10, 121, 680–1.

113. Wünderich, *Biografía*, 116.

114. Schroeder, "'To Defend,'" 108.

115. O'Brien, *Mission*, 71; Gould, *Equals*, 67, 37.

116. O'Brien, *Mission*, 74.

117. My translation. Sandino to Munguia, El Chipote, October 22, 1927, E-001, C-003, 000088, ACS.

118. Zelaya to "manager, Standard Fruit Co.," Puerto Castilla, September 2, 1927, 817.00/5041, Nicaragua 1910–1929.

119. Veitch to Foreign Dept. in New Orleans, Puerto Cabezas, August 27, 1927, 817.00/5041, Nicaragua 1910–1929.

120. Munro to secretary of state, Managua, January 12, 1928, 817.5045/16, Nicaragua 1910–1929.

121. My translation. Cruz, oral history.

122. "Sandino," *Literary Digest*, February 4, 1928, 46.

123. My translation. Sandino, message to workers and peasants of Nicaragua and Latin America, Veracruz, Mexico, February 26, 1930, E-001, C-005, 000242, ACS.

124. Instituto, *Ahora*, 186.

125. My translation. Cited in Instituto, *Ahora*, 186.

126. My translation. Hernández Blandón, oral history. A similar story is that of Romero, oral history.

127. My translation. Rugama, oral history.
128. Rivas, oral history.
129. Emphasis in original. Sandino, "Manifesto to Nicaraguan Compatriots," ca. July 14, 1927, in *Sandino*, comp. Ramírez, trans. Conrad, 79.
130. My translation. Paraphrased by Veles, oral history.
131. Flores Gladys, oral history.
132. O'Brien, *Mission*, 74–5.
133. Evelyn Trent, "Californian's Mine Is Seized in Nicaragua," *San Francisco Chronicle*, February 19, 1928, 1F; Schroeder, "'To Defend,'" 212; Floyd to commanding officer, San Albino, August 2, 1927, folder Nicaragua, San Albino Mine, box 30, O&T. See also "Sandino Took Mine to Finance 'War,'" *San Francisco Chronicle*, February 1, 1928.
134. Editorial, "Get Sandino!" *Washington Post*, January 3, 1928; Evelyn Trent, "Californian's Mine Is Seized in Nicaragua," *San Francisco Chronicle*, February 19, 1928, 1F.
135. Sandino to manager of La Luz and Los Angeles mines, La Luz, April 29, 1928, folder Nicaragua La Luz Mine, box 26, O&T.
136. Wünderich, *Costa*, 47.
137. Eudiviges Herrera Siles, interview with Shroeder, Estelí, October 1990, in "'To Defend,'" 133.
138. Graae, Puerto Cabezas, May 14, 1928, 817.00/5739, Nicaragua 1910–1929.
139. Thompson to Larsen, April 17, 1928, file A3380, reference 12746, FO 371.
140. Max Stern, "Nicaragua Stands Nineteenth in Latin Countries in Which America Boasts Investments," *San Francisco Chronicle*, February 23, 1928. Other investments were in mahogany, coffee, sugar, and gold.
141. My translation. Sandino to Carbajal and Chavarria, Headquarters of EDSNN, January 8, 1932, folder Nicaragua—Bandit Correspondence (Miscellaneous, Jefes, etc.), box 18, O&T.
142. Macaulay, *Affair*, 108.
143. Navarro-Génie, *Augusto*, 26.
144. Román, *Maldito país*, 118.
145. Merritt, "Patrol," 40.
146. Pineda Cordero, oral history. Gould, *To Die*, 157–8, also noted Sandino's inability to distinguish between indigenous peoples in the Segovias and in the east.
147. Gould, *To Die*, 159–60.
148. Hale largely revised a school of historical thought that argued that Miskitos hated Sandino, in *Resistance*. See mostly 53–4.
149. Gould, *To Die*, 157.
150. Beals, "With Sandino," 205.
151. Brooks, "US Marines," 320. Confirming this help as guides is Nasario Ortega Aldaba and others in Instituto, *Ahora*, 35.
152. Fletcher to American minister in Nicaragua, Bluefields, May 17, 1928, 817.00/5739, Nicaragua 1910–1929.
153. Román, *Maldito país*, 118. Some former Sandinistas recalled that palmazones were named so because they killed, or "palmaban," those they captured; others that palmazones could be as old as 16. See Instituto, *Ahora*, 212, 213.
154. Ramírez, "Kid," 70.
155. My translation. Instituto, *Ahora*, 214.
156. Linton Wells, "Marine Planes Again Targets in Sandino Attack," *NYHT*, July 21, 1927, FDRL, 1.
157. Sandino to Turcios, *El Chipote*, September 2, 1928, folder 2dBrig—B-2 Int. Repts., box 4, Nicaragua 1927–1933.
158. Cited in Paige, *Coffee*, 170.
159. My translation. Cited in Amador, *Exilio*, 29–30.
160. My translation. Sandino, declarations for the *New York World*, Mexico City, January 28, 1930, E-001, C-004, 000215, ACS.
161. Sandino to manager of La Luz and Los Angeles mines, La Luz, April 29, 1928, folder Nicaragua La Luz Mine, box 26, O&T.

162. My translation. Sandino, manifesto, Segovias, September 15, 1931, folder C [unlabeled] 1 of 2, box 1, GN-2 1928–1932.
163. Sandino, decree, *El Chipote*, November 14, 1927, E-001, C-004, 000205, ACS.
164. My translation. Juan Pablo Ramírez Velázquez cited in Instituto, *Ahora*, 118. Five *cortes* are described in Bolaños Geyer, *El iluminado*, 33.
165. My translation. Francisco Lara López cited in Instituto, *Ahora*, 125.
166. Cited in Schroeder, "'To Defend,'" 298.
167. Román, *Maldito país*, 119–20; Sociedad, *La verdad*, 27–8.
168. Altamirano to Herrera, November 12, 1930, folder C [unlabeled] 2 of 2, box 1, GN-2 1928–1932; Castillo Girón, oral history; Cerro Castellón, oral history.
169. Wünderich, *Biografía*, 111. Wünderich assigned to Altamirano the characteristics of a "social bandit."
170. My translation. Cited in Román, *Maldito país*, 166.
171. My translation. Cited in Arrieta, ¡*Habla Sandino!*, 15.
172. Eberhardt to secretary of state, Managua, July 20, 1927, 817.00/4940, Nicaragua 1910–1929; Pineda Cordero, oral history; Schroeder, "'To Defend,'" 223.
173. My translation. De Belausteguigoitia, *Con Sandino*, 9.
174. Sandino, bulletin of operation, July 16, 1931, folder Nicaragua—Bandits, Activities of, box 18, O&T.
175. Sandino cited in Zimmermann, *Sandinista*, 159.
176. Román, *Maldito país*, 182, 184.
177. Tercero González, oral history; Bendaña, *Mística*, 197.
178. Cited in Román, *Maldito país*, 86; Sandino, "Circular Para El Ejército y Vecinos Pacificos," *El Chipote*, November 30, 1927, E-001, C-004, 000191, ACS; De Belausteguigoitia, *Con Sandino*, 189; Benson to commander, June 5, 1930, folder Nicaragua—Bandits, Activities of, box 18, O&T.
179. "Sandino," *Literary Digest*, February 4, 1928, 44; Alexander Montoya, oral history.
180. Evelyn Trent, "Californian's Mine Is Seized in Nicaragua," *San Francisco Chronicle*, February 19, 1928, 2F.
181. For evidence of rape, see "Statement by Toribio Mendez . . . ," in Reagan, Ocotal, February 11, 1929, folder 11th Regiment R-2 Reports (May 1927–July 1929), box 26, Nicaragua 1927–1932; for looting, see Cruse, San José, July 1, 1930, 817.00/6736, Nicaragua 1930–1944. See also Schroeder, "'To Defend,'" 497.
182. My translations. Sandino manifesto, San Albino Mine, July 1, 1927, E-001, C-005, 000229, ACS.

Chapter 8

1. Memo to brigade intelligence officer, Santo Domingo, December 22, 1921, legajo 37, 1921–22, GM.
2. "Hatred and fear of the Marines" and their constabularies, wrote Calder, overshadowed "all other factors," in "Caudillos," 4 (1978): 662. See also Kelsey, "Intervention," 187.
3. Miller, oral history.
4. Welles used the phrase in *Vineyard*, 806.
5. Bennett to attorney general of Cap-Haïtien, Borgne, March 20, 1916, folder Interior, Department of, from, 1 of 2, box 2, Corr. 1916–1919.
6. My translation. Gaillard, *Péralte*, 32.
7. Gaillard, *Péralte*, 34–7. See also Gaillard, *Hinche*, 32.
8. Delage to minister of foreign affairs, Port-au-Prince, April 12, 1919, dossier 9, Haiti 1918–1940; Senate, *Hearings*, vol. 2, 858–9, 876–7.
9. Evans statement, Senate, *Hearings*, vol. 1, 246.
10. Mejía estimated that Hato Mayor saw over 300 summary executions during the occupation, in *Lilís*, 158.
11. Thorpe to brigade commander, May 30, 1918, folder 20, box 2, Pendleton Papers.
12. Kingsbury to brigade commander, Santo Domingo, September 30, 1918, folder Dominican Republic, Santa [*sic*] Domingo, 1918, Dominican Republic, Geographical Files, Reference Branch, MCH; Langley, *Banana Wars*, 147.

13. For instance, Toruño Reyes, oral history.
14. For stories of Lee, see Alemán Bolaños, *Sandino*, 182–7; Amador, *Exilio*, 31.
15. My translation. Cana Araúz, oral history.
16. The handbill is in Berkeley to commander Special Services Squadron, [ca. January 26, 1932], folder Nicaragua—Bandit Propaganda, and miscellaneous, box 19, O&T.
17. Boedecker González, oral history; Angelina Rugama and Secondino Hernández Blandón cited in Schroeder, "'To Defend,'" 425, 430. Grossman found ten of these claims, in "'La Patria,'" 659.
18. Salvatierra, *Sandino*, 64. Others denied that the marines killed children: Osoba Izaguerri, oral history; Toruño Reyes, oral history.
19. "Dumb Man Shot for Not Speaking," *Daily Herald*, May 25, 1928, file A3642, reference 12745, FO 371.
20. Thorpe to brigade commander, May 30, 1918, folder 20, box 2, Pendleton Papers.
21. Berle to Knapp, Santo Domingo, May 31, 1918, legajo 20, 1920–1921, GM.
22. UP, *Memoir*, 9.
23. Vincent statement, Senate, *Hearings*, vol. 1, 30–2.
24. Baker testimony, Turner to the brigade commander, November 3, 1919; folder Investigations, Haiti, extra copies; box 2, Operations 1915–1921.
25. My translation. Cuadra, *Contra Sandino*, 25.
26. London to Chamberlain, December 2, 1929, file A496, reference 13470, FO 371.
27. Marchand to Borah, Bluefields, January 25, 1928, file A4574, reference 12746, FO 371. See also Marchand to Borah, Bluefields, May 18, 1928, folder Nicaragua 1927–1928 (2), box 257, Borah Papers, and "Dumb Man Shot for Not Speaking," *Daily Herald*, May 25, 1928, file A3642, reference 12745, FO 371. According to one Sandinista, marines also used the electric chair against him: Contreras Dávila, oral history.
28. Marchand to Borah, Bluefields, March 12, 1928, file A4574, reference 12746, FO 371.
29. Brooks, "Rebellion," 222–8.
30. The details exist in Senate, *Hearings*, vol. 1. An example of a court-martial is Folder Confidential Order (27Sep19–18Apr20), box 1, First Brigade.
31. Feland cited in Harold Denny, "Our Marines Must Guard Nicaraguans," *NYT*, June 1, 1928, 27.
32. An example is Snowden to secretary of the navy, Santo Domingo, May 4, 1920, folder 42, box 31, MGSD.
33. It was in December 1927, Denny, *Dollars*, 345.
34. Angell, statement, Senate, *Hearings*, vol. 2, 1514.
35. Folder Adams, Donald V. Pfc. (11Jul32–10Aug34), box 1, First Brigade.
36. My translation. Cited in Instituto, *Ahora*, 77.
37. "Dumb Man Shot for Not Speaking," *Daily Herald*, May 25, 1928, file A3642, reference 12745, FO 371.
38. My translation. "Un episodio de la guerra en Nicaragua," *La Opinión*, February 14, 1928, E-001, C-007, 000372, ACS.
39. Báez interviewed in Castro García, *Intervención*, 38–9.
40. Ferreras, *Enfoques*, 246.
41. Santana and Santana to the Department of Interior and Police, Santo Domingo, November 1, 1921, and residents of Los Llanos to Robison, Santo Domingo, November 7, 1921, both in legajo 2, 1919, GM.
42. Harllee to commanding general, San Pedro de Macorís, December 8, 1921, legajo 2, 1919, GM; Kincade to district commander, San Pedro de Macorís, November 10, 1921, legajo 2, 1919, GM.
43. Robison to Fiallo, Santo Domingo, November 5, 1921, legajo 2, 1919, GM.
44. Harlee, "Attention People," October 30, 1921, La Paja, in *Fifteenth Regiment Newsletter* (San Pedro de Macorís), no. 2, November 12, 1921, box 1, Newspapers 1914–1923. This talk recurred in several towns.
45. My translation. Instituto, *Ahora*, 80. Ramírez repeated the accusation in "Kid," 74.
46. Willey cited in Hanna to secretary of state, Managua, June 6, 1930, 817.00/6673, Nicaragua 1930–1944; Thurston to Sayre, Washington, July 17, 1930, 817.00/6714, Nicaragua 1930–1944.
47. Craige, *Cannibal Cousins*, 124.

48. My translation. Interviewed on February 27, 1982, in Gaillard, *Péralte*, 35.

49. Gover to Brigade Commander, Gonaives, September 2, 1919, folder Brigade Commander—Correspondence, box 5, Gendarmerie.

50. Pfeiffer, oral history; Roorda, *Dictator*, 21.

51. Pfeiffer, oral history, 30–1.

52. Kuant to "Primer Jefe de las Fuerzas Americanas en Nicaragua," Matagalpa, April 24, 1928, folder Civilians, Complaints of, box 1, Civilian Complaints.

53. My translation. Joya Dávila, oral history.

54. Uriarte, oral history.

55. Munro, *Intervention*, 317; Senate, *Hearings*, vol. 2, 1117–19, 1136–49. See also Ferreras, *Enfoques*, 251–3.

56. My translation. De Lara to secretary of state of interior and police, San Francisco de Macorís, March 1, 1920, legajo 51, 1920, IP.

57. Mejía, *Lilís*, 158.

58. Court of Inquiry, finding of facts, opinion, and recommendation, Moca, August 3, 1920, folder 16, 1–10 Courts and Boards, box 40, MGSD.

59. Snowden, memo to secretary of the navy, November 19, 1920, legajo 17, 1920, GM.

60. Thoby used the term in a letter to Borah, Port-au-Prince, June 12, 1929, folder Haiti 1927–1928, box 247, Borah Papers. The most public use of the statistic was in UP, *Memoir*, 20. Heinl, Jr., and Heinl called these "statistical whoppers" in *Written in Blood*, 470. Yet the numbers were repeated: Moral, *Paysan*, 66; Millet, *Paysans*, 67.

61. "Contents of Procees [*sic*] Verbal (Prison Report Cape Haitien) as remembered by Mr. Auguste Nemours, Lawyer and Conseiller d'Etat, and member of the Prison Investigating Committee," September 3, 1921, folder Haiti opns. Reports, Intelligence Summaries (1921–1924), box 3, GC. The original accusation was Ligue du Bien Public letter to Minister of the Interior, undated, folder Haiti opns. Reports, Intelligence Summaries (1921–1924), box 3, GC.

62. Sandino, "Resolution Number 20: Confiscation of North American Properties," January 8, 1928, *Sandino*, comp. Ramírez, trans. Conrad, 156.

63. Perkins, *Las Cahobas*, August 5, 1920, folder Confidential Order (27Sep19–18Apr20), box 1, First Brigade.

64. White to Cumberland, Washington, March 28, 1928, 817.00/5649, Nicaragua 1910–1929.

65. Bourke, oral history.

66. My translation. Sandino to López, Ciudad Sandino, June 25, 1927, E-001, C-003, 000087, ACS.

67. Statement of Cuebeas, Port-au-Prince, May 9, 1922, folder Claims + Complaints of Natives 2 of 3, box 3, Corr. 1915–1926.

68. Kelsey, "Intervention," 142.

69. Montoya to the commanding officer of the marine detachment, Matagalpa, May 3, 1928, folder Civilians, Complaints of, box 1, Civilian Complaints.

70. Behrenz to commanding general, Managua, May 24, 1929, folder Native Grievances 2 of 2, box 7, Corr. 1928–1930.

71. My translation. Lopez to Feland, Jinotega, March 20, 1929.

72. Gross to Kellogg, July 19 and 20, 1927, 838.00/2356 and 838.00/2373, Haiti 1910–1929.

73. Frank, *Roaming*, 238.

74. Martin to commanding officer, Juigalpa, August 17, 1928, folder Chontales, box 2, Corr. 1928–1930.

75. Mehlinger to commanding officer, Granada, January 27, 1929, folder "Granada," box 3, Corr. 1928–1930.

76. McPherson, "Personal Occupations," 587–8.

77. My translation. *El Diario*, November 22, 1916, in Castro García, *Intervención*, 33.

78. "Los Desplantes de Hato Mayor," *Listín Diario*, January 5, 1921, in file A2576, reference 5576, FO 371. Knight inaccurately reported that the marines burned the shop because it would not sell them alcohol, in *Americans*, 109.

79. "Marines who Abused Countrywomen," *Diario Moderno* [Matagalpa?] of March 7, 1930, folder Nicaragua, Treatment of Natives 1930, box 5, Corr. 1928–1930.

80. For examples, see Amador, *Derrota militar*, 41; and Araúz Pineda, unpublished autobiography, E-001, C-006, 000323, ACS.

81. Pellerano Alfau, ordinance, October 23, 1917, legajo 16, 1917, IP; acting military governor to secretary of the navy, Santo Domingo, July 25, 1918, folder 15, box 7, MGSD.

82. Buckley testimony, Port-au-Prince, July 6, 1918, folder 15, box 7, MGSD.

83. Bessman, oral history, 27.

84. Beadle to commanding general, Managua, August 17, 1928, folder Nic[aragua] Nat[ional] GD. Det., box 5, Corr. 1928–1930.

85. Lee, "Indoctrination . . . ," October 30, 1922, 839.00/2689, DR 1910–1929.

86. My translation. Cited in De Belausteguigoitia, *Con Sandino*, 182.

87. Castor, *Occupation*, 17.

88. Cited in Dubois, *Aftershocks*, 208.

89. Castor counted "at least thirty-three agrarian bills" passed from 1915 to 1930, in "Occupation," 266. She cited no source.

90. Balch, ed., *Occupied Haiti*, 74.

91. Michiel Baud, "The Struggle for Autonomy: Peasant Resistance to Capitalism in the Dominican Republic, 1870–1924, in *Labour*, ed. Cross and Heuman, 127–8; Castor, "Occupation," 266. Calder made the claim that sugar companies took land through "outright purchase, cajolery, tricks, threats, violence, and legal maneuvers," yet provided no evidence. He cited one document showing that in 1922, "military officials found that a significant percentage to be men who had recently lost their land," but I could not trace the citation. In Calder, "Caudillos," 657.

92. Franks, "*Gavilleros*," 164.

93. Derby, "Haitians," 509.

94. Castro García, *Intervención*, 22–3; Ayala, *Kingdom*, 103–4, 145; Knight, *Americans*, 118.

95. Brady to Snowden, New York, March 17, 1920, legajo 61, 1918–1920, GM.

96. D'Alencour cited 100 newspaper articles to demonstrate the higher number, in statement, Port-au-Prince, March 6, 1930, folder Depositions, March 6, 1930, box 1069, President's Comm. Yet De la Rue said such newspaper articles were pure propaganda and cited the lower number, in "Report on Current Conditions . . . ," March 12, 1930, folder Itinerary, 1929–1930, box 1070, President's Comm. According to agrarian historian Moral, resistance to this drive "forms one of the principal themes of the resistance to the occupation" from 1926 to 1930: *Paysan*, 65.

97. Balch, ed., *Occupied Haiti*, 70.

98. My translations. "L'Union Nationaliste et la masse paysanne," mémoire of Union Nationaliste to president and secrétaires d'état, and "Questionnaire auquel ont été soumis les dépossédés conformément à la 'dite Loi,'" both in UN, *Dépossessions*, 4, 10, 25–6. The UN, presided by Thoby, may have been the same as the UP, for which Thoby was general secretary. Corvington, *1922–1934*. This pamphlet is its only surviving publication and one of its few acts, at least under that name.

99. My translation. "Plus de restriction au droit de propriété pour les Compagnies Etrangères," *Le Nouvelliste*, February 25, 1925, 1.

100. My translation. Marcellus et al. to Hoover, Fort-Liberté, November 23, 1929, 838.00/2726, Haiti 1930–1939.

101. Deputy general receiver to director general of contributions, November 19, 1929, folder Itinerary, 1929–1930, box 1070, President's Comm.

102. My translation. Sánchez González to Fuller, San Pedro, August 11, 1920, legajo 68, 1920, IP. See also Roberto Cassá, "Campiña: un caso aislado de lucha agraria," *Isla Abierta*, in *Hoy*, July 14, 1990, 7–9.

103. O'Connor to Fuller, Los Llanos, March 4, 1920, legajo 50, 1920, IP.

104. My translation. Cited from *El Cable*, May 21, 1921, reproduced in Quiterio Berroa, "Hurgando y Glosando," *L . . . . .* (Santo Domingo), June 5, 1921; Michiel Baud, "The Struggle for Autonomy: Peasant Resistance to Capitalism in the Dominican Republic, 1870–1924, in *Labour*, ed. Cross and Heuman, 130.

105. Russell to Kellogg, January 18, 1928, 838.00/2437, Haiti 1910–1929. See also Russell, annual report, January 3, 1928, 838.00/2463a, Haiti 1910–1929.

106. [Berle?] to secretary of state for justice and public instruction, Santo Domingo, May 13, 1918, folder Santo Domingo 1918, box 3, Berle Papers, FDRL.

107. Franks, "Gavilleros," 163.

108. Frank, Roaming, 232.

109. Williams to all officers, Port-au-Prince, March 26, 1918, folder 3rd Company Correspondence, box 9, Gendarmerie.

110. Turits, Foundations, 77.

111. Snowden to Department of Interior and Police, September 28, 1920, legajo 391, 1920, IP.

112. El Cable, May 21, 1921, reproduced in Quiterio Berroa, "Hurgando y Glosando," L . . . . . (Santo Domingo), June 5, 1921; Michiel Baud, "The Struggle for Autonomy: Peasant Resistance to Capitalism in the Dominican Republic, 1870–1924, in Labour, ed. Cross and Heuman: 130. Vega assessed that the 1920 law made the landowning system "much more secure, simple, and logical" and called it "the only positive and durable contribution that the North American intervention left us": my translation, Derecho, 353.

113. Russell, "Seventh Annual Report of the American High Commissioner at Port au Prince, Haiti, to secretary of state, 1928," (Washington, D.C.: USGPO, 1929), FDRL.

114. Clarence K. Streit, "Land Use Issue to Front in Haiti," NYT, April 8, 1928.

115. Coolidge to Kellogg and Coolidge to Shipstead, both May 3, 1927, case file 162, reel 87, series 1, Coolidge Papers.

116. Balch, ed., Occupied Haiti, 142, 74, 75. See also Moral, Paysan, 64, and Munro, United States, 99–100.

117. Moral, Paysan, 70–1. See also Castor, Occupation, 98. Castor has similar numbers but points to them as emigration only, which she estimates to be a third to half of the total. Estimates are also difficult because of the seasonal nature of the work, many Haitians coming back from Cuba every year.

118. "La question agraire dans le Nord: Un intéressant rapport de M. Georges Séjourné," in UN, Dépossessions, 15.

119. Moral, Paysan, 69.

120. Simpson especially noted how the largest US buyouts of land came after the largest migrations to Cuba, in "Haitian," 516. In addition, the land was largely unused when they took it over and the companies employed thousands of workers.

121. Millet, Paysans, 57–8.

122. Castor, Occupation, 97.

123. Corvington, 1915–1922, 90.

124. My translation. Anonymous letter to Le Matin, December 5, 1917, reproduced in Gaillard, Hinche, 71.

125. Thorpe to brigade commander, May 30, 1918, folder 20, box 2, Pendleton Papers.

126. McLean to commandant, Santo Domingo, January 29, 1919, legajo 379, 1919, IP. See also McLean to procurador general, Santo Domingo, January 28, 1919, legajo 379, 1919, IP.

127. Cited in Calder, Impact, 85.

128. Munro, United States, 100.

129. Posner, "Marines," 245–6.

130. "Dissolution Retentissante," Le Nouvelliste, May 5, 1927, file A3593, reference 11995, FO 371.

131. Suzy Castor, Occupation, 69.

132. Calder, Impact, 55.

133. Butler statement, Senate, Hearings, vol. 1, 514.

134. McLean, quarterly report, [19 August?] 1919, legajo 9, 1919, IP.

135. McCrocklin, Garde, 137.

136. McCrocklin, Garde, 56, 58.

137. Fuller and Cosmas, Marines, 46–7; entry of December 23, 1924, Folder Diary, 1924–1933, box 2, correspondence and papers—additions, 1920–1941, 83/153, Chapman Papers.

138. Examples include Dunn to Johnson, April 7, 1919, box 14, ASN; chief of the Gendarmerie to brigade commander, Port-au-Prince, August 4, 1920, folder Bandits, Reports on—June 20 - May 21, box 4, Gendarmerie.

139. Chief of the Gendarmerie to brigade commander, Port-au-Prince, August 4, 1920, folder Bandits, Reports on—June 20 - May 21, box 4, Gendarmerie. The year was July 1, 1919, to June 30, 1920. The next year the numbers were smaller but still proportional: chief of the Gendarmerie to brigade commander, Port-au-Prince, July 15, 1920, folder Brigade Commander, Annual Report to (July 1, 1920–June 30, 1921), box 4, Gendarmerie.

140. De la Batie to minister of foreign affairs, Port-au-Prince, June 6, 1917, dossier 6, Haiti 1897–1918.

141. See Gaillard, *Hinche*, 82–3; Woods, report, September 1, 1923, 838.00/1965, Haiti 1910–1929.

142. Translation by author. Cited in Gaillard, *Péralte*, 38.

143. Knapp to secretary of the navy, October 25, 1920, folder Haiti opns. Reports, Intelligence Summaries (1920–1921), box 3, GC.

144. Thorpe to Pendleton, Seibo, May 11, 1918, folder 20, box 2, Pendleton Papers.

145. My translation. Limardo to secretary of interior and police, Puerto Plata, December 10, 1920, legajo 406, 1921, IP.

146. McLean, quarterly report, [19 August?] 1919, legajo 9, 1919, IP.

147. Schmidt, *Occupation*, 87.

148. Lundius and Lundahl, *Peasants*, 97. A historian of the Gendarmerie listed the reasons that the elite soon resigned: "dislike of wearing the uniform on an enlisted man, irritation at being instructed by foreigners, dislike of obeying orders, family condemnation because they had joined the replacement for the hated old Haitian Army, and finally the plain, elemental fear of being shot at by cacos": McCrocklin, *Garde*, 92.

149. Russell, undated, folder Inderdepartmental Correspondence Santo Domingo, box 21, ASN.

150. Knapp to commander, Santo Domingo, June 14, 1918, legajo 0, 1918, IP. A dozen copies of the Spanish version have survived, suggesting the wide distribution of the letter.

151. For background on the Dominican-Haitian border, see Derby, "Haitians," 489, 499, 513.

152. McLean, quarterly report, [19 August?] 1919, legajo 9, 1919, IP.

153. Gaillard, *La guérilla*, 123–4.

154. Gaillard, *Péralte*, 178.

155. Cole to expeditionary commander, Cap-Haïtien, June 27, 1916, folder [Bandits—Civil?], box 1, Exp. Comm.; Thorpe to regimental commander, San Pedro de Macorís, July 25, 1918, folder Santo Domingo, Contacts, Reports of, box 2, Occupation 1916–1924.

156. Ducoudray, *Los "Gavilleros,"* 90. Confirming Gil is Gaillard, *République*, 268. On Louis, see McLean to commandant, San Pedro de Macorís, July 8, 1918, legajo 28, 1918, IP.

157. For example, Lansing to American legation in Santo Domingo, September 10, 1915, 838.00/1307a, Haiti 1910–1929.

158. Hooker to department commander, Department of the North, April 23, 1920, folder Bandit Activities and Descriptions, box 3, Gendarmerie.

159. McLean, quarterly report, [19 August?] 1919, legajo 9, 1919, IP; Brigade USMC at Port-au-Prince to commandant, June 12, 1919, 838.00/1584, Haiti 1910–1929.

160. My translation. Cited in *Le Temps*, June 27, 1934, reproduced in Gaillard, *Premier écrasement*, 144. See also Derby, "Haitians," 503.

161. Portis to battalion commander, Barahona, August 19, 1919, folder Santo Domingo, Contacts, Reports of, box 2, Occupation 1916–1924.

162. [Johnson?] to secretary of state, Santo Domingo, August 19, 1915, 838.00/1263, Haiti 1910–1929; Desiderio Arias, for instance, aided *caco* Charles Zamor in October 1915, allegedly in a plot to assassinate Dartiguenave: Russell to secretary of state, Santo Domingo, October 30, 1915, 838.00/1362, Haiti 1910–1929. Arias's ministry of war also supported Bobo: Boot, *Savage*, 157. See also Lansing to American legation in Santo Domingo, September 10, 1915, 838.00/1307a, Haiti 1910–1929.

163. Caperton testimony, Senate, *Hearings*, vol. 1, 402.

164. Derby, "Haitians," 505.

165. McLean to commandant, Santo Domingo, December 16, 1919, legajo 40, 1919, IP; Pichardo to Russell, Santo Domingo, March 29, 1916, in Russell to Lansing, March 29, 1916, 839.00/1800, DR 1910–1929.

166. Magloire to Ramsey, Santo Domingo, November 30, 1921, legajo 429, 1921, IP.
167. McLean to commandant, Santo Domingo, September 22, 1919, legajo 216/240, 1919, IP.
168. Derby, "Haitians." 501.
169. McDougal to secrétaire d'état au Département de l'Intérieur, Port-au-Prince, December 29, 1922, folder Dept of South, Command Affairs, box 7, Gendarmerie.
170. Hanna to secretary of state, Managua, June 8, 1930, 817.00/6656, Nicaragua 1930–1944.
171. Cited in House hearings, Washington, February 3, 1931, 817.00/7029, Nicaragua 1930–1944.
172. Grossman, "'Hermanos,'" 154.
173. My translation. Cited in Román, Maldito país, 94. See also Moreno Palacios, oral history; Navy, report, Tegucigalpa, June 15, 1932, folder Nicaragua—Bandits, Activities of, box 18, O&T.
174. Smith et al., Review, 30.
175. Cruse, San José, May 21, 1930, 817.00/6697, Nicaragua 1930–1944; Office of Naval Intelligence, report, Tegucigalpa, December 29, 1931, folder Nicaragua—Bandits, Activities of, box 18, O&T.
176. Cuadra to Matthews, March 11, 1932, folder Misc. Confidential Data, box 1, GN-2 1932.
177. Munro to secretary of state, Managua, November 24, 1927, 817.00/5155, Nicaragua 1910–1929.
178. Navy to Morgan, Washington, September 27, 1928, 817.00/6006, Nicaragua 1910–1929.
179. Macaulay, Affair, 148.
180. Geyer to American minister in Tegucigalpa, Tegucigalpa, January 26, 1931, folder Correspondence, American Minister to Nicaragua (Conf.), box 21, O&T.
181. Blas Henríquez to the president of Honduras, April 14, 1929, E-001, C-006, 000353, ACS.
182. Hanna to secretary of state, Managua, May 3, 1930, 817.00/6622, Nicaragua 1930–1944.
183. Smith et al., Review, 29.
184. Sandino to León Díaz, El Chipote, December 1, 1927, E-001, C-001, 000043, ACS; report to the president of Honduras, January 27, 1931, E-001, C-006, 000353, ACS.
185. Munro to White, June 28, 1928, folder Munro, Dana G. 1928, box 8, White Papers; Hanna to secretary of state, Managua, May 3, 1930, 817.00/6622, and June 12, 1930, 817.00/6678, both in Nicaragua 1930–1944. The exception was Munro to White, Tegucigalpa, July 22, 1928, folder Munro, Dana G. 1928, box 8, White Papers.
186. Hanna to secretary of state, Managua, June 12, 1930, 817.00/6678, Nicaragua 1930–1944.
187. Geyer to American minister in Tegucigalpa, Tegucigalpa, January 26, 1931, folder Correspondence, American Minister to Nicaragua (Conf.), box 21, O&T.
188. Cuadra to Matthews, March 11, 1932, folder Misc. Confidential Data, box 1, GN-2 1932.
189. Navy to Morgan, Washington, September 27, 1928, 817.00/6006, Nicaragua 1910–1929.
190. Cited in editorial, "Unselfish Intervention," NYT, December 5, 1916, 10.
191. Berle to Knapp, Santo Domingo, May 31, 1918, legajo 20, 1920–1921, GM.
192. Ledger to Curzon of Kedleston, December 31, 1920, file 430, reference 5575, FO 371.
193. Kouri and forty-five others, petition, Port-au-Prince, January [1921], 838.00/1770, Haiti 1910–1929.
194. Simpson, "Haitian," 500; Simpson, "Social Structure," 646.
195. Berle to Knapp, Santo Domingo, May 31, 1918, legajo 20, 1920–1921, GM. Munro reached the same conclusion in Intervention, 543.
196. McManus to Pendleton, April 1, 1918, 839.00/2082, DR 1910–1929.
197. McCrocklin, Garde, 49.
198. Cited in Russell, "Seventh Annual Report of the American High Commissioner at Port au Prince, Haiti, to secretary of state, 1928," (Washington, D.C.: USGPO, 1929), FDRL.
199. Rockey to chief of the Gendarmerie, Mirebalais, August 15, 1920, folder Bandit Activities and Descriptions, box 3, Gendarmerie. For Dominican evidence see district commander to commanding general, San Pedro de Macorís, December 8, 1921, legajo 74, 1917–1921, GM; Lee to major general commandant in Washington, Santo Domingo, July 5, 1922, folder Santo Domingo, Contacts, Reports of, box 2, Occupation 1916–1924.

Chapter 9

1. Welles, *Vineyard*, 818.
2. My translation from a Spanish translation. "Discurso del Gobernador Militar . . . ," *Listín Diario*, June 30, 1919.
3. Berle to Knapp, Santo Domingo, May 31, 1918, legajo 20, 1920–1921, GM.
4. Calder agrees that "neither in Cuba, Haiti, nor Nicaragua [nor his own object of study, the Dominican Republic] did US intervention change the fundamental characteristics of those societies," in *Impact*, 242.
5. Calder, *Impact*, 241; Corvington, *1915–1922*, 224.
6. My translation. "La Vida en Provincias: De Samaná," *Listín Diario* (Santo Domingo), September 15, 1922, 6.
7. Calder, *Impact*, 241; Ruck, *Tropic*.
8. Gobat, *Confronting*, 63.
9. Ham, "Americanizing," 187.
10. Melhorn, oral history.
11. Ham, "Americanizing," 188.
12. Keyser, Managua, November 30, 1924, folder Nicaragua Intell. Summaries (1921–1925), box 7, GC.
13. Ruck, *Tropic*, 24.
14. Cited in Derby, "Magic of Modernity," 108.
15. Klein, *Sugarball*, 17.
16. Báez Vargas cited in Ruck, *Tropic*, 26.
17. My translation. "El base–ball en castellano," *Letras* (Santo Domingo), August 25, 1918, 15–6. AGN.
18. Lerebours, "Indigenist Revolt," 713.
19. Hoffman, "États–Unis," 297.
20. Hoffman, "États–Unis," 297; Wucker, *Cocks*, 190.
21. Calder, *Impact*, 241.
22. Ferreras, *Enfoques*, 13–7.
23. Conrady, "Roman haïtien," 93.
24. Hoffman, "États–Unis," 299, 301; Conrady, "Roman haïtien," 118–27. Dash also wrote that Haitians offered "stately and sonorous alexandrines and high-sounding language as a way of asserting links with Europe and demonstrating Haiti's sophisticated intellectual culture in the face of national humiliation," in *Haiti*, 38.
25. Danache, *Président*, 63–4.
26. Lerebours, "Indigenist Revolt," 713–4.
27. Derby, "Magic of Modernity," 86, 92, 95.
28. Calder, *Impact*, 88; Mayes, "Dominican Feminism," 357; Kelsey, "Intervention," 170; Derby, "Magic of Modernity," 55–6.
29. My translation. Read, *Civilizadores*, 105, 111.
30. My translation. "La Vida en Provincias: De Samaná," *Listín Diario*, September 15, 1922, 6.
31. Averill, "Dance Bands," 210.
32. Gobat, *Confronting*, 177, 186–9, 254.
33. Skinner to jefe director, Chinandega, March 30, 1932, folder Nicaragua—Bandits, Activities of, box 18, O&T.
34. Editorial, "Hoover's Problem in Haiti," *The New Republic* 61: 785 (December 18, 1929): 83.
35. U.S. Army, *Military Government*, 45, 46; Vega, *Derecho*, 346–7.
36. U.S. Army, *Military Government*, 46–8.
37. Frank, *Roaming*, 244, 245.
38. U.S. Army, *Military Government*, 46. Vega attributed the decision not to Americanize to Dominican resistance but gave no instance of it, and none exists in the record: *Derecho*, 347.
39. My translation. "Declaración del Sr. Manuel Maria Velez, Síndico Municipal," no date or place, in Keimling to post commander, Santo Domingo, June 11, 1920, legajo 71, 1920, IP.
40. U.S. Army, *Military Government*, 49.
41. Calder, *Impact*, 38–9.

42. My translation. Bordas, "Un escándalo más," *Listín Diario*, May 18, 1921, reproduced in Bordas, *Frente*, 13.
43. Barré-Ponsignon to minister of foreign affairs, Santo Domingo, May 20, 1921, dossier 5, DR 1918–1940.
44. Calder, *Impact*, 38–9.
45. Grant to district commander, Léogâne, November 11, 1916, folder Leogane, Sub-Dist. of, Mo. Rpts., box 10, Gendarmerie.
46. Mayer to secretary of state, October 30, 1917, 838.00/1496, Haiti 1910–1929.
47. Pamphile, *L'éducation*, 37; Heinl, Jr., and Heinl, *Written in Blood*, 490.
48. Inman, "Hard Problems," 341.
49. Cook, "Dantes Bellegarde," 125–6.
50. Pamphile, *L'éducation*, 45–6, 85, 115. Others were Fleury Féquière, Auguste Magloire, and Jean Price-Mars. See Féquière, *L'éducation*; Bellegarde, *Haïti Heureuse*; Bellegarde, *Résistance*.
51. Transcript of interview with Bellegarde, Port-au-Prince, March 3, 1930, folder Depositions, 1930 March 3, box 1069, President's Comm.
52. Both cited in Pamphile, "Policy–Making," 100, 99.
53. Russell to Forbes, Port-au-Prince, March 13, 1930, folder Russell, John H., 1930 19 March 30, 2013–2014, box 1073, President's Comm. One Haitian historian agreed, condemning Bellegarde because he "continued at the end of each month to show up at the Bank teller to collect the price for his passive resistance, his useless resistance": my translation, Blanchet, *Peint*, 13.
54. Transcript of interview with Freeman, Port-au-Prince, March 13, 1930, folder Courts, 1929–1930 & Undated, box 1069, President's Comm.
55. Pamphile, "Policy–Making," 104.
56. Service Technique, *Programme*, 14.
57. Thoby to Borah, Port-au-Prince, May 29, 1929, folder Haiti 1928–1929, box 271, Borah Papers.
58. Transcript of interview with Freeman, Port-au-Prince, March 13, 1930, folder Courts, 1929–1930 & Undated, box 1069, President's Comm.
59. Velten to minister of foreign affairs, Port-au-Prince, February 8, 1926, dossier 12, Haiti 1918–1940.
60. Transcript of interview with Freeman, Port-au-Prince, March 13, 1930, folder Courts, 1929–1930 & Undated, box 1069, President's Comm.
61. Pamphile, *African Americans*, 109.
62. "Digest of the Report of the United States Commission on Education in Haiti, by G. Lake Imes, Secretary of the Commission," Department of State, November 29, 1930, folder Report of Investigation March 10, 1919–March 13, 2020, Haiti, Geographical Files, Reference Branch, MCH.
63. Apart from Moton, the commissioners were Dr. Mordecai W. Johnson, President, Howard University; Professor Le M. Favrot, Field Agent of the General Education Board; B. F. Hubert, President, Georgia State Industrial College; and Dr. W. T. B. Williams, Dean, College at Tuskegee and Field Agent of the Jeanes and Slater Boards. Five others accompanied the party. Among the commissioners only Favrot was white: R. R. Moton letter to Hoover, February 20, 1930, folder Countries—Haiti Haitian Commission, Moton Commission, box 989, Foreign Affairs, PP.
64. Cited in Pamphile, *African Americans*, 124.
65. "Digest of the Report of the United States Commission on Education in Haiti, by G. Lake Imes, Secretary of the Commission," Department of State, November 29, 1930, folder Report of Investigation 10 Mar 1919–13 Mar 20, Haiti, Geographical Files, Reference Branch, MCH.
66. Munro to secretary of state, Port-au-Prince, December 13, 1930, folder Munro, Dana G. 1929–1930, box 8, White Papers; Shannon, *Jean Price-Mars*, 94–5.
67. Munro, *United States*, 95.
68. "Digest of the Report . . . ," Department of State, November 29, 1930, folder Report of Investigation 10 Mar 1919–13 Mar 20, Haiti, Geographical Files, Reference Branch, MCH; Douglas, "Haiti II," 371.

69. Spector, *Forbes*, 173.
70. Agel to minister of foreign affairs, Port-au-Prince, July 26, 1923, dossier 11, Haiti 1918–1940.
71. My translation. François-Marie, Le Nouvelliste, March 6, 1919, cited in Gaillard, Péralte, 66.
72. Castor, *Occupation*, 78.
73. Kelsey, "Intervention," 122.
74. My translation. Cham to Williams, Port-au-Prince, March 20, 1918, folder Department of Interior, Corres. from, box 8, Gendarmerie.
75. Russell, daily diary report, May 9, 1920, 838.00/1641, Haiti 1910–1929.
76. My translation. La Gouaze cited in Vézina, memcon, March 2, 1930, folder Depositions, March 1, 1930, box 1069, President's Comm.
77. Statement of Le Sidanier, Senate, *Hearings*, vol. 2, 849–53.
78. Stabler to Latin-American Division, Washington, September 17, 1918, 838.00/1550, Haiti 1910–1929.
79. Kersuzan to Lansing, Washington, September 17, 1918, 838.00/1551, Haiti 1910–1929.
80. Pamphile, *Croix*, 47–54, 138.
81. Harold Denny, "Church Joins Haiti in Demand We Quit," *NYT*, March 8, 1930, 1.
82. Clergy of Haiti, Port-au-Prince, ca. 1930, folder Clergy, Undated, box 1068, President's Comm.
83. Vézina, memcon, March 2, 1930, folder Depositions, March 1, 1930, box 1069, President's Comm.; Castor, *Occupation*, 79.
84. The hookworm campaign of the Rockefeller Foundation from 1914 to 1928 threatened the authority and methods of popular healers. See Peña Torres and Palmer, "Rockefeller," 59–60. The foundation, however, was not an official arm of the US occupation.
85. League cited in Kinloch Tijerino, "Identidad nacional," 181.
86. Gobat, *Confronting*, 175–87.
87. Canuto, "Circular to Curates and Chaplain," Granada, August 18, 1927, in Munro to Kellogg, Managua, January 16, 1928, 817.00/5359, Nicaragua 1910–1929.
88. *Primer censo*, 139. The clergy were mostly Dominicans with a few Spanish Franciscans. Kelsey, "Intervention," 174.
89. Derby, "Magic of Modernity," 78.
90. My translation. "Restauración," *El eco mariano*, August 20, 1916, 1.
91. My translation. De Noel Henríquez et al., *Al pueblo*, pamphlet collection, AGN.
92. Editorial "Mosaico Luminoso," *Listín Diario*, in Deschamps, *El espíritu*, 25.
93. One version of the story is in Tulio M. Cestero, "American Rule in Santo Domingo," *The Nation*, July 17, 1920, 78.
94. Kelsey, "Intervention," 174.
95. Snowden to secretary of the navy, Santo Domingo, April 10, 1920, and Nouel to Snowden, Santo Domingo, April 28, 1920, both in folder 42, box 31, MGSD.
96. My translation. Barré-Ponsignon to minister of foreign affairs, Santo Domingo, October 12, 1920, dossier 5, DR 1918–1940.
97. My translation. Barré-Ponsignon to minister of foreign affairs, Santo Domingo, August 19, 1922, dossier 2, DR 1918–1940. Derby argued that "the coronation expressed a worldview at odds with the utilitarian pragmatism of the U.S. Military; one that privileged morality over money, renewal over decline, and divine hierarchy over social democracy": "Magic," 78, 79.
98. For an example of Vodou in Restauración where a city councillor takes part, see Hurst to the director, Monte Cristo, February 24, 1920, legajo 32, 1919, IP; [Johnson?] to Tracey, Petit Goâve, August 21, 1918, folder Confidential File, box 5, Gendarmerie.
99. Agel to minister of foreign affairs, Port-au-Prince, February 9, 1921, dossier 4, Haiti 1918–1940.
100. Millet, *Paysans*, 69–70.
101. Lundius and Lundahl, *Peasants*, 107.
102. Kuser, *Haiti*, 57.
103. Cited in Dessez, oral history.
104. Millet, *Paysans*, 70.
105. Kuser, *Haiti*, 56.

106. McDougal to commanders of North, South, and Central Departments, and chief of police of Port-au-Prince, Port-au-Prince, November 13, 1924, folder Garde d'Haiti [Misc. Corres. 1924–1932], box 4, Corr. 1915–1926.

107. Scott to chief of the Gendarmerie, Hinche, January 13, 1925, folder 4th Drawer—G-2 1925 Voodooism, box 1, Road Reports.

108. Weller to district commander, Le Trou, April 21, 1925, box 1, Corr. 1923, 1925.

109. Butler, Gimlet, 239. Wirkus also allowed Vodou to survive in La Gonâve, in Seabrook, Magic Island, 193.

110. Folder Bellegarde, Cadeus (28Dec19–22Sep20), box 1, First Brigade.

111. See the statements in folder Bellegarde, Cadeus (28Dec19–22Sep20), box 1, First Brigade.

112. Russell, daily diary report, April 1, 1920, 838.00/1634, Haiti 1910–1929, RG 59, NARA II; Russell to Knapp, December 4, 1920, folder Confidential Letter of Admiral Knapp 12–4–20 advising of audience with President of Haiti, case of Voudou Priest, Cedeus Bellegarde, remarks of the President on unsettled conditions in Port-au-Prince, box 1, Corr. 1918–1921.

113. My translation; emphasis in original. Constant Vieux, "L'histoire du rapport de l'Amiral Knapp: Le cannibalisme à Haiti," Le Courrier Haïtien, February 9, 1921, in dossier 4, Haiti 1918–1940.

114. Little to brigade commander, Port-au-Prince, January 22, 1921, folder Untitled, box 1, Corr. 1921–1923.

115. Cassá, "Movimientos," 187, 185–6; San Miguel, "Historias," 113, 112–21; Lundius and Lundahl, Peasants, 50, 71.

116. Kilgore, March 24, 1921, folder Santo Domingo—Intell. Summaries 1921, box 5, GC.

117. "Engagement with Dominican Bandits at Las Canitas," April 7, 1917, folder Miscellaneous Records 1916–1922, 1932–1940, box 1, Occupation 1916–1924.

118. Lundius and Lundahl, Peasants, 93–9, 109–10, 77.

119. Cassá, "Movimientos," 189; Roberto Cassá, "Persecución y muerte de Oliborio Mateo," Isla Abierta, in Hoy, October 9, 1993, 4; San Miguel, "Historias," 117; Michiel Baud, "The Struggle for Autonomy: Peasant Resistance to Capitalism in the Dominican Republic, 1870–1924," in Labour, ed. Cross and Heuman, 133.

120. Marine newspaper cited in Lord, "'Imperative Obligation,'" 152.

121. Examples of their reports include Thorpe, field order, San Juan, January 15, 1918; Thorpe, field order, Camp Olivorio, Top Mount Colorao, January 19, 1918; Thorpe to Brigade Commander, San Juan, January 23, 1918; and Byrd to battalion commander, Dos Rios, March 3, 1919, all in folder Santo Domingo, Contacts, Reports of, box 2, Occupation 1916–1924; also Feeley to director, Azua, January 20, 1919, legajo 379, 1919, IP; Robertson to district commander, Azua, January 28, 1920, folder 24, box 3, Pendleton Papers; and Bales to director, San Juan, December 25, 1920, and McLean to commandant, Santo Domingo, January 11, 1921, both in legajo 34, 1919, IP.

122. Williams to the director, July 8, 1922, folder Santo Domingo, Contacts, Reports of, box 2, Occupation 1916–1924.

123. Lundius and Lundahl, Peasants, 120, 34.

124. Historians have noted how anti-imperialism has long had a racial and ethnic component. For instance, Thomas Miller Klubock, "Nationalism, Race, and the Politics of Imperialism: Workers and North American Capital in the Chilean Copper Industry," in Reclaiming, ed. Joseph, 232.

125. Calder, "Caudillos," 664.

126. Dickinson to Elizabeth, Managua, July 5, 1929, Dickinson Letters.

127. Bendaña warns that Sandino was not as obsessed with race as Vasconcelos and that he was more concerned with exploitation, in Mística, 98.

128. Frazier, "Dawn," 2. Gould, however, warns in To Die, 17, that the census may be "profoundly misleading," especially its count of pure Indians.

129. My translations. Sandino to Ramires [Ramírez?], Telpaneca, June 17, 1927, E-001, C-003, 000155, ACS.

130. Calder, Impact, xxvii.

131. My translation. Vicente Galván, Conrado Sánchez, Manuel A. Patin Maceo, and Lirio H. Galván, "Al Señor Ministro Americano," in Alfau Durán, ed. Incháustegui and Delgado Malagón, 544–6.

132. Cestero to Wilson, Washington, April 1, 1920, legajo Papeles 1919–1920, Tomo 1, Cestero Archive.
133. Statement of Perez, Senate, *Hearings*, vol. 2, 967. See also Fabio Fiallo et al., "A los extranjeros residents en el territorio nacional," Santo Domingo, June 19, 1921, in *Alfau Durán*, ed. Incháustegui and Delgado Malagón, 609.
134. My translation. García Godoy, *El derrumbe*, 55.
135. Cited in Sagás, *Race*, 40. See also Herrera Rodríguez, "Desocupación," 123–38.
136. My translation. Vincent, *En posant*, 4–5, 14.
137. Morand, *Hiver caraïbe*, 132, 122.
138. Coyle, "Service," 343; Munro, *Intervention*, 358–9.
139. Schmidt, *Occupation*, 136.
140. My translation. Morand, *Hiver caraïbe*, 113; Harold N. Denny, "Haiti—A Problem Unsolved. IV. Heredity that Hampers Agreement," *NYT*, July 2, 1931, dossier 14, Haiti 1918–1940.
141. Balch, ed., *Occupied Haiti*, 119.
142. Miller, oral history, 24.
143. Seabrook, *Magic Island*, 193.
144. Wirkus and Dudley, *White King*, 73.
145. Kelsey, "Intervention," 123–4.
146. [Shepard?] Cap-Haïtien, July 22, 1926, folder Intelligence Reports Nord 2 of 2, box 1, Intel. Reports 1926–1927.
147. My translation. Bellegarde, *L'occupation*, 20.
148. My translation. Roumer cited in Fabre, "La *Revue*," 32.
149. Vincent, *En posant*, 21–3. One marine recalled that Haitians had "37 variations of color," in Dessez, oral history, 94.
150. My translation. Vincent, *En posant*, 152, 153.
151. "The color issue:" wrote Danache, "it's the only one that really moves us to the greatest injustices, the worst extremes." My translation, in *Président*, 20; Dessez, oral history, 94.
152. Melhorn, oral history, 39.
153. Hughes, *Autobiography*, 59, 61.
154. Phillips to McCormick, Washington, July 13, 1923, 838.00/1950, Haiti 1910–1929.
155. Leyburn, *Haitian People*, ix, xi.
156. Russell to Kellogg, February 14, 1928, 838.00/2443, Haiti 1910–1929.
157. My translation. Agel to minister of foreign affairs, Port-au-Prince, July 10, 1922, dossier 5, Haiti 1918–1940.

Chapter 10

1. Simpson, "Social Structure," 640. Around the same time Lobb estimated the elite to number from 20,000 to several hundred thousand, in "Caste," 25.
2. Lozano, *Dominación*, 216.
3. *Report Covering Haiti Prepared in the Division of Latin American Affairs*, January 1, 1930, folder Haiti Report, 1930 pp. 1–106, box 14, White Papers, 40.
4. Simpson, "Social Structure," 640.
5. Kilgore, March 2, 1921, folder Santo Domingo—Intell. Summaries (1921), box 5, GC.
6. De la Batie to minister of foreign affairs, Port-au-Prince, December 11, 1916, dossier 6, Haiti 1897–1918.
7. Álvarez, *Mujeres*, 21.
8. My translation. De la Batie to minister of foreign affairs, Port-au-Prince, December 11, 1916, dossier 6, Haiti 1897–1918.
9. Catlin cited in Inman, "Hard Problems," 340.
10. My translation. "Comment est dépeinte notre situation dans un journal américain," *Le Nouvelliste*, January 9, 1925, 1.
11. Shannon, *Jean Price-Mars*, 64.
12. My translation. Delage to minister of foreign affairs, Port-au-Prince, March 7, 1919, dossier 9, Haiti 1918–1940.
13. Its leaders were Timothé Paret, Piou, Elias Eli, H. Pauléus Sannon, Seymour Pradel, Price-Mars, Edmond Lespinasse, Dr. Gaton Dalencour, Louis Edouard Pouget, Constantin

Mayard, Sténio Vincent, Antoine C. Sansaricq, and Annibal Hilaire. See Bailly-Blanchard to secretary of state, June 1, 1918, 838.00/1520, Haiti 1910–1929.

14. Schmidt, *Occupation*, 189.
15. R. Cruz Torez, "Boicoteo," *El Anuncio*, February 22, 1921.
16. Blancpain, *Haïti*, 245.
17. Memo to Butler, "Deputies Elected January 15, 1917," undated, folder Elec. of Cand&Ref. data (6Nov16–22Dec19), box 2, First Brigade.
18. De la Batie to minister of foreign affairs, Port-au-Prince, June 6, 1917 and July 2, 1917, both in dossier 6, Haiti 1897–1918.
19. Knapp to Daniels, June 9, 1917, 838.00/1464, Haiti 1910–1929; Mayer to secretary of state, October 30, 1917, 838.00/1496, Haiti 1910–1929.
20. Butler to Thomas Butler, May 16, 1917, in *Letters*, ed. Cipriano Venzon, 193.
21. Daniels to secretary of state, April 9, 1917, 838.00/1444, Haiti 1910–1929.
22. Ménos to Lansing, Washington, September 4, 1915, 838.00/1284, Haiti 1910–1929.
23. De la Batie to minister of foreign affairs, Port-au-Prince, August 10, 1916, dossier 6, Haiti 1897–1918.
24. Cole cited in McCrocklin, *Garde*, 71.
25. Heinl, Jr., and Heinl, *Written in Blood*, 446.
26. Smith, "Bainbridge Colby," 61.
27. Welles to the under secretary, August 20, 1920, 838.00/1684, Haiti 1910–1929. The seven recommendations were the following:

   1. Organize a purely national armed Gendarmerie.
   2. Give U.S. marines a simple military mission, not administrative or judicial, evacuating others as soon as the Gendarmerie would be in place.
   3. Respect Haitian sovereignty and public freedoms.
   4. Assist with U.S. funds for economic development.
   5. Cooperate with Haiti on administrative matters; determine attributions of U.S. financial advisor.
   6. Determine what Haitians can spend without U.S. control.
   7. Appoint a single agent as financial advisor and customs administrator.

28. Agel to minister of foreign affairs, Port-au-Prince, April 6, 1921, dossier 4, Haiti 1918–1940.
29. Dartiguenave to Denby, March 27, 1921, 838.00/1837, Haiti 1910–1929. Johnson called him "bitterly rebellious at heart as is every good Haitian," in "Haiti I," 237.
30. My translation. Paraphrased by Bellegarde, cited in Gaillard, *La guérilla*, 196.
31. Dartiguenave to Denby, March 27, 1921, 838.00/1837, Haiti 1910–1929.
32. Sylvain, *Dix années*, vii.
33. Corvington, *1915–1922*, 246; Brissman, "Interpreting," 283.
34. Kelsey, "Intervention," 188.
35. White, "Danger," 232.
36. Russell to Kellogg, Port-au-Prince, April 14, 1925, 838.00/2097, Haiti 1910–1929.
37. The group was made up of twenty-two marines and one hospital apprentice 1st class. Underhill, Managua, February 28, 1921, folder Nicaragua—Legations, Foreign Correspondence, miscellaneous, box 26, O&T.
38. "Marines Sentenced for Managua Raid," *NYT*, February 27, 1921, 2.
39. It is not clear if either of these lasted, how they differed, or what they did: Calder, *Impact*, 14, 198.
40. The holdout was *Le Nouvelliste*, which was, strangely enough, among the most anti-occupation. Entry of February 18, 1921, Russell, daily diary report, February 19, 1921, 838.00/1755, Haiti 1910–1929.
41. Corvington, *1915–1922*, 253.
42. My translation. Agel to minister of foreign affairs, Port-au-Prince, May 26, 1921, dossier 4, Haiti 1918–1940. See also Jolibois Fils, circular letter, Port-au-Prince, March 20, 1922, 838.00/1857, Haiti 1910–1929.
43. Berroa, "Hurgando," AGN, 2–3.

44. "Hayti Peaceful and Prosperous, Says Gen. Russell," *NYHT*, March 10, 1926, file A1586, reference 11141, FO 371.

45. [Craige?], Port-au-Prince, August 23, 1927, folder Secret + Confidential Reports of Chief of Police 1927–G-2, box 1, COCP.

46. Derby, "Haitians," 501.

47. Cassá, "Movimientos," 204.

48. Russell to chief of naval operations, January 18, 1921, folder Haiti opns. Reports, Intelligence Summaries (1920–1921), box 3, GC; Russell to Hughes, June 6, 1924, 838.00/2027, Haiti 1910–1929.

49. See García Godoy to Snowden, La Vega, October 7, 1919, and Snowden to García Godoy, Santo Domingo, October 14, 1919, both in folder 41, box 16, MGSD.

50. Feland, Special Order December 69, 2022, 1919, legajo 109, 1917–1922, GM; Fiallo, *Crime*, 40.

51. Castro García, *Intervención*, 44.

52. Balch, ed., *Occupied Haiti*, 146; Calder, *Impact*, 197; "Les Victimes de M. Louis Borno," *La Poste*, March 31, 1925, listed eighteen prisoners: from *L'Opinion Nationale*, August Albert and Emmanuel Paul; from *Le Nouvelliste*, Ernest Chauvet, Fred. Duvigneaud, and Suirard Villard; from *La Poste*, Louis-Edouard Pouget, Clément Juste, Décimus Heurtelou, and François M. Vincent; from *Le Courrier Haïtien*, Jolibois Fils, Georges Petit, Oscar Savain, Philéas Lemaire, Ottanès Duplessy, Elie Guérin, Antoine Pierre-Paul, Albert Siméon, and Alcius Charmant.

53. "Hayti Peaceful and Prosperous, Says Gen. Russell," *NYHT*, March 10, 1926, file A1586, reference 11141, FO 371; Kelsey, "Intervention," 184. A clear example of libel is Ellis Cambiaso, *Monstruos*.

54. Munro to White, December 15, 1923, 838.00/1999, Haiti 1910–1929.

55. Woods, Cap-Haïtien, September 1, 1923, 838.00/1965, Haiti 1910–1929.

56. Feland to Daniels, Santo Domingo, July 29, 1920, folder 4 Admiral Snowden Personal File, box 30, MGSD. This document also lists the names and sentences of editors arrested in June 1920: Luis C. Del Castillo, Rafael Emilio Sanabia, Américo Lugo, Fabio Fiallo, Manuel Flores Cabrera, Vicente R. Tolentino, Luis Arzeno Colon, and Manuel Alexis Liz.

57. Velten to minister of foreign affairs, Port-au-Prince, February 16, 1925, dossier 11, Haiti 1918–1940; "Le Sagittaire" [pseud. Jolibois Fils], "Fléchette," *Courrier Haïtien*, June 12, 1924, 838.00/2028, Haiti 1910–1929; "Les Victimes de M. Louis Borno," *La Poste*, March 31, 1925.

58. Russell to secretary of state, Port-au-Prince, December 23, 1929, folder Biographies, Haitian, box 1068, President's Comm.

59. Morand, *Hiver caraïbe*, 87.

60. Mme Pierre-Paul to Coolidge, [19 April] 1924, 838.00/2018, Haiti 1910–1929.

61. One example is Regalado, *Via-crucis*, 16–35.

62. Barré-Ponsignon to minister of foreign affairs, Santo Domingo, August 31, 1920, dossier 5, DR 1918–1940.

63. My translation. Fiallo, "Oidme Todos," undated, in dossier 5, DR 1918–1940.

64. Fiallo, *Crime*, 40, 41, 63.

65. My translation from the French. Note by Lugo, in Barré-Ponsignon to minister of foreign affairs, Santo Domingo, August 31, 1920, dossier 5, DR 1918–1940.

66. My translation. Cited in Barré-Ponsignon to minister of foreign affairs, Santo Domingo, November 25, 1920, dossier 2, DR 1918–1940.

67. The torturer, who did not deny the accusations, was Ramón Ulises Escobosa. The proceedings are in McReynolds, Santo Domingo, November 17, 1920, legajo 17, 1920, GM. See also Snowden to secretary of the navy, November 19, 1920, legajo 17, 1920, GM.

68. My translation. Barré-Ponsignon to minister of foreign affairs, Santo Domingo, November 25, 1920, dossier 2, DR 1918–1940.

69. Cited in McReynolds, *Santo Domingo*, November 17, 1920, legajo 17, 1920, GM.

70. My translation. Barré-Ponsignon to minister of foreign affairs, Santo Domingo, November 25, 1920, dossier 2, DR 1918–1940.

71. My translation. Berroa, "Hurgando," May 8, 1921, AGN.

72. Unauthored, August 1, 1930, folder Jolibois, Joseph Fils, box 14, Gendarmerie.

73. Cooper, "Withdrawal," 88.

74. Jolibois, electoral flyer, [ca. August 6, 1930], folder Jolibois, Joseph Fils, box 14, Gendarmerie.

75. Scholars have minimized the links: Brissman, "Interpreting," 208; Castor, *Occupation*, 158; Cassá, "Movimientos," 196. Those who have suggested support presented no evidence: Graham Cosmas, "*Cacos* and *Caudillos*: Marines and Counterinsurgency in Hispaniola, 1915–1924," in *New Interpretations*, ed. Roberts and Sweetman, 294; Corvington, *1915–1922*, 98–9; Kuser, *Haiti*, 24.

76. Gobat, *Confronting*, 240, 255.

77. Gobat, "Nicaragua," 158.

78. Munro to Kellogg, Managua, January 9, 1928, 817.00/5233, Nicaragua 1910–1929.

79. Calder, *Impact*, xvii.

80. Randall to Pendleton, Santo Domingo, 13 August [1917?], folder 19, box 2, Pendleton Papers.

81. My translation. Thorpe to regimental commander, Bayaguana, September 8, 1918, folder Dominican Republic, Santa [*sic*] Domingo, 1918, Dominican Republic, Geographical Files, Reference Branch, MCH.

82. Russell to secretary of state, Santo Domingo, May 30, 1918, 839.00/2091, DR 1910–1929.

83. Ellis, August 31, 1920, folder D-28 Dominican Rep. Intelligence Summaries, box 8, O&T.

84. Kelsey, "Intervention," 179.

85. Junta de Defensa Nacional to Peguero, translation, Santo Domingo, August 30, 1920, folder Santo Domingo—Intell. Summaries 1921, box 5, GC.

86. Unsigned [August Magloire?] to Péralte, Port-au-Prince, October 8 and 11, 1918, and [Charlemagne's brother?] letter to Péralte, Port-au-Prince, June 27, 1919, all in folder Bandit Activities and Descriptions, box 3, Gendarmerie.

87. Buckley to Russell, October 3, 1919, and Russell to chief of the Gendarmerie, Port-au-Prince, December 1, 1919, both in folder Brigade Commander—Correspondence, box 5, Gendarmerie.

88. Russell to major general commandant, December 11, 19[19?], folder Haiti opns. + training (1915–1920), box 2, GC.

89. Wise to Russell, November 24, 1919, folder Brigade Commander—Correspondence, box 5, Gendarmerie.

90. Agel to minister of foreign affairs, Port-au-Prince, November 18 and 19, 1919, both in dossier 9, Haiti 1918–1940.

91. Agel to minister of foreign affairs, Port-au-Prince, January 17, 1920, dossier 9, Haiti 1918–1940.

92. "Intérior," two letters to Benoît Batraville, Port-au-Prince, December 1919, folder [Action Reports], 1919–1922, box 1, Corr. 1916–1919.

93. Entry of January 15, 1920, Russell, daily diary report, January 19, 1920, 838.00/1618, Haiti 1910–1929.

94. "Intérior" to Batraville, Port-au-Prince, December 1919 (first letter), folder [Action Reports], 1919–1922, box 1, Corr. 1916–1919.

95. Corvington, *1915–1922*, 99.

96. Entry of January 15, 1920, Russell, daily diary report, January 19, 1920, 838.00/1618, Haiti 1910–1929.

97. Wise, *A Marine*, 313.

98. Russell to major general commandant, December 11, 19[19?], folder Haiti opns. + training (1915–1920), box 2, GC; Russell, statement, [1920], folder Investi[gation] Haitien Affai[rs], box 1, Corr. 1918–1921.

99. Knapp to Opnav, aboard USS *New Hampshire*, December 10, 1920, 838.00/1727, Haiti 1910–1929.

100. My translation. Corvington, *1915–1922*, 212, 213.

101. UP, *Memoir*.

102. My translation. Flyer, "Protesta de la Unión Nacional Dominicana," December 24, 1920, in Ledger to Curzon of Kedleston, December 31, 1920, file 430, reference 5575, FO 371.

103. On the Dominican case Calder did the most, but mostly noted the support of local officials for caudillos and the difficulty in replacing them, in *Impact*, 136. On Nicaragua an exception is Gobat, *Confronting*.

104. Scott discussed the concept of "the state as claimant," in *Moral Economy*, Chapter 4. San Miguel also made this argument in "Resistance," 48.

105. R. L. Shepard, May 17, 1921, folder [Intelligence Reports–1921] Folder 1 of 2, box 4, Corr. 1915–1926. Such a dynamic seems to have occurred in revolutionary Mexico, as Hart found in *Empire*, 275. In relatively egalitarian communities, municipal political chiefs often defended peasants when they saw them threatened by US investors.

106. Bickel, *Mars Learning*, 112.

107. Gendarmerie d'Haiti, "A Brief Sketch of the Gendarmerie d'Haiti," Port-au-Prince, March 25, 1921, folder Gendarmerie d'Haiti (History) 33.11, box 12, Gendarmerie.

108. Inman, "Hard Problems," 339.

109. My translation. Constantin Mayard to all magistrats communaux of Haiti, Port-au-Prince, January 21, 1916, folder Correspondence: 1916, box 6, Butler Papers.

110. Shepard, May 17, 1921, folder [Intelligence Reports–1921] Folder 1 of 2, box 4, Corr. 1915–1926.

111. Gendarmerie d'Haïti, "A Brief Sketch of the Gendarmerie d'Haïti," Port-au-Prince, March 25, 1921, folder Gendarmerie d'Haiti (History) 33.11, box 12, Gendarmerie.

112. Wise, *A Marine*, 132, 134.

113. District commander to chief of the Gendarmerie, Hinche, March 14, 1921, folder Summary of—Gendarmerie–1921, box 1, Corr. 1915–1926.

114. Silverthorn, oral history.

115. Snowden to Rowe, Santo Domingo, March 2, 1920, folder unmarked, box 30, MGSD.

116. Vega, *Derecho*, 342.

117. Álvarez, *Mujeres*, 21.

118. My translation. Knapp, aboard the USS *Olympia*, Santo Domingo, December 4, 1916, legajo 54, 1921–1922, GM.

119. Snowden to Rowe, Santo Domingo, March 2, 1920, folder unmarked, box 30, MGSD.

120. Cited in Perkins, *Constraint*, 118.

121. Feland to Snowden, Santo Domingo, August 17, 1920, folder 4 Admiral Snowden Personal File, box 30, MGSD.

122. Examples include Rixey to president of ayuntamiento of Jovero, Santo Domingo, December 15, 1920, legajo 74, 1920, IP; and Davis to ayuntamiento of San Pedro de Macorís, San Pedro de Macorís, December 7, 1917, legajo 5527, 1917, Municipio.

123. De J. Lluveres, [February 6, 1921?], legajo 397, 1921, IP.

124. LaDuke to the secretary of the interior and police, Seibo, May 8, 1922, legajo 436, 1922, IP.

125. See Baugham, "Occupation," 2309.

126. Ramírez to McKelvey [McKelvy?], San Juan, September 3, 1917, legajo 48, 1917–1924, GM.

127. Kinloch Tijerino, "Identidad nacional," 164, 168.

128. Grossman, "'Hermanos,'" 15, 154.

129. Munro to secretary of state, Managua, October 17, 1927, 817.00/5121, Nicaragua 1910–1929.

130. Sandino to Turcios, March 14, 1928, El Chipotón, published in *El Libertador* April 1928, 4, in Office of Naval Intelligence memo, July 5, 1928, folder Sandino, box 1, Corr. 1927–1932.

131. Buckalew to inspector GND [Taylor?], San Francisco de Macorís, October 10, 1918, legajo 71, 1918, IP.

132. McLean to commandant, Santo Domingo, June 11 and May 7, 1919, legajo 379, 1919, IP.

133. Adams to commanding officer, Santo Domingo, December 16, 1916, folder Dominican Republic, Santo Domingo, 1916, Dominican Republic, Geographical Files, Reference Branch, MCH.

134. Translation by author. Silverio to McKelvy, Azua, September 29, 1917, legajo 359, 1917, IP.

135. Flynn to district commander, Anse-à-Veau, October 31, 1922, folder Dept of South, Command Affairs, box 7, Gendarmerie.

136. My translation. Peguero to Ariza, San Juan, December 11, 201922, legajo 100, 1922, IP.
137. Caraballo to secretary of interior and police, Consuelo, May 16, 1922, legajo 22, 1917–1922, GM. Other examples include Raymond to chief of the Gendarmerie, Lascahobas, October 29, 1919, folder 17th Co, District Commander Reports, box 10, Gendarmerie; and [Michel?] to chief of the Gendarmerie, Port-au-Prince, November 21, 1919, folder Complaints from Citizens (1918–1919), 1 of 3, box 1, Corr. 1916–1919.
138. Kieren to commanding officer, Estelí, December 28, 1928, folder "Estelí" 2 of 2, box 3, Corr. 1928–1930.
139. Hooker to McConnico, Bluefields, October 12, 1927, 817.00/5158, Nicaragua 1910–1929.
140. Munro to secretary of state, Managua, October 17, 1927, 817.00/5121, Nicaragua 1910–1929.
141. Gobat, *Confronting*, 205–6.
142. Munro to secretary of state, Managua, November 4, 1927, 817.00/5161, Nicaragua 1910–1929.
143. Munro to Kellogg, Managua, January 16, 1928, 817.00/5347, Nicaragua 1910–1929.
144. Gobat, *Confronting*, 215, 208, 210, 211.
145. Carlson, "Guardia Nacional," 7.
146. Gobat, *Confronting*, 220, 215, 217, 218.
147. Stimson to Hanna, Washington, October 29, 1929, 817.00/6433, Nicaragua 1910–1929.
148. Kelsey, "Intervention," 176.
149. Williams to Chandler, January 12, 1917, legajo 360, 1917, IP.
150. Other examples include Norris to the colonel commandant, San Francisco de Macorís, June 23, 1921, legajo 410, 1921, IP.
151. Thorpe to regimental commander, September 6, 1918, legajo 371, 1918, IP.
152. McManus to Pendleton, Santo Domingo, April 2, 1918, legajo 20, 1920–1921, GM.
153. Herrera to the secretary of the interior and police, Duvergé, August 1, 1922, and Perez Cuevas to the secretary of the interior and police, Duvergé, May 23, 1922, both in legajo 437, 1922, IP.
154. My translation. Anonymous to Knapp, Santo Domingo, February 1917, folder 16 to 16–49, box 2, MGSD.
155. My translation. Citizens of San Pedro de Macorís to governor of San Pedro Province, October 11, 1921, legajo 429, 1921, IP.
156. My translations. Lora, June 8, 1917, legajo 1157, 1918, IP.
157. My translation. Rixey to presidents of ayuntamientos, Santo Domingo, December 17, 1920, legajo 96, 1922, IP.
158. Roben to Bearss, Santo Domingo, March 13, 1917, legajo 8, 1917, IP.
159. Reid to the commanding general, San Pedro de Macorís, May 10, 1921, legajo 406, 1921, IP.
160. Williams to director, San Pedro de Macorís, June 3, 1921, legajo 408, 1921, IP.
161. My translations. Guillaume to the president of Haiti, Cap-Haïtien, undated, and "Artaud" to the president of Haiti, Cap-Haïtien, undated, both in folder Department of Cape, Corres. from, box 6, Gendarmerie.
162. Snowden to Rowe, Santo Domingo, March 2, 1920, folder unmarked, box 30, MGSD.
163. Lane, "Civil Government," 135.
164. Sosa Jiménez, *Hato Mayor*, 268, 267–72.
165. Contín Alfau gave several examples but provided no evidence for the high number, in *El Hato*, 139. See also *passim* 119–32 for cases of abuse.
166. Davis to brigade adjutant, San Pedro de Macorís, December 14, 1917, legajo 23, 1918, IP.
167. Kneeland to parents, Hato Mayor, June 15, 1919, Kneeland Letters.
168. Sosa Jiménez, *Hato Mayor*, 307, 311, 341.
169. Chandler to Pendleton, Santo Domingo, December 21, 1916, legajo 354, 1916, IP.
170. McLean to commandant, Santo Domingo, January 22, 1918, legajo 371, 1918, IP; Davis to brigade adjutant, San Pedro de Macorís, December 14, 1917, legajo 23, 1918, IP.
171. McLean to commandant, Santo Domingo, January 22, 1918, legajo 371, 1918, IP.
172. McLean to Department of Justice, Santo Domingo, January 15, 1918, legajo 1157, 1918, IP.
173. This was, again, the exacerbation of an ongoing trend: Franks, "*Gavilleros*," 160.

174. Etienne [Gill?], memo to secretary of interior and police, Saint-Michel de l'Attalaye, February 16, 1916, folder Interior, Department of, 2 of 2, box 2, Corr. 1916–1919.
175. My translation. Vincent to Butler, October 9, 1916, folder Interior, Department of, from, 1 of 2, box 2, Corr. 1916–1919.
176. My translation. Limardo to secretary of interior and police, Puerto Plata, October 8, 1921, legajo 422, 1921, IP.
177. Bordnave to district commander, June 12, 1919, folder Hq. 10th Co. Gonaives, box 9, Gendarmerie.
178. See folder Interior, Department of, 2 of 2, box 2, Corr. 1916–1919.
179. T. D. Beven to the inspector, GND, San Pedro de Macorís, December 22, 1919, legajo 48, 1920, IP.
180. Frank, *Roaming*, 249.
181. Kelsey, "Intervention," 109–202.
182. Lane, July 11, 1918, legajo 28, 1918, IP.
183. McLean, quarterly report, [19 August?] 1919, legajo 9, 1919, IP.
184. Angulo Guridi to secretary of interior and police, Monte Plata, October 4, 1920, legajo 394, 1920, IP.
185. No document indicates why. One possible reason is that its legal authority was less and so marines did not bother going through Haitian politicians. Another might be tied to race, in that occupiers were generally less optimistic about the impact of their reforms on blacks. A third reason might be that marines themselves engaged in gambling and cockfights: Ennis, oral history.
186. Baxter to Rowe, May 19, 1920, 839.00/2265, DR 1910–1929.
187. Otero et al. to ayuntamiento of San Pedro de Macorís, San Pedro de Macorís, December 3, 1917, legajo 5527, 1917, Municipio.
188. Carbonell et al. to ayuntamiento of San Pedro de Macorís, San Pedro de Macorís, November 28, 1917, legajo 5527, 1917, Municipio; Fuller to Angulo Guridi, Santo Domingo, October 6, 1920, legajo 5527, 1917, Municipio.
189. Angulo Guridi to Fuller, Monte Plata, October 4, 1920, legajo 394, 1920, IP;
190. Governor of the province of Santiago to secretary of interior and police, April 1, 1922, legajo 90, 1922, IP.
191. Beven to Knoechel, Seybo, June 10, 1919, legajo 387, 1919, IP.
192. Ennis, oral history.
193. Frank, *Roaming*, 249.
194. Hamet to district commander, San Pedro de Macorís, June 15, 1919, folder Santo Domingo—Operations Reports, 8 Sept 18–15 Jun 19, box 2, Occupation 1916–1924.
195. Carbonell et al. to ayuntamiento of San Pedro de Macorís, San Pedro de Macorís, November 28, 1917, legajo 5527, 1917, Municipio.
196. Otaro et al. to ayuntamiento of San Pedro de Macorís, San Pedro de Macorís, December 3, 1917, legajo 5527, 1917, Municipio.
197. My translation. Lora, June 8, 1917, legajo 1157, 1918, IP.
198. Thorpe to regimental commander, September 6, 1918, legajo 371, 1918, IP.
199. Van Hoose, June 7, 1920, legajo 20, 1920–1921, GM.
200. Shepard, May 17, 1921, folder [Intelligence Reports–1921] Folder 1 of 2, box 4, Corr. 1915–1926.
201. McLean, quarterly report, [19 August?] 1919, legajo 9, 1919, IP.
202. Cited in Bailly-Blanchard to secretary of state, March 18, 1919, 838.00/1566, Haiti 1910–1929.
203. My translation. Brisson to secretary of interior, Port-au-Prince, March 4, 1916, folder Interior, Department of, 2 of 2, box 2, Corr. 1916–1919.
204. My translation. Barré-Ponsignon to minister of foreign affairs, Santo Domingo, February 14, 1920, dossier 2, DR 1918–1940.
205. Rimpel to the prefect of Port-au-Prince, Mirebalais and Lascahobas, Belladere, April 19, 1922, folder Dept of South, Command Affairs, box 7, Gendarmerie.
206. My translation. Inhabitants of Las Matas de Farfán petition to minister of interior and police, Las Matas de Farfan, May 12, 1919, legajo 30, 1919, IP.

207. My translation. Hernando F. to secretary of sanidad and beneficiencia, Jarabacoa, February 7, 1921, legajo 400, 1921, IP.
208. President of the ayuntamiento of Samaná to Rixey, March 5, 1921, legajo 404, 1921, IP.
209. My translation. Peguero to Department of Interior and Police, San Juan, June 21, 1921, legajo 409, 1921, IP.
210. Gaspar to area commander, Estelí, August 17, 1932, folder Jefe Dir., Law Sect. Investigations 2Nov31–27Dec32, box 37, Nicaragua 1927–1933.
211. Polanco et al. to Pendleton, Santo Domingo, July 9, 1918, and Rixey to president of ayuntamiento of Samaná, Santo Domingo, March 12, 1921, both in legajo 1, 1917–1920, GM.
212. Polanco et al. to Pendleton, Santo Domingo, July 9, 1918, legajo 1, 1917–1920, GM.
213. Knapp, to "Pedro Polanco and the other Signers," Santo Domingo, October 4, 1918, legajo 1, 1917–1920, GM.
214. Kelsey, "Intervention," 169; Calder, Impact, 46.
215. Orme to general receiver, Puerto Plata, March 10, 1922, legajo 3, 1922, GM. See also Hayden to Department of Interior and Police, July 25, 1919, legajo 9, 1919, IP.
216. Scott, Moral Economy, 91.
217. Cassá, "Movimientos," 179.
218. Frank, Roaming, 231.
219. San Miguel, "Resistance," 49. For an example, see Snowden to Rowe, Santo Domingo, March 2, 1920, folder unmarked, box 30, MGSD.
220. "Wilson Takes Step to Give Up Control in Santo Domingo," NYT, December 25, 1920, 3.
221. Seabrook, Magic Island, 172.
222. "Quarterly Report," August 28, 1919, 839.00/2153, DR 1910–1929.
223. Vega, Derecho, 349. The property tax was Executive Order No. 282.
224. Primer censo, 141.
225. Knapp to Department of Interior and Police, Santo Domingo, June 2, 1917, legajo 359, 1917, IP.
226. Snowden to Fairchild, August 4, 1919, folder 41, box 16, MGSD; Calder, Impact, 111.
227. Polanco and nine others, petition to the ayuntamiento of Samaná, El Limón, November 8, 1921, legajo 425, 1921, IP. The legajo contains several similar letters.
228. Derby largely misunderstood this by stating that elites shared the view of occupiers that taxes equaled modernity, in "Haitians," 504. Calder more accurately noted much "elite distress" over the land law, in "Varieties," 111.
229. Cruz Torres to Fuller, San Francisco de Macorís, June 29, 1919, legajo 386, 1919, IP; Loomis to secretary of Hacienda y Comercio, Santo Domingo, December 29, 1920, and Oliver to Loomis, undated, both in legajo 12, 1922, GM.
230. Lake to military governor, Santo Domingo, February 24, 1922, legajo 2, 1922, GM.
231. My translation. Colsón, Principios, 10, 9–11.
232. Chamber of Commerce to military governor, October 17, 1921, legajo 9, 1921, GM. See also Pastoriza to the Military Government, Santiago, January 1922, legajo 45, 1918–1922, GM; property owners of Santiago petition to the military governor, Santiago, November 14, 1921, legajo 425, 1921, IP (two more petitions are in the same legajo); residents of San José petition to Robison, February 20, 1922, legajo 2, 1922, GM; and Díaz et al. to military governor, Samaná, November 15, 1921, legajo 12, 1922, GM.
233. Commanding officer to Department of Interior and Police, Barahona, August 9, 1917, legajo 13, 1917, IP.
234. Moses to the military governor, October 1, 1921, legajo 417, 1921, IP.
235. Moses to Cordero y Bido, Santo Domingo, June 8, 1922, legajo 436, 1922, IP; Ramírez to Department of Interior and Police, Seybo, August 21, 1922, legajo 103, 1922, IP.
236. My translation. Belas to Department of Interior and Police, Seybo, undated, legajo 103, 1922, IP.
237. Cervantes to Department of Interior and Police, August 31, 1921, and Cabral to Department of Interior and Police, Guayubín, September 5, 1921, both legajo 420, 1921, IP; De Castro to Department of Interior and Police, Azua, July 9, 1920, legajo 57, 1920, IP; Taveras to Department of Interior and Police, Cotuy, February 23, 1921, legajo 403, 1921, IP.
238. Robison to unknown recipient, October 25, 1921, legajo 57-A, 1917–1921, GM.

239. Robison to Bonnelly and Pichardo, November 28, 1921, legajo 425, 1921, IP.
240. Gould to district provost marshal, March 21, 1922, and Johnson to military governor, Santo Domingo, March 16, 1922, both in legajo 2, 1922, GM.
241. Lyman to Lake, March 6, 1922, legajo 2, 1922, GM.
242. San Miguel, "Resistance," 51.
243. Loomis to Robison, Santo Domingo, January 12, 1922, legajo 2, 1922, GM.
244. Unión Agrícola No. 4 to Sheard, Jaya, January 24, 1919, legajo 31, 1919, IP.
245. Moses to the síndico of San Juan, Santo Domingo, September 21, 1922, legajo 14, 1922, IP.
246. Moses to Rodríguez, Santo Domingo, May 29, 1922, legajo 436, 1922, IP.
247. My translation. Brouwer to Moses, San Pedro de Macorís, September 16, 1922, legajo 436, 1922, IP.
248. My translation. Vallejo to the secretary of the interior and police, Los Llanos, September 11, 1922, legajo 83, 1922, IP.
249. Lane, "Civil Government," 133; Calder, Impact, 74.
250. Moya Pons, "Import–Substitution," 541.
251. Shoe and leather industry to military governor, Santo Domingo, September 16, 1919, legajo 34, 1919, IP.
252. Scott to Hughes, February 12, 1924, 838.00/2005, Haiti 1910–1929.
253. Diary of Cole, in Daniels to secretary of state, June 5, 1917, 838.00/1439, Haiti 1910–1929.
254. Millet, Paysans, 68.
255. Kelchner, "A Résumé of the Political Events in Haiti For the Year 1930," undated, in McGurk to secretary of state, Port-au-Prince, April 18, 1931, 838.00/2954, Haiti 1930–1939.
256. Kelsey, "Intervention," 176.
257. Moral, Paysan, 65.
258. Dunn to secretary of state, Port-au-Prince, August 27, 1923, 838.00/1960, Haiti 1910–1929.
259. "Raid Arouses Wet Hayti; Mob Routs Revenue Men," NYHT, ca. April 7, 1931. See also Munro to secretary of state, Port-au-Prince, April 4, 1931, 838.00/2946, Haiti 1930–1939.
260. Fegan to Evans, Cap-Haïtien, May 21, 1930, 838.00/2832, Haiti 1930–1939.
261. Grummon to secretary of state, Port-au-Prince, July 29, 1930, 838.044/60, Haiti 1930–1939.
262. Josephus Daniels, "The Problem of Haiti," Saturday Evening Post, July 12, 1930, 36.
263. Examples include Ramírez to De Jesús Lluberes, Seybo, September 22, 1921, legajo 418, 1921, IP.
264. Baugham, "Occupation," 2308–9.
265. Davis, "Indoctrination," 156.

Chapter 11

1. An exception is Betances, "Social Classes," 35.
2. My translation. Henríquez y Carvajal to Fache, on board SS Brazos, December 14, 1916, and Henríquez y Carvajal to Fache, New York City, December 20, 1916, both in dossier 7, DR 1897–1918.
3. My translation. Henríquez Ureña, Los yanquis, 243.
4. My translation. Del Castillo to Cestero, Santo Domingo, October 1, 1916, legajo Cartas de dominicanos y acerca de asuntos de la Rep. Dominicana, 1896–1917, Cestero Archive.
5. Henríquez y Carvajal to Henríquez Ureña, New York City, December 22, 1916, in Henríquez Ureña, Epistolario, 641; Henríquez y Carvajal, January 12, 1917, 839.00/1982, DR 1910–1929; Henríquez y Carvajal to Henríquez Ureña, Washington, January 12, 1917, in Henríquez Ureña, Epistolario, 644–5. See also Calder, Impact, 183.
6. Henríquez Ureña to Henríquez y Carvajal, New York City, September 18, 1916, in Henríquez Ureña, Epistolario, 635.
7. McLean to commandant, Santo Domingo, March 5, 1919, legajo 72 and 117, 1918–1921, GM.
8. Federico Henríquez y Carvajal, "Post–Scriptum," in Fiallo, Crime, 80.
9. The eleven were Max Henríquez Ureña, Fernando Abel Henríquez (Francisco's nephew, very likely Federico's son), Alcibiades Franco, Alfredo del Prado, Tomás Puyans, Teobaldo

Rosell Silveira, Dr. Francisco Mercer, Eduardo Abril Amores, Daniel Serra Navas, Carlos de la Torre, and Antonio Fadhel. On December 30, 1918, they joined larger groups in founding the Comités. The Santiago committee included Emilio Bacardí Moreau. The one in Havana included Manuel Sanguily and Emilio Roig de Leuchsenring. Smaller sub-committees formed in other towns of Oriente Province. Federico Henríquez y Carvajal, "Post-Scriptum," in Fiallo, *Crime*, 83–6.

10. My translation. Henríquez to chargé d'affaires of the Ministry of Foreign Relations, Santiago de Cuba, January 30, 1919, legajo 72 and 117, 1918–1921, GM.

11. US vice consul in Cuba to secretary of state, Antilla, Cuba, June 24, 1919, 839.00/2140, DR 1910–1929; "Brillante inauguración del Comité pro Santo Domingo en Banes," *Diario de Cuba*, January 21, 1919, in US vice consul in Cuba to secretary of state, Antilla, Cuba, June 24, 1919, 839.00/2140, DR 1910–1929.

12. Handwritten report, unsigned and undated [probably 1919], legajo 37, 1921–1922, GM; Henríquez Ureña, *Los yanquis*, 244, 245; Henríquez y Carvajal, "Al pueblo dominicano," Santiago de Cuba, November 20, 1919, in *Alfau Durán*, ed. Incháustegui and Delgado Malagón: 584–6.

13. "Sección Internacional Reunión Magna de Dominicanos," *La Nación*, November 6, 1919, in 839.00/2305, DR 1910–1929; "Pro–Santo Domingo," *Letras Antillanas*, January 19, 1919, in US vice consul in Cuba to secretary of state, Antilla, Cuba, June 24, 1919, 839.00/2140, DR 1910–1929.

14. My translation. Comité Pro-Santo Domingo de la Provincia de Oriente, communiqué, Santiago de Cuba, December 30, 1918, legajo 72 and 117, 1918–1921, GM.

15. My translation from French. Henríquez y Carvajal to Stabler, Paris, May 28, 1919, 839.00/2076, DR 1910–1929.

16. Grew to Polk, April 25, 1919, 839.00/2134, DR 1910–1929.

17. My translation. Henríquez y Carvajal to Henríquez Ureña, Paris, April 8, 1919, in Henríquez Ureña, *Epistolario*, 651.

18. Henríquez y Carvajal to Stabler, Paris, May 28, 1919, 839.00/2076, DR 1910–1929; Henríquez y Carvajal, "Al pueblo dominicano," Santiago de Cuba, November 20, 1919, in *Alfau Durán*, ed. Incháustegui and Delgado Malagón: 584–6.

19. Grew to Polk, April 25, 1919, 839.00/2134, DR 1910–1929.

20. My translation. Roig de Leuchsenring, *La ocupación*, 58. For similar hypocrisy arguments, see Colsón, *Principios*.

21. Asociación, *Juventud*.

22. My translation. "La Soberanía Dominicana," *Diario de Cuba*, February 18, 1919, in US vice consul in Cuba to secretary of state, Antilla, Cuba, June 24, 1919, 839.00/2140, DR 1910–1929.

23. Fiallo, *Crime*, 29.

24. Comment by "R. S.," August 9, 1919, on extract from parliamentary debate, August 11, 1919, file 115728, reference 3803, FO 371.

25. US mission in Paris to secretary of state, March 14, 1919, 838.00/1563, Haiti 1910–1929.

26. Jiménez to Cestero, La Marianita, August 23, 1918, legajo Papeles 1919–1920, Tomo 1, Cestero Archive.

27. My translation. Cestero to Jiménez, New York, October 8, 1918, legajo Papeles 1919–1920, Tomo 1, Cestero Archive.

28. My translation. Henríquez y Carvajal to Cestero, October 9, 1919, legajo Papeles 1919–1920, Tomo 1, Cestero Archive.

29. Henríquez Ureña, *Los yanquis*, 247.

30. Dunn, September 8, 1919, 839.00/2149, DR 1910–1929.

31. Translation by the Dominicans. Henríquez y Carvajal to Lansing, October 27, 1919, legajo Papeles 1919–1920, Tomo 1, Cestero Archive. A summary of Henríquez's plan is "Al pueblo dominicano," Santiago de Cuba, November 20, 1919, in *Alfau Durán*, ed. Incháustegui and Delgado Malagón: 584–6.

32. Dunn, September 8, 1919, 839.00/2149, DR 1910–1929.

33. Philipps to secretary of the navy, September 6, 1919, 839.00/2147, DR 1910–1929.

34. Both citations from Welles, *Vineyard*, 822.

35. Cestero, notes of meeting with Daniels, Washington, April 8, 1920, legajo Papeles 1919–1920, Tomo 1, Cestero Archive.
36. Cestero to Wilson, Washington, April 1, 1920, 839.00/2200, DR 1910–1929.
37. Calder, *Impact*, 200; Nouel to Russell, Santo Domingo, December 29, 1919, 839.00/2206, DR 1910–1929. On the Nouel letter see also Alfau Durán, "La palabra," 661–9. Cestero to secretary of state, Washington, March 27, 1920, 839.00/2197, DR 1910–1929.
38. "Flag San Domingo" to secretary of the navy, [April 12, 1920?], 839.00/2203, DR 1910–1929.
39. Fiallo, *Crime*, 33; Grew to Polk, April 25, 1919, 839.00/2134, DR 1910–1929.
40. My translation. "Palabras pronunciadas por Tulio M. Cestero el 5 de julio en Nueva York," *Letras*, August 11, 1918, 7, AGN.
41. My translation. Cestero to Henríquez y Carvajal, Washington, December 20, 1919, legajo Papeles 1919–1920, Tomo 1, Cestero Archive.
42. Barré-Ponsignon to minister of foreign affairs, Santo Domingo, September 22, 1920, dossier 2, DR 1918–1940.
43. Long to secretary of state, Havana, May 6, 1920, 839.00/2208, DR 1910–1929.
44. Buck to secretary of state, Antilla, Cuba, April 21, 1920, 839.00/2205, DR 1910–1929.
45. Henríquez Ureña to Cestero, Santiago de Cuba, December 12, 1919, legajo Papeles 1919–1920, Tomo 1, Cestero Archive.
46. My translation. Henríquez y Carvajal to Cestero, New York, November 29, 1920, legajo Papeles 1921–1922, Tomo II, Cestero Archive. The three times were following the Knapp proclamation of November 1916, during the Versailles conference, and after his return to the United States. Federico himself said the CND met in October 1919, but more likely he meant 1920: Henríquez y Carvajal, "Post-Scriptum," in Fiallo, *Crime*, 88.
47. Henríquez Ureña to Cestero, Buenos Aires, February 1, 1921, legajo Papeles 1921–1922 Tomo II, Cestero Archive; Cox, "'Yankee Imperialism,'" 256.
48. "Memoria que presenta al Presidente de Jure de la República Dominicana Doctor Francisco Henríquez y Carvajal, el Señor Tulio M. Cestero, de la Misión que cumplió en Perú, Chile, Argentina, Uruguay, y Brazil, de Enero a Mayo de 1921," Washington, July 7, 1921, legajo Papeles 1921–1922 Tomo II, Cestero Archive.
49. My translation. Enriquillo Henríquez to Cestero, Havana, January 27, 1921, legajo Cartas de Henríquez y C (Fco y Fed.), Max Henríquez U., E. Henríquez, E. Ap. Henríquez, G. J. Henríquez y A. S. Nolasco, Cestero Archive.
50. Henríquez Ureña to Cestero, Buenos Aires, February 1, 1921, legajo Papeles 1921–1922 Tomo II, Cestero Archive. See also Henríquez Ureña to Cestero, Buenos Aires, February 26, 1921, legajo Papeles 1921–1922 Tomo II, Cestero Archive; and Smith, "Bainbridge Colby," 56–78.
51. Calder, "Varieties," 111; Smith, "Bainbridge Colby," 73.
52. Matte Gomaz, and Yrigoyen cited in "Memoria . . . ," Washington, July 7, 1921, legajo Papeles 1921–1922 Tomo II, Cestero Archive.
53. Welles, *Vineyard*, 830.
54. Ramsey, Santo Domingo, March 1, 1921, folder D-17 Dominican Rep. Guardia Nacional Intelligence Sum., box 8, O&T.
55. Oficina de Información, UND, circular, *Unidad*.
56. Calder, *Impact*, 203; Welles, *Vineyard*, 829.
57. Cited in Juarez, "Withdrawal," 156.
58. Spencer to secretary of state, Madrid, July 4, 1922, 839.00/2547, DR 1910–1929; Calder, *Impact*, 188; Juarez, "Withdrawal," 183.
59. My translation. Deschamps, *El espíritu*, 5, 17.
60. "Asks U.S. to Quit Santo Domingo," *Washington Post*, September 11, 1919, n. p.
61. Oficina de Información, UND, *Important Message*; Deschamps, *El espíritu*, 7. The text of the 1919 Congressional statement is: "The undersigned, Congressmen and Senators of the Spanish Parliament, openly and wholly in accordance, believe that it would be now opportune for the Spanish Government to amicably express to the Washington Government the desire of the Dominican Republic to have the regime of right re–established there, which has been annulled by the military occupation to which said country is at present subject,

and that the Spanish Government itself should also use its good services near the American Government, fulfilling with this a high moral duty as regards the Dominican people and as an act of cordial friendship towards the Government of the United States," in Gaudier to Snowden, Palma de Mallorca, Spain, July 6, 1920, folder 4 Admiral Snowden Personal File, box 30, MGSD.

62. Juarez, "Withdrawal," 169, 183.

63. Editorial, "América en la Universidad Internacional de Barcelona," *Mercurio*, September 1920, in Deschamps, *El espíritu*, 24.

64. My translation. Henríquez y Carvajal to Henríquez García, Washington, May 7, 1921, in Henríquez García, *Cartas*, 26.

65. Mason to Cestero, Washington, April 27, 1920, and Cestero to Mason, Havana, June 17, 1920, legajo Papeles 1919–1920, Tomo 1, Cestero Archive.

66. Calder, *Impact*, 201.

67. Knowles to Hughes, New York, April 12, 1922, 839.918/17; Knowles to Fletcher, New York, February 15, 1922, 839.918/13; Knowles to Davis, January 13, 1921, 839.00/2321; Knowles to Davis, January 30, 1921, 839.00/2326; Colby cited in Knowles to Colby, February 24, 1921, 839.00/2348; Knowles to Harding, New York, February 25, 1921, 839.00/2471, all in DR 1910–1929.

68. Maguire to military governor, Santo Domingo, May 3, 1922, folder 14, 201–25, Commanding General, USMC, box 49, MGSD. Another source says he received $1,000 per week but did not specify for how many weeks: "Information furnished by the Provost Marshal's Office," Santo Domingo, December 22, 1921, legajo 37, 1921–1922, GM.

69. Knowles to Fletcher, New York, July 25, 1921, 839.00/2471, DR 1910–1929.

70. Knowles to Borah, New York, April 6, 1922, folder 1921–1921 Haiti and Caribbean Situation, box 113, Borah Papers.

71. Calder, "Varieties," 109; Laurence Todd, "Startling Exposure of American Ruthlessness in Dominican Republic," *Butte Bulletin*, February 24, 1922, in Knowles to Borah, New York, April 6, 1922, folder 1921–1921 Haiti and Caribbean Situation, box 113, Borah Papers; Laurence Todd, "U.S. Imperialism Tortures in San Domingo," *Telegram*, March 4, 1922, in Knowles to Borah, New York, April 6, 1922, folder 1921–1921 Haiti and Caribbean Situation, box 113, Borah Papers; "Declares Marines Abused Dominicans," *NYT*, August 15, 1921, 2; "Condemns Dominican Rule," *NYT*, February 17, 1922, 3.

72. Maguire to military governor, Santo Domingo, May 3, 1922, folder 14, 201–25, Commanding General, USMC, box 49, MGSD.

73. Miller to military governor, December 22, 1921, legajo 37, 1921–1922, GM.

74. "Assail Our Record in Ruling Latins," *NYT*, May 21, 1920, 16.

75. Oficina de Información, UND, circular, *El problema*.

76. Gompers to Kunhardt, Washington, November 4, 1916, folder 29, box 8, MGSD.

77. Fay to military governor, Santo Domingo, February 2, 1922, folder 13, 1–25 Brigade Intelligence Officer, box 48, MGSD.

78. "Quarterly Report," January 1, 1920, 839.00/2193, DR 1910–1929.

79. Gompers to Wilson, Mexico City, January 8, 1921, 839.00/2386, DR 1910–1929; Henríquez y Carvajal, "Carta del Presidente Henríquez," *Listín Diario*, March 8, 1921.

80. Oficina de Información, UND, *El Congreso*. See also Cestero to Brady and McAndrews, Washington, April 7, 1920, legajo Papeles 1919–1920, Tomo 1, Cestero Archive.

81. Wilson to Davis, Washington, January 20, 1921, 839.00/2386, DR 1910–1929.

82. Kunhardt paraphrased in Lake to provost marshal, Santo Domingo, January 28, 1922, folder 13, 1–25 Brigade Intelligence Officer, box 48, MGSD.

83. García Muñiz and Giovannetti, "Garveyismo," 127–34.

84. Van Putten to secretary of interior and police, San Pedro de Macorís, December 23, 1919, legajo 43, 1919, IP.

85. Hennessy to secretary of interior and police, San Pedro de Macorís, February 6, 1921, legajo 405, 1921, IP.

86. Beer to Moses, San Pedro de Macorís, September 13, 1921, legajo 420, 1921, IP.

87. My translation. Warfield to the Department of Foreign Relations, April 28, 1922, legajo 90, 1922; Fuller to Van Putten, Santo Domingo, December 27, 1919, legajo 43, 1919; De Jesús

Lluveres to Peguero, San Pedro, January 24, 1922, legajo 90, 1922; military governor to the Department of Interior and Police, March 22, 1922, legajo 90, 1922, all in IP.

88. Russell, daily diary report, July 12, 1920, 838.00/1651, Haiti 1910–1929.

89. My translation. Russell to Hughes, October 31, 1924, 838.00/2049; and Scott to Kellogg, October 27, 1925, 838.00/2165, both in Haiti 1910–1929; Plummer, *Psychological Moment*, 123; Russell to Hughes, November 11, 1924, 838.00/2051, Haiti 1910–1929.

90. *Les Annales Capoises*, October 30, 1924, cited in Pamphile, *African Americans*, 132.

91. Winkler-Morey, "Good Neighbors," 87–103; Rosenberg, *Missionaries*, 127; Lerebours, "Indigenist Revolt," 713–4.

92. Blackwood to Wise, Port-au-Prince, September 22, 1919, folder Complaints from Citizens (1918–1919), 1 of 3, box 1, Corr. 1916–1919.

93. Munro to White, Washington, April 19, 1929, 838.00/2523, Haiti 1910–1929; Rosenberg, *Missionaries*, 127.

94. Lawson, petition to Coolidge, New York, December 14, 1925, 838.00/2178, Haiti 1910–1929.

95. "Bishop Hurst Calls for Haitian Inquiry," *NYT*, November 10, 1920, 3.

96. Munro to White, May 19, 1924, 838.00/2024, Haiti 1910–1929.

97. The NAACP did not completely ignore the Dominican Republic. It prepared a full day of activities on its behalf for its August 1922 convention in New York City: Robison to Department of Foreign Relations, Santo Domingo, May 25, 1922, legajo 120, 1920–1922, GM.

98. DuBois, "Hayti," 291.

99. DuBois, "Hayti," 291; *Le Nouvelliste*, October 20, 1915, cited in Gaillard, *Premier écrasement*, 153; Pamphile, *African Americans*, 104, 122. One such letter was Williams to Wilson, Cincinnati, February 8, 1916, 711.38/66, U.S.-Haiti 1910–1929.

100. Storey to Hughes, Boston, June 6, 1921, 838.00/1780, Haiti 1910–1929; Johnson, *Gruening*, 37.

101. Plummer, "Response," 139.

102. Arthur Spingarn, "Under American Rule in Haiti," *The World*, February 7, 1925. A similar case was that of Jolibois Fils: Thoby to Spingarn, Port-au-Prince, May 1, 1923, folder Thoby, Perceval (On Haiti) 1923–1927; Sylvain to Spingarn, Port-au-Prince, May 30 and June 12, 1923, folder Sylvain, Georges (On Haiti) 1923–1924, and undated; Thoby to Spingarn, Port-au-Prince, July 4, 1923, folder Thoby, Perceval (On Haiti) 1923–1927, all in box 4, Spingarn Papers.

103. Cited in Cook, "Dantes Bellegarde," 134.

104. Delpar, *Vogue*, 93, 193, 195, 8, 9.

105. Freeman to Beals, October 20, 1931, folder Beals, Carleton, box 14, Freeman Papers.

106. My translation. From *Le Nouvelliste*, October 20, 1915, cited in Gaillard, *Premier écrasement*, 153.

107. White, *Will Rogers*, 16.

108. Blassingame, "The Press," 29–37.

109. My translation. *Le Nouvelliste*, October 20, 1915, cited in Gaillard, *Premier écrasement*, 153.

110. Rosenberg, *Missionaries*, 126. The few who opposed the occupation in its first four years included Jane Addams and the Women's Peace Party, Du Bois and the *Crisis*, and Lovett Fort-Whiteman of the *Messenger*. See Renda, *Taking Haiti*, 19 and Suggs, "Response," 33–45.

111. Johnson, *Autobiography*.

112. Levy, *Johnson*, 202–3.

113. Biographers disagree on the point: Levy, *Johnson*, 204; Pamphile, *African Americans*, 109. But Johnson himself said he was in Haiti from March 21 to May 21 or 22, 1920, in Senate, *Hearings*, vol. 1, 779.

114. My translation. Danache, *Président*, 99.

115. Pamphile, "NAACP," 118; Plummer, "Response," 132.

116. Johnson, "Truth," 217–24; Johnson, "Haiti II," 265–7. For more writings and speeches, see Wilson, ed., *Search*.

117. Johnson, "Truth," 220–2.

118. Johnson, "Haiti and Our Latin–American Policy," delivered at the "World Tomorrow Dinner," New York City, March 31, 1924, in *Search*, ed. Wilson, 113.

119. Plummer, "Response," 132.

120. Levy, *Johnson*, 203.

121. Harding cited in Schoultz, *Beneath*, 255; Pamphile, "NAACP," 94, 113–4; Sherman, "Harding," 156; Grieb, *Harding*, 2.

122. Rosenberg, *Missionaries*, 124.

123. Juarez, "Withdrawal," 153.

124. Heinl, Jr., and Heinl, *Written in Blood*, 469; Grieb, *Harding*, 69; Rosenberg, *Missionaries*, 124.

125. Entry for November 27, 1920, Russell, USMC, daily diary report, November 29, 1920, 838.00/1725, Haiti 1910–1929.

126. "Santo Domingo," 528. See also Onlooker, "America's Ireland," 231–4.

127. Delgadillo, "Destiny and Democracy," 11.

128. Johnson, *Gruening*, 36.

129. Bellegarde, *Résistance*, 70.

130. Perkins to brigade commander, Port-au-Prince, July 26, 1920 and December 13, 1921, and Villars to brigade commander, Port-au-Prince, December 17, 1921, all in folder Investi[gation] Haitien Affai[rs], box 1, Corr. 1918–1921; Russell, "Some Truths about Haiti," unaddressed memo, August 7, 1920, folder Haiti opns. + training (1915–1920), box 2, GC.

131. Seligmann, "Conquest," 35–6.

132. No title or author, *The Nation*, February 23, 1921, 277–8; the original is UP, *Memoir*; Pamphile, "NAACP," 118.

133. Villard to Roosevelt, July 7, 1920, box 41, ASN; Johnson, *Gruening*, 31.

134. Blassingame, "The Press," 42.

135. Williams to Snowden, Santiago, December 17, 1920, folder 4 Admiral Snowden Personal File, box 30, MGSD.

136. Unsigned memo, Washington, DC, June 24, 1921, folder Haiti opns. Reports, Intelligence Summaries (1920–1921), box 3, GC.

137. Rosenberg, *Missionaries*, 126; Posner, "Marines," 262.

138. Agel to minister of foreign affairs, Port-au-Prince, March 15, 1921, dossier 4, Haiti 1918–1940; Sannon, Vincent, and Thoby to Hughes, New York, April 13, 1921, 838.00/1765, Haiti 1910–1929; Pamphile, "NAACP," 96–7.

139. Senate, *Hearings*, vol. 1, 3–4.

140. A summary is in "Haitian Delegates Want Us to Get Out," *NYT*, May 9, 1921, 17.

141. Welles to Schoenrich, April 16, 1921, folder Haiti 1920–1922, box 178, Welles Papers.

142. Bellegarde cited in Cook, "Dantes Bellegarde," 132, 130. See also interview with Bellegarde, "Latin America Against the Hegemony of the United States," *Le Temps* (Port-au-Prince), September 20–21, 1927, in Russell to secretary of state, October 27, 1927, 838.00/2412, Haiti 1910–1929.

143. Cook, "Dantes Bellegarde," 130.

144. "Defends Our Haiti Action," *NYT*, July 3, 1924, 17; Russell to Hughes, secretary of state, October 1, 1924, 838.00/2040, Haiti 1910–1929.

145. Much of the July 1, 1924, speech is reproduced in "La République de Haiti demande à être libérée des troupes américaines," *Le Nouvelliste*, July 24, 1924, in folder Newspaper Clippings (1–28Jul24), box 3, First Brigade; "La Presse Française enfin s'intéresse à la Cause Nationale Haïtienne," *Le Nouvelliste*, January 12, 1925, 1.

146. Frost to Department of State, Marseille, September 26, 1924, 838.00/2041, Haiti 1910–1929.

147. Yannick Wehrli, "Latin America in the League of Nations: Bolivar's Dream Come True?" in Auroi and Helg, *Latin America*, 67–82.

148. Cited in Munro, *Intervention*, 54.

149. Brissman, "Interpreting," 293.

150. Hudicourt to Coolidge, Washington, May 21, 1925, 838.00/2119; Hudicourt to Kellogg, Washington, May 21, 1925, 838.00/2114; Russell to Kellogg, June 20, 1925, 838.00/2131; and Merrell to Kellogg, July 18, 1925, 838.00/2143, all in Haiti 1910–1929.

151. "La République de Haiti demande à être libérée des troupes américaines," Le Nouvelliste, July 24, 1924, and "Une grande victoire morale—détails sur l'action de Bellegarde," *Le Nouvelliste*, July 29, 1924, both in folder Newspaper Clippings (1–28Jul24), box 3, First Brigade.

152. "Rejects Plea for Haiti," *NYT*, March 25, 1925, 33.
153. "Une grande victoire morale," *Le Nouvelliste*, July 29, 1924, in folder Newspaper Clippings (1–28Jul24), box 3, First Brigade.
154. Corvington, *1915–1922*, 213.
155. Welles to Hughes, Washington, March 24, 1921, 838.00/1833, Haiti 1910–1929.
156. Russell to Kellogg, Port-au-Prince, November 13, 1925, 838.00/2169, Haiti 1910–1929; biography of Thoby, unsigned and undated, 838.00/2585, Haiti 1910–1929.
157. There was one possible exception: Abel Théard, the chargé in London. See Delage to minister of foreign affairs, Port-au-Prince, September 20, 1919, dossier 9, Haiti 1918–1940.
158. Corvington, *1915–1922*, 214.
159. My translation. "La leçon d'un échec," *Le Courrier Haïtien*, July 1924, in folder Newspaper Clippings (1–28Jul24), box 3, First Brigade.
160. For more, see McPherson, "Jolibois Fils," 120–47.
161. Cohen, G-2 report, October 11, 1928, 838.00/2489, Haiti 1910–1929.
162. Welles, [February 13?] 1922, 838.00/1845, Haiti 1910–1929.
163. Posner, "Marines," 264; Juarez, "Withdrawal," 159.
164. Barnett to Russell, Washington, October 2, 1919, folder 9, box 2, Russell Papers. See also Barnett's testimony in Senate, *Hearings*, vol. 1, 424–43.
165. Barnett wrote that almost all the killings were by gendarmes, not marines; only a few were truly "indiscriminate"; half had occurred during a caco attack on Port-au-Prince; there were 2,250 rather than the 3,250 he initially reported; and otherwise marines maintained law and order: "Reports Unlawful Killing of Haitians by Our Marines," *NYT*, October 14, 1920, 1, 3; "Barnett Modifies Haitian Charges," *NYT*, October 28, 1920, 17.
166. Pamphile, "NAACP," 95.
167. Cited in Senate, *Hearings*, vol. 1, 432.
168. Emphasis in original. Hickey and Williams to all officers, Port-au-Prince, June 18, 1919, folder Report of Investigation 10 Mar 1919–13 Mar 20, Haiti, Geographical Files, Reference Branch, MCH.
169. U.S. Army, *Military Government*, 14.
170. Officers of the Court of Inquiry were Admiral Henry T. Mayo, Read-Admiral James H. Oliver, Major-General Wendell C. Neville of the Marine Corps, and Major Jesse F. Dyer as Judge Advocate.
171. UP, *Memoir*, 17; Corvington, *1915–1922*, 114.
172. Agel to minister of foreign affairs, Port-au-Prince, November 14, 1920, dossier 10, Haiti 1918–1940.
173. Corvington, *1915–1922*, 115.
174. Mayo Court of Inquiry, "Report of Inquiry into Haitian Matters–1920," October 19, 1920, folder Rpt of Inquiry into Haitian matter, box 18, Gendarmerie.
175. Sherman, "Harding," 154.
176. "La Commission d'Enquête ayant refusé de m'entendre, je rends ma déposition publique, nous dit Monsieur Ph. Lacroix," *Le Courrier Haïtien*, November 27, 1920, dossier 3, Haiti 1918–1940; J. J. R. Providence, "Plaintes et dénonciations," *Le Courrier Haïtien*, December 1, 1920, in dossier 3, Haiti 1918–1940.
177. "Haitian Protest Nonsense, Declares Navy Secretary," *NYHT*, May 12, 1921, in dossier 4, Haiti 1918–1940; Jusserand to minister of foreign affairs, Washington, December 20, 1920, dossier 3, Haiti 1918–1940; "Weeps in Denying Murder of Haitians," *NYT*, November 20, 1920, 4.
178. Shepard, Port-au-Prince, January 31, 1921, folder Haiti opns. Reports, Intelligence Summaries (1920–21), box 3, GC.
179. The Committee was composed of McCormick, Philander Knox (R-Penn.), Atlee Pomerene (D-Ohio), Tasker Oddie (R-Nev.), William King (D-Utah), and clerk Elisha Hanson. Andrieus A. Jones (D-N.M.) later replaced King. Senate, *Hearings*, vols. 1 and 2.
180. "2,500 Slain in Haiti, Major Turner Says," *NYT*, October 27, 1921; NAACP, press release, March 22, 1922, folder Haiti-Santo Domingo Press Releases 1922, news clippings, box 4, Subject File, Storey Papers; Agel to minister of foreign affairs, Port-au-Prince, December 8, 1921, dossier 4, Haiti 1918–1940. A Dominican publication also gathered all testimony by Dominicans: Hopelman and Senior, eds., *Documentos*.

181. Agel to minister of foreign affairs, Port-au-Prince, December 8, 1920, dossier 10, Haiti 1918–1940; Geddes to Curzon of Kedleston, May 12, 1922, file A3343, reference 7217, FO 371. For historical appraisals see McCrocklin, *Garde*, 151–2; Pamphile, "NAACP," 98.

182. "La opinión del Senador McCormick sobre la intervención en Haiti y Santo Domingo," [April?] 1921, 839.00/2385, DR 1910–1929; NAACP, press release, March 22, 1922, folder Haiti-Santo Domingo Press Releases 1922, news clippings, box 4, Subject File, Storey Papers.

183. Torrey to commanding officers, Port-au-Prince, August 15, 1921, folder 3rd Company Correspondence, box 9, Gendarmerie; Robison to commanding general, December 20, 1921, and Lyman to commanding general, Santiago, January 4, 1922, both in legajo 37, 1921–1922, GM.

184. Robison to Howe, December 22, 1921, legajo 37, 1921–1922, GM.

185. Johnson, *Peace Progressives*, 226.

186. "Arrivée de la Commission Sénatoriale," *Le Matin*, November 29, 1921; "Pancartes," *Le Courrier Haïtien*, November 29, 1921, recorded every banner's writings; Johnson, *Peace Progressives*, 226.

187. My translation. Barré-Ponsignon to minister of foreign affairs, Santo Domingo, December 17, 1921, dossier 2, DR 1918–1940.

188. Knight, *Americans*, 119.

189. Senate, *Hearings*, vol. 2, *passim* 947–1125.

190. Rossell to major general commandant, Anderson, S.C., September 12, 1921, folder Haiti opns. Reports, Intelligence Summaries (1920–1921), box 3, GC.

191. Cited in Senate, *Hearings*, vol. 2, 1210–1, 1251, 1275.

192. Senate, *Hearings*, vol. 2, 1125.

193. My translation. Paraphrased by George Lespinasse in Agel to minister of foreign affairs, Port-au-Prince, December 8, 1921, dossier 4, Haiti 1918–1940.

194. McCormick to Hughes, Santo Domingo, December 14, 1921, 838.00/1825 ½, Haiti 1910–29.

195. My translation. Barré-Ponsignon to minister of foreign affairs, Santo Domingo, December 1, 1921, dossier 5, DR 1918–1940.

196. Barré-Ponsignon to minister of foreign affairs, Santo Domingo, December 23, 1921, dossier 5, DR 1918–1940.

197. Memo to brigade intelligence officer, Santo Domingo, December 22, 1921, legajo 37, 1921–1922, GM.

198. Grieb, "Harding," 428.

199. McCormick, "Failure," 615.

200. Harding to Thomas, Washington, February 20, 1922, folder 1921–1921 Haiti and Caribbean Situation, box 113, Borah Papers.

201. "Urges Maintaining Our Troops in Haiti," *NYT*, June 27, 1922; Heinl, Jr., and Heinl, *Written in Blood*, 472.

202. Cited in Owen, "Address to the Secretary of State of the United States against the American Occupation of Haiti," Washington, April 27, 1922, in King to Hughes, Washington, D.C., April 27, 1922, 838.00/1867, Haiti 1910–1929; NPGL, press release, April 29, 1922, 838.00/1873, Haiti 1910–1929.

203. Cited in Owen, "Address to the Secretary of State of the United States against the American Occupation of Haiti," Washington, April 27, 1922, and FPA, "The seizure of Haiti by the United States," both King to Hughes, Washington, April 27, 1922, 838.00/1867, Haiti 1910–1929; Johnson, *Gruening*, 42.

204. Juarez, "Withdrawal," 170.

205. Heinl, Jr., and Heinl, *Written in Blood*, 472.

206. "U.S. Invaded Hayti to Exploit Riches, Declares Borah," *New York World*, May 2, 1922; "Borah Sees Haiti Prey of Our Greed," *NYT*, May 2, 1922; NAACP, press release, May 5, 1922, folder Haiti-Santo Domingo Press Releases 1922, news clippings, box 4, Subject File, Storey Papers; Rosenberg, *Missionaries*, 125.

207. Borah and the *Times* cited in Juarez, "Withdrawal," 171.

208. Agel to minister of foreign affairs, Port-au-Prince, June 1, 1922, dossier 5, Haiti 1918–1940.

209. Mayer to Hughes, July 30, 1921, 839.00/2451, DR 1910–1929.
210. Cited in "Urges Maintaining Our Troops in Haiti," *NYT*, June 27, 1922.
211. Emphasis in original. Dubois, editorial, *The Crisis*, June 1922, 60.
212. Russell, "Regarding a Constructive Policy for Haiti," October 1, 1921, 838.00/1842; Welles to Hughes, Washington, August 29, 1921, 838.00/1806; and Welles, [13 February?] 1922, 838.00/1845, all in Haiti 1910–1929.
213. Inman, "Imperialistic," 107–6; Welles, "Imperialistic?" 412–23; Woods, "'Imperialistic America,'" 55–68; Rosenberg, *Missionaries*, 131–5. See also Inman, "Hard Problems," 338–42; Inman, "Occupation," 342–8.
214. Inman, "Imperialistic," 107, 112, 114.
215. Woods, "'Imperialistic America,'" 68, 58, 62, 65–7.
216. My translation. UP, *Séance*, 5.
217. Hanson, "Welles," 3, 30, 34.
218. Fiallo, *Crime*, 55.
219. Colby to Daniels, Washington, November 27, 1920, in State, FRUS, 1920: 2, 136. For more examples, see Juarez, "Withdrawal," 167; Munro, "Withdrawal," 1; White to Welles, February 17, 1923, 839.00/2686a, DR 1910–1929.
220. Welles, "Imperialistic?," 412, 413, 418–19. For a similar defense, see Norton, "Imperialism," 210–18.
221. San Miguel was perhaps the only historian to also come to this conclusion, in "Resistance," 54–5.
222. Vega, *Derecho*, 350.
223. J. Belisario Curiel, "La carga se hace mas pesada," *El Anuncio*, February 9, 1922, in legajo 2, 1922, GM.
224. Chamber of Commerce, Industry and Agriculture of San Pedro de Macorís to military governor, October 1, 1921, legajo 9, 1921, GM.
225. Bosch, *Dictaduras*, 130.
226. Robison to unknown recipient, October 25, 1921, legajo 57-A, 1917–1921, GM.
227. Chamber of Commerce, Industry and Agriculture of San Pedro de Macorís to military governor, October 1, 1921, legajo 9, 1921, GM.
228. My translation. Henríquez y Carvajal to Henríquez García, Washington, December 9, 1920, in Henríquez García, *Cartas*, 11.
229. Snowden to Russell, Santo Domingo, December 2, 1919, folder unmarked, box 13, MGSD.
230. Advisory Council, Memorandum No. 1 to Snowden, November 12, 1919; and Advisory Council, Memorandum No. 3 to Snowden, December 16, 1919, both in folder 42–3 Secretary of the Navy (Operations), box 31, MGSD.
231. Snowden to secretary of the navy, Santo Domingo, January 17, 1920; Advisory Council, Memorandum No. 2 to Snowden, December 3, 1919, both in folder 42–3 Secretary of the Navy (Operations), box 31, MGSD.
232. Welles, *Vineyard*, 825–6.
233. Brewer to secretary of state, Santo Domingo, January 10, 1920, 839.00/2185, DR 1910–1929.
234. "Quarterly Report," January 1, 1920, 839.00/2193, DR 1910–1929.
235. Brewer to secretary of state, Santo Domingo, March 21, 1920, 839.00/2199, DR 1910–1929.
236. My translation. Barré-Possignon to minister of foreign affairs, Santo Domingo, April 22, 1920, dossier 2, DR 1918–1940; Calder, *Impact*, 194. Its president was Emiliano Tejera and its secretary, Antonio Hoepelman, a journalist and former deputy.
237. Feliz to Department of Interior and Police, January 8, 1920, legajo 413, 1920–1921, IP.
238. Welles, *Vineyard*, 828.
239. Munro, *Intervention*, 322.
240. My translation. Barré-Possignon to minister of foreign affairs, Santo Domingo, April 3, 1920, dossier 2, DR 1918–1940.
241. De Noel Henríquez et al., *Al pueblo*.
242. Ellis, July 31, 1920, folder D-28 Dominican Rep. Intelligence Summaries, box 8, O&T.
243. Lake to Snowden, Santo Domingo, July 20, 1920, legajo 40-A, 1920, GM; Snowden to Swan, Santo Domingo, June 23, 1920, folder unmarked, box 30, MGSD; Feland to Daniels, Santo Domingo, July 29, 1920, 839.00/2226, DR 1910–1929.

244. Ellis, August 31, 1920, folder D-28 Dominican Rep. Intelligence Summaries, box 8, O&T; Snowden to secretary of the navy, Santo Domingo, May 10, 1920, folder 42, box 31, MGSD; Van Hoose, June 8, 1920, legajo 20, 1920–1921, GM.

245. "Wilson Takes Step to Give Up Control in Santo Domingo," *NYT*, December 25, 1920, 1.

246. Cited in Juarez, "Withdrawal," 163.

247. "Quarterly Report," January 2, 1921, 839.00/2352; Henríquez y Carvajal to Welles, New York, January 6, 1921, 839.00/2341; and Brewer to secretary of state, July 16, 1920 839.00/2216, all in DR 1910–1929.

248. Calder, *Impact*, 206–7; Fiallo, *Crime*, 51–3.

249. Frisbie, "Reasons for the Increase in the Bandit Activity in the Eastern District," January 20, 1921, folder D-28 Dominican Rep. Intelligence Summaries, box 8, O&T; Kilgore, March 24, 1921, folder Santo Domingo—Intell. Summaries 1921, box 5, GC.

250. Fiallo, *Crime*, 54.

251. Some historians have seen his policy as a precursor of the Good Neighbor Policy. Grieb, for example, argued that, instead of the big stick, "Harding emphasized a more measured, pragmatic approach." In *Harding*, x.

252. Pamphile, "NAACP," 98.

253. Grieb, *Harding*, 64.

254. Feland to Snowden, Washington, November 30, 1920, folder 4 Admiral Snowden Personal File, box 30, MGSD.

255. Peynado to Henríquez y Carvajal, Santo Domingo, November 28, 1919; and Henríquez y Carvajal to Cestero, Santiago de Cuba, December 8, 1919, both in legajo Papeles 1919– 1920, Tomo 1, Cestero Archive.

256. My translation. Henríquez y Carvajal to Henríquez García, New York, January 1 and February 1, 1921, in Henríquez García, *Cartas*, 15, 17.

257. Henríquez y Carvajal to Henríquez Ureña, Santiago de Cuba, March 30, 1921, in Henríquez Ureña, *Epistolario*, 695–700.

258. Snowden to secretary of the navy, June 20, 1921, 839.00/2422, DR 1910–1929.

259. Barré-Ponsignon to minister of foreign affairs, Santo Domingo, July 20, 1921, dossier 2, DR 1918–1940.

260. Quiñones to De Jesús Lluveres, Moca, June 30, 1921, legajo 412, 1921, IP.

261. Rixey to commanding general, Santo Domingo, June 26, 1921, legajo 40, 1917–1919, GM.

262. Russell to Hughes, June 20, 1921, 839.00/2404, DR 1910–1929.

263. Aristoteles, "Reunión Ayuntamientos," *Listín Diario*, July 9, 1921; petitions from Monte Cristi, Jarabacoa, San José de las Matas, Jimentel, La Vega, Guayubín, Sánchez, Moca, Castillo, Puerto Plata, Salcedo, Altamirana, Bajabonico, San Francisco de Macorís, Samaná, Valverde, Cotuí, Sabaneta, Sabana de la Mar, Jánica, Peña, Constanza, Restauración, and Santiago, all in legajo 410, 1921, IP.

264. Editorial, "Mas unidos que nunca," *Listín Diario*, June 16, 1921, in 839.00/2437, DR 1910–1929.

265. Moses to all provincial governors, Santo Domingo, July 22, 1921, legajo 412, 1921, IP; military governor to Department of Hacienda y Comercio, August 3, 1921, legajo 107, 1917–1922, GM.

266. Barré-Ponsignon to minister of foreign affairs, Santo Domingo, August 27, 1921, dossier 2, DR 1918–1940.

267. My translation. Américo Lugo, "Reto cívico," *Tiempo*, June 16, 1921, in 839.00/2437, DR 1910–1929; *Constitución*.

268. Russell to Hughes, June 20, 1921, 839.00/2404, DR 1910–1929.

269. My translation. "PROTESTA de la JUNTA DE ABSTENCION ELECTORAL . . . ," July 18, 1921, dossier 5, DR 1918–1940. It is reproduced as Américo Lugo et al., "Protesta de la Junta de Abstención Electoral," Santo Domingo, July 18, 1921, in *Alfau Durán*, ed. Incháustegui and Delgado Malagón: 611–4.

270. Dr. Juan B. Pérez, "Habla el Doctor Juan B. Pérez," *Listín Diario*, July 1, 1921. See also López Méndez, "El pueblo," 276.

271. Kelsey, "Intervention," 193.

272. My translation. Henríquez to Cestero, San Pedro de Macorís, August 31, 1921, legajo Cartas de Henríquez y C (Fco y Fed.), Max Henríquez U., E. Henríquez, E. Ap. Henríquez, G. J. Henríquez y A. S. Nolasco, Cestero Archive.

273. My translation. Barré-Ponsignon to minister of foreign affairs, Santo Domingo, July 20, 1921, dossier 2, DR 1918–1940.

274. Barré-Ponsignon to minister of foreign affairs, Santo Domingo, August 27, 1921, dossier 2, DR 1918–40.

275. Editorial, "Cambio de timonel," *Listín Diario*, June 29, 1921, in 839.00/2427, DR 1910–1929. See also Kilgore, Santo Domingo, August 31, 1921, folder Santo Domingo—Intell. Summaries (Aug.–Oct. 1921), box 6, GC; Gustavo Julio Henríquez, letter to Cestero, San Pedro de Macorís, June 28, 1921, legajo Cartas de Henríquez y C (Fco y Fed.), Max Henríquez U., E. Henríquez, E. Ap. Henríquez, G. J. Henríquez y A. S. Nolasco, Cestero Archive.

276. De Jesús Lluveres, "MEMORANDUM . . . with regard to POLITICAL SITUATION," September 1921, legajo 418, 1921, IP.

277. Ramsey, Santo Domingo, April 1, 1921, folder D-17 Dominican Rep. Guardia Nacional Intelligence Sum, box 8, O&T.

278. Kilgore, Santo Domingo, June 30, 1921, folder Santo Domingo—Intell. Summaries May–Aug. 1921, box 5, GC.

279. Knowles to Fletcher, New York, July 25, 1921, 839.00/2471, DR 1910–1929.

280. Welles to Fletcher, Washington, August 29, 1921, 839.00/2471, DR 1910–1929.

281. "Reproducción suplicada: Conferencia Nacionalista de Puerto Plata," *Listín Diario*, January 31, 1922 [correct date is 1921]. Those who signed on included Francisco Henríquez y Carjaval; Horacio Vásquez, director of the Partido Nacional; Enrique Jiménes, director of the Partido Unionista; and Luis Felipe Vidal, director of the Partido Legalista; Francisco Henríquez y Carvajal, "De Presidente a Presidente," *Pluma y Espada*, January 19, 1922.

282. My translation. Cestero to Henríquez y Carvajal, Santo Domingo, January 26, 1922, legajo Papeles 1921–1922 Tomo II, Cestero Archive.

283. Kilgore, September 30, 1921, folder D-28 Dominican Rep. Intelligence Summaries, box 8, O&T.

284. Robison to secretary of the navy, Santo Domingo, December 30, 1921, folder 43, 76–100 Secretary of the Navy (Operations), box 44, MGSD.

285. My translation. "Habla el Sr. Fed. Velásquez [sic] H.," *Listín Diario*, May 19, 1922.

286. Henríquez y Carvajal, "Importante Carta del Doctor Fco. Henríquez y Carvajal," *Listín Diario*, February 6, 1922. Also present were Jacinto de Castro and Enrique Jiménes.

287. My translation; emphasis in original. Bordas, "De la Hora: Organización de partidos," *La Información*, November 7, 1921, reproduced in Bordas, *Frente*, 42.

288. Henríquez Ureña, *Epistolario*, *passim* 671–90.

289. Calder, *Impact*, 219.

290. Cited in DeConde, *Latin-American Policy*, 5.

291. Robison to Pellermo Sarda and Brache, Santo Domingo, 2[1?] June 1921, legajo 107, 1917–1922, GM.

292. Welles, *Vineyard*, 847, 852.

293. Cabral et al. to Robison, Santo Domingo, February 23, 1922, 839.00/2497, DR 1910–1929.

294. "Quarterly Report," August 28, 1919, 839.00/2153, and "Quarterly Report," April 22, 1922, 839.00/2528, both in DR 1910–1929; Maguire, Santo Domingo, January 24, 1922, folder Santo Domingo Intell. Summaries (Dec. 19March 21, 1922), box 6, GC.

295. Knight, *Americans*, 102.

296. Hughes to Hoover, New York, January 23, 1930, folder Commission Personnel 1930 January, box 1068, President's Comm.

297. Welles to Hughes, October 11, 1921, 839.00/2452, DR 1910–1929.

298. The 19 percent figure included fees. "Dominicans Want to Handle Finance," *Christian Science Monitor*, January 5, 1922, in 839.00/2468, DR 1910–1929.

299. Hughes to Harding, February 2, 1922, 839.00/2461, DR 1910–1929; Harding to Hughes, February 6, 1922, 839.00/2462, DR 1910–1929.

300. Welles, *Vineyard*, 853.

301. "Quarterly Report," July 15, 1922, 839.00/2577, DR 1910–1929.

302. Calder, *Impact*, 222–3.

303. My translation. Peynado to Cestero, Washington, March 25, 1922, in *Papeles*, ed. Balcacér, 379. See also Hughes to Harding, March 30, 1922, 839.00/2462, DR 1910–1929.

304. Federico Velázquez, "El Sr. Fed. Felazquez [*sic*] H. da cuenta de su misión a Washington," *Listín Diario*, July 26, 1922.

305. Welles to secretary of state, Santo Domingo, August 1, 1922, folder 06 Dominican Republic, 1923–24, Outgoing Telegrams, box 157, Welles Papers.

306. Welles to secretary of state, Santo Domingo, August 29, 1922, 839.00/2590, DR 1910–1929.

307. Rafael Damirón, "También el Maestro," *Listín Diario*, September 4, 1922; Welles to secretary of state, Santo Domingo, August 1, 1922, folder 06 Dominican Republic, 1923–24, Outgoing Telegrams, box 157, Welles Papers; Welles to Hughes, Santo Domingo, October 17, 1922, 839.00/2643, DR 1910–1929.

308. My translation. Lugo, *Plan*, 4. See also Lugo, *Nacionalismo*; *Conferencia*; and Mejía, *Al rededor*.

309. Welles to White, November 23, 1923, folder 04 Dominican Republic, 1923, box 157, Welles Papers.

310. Welles to secretary of state, Santo Domingo, August 7, 1922, folder 06 Dominican Republic, 1923–24, Outgoing Telegrams, box 157, Welles Papers.

311. Welles to White, April 23, 1923, folder 04 Dominican Republic, 1923, box 157, Welles Papers; Welles to secretary of state, Santo Domingo, April 5, 1923, 839.00/2693, DR 1910–1929.

312. Welles to Hughes, December 15, 1923, 839.00/2780, DR 1910–1929.

313. My translation. Federico Velázquez H., "Habla el Sr. FedericoVelázquez [*sic*] H.," *Listín Diario*, December 9, 1922, in Russell to Welles, December 9, 1922, 839.00/2667, DR 1910–1929.

314. Russell to secretary of state, July 12, 1923, 839.00/2725, DR 1910–1929. See also Hughes to U.S. legation, August 3, 1923, 839.00/2726a, DR 1910–1929; and Russell to Hughes, August 12, 1923, 839.00/2730, DR 1910–1929.

315. Russell to Hughes, September 11, 1923, 839.00/2736, DR 1910–1929.

316. Welles to secretary of state, Santo Domingo, April 17, 1923, 839.00/2700, and April 18, 1923, 839.00/2701, both in DR 1910–1929.

317. Dominican historian Ortega Frier accused Welles of engineering the Vásquez-Velázquez alliance in *Memorandum*, 56.

318. Welles to secretary of state, Santo Domingo, April 30, 1923, 839.00/2709, DR 1910–1929.

319. Wilson to Curzon of Kedleston, February 25, 1924, file A1779, reference 9548, FO 371. It is unlikely that Peynado received $100,000 from the sugar magnates since he ran out of funds a month before the election and spent all his own money, bringing him to the edge of resigning: Welles to White, February 19, 1924, folder 04 Dominican Republic, 1923, box 157, Welles Papers. Months before the election, a Peynado aide came to Welles begging for money since the sugar corporations were giving the new *alliance* their contributions. Welles immediately "terminated" the interview: Welles, diary entry, September 22, 1923, folder 04 Dominican Republic, 1923, box 157, Welles Papers.

320. My translation; italics in English in the original. Américo Lugo, "La política de cooperación solo es favorable al Yanqui," *La Información* (Santiago), March 12, 1924, in Welles to secretary of state, April 9, 1924, 839.00/2829, DR 1910–1929.

321. Final election results are in Welles to secretary of state, April 2, 1924, 839.00/2827; Russell to Hughes, September 7, 1923, 839.00/2737, both in DR 1910–1929.

322. Barré-Ponsignon to minister of foreign affairs, Santo Domingo, October 4, 1924, dossier 5, DR 1918–1940.

323. Munro, *United States*, 60.

324. Cited in entry of December 21, 1924; see also entry of December 23, both in folder Diary, 1924–1933, box 2, correspondence and papers—additions, 1920–1941, 83/153, Chapman Papers.

325. Cited in Velten to minister of foreign affairs, Port-au-Prince, July 12, 1924, dossier 5, Haiti 1918–1940.

326. Moses to the military governor, December 31, 1921, legajo 433, 1921, IP.

327. Vance to Wilson, October 25, 1920, 839.00/2353, DR 1910–1929.

Chapter 12

1. Beaulac, *Career,* 108.

2. Wise, *A Marine,* 332.

3. Manager of All America Cables to Sanders, Washington, April 12, 1927, case file 162, reel 87, series 1, Coolidge Papers.

4. Tulchin, *Aftermath,* 206–33.

5. Fejes, *Imperialism,* 18–24.

6. Thomas H. Healy, "New Era Thought Begun in Interamerican Affairs," *Sunday Star,* August 10, 1930, folder General Subjects Latin American Republics 1929, box 1018, Foreign Affairs, PP.

7. Haring, *South America,* 15.

8. Fejes, *Imperialism,* 25; Schwoch, *Radio,* 21–3.

9. Haring, *South America,* 15.

10. Espinosa, *Beginnings,* 59; "Plane and Ship Lines United to Link Americas," *Christian Science Monitor,* May 7, 1929, 20.

11. My translation. Román, *Maldito país,* 17.

12. Howard to Chamberlain, December 31, 1926, file A153, reference 11969, FO 371.

13. Cited in White, *Will Rogers,* 101.

14. Schroeder, "Bandits," 67–86.

15. Graham A. Cosmas, "*Cacos* and *Caudillos:* Marines and Counterinsurgency in Hispaniola, 1915–1924," in *New Interpretations,* ed. Roberts and Sweetman, 296.

16. Baylen, "Sandino," 407.

17. Historians also pursued the debate: Baylen, "Sandino," 394–419.

18. Cited in Miller, oral history, 29.

19. Batson, *Paradise,* 18.

20. Lieutenant T. J. Kilcourse, diary entry, December 31, 1927, cited in Schroeder, "'To Defend,'" 376.

21. Cited in Cummins, *Quijote,* 116.

22. De la Selva, "Sandino," 64.

23. Cited in "Nicaragua's Bloody "Peace," *Literary Digest,* January 14, 1928, 8. See also "Sandino, of Nicaragua: Bandit or Patriot?" *Literary Digest,* February 4, 1928, 42–50.

24. Delpar, *Vogue,* 30; Hart, *Empire,* 367.

25. My translation. Beals, *Banana,* 106.

26. Williams, *Radical Journalists,* 84; Rosenberg, *Missionaries,* 142. A document contains evidence of Beals accepting money from the Mexican government: Eberhardt to Kellogg, Managua, February 2, 1928, 817.00/5366, Nicaragua 1910–1929. Another said he received support from his brother Sócrates from Brooklyn, which probably would come from the Communist Party: Schmidt, Managua, February 12, 1928, folder 2d Brigade B-2 Intelligence Reports (1Feb1927–1926Feb1928), box 6, Nicaragua 1927–1932.

27. Beals, *Banana,* 115.

28. Beals, "With Sandino," 340–1.

29. Carleton Beals, "Carta de Carleton Beals para Froylán Turcios," Mexico City, May 10, 1928, in *Ariel,* June 15, 1928, 1260.

30. The article he referred to was Beals, "With Sandino," 204–5.

31. "Testimony of the Major General Commandant before the Senate Committee of Foreign Relations," February 18, 1928, folder Nicaragua—U.S. Senate Inquiry, box 30, O&T, 64–5.

32. Beals, *Banana,* 116.

33. Cited in Baylen, "Sandino," 406.

34. "Can We Get Out of Nicaragua?" *The Nation,* 126: 3268, February 22, 1928, 201.

35. Cited in "Nicaragua's Bloody 'Peace,'" *Literary Digest,* January 14, 1928, 8.

36. Cited in Sheesley, *Streets,* xvii.

37. Cited in Beals, "With Sandino," 204.

38. Denny, *Dollars*, 6.
39. For a broader discussion of this dynamic, see Alan McPherson, "Americanism against American Empire," in *Americanism*, ed. Kazin and McCartin, 169–91.
40. Cited in "Nicaragua's Bloody "Peace," *Literary Digest*, January 14, 1928, 8.
41. Cited in Cummins, *Quijote*, 38.
42. Editorial, "Why?" *Boston Daily Globe*, January 10, 1927, reproduced in Cong. Rec., 69th Cong., 2nd Sess., vol. 68, part 2 (Washington: USGPO, 1927).
43. Kerr to Chamberlain, Guatemala City, January 5, 1927, file A328, reference 11969, FO 371.
44. Mallet to Chamberlain, Buenos Aires, January 14, 1927, file A880, reference 11969, Scott to Chamberlain, Montevideo, March 15, 1927, file A2127, reference 11970, and Harrington to Kerr, San Salvador, January 17, 1927, file A743, reference 11969, all in FO 371; Davis to Kellogg, San José, February 8, 1928, 817.00/5414, and Frost to Kellogg, Santo Domingo, July 22, 1927, 817.00/4967, both in Nicaragua 1910–1929. Amador, *Derrota militar*, 59, listed the most sympathetic Latin American and European publications: *Ariel*, Honduras, director Don Froylán Turcios; *Repertorio Americano*, Costa Rica, Joaquín García Monge; *Amauta*, Peru, José Carlos Mariátegui; *Eurindia*, Mexico, Horacio Espinoza Altamirano; *El Machete* and El *Libertador*, Mexico, Julio Antonio Mella, Diego Rivera, and David Alfaro Siqueiros; *Libertad and Avance*, Cuba; *Claridad* and La *Vanguard*, Buenos Aires, Argentina; *Zig Zag*, Chile; *Le Monde*, Paris; and *Cenit*, Madrid.
45. Collier to Kellogg, Santiago de Chile, January 13, 1928, 817.00/5267, Nicaragua 1910–1929.
46. "The Great Demonstration of Students and Workmen which Took Place Yesterday," *Diario Latino*, January 14, 1927, file A743, reference 11969, FO 371.
47. Ghiraldo, *Yanquilandia*; Soto Hall, *Sombra*.
48. Manuel Antonio Valle, "Viva Sandino," *The Living Age*, translated from *Nosotros* (Buenos Aires), 243 (November 1932): 243, 244, 245, 248.
49. Cited in "Disputes Moncada on Our Occupation," *NYT*, December 19, 1929, 8.
50. "The Great Demonstration of Students and Workmen which Took Place Yesterday," *Diario Latino*, January 14, 1927, file A743, reference 11969, FO 371.
51. Caffery to secretary of state, San Salvador, May 31, 1928, 817.00/5750, Nicaragua 1910–1929.
52. My translation. Allessandri to Borah, Santiago de Chile, January 17, 1927, folder Nicaragua 1926–1927 (1), box 234, Borah Papers.
53. Beals, "With Sandino," 204–5.
54. Caffery to Kellogg, San Salvador, May 4, 1928, 817.00/5617, Nicaragua 1910–1929.
55. Vasconcelos failed to show; Haya did make it to Nicaragua the following year but got no farther than the port of Corinto: Bendaña, *Mística*, 83.
56. Kellogg to U.S. embassy in Buenos Aires, Washington, December 31, 1927, 817.00/5208, Nicaragua 1910–1929. See also Kellogg to U.S. embassy in Buenos Aires, Washington, December 29, 1927, 817.00/5207a; Kellogg to U.S. embassy in Buenos Aires, Washington, December 23, 1927, 817.00/5207a; and Collier to Kellogg, Santiago de Chile, January 12, 1928, 817.00/5249, all in Nicaragua 1910–1929.
57. Bliss to Kellogg, Buenos Aires, January 11, 1928, 817.00/5352, Nicaragua 1910–1929.
58. *La Acción*, January 31, 1928, reproduced in White to McFadden, Washington, June 4, 1928, 817.00/5723; Dr. Anastasi cited in Bliss to Kellogg, Buenos Aires, March 17, 1928, 817.00/5555; and Mallen to State Department, New York, May 15, 1928, 817.00/5722, all in Nicaragua 1910–1929.
59. "World," 88–9.
60. "Contre l'intervention américaine à Haïti," *Gazette Rouge de Léningrad*, December 13, 1929, dossier 13, Haiti 1918–1940.
61. Haring, "South America," 146–52.
62. Haring, "Two Americas," 376; Diffie, "Hispanidad," 457–8.
63. Winkler-Morey, "Good Neighbors," 7, 14–5.
64. Beman, ed., *Intervention*, v.
65. Munro, *Intervention*, 112.
66. Knight, *Americans*, ix; Delpar, *Looking South*, 104. The other books were Jenks, *Cuban Colony*; Marsh, *Bolivia*; Rippy, *Colombia*; and Diffie and Diffie, *Porto Rico*. See also Kepner and Soothill, *Banana Empire*.

67. Nearing and Freeman, *Dollar Diplomacy*, see Chapter 5 especially; Rosenberg, *Missionaries*, 144–5.
68. Park, *Underdevelopment*, 4.
69. Munro, *Intervention*, 531, 533.
70. Haring, *South America*. Similar books were Beman, ed., *Intervention*; Hopkins and Alexander, *Machine-Gun*. See also Delpar, *Looking South*, 103–4.
71. Rosenberg, *Missionaries*, 145, 146; Beman, ed., *Intervention*.
72. Espinosa, *Beginnings*, 51, 59.
73. Gulick et al. to president of the United States, April 26, 1922, 838.00/1868, Haiti 1910–1929.
74. British Library of Information, February 20, 1926, file A1172, reference 11141, FO 371.
75. Balch to Coolidge, April 1, 1926, 838.00/2212, Haiti 1910–1929; Balch to Forbes, February 14, 1930, folder Commission Correspondence, 1930 February, box 1068, President's Comm.; Johnson, *Peace Progressives*, 217; Winkler-Morey, "Good Neighbors," 187; Rosenberg, *Missionaries*, 130; Balch, ed., *Occupied Haiti*; Wilbur, letter to Clark, April 30, 1926, 838.00/2243, Haiti 1910–1929.
76. Dewey et al. to Hoover, February 26, 1930, 817.00/6551, Nicaragua 1930–1944.
77. Libby to Kellogg, Washington, January 3, 1928, 817.00/5219, Nicaragua 1910–1929.
78. Cited in Howlett, "Neighborly Concern," 44.
79. Howlett, "Neighborly Concern," 20–4.
80. Howlett, "Neighborly Concern," 24–5.
81. Beals, "With Sandino," 288.
82. Munro to Kellogg, Managua, December 31, 1927, 817.00/5270, and December 30, 1927, 817.00/5193, both in Nicaragua 1910–1929.
83. Munro to Kellogg, Managua, December 31, 1927, 817.00/5270, Nicaragua 1910–1929.
84. Cited in Howlett, "Neighborly Concern," 34.
85. Cited in Howlett, "Neighborly Concern," 38.
86. Cooper to Borah, Everett, Washington, April 21, 1928, folder Nicaragua 1927–1928 (2), box 257, Borah Papers.
87. Reynolds to Hoover, Ventura, California, January 14, 1931, folder Countries—Nicaragua Correspondence, 1930–1933, box 992, Foreign Affairs, PP.
88. Munro, *United States*, 13.
89. Johnson's overview of this group and their historiography is in *Peace Progressives*, 3–8.
90. "Nicaragua and After," 70.
91. Johnson, *Peace Progressives*, 115–16.
92. Cummins, *Quijote*, 114.
93. Johnson, *Peace Progressives*, 132.
94. Borah to Story [*sic*], Washington, April 13, 1922, folder 1921–1921 Haiti and Caribbean Situation, box 113, Borah Papers.
95. Senator Burton K. Wheeler, "Why Are We in Nicaragua?" *Plain Talk* (May 1928), reproduced in Cong. Rec., 70th Cong., 1st Sess., vol. 69, part 6 (Washington: USGPO, 1928): 6521–4.
96. Cong. Rec., 67th Cong., 2nd Sess., vol. 62, part 4. (Washington: USGPO, 1922), 3467; Delgadillo, "Destiny and Democracy," 145. Hughes explained to senators that a high commissioner did not enjoy the same status as an ambassador extraordinary and therefore did not need senatorial confirmation: Nelson to Storey, New York, April 17, 1922, folder Corres. Haiti-Santo Domingo Mar-Apr 1922, box 4, Subject File, Storey Papers.
97. Johnson, *Peace Progressives*, 130.
98. "Borah Sees Haiti Prey of Our Greed," *NYT*, May 2, 1922.
99. The term is from Johnson, *Peace Progressives*.
100. For example, Hudicourt to Borah, Port-au-Prince, March 31, 1922, folder 1921–1921 Haiti and Caribbean Situation, box 113, Borah Papers; Cong. Rec., 67th Cong., 2nd Sess., vol. 62, part 7. (Washington: USGPO, 1922), 7222–4.
101. "Retour de Me Pierre Hudicourt; Une conversations avec lui," *Le Nouvelliste*, January 13, 1925, 1; White, Washington, May 22, 1925, 838.00/2124, Haiti 1910–1929.
102. Cumberland to Gross, Port-au-Prince, March 29, 1927, 838.00/2309, Haiti 1910–1929.
103. Bingham, *Obsolete Shibboleth*.
104. "Favors Investigation of Our Haitian Policy," *NYT*, February 3, 1921, 11.

105. Cong. Rec., 67th Cong., 2nd Sess., vol. 62, part 2. (Washington: USGPO, 1922), 1385.
106. "Would Evacuate Haiti," *NYT*, March 11, 1922, 8.
107. Salles to minister of foreign affairs, Port-au-Prince, March 30, 1927, dossier 6, Haiti 1918–1940; Corvington, 1922–1934, 306.
108. Blair to Welles, February 17, 1922, folder Haiti 1920–1922, box 178, Welles Papers.
109. Rosenberg, *Missionaries*, 139, 141.
110. Cited in Johnson, *Peace Progressives*, 129.
111. Tierney, "United States," 214, 218.
112. Peavey to Kellogg, Washburn, Wisconsin, July 19, 1927, 817.00/4939, Nicaragua 1910–1929.
113. Johnson, *Peace Progressives*, 2, 135–40.
114. Borah, "Adverse Report," March 6, 1928, file A2199, reference 12746, FO 371.
115. See correspondence between McCormick and Coolidge/Hughes, June 30, 1923, 838.00/1950, July 16, 1923, 838.00/1950, January 13, 1924, 838.00/1997, January 19, 1924, 838.00/1998, February 6, 1924, 838.00/2000, February 9, 1924, 838.00/2004, and February 21, 1924, 838.00/2004, Haiti 1910–1929; and correspondence between Shipstead and Coolidge/Kellogg, April 27, 1927 and August 24, 1927, 838.00/2313, Haiti 1910–1929.
116. Morgan, Washington, May 21, 1928, 817.00/5676, Nicaragua 1910–1929.
117. "War," 311.
118. Kellogg to U.S. legation in Managua, Washington, March 3, 1928, 817.00/5444a, Nicaragua 1910–1929.
119. US investments increased from $1.65 billion to $5.43 billion, Gellman, *Good Neighbor*, 6–7; Pearce, *Under*, 17. Exports increased from $348 million in 1913 to $986 million in 1929, Ferrell, *Presidency*, 122.
120. Tulchin, *Aftermath*, 74.
121. Oliver McKee, Jr., "Our Latin–American Trade Again Comes into Focus," *NYT*, November 25, 1928.
122. Munro, *United States*, 12.
123. "Dennis Will Join Banking Concern," *Washington Star*, June 5, 1927.
124. Schulzinger, "Diplomatic Mind," 3–16, 218.
125. Munro, *United States*, 15.
126. Gellman, *Good Neighbor*, 4; Macaulay, *Affair*, 142.
127. Juarez, "Withdrawal," 168; Gruening, *Many Battles*, 160.
128. Cooper, "Withdrawal," 86.
129. My translation. Pedro Henríquez Ureña, "El hermano definidor," *El Independiente*, January 8, 1924, in Welles to secretary of state, January 19, 839.00/2794, DR 1910–1929.
130. Sandino to the *New York World*, ca. January 16, 1928, in *Sandino*, comp. Ramírez, trans. Conrad, 157.
131. My translation. José Vasconcelos, "Disparos Reveladores," *El Universal*, January 16, 1928.
132. Cited in Traphagen, "Diplomacy," 309.
133. Ellis, *Kellogg*, 99.
134. White to Davis, March 2, 1928, folder Davis, Roy T. 1927–1930, box 4, White Papers; Ferrell, *Presidency*, 139.
135. My translation. Amador, *Derrota militar*, 45.
136. Cummins, *Quijote*, 30.
137. Cited in Raymond Leslie Buell, "Our Changing Policy toward Latin America," *NYT*, March 16, 1930, XX3; Grandin, *Workshop*, 32.
138. Historians disagree on the reception given his speech in Havana: Ferrell, *Presidency*, 141; Grandin, *Workshop*, 32.
139. Hughes cited in Cooper, "Withdrawal," 86.
140. Salisbury, *Anti-Imperialism*, 121.
141. My translation. Arguello Bolaños to Arguello, Havana, February 19, 1928, folder Munro, Dana G. 1928, box 8, White Papers.
142. White to Davis, March 2, 1928, folder Davis, Roy T. 1927–1930, box 4, White Papers.
143. Ferrell, "Repudiation," 669.
144. Raymond Leslie Buell, "Our Changing Policy toward Latin America," *NYT*, March 16, 1930, XX3.

145. Cited in Cummins, *Quijote*, 41.
146. Hoover, *Memoirs*, 210.
147. DeConde, *Latin-American Policy*, 6.
148. Roosevelt, "Democratic View," 583, 584.
149. Cummins, *Quijote*, 130.
150. The trip stopped in Honduras, El Salvador, Nicaragua, Costa Rica, Ecuador, Peru, Chile, Argentina, Uruguay, and Brazil.
151. Amador, *Gustavo Machado*, 40.
152. My translation. "'Este país me da la impresión de ser la gran canasta de pan del mundo,'" *Crítica*, December 13, 1928.
153. "Plot Against Mr. Hoover?" *Buenos Aires Herald*, December 12, 1928, 1; "La policia prosigue la tarea a fin de conocer todos los datos del atentado que se preparaba," *La Nación* (Buenos Aires), December 13, 1928.
154. George Manning, "Charge Press Censorship on Hoover Good–Will Trip to South," *The Editor and Publisher and the Fourth Estate*, January 12, 1928, reproduced in Cong. Rec., 1929, 2109–10, folder Latin American Trip: Censorship, box 168, CTP.
155. Baker, "Mission of Tour," undated, folder Latin American Trip: Purpose of Trip, box 170, CTP.
156. Press meeting called by Hoover in his stateroom, aboard the USS *Maryland*, November 20, 1928, folder Latin American Trip: Press, box 170, CTP.
157. "Extracts for [from?] speeches made by President-elect Hoover on his 1928 trip to South America, emphasizing his Policy of 'Good Neighbor,'" folder Latin American Trip: Purpose of Trip, box 170, CTP.
158. Interviewed by *La Nación*, reproduced in "The Hoover Idea on Argentina," *The Review of the River Plate*, December 21, 1928, 13–9.
159. Cited in Black, *Good Neighbor*, 54.
160. For examples, see "Hoover to See"; Simonds, "South Americanus," 67–71; Edwin S. McIntosh, "Hoover's Latin–American Tour Appraised as to Its Net Results," *NYHT*, January 13, 1929; *La Argentina Económica* (Buenos Aires), November 15, 1928; Editorial, "Mr. Hoover," *El Imparcial*, December 10, 1928, 4; "'Ninguna nación tiene derecho a ejercer función tutelares ni de policía sobre otra,' declara Hoover," *La Nación*, December 17, 1928, 7; Editorial, "Our Distinguished Visitor," *Buenos Aires Herald*, December 13, 1928, 6.
161. Munro, "Withdrawal," 5.
162. Bellegarde, *L'occupation*.
163. Cited in Millett, *Searching*, 66.

Chapter 13

1. English translation of Irias et al. to Langhorne, September 1, 1912, 817.00/1991, Nicaragua 1910–1929.
2. White to secretary of state, Tegucigalpa, November 5, 1912, 817.00/2139, Nicaragua 1910–1929.
3. Salisbury, *Anti-Imperialism*, 11.
4. See, for example, López, *Conquest*, n.p.
5. Haggard to Grey, Guatemala City, February 14, 1913, file A11091, reference 1583, FO 371.
6. Nalty, *Marines*, 10.
7. Powell, "Relations," 57–60.
8. "Nicaraguan Crisis May Call for Force," *NYT*, September 17, 1916, sec. 1, p. 8; Salisbury, *Anti-Imperialism*, 14–7.
9. Cong. Rec., 62nd Cong., 3rd Sess., vol. 49, part 3. (Washington: USGPO, 1913), 2683.
10. "'Moral Mandate,'" 506. See also Turner, "Nicaragua," 646–8; "Brown Bros.," 667
11. Foner, *Labor*, 93.
12. Cited in "Keeping," 286.
13. Taylor to secretary of the navy, Managua, January 27, 1922, roll 30, OCNO/OSN.
14. Musicant, *Banana Wars*, 286.

15. Marston, Managua, January 31, 1924, folder Nicaragua Intell. Summaries (1921–1925), box 7, GC.

16. Hughes to Thurston, Washington, October 8, 1923, roll 30, OCNO/OSN.

17. Munro, *United States*, 185–6.

18. Keyser, Managua, January 31, 1925, folder Nicaragua Intell. Summaries (1921–25), box 7, GC.

19. Musicant, *Banana Wars*, 288. See also Kamman, *Search*, 28–34.

20. Musicant, *Banana Wars*, 288.

21. Unnamed advocate cited in Denny, *Dollars*, 337.

22. Beaulac, *Career*, 114.

23. Hodges, *Sandino's Communism*, 3, 14, 7, 13.

24. My translation. Veles, oral history.

25. Cited in Hodges, *Sandino's Communism*, 42.

26. Selser, "Antimperialismo," 12. "Continentalist" intellectuals included Manuel Ugarte, Vicente Sáenz, José Ingenieros, Isidro Fabela, Manuel Sanguily, and Alfredo L. Palacios.

27. Sandino to Turcios, El Chipotón, June 10, 1928, *Sandino*, comp. Ramírez, trans. Conrad, 202, 203.

28. Navarro-Génie, *Augusto*, 56.

29. My translation. Sandino cited in Román, *Maldito país*, 23.

30. Santos López in Instituto, *Ahora*, 190–2.

31. Trelawney-Ansell, *Nine Lives*. Trelawney himself was British, and Sandino had him train a "batch of men coming from New Orleans—mostly Americans," 198.

32. Amador, *Derrota militar*, 61.

33. The city of Santo Domingo and the Partido Nacionalista gave him 1,000 pesos each; lawyer Enrique Henríquez gave 200 pesos; and San Pedro and La Romana gave 100 pesos each. Gilbert, *Junto*, 16; Young to secretary of state, Santo Domingo, December 14, 1928, 817.00/6156, Nicaragua 1910–1929.

34. My translation. Gilbert, *Junto*, passim 17–43, 269–73. Sandino, pronouncement, El Chipotón, November 5, 1928, and Sandino, credential, El Chipotón, February 13, 1930, both in E-001, C-002, 000070, ACS.

35. Sandino to Turcios, El Chipote, September 8 and 20, and December 29, 1927, all in E-001, C-002, 000080, ACS.

36. For example, see *Revista Ariel*, June 15, 1928.

37. Navarro-Génie, *Augusto*, 52.

38. Turcios to Sandino, El Chipote, October 11, 1927, E-001, C-002, 000429, ACS. See also Max Jordan, "The Sandino Legend," *Berliner Tageblatt*, December 22, 1929, translation, in Schurman to secretary of state, Berlin, January 10, 1929, 817.00/6191, Nicaragua 1910–1929.

39. Beals, "With Sandino," 205.

40. Eberhardt to secretary of state Kellogg, Managua, July 31, 1928, 817.00/5929, Nicaragua 1910–1929.

41. Max Jordan, "The Sandino Legend," *Berliner Tageblatt*, December 22, 1929.

42. McPherson, *Yankee No!*, 13.

43. Navy Department to Morgan, Washington, September 27, 1928, 817.00/6006, Nicaragua 1910–1929.

44. Navarro-Génie, *Augusto*, 52.

45. Amador, *Gustavo Machado*, 53.

46. Eberhardt to Kellogg, Managua, February 11, 1928, 817.00/5393, Nicaragua 1910–1929; Cruse to War Department, May 14, 1928, 817.00/5744, Nicaragua 1910–1929; Buchenau, *Shadow*, 178.

47. The chief of staff was General José Alvarez and the consul general was Arturo M. Elias: Halpin to assistant chief of staff, War Department, Ft. Sam Houston, Texas, February 16, 1928, 817.00/5456, Nicaragua 1910–1929. See also Reagan, October 13, 1929, folder 5thRgt—R-2 Int. Rpts.-21Mar-17Dec29, box 20, Nicaragua 1927–1933.

48. Morrow to Kellogg, Mexico City, April 11, 1928, 817.00/5568, Nicaragua 1910–1929.

49. Chargé d'affaires to the secretary and undersecretary of state, San Salvador, November 1, 1928, folder State Dept. Agents, box 1, Corr. 1927–1932.

50. Cruse, unaddressed, June 18, 1928, 817.00/5858, Nicaragua 1910–1929. For proof that Turcios sent medical supplies, see Turcios to All-American Anti-Imperialist League, Tegucigalpa, April 7, 1928, 817.00/5722, Nicaragua 1910–1929.
51. My translation. Portes Gil cited in Portes Gil, "Sandino," 13. See also Buchenau, *Shadow*, 179, 178.
52. Thompson, intelligence report, Mexico City, March 23, 1928, 817.00/5562, Nicaragua 1910–1929.
53. Cruse, unaddressed, June 18, 1928, 817.00/5858, Nicaragua 1910–1929.
54. Thompson, intelligence report, Mexico City, March 23, 1928, folder Nicaragua—Sandino, Mexican aid to, box 30, O&T; Cruse, intelligence report, Tegucigalpa, July 18, 1928, folder Misc. 1928, box 1, Corr. 1927–1932; Cerdas, *APRA*, 70.
55. The founding groups of MAFUENIC and some of their foreign leaders were the International League against Imperialism and for National Independence and its Mexican representative, Venezuelan lawyer Gustavo Machado; the International Workers Aid Association; the Anti-Imperialistic League of the Americas; UCSAYA; the International League in Behalf of Persecuted Strugglers; the Anti-Clerical Federation of Mexico; the International Workers for Knowledge; the Haitian Patriotic Union, represented by J. Jolibois Fils; the United R. R. Association; the Countryside National League; and the Miners' Federation of Jalisco. See Thompson, report, Mexico City, March 23, 1928, folder Nicaragua—Sandino, Mexican aid to, box 30, O&T.
56. Amador, *Derrota militar*, 60.
57. My translation. Cited in Amador, *Gustavo Machado*, 43.
58. Flyer, Sandino, to fifteen Latin American republics, distributed in Veracruz, November 1928, serie cartas abiertas, sub-sección correspondencia, sección fondo personal, box 1, CS; Sandino postcards by MAFUENIC, E-001, C-005, 000262, ACS.
59. My translation. Machado cited in Comisión, *Machado*, 4, 8.
60. "Horrorosa 'Carnicera,'" *El Día*, January 2, 1929, 817.00/6175, Nicaragua 1910–1929.
61. Amador, *Gustavo Machado*, 49.
62. Reagan, Ocotal, December 2, 1928, folder 11th Regiment R-2 Reports (May 1927–July 1929), box 26, Nicaragua 1927–1932; Feland to major general commandant, Managua, February 12, 1929, folder Nicaragua—Bandits, Activities of, box 18, O&T.
63. Román, *Maldito país*, 11, 18.
64. My translation. "La Liga Anti-Imperialista puso a la venta sellos para defender a Sandino," *La Prensa*, January 31, 1928, E-001, C-007, 000375, ACS.
65. White to Schoenfeld, Mexico City, June 6, 1928, folder Schoenfeld, H. F. Arthur 1928–31, box 10, White Papers.
66. "Motín sandinista en Brooklyn," *La Opinión*, January 15, 1928, E-001, C-007, 000372, ACS.
67. Office of the Solicitor to "LA," [29?] March 1928, 817.00/5542, Nicaragua 1910–1929.
68. New to Kellogg, Washington, April 16, 1928, 817.00/5591, Nicaragua 1910–1929.
69. Cummins, *Quijote*, 127; Grossman, "'Hermanos,'" 398.
70. Thatcher, finding, May 16, 1928, 817.00/5669, Nicaragua 1910–1929.
71. Arrieta, ¡*Habla Sandino!*, 23.
72. Sócrates Sandino to Gregorio Sandino, New York, June 21, 1926, E-001, C-001, 000019; Sócrates Sandino to América Tiffer, New York, April 15, 1927 and November 18, 1926 (my translation), E-001, C-001, 000020, all in ACS.
73. Sócrates Sandino to Gregorio Sandino, Brooklyn, May 18, 1927, E-001, C-001, 000417, ACS.
74. My translation. Sócrates Sandino to Gregorio Sandino, Brooklyn, July 30, 1927, E-001, C-001, 000417, ACS.
75. "Sandino," *Literary Digest*, February 4, 1928, 46. See also "Un hermano del General Sandino hará importantes revelaciones el domingo," *La Prensa*, January 14, 1928, E-001, C-007, 000375, ACS.
76. Arrieta, ¡*Habla Sandino!*, 23.
77. Larsen, Managua, April 30, 1928, folder 5th Regiment R-2 (Intelligence) Reports (June 1927–Oct 1928), box 15, Nicaragua 1927–1932.

78. "Socrates Sandino, Brother of the Nicaraguan Leader, Disembarked Yesterday in the Port of Veracruz and Left for Mexico," *Excelsior*, June 29, 1928, translation, 817.00/5800, Nicaragua 1910–1929; "'Mi hermano irá con gusto a la muerte por salvar el nombre de Nicaragua,'" *La Prensa*, January 23, 1928, E-001, C-007, 000375, ACS.

79. Sócrates Sandino to América Tiffer, Mérida, January 15, 1930, E-001, C-001, 000021, ACS.

80. Cruse, intelligence report, San José, October 23, 1930, 817.00/6855, Nicaragua 1930–1944; Hanna to McDougal, November 11, 1930, folder Correspondence, American Minister to Nicaragua (Conf.), box 21, O&T.

81. O'Leary to jefe director, Corinto, November 13, 1930, folder Sandino, Socrates, box 10, Corr. 1929–1931.

82. Argos, letter, San Salvador, January 16, 1931, folder Sandino, Socrates, box 10, Corr. 1929–1931.

83. Cerda to Hunt, Danlí, August 14, 1931, folder Tijerino, Toribio, box 11, Corr. 1929–1931.

84. My translations. Veles, oral history.

85. For instance Sandino to Portes Gil and Hoover, El Chipotón, March 20, 1929, E-001, C-003, 000161; and Sandino, drawing, El Chipotón, March 28, 1929, E-001, C-004, 000208, both in ACS. See also Campos Ponce, *Los yanquis*, 104.

86. *La Crítica* cited in White to secretary of state, Buenos Aires, April 12, 1929, 817.00/6304, Nicaragua 1910–1929.

87. Amador, *Derrota militar*, 73, 75.

88. Cohen, G-2 Report, May 22, 1928, folder Misc. 1928, box 1, Corr. 1927–1932; Salisbury, *Anti-Imperialism*, 100–2.

89. Cerdas, *APRA*, n. p., 77.

90. Cerdas, *APRA*, 70; Frazier, "Dawn," 440. Amador, *Derrota militar*, 60; Comisión, *Machado*, 6.

91. My translation. Bukharin cited in Amador, *Derrota militar*, 63. See also Comintern message to Sandino and Nicaraguan workers, n. d., E-001, C-004, 000212, ACS.

92. Amador, *Derrota militar*, 70. To this day no one has debunked the flag. Even Grandin believed its provenance, in *Workshop*, 32.

93. Amador, *Exilio*, 26; Amador, *Derrota militar*, 70.

94. Román, *Maldito país*, 19.

95. Langley, *Banana Wars*, 188.

96. My translation. Sandino to Guadalupe Rivera, El Chipotón, January 7, 1929, E-001, C-002, 000058, ACS.

97. Binder, "Front," 90. See also Munro, "Establishment," 704.

98. Dodd, "Nicaraguan Politics," 173.

99. Sandino, letter, August 28, 1928, folder 5thRgt—R-2 Int. Rpts.-19Aug-28 Oct28, box 20, Nicaragua 1927–1933; Cummins, *Quijote*, 34; "American Electoral Mission in Nicaragua," in London to Willert, January 10, 1929, file A224, reference 13470, FO 371; Joes, *Guerrilla Warfare*, 135–6.

100. Cruse, "Sandino Situation," August 13, 1928, folder Nicaragua (1927–1928), box 2, GC; Mairena Hernández to Miralda, El Chipotón, August 22, 1928, folder Nicaragua (1927–1928), box 2, GC; Gilbert, *Junto*, 29.

101. Eberhardt to Kellogg, Managua, July 31, 1928, 817.00/5929, Nicaragua 1910–1929; U.S. chargé d'affaires to the secretary and undersecretary of state, San Salvador, November 1, 1928, folder State Dept. Agents, box 1, Corr. 1927–1932.

102. Román, *Maldito país*, 132. More Sandino invective against Turcios is in Sandino to unknown recipient, Mérida, October 16, 1929, E-001, C-002, 000429, ACS.

103. Aymé-Martin to minister of foreign affairs, Guatemala, February 22, 1929, dossier 71, Cent. Am. 1918–1940.

104. Cited in "La política americana de Sandino," *El Diario de Yucatán*, July 2, 1929, in Villanueva, *Yucatán*, 33.

105. Sandino to Mairena Hernández, El Chipote, January 7, 1929, E-001, C-002, 000081, ACS; Sandino, interview with *El Dictamen*, October 1929, in *Sandino*, comp. Ramírez, trans. Conrad, 276; de Lambert to secretary of state, San Salvador, February 4, 1929, 817.00/6209, Nicaragua 1910–1929; Turcios to Sandino, in Wünderich, *Biografía*, 169.

106. Portes Gil, "Sandino," 14.

107. Macaulay, *Affair*, 149. A detailed itinerary is in unsigned, intelligence report, Ocotal, June 30, 1929, folder 11th Regiment R-2 Reports (May 1927–July 1929), box 26, Nicaragua 1927–1932.

108. Buchenau, *Shadow*, 180.

109. Sandino, interview with *El Dictamen*, October 1929, *Sandino*, comp. Ramírez, trans. Conrad, 276–7.

110. My translation. Sandino to Laborde, Mérida, January 1930, E-001, C-003, 000142, ACS.

111. Cruse, intelligence report, San José, April 12, 1929, 817.00/6305, Nicaragua 1910–1929.

112. Hanna to White, Managua, September 24, 1929, folder Hanna, Matthew E. 1927–1929, box 5, White Papers.

113. Treatments of Sandino's year in Mexico include Román, *Maldito país*, 110–3; Bendaña, *Mística*, 79–81; Campos Ponce, *Los yanquis*, 13–6; Arguello Bolanos, "Vende Patria," 24–35; Brooks, "Rebellion," 248; Frazier, "Dawn," 436; and especially Villanueva, *Yucatán*.

114. Zimmermann, *Sandinista*, 159; Spenser, *Impossible Triangle*, 152–3; Poppino, *International Communism*, 153; Herman, *Comintern*, 17.

115. Navarro-Génie, *Augusto*, 63.

116. Amador, *Derrota militar*, 96.

117. Acosta to Portes Gil, Veracruz, July 1, 1929, serie expedientes, sub-sección girada Sandino por Mexico, sección EDSN, box 2, CS.

118. [Arriagal?] to Portes Gil, Mérida, August 1, 1929, serie expedientes, sub-sección girada Sandino por Mexico, sección EDSN, box 2, CS. Navarro-Génie claimed that 2,000 pesos arrived every month, in *Augusto*, 63, but Sandino himself in January 1930 complained of a months-long wait for such a one-time amount: Sandino to Zepeda, Mérida, January 25, 1930, E-001, C-002, 000083, ACS.

119. For instance, Sandino, "Observando," *Diario de Yucatán*, July 21, 1929, reproduced in Villanueva, *Yucatán*, 73–4.

120. Villanueva, *Yucatán*, 306; Navarro-Génie, *Augusto*, 87.

121. "El drama," 17–26. In E-001, C-008, 000411, ACS, 21.

122. Villanueva, *Yucatán*, 20–1; Navarro-Génie, *Augusto*, 63–4.

123. Román, *Maldito país*, 111.

124. Navarro-Génie, *Augusto*, 69; García Salgado, *Yo estuve*, 82. Others claimed Sandino received no weapons at all: Campos Ponce, *Los yanquis*, 116–7.

125. My translation. Sandino to Zepeda, Mérida, March 4, 1930, E-001, C-002, 000083, ACS.

126. "Investigate Story Sandino Took Bribe," *NYT*, December 26, 1929, 12; Hodges, *Foundations*, 101.

127. Navarro-Génie, *Augusto*, 68.

128. Bendaña, *Mística*, 80.

129. Sandino to Sócrates Sandino, Mérida, September 24, 1929, GS; Navarro-Génie, *Augusto*, 74.

130. Cerdas, *APRA*, 112.

131. Carlson, "Guardia Nacional," 10; Cruse, intelligence report, San José, October 2, 1930, 817.00/6835, Nicaragua 1930–1944.

132. My translation. Sócrates Sandino to América Tiffer, Mexico City, June 30, 1930, E-001, C-001, 000021, ACS. In October Sócrates ended up in El Salvador after being arrested by Honduran police, stripped of all his possessions, and deported. He claimed that Tegucigalpa's police chief had orders from the Honduran president, who in turn responded to US diplomatic complaints against Sócrates. He secreted himself to Costa Rica, then back to El Salvador, begging his parents for money. By summer 1931 he was back with his brother in the Segovias: Sócrates to Gregorio Sandino, La Unión, El Salvador, October 21, 1930, E-001, C-001, 000417, ACS; Sócrates to América Tiffer, aboard a ship, [between October 22 and December 31] 1930, and San Salvador, May 28, 1931, both in E-001, C-001, 000021, ACS.

133. De Paredes to Portes Gil, Mexico City, February 7, 1931, E-001, C-006, 000333, ACS.

134. Sandino, communiqué, October 20, 1931, in *Sandino*, comp. Ramírez, trans. Conrad, 388.

135. Munro, Washington, September 4, 1929, 817.00/6404, Nicaragua 1910–1929. See also Grossman, "'Hermanos,'" 420.

136. Grossman, "'Hermanos,'" 632.

137. My translation. Sandino, manifesto, El Chipotón, November 20, 1930, E-001, C-005, 000233, ACS.
138. Macaulay, *Affair*, 135; Holden, *Armies*, 91.
139. My translation. Sandino, manifesto, El Chipotón, February 15, 1931, E-001, C-005, 000234, ACS.
140. Mora Lomeli, "Pensamiento," 44, 47; Wünderich, *Biografía*, 138.
141. Bendaña, *Mística*, 113.
142. My translation. Sandino cited in Román, *Maldito país*, 88.
143. Román, *Maldito país*, 88.
144. Macaulay, *Affair*, 214; Navarro-Génie, *Augusto*, 93.
145. My translation. Román, *Maldito país*, 177.
146. Navarro-Génie, *Augusto*, 94, 95.
147. My translation. De Belausteguigoitia, *Con Sandino*, 145, 146.
148. Navarro-Génie, *Augusto*, 91; Wünderich, *Biografía*, 136.
149. Bendaña, *Mística*, 132; Bolaños Geyer, *Sandino*, 49.
150. My translation. Bolaños Geyer, *Sandino*, 44–5.
151. Schroeder, "'To Defend,'" 307, 243.
152. Michael J. Schroeder, "The Sandino Rebellion Revisited," in *Close Encounters*, ed. Joseph, LeGrand, and Salvatore: 227.
153. My translation. Román, *Maldito país*, 139–45.
154. Grossman, "'Hermanos,'" 571–2.
155. Schroeder, "'To Defend,'" 254.
156. Lopez to Altamirano, July 16, 1930, folder Nicaraguan Bandit Jefes—Correspondence—A to G, box 19, O&T.
157. Arrieta, ¡*Habla Sandino!*, 18, 21, 22; De la Selva, *Sandino*, 12.
158. "Sandino Propone al Gral. Moncada la Segregación de la Rep.," *El Comercio*, January 15, 1929, 1; "Brief Notice of Sandino's Career," *Panama América*, February 24, 1934, in *Sandino*, comp. Arellano, 10; Smith et al., *Review*, 21; and even in Schroeder, "'To Defend,'" 245; Brooks, "Rebellion," 253.
159. Sandino, Bulletin of Operation, headquarters of EDSNN, July 16, 1931, folder Nicaragua—Bandits, Activities of, box 18, O&T.
160. Wünderich, *Biografía*, 101.
161. Willey to Hanna, Matagalpa, November 18, 1930, 817.00/6512, Nicaragua 1910–1929; Hanna to secretary of state, Managua, November 25, 1930, 817.00/6512, Nicaragua 1910–1929; Sandino, report, El Chipotón, August 20, 1931, E-001, C-005, 000235, ACS.
162. Bickel, *Mars Learning*, 163.
163. Chancery of British legation to American Department, Managua, January 15, 1932, file A7406, reference 15816, FO 371, PRO.
164. My translation. Butters to Matthews, Berkeley, February 16, 1932, folder Nicaragua, San Albino Mine, box 30, O&T.
165. Cited in Brooks, "Rebellion," 277.
166. The statistic is from 1928, so the numbers were probably slightly higher in 1931. Munro to Kellogg, Managua, December 28, 1928, 817.00/5265, Nicaragua 1910–1929.
167. Brooks, "Rebellion," 281.
168. My translation; emphasis in original. Blandón cited in Wünderich, *Costa*, 67, 68–74, 78–9.
169. Brugière, "Whither," 127–9, 148, in 817.00/7153, Nicaragua 1930–1944. See also Smith et al., *Review*, 37;
170. Pfaeffle, Managua, August 2, 1931, folder Nicaragua—Bandits, Activities of, box 18, O&T.
171. O'Brien, *Mission*, 76.
172. Gobat, *Confronting*, 63.
173. Brooks, "Rebellion," 153–4, 160, 161, 241, 292.
174. O'Brien, *Mission*, 241.
175. Legouillard to Ministry of Foreign Affairs, Guatemala, August 11, 1932, dossier 71, Cent. Am. 1918–1940.
176. Beaulac, Managua, July 15, 1929, 817.00/6380, Nicaragua 1910–1929; "Nicaragua and the United States," 4.

177. Previous historians have been cautious in appreciating public disenchantment. DeConde, for example, said that "the criticism which American intervention in Nicaragua had long drawn, both in the United States and in Latin America, *probably* had some influence on the Hoover administration's determination to withdraw the Marines at this time" (my emphasis), *Latin-American Policy*, 82.

178. Dennis, "Nicaragua," 496.

179. Wilson, Washington, February 3, 1932, 817.00/7323, Nicaragua 1930–1944.

180. Dore, *Myths*.

181. Hanna to Stimson, Managua, January 7, 1931, 817.00/6940, Nicaragua 1930–1944.

182. Hanna to Stimson, Managua, January 5, 1931, 817.00/6921, Nicaragua 1930–1944.

183. Joes, *Guerrilla Warfare*, 139.

184. Macaulay, *Affair*, 183.

185. Hanna to Stimson, Managua, January 7, 1931, 817.00/6940, Nicaragua 1930–1944.

186. Stimson to Adams, Washington, January 28, 1931, 817.00/6962, Nicaragua 1930–1944.

187. Richey to Stimson, Washington, January 2, 1931, 817.00/6918, Nicaragua 1930–1944.

188. McDermott, Washington, February 13, 1931, 817.00/7004, Nicaragua 1930–1944.

189. Hanna to Stimson, Managua, June 4, 1929, 817.00/6331, and November 2, 1929, 817.00/6451, both in Nicaragua 1910–1929; Samuelson to US minister, San Francisco de Cuajniquilapa, December 6, 1929, folder American Minister, box 1, Corr. 1928–1930.

190. Metcalf to manager of Bonanza Mining Co., February 19, 1930, folder 5thRgt—East Area Cor.-3May29–2May30, box 24, Nicaragua 1927–1933. Metcalf calculated that security around Puerto Cabezas cost the marines $5,000 per month, in Puerto Cabezas, March 11, 1930, folder 5thRgt—East Area Study-8Aug29–11May30, box 25, Nicaragua 1927–1933.

191. Williams cited in Beaulac to Stimson, Managua, April 9, 1930, 817.00/6638, Nicaragua 1930–1944.

192. Metcalf to Moss, Puerto Cabezas, July 26, 1929, Potter to London, Matagalpa, October 24, 1929, and Metcalf, Puerto Cabezas, March 11, 1930, all in folder 5thRgt—East Area Study-8Aug29–11May30, box 25, Nicaragua 1927–1933.

193. Hanna to secretary of state, April 15, 1930, 817.00/6586; and Beaulac to Stimson, Managua, April 9, 1930, 817.00/6638, Nicaragua 1930–1944.

194. White for Stafford to area commander, Matagalpa, June 16, 1930, folder Matagalpa Dist., Intelligence and Patrol Reports, 25May29–21Sept30, box 35, Nicaragua 1927–1933.

195. Muller to Munro, New Orleans, November 8, 1930, folder Correspondence, American Minister to Nicaragua (Conf.), box 21, O&T. There is a handful of letters such as this one at this time.

196. Stimson diary, April 15, 1931, cited in Stimson and Bundy, *Active Service*, 182.

197. Stimson to Coolidge, April 29, 1931, 817.00/7111A, Nicaragua 1930–1944.

198. Leach, "Memorandum on Political Situation in Nicaragua," Managua, April 2, 1932, file A2721, reference 15816, FO 371.

199. Max Jordan, "Nicaragua's Sad Capital," *Berliner Tageblatt*, December 15, 1929, translation, in Schurman to secretary of state, Berlin, January 10, 1929, 817.00/6191, Nicaragua 1910–1929.

200. Max Stern, "The Nicaraguan Affair," draft in folder The Nicaraguan Affair, box 1, Stern Papers.

201. Comité Ejecutivo Central del Partido Trabajador Nicaragüense, "A la juventud obrera y campesina de Nicaragua," October 21, 1932, folder Nicaragua—Communists, Anti-American & Red Propaganda, box 20, O&T.

202. Erskine, oral history.

203. De la Selva to Stimson, Washington, December 2, 1929, 817.00/6478; and Hanna to Stimson, Managua, October 3, 1929, and enclosures 1 and 4, 817.00/6422, both in Nicaragua 1910–1929.

204. White to Hanna, October 14, 817.00/6422; De la Selva to Stimson, Washington, December 2, 1929, 817.00/6478, both in Nicaragua 1910–1929. Disputing some details but confirming most of the story was Vogel to US chargé d'affaires, Managua, January 7, 1930, 817.00/6553, Nicaragua 1930–1944.

205. See, for instance, Beaulac to secretary of state, Managua, February 24, 1932, 817.00/7345; and Wilson, Washington, April 12, 1932, 817.00/7387, Nicaragua 1930–1944.

206. Stimson to Hanna, January 3, 1931, 817.00/6901, Nicaragua 1930–1944.

207. Carlson to jefe director, Managua, October 14, 1932, folder Misc. Confidential Data, box 1, GN-2 1932; Matthews to major general commandant, October 14, 1932, folder Financial Reports (1923–32), box 1, GC.

208. De la Selva to Stimson, Washington, December 2, 1929, 817.00/6478, Nicaragua 1910–1929.

209. Carlson to jefe director, Managua, November 4, 1932, folder Jefe Dir. Elections Confidential Corresp. 1932, box 35, Nicaragua 1927–1933.

210. Arrieta, ¡Habla Sandino!, 18.

211. White to Hanna, Washington, November 9, 1929, 817.00/6443; and Hanna, memo to secretary of state, Managua, August 14, 1929, 817.00/6389, both in Nicaragua 1910–1929.

212. Max Stern, "The Nicaraguan Affair," draft in folder The Nicaraguan Affair, box 1, Stern Papers.

213. Fuller to secretary of the navy, March 4, 1931, 817.00/7029, Nicaragua 1930–1944.

214. US legation, Managua, June 18, 1930, 817.00/6709, Nicaragua 1930–1944.

215. Leach memo, November 25, 1932, file A8386, reference 15816, FO 371; De la Selva, Sandino, 12.

216. Sandino to his officers, headquarters of the EDSNN, May 2, 1932, E-001, C-001, 000048; Sandino to Idiáquez and Irías, headquarters, Las Segovias, November 1932, E-001, C-003, 000117, both in ACS; Leach, November 25, 1932, file A8386, reference 15816, FO 371.

217. Sacasa and other signatories, peace agreement, Managua, February 2, 1933, E-001, C-004, 000200, ACS.

218. My translation. Paraphrased by Reyes Fuentes in Instituto, Ahora, 243.

219. Instituto, Ahora, 252.

220. García to Sandino, Matagalpa, March 1933, E-001, C-001, 000024, ACS.

221. "El general Augusto César Sandino es lanzado como candidato a la presidencia," Masaya, February 2, 1934, E-001, C-006, 000341, ACS.

222. Baylen, "Sandino," 118–9.

223. Cited in Gobat, Confronting, 261, 232, 234.

224. Baylen, "Sandino," 121–5; Guardia to Sacasa, Jinotega, November 13, 1933, Sacasa Archive.

225. Leach to Birch, Managua, February 12, 1934, file A1609 reference 17497, FO 371.

226. Erskine, oral history.

227. My translation. Cited in "El Sr. Salvatierra relata la trágica muerte de Sandino," Patria, May 16, 1934, GS.

228. Mercier to minister of foreign affairs, Guatemala, February 28, 1934, dossier 72, Cent. Am. 1918–1940.

229. Gobat, Confronting, 264.

230. Schroeder, "'To Defend,'" 10.

231. Uriarte, oral history; Duarte, oral history.

232. Salvatierra to Sacasa, New York, November 11, 1934, GS.

233. For examples, editorial, "El General Augusto C. Sandino ha muerto," El Centroamericano, February 23, 1934; and editorial, "La Muerte de Sandino," El Cronista, February 24, 1934, both in GS.

234. Hanna to Stimson, Managua, November 4, 1932, 817.00/7614; and Chamorro cited in Hanna to Stimson, Managua, November 19, 1932, 817.00/7637, both in Nicaragua 1930–1944.

Chapter 14

1. Streit, "Haiti," 626.

2. Douglas, "Haiti I," 256, 255.

3. Schmidt, Occupation, 127.

4. Theodore Joslin, "Hayti a Long Job," Boston Transcript, April 16, 1923, file A2523, reference 8463, FO 371.

5. My translation. "Retour de Me Pierre Hudicourt; Une conversation avec lui," *Le Nouvelliste*, January 13, 1925, 1.

6. For instance, Coffenberg to department commander, Mirebalais, May 26, 1922, folder Dept of South, Command Affairs, box 7, Gendarmerie.

7. Corvington, *1922–1934*, 198.

8. Danache, *Président*, 125.

9. Munro, *United States*, 309.

10. Cited in Cooper, "Withdrawal," 85.

11. Russell to Hughes, Port-au-Prince, August 5, 1922, 838.00/1897, Haiti 1910–1929.

12. See, for instance, Russell to Hughes, Port-au-Prince, August 5, 1922; Phillips to Russell, Washington, [28?] August 1922; Russell to secretary of state, Port-au-Prince, August 26, 1922; and Phillips to Russell, Washington, August 29, 1922, all in 838.00/1897, Haiti 1910–1929.

13. Russell to Hughes, Port-au-Prince, September 7, 1922, 838.00/1896, Haiti 1910–1929.

14. Woods, July 7, 1923, 838.00/1954; Russell to Kellogg, Port-au-Prince, December 11, 1925, 838.00/2182; and Russell to Kellogg, Port-au-Prince, November 13, 1925, 838.00/2169, all in Haiti 1910–1929; Corvington, *1922–1934*, 200.

15. Woods, July 7, 1923, 838.00/1954; and Dunn to secretary of state, Port-au-Prince, September 1, 1923, 838.00/1964, both in Haiti 1910–1929.

16. Merrell to Kellogg, August 27, 1925, 838.00/2149, Haiti 1910–1929.

17. My translation. Sylvain to Spingarn, Port-au-Prince, 14 September [1923?], folder Sylvain, Georges (On Haiti) 1923–1924, and undated, box 4, Spingarn Papers.

18. Sylvain to Villard, Port-au-Prince, September 25, 1923, folder 1922–1923 Haiti, box 133, Borah Papers.

19. White, Washington, May 22, 1925, 838.00/2124; Munro to White, Washington, September 27, 1923, 838.00/1977; Haitian minister to Washington, September 29, 1923, 838.00/1978, all in Haiti 1910–1929.

20. Scott to Kellogg, November 1, 1927, 838.00/2419, Haiti 1910–1929.

21. Albert et al., petition, June 30, 1925, 838.00/2146, Haiti 1910–1929.

22. UP, "Protestation," Port-au-Prince, February 1, 1927. Signed by Perceval Thoby, Victor Chauvin, Jolibois Fils, A. Pierre Paul, and about ten others, in dossier 6, Haiti 1918–1940.

23. Craige, Port-au-Prince, September 19, 1927, folder Secret + Confidential Reports of Chief of Police 1927–G-2, box 1, COCP.

24. Cumming to chief of the Gendarmerie, headquarters of Petit Goâve, October 31, 1923, folder Summary of, GD'H 1923 Folder 1 of 2, box 1, Corr. 1915–1926.

25. Russell, January 11, 1928, 838.00/2432, Haiti 1910–1929.

26. Magowan to Henderson, May 5, 1931, file A2898, reference 15093, FO 371.

27. Shannon, *Jean Price-Mars*, 27, 7–20; Gaillard, *République*, 220; Price-Mars, *Une étape*.

28. Nicholls, "Ideology," 3–26; Lerebours, "Indigenist Revolt," 711–25; Smith, "Shades, 24–5.

29. Shannon, *Jean Price-Mars*, 71.

30. Nicholls, "Ideology," 3–26.

31. Corvington, *1915–1922*, 220.

32. Corvington, *1922–1934*, 21.

33. Heinl, Jr., and Heinl, *Written in Blood*, 492; Roumain, *Masters*.

34. Murray to the commandant of the Garde d'Haïti, June 21, 1929, folder [Police Memoranda] 12, box 1, COCP.

35. Shannon, *Jean Price-Mars*, 81.

36. Fowler, "Shared Vision," 86.

37. My translation. Haitian customs employees, circular, Port-au-Prince, December 1929, folder Strike and General Info File #3, box 19, Gendarmerie.

38. Headquarters of First Brigade, unsigned memo, Port-au-Prince, January 24, 1931, folder Haiti (1930–31), box 4, GC.

39. Cited in Heinl, Jr., and Heinl, *Written in Blood*, 429.

40. Fegan to Evans, Cap-Haïtien; and R. L., "Inauguration of the 'Ligue of the Patriotic Young People,'" both April 24, 1930, 838.00/2806, Haiti 1930–1939.

41. Lerebours, "Indigenist Revolt," 720.

42. Brissman, "Interpreting," 322–3.
43. The UP and the Ligue Haitienne Pour la Défense des Droits de L'Homme et du Citoyen. See Merrell, "Political Parties in Haiti," June 6, 1925, 838.00/2127, Haiti 1910–1929.
44. Nicholls, "Ideology," 7.
45. Corvington, 1922–1934, 117.
46. Munro to White, March 16, 1929, folder Elections, 1929–30 & Undated, box 1069, President's Comm.
47. Stimson to U.S. legation in Port-au-Prince, April 11, 1929, folder Elections, 1929–30 & Undated, box 1069, President's Comm; White to Stimson, Washington, October 30, 1929, 838.00/2601, Haiti 1910–1929; White to Stimson, May 10, 1929, folder Elections, 1929–30 & Undated, box 1069, President's Comm.
48. Stimson to Hoover, September 30, 1929, folder Countries—Haiti Haitian Commission, 1929, box 989, Foreign Affairs, PP.
49. Office of the Chief of Police, "Substance of Report Submitted by Paul #8," Port-au-Prince, October 7, 1929, folder Intelligence Rpts, Secret Agent #2—Paul, box 13, Gendarmerie.
50. My translation. Wiet to minister of foreign affairs, Port-au-Prince, November 17, 1929, dossier 13, Haiti 1918–1940; De Bekker to Borah, December 8, 1929, folder Haiti 1929–1930, box 292, Borah Papers.
51. "Summary of Strike," in Compendium of Information on the Garde d'Haiti, folder Garde d'Haïti, Compendium of Information on the, Undated, box 1070, President's Comm; Heinl, Jr., and Heinl, Written in Blood, 504.
52. The other organizations were the Union Nationaliste des Jeunes and the Collaboration Patriotique des Jeunes. Corvington, 1922–1934, 200; Brissman, "Interpreting," 312; Pamphile, L'éducation, 228.
53. My translation. Wiet to minister of foreign affairs, Port-au-Prince, November 17, 1929, dossier 13, Haiti 1918–1940. See also Annex No. 5, "Agents Américains du Service Technique de l'Agriculture et de l'Enseignement Professionel en Haïti," dossier 13, Haiti 1918–1940; Heinl, Jr., and Heinl, Written in Blood, 504.
54. My translation. Haitian students, announcement, Port-au-Prince, September 17, 1930, folder Haiti, 1928–1931—Haitiana, box 20, Smith Papers.
55. Magowan to Henderson, December 12, 1929, file A326, reference 14225, FO 371.
56. Cutts to major general commandant, December 4, 1929, folder Haiti (1929–30), box 3, GC.
57. My translation. Paraphrased in Noël, 1930, folder Recommendations and Suggestions Submitted to Commission, Undated, box 1073, President's Comm.
58. Wiet to minister of foreign affairs, Port-au-Prince, November 23, 1929, dossier 13, Haiti 1918–1940; Savaille, La grève, 42; Wiet to minister of foreign affairs, Port-au-Prince, December 1, 1929, dossier 13, Haiti 1918–1940.
59. Magowan to Henderson, December 12, 1929, file A326, reference 14225, FO 371; Munro, United States, 311.
60. Russell, "Eighth Annual Report of the American High Commissioner at Port-au-Prince, Haiti, to Secretary of State, 1929" (Washington, D.C.: USGPO, 1930), FDRL, 9.
61. "Black Haiti a Republic of Many Revolutions," NYT, December 15, 1929, XX6.
62. Cutts to major general commandant, December 4, 1929, folder Haiti (1929–30), box 3, GC.
63. Daniels to Hull, September 9, 1933, in Documentary History, ed. McJimsey, 292–5.
64. Millet, Paysans, 112–3.
65. Cutts to major general commandant, December 4, 1929, folder Haiti (1929–30), box 3, GC.
66. Russell to Stimson, Port-au-Prince, December 3, 1929, 838.5045/1, Haiti 1910–1929.
67. Pratt and Swink cited in "Summary of Strike," report in Compendium of Information on the Garde d'Haiti, folder Garde d'Haïti, Compendium of Information on the, Undated, box 1070, President's Comm.
68. Schmidt, Occupation, 200. Historians have presented varying tallies: from six killed and twenty-eight wounded in McCrocklin, Garde, 192, to twenty-two killed and fifty-one wounded in Millet, Paysans, to twenty-five dead and seventy-five wounded in Plummer, Psychological Moment, 118.
69. De Bekker, "The Massacre," 310.
70. My translation. Condé, Des Cayes, 47.

71. My translation. Numa, *Antoine Simon*, 82–4; memcon between Mayard and Fletcher, Port-au-Prince, undated March 1930, folder Depositions, undated, box 1069, President's Comm.

72. My translation. Workers of Torbeck, address to Borno, February 17, 1929, cited in Condé, *Des Cayes*, 87.

73. My translation. Numa, *Antoine Simon*, 85–6.

74. Welles, [25?] December 1928, folder 03 Speeches & Writings, 1928–1950 Pan American Situation December 1928, box 194, Welles Papers.

75. Schmidt, *Occupation*, 204.

76. British Library of Information, memo, "U.S.A. Press to December 10, 1929," December 13, 1929, file A8860, reference 13485, FO 371; ACLU to Stimson, December 9, 1929, folder Correspondence—Save Haiti League, box 112–2, Conservatory Papers.

77. Manning to Hoover, Chicago, December 11, 1929, 838.00/2677, Haiti 1910–1929.

78. Boot, *Savage*, 179.

79. Stimson to all diplomatic missions in Latin America, December 21, 1929, 838.00/2663A, Haiti 1910–1929. From 838.00/2654 to 838.00/2668 are the responses.

80. Matthews to secretary of state, Bogotá, December 14, 1929, 838.00/2695, Haiti 1930–1939.

81. Guggenheim to Stimson, Havana, December 23, 1929, 838.00/2678, Haiti 1910–1929. See also O'Hare, G-2 report, "Susceptibility of Public to Propaganda Effort," December 24, 1929, 838.00/2709, Haiti 1930–1939.

82. Hoover, *Memoirs*, 333.

83. Woods, "'Imperialistic America,'" 61–2.

84. Hoover, *Memoirs*, 331, 335.

85. Munro, *United States*, 310.

86. McCrocklin, *Garde*, 195.

87. Cited in British Library of Information, "U.S.A. Press to December 10, 1929," December 13, 1929, file A8860, reference 13485, FO 371.

88. My translation. Wiet to minister of foreign affairs, Port-au-Prince, March 1, 1930, dossier 13, Haiti 1918–1940.

89. Cited in British Library of Information, "U.S.A. Press to December 10, 1929," December 13, 1929, file A8860, reference 13485, FO 371.

90. Heinl, Jr., and Heinl, *Written in Blood*, 497.

91. Stimson to Russell, December 5, 1929, folder Countries—Haiti Correspondence, 1928–1929, box 989, Foreign Affairs, PP.

92. My translation. Cited in Blancpain, *Haïti*, 290.

93. British Library of Information, "Central America—Hayti," January 10, 1930, file A612, reference 14225, FO 371.

94. Cited in "President Seeks Plan to Complete Haiti Obligation," *U.S. Daily News*, February 5, 1930, which reproduces the statement in total.

95. White to Stimson, December 7, 1929, and Russell to Stimson, Port-au-Prince, December 8, 1929, both in folder Countries—Haiti Haitian Commission, 1929, box 989, Foreign Affairs, PP.

96. Hughes to McCormick, February 6, 1924, case file 162, reel 87, series 1, Coolidge Papers.

97. Spector, *Forbes*, 50–3.

98. Hoover, February 7, 1930, folder Countries—Haiti Haitian Commission, Correspondence 1930, January–February, box 989, Foreign Affairs, PP; Cooper, "Withdrawal," 92; Schmidt, *Occupation*, 208.

99. Forbes's Journal on Haiti, December 1929 to October 1931, General Accessions 342, HHL, 12.

100. Swink to Evans, February 10, 1930, folder Strike and General Info File #3, box 19, Gendarmerie.

101. Evans to Russell, Port-au-Prince, February 18, 1930, 838.00/2747, Haiti 1930–1939.

102. My translation. Wiet to minister of foreign affairs, Port-au-Prince, February 14, 1930, dossier 13, Haiti 1918–1940.

103. Murray to Evans, February 12, 1930, folder Strike and General Info File #3, box 19, Gendarmerie.

104. Russell to Stimson, Port-au-Prince, February 14, 1930, 838.00/2739, Haiti 1930–1939.

105. Harold Denny, "Haiti Board Greeted with Quiet Protest," *NYT*, March 1, 1930, 1.
106. Evans to "all members of the constabulary detachments," January 24, 1930, in Evans to the President's Commission, March 5, 1930, folder Garde News Digest, 1930 March 1–5, box 1070, President's Comm.; "Agitators under Surveillance (Undated)" [ca. March 5, 1930], folder Agitators under Surveillance, box 1, Gendarmerie.
107. Russell, General Order No. 20, Port-au-Prince, February 27, 1930, folder Strike and General Info File #3, box 19, Gendarmerie.
108. Chief of police to commandant of the Garde d'Haïti, Port-au-Prince, February 28, 1930, folder Strike and General Info File #3, box 19, Gendarmerie; Wiet to minister of foreign affairs, Port-au-Prince, March 1, 1930, dossier 13, Haiti 1918–1940.
109. The Comité Fédératif des Groupements Patriotiques d'Haïti represented the following organizations: UP, Ligue des Droits de l'Homme et du Citoyen, Ligue d'Action Social Haïtienne, Ligue Nationale d'Action Constitutionnelle, Ligue de Défense Nationale, Ligue de Jeunesse Patriote, Parti National Travailliste, and UN. See interview with Rigal, Port-au-Prince, March 3, 1930, folder Depositions, 1930 March 1, box 1069, President's Comm.; Russell to secretary of state, Port-au-Prince, March 17, 1930, 838.00 Commission of Investigation/108, Haiti 1930–1939. See also Cooper, "Withdrawal," 93.
110. Cited in Kelchner, "A Résumé of the Political Events in Haiti For the Year 1930," undated, in McGurk to secretary of state, Port-au-Prince, April 18, 1931, 838.00/2954, Haiti 1930–1939.
111. Wiet to minister of foreign affairs, Port-au-Prince, March 1, 1930, dossier 13, Haiti 1918–1940.
112. Harold Denny, "Haiti Board Greeted with Quiet Protest," *NYT*, March 1, 1930, 1; Magowan to Henderson, March 3, 1930, file A2216, reference 14225, FO 371.
113. Fletcher, "Quo Vadis," 541.
114. Forbes's Journal on Haiti, December 1929 to October 1931, General Accessions 342, HHL, 28.
115. Russell to secretary of state, Port-au-Prince, March 6, 1930, 838.00/2750, Haiti 1930–1939.
116. Heinl, Jr., and Heinl, *Written in Blood*, 499. See also List of Witnesses before Forbes Commission in Haiti, folder Witnesses Before Commission, 1930 March 1–14, box 1074, President's Comm.
117. Fletcher, "Quo Vadis," 542; Magowan to Henderson, March 12, 1930, file A2227, reference 14225, FO 371. For examples, see interviews with Pierre-Paul and Price-Mars, Port-au-Prince, March 6, 1930, folder Depositions, 1930 March 6, interview with Velaire, Port-au-Prince, March 7, 1930, folder Courts, 1929–30 & Undated, and interview with Rampy, Port-au-Prince, March 7, 1930, folder Depositions, 1930 March 7, all in box 1069, President's Comm.
118. Interview with Velaire, Port-au-Prince, March 7, 1930, folder Courts, 1929–30 & Undated, interview with Ricot, Port-au-Prince, March 7, 1930, folder Depositions, 1930 March 7, both in box 1069, President's Comm. Doctors' testimony is "Mémoire à la Commission du Président Hoover," March 7, 1930, folder Commission Petitions, 1930 March 7–12, box 1068, President's Comm.
119. Interview with Cauvin, March 5, 1930, folder Depositions, 1930 March 5, box 1069, President's Comm.
120. La Presse, March 3, 1930, folder Press Clippings: La Presse (anti-Government), 1930 March 1–10, box 1071, President's Comm.
121. "Our Greetings to the Commission," *Le Nouvelliste*, February 28, 1930, 1, in Magowan to Henderson, March 3, 1930, file A2216, reference 14225, FO 371.
122. "Quize milles femmes debout réclament la libération du territoire," *Haïti-Journal*, March 4, 1930, 1.
123. Several of these responses are in "Les Nationalistes répondent à Russell," *L'Action* [undated], folder Press Clippings: L'Action, 1930, March 1–13, box 1071, President's Comm.
124. Forbes's Journal on Haiti, December 1929 to October 1931, General Accessions 342, HHL, 48. The commission went to Pont Beudet, Mirabelais, Las Canobas, Thomonde, Hinche, Saint-Michel, Maïssade, and Cap-Haïtien.
125. Magowan to Henderson, March 3, 1930, file A2216, reference 14225, FO 371.

126. Forbes to Hoover, March 7, 1930, folder Plan of Commission, 1930 March 1–10, box 1070, President's Comm.
127. Russell to secretary of state, Port-au-Prince, March 6, 1930, 838.00/2750, Haiti 1930–1939.
128. Forbes's Journal on Haiti, December 1929 to October 1931, General Accessions 342, HHL, 44.
129. Fletcher, "Quo Vadis," 544–5; Wiet to minister of foreign affairs, Port-au-Prince, March 17, 1930, dossier 13, Haiti 1918–1940.
130. Commission to Hoover and acting secretary of state, March 14, 1930, folder Plan of Commission, March 1–10, 1930, box 1070, President's Comm.
131. Forbes to secretary of state, March 15, 1930, folder Plan of Commission, 1930 March 1–10, box 1070, President's Comm.
132. "Our Greetings to the Commission," *Le Nouvelliste*, February 28, 1930, 1. For more detail, see Franklin Waltman, Jr., "Haiti Virtually Run by U.S. Officials," *Baltimore Sun*, March 25, 1930, dossier 13, Haiti 1918–1940.
133. Interview with Seide, Port-au-Prince, March 7, 1930, folder Depositions, 1930 March 7, box 1069, President's Comm.
134. Vézina, memcon with Le Gouaze, March 2, 1930, folder Depositions, 1930 March 1, box 1069, President's Comm.
135. "Our Greetings to the Commission," *Le Nouvelliste*, February 28, 1930, 1.
136. Statement by Léger, March 4, 1930, folder Depositions, 1930 March 4, box 1069, President's Comm.
137. My translation; italics in English in original. Ligue Nationale D'Action Constitutionnelle to Forbes Commission, March 8, 1930, folder Commission Petitions, 1930 March 7–12, box 1068, President's Comm.
138. Fletcher, "Quo Vadis," 547.
139. Office of the Financial Adviser-General Receiver, "Report on Current Conditions . . . ," March 12, 1930, folder Itinerary, 1929–30, box 1070, President's Comm.
140. Cited in Streit, "Haiti," 623.
141. Harold N. Denny, "Haiti—A Problem Unsolved. I. Work of the Commission," *NYT*, June 29, 1931; Denny, "Haiti—A Problem Unsolved. II. Causes of Present Fiction," *NYT*, June 30, 1931; and Denny, "Haiti—A Problem Unsolved. III. A Stalemate in Negotiation," *NYT*, July 1, 1931.
142. Interview with Freeman, Port-au-Prince, March 13, 1930, folder Courts, 1929–30 & Undated, box 1069; and Russell to Forbes, Port-au-Prince, March 13, 1930, folder Russell, John H., 1930 March 13–14, box 1073, both in President's Comm.
143. "Our Greetings to the Commission," *Le Nouvelliste*, February 28, 1930, 1.
144. Roy to Vézina, June 12, 1930, folder Countries—Haiti Correspondence, 1930 May-1932, box 989, Foreign Affairs, PP.
145. Russell to Forbes, Port-au-Prince, March 13, 1930, 838.00 Commission of Investigation/107, Haiti 1930–1939.
146. Forbes's Journal on Haiti, December 1929 to October 1931, General Accessions 342, HHL, 35.
147. Fletcher, "Quo Vadis," 539.
148. Cited in Grant to De la Rue, March 12, 1930, folder Rue, Syndey de la, Financial Service Testimony Exhibits, 1930, box 10, White Papers.
149. Forbes's Journal on Haiti, December 1929 to October 1931, General Accessions 342, HHL, 48.
150. De la Rue to White, Port-au-Prince, March 17, 1930, folder Haiti General 1929–30, box 14, White Papers.
151. Commission, March 21, 1930, folder Plan of Commission, 1930 March 11–24 & Undated, box 1071, President's Comm. Summarized here are the nine recommendations: 1) Haitianize; 2) retain only non-racist US citizens; 3) recognize temporary president when elected; 4) recognize president who will be elected by legislature; 5) abolish office of high commissioner; 6) have minister to Haiti carry out early Haitianization, even if inefficient; 7) begin gradual withdrawal of marines; 8) limit US intervention to that provided by Treaty or

specific agreement; and 9) have new minister to Haiti negotiate all other matters for reducing intervention.

152. Forbes's Journal on Haiti, December 1929 to October 1931, General Accessions 342, HHL, 57, 63.

153. Editorial, *The Nation*, March 26, 1930, folder Press Clippings—American 1930 March 11–26, box 1072, President's Comm.

154. Murray to commandant of the Garde d'Haïti, March 19, 1930, folder Strike and General Info File #3, box 19, Gendarmerie.

155. Magowan to Henderson, May 3, 1930, file A3843, reference 14225, FO 371; Murray, Port-au-Prince, April 30, 1930, folder Intelligence Rpts, Secret Agent #2—Paul, box 13, Gendarmerie.

156. Grummon to secretary of state, Port-au-Prince, May 22, 1930, 838.00/2831, Haiti 1930–1939.

157. Roy cited in Grummon to secretary of state, Port-au-Prince, June 7, 1930, 838.00/2838, Haiti 1930–1939.

158. Magowan to Henderson, October 7, 1930, file A6778, reference 14225, FO 371.

159. Cutts to major general commandant, October 17, 1930, folder Haiti (1929–30), box 3, GC.

160. Murray to commandant of the Garde d'Haïti, Port-au-Prince, October 13 and 20, 1930, folder [Police Memoranda] 25, box 1, COCP.

161. Williams to U.S. high commissioner, September 26, 1930, folder Haiti (1929–30), box 3, GC.

162. My translation. Wiet to minister of foreign affairs, Port-au-Prince, June 5, 1930, dossier 13, Haiti 1918–1940.

163. Murray to commandant of the Garde d'Haïti, Port-au-Prince, October 20, 1930, folder [Police Memoranda] 25, box 1, COCP.

164. Cutts to major general commandant, October 30, 1930, folder Haiti (1929–30), box 3; and November 29, 1930, folder Haiti (1930–31), box 4, both in GC; "Foe of Occupation Is Haitian President; Vincent Election by the National Assembly," *NYT*, November 19, 1930, 1; Editorial, "Haiti's New President," *NYT*, November 20, 1930, 25.

165. My translation. Wiet to minister of foreign affairs, Port-au-Prince, April 2, 1931, dossier 7, Haiti 1918–1940.

166. Stimson, April 22, 1931, reel 3, vol. 16; and September 30, 1931, reel 3, vol. 18, both in Stimson Diaries, FDRL.

167. My translation. Sannon, *Six mois*, I, III.

168. My translation. Sannon, *Six mois*, III; Shannon, *Jean Price-Mars*, 108; Vincent, *Efforts*, 9.

169. Emphasis in original. "Search Our History, Whites!" *Le Petit Impartial*, August 14, 1930, in Grummon to secretary of state, Port-au-Prince, August 23, 1930, 838.00/2877, Haiti 1930–1939.

170. Shannon, *Jean Price-Mars*, 109.

171. Farrell, summary of intelligence, December 29, 1931, folder Haiti (1931–32), box 4, GC.

172. My translation. "Rapport de la Commission de l'Assemblée Nationale rejetant à l'unanimité le principe du nouveau Traité," *Le Nouvelliste*, September 13, 1932, in file A6893, reference 15840, FO 371.

173. Grummon to secretary of state, Port-au-Prince, August 29, 1930, 838.00/2881, Haiti 1930–1939. British and French diplomats reached similar conclusions: Shepherd to Henderson, March 23, 1934, file A2993, reference 17526, FO 371; Wiet to minister of foreign affairs, Port-au-Prince, October 15, 1932, dossier 7, Haiti 1918–1940.

174. Munro to White, Port-au-Prince, January 9, 1931, folder Munro, Dana G. 1931, box 8, White Papers.

175. Hibbert paraphrased in Scott, Washington, March 24, 1931, 838.00/2945, Haiti 1930–1939.

176. Shepherd to Henderson, March 23, 1934, file A2993, reference 17526, FO 371.

177. Wood, Cap-Haïtien, September 16, 1932, 838.00/3103, Haiti 1930–1939.

178. Matthews, "Policy," 810.

179. Cited in Farrell, summary of intelligence, April 29, 1932, folder Haiti (1931–32), box 4, GC.

180. Phillips to Roosevelt, November 28, 1933, folder Haiti, box 39, President's Secretary's File, FDRL; White to Bellegarde, November 13, 1933, in Bellegarde microfilm, Bellegarde

Papers; Blake to Roosevelt, December 15, 1933, folder Women's International League for Peace and Freedom, President's Personal File 928, FDRL.

181. White to Bellegarde, November 13, 1933, in Bellegarde microfilm, Bellegarde Papers.

182. White, Washington, April 5, 1933, 838.00/3127, Haiti 1930–1939.

183. Gruening, "At Last," 700.

184. Roosevelt and Vincent, joint statement, April 17, 1934, folder Haiti 1933–1934, Official File 162, Papers as President; and Roosevelt, "Address of the President," Cap-Haïtien, July 5, 1934, box 18, Speeches, President's Personal File, both in FDRL.

185. My translation. Maurice Liautaud, "La Désoccupation Militaire du Pays," Haïti-Journal, August 16, 1934.

186. Gruening, Many Battles, 162.

Conclusion

1. Craig, oral history, 29.

2. Most recently Edelstein compared dozens of modern occupations and labeled those in Haiti and the Dominican Republic "failures," in "Hazards," 86. See also Ferguson, Colossus, 58; and Calder, Impact, 252. The only historian who has argued for the overall success of these occupations was Boot, and his argument was about short-term military success: Savage, 180. Langley argued the opposite, that marine wars in the circum-Caribbean failed because they rested on the use of force, in Banana Wars, 219.

3. On Nicaragua there is indeed a heated argument. The classic view is that Sandino "defeated" the United States because its soldiers left, for instance, in Amador, Exilio, 6; see also Amador, Derrota militar. More pessimistic were Bolaños Geyer, El iluminado, 36, and Schroeder, "'To Defend,'" 528–34. Grossman disagreed, saying Sandino and his army "were at the height of their military and political power at the end of the war," in "'La Patria,'" 270; Grandin characterized the Sandino-Marine Corps confrontation as a "draw," in Workshop, 31; Bickel spoke of a "stalemate," in Mars Learning, 160; Macaulay wrote that Sandino failed politically because he did not destroy his enemy, in Affair, 10.

4. Chapman, "The United States," 88.

5. Cooper, "Withdrawal," 98–9.

6. The number includes those killed in action and who died of wounds: five in Nicaragua in 1912, seventeen in the Dominican Republic in 1916–1920, ten in Haiti in 1915–1934, and forty-seven in Nicaragua in 1926–1933. The casualty rates of the occupations can also include those of the constabularies, not much higher than those of US forces. The most authoritative source for US casualties is "Casualties," 1067. See slightly different numbers in unsigned, undated, "Casualties of U.S. Marine Corps during American Occupation of Dominican Republic, and Republic of Haiti," folder Dom. Rep. Strengths + Casualties, Dominican Republic, Geographical Files, Reference Branch, MCH, and Boot, Savage, 252. For individual countries, see "Haiti Casualties 1915–1934," September 28, 1934, folder Misc. Reports (1915–1934), box 3, First Brigade; Dennis, "Nicaragua," 499; and Joes, Guerrilla Warfare, 140. For the financial estimates, "U.S. Marine Head Urges They Stay in Nicaragua," NYHT, February 10, 1931, which added up the costs to the US Treasury of the three occupations—granted, before two of them ended—and they came up to $8,941,826. See also Cheatham, memo to chief of naval operations, June 23, 1930, and Jahnke, letter to secretary of state, July 14, 1930, both in folder Haiti—Occupations 1915–1934, Haiti, Geographical Files, Reference Branch, MCH. Knight came up with wildly different figures, at least $12 million just for the Dominican occupation, including the sinking of the USS Memphis at a cost of $6 million, in Americans, 10. Cummins reported $20 million for the Nicaragua occupation, in Quijote, 137.

7. For Sandinistas, Grossman, "'Hermanos,'" 199.

8. Calder is an exception, saying the urban Dominican campaign was "the primary cause of the withdrawal." His evaluation of the rural insurgency is more contradictory: he wrote that the peasants of the east "successfully waged a guerrilla war against the forces of the U.S. military government," yet also that they were "the last gasp of a declining political system," in Impact, 182, 115, 181. He is more categorical toward the end: "Resistance to the occupation was a

primary factor in bringing it to an end. In different ways, this was true both of the peasants' war against the marines in the east and of the nationalists' political-intellectual campaign of protest," 246.

9. Munro, *Intervention*, 543.
10. Miller, "Spurs," 44. See also Kepner and Soothill, *Banana Empire*, 344.
11. Boza Gutiérrez, *Memorias*, 75.
12. "Haitians Protest," 298.
13. Logan et al., "The Contributions of Negroes in the Dominican Republic, Haiti, and Cuba to Hemispheric Solidarity as Conditioned by the Agrarian Problems in Each," 1942, folder 16, box 166-37, Logan Papers.
14. Brissman, "Interpreting," 4.
15. Dempsey and Fontaine, *Fool's Errand*, 70.
16. Cited in Buell, "Intervention," 70.
17. My translation. Vincent, *En posant*, 292.
18. Simpson, "Social Structure," 649.
19. My translation. Beals, *Banana*, 108.
20. "Léger," perhaps the brother of Agel Léger, cited in Miller, oral history, 22.
21. Schoultz, *Beneath*, 248.
22. Buell, "Intervention," 70.
23. Ducoudray, "Epopeya," 39.
24. For instance, Tercero González, oral history.
25. Zimmermann, *Sandinista*, 26–7, 61, 73. The book argues that Fonseca's two great influences were Ché Guevara and Sandino.
26. Camacho Navarro, *Usos*.
27. Salomón de la Selva, "Sandino," *Latin American Digest*, February 26, 1934, reproduced in De la Selva, *Sandino*, 14–6.
28. My translation. Firschnaler to Gregorio Sandino and Doña América, San Salvador, El Salvador, February 26, 1938, GS.
29. My translation. Sandino to Firschnaler, San Salvador, El Salvador, March 1, 1938, GS.
30. *Hombres Libres*.
31. *Hombres Libres*. A study of four different types of Sandino memory-making is Campbell-Jeffrey, "Social Movement Theory."
32. My translation. Mejía, *Lilís*, 158.
33. Chamorro, *Orígenes*, 2.
34. Werleigh cited in Michel, *Péralte*, 50.
35. Wilentz, *Rainy Season*, 78. Alexis, "Nationalism," features many more examples of Péralte in Haitian memory.
36. Other pro-Sandino children's literature included Instituto de Estudio del Sandinismo, *Padre*; Rius, *Hermano*.
37. My translation. Bolaños Geyer, *El iluminado*, 13.
38. Wilentz, *Rainy Season*, 79.
39. Williams, *Tragedy*, 1–13; Grandin, *Workshop*. See also Hart, *Empire*, 5.

BIBLIOGRAPHY

Archives

DOMINICAN REPUBLIC

Archivo General de la Nación, Santo Domingo
  Fondo Gobierno Militar
  Fondo Municipio
  Fondo Secretaría de Estado de Interior y Policía
Archivo de Tulio Cestero, Universidad Autónoma de Santo Domingo
  Fondo Antiguo
Archivo Vetilio Alfau Durán, Santo Domingo

FRANCE

Archives Diplomatiques, Ministère des Affaires Étrangères, Paris
  Correspondance Politique et Commerciale 1914–1940
    Centre Amérique, Amérique 1918–1940
    Haïti, Amérique 1918–1940
    République Dominicaine, Amérique 1918–1940
  Correspondance Politique et Commerciale/Nouvelle Série 1897–1918
    Haïti
    République Dominicaine
  Correspondance Politique et Commerciale/Série Nouvelle 1897 à 1918
    Nicaragua

NICARAGUA

Archivo Nacional de Nicaragua, Managua
  Fondo Colección Sandino
Centro de Historia Militar, Managua
  Collección ACS (Augusto César Sandino)
  Collección BZ (Benjamín Zeledón)
Instituto de Historia de Nicaragua y Centroamérica, Managua
  Archivo de Gregorio Sandino
  Archivo de Juan B. Sacasa

UNITED KINGDOM

Public Record Office, Kew
  Foreign Office 370
  Foreign Office 371

UNITED STATES

Bancroft Library, University of California-Berkeley
  Charles Edward Chapman Papers
  Fred Ludwig Morris Papers
  Max Stern Papers
Franklin D. Roosevelt Library, Hyde Park, N. Y.
  Adolf Berle Papers
  Papers as Assistant Secretary of the Navy
  Papers as President
  President's Personal File
  President's Secretary's File
  Stimson Diary
  Sumner Welles Papers
  U.S. Navy Dispatches March 1912–August 1914
Herbert Hoover Library, West Branch, Iowa
  Calvin Coolidge Papers
  Campaign and Transition Papers
  Francis White Papers
  Letters of Dwight Dickinson
  President's Commission for Study & Review of Conditions in Haiti
  Presidential Papers
Hoover Institution, Stanford University, California
  Diary, Charles Dudley Rhodes
  Kneeland Letters
  Papers of Joseph Freeman
  Unpublished manuscript by Captain Edward Beach, U.S. Navy, 1941
Library of Congress, Manuscript Division
  Papers of Arthur B. Spingarn, 1850–1968
  Papers of Moorfield Storey
  Papers of William Banks Caperton
  Papers of William E. Borah
  Washington Conservatory of Music Papers
Marine Corps Archives and Special Collections, Gray Research Center, Quantico, Virginia
  Papers of John H. Russell
  Papers of Joseph H. Pendleton
  Papers of Oliver P. Smith
  Papers of Smedley Butler
Marine Corps Historical Division, Marine Corps Base, Quantico, Virginia
  Geographical Files, Reference Branch
Moorland-Spingarn Research Center, Howard University, Washington, D.C.
  Bellegarde Papers
  Rayford D. Logan Papers
Operational Archives Branch, Naval Historical Center, Washington, D.C.
Southern Historical Collection, University of North Carolina at Chapel Hill
  William P. Upshur Letters
U.S. National Archives and Records Administration, Washington, D.C.
  Record Group 38, Records of the Office of the Chief of Naval Operations
    Military Government of Santo Domingo

Record Group 127, Records of the United States Marine Corps
    Correspondence of the Gendarmerie d'Haiti 1923, 1925
    Correspondence of the Office of the Chief of Police, Gendarmerie d'Haiti, 1927–1934
    Correspondence Relating to Bandit Prisoners, 1929–1931
    Correspondence Relating to Civilian Complaints in the District of Matagalpa at Jinotega, 1928
    Correspondence Relating to Subjects Not in the Regular Series of General Correspondence, 1918–1921
    General Correspondence, 1907–1936
    General Correspondence of Headquarters, Gendarmerie d'Haiti 1916–1919
    General Correspondence of the 2nd Brigade, 1928–1930
    General Correspondence of the Chief of the Gendarmerie, 1921–1923
    General Correspondence of the Expeditionary Commander and 1st Brigade, 1915–1920
    General Correspondence of the Gendarmerie d'Haiti 1915–1926
    Headquarters, Historical Section, Records Relating to Marine Corps Units in Nicaragua, 1927–1933
    Intelligence Reports from the Department of the North, 1926–1927
    Miscellaneous Collection of Records Relating to the Marine Occupation of Santo Domingo (Dominican Republic), 1916–1924
    Miscellaneous Correspondence of the 2nd Brigade, 1927–1932
    Miscellaneous Records Relating to Marine Activities in the pre-World War II era, 1912–1979
    Operations and Training Division, Intelligence Section, 1915–1934
    Original and Microfilmed World War I and Inter-War Era Newspapers, 1914–1923
    Records of the First Provisional Brigade in Haiti, 1915–1934
    Records of the Gendarmerie d'Haiti, 1915–1934
    Reports Received from Marine Units in Nicaragua, 1927–1932
    Reports Relating to U.S. Navy and Marine Corps Operations in Haiti and Santo Domingo, 1915–1921
    Road Reports of Headquarters Gendarmerie d'Haiti, 1916–1921
    Selected Correspondence of the Intelligence Department (GN-2), 1928–1932
    Special Correspondence of the Chief of the Gendarmerie d'Haiti, 1919–1920
U.S. National Archives and Records Administration, College Park, Maryland
    Record Group 59, General Records of the Department of State
    Central Decimal Files Relating to Internal Affairs of Haiti, 1910–1929
    Central Decimal Files Relating to Internal Affairs of Haiti, 1930–1939
    Central Decimal Files Relating to Internal Affairs of Nicaragua, 1910–1929
    Central Decimal Files Relating to Internal Affairs of Nicaragua, 1930–1944
    Central Decimal Files Relating to Internal Affairs of the Dominican Republic, 1910–1929
    Central Decimal Files Relating to Political Relations Between the U.S. and Haiti, 1910–1929
    Record Group 80, General Records of the Department of the Navy
    Secret and Confidential Correspondence of the Office of the Chief of Naval Operations and the Office of the Secretary of the Navy, 1919–1927

Oral Histories

Ejército Soberano de la Defensa Nacional de Nicaragua, oral history tapes, Instituto de Estudio del Sandinismo, Centro de Historia Militar, Managua, Nicaragua
    Boedecker González, Luis. By Susana Morales, 1 and 4 July 1983
    Cana Araúz, Luisa. By Vera Patricia Ibana, n. d.
    Castillo Castilblanco, Mónico. Interviewer unknown, 16 July 1983
    Castillo Girón, Leonidas. By Ines Avanda, 11 July 1980
    Cerro Castellón, José M. By Susana Morales, 28 October 1983
    Ceteño Fonseca, Francisco. By Auxiliadora Rosales, 26 July 1983
    Contreras Dávila, Agustín. By Auxiliadora Rosales, 13 September 1983

Cruz, Gabriel. By Ligia María Peña, 4 November 1986
Duarte, Gregorio. By José Vallecillo, 8 July 1980
Flores Gladys, José. By Auxiliadora Rosales, 10 July 1983
González, Sinforozo. By Susana Morales, 12 March 1983
Hernández Blandón, Secundino. By Auxiliadora Rosales, 14 May 1983
Ortiz, José. By Chuno Blandón, n.d.
Osoba Izaguerri, Aurelio. Interviewer unknown, 6 July 1983
Pineda Cordero, Jesús. By Sandra Carrasquilla, 3 November 1986
Ramírez, Juan Pablo. By Guillermo Rodríguez, 17 May 1980
Rivas, Mercedes. By Wilfredo Ortíz, 16 July 1983
Rodríguez Casco, Anastacio. By Auxiliadora Rosales, 21 September 1983
Romero, Felipe. By Susana Morales, 20 April 1983
Rugama, Gerardo. By Auxiliadora Rosales, 9 July 1983
Salgado Castellano, Juan J. By Ligia María Peña, 4 November 1986
Sandino Pérez, Soledad. By Susana Morales, n.d.
Tercero González, Calixto. By Susana Morales and Auxiliadora Rosales, 24 February 1984
Toruño Reyes, Heriberto. By Susana Morales, 20 August 1983
Uriarte, Engracia. By Susana Morales, 22 August 1983
Veles, José. By Susana Morales, 13 August 1983
Zalaya, Tiburcio. By Susana Morales, 13 September 1983
Marine Corps Audiovisual Research Archives, Marine Corps Base, Quantico, Virginia.
Bessman, Leonard. By E. M. Coffman, 3 August 1989
Bourke, Thomas E., Lieut. Gen. USMC. By Lloyd E. Tatem, 16 July 1969
Craig, Edward A., Lieut. Gen. USMC. By L. E. Tatem, 16 May 1968
Dawson, Marion L., Maj. Gen. USMC. By Thomas E. Donnelly, 1 December 1970
Del Valle, Pedro, Lieut. Gen. USMC. By Benis Frank, 15 November 1966
Dessez, Lester A., Brig. Gen. USMC. By Thomas E. Donnelly, 16 June 1970
Ennis, Thomas G., Maj. Gen. USMC. By Thomas E. Donnelly, 22 March 1971
Erskine, Graves B., Gen. USMC. By Benis M. Frank, October 1969–March 1970
Miller, Ivan W., Brig. Gen. USMC. By Thomas E. Donnelly, 10 December 1970
Montoya, Alfonso Alexander. By Roberto Cajina, 23 February 1983
Munn, John C., Lieut. Gen. USMC. By Thomas E. Donnelly, 3–4 December 1970
Pfeiffer, Omar T., Maj. Gen. USMC. By Lloyd E. Tatem, 24 May 1968
Silverthorn, Merwin H., Lieut. Gen. USMC. By Benis M. Frank, 28 February 1969
Smith, Julian C., Gen. USMC. By C. W. Harrison, 13 January 1958

Newspapers

Ariel (Tegucigalpa)
Baltimore Sun
Berliner Tageblatt
Boston Transcript
Buenos Aires Herald
Butte Bulletin
Boston Daily Globe
Christian Science Monitor
Crítica (Buenos Aires)
Des Moines Register
Diario de Cuba (Santiago)
Diario Latino (San Salvador)
Diario Moderno (Managua)
Ecos del valle (Baní, Dominican Republic)
El Anuncio (San Francisco de Macorís, Dominican Republic)

El Centroamericano (León, Nicaragua)
El Comercio (Managua)
El Cronista (León, Nicaragua)
El Día (Ciudad Juárez, Mexico)
El Diario de Yucatán (Mérida)
El Dictamen (Veracruz, Mexico)
El Eco Mariano (Puerto Plata, Dominican Republic)
El Imparcial (Mexico City)
El Independiente (Mexico City)
El Libertador (Mexico City)
El Tiempo (Santo Domingo)
El Universal (Mexico City)
Excelsior (Bluefields, Nicaragua)
Gazette Rouge de Léningrad
Haïti-Journal (Port-au-Prince)
Hoy (Santo Domingo)
La Argentina Económica (Buenos Aires)
L'Action (Port-au-Prince)
La Información (Santiago, Dominican Republic)
La Nación (Buenos Aires)
La Nación (Havana)
La Opinión (Los Angeles)
La Poste (Port-au-Prince)
La Prensa (New York)
La Presse (Port-au-Prince)
La Razón (Buenos Aires)
Le Matin (Port-au-Prince)
Le Nouvelliste (Port-au-Prince)
Le Petit Impartial (Port-au-Prince)
Letras Antillanas (Antilla, Cuba)
Letras (Santo Domingo)
Les Annales Capoises (Cap-Haïtien)
Listín Diario (Santo Domingo)
New York Herald Tribune
New York Times
New York World
Panama América (Panama City)
Patria (San Salvador)
Renacimiento (Santo Domingo)
San Francisco Chronicle
Telegram (Boston)
The Review of the River Plate (Buenos Aires)
U.S. Daily News
Washington Post
Washington Star

Works Cited

Adler, Selig. "Bryan and Wilsonian Caribbean Penetration." *Hispanic American Historical Review* 20, no. 2 (May 1940): 198–226.
Alfau Durán, Vetillo. "La palabra del Pastor: Una verdadera carta magna." *Boletín del Archivo General de la Nación* (September–December 2005): 661–9.
Alvarez, Sonia E., Evelina Dagnino, and Arturo Escobar, eds. *Cultures of Politics, Politics of Cultures: Re-visioning Latin American Social Movements*. Boulder, Colo.: Westview Press, 1998.

Álvarez, Virtudes. *Mujeres del 16.* Santo Domingo: Mediabyte, 2005.

Amador, Armando. *El exilio y las banderas de Nicaragua.* Mexico City: Federación Editorial Mexicana, 1987.

Amador, Armando. *Nicaragua y Sandino: Las banderas de Gustavo Machado.* Caracas: Ediciones Centauro, 1984.

Amador, Armando. *Sandino y la derrota militar de los Estados Unidos en Nicaragua.* Mexico City: Federación Editorial Mexicana, 1987.

Anderson, Benedict. *Java in a Time of Revolution: Occupation and Resistance, 1944–1946.* Ithaca, N.Y.: Cornell University Press, 1972.

Arguello Bolanos, Horacio. "Los Vende Patria: Genios y Hombres." *Revista Conservadora,* October 1960, 24–35.

Arrieta, Nicolás. *¡Habla Sandino!* Masaya, Nicaragua: n.p., 1971.

Asociación de Jóvenes Dominicanos. *A la juventud del país.* Santiago, Dominican Republic: n.p., 1921.

Asprey, Robert B. "The Court-Martial of Smedley Butler." *Marine Corps Gazette,* December 1959, 28–34.

Auroi, Claude, and Aline Helg, eds, *Latin America 1810–2010: Dreams and Legacies.* London: Imperial College Press, 2011.

Averill, Gave. "Haitian Dance Bands, 1915–1970: Class, Race, and Authenticity." *Latin American Music Review* 10, no. 2 (Autumn 1989): 203–35.

Ayala, César. *American Sugar Kingdom: The Plantation Economy of the Spanish Caribbean, 1898–1934.* Chapel Hill: University of North Carolina Press, 1999.

Balcacér, Juan Daniel, ed. *Papeles y escritos de Francisco José Peynado (1867–1933), prócer de la Tercera República.* Vol. 1. Santo Domingo: Fundación Peynado Alvarez, 1994.

Balch, Emily G., ed. *Occupied Haiti.* New York: Garland, 1972. Original, New York: Writers Publishing Company, 1927.

Batson, Alfred. *Vagabond's Paradise.* Boston: Little, Brown, 1931.

Baugham, C. C., Commander USN. "United States Occupation of the Dominican Republic." *U.S. Naval Institute Proceedings* (December 1925): 2306–27.

Baylen, Joseph O. "Sandino: Death and Aftermath." *Mid-America,* April 1954, 118–9.

Baylen, Joseph O. "Sandino: Patriot or Bandit?" *Hispanic American Historical Review* 31, no. 3 (August 1951): 394–419.

Beach, Edward. "From Annapolis to Scapa Flow: The Autobiography of a Naval Officer." Unpublished manuscript. U.S. Navy, 1941. Hoover Institution Archives, Stanford, California.

Beals, Carleton. *Banana Gold.* Translated by Luciano Cuadra. Managua: Nueva Nicaragua, 1983. Original, Philadelphia: Lippincott, 1932.

Beals, Carleton. "Carta de Carleton Beals para Froylán Turcios." *Revista Ariel,* June 15, 1928, 1260.

Beals, Carleton. "With Sandino in Nicaragua I. To the Nicaraguan Border." *The Nation,* February 22, 1928, 204–5.

Beals, Carleton. "With Sandino in Nicaragua IV. Sandino Himself." *The Nation,* March 14, 1928, 288–9.

Beals, Carleton. "With Sandino in Nicaragua VI. Sandino—Bandit or Patriot?" *The Nation,* March 28, 1928, 340–1.

Beaulac, Willard L. *Career Ambassador.* New York: Macmillan, 1951.

Bellegarde, Dantès. *L'occupation américaine d'Haïti: ses conséquences morales et économiques.* Port-au-Prince: Chéraquit, 1929.

Bellegarde, Dantès. *Pour une Haïti heureuse. Vol II: Par l'éducation et le travail.* Port-au-Prince: Chéraquit, 1929.

Bellegarde, Dantès. *La résistance haïtienne: L'occupation américaine d'Haïti.* Montréal: Éditions Beauchemin, 1937.

Beman, Lamar T., ed. *Intervention in Latin America.* New York: H. W. Wilson, 1928.

Bendaña, Alejandro. *La mística de Sandino.* Managua: Centro de Estudios Internacionales, 1994.

Berroa, Quiterio. "Hurgando y Glosando," *L . . . . .* (Santo Domingo), February 27, 1921, 1–3.

Best, Richard A., Jr. *The U.S. Occupation of Haiti, 1915–1934*. Congressional Research Service Report for Congress. Bethesda, Md.: University Publications of America, 1994.

Betances, Emilio. "Social Classes and the Origin of the Modern State: The Dominican Republic, 1844–1930." *Latin American Perspectives* 22, no. 3 (Summer 1995): 20–40.

Bickel, Keith B. *Mars Learning: The Marine Corps Development of Small Wars Doctrine, 1915–1940*. Boulder, Colo.: Westview Press, 2001.

Binder, Carroll. "On the Nicaraguan Front: How the American Intervention Looks to an Eye-Witness." *New Republic*, March 16, 1927, 87–90.

Bingham, Hiram, III. *The Monroe Doctrine: An Obsolete Shibboleth*. New Haven, Conn.: Yale University Press, 1915.

Black, George. *The Good Neighbor: How the United States Wrote the History of Central America and the Caribbean*. New York: Pantheon Books, 1988.

Blanchet, Jules. *Peint par lui-même: La résistance de M. Dantès Bellegarde*. Port-au-Prince: V. Valcin, 1938.

Blancpain, François. *Haïti et les Etats-Unis 1915–1934: Histoire d'une occupation*. Paris: L'Harmattan, 1999.

Blassingame, John W. "The Press and American Intervention in Haiti and the Dominican Republic, 1904–1920." *Caribbean Studies* 9, no. 2 (July 1969): 27–43.

Bolaños Geyer, Alejandro. *El iluminado*. Masaya, Nicaragua: Bolaños Geyer, 2001.

Bolaños Geyer, Alejandro. *Sandino*. Masaya, Nicaragua: n.p., 2002.

Boot, Max. *The Savage Wars of Peace: Small Wars and the Rise of American Power*. New York: Basic Books, 2002.

Bordas, J. R. *Frente al imperialismo*. Santo Domingo: E. M. Casanova, 1923.

Borgen, José Francisco. *Una vida a la orilla de la historia*. Managua: Dilesa, 1979.

Bosch, Juan. *Las dictaduras dominicanas*. Santo Domingo: Alfa & Omega, 1988.

Boza Gutiérrez, Francisco. *Memorias de un soldado: Nicaragua y la Guardia Nacional: 1928–1979*. Managua: PAVSA, 2002.

Brierre, Jean F. *Le petit soldat: causerie prononcée à l'Association des étudiants en Droit*. Port-au-Prince: Imprimerie Haïtienne, 1934.

Brissman, D'Arcy M. "Interpreting American Hegemony: Civil Military Relations during the United States Marine Corps' Occupation of Haiti, 1915–1934." PhD diss., Duke University, 2001.

Brooks, David C. "Rebellion from Without: Culture and Politics along Nicaragua's Atlantic Coast in the Time of the Sandino Revolt, 1926–1934." PhD diss., University of Connecticut, 1998.

Brooks, David C. "US Marines, Miskitos and the Hunt for Sandino: The Rio Coco patrol in 1928." *Journal of Latin American Studies* 21, no. 2 (May 1989): 311–42.

Brown, George W. "Haiti and the United States." *Journal of Negro History* 8, no. 2 (April 1923): 134–52.

Brown, Philip M. "The Armed Occupation of Santo Domingo." *American Journal of International Law* 11, no. 2 (April 1917): 394–9.

Brugière, E. "Whither Nicaragua Now?" *Chile Pan-Am*, May 1931, 127–9, 148.

Buchenau, Jürgen. *In the Shadow of the Giant: The Making of Mexico's Central American Policy, 1876–1930*. Tuscaloosa: University of Alabama Press, 1996.

Buell, Raymond Leslie. *The American Occupation of Haiti*. New York: Foreign Policy Association Special Number, November 27–December 12, 1929.

Buell, Raymond Leslie. "The Intervention Policy of the United States." *Annals of the American Academy of Political and Social Science* 138 (July 1928): 69–73.

Burns, E. Bradford. *The Poverty of Progress: Latin America in the Nineteenth Century*. Berkeley: University of California Press, 1980.

Butler, Smedley D. "America's Armed Forces: 2. 'In Time of Peace': The Army." *Common Sense*, November 1935, 8–12.

Butler, Smedley D. *Old Gimlet Eye: The Adventures of Smedley D. Butler as told to Lowell Thomas*. New York: Farrar & Rinehart, 1933.

Calder, Bruce J. "Caudillos and *Gavilleros* versus the United States Marines: Guerrilla Insurgency during the Dominican Intervention, 1916–1924." *Hispanic American Historical Review* 58, no. 4 (1978): 649–75.

Calder, Bruce J. *The Impact of Intervention: The Dominican Republic during the U.S. Occupation of 1916–1924.* Austin: University of Texas Press, 1984.

Calder, Bruce J. "Varieties of Resistance to the United States Occupation of the Dominican Republic, 1916–1924." *SECOLAS Annales* 11 (March 1980): 103–36.

Calhoun, Frederick S. *Power and Principle: Armed Intervention in Wilsonian Foreign Policy.* Kent, Ohio: Kent State University Press, 1986.

Callcott, Wilfrid H. *The Caribbean Policy of the United States, 1890–1920.* Baltimore, Md.: Johns Hopkins University Press, 1942.

Camacho Navarro, Enrique. *Los usos de Sandino.* Mexico City: Universidad Nacional Autónoma de México, 1991.

Campbell-Jeffrey, Nancy. "Social Movement Theory and the Reconstruction of the Past: A Case Study of Augusto César Sandino and the Frente Sandinista de Liberación Nacional." PhD diss., University of Texas at Austin, 2005.

Campos Ponce, Xavier. *Los yanquis y Sandino.* Mexico: n.p., 1962.

"Can We Get Out of Nicaragua?" *The Nation,* February 22, 1928, 201–2.

Carlson, Evans F., Cap. USMC. "The Guardia Nacional de Nicaragua." *Marine Corps Gazette,* August 1937, 7–20.

Carlton, Eric. *Occupation: The Policies and Practices of Military Conquerors.* Savage, Md.: Barnes & Noble Books, 1992.

Carter, C. B. "The Kentucky Feud in Nicaragua: Why Civil War Has Become Her National Sport." *World's Work,* July 1927, 312–21.

Castor, Suzy. "The American Occupation of Haiti (1915–34) and the Dominican Republic, 1916–24." *Massachusetts Review* (Winter–Spring 1974): 253–75.

Castor, Suzy. *L'occupation américaine d'Haïti.* Port-au-Prince: Maison Henri Deschamps, 1988.

Cassá, Roberto. "Movimientos sociales durante la intervención militar norteamericana en República Dominicana." *Ecos* (Dominican Republic) 6, no. 8 (1998): 177–206.

Castro, Pedro. "El caudillismo en América Latina, ayer y hoy." *Política y Cultura* 27 (Spring 2007): 9–29.

Castro García, Teófilo. *Intervención yanqui, 1916–1924.* Santo Domingo: Editora Taller, 1978.

Cerdas, Rodolfo. *Sandino, el APRA y la Internacional Comunista.* Lima: EDIMSSA, 1983.

Cestero, Tulio M. "American Rule in Santo Domingo." *The Nation,* July 17, 1920, 78–9.

Challener, Richard D. *Admirals, Generals, and American Foreign Policy, 1898–1914.* Princeton, N.J.: Princeton University Press, 1973.

Chamorro, Pedro Joaquín. *Orígenes de la intervención americana en Nicaragua.* Managua: Editorial La Prensa, 1951.

Chapman, Charles E. "The United States and the Dominican Republic." *Hispanic American Historical Review* 7, no. 1 (February 1927): 84–91.

Charlip, Julie A. *Cultivating Coffee: The Farmers of Carazo, Nicaragua, 1880–1930.* Athens: Ohio University Press, 2003.

Chasteen, John C. *Heroes on Horseback: A Life and Times of the Last Gaucho Caudillos.* Albuquerque: University of New Mexico Press, 1995.

Chomsky, Aviva, and Aldo Lauria-Santiago, eds. *Identity and Struggle at the Margins of the Nation-State: The Laboring Peoples of Central America and the Hispanic Caribbean.* Durham, N.C.: Duke University Press, 1998.

Cipriano Venzon, Anne, ed. *Letters of a Leatherneck, 1898–1931.* New York: Praeger, 1992.

Colsón, Jayme. *Principios de representación.* Pamphlet.

Comisión de Información de la Representación en Cuba, del Frente Sandinista de Liberación Nacional. *Gustavo Machado nos habla de Augusto C. Sandino.* N.p., [1976?].

Condé, Georges. *La ville des Cayes.* Port-au-Prince: Imprimeur II, 2002.

Conferencia dictada por el Doctor Américo Lugo en el teatro Colón de Santiago de los Caballeros el día 25 de Junio de 1922. Santo Domingo: Rafael V. Montalvo, 1922.

Conrad, Robert Edgar, ed. and trans., and Sergio Ramírez, ed. *Sandino: The Testimony of a Nicaraguan Patriot, 1921–1934.* Princeton, N.J.: Princeton University Press, 1990.

Considine, Bob. "The Marines Have Landed." *American Weekly [Washington Post & Times Herald]*, October 5, 1958, 7–9.

Constitución de la Junta de Abstención Electoral de la Provincia de Santo Domingo. Santo Domingo: Rafael V. Montalvo, [1921?].

Contín Alfau, Melchor. *El Hato Mayor del Rey: reseña histórico-geográfica tradicional y religiosa.* Santo Domingo: Taller, 1991.

Conrady, Nancy J. "Le roman haïtien d'expression française et l'occupation américaine de 1915–1934: Trois décennies d'histoire vues par quatre romanciers haïtiens engagés (Stéphane Alexis, Annie Desroy, Léon Laleau, Mme Virgile Valcin)." PhD diss., Middlebury College French School, 1995.

Cook, Mercer. "Dantes Bellegarde." *Phylon* 1, no. 2 (2nd qtr.) 1940: 125–35.

Cooper, Donald B. "The Withdrawal of the United States from Haiti, 1928–1934." *Journal of Inter-American Studies* 5, no. 1 (January 1963): 83–101.

Corvington, Georges. *Port-au-Prince au cours des ans.* Vol. 5: *La capitale d'Haïti sous l'occupation, 1915–1922.* Port-au-Prince: Henri Deschamps, 1984.

Cox, Isaac J. "'Yankee Imperialism' and Spanish American Solidarity: A Colombian Interpretation." *Hispanic American Historical Review* 4, no. 2 (May 1921): 256–65.

Coyle, Randolph, Cap. USMC. "Service in Haiti." *Marine Corps Gazette*, December 1916, 343–8.

Craige, John H. *Cannibal Cousins.* New York: Minton, Balch, 1934.

Croly, Herbert. *The Promise of American Life.* New York: Macmillan, 1909.

Cross, M., and G. Heuman, eds. *Labour in the Caribbean: From Emancipation to Independence.* London: Warwick University Caribbean Studies, 1988.

Cuadra, Guillermo. "Memorias de un ex-oficial de la Guardia Nacional." *Revista Conservadora*, March 1962, supplement.

Cuadra, Manolo. *Contra Sandino en la montaña.* Managua: n.p., 1942.

Cummins, Lejeune. *Quijote on a Burro: Sandino and the Marines, a Study in the Formulation of Foreign Policy.* Mexico City: La Impresora Azteca, 1958.

Danache, B. *Le président Dartiguenave et les Américains.* 2nd ed. Port-au-Prince: Les Editions Fardin, 1984.

Dash, J. Michael. *Haiti and the United States: National Stereotypes and the Literary Imagination.* 2nd ed. New York: St. Martin's Press, 1997.

Daugherty, Leo J., III. "Reminiscences of a Rio Coco Marine." *Sentinel* (Marine Corps Heritage Foundation), Winter 2000, 3–5.

Davis, Burke. *Marine! The Life of Lt. Gen. Lewis B. (Chesty) Puller, USMC (Ret).* Boston: Little, Brown, 1962.

Davis, Henry C., Lt. Col. USMC, "Indoctrination of Latin–American Service," *Marine Corps Gazette*, June 1920: 154–61.

De Bekker, L. J. "The Massacre at Aux Cayes." *The Nation*, March 12, 1930, 310.

De Belausteguigoitia, Ramón. *Con Sandino en Nicaragua: la hora de la paz.* Managua: Nueva Nicaragua, 1981. Original, Madrid: n.p., 1934.

DeConde, Alexander. *Herbert Hoover's Latin-American Policy.* Stanford, Calif.: Stanford University Press, 1951.

De la Fuente, Ariel. *Children of Facundo: Caudillo and Gaucho Insurgency during the Argentine State-Formation Process (La Rioja, 1853–1870).* Durham, N.C.: Duke University Press, 2000.

De la Selva, Salomón. "Sandino." *The Nation*, January 18, 1928, 64.

De la Selva, Salomón. *Sandino: Free Country or Death.* Managua: Biblioteca Nacional de Nicaragua, 1984.

De León, Carlos V. *Casos y cosas de ayer: narraciones históricas sobre la primera ocupación militar de la República Dominicana por las fuerzas navales de los Estados Unidos de América años 1916 a 1924, y otros relatos.* Santo Domingo: Imprenta Núñez, 1972.

Delgadillo, Charles Edward. "Destiny and Democracy: Liberals, Reform, and U.S. Foreign Policy, 1914–1941." PhD diss., University of California-Santa Barbara, 2010.

Delpar, Helen. *The Enormous Vogue of Things Mexican: Cultural Relations between the United States and Mexico, 1920–1935.* Tuscaloosa: University of Alabama Press, 1992.

Delpar, Helen. *Looking South: The Evolution of Latin Americanist Scholarship in the United States, 1850–1975.* Tuscaloosa: University of Alabama Press, 2008.

Dempsey, Gary T., and Roger W. Fontaine. *Fool's Errand: America's Recent Encounters with Nation Building.* Washington, D.C.: CATO Institute, 2001.

Dennis, Laurence. "Nicaragua: In Again Out Again." *Foreign Affairs* 10 (April 1931): 496–500.

Denny, Harold N. *Dollars for Bullets: The Story of American Rule in Nicaragua.* Westport, Conn.: Greenwood Press, 1929.

De Noel Henríquez M., Rosa, et al. *Al pueblo dominicano.* Pamphlet.

Department of the Navy. "List of Expeditions, 1901–1929," http://www.history.navy.mil/library/online/haiti_list_exp.htm. Last accessed August 16, 2013.

Derby, Lauren H. "Haitians, Magic, and Money: Raza and Society in the Haitian-Dominican Borderlands, 1900 to 1937." *Comparative Studies in Society and History* 36, no. 3 (July 1994): 488–526.

Derby, Lauren H. "The Magic of Modernity: Dictatorship and Civic Culture in the Dominican Republic, 1916–1962." PhD diss., University of Chicago, 1998.

Derby, Lauren H. *The Dictator's Seduction: Politics and the Popular Imagination in the Era of Trujillo.* Durham, N.C.: Duke University Press, 2009.

Deschamps, Enrique. *El espíritu de España en la liberación de la República Dominicana, 1916–1924.* Caracas: Tipografia Universal, 1928.

Diffie, Bailey W. "The Ideology of Hispanidad." *Hispanic American Historical Review* 23, no. 3 (August 1943): 457–82.

Diffie, Bailey, and Justice Whitfield Diffie. *Porto Rico: A Broken Pledge.* New York: Vanguard, 1931.

Dodd, Thomas J., Jr. "United States in Nicaraguan Politics: Supervised Elections, 1927–1932." PhD diss., George Washington University, 1966.

Dore, Elizabeth. *Myths of Modernity: Peonage and Patriarchy in Nicaragua.* Durham, N.C.: Duke University Press, 2006.

Dospital, Michelle. *Siempre más allá: el movimiento Sandinista en Nicaragua, 1927–1934.* Managua: IHN/CEMCA, 1996.

Douglas, Paul H. "The American Occupation of Haiti I." *Political Science Quarterly* 42, no. 2 (June 1927): 228–58.

Douglas, Paul H. "The American Occupation of Haiti II." *Political Science Quarterly* 42, no. 3 (September 1927): 368–96.

Dubois, Laurent. *Haiti: The Aftershocks of History.* New York: Metropolitan Books, 2012.

Ducoudray, Felix Servio. "Una epopeya ignorada: fueron bandidos los guerrilleros anti-Yanquis de 1916?" *Ahora,* July 15, 1974, 36–43.

Ducoudray, Felix Servio. *Los "Gavilleros" del Este: Una epopeya calumniada.* Santo Domingo: UASD, 1976.

Edelstein, David. *Occupational Hazards: Success and Failure in Military Occupation.* Ithaca, N.Y.: Cornell University Press, 2008.

Edelstein, David. "Occupational Hazards: Why Military Occupations Succeed or Fail." *International Security* 29, no. 1 (Summer 2004): 49–91.

Editorial. "Big Brother or Big Bully." *The Nation,* July 14, 1926, 25.

Editorial. "Hoover's Problem in Haiti." *New Republic,* December 18, 1929, 82–3.

Editorial. *The Nation,* March 26, 1930, n.p.

"El drama de Nicaragua," *Revista Forum* (Peru), September 1978, 17–26.

Ellis, L. Ethan. *Frank B. Kellogg and American Foreign Relations, 1925–1929*. New Brunswick, N.J.: Rutgers University Press, 1961.

Ellis Cambiaso, Federico. *Los cuatro monstruos de la anexión*. Santo Domingo: Rafael V. Montalvo, 1922.

Espinosa, J. Manuel. *Inter-American Beginnings of U.S. Cultural Diplomacy, 1936–1948*. Washington, D.C.: U.S. Government Printing Office, 1976.

Fabre, Michel J. "La *Revue Indigène* et le mouvement nouveau noir." *Revue de littérature comparée* 1 (January–March 1977): 30–9.

Fejes, Fred. *Imperialism, Media, and the Good Neighbor: New Deal Foreign Policy and United States Shortwave Broadcasting to Latin America*. Norwood, N.J.: Ablex, 1986.

Féquière, Fleury. *L'éducation haïtienne*. Port-au-Prince: Imprimerie de l'Abeille, 1906.

Ferguson, Niall. *Colossus: The Rise and Fall of the American Empire*. New York: Penguin Books, 2004.

Ferrell, Robert H. *The Presidency of Calvin Coolidge*. Lawrence: University of Kansas Press, 1998.

Ferrell, Robert H. "Repudiation of a Repudiation." *Journal of American History*, March 1965, 669–73.

Ferreras, Ramón Alberto. *Enfoques de la intervención militar norteamericana a la RD (1916–1924)*. Santo Domingo: Editorial del Nordeste, 1984.

Fiallo, Fabio. *The Crime of Wilson in Santo Domingo*. Havana: Arellano, 1940.

Fletcher, Henry P. "Quo Vadis Haiti." *Foreign Affairs* 8, no. 4 (1930): 533–48.

Foner, Philip S. *U.S. Labor Movement and Latin America: A History*. South Hadley, Mass.: Bergin & Garvey, 1988.

Fowler, Carolyn. "The Shared Vision of Langston Hughes and Jacques Roumain." *Black American Literature Forum* 15, no. 3 (Autumn 1981), 84–8.

Frank, Harry. "The Death of Charlemagne." *Century Magazine*, May 1920, 22–35.

Frank, Harry. *Roaming through the West Indies*. New York: Century, 1920.

Franks, Julie. "The *Gavilleros* of the East: Social Banditry as Political Practice in the Dominican Sugar Region, 1900–1924." *Journal of Historical Sociology* 8, no. 2 (June 1995): 158–81.

Frazier, Charles E., Jr. "The Dawn of Nationalism and Its Consequences in Nicaragua." PhD diss, University of Texas, 1958.

Fuller, Stephen, M. CPT USMCR, and Graham A. Cosmas. *Marines in the Dominican Republic 1916–1924*. Washington, D.C.: History and Museums Division Headquarters, U.S. Marine Corps, 1974.

Gaillard, Roger. *Les blancs débarquent*. Vol. 3: *Premier écrasement du cacoïsme: 1915*. N.p., 1981.

Gaillard, Roger. *Les blancs débarquent*. Vol. 4: *La République autoritaire, 1916–1917*. N.p., 1981.

Gaillard, Roger. *Les blancs débarquent*. Vol. 5: *Hinche mise en croix, 1917–1918*. N.p., 1982.

Gaillard, Roger. *Les blancs débarquent*. Vol. 6: *Charlemagne Péralte le caco, 1918–1919*. N.p., 1982.

Gaillard, Roger. *Les blancs débarquent*. Vol. 7: *La guérilla de Batraville, 1919–1934*. N.p., 1983.

García Godoy, Federico. *El derrumbe*. Santo Domingo: UASD, 1975. Original, n.p., 1916.

García Muñiz, Humberto, and Jorge Giovannetti. "Garveyismo y racismo en el Caribe: El caso de la población cocola en la República Dominicana." *Clío* (Dominican Republic) 168 (2004): 118–202.

García Salgado, Andres. *Yo estuve con Sandino*. Mexico City: Editorial Color, 1979.

Gellman, Irwin F. *Good Neighbor Diplomacy: United States Policies in Latin America, 1933–1945*. Baltimore, Md.: Johns Hopkins University Press, 1979.

Gellner, Ernest. *Nations and Nationalism*. Ithaca, N.Y.: Cornell University Press, 1983.

Ghiraldo, Albert. *Yanquilandia bárbara: la lucha contra el imperialismo*. Madrid: n.p., 1929.

Gilbert, Gregorio Urbano. *Junto a Sandino*. Santo Domingo: UASD, [1979?].

Gilbert, Gregorio Urbano. *Mi lucha contra el invasor yanqui de 1916*. Santo Domingo: UASD, 1975.

Go, Julian. *American Empire and the Politics of Meaning: Elite Political Cultures in the Philippines and Puerto Rico during U.S. Colonialism*. Durham, N.C.: Duke University Press, 2008.

Gobat, Michel. *Confronting the American Dream: Nicaragua under U.S. Imperial Rule*. Durham, N.C.: Duke University Press, 2005.

Gobat, Michel. "Granada's Conservative Revolutionaries: Anti-Elite Violence and the Nicaraguan Civil War of 1912." Presented at the Third Central American Congress of History, San José, Costa Rica, July 15–18, 1996.

Gobat, Michel. "Nicaragua perdió la partida, la ganó la oligarquía. Le élite nicaragüense y la intervención financiera de los Estados Unidos en Nicaragua, 1912–1926," *Revista de Historia* (Nicaragua) 5/6 (1995): 58–71.

Goldwert, Marvin. *The Constabulary in the Dominican Republic and Nicaragua: Progeny and Legacy of United States Intervention.* Gainesville: University of Florida Press, 1962.

Gómez, Juan. "The Gallant Dominicans." *American Mercury,* May 1929, 89–95.

González Canalda, María Filomena. "Incursiones de gavilleros: tiempo y lugar, 1904–1916." *Clío* (Dominican Republic): 103–17.

González Canalda, María Filomena. *Línea noroeste: testimonio del patriotismo olvidado.* San Pedro de Macorís, Dominican Republic: Universidad Central del Este, 1985.

Gould, Jeffrey L. *To Lead as Equals: Rural Protest and Political Consciousness in Chinandega, Nicaragua, 1912–1979.* Chapel Hill: University of North Carolina Press, 1990.

Gould, Jeffrey L. *To Die in This Way: Nicaraguan Indians and the Myth of Mestisaje, 1880–1965.* Durham, N.C.: Duke University Press, 1998.

Grandin, Greg. *Empire's Workshop: Latin America, the United States, and the Rise of the New Imperialism.* New York: Metropolitan Books, 2006.

Gray, John A., Maj. USMC. "The Second Nicaraguan Campaign." *Marine Corps Gazette,* February 1933, 36–41.

Greathouse, R. H. "King of the Banana Wars." *Marine Corps Gazette,* June 1960, 29–33.

Greer, Virginia L. "State Department Policy in Regard to the Nicaraguan Election of 1924." *Hispanic American Historical Review* 34 (November 1954): 445–67.

Grieb, Kenneth J. *The Latin American Policy of Warren G. Harding.* Fort Worth: Texas Christian University Press, 1976.

Grieb, Kenneth J. "Warren G. Harding and the Dominican Republic U.S. Withdrawal, 1921–1923." *Journal of Inter-American Studies* 11, no. 3 (July 1969): 425–40.

Grossman, Richard. "'Hermanos en la Patria': Nationalism, Honor and Rebellion: Augusto Sandino and the Army in Defense of the National Sovereignty of Nicaragua, 1927–1934." PhD diss., University of Chicago, 1996.

Grossman, Richard. "'La Patria es nuestra madre': Género, patriarcado y nacionalismo dentro del Movimiento Sandinista, 1927–1934." Paper presented at the Third Congreso Centroamericano de Historia, San José, Costa Rica, July 15–18, 1996.

Grossman, Richard. "Solidarity with Sandino: The Anti-Intervention and Solidarity Movements in the United States, 1927–1933." *Latin American Perspectives* 36, no. 67 (November 2009): 67–79.

Gruening, Ernest. "At Last We're Getting Out of Haiti." *The Nation,* June 20, 1934, 700–1.

Gruening, Ernest. *Many Battles: The Autobiography of Ernest Gruening.* New York: Liveright, 1973.

Gutiérrez S., Tomás J., ed. *Protestantismo y política en América Latina y el Caribe.* Lima: CEHILA, 1996.

Gutmann, Matthew C. "Rituals of Resistance: A Critique of the Theory of Everyday Forms of Resistance." *Latin American Perspectives* 20, no. 2 (Spring 1993): 74–92.

Guzmán, Avelino. *Ocupación militar norteamericana 1916–1924: aspecto jurídico de la Convención dominico-americana de 1907.* 2nd ed. Santiago, Dominican Republic: Editora Teófilo, 1999.

"Haitians Protest N.A.A.C.P. Resolution." *The Crisis,* October 1935, 298.

Hale, Charles R. *Resistance and Contradiction: Miskitu Indians and the Nicaraguan State, 1894–1987.* Stanford, Calif.: Stanford University Press, 1994.

Ham, Clifford D. "Americanizing Nicaragua: How Yankee Marines, Financial Oversight, and Baseball Are Stabilizing Central America." *Review of Reviews,* February 1916, 185–91.

Hanson, Gail. "Sumner Welles and the American System: The United States in the Caribbean, 1920–1940." PhD diss., State University of New York at Stony Book, 1990.

Haring, Clarence H. "South America and Our Policy in the Caribbean." *Annals of the Academy of Political and Social Science* 132 (July 1927): 146–52.

Haring, Clarence H. *South America Looks at the United States.* New York: Macmillan, 1928.

Haring, Clarence H. "The Two Americas." *Foreign Affairs* (April 1927): 364–78.

Harris, Louis K., and Victor Alba. *The Political Culture and Behavior of Latin America.* Kent, Ohio: Kent State University Press, 1974.

Harrison, Benjamin T. *Dollar Diplomat: Chandler Anderson and American Diplomacy in Mexico and Nicaragua.* Pullman: Washington State University Press, 1988.

Hart, John Mason. *Empire and Revolution: The Americans in Mexico since the Civil War.* Berkeley: University of California Press, 2002.

Hayes, Carlton J. H. *Essays on Nationalism.* New York: MacMillan, 1937.

Hazlet, Raymond L. "United States Foreign Policy in Nicaragua, 1909–1928." Master's thesis, University of California-Berkeley, 1927.

Healy, David. *Gunboat Diplomacy in the Wilson Era: The U.S. Navy in Haiti, 1915–1916.* Madison: University of Wisconsin Press, 1976.

Healy, David. *Rise to Hegemony: The United States in the Caribbean, 1898–1917.* Madison: University of Wisconsin Press, 1988.

Heinl Jr., Robert Debs, and Nancy Gordon Heinl. *Written in Blood: The Story of the Haitian People 1492–1971.* Boston, Mass.: Houghton Mifflin, 1978.

Henríquez García, Enriquillo. *Cartas del Presidente Francisco Henríquez y Carvajal.* Santo Domingo: Sánchez, 1970.

Henríquez Ureña, Familia. *Epistolario.* Santo Domingo: Secretaría de Estado de Educación, 1994.

Henríquez Ureña, Max. *Los yanquis en Santo Domingo: la verdad de los hechos comprobada por datos y documentos oficiales.* Santo Domingo: Editora de Santo Domingo, 1977. Original, Madrid: n.p., 1929.

Henríquez y Carvajal, Francisco. "De Presidente a Presidente," *Pluma y Espada,* January 19, 1922, n.p.

Herman, Daniel. *The Comintern in Mexico.* Washington, D.C.: Public Affairs Press, 1974.

Herrera Rodríguez, Rafael D. "Le desocupación militar norteamericana de 1924 vista por Américo Lugo." *Clío* 176 (July–December 2008): 123–38.

Hill, Roscoe. "Los Marinos en Nicaragua, 1912–1925." *Revista Conservadora del Pensamiento Centroamericano,* December 1971, 2–11.

"History of Flag Career of Rear Admiral W.B. Caperton, U.S. Navy Commencing January 5, 1915," http://www.history.navy.mil/library/online/haiti_cap.htm. Last accessed May 20, 2013.

Hobsbawm, Eric. *Bandits.* New York: New Press, 2000.

Hodges, Donald C. *Intellectual Foundations of the Nicaraguan Revolution.* Austin: University of Texas Press, 1986.

Hodges, Donald C. *Sandino's Communism: Spiritual Politics for the Twenty-First Century.* Austin: University of Texas Press, 1992.

Hoffman, Léon-François. "Les États-Unis et les Américains dans les lettres haïtiennes." *Etudes Littéraires* 13, no. 2 (August 1980): 289–312.

Holden, Robert H. *Armies without Nations: Public Violence and State Formation in Central America, 1821–1960.* New York: Oxford, 2004.

Holden, Robert H. "Constructing the Limits of State Violence in Central America: Towards a New Research Agenda." *Journal of Latin American Studies* 28, no. 2 (May 1996): 435–59.

Holmes, Capt. Maurice G. "With the Horse Marines in Nicaragua." *Marine Corps Gazette* 68, no. 2, February 1984, 36–43.

Hoover, Herbert. *The Memoirs of Herbert Hoover: The Cabinet and the Presidency, 1920–1933.* New York: Macmillan, 1952.

"Hoover to See South America First." *Literary Digest,* November 24, 1928, n.p.

Hopelman, Antonio, and Juan A. Senior, eds. *Documentos históricos que se refieren a la intervención armada de los Estados Unidos de Norte América y la implantación de un Gobierno Militar Americano en la República Dominicana.* 2nd ed. Santo Domingo: Librería Dominicana, 1973. Original, n.p., 1922.

Hopkins, J. A. H., and Melinda Alexander. *Machine-Gun Diplomacy.* New York: Lewis Copeland, 1928.

Howlett, Charles F. "Neighborly Concern: John Nevin Sayre and the Mission of Peace and Good-will to Nicaragua, 1927–28." *Americas* 45, no. 1 (July 1988): 19–46.

Hudson, Peter James. "Dark Finance: An Unofficial History of Wall Street, American Empire and the Caribbean, 1889–1925." PhD diss., New York University, 2007.

Hughes, Langston. *Autobiography: I Wonder as I Wander.* Vol. 13: *The Collected Works of Langston Hughes,* edited by Joseph McClaren. Columbia: University of Missouri Press, 2003.

Hurston, Zora N. *Tell My Horse.* New York: J. B. Lippincott, 1938.

Incháustegui, Arístides, and Blanca Delgado Malagón, eds. *Vetilio Alfau Durán en Anales: escritos y documentos.* Santo Domingo: Banco de Reservas, 1997.

Inman, Samuel G. "Hard Problems in Haiti." *Current History,* 1920, 338–42.

Inman, Samuel G. "The American Occupation of Haiti." *Current History,* 1920, 342–8.

Inman, Samuel G. "Imperialistic America." *Atlantic Monthly,* July 1924, 107–16.

Instituto de Estudio del Sandinismo. *Ahora sé que Sandino manda.* Managua: Editorial Nueva Nicaragua, 1986.

Instituto de Estudio del Sandinismo. *Augusto C. Sandino, Padre de la Revolución Popular Sandinista y Antimperialista.* Managua: Nueva Nicaragua, 1985.

"Iraqi Public Opinion and the Occupation," *Global Policy Forum* http://www.globalpolicy.org/component/content/article/168/37143.html, last accessed May 20, 2013.

Jenks, Leland. *Our Cuban Colony, a Study in Sugar.* New York: Vanguard, 1928.

Joes, Anthony J. *America and Guerrilla Warfare.* Lexington: University Press of Kentucky, 2000.

Johnson, James W. *Along this Way: The Autobiography of James Weldon Johnson.* New York: Da Capo Press, 2000. Original, n.p., 1933.

Johnson, James W. "Self-Determining Haiti I: The American Occupation." *The Nation,* August 28, 1920, 236–8.

Johnson, James W. "Self-Determining Haiti II: What the United States Has Accomplished." *The Nation,* September 4, 1920, 265–7.

Johnson, James W. "The Truth about Haiti: An N.A.A.C.P. Investigation." *The Crisis,* September 1920, 217–24.

Johnson, Robert D. *Ernest Gruening and the American Dissenting Tradition.* Cambridge, Mass.: Harvard University Press, 1998.

Johnson, Robert D. *The Peace Progressives and American Foreign Relations.* Cambridge, Mass.: Harvard University Press, 1995.

Joseph, Gilbert M., Catherine C. LeGrand, and Ricardo D. Salvatore, eds. *Close Encounters of Empire: Writing the Cultural History of U.S.–Latin American Relations.* Durham, N.C.: Duke University Press, 1998.

Joseph, Gilbert M., and Daniel Nugent, eds. *Everyday Forms of State Formation: Revolution and the Negotiation of Rule in Modern Mexico.* Durham, N.C.: Duke University Press, 1994.

Joseph, Gilbert M. "On the Trail of Latin American Bandits: A Reexamination of Peasant Resistance." *Latin American Research Review* 25, no. 3 (1990): 7–53.

Joseph, Gilbert M., ed. *Reclaiming the Political in Latin American History: Essays from the North.* Durham, N.C.: Duke University Press, 2001.

Juarez, Joseph R. "United States Withdrawal from Santo Domingo." *Hispanic American Historical Review* 42, no. 2 (May 1962): 152–90.

Kamman, William. *A Search for Stability: United States Diplomacy toward Nicaragua, 1925–1933.* Notre Dame, Ind.: University of Notre Dame Press, 1968.

Kazin, Michael, and Joseph A. McCartin, eds. *Americanism: New Perspectives of the History of an Ideal.* Chapel Hill: University of North Carolina Press, 2006.

Keck, Margaret E., and Kathryn Sikkink. *Activists beyond Borders: Advocacy Networks in International Politics.* Ithaca, N.Y.: Cornell University Press, 1998.

"Keeping the Peace in Nicaragua." *Literary Digest,* August 24, 1912, 286.

Kelsey, Carl. "The American Intervention in Haiti and the Dominican Republic." *Annals of the American Academy of Political and Social Science* 100 (March 1922): 110–202.

Kepner, Charles David, Jr., and Jay Henry Soothill. *The Banana Empire: A Case Study of Economic Imperialism.* New York: Russell & Russell, 1967. Original, Vanguard Press, 1935.

Kinloch Tijerino, Frances. "Identidad nacional e intervención extranjera. Nicaragua, 1840–1930." *Revista de Historia* (January–February 2002): 163–89.

Klein, Alan. *Sugarball: The American Game, the Dominican Dream.* New Haven, Conn.: Yale University Press, 1991.

Knight, Melvin M. *The Americans in Santo Domingo.* New York: Vanguard Press, 1928.

Kuser, John D. *Haiti: Its Dawn of Progress after Years in a Night of Revolution.* Westport, Conn.: Negro Universities Press, 1921.

La comisión nacionalista en Washington. Ciudad Trujillo: La Opinión, 1939.

Lane, Rufus H., Col. USMC. "Civil Government in Santo Domingo in the Early Days of the Military Occupation." *Marine Corps Gazette,* June 1922, 127–46.

Langley, Lester D. *The Banana Wars: United States Intervention in the Caribbean, 1898–1934.* Wilmington, Del.: Scholarly Resources, 2002. Original, Lexington: University Press of Kentucky, 1983.

Langley, Lester D. *The United States and the Caribbean in the Twentieth Century.* Athens: University of Georgia Press, 1985.

Legrand, Catherine C. "Informal Resistance on a Dominican Sugar Plantation during the Trujillo Dictatorship." *Hispanic American Historical Review* 75, no. 4 (November 1995): 555–96.

Lerebours, Michel-Philippe. "The Indigenist Revolt: Haitian Art, 1927–1944." *Callaloo* 15, no. 3 (Summer 1992): 711–25.

"Less Than A Day's Automobile Casualties," *U.S. Naval Institute Proceedings,* July 1932, 1067.

Levine, Daniel H., ed. *Constructing Culture and Power in Latin America.* Ann Arbor: University of Michigan Press, 1993.

Levy, Eugene. *James Weldon Johnson: Black Leader, Black Voice.* Chicago, Ill.: University of Chicago Press, 1973.

Leyburn, James G. *The Haitian People.* New Haven, Conn.: Yale University Press, 1966. Original, Yale University Press, 1941.

Lobb, John. "Caste and Class in Haiti." *American Journal of Sociology* 46, no. 1 (July 1940): 23–34.

Longley, Kyle. *In the Eagle's Shadow: The United States and Latin America.* Wheeling, Ill.: Harlan-Davidson, 2002.

López, Jacinto. *The Conquest of Nicaragua by the United States: Letter to President Taft.* New York: Press of William Fitzpatrick, 1913.

López Méndez, R. Vargas. "El pueblo dominicano frente a la intervención norteamericana." *Boletín del Archivo General de la Nación* 31, no. 115 (May–August 2006): 275–98.

Lord, Rebecca. "An 'Imperative Obligation': Public Health and the United States Military Occupation of the Dominican Republic." PhD diss., University of Maryland, College Park, 2002.

Lowenthal, Abraham F., ed. *Exporting Democracy: The United States and Latin America.* Baltimore, Md.: Johns Hopkins University Press, 1991.

Lozano, Wilfredo. *La dominación imperialista en la República Dominicana, 1900–1930.* Santo Domingo: UASD, 1976.

Lugo, Américo. *El nacionalismo dominicano.* Santiago: La Información, 1923.

Lugo, Américo. *El Plan de Validación Hughes-Peynado.* Santo Domingo: La Cuna de América, 1922.

Lugo, Américo. *La intervención americana.* Santo Domingo: 1916.

Lundius, Jan, and Mats Lundahl. *Peasants and Religion: A Socioeconomic Study of Dios Olivorio and the Palma Sola Movement in the Dominican Republic.* New York: Routledge, 2000.

Macaulay, Neill. *The Sandino Affair.* Chicago, Ill.: Quadrangle Books, 1967.

Marsh, Margaret. *The Bankers in Bolivia.* New York: Vanguard, 1928.

Matthews, John M. "Roosevelt's Latin-American Policy." *American Political Science Review* 29, no. 5 (October 1935): 805–20.

Mayes, April. "Why Dominican Feminism Moved to the Right: Class, Colour and Women's Activism in the Dominican Republic, 1880s–1940s." *Gender & History* 20, no. 2 (August 2008): 349–71.

McCormick, Medill. "Our Failure in Haiti." *The Nation,* December 1, 1920, 615–6.

McCrocklin, James H. *Garde d'Haïti: Twenty Years of Organization and Training by the United States Marine Corps.* Annapolis, Md.: United States Naval Institute, 1956.

McJimsey, George T., ed. *Documentary History of the Franklin D. Roosevelt Presidency*. Vol. 19: *Cuba, the Good Neighbor Policy, and the Abrogation of the Platt Amendment*. Lanham, Md.: University Press of America, 2003.

McKim, Robert, and Jeff McMahan, eds. *The Morality of Nationalism*. New York: Oxford University Press, 1997.

McPherson, Alan. "Artful Resistances: Song, Literature, and Representations of U.S. Occupations in Nicaragua and Hispaniola." *Latin Americanist* 56, no 2 (June 2012): 93–117.

McPherson, Alan. "Foreigners under U.S. Occupations in the Caribbean," *International History Review* 35, no. 1 (March 2013): 100–20.

McPherson, Alan. "The Irony of Legal Pluralism in U.S. Occupations," *American Historical Review* 117, no. 4 (October 2012): 1149–72.

McPherson, Alan. "Joseph Jolibois Fils and the Flaws of Haitian Resistance to U.S. Occupation." *Journal of Haitian Studies* 16, no. 2 (Fall 2010): 120–47.

McPherson, Alan. "Personal Occupations: Women's Responses to U.S. Military Occupations in Latin America." *Historian* 72, no. 3 (Fall 2010): 568–98.

McPherson, Alan. *Yankee No! Anti-Americanism in U.S.-Latin American Relations*. Cambridge, Mass.: Harvard University Press, 2003.

Mejía, Félix E. *Al rededor y en contra del Plan Hughes-Peynado*. Santo Domingo: Gran Librería Selecta, 1922.

Mejía, Luis F. *De Lilís a Trujillo: historia contemporánea de la República Dominicana*. Caracas: Editorial Elite, 1944.

Merritt, Edson. "The Coco River Patrol: Operations of a Marine Patrol along the Coco River in Nicaragua." *Marine Corps Gazette*, August 1936, 18–23, 38–48.

Michel, Georges. *Charlemagne Péralte and the First American Occupation of Haiti*. Translated by Douglas Henry Daniels. Dubuque, Iowa: Kendall/Hunt, 1996.

Miller, Charles J. "Diplomatic Spurs: Our Experiences in Santo Domingo." *Marine Corps Gazette*, February 1935, 43–50.

Miller, Charles J. "Diplomatic Spurs: Our Experiences in Santo Domingo." *Marine Corps Gazette*, August 1935, 35–55.

Millet, Kethly. *Les paysans haïtiens et l'occupation américaine d'Haïti, 1915–1930*. La Salle, Québec: Collectif Paroles, 1978.

Millett, Richard L. *Searching for Stability: The U.S. Development of Constabulary Forces in Latin America and the Philippines*. Fort Leavenworth, Kans.: Combat Institute Studies Press, 2010.

Mintz, Sidney. "The Rural Proletariat and the Problem of Rural Proletarian Consciousness." *Journal of Peasant Studies* 1, no. 3 (April 1974): 291–325.

Moncada, José María. "Nicaragua and American Intervention." *Outlook*, December 14, 1927, 460–2, 477.

Montague, Ludwell L. *Haiti and the United States 1714–1938*. Durham, N.C.: Duke University Press, 1940.

Moore, Margaret. *The Ethics of Nationalism*. New York: Oxford University Press, 2001.

Mora Lomeli, Raul H. "Pensamiento de Sandino ante la religión de su tiempo." *Revista Encuentro*, 1984, 43–58.

Moral, Paul. *Le paysan haïtien: étude sur la vie rurale en Haïti*. Paris: G. P. Maisonneuve & Larose, 1961.

Morand, Paul. *Hiver caraïbe, documentaire*. Paris: Flammarion, 1929.

Moya Pons, Frank. "Import-Substitution Industrialization Policies in the Dominican Republic, 1925–1961." *Hispanic American Historical Review* 70, no. 4 (November 1990): 539–77.

Morelli, Federica. "Entre ancien et nouveau régime: L'histoire politique hispano-américaine du XIXe siècle." *Annales. Histoire, Sciences Sociales* 59e Année, 4 (July–August 2004): 759–81.

Munro, Dana G. "The American Withdrawal from Haiti, 1929–1934." *Hispanic American Historical Review* 49, no. 1 (February 1969): 1–26.

Munro, Dana G. "The Establishment of Peace in Nicaragua." *Foreign Affairs* 11, no. 4 (July 1933): 696–705.

Munro, Dana G. *The Five Republics of Central America: Their Political and Economic Development and their Relationship with the United States*. New York: Russell & Russell, 1967.

Munro, Dana G. *Intervention and Dollar Diplomacy in the Caribbean 1900–1921*. Princeton, N.J.: Princeton University Press, 1964.

Munro, Dana G. *The United States and the Caribbean Republics 1921–1933*. Princeton, N.J.: Princeton University Press, 1974.

Musicant, Ivan. *The Banana Wars: A History of United States Military Intervention in Latin America from the Spanish-American War to the Invasion of Panama*. New York: Macmillan, 1990.

Nabulsi, Karma. *Traditions of War: Occupation, Resistance, and the Law*. New York: Oxford University Press, 1999.

Nalty, Bernard C. *The United States Marines in Nicaragua*. Rev. ed. Washington, D.C.: Historical Branch, G-3 Division, Headquarters, U.S. Marine Corps, 1968.

Navarro-Génie, Marco A. *Augusto "César" Sandino: Messiah of Light and Truth*. Syracuse, N.Y.: Syracuse University Press, 2002.

Nearing, Scott, and Joseph Freeman. *Dollar Diplomacy: A Study in American Imperialism*. New York: Modern Reader, 1969. Original, n.p.: B. W. Huebsch, 1925.

"Nicaragua and After." *The Nation*, July 24, 1913, 70.

"Nicaragua and the United States." *Information Service* (Federal Council of the Churches of Christ in America), April 4, 1931, 4.

"Nicaragua's Bloody 'Peace.'" *Literary Digest*, January 14, 1928, 8.

Nicholls, David. "Ideology and Political Protest in Haiti, 1930–1946." *Journal of Contemporary History* 9, no. 4 (October 1974): 3–26.

Niles, Blair. *Black Haiti: A Biography of Africa's Eldest Daughter*. New York: G. P. Putnam's Sons, 1926.

No title or author, *The Nation*, February 23, 1921, 277–8.

Norton, Henry K. "American Imperialism in the Indies." *World's Work*, December 1925, 210–8.

Numa, Edgar N. *Antoine Simon et la "fatalité historique."* N.p.

O'Brien, Thomas. *The Revolutionary Mission: American Enterprise in Latin America, 1900–1945*. Cambridge: Cambridge University Press, 1996.

Oficina de Información, UND. *An Important Message Addressed to His Majesty the King of Spain*. Barcelona, March 10, 1921.

Oficina de Información, UND. *El Congreso Obrero reunido en Mexico trabaja por la independencia de Santo Domingo*. January 18, 1921.

Oficina de Información, UND. *El problema del Caribe y la "League of Free Nations."* [December 1920?].

Oficina de Información, UND. *Unidad de acción de España y los países de américa en pro de la independencia dominicana*. March 12, 1921.

An Onlooker. "America's Ireland: Haiti-Santo Domingo." *The Nation*, February 21, 1920. 231–4.

Ortega Frier, José. *Memorandum relativo a la intervención del señor Benjamín Sumner Welles en la República Dominicana*. 3rd ed. Santo Domingo: Taller, 1983.

"Our 'Moral Mandate' in Nicaragua." *Literary Digest*, September 28. 1912, 505–6.

Pagano, Dom A. *Bluejackets*. Boston: Meador, 1932.

Paige, Jeffrey M. *Coffee and Power: Revolution and the Rise of Democracy in Central America*. Cambridge, Mass.: Harvard University Press, 1997.

Pamphile, Leon D. "America's Policy-Making in Haitian Education, 1915–1934." *Journal of Negro Education* 54, no. 1 (1985): 99–108.

Pamphile, Leon D. *La croix et le glaive: l'église catholique et l'occupation américaine d'Haïti, 1915–1934*. Port-au-Prince: Editions des Antilles, 1991.

Pamphile, Leon D. *L'éducation en Haïti sous l'occupation américaine 1915–1934*. Port-au-Prince: Imprimerie des Antilles, 1988.

Pamphile, Leon D. *Haitians and African Americans: A Heritage of Tragedy and Hope*. Gainesville: University Press of Florida, 2001.

Pamphile, Leon D. "The NAACP and the American Occupation of Haiti." *Phylon* 47, no. 1 (1st Qtr., 1986): 91–100.

Park, James W. *Latin American Underdevelopment: A Historical Perspective in the United States, 1870–1965*. Baton Rouge: Louisiana State University Press, 1995.

Pearce, Jenny. *Under the Eagle: U.S. Intervention in Central America and the Caribbean*. Boston: South End Press, 1982.

Pei, Minxin. "Lessons from the Past." *Foreign Policy* 137 (July–August 2003): 52–5.

Peña Torres, Ligia M., and Steven Palmer. "A Rockefeller Foundation Health Primer for US-Occupied Nicaragua, 1914–1928." *Canadian Bulletin of Medical History* 25, no. 1 (2008): 43–69.

Pérez, Louis A., Jr. *Lords of the Mountain: Social Banditry and Peasant Protest in Cuba, 1878–1918*. Pittsburgh, Penn.: University of Pittsburgh Press, 1989.

Perkins, Whitney T. *Constraint of Empire: The United States and Caribbean Interventions*. Westport, Conn.: Greenwood Press, 1981.

Pfoh, Emanuel. "La formación del Estado Nacional en América Latina y la cuestión del clientelismo político." *Revista de Historia de América* (January–December 2005): 129–48.

Pierce, Philip N., Lt. Col. USMC, and Lt. Col. Frank O. Hough, USMCR. *The Compact History of the United States Marine Corps*. New York: Hawthorn Books, 1964.

Pierre-Paul, Antoine. *Première protestation armée contre l'intervention américaine de 1915 et 260 jours dans le maquis*. N.p.

Pinney, Edward L., ed. *Comparative Politics and Political Theory: Essays Written in Honor of Charles Baskervill Robson*. Chapel Hill: University of North Carolina Press, 1966.

Plummer, Brenda G. "The Afro-American Response to the Occupation of Haiti, 1915–1934." *Phylon* (June 1982): 125–43.

Plummer, Brenda G. *Haiti and the United States: The Psychological Moment*. Athens: University of Georgia Press, 1992.

Poppino, Rollie E. *International Communism in Latin America: A History of the Movement, 1917–1963*. London: Collier-Macmillan, 1964.

Portes Gil, Emilio. "Sandino visto por un presidente mexicano." *Revista Conservadora*, July 1962, 12–7.

Posner, Walter H. "American Marines in Haiti, 1915–1922." *The Americas* 20, no. 3 (January 1964): 231–66.

Powell, Anna I. "Relations between the United States and Nicaragua, 1898–1916." *Hispanic American Historical Review* 8, no. 1 (February 1928): 43–64.

Price-Mars, Jean. *Une étape de l'évolution haïtienne*. Port-au-Prince: La Presse, n. d.

Primer censo nacional de la República Dominicana, 1920. Santo Domingo: UASD, 1975. Original, Santo Domingo: Gobierno Provisional de la República Dominicana, 1923.

Pye, Lucian W., and Sidney Verba, eds. *Political Culture and Political Development*. Princeton, N.J.: Princeton University Press, 1965.

Ramírez, Sergio, ed. *Augusto C. Sandino: el pensamiento vivo*. 2nd ed. Tome 1. Managua: Nueva Nicaragua, 1984.

Ramírez, Sergio. "The Kid from Niquinohomo." *Latin American Perspectives* 16, no. 3 (Summer 1989): 48–82.

Read, Horacio. *Los civilizadores: novela de la ocupación militar en Santo Domingo*. [Havana?]: El Paladion, 1924.

Regalado, Doroteo. *De mi via-crucis (A través de la ocupación norteamericana)*. La Vega, Dominican Republic: Imprenta el Progreso, 1922.

Renda, Mary A. *Taking Haiti: Military Occupation and the Culture of U.S. Imperialism*. Chapel Hill: University of North Carolina Press, 2001.

"The Republic of Brown Bros." *The Nation*, June 7, 1922, 667.

Rippy, Fred. *The Capitalists and Colombia*. New York: Vanguard, 1931.

Rius [Eduardo del Río]. *El hermano Sandino*. Mexico City: Grijalbo, 1988.

Roberts, William R., and Jack Sweetman, eds. *New Interpretations in Naval History*. Annapolis, Md.: Naval Institute, 1991.

Rodríguez Bonilla, Manuel. *La batalla de La Barranquita*. Santo Domingo: UASD, 1987.

Rodríguez Demorizi, Emilio. *Lengua y folklore de Santo Domingo*. Santiago: UCMM, 1975.

Roig de Leuchsenring, Emilio. *La ocupación de la República Dominicana por los Estados Unidos y el derecho de las pequeñas nacionalidades de América*. Havana: Imprenta "El Siglo," 1919.

Román, José. *Maldito país*. Managua: Ediciones El Pez y la Serpiente, 1983.

Roorda, Eric P. *The Dictator Next Door: The Good Neighbor Policy and the Trujillo Regime in the Dominican Republic, 1930–1945*. Durham, N.C.: Duke University Press, 1998.

Rosenberg, Emily S. *Financial Missionaries to the World: The Politics and Culture of Dollar Diplomacy 1900–1950*. Durham, N.C.: Duke University Press, 2003.

Roosevelt, Franklin. "Our Foreign Policy: A Democratic View." *Foreign Affairs* 6, no. 4 (July 1928): 573–86.

Roumain, Jacques. *Masters of the Dew*. Oxford, UK: Heinemann, 1997. Original, n.p., 1944.

Ruck, Rob. *The Tropic of Baseball: Baseball in the Dominican Republic*. Lincoln: University of Nebraska Press, 1998.

Ruiz Chataing, David. "Caudillos y caudillismo en la historiografía." *Boletín de la Academia Nacional de la Historia* 91, no. 361 (January–March 2008): 101–44.

Sagás, Ernesto. *Race and Politics in the Dominican Republic*. Gainesville: University Press of Florida, 2000.

Saint-Amand, J. *Le code rural d'Haïti*. Port-au-Prince: Imprimerie Edmont Chenet, 1913.

Salisbury, Richard V. *Anti-Imperialism and International Competition in Central America, 1920–1929*. Wilmington, Del.: Scholarly Resources, 1989.

Salisbury, Richard V. "Mexico, the United States, and the 1926–1927 Nicaraguan Crisis." *Hispanic American Historical Review* 66, no. 2 (May 1986): 319–39.

Salvatierra, Sofonias. *Sandino o la tragedia de un pueblo*. 2nd ed. Managua: Maltez, 1980. Original, Madrid: Europa Libertad, 1934.

"Sandino, of Nicaragua: Bandit or Patriot?" *Literary Digest*, February 4, 1928, 42, 44–50.

Sandino, A. C. *General de Hombres Libres*. Havana: Imprenta Nacional de Cuba, Ediciones Juveniles, 1962.

San Miguel, Pedro L. "Historias de gringos y campesinos: una revisita de la ocupación estadunidense de la República Dominicana, 1916–1924." *Secuencia: Revista de historia y ciencias sociales* no. 55 (January–April 2003): 107–41.

San Miguel, Pedro L. "Peasant Resistance and State Demands in the Cibao during the U.S. Occupation." Translated by Phillip Berryman. *Latin American Perspectives* 86, no. 3 (Summer 1995): 41–62.

Sannon, H. P. *Six mois de ministère*. Port-au-Prince: Héraux, 1936.

"Santo Domingo." *The Nation*, December 7, 1916, 528.

Savaille, Rulhière. *La grève de 29 (la première grève des étudiants haïtiens)*. Port-au-Prince: Ateliers Fardin, 1979.

Schmidt, Hans. *The United States Occupation of Haiti, 1915–1934*. N.p., 1971. Reprint with a foreword by Stephen Solarz, New Brunswick, N.J.: Rutgers University Press, 1995.

Schoultz, Lars. *Beneath the United States: A History of U.S. Policy toward Latin America*. Cambridge, Mass.: Harvard University Press, 1998.

Schroeder, Michael J. "Bandits and Blanket Thieves, Communists and Terrorists: The Politics of Naming Sandinistas in Nicaragua, 1927–1936 and 1979–1990." *Third World Quarterly* 26, no. 1 (2005): 67–86.

Schroeder, Michael J. "Horse Thieves to Rebels to Dogs: Political Gang Violence and the State in the Western Segovias, Nicaragua, in the Time of Sandino, 1926–1934," *Journal of Latin American Studies* 28 (1996): 383–434.

Schroeder, Michael J. "'To Defend Our Nation's Honor': Toward a Social and Cultural History of the Sandino Rebellion in Nicaragua, 1927–1934." 2 vols. PhD diss., University of Michigan, 1993.

Schulzinger, Robert D. "The Making of the Diplomatic Mind: The Training, Outlook, and Style of United States Foreign Service Officers, 1906–1928." PhD diss., Yale University, 1971.

Schwoch, James. *The American Radio Industry and Its Latin American Activities, 1900–1939.* Urbana: University of Illinois Press, 1990.

Scott, James C. *Domination and the Arts of Resistance: Hidden Transcripts.* New Haven, Conn.: Yale University Press, 1990.

Scott, James C. *The Moral Economy of the Peasant: Rebellion and Subsistence in Southeast Asia.* New Haven, Conn.: Yale University Press, 1976.

Seabrook, William B. *The Magic Island.* New York: Paragon House, 1989. Original, New York: Harcourt, Brace, 1929.

Seligmann, Herbert J. "The Conquest of Haiti." *The Nation,* July 10, 1920, 35–6.

Selser, Gregorio. "El antimperialismo de Sandino." *Cuadernos del Tercer Mundo,* August 1979, 11–4.

Selser, Gregorio. *La restauración conservadora y la gesta de Benjamín Zeledón: Nicaragua-USA, 1909/1916.* Managua: Aldilá, 2001.

Selser, Gregorio. *Sandino: general de hombres libres.* 2 vols. Buenos Aires: Editorial Triángulo, 1959.

Service Technique du Département de L'Agriculture et de L'Enseignement Professionel. *Programme de L'École Centrale 1929–1930.* Port-au-Prince: Service Technique, October 1, 1929.

Shadid, Anthony. *Night Draws Near: Iraq's People in the Shadow of America's War.* New York: Picador, 2006.

Shannon, Magdaline W. *Jean Price-Mars, the Haitian Elite and the American Occupation, 1915–1935.* New York: St. Martin's Press, 1996.

Sheesley, Joel C. *Sandino in the Streets.* Translated and edited by Wayne G. Bragg. Bloomington: Indiana University Press, 1991.

Sherman, Richard B. "The Harding Administration and the Negro: An Opportunity Lost." *Journal of Negro History* 49, no. 3 (July 1964): 151–68.

Shumway, Jeffrey M. "Juan Manuel de Rosas: Authoritarian Caudillo and Primitive Populist." *History Compass* 2 (2004): 1–14.

Simonds, Frank H. "Hoover, *South Americanus.*" *Review of Reviews,* February 1929, 67–71.

Simpson, George E. "Haiti's Social Structure." *American Sociological Review* 6, no. 5 (October 1941): 640–9.

Simpson, George E. "Haitian Peasant Economy." *Journal of Negro History* 25, no. 4 (October 1940): 498–519.

Smith, Daniel. "Bainbridge Colby and the Good Neighbor Policy, 1920–1921." *Mississippi Valley Historical Review* 50, no. 1 (June 1963): 56–78.

Smith, Julian C., Maj. USMC, et al. *A Review of the Organization and Operations of the Guardia Nacional de Nicaragua.* Quantico, Va.: United States Marine Corps, 1937.

Smith, Matthew J. "Shades of Red in a Black Republic: Radicalism, Black Consciousness, and Social Conflict in Postoccupation Haiti, 1934–1957." PhD diss., University of Florida, 2002.

Sociedad Pro-Investigación de la Verdad Histórica Sobre el Sandinismo, *La verdad histórica sobre el sandinismo.* N.p.: 1947.

Sosa Jiménez, Manuel A. *Hato Mayor del Rey, su sitial en la historia dominicana.* Santo Domingo: Taller, 1993.

Soto Hall, Máximo. *La sombra de la Casa Blanca.* Buenos Aires: El Ateneo, 1927.

Spector, Robert M. *W. Cameron Forbes and the Hoover Commissions to Haiti, 1930.* Lanham, Md.: University Press of America, 1985.

Spenser, Daniela. *The Impossible Triangle: Mexico, Soviet Russia, and the United States in the 1920s.* Durham, N.C.: Duke University Press, 1999.

Stern, Steve, ed. *Resistance, Rebellion, and Consciousness in the Andean Peasant World, 18th to 20th Centuries.* Madison: University of Wisconsin Press, 1987.

Stimson, Henry L., and McGeorge Bundy. *On Active Service in Peace and War.* New York: Harper & Brothers, 1948.

Streit, Clarence K. "Haiti: Intervention in Operation." *Foreign Affairs* 6 (July 1928): 615–32.

Suggs, Henry L. "The Response of the African American Press to the United States Occupation of Haiti, 1915–1934." *Journal of Negro History* 73, no. 1/4 (Winter–Autumn 1988): 33–45.

Sylvain, Georges. *Dix années de lutte pour la liberté, 1915–1925*. Port-au-Prince: Editions Henri Deschamps, n.d.

Tierney Jr., John J. "The United States and Nicaragua, 1927–1932: Decisions for De-Escalation and Withdrawal." PhD diss., University of Pennsylvania, 1969.

Tillman, Ellen D. "Dollar Diplomacy by Force: Military Experimentation in the U.S. Dominican Occupation, 1900–1924." Unpublished manuscript, 2012.

Traphagen, Jeanne C. "The Inter-American Diplomacy of Frank B. Kellogg." PhD diss., University of Minnesota, 1956.

Trelawney-Ansell, Edward C. [Joseph Crad]. *I Had Nine Lives: Fighting for Cash in Mexico and Nicaragua*. London: Sampson Low, Marston, 1938.

Tulchin, Joseph S. *The Aftermath of War: World War I and U.S. Policy toward Latin America*. New York: New York University, 1971.

Turits, Richard L. *Foundations of Despotism: Peasants, the Trujillo Regime, and Modernity in Dominican History*. Stanford, Calif.: Stanford University Press, 2003.

Turner, John K. "Nicaragua." *The Nation*, May 31, 1922, 646–8.

UN. *Dépossessions*. Port-au-Prince: Imprimerie de *La Presse*, 1930.

UP. *Memoir on the Political, Economic, and Financial Conditions Existing in the Republic of Haiti under the American Occupation*. N.p., May 1, 1921.

UP. *Séance publique du 16 février 1925*. Port-au-Prince, 1925.

U.S. Army School for Military Government and Administration, 2nd section, group V. *The United States Military Government in the Dominican Republic 1916 to 1922: A Case History*. New York: August 14, 1943.

U.S. Congress. Senate. *Hearings before a Select Committee on Haiti and Santo Domingo*. 67th Congress, 1st and 2nd sessions, vol. 1: 1921. Washington: U.S. GPO, 1922.

U.S. Department of State. *A Brief History of the Relations between the United States and Nicaragua, 1909–1928*. Washington, D.C.: USGPO, 1928.

Valle, Manuel Antonio. "Viva Sandino." *The Living Age*, November 1932, 243–8.

Van Young, Eric V. "To See Someone Not Seeing: Historical Studies of Peasants and Politics in Mexico." *Mexican Studies/Estudios Mexicanos* 6, no. 1 (Winter 1990): 133–59.

Vayssière, Pierre. *Auguste César Sandino, ou l'envers d'un mythe*. Paris: Editions du CNRS, 1988.

Vayssière, Pierre. *Nicaragua: les contradictions du sandinisme*. Paris: Editions du CNRS, 1985.

Vega B., Wenceslao. *Historia del Derecho Dominicano*. Santo Domingo: INTEC, 1986.

Villanueva, Carlos. *Sandino en Yucatán, 1929–1930*. Mexico City: Secretaría de Educación Pública, 1988.

Vincent, Sténio. *Efforts et résultats*. Port-au-Prince: Imprimerie de L'État, [1939].

Vincent, Sténio. *En posant les jalons . . .* Tome 1. Port-au-Prince: Imprimerie de L'État, 1939.

"War in Nicaragua." *The Nation*, March 21, 1928, 311.

Welles, Sumner. "Is America Imperialistic?" *Atlantic Monthly*, September 1924, 412–23.

Welles, Sumner. *Naboth's Vineyard: The Dominican Republic, 1844–1924*. 2 vols. Mamaroneck, N.Y.: Paul P. Appel, 1966.

"What the World Thinks of America." *The Nation*, January 26, 1927, 88–9.

Whisnant, David. *Rascally Signs in Sacred Places: The Politics of Culture in Nicaragua*. Chapel Hill: University of North Carolina Press, 1995.

Whitaker, Arthur P. *The Western Hemisphere Idea: Its Rise and Decline*. Ithaca, N.Y.: Cornell University Press, 1954.

White, Richard. *Will Rogers: A Political Life*. Lubbock: Texas Tech University Press, 2011.

White, Walter. "Danger in Haiti." *The Crisis*, July 1931, 231–2.

Wiarda, Howard J. *The Soul of Latin America: The Cultural and Political Tradition*. New Haven, Conn.: Yale University Press, 2001.

Wilentz, Amy. *The Rainy Season: Haiti since Duvalier*. New York: Simon and Schuster, 1990.

Williams, Virginia. *Radical Journalists, Generalist Intellectuals, and U.S.-Latin American Relations*. Lewiston, N.Y.: Edwin Mellen Press, 2001.

Williams, William A. *The Tragedy of American Diplomacy*. New York: Dell, 1962.

Wilson, Sondra Kathryn, ed. *In Search of Democracy: The NAACP Writings of James Weldon Johnson, Walter White, and Roy Wilkins, 1920–1977.* New York: Oxford University Press, 1999.

Winkler-Morey, Anne R. "Good Neighbors: Popular Internationalists and United States' Relations with Mexico and the Caribbean Region (1918–1929)." PhD diss., University of Minnesota, 2001.

Wirkus, Faustin, and Taney Dudley. *The White King of La Gonave.* Garden City, N.Y.: Doubleday, Doran, 1931.

Wise, Frederic M., Col. USMC. *A Marine Tells it to You: As told to Meigs O. Frost.* New York: J. H. Sears, 1929.

Wolf, Eric, and Edward Hansen. "Caudillo Politics: A Structural Analysis." *Comparative Studies in Society and History* 9 (January 1967): 168–79.

Wolfe, Justin. *The Everyday Nation-State: Community & Ethnicity in Nineteenth-Century Nicaragua.* Lincoln: University of Nebraska Press, 2007.

Woods, Kenneth. "'Imperialistic America': A Landmark in the Development of U.S. Policy toward Latin America." *Inter-American Economic Affairs* 21 (Winter 1967): 55–72.

Wucker, Michele. *Why the Cocks Fight: Dominicans, Haitians, and the Struggle for Hispaniola.* New York: Hill and Wang, 1999.

Wünderich, Volker. *Sandino en la Costa: de las Segovias al litoral Atlántico.* Managua: Nueva Nicaragua, 1989.

Wünderich, Volker. *Sandino: una biografía política.* Managua: Nueva Nicaragua, 1995.

Yerxa, Donald. "The United States Navy in Caribbean Waters during World War I." *Military Affairs* 51, no. 4 (October 1987): 182–7.

Zeledón, Sergio Alejandro. "Fighting Intervention in Nicaragua in the Age of British-American Conflict 1820–1920: Dr. and General Benjamin F. Zeledón, Supreme Chief of Government of Nicaragua in Rebellion 1909–1912." PhD diss., University of California-Berkeley, 2010.

Zeller, Neici M. "The Appearance of All, the Reality of Nothing: Politics and Gender in the Dominican Republic, 1880–1961." PhD diss., University of Illinois at Chicago, 2010.

Zimmermann, Mathilde. *Sandinista: Carlos Fonseca and the Nicaraguan Revolution.* Durham, N.C.: Duke University Press, 2000.

Zissa, Robert. "Nicaragua–1912." *Leatherneck,* July 1984, 24–8.

INDEX

Note: Page numbers in *italics* indicate figures; letter 'n' refers to notes.

CPSIA information can be obtained
at www.ICGtesting.com
Printed in the USA
BVHW030100230120
570246BV00003B/148